The Best of the Best from

CAMPAIGNS & ELECTIONS

THE ROAD TO VICTORY

The Complete Guide to Winning in Politics

Edited by Ron Faucheux

KENDALL/HUNT PUBLISHING COMPANY
4050 Westmark Drive   Dubuque, Iowa 52002

Copyright © 1995 by Campaigns & Elections Publishing Company

ISBN 0-7872-0744-6

All rights reserved. No part of this publication may be reproduced, stored in a retrieval system, or transmitted, in any form or by any means, electronic, mechanical, photocopying, recording, or otherwise, without the prior written permission of the copyright owner.

Printed in the United States of America

10 9 8 7 6 5 4 3 2 1

CONTENTS

★ ★ ★

Introduction v

1: Strategy, Message, and Planning 1

2: Campaign Technology: Computers, Database Management, and Voter Files 65

3: Public Opinion, Issues, and Opposition Research 86

4: Targeting and Demographics 139

5: Fundraising: Strategies and Techniques 189

6: Scheduling, Campaign Administration, and Post-Election 239

7: Direct Mail: Strategies and Techniques 271

8: Telephone Direct Contact: Strategies and Techniques 317

9: Television and Radio Advertising 331

10: Print Advertising and Campaign Materials 400

11: Candidate Preparation and Presentation 423

12: Dealing with the News Media 481

13: Initiatives, Referenda, and Grassroots Lobbying 515

14: Recruiting, Mobilizing, and Activating Volunteers 538

15: Voter Registration and Turnout Programs 553

16: Perspectives on Modern Campaigning 569

Introduction
Ron Faucheux

★ ★ ★

There's nothing quite like political campaigns.

They bring out the best and worst in people. They offer participants a cross-section glimpse of society that is both penetrating and unique. They demand much, usually too much. By nature of the process, they yield more losers than winners. They may be messy, confusing, and ephemeral, and occasionally silly, mindless, and ferocious, but they provide the pivot upon which our democracy turns. Without them, free government for, by, and of the people could not exist.

The chapters of this book have been adapted from articles that have been published by *Campaigns & Elections* and *Campaign* magazines. (Since March 1993, *Campaign* has been incorporated within *Campaigns & Elections*.) As you read them, you must always remember the First Rule of Political Campaigning: There are no rules. While the events, strategies, successes, and failures of past combat may be highly instructive and fascinating, each campaign has its own heart and soul. It must be judged and gauged around singular circumstances. There are no magic wands in the campaign management business; there is no supernatural formula.

In the end, political campaigns are about eight things:

First, *people*. This includes voters as well as candidates. Their imperfections and biases shape the limits of what *can* be done as opposed to what *should* be done.

Second, *strategy*. Before you can win a campaign, in war or politics, you need a plan that explains how to accomplish your goals based on practical realities and sound timing.

Third, *messages*. Every campaign, no matter how small or obscure, needs a rationale.

Fourth, *issues*. Yes, Virginia, there are issues in politics. And they're important even in a world of well-crafted imagery and finely-tuned spin control. Issues frequently determine how people vote. They set the stage for drawing the line between political choices.

Fifth, *coalitions*. Electoral majorities are usually forged by bringing people together who, as individuals and groups, often disagree. This means using your messages and issues to draw the right line around the right constituencies.

Sixth, *cues*. Voters rarely know every little detail about every candidate's philosophy, credentials, or platform. More basic candidate characteristics—incumbency, party, race, region, gender, occupation, group affiliation—signal to voters key distinctions that matter to them. Around those distinctions, votes are accumulated.

Seventh, *organization*. Political support must be nurtured, identified, recruited, and activated. Limited capital must be optimized. *Ad hoc* assemblages of human resources, often under the most chaotic and emotionally charged conditions, must be managed.

Eighth, *money*. Called the mother's milk of politics, money determines how, when, and where a candidate can deliver his or her message. In a world where the average person is exposed to over 20,000 advertising messages and sales pitches a week, effective political communication needs both reach and frequency to break through this dense labyrinth of noise and news.

Modern Campaigns and Political Science

Modern campaigning, and the impact of technology upon methods of communications and information processing, is changing basic notions of political science and straining old definitions and theoretical constructs.

Take the idea of participation, for example. There was a time when people had to *do* something before they were counted as political participants; they had to vote, work in a campaign, run for office, contribute money, or whatever. Now, all they have to do is be part of a voter pool that is sampled for a public opinion survey. Poll results, both private and public, may determine whether prospective candidates run or not, whether potential supporters play or pull back, whether certain policy proposals are unveiled, and whether underdogs gain momentum because of unexpected strength or lose steam because of revealed weakness. Just *being there*, as part of the universe that is randomly sampled, now matters.

As voting is made easier through more liberal registration rules allowing election-day sign-up, "motor voter" opportunities, voting-by-mail, and pre-election early voting, enhanced efforts have to be made to target individuals, and not just ideological or demographic groups, and to stimulate their mobilization. This is part of an organizational procedure that is shaping the contours of public participation.

Better voter lists, accessible through computer disk and enhanced with a variety of useful information, makes more precise targeting possible. It also affords the opportunity for quicker communications, whether it's to seek small financial donors, build an election-day turnout mechanism, or mobilize grassroots activists.

Concepts involving mass-elite linkages, in the world of cyberspace communication, are also being altered by technology. The masses have greater and speedier access to information about politics and public policy than the elites did just a few years ago. How this will transform the political arena has yet to be fully fathomed.

Movements for direct democracy and increased use of initiatives and referenda modify not only the relationship between elites and masses, but also the function of representative government. Campaign finance regulations imposed by federal, state, and local governments have professionalized the money-chase in politics, shifting influence toward interest groups who are permanently organized to prospect and reap contributions from established constituencies.

Analytical models such as "critical elections" theory and "secular realignment"—proffered as tools to define enduring partisan shifts—are also affected. Better and more extensive survey research affords partisans of every stripe a clearer view of public attitudes, wants, and fears. Use of more information-oriented attack advertising and a plethora of rapid response tactics, made possible by fax machines, on-line data services, and satellite technology, has revolutionized the timetable of politics. Mass communications and micro-processors have not only altered the pace of political change but have altered influence channels. The concept of political activism is being recast, begging worn definitions of "amateurs" and "professionals" and how they relate to one another.

On the one hand, these trends have opened the door of participation and influence to more and more average citizens, making activism more programmable. On the other hand, the process is becoming so sophisticated, amateurs need not apply when it comes to the management of it.

Professionalism + Technology = Speed

While all of these trends may not have fundamentally changed the nature of political campaigning in recent years, they have done two things that are undeniable: made campaigning more professional and considerably accelerated its pace. Campaign cycles once measured in months and weeks are now measured in hours and minutes.

Technology, and the regulation of money to pay for it, drives this professionalism. It has also made the political campaign industry more specialized and competitive.

Ironically, a down side of this professionalism has been to make campaigning decidedly less civil. There is a declining sense of propriety in our politics, an abandonment of standards.

This new incivility goes not to the dishonesty of the game, but to its dignity. Corruption is a moral question, and when it goes too far, a legal one. The issue of civility centers on the manner of personal conduct, and today's candidate-centered campaigns make the importance of that conduct more obvious than ever.

Too many contemporary campaigners are allowing the stress of media inquiry and rapid-fire technology to rob them of their dignity. They think you have to be vicious to win. But if they looked at some of the real masters—Ronald Reagan, John Kennedy, and Franklin Roosevelt, like Lincoln and Jefferson before them—they would learn a lot about hitting the opposition where it hurts and doing it without demeaning oneself. "There you go again!" Reagan chided the hapless Jimmy Carter; "We've had the New Deal and the Fair Deal, but before Mr. Nixon deals, somebody better cut the cards" mocked JFK in 1960; "Not content with attacks on me, my wife, or my sons, they now include my little dog Fala" was FDR's cheerful way to taunt political adversaries.

You can attack without being malicious. Spitefulness degrades the attacker and diminishes the process. It feeds media obsession with candidate flaws. It trivializes debate. Public figures are mortal humans; as such, they all have defects. Indeed, if they could be recalled like cars, they would all have to go back to the factory. Every one of them is subject to being picked apart, which is fine. But when the sundering becomes excessive, and contorts context, democracy is the true victim. It drives out good people and keeps new blood from entering public life. And that is a tragedy.

Political competition, like war, is not for the squeamish or thin-skinned. It is hard and bloody. As it should be. Partisan and issue advancement often demands implacable resolve and ardent advocacy. The best political leaders have been tough operators, able to throw as many punches as they take. But when they fight, they always do it with civility—as if, as it was once observed, the whole world marks their demeanor. We are quickly losing that in our campaigns and in the press coverage of our politics. We must regain it before it is gone forever.

A Continuous Process

One of the most striking things that has happened to politics in recent years has to do with its calendar. There's no such thing as an *off* year anymore. There may be even and odd numbered years, but the process of campaigning and electing is now continuous. Every week, in both even and odd years, there's a federal, state, or local election somewhere in the United States (not to mention the other 95 percent of the world); every hour, a candidacy is launched; every day, signatures are gathered to put an issue on a ballot.

Not only have elections become ceaseless, but the time it takes to plan a campaign has been extended. By Labor Day of an odd year, hundreds of incumbent members of Congress, governors, down-ballot officials, and legislators will have hired consultant teams for their re-elections to be held the next year. Many challengers are in full swing many, many months—even years—before election day.

"Campaign" is now a metaphor not just for candidates running against one another, but also for ballot propositions, grassroots lobbying, issue advocacy, corporate crisis management, franchise and proxy fights, and union workplace contests. These bouts are endless and usually expensive in time, talent, and money. Significantly, they more and more utilize the skills of campaign professionals and the disciplines of political strategy and technique.

Road to Victory

Like a good candidate, this volume is brought to you by popular demand. Over the years, thousands of our readers and seminar participants, candidates and political consultants, party officials and association executives, professors and students in undergraduate and graduate schools, have requested that we put together the "best of the best" from *Campaigns & Elections* into one book.

Special thanks to the many people who have made this project possible. Appreciation is extended to the authors of the articles that appear in these chapters. While they represent varying points of view from widely differing perspectives, each of them have contributed substantially to a better professional understanding of the political campaign process by their experiences and their willingness to commit their knowledge and insights to paper.

Even though a number of articles in this book are somewhat dated, they were included to show the evolutionary process of how various tactics were refined and implemented over time. In some instances, where possible, time-bound references were deleted; when necessary to explain context, they were kept.

Thanks to Abigail Fairbanks Emerson, whose drive and determination made this book a reality; to the entire staff of *Campaigns & Elections*, to David and Lynn Beiler, John Persinos, Rita Kefalas, and to the many editors, editorial advisers, staff writers, and interns who over the years developed these chapters through their hard work and sheer love of the process; and to our publisher Kendall/Hunt for making it possible, along with their outstanding editing, production, and marketing staff; and last but not least, to Stanley Foster Reed, the man who started it all, the visionary who founded *Campaigns & Elections* in 1980.

The road to victory is a long, arduous one. But it must begin with a first step. We hope in some way, this volume will make that first step a little easier for all who dare it.

1

Strategy, Message, and Planning

★ ★ ★

✓ Developing the Right Message

Ron Faucheux

You can't talk campaign politics anymore without talking about The Message. It has become the Holy Grail of electoral strategy, the sacred epistle of political communications. It is a term that stands for what every winning campaign must have. Your TV, radio, newspaper, and direct mail must communicate it. Your speeches, soundbites, and press interviews must reinforce it.

Every campaign manual and political consultant will refer to The Message—and they'll do it over and over again. It is essential, they will tell you, not only to have one but to stick to it. Bill Clinton had a clear, consistent message in 1992 and he's now in the White House; George Bush didn't, and he's now doing a lot of baby-sitting. The Message. It's more than a buzz word.

If you want to run for office, or want to pass a ballot proposition, make sure you have the right message at the right time. A misplaced message may be worse than none at all.

So now you know you need one, your next question is probably: Well, what is it?

Put simply, The Message is your rationale for running, it's the most compelling reasons why voters should vote for you and not for the opposition.

Effective messages set up a choice: Candidate A versus Candidate B. Unless it's a retention referendum, where voters get to vote an incumbent judge up or down, candidate elections are about choices between two or more people. When voters cast ballots for a candidate, they're not deciding whether that candidate is good or bad, popular or unpopular, perfect or flawed. They're choosing that candidate over another one. They're exercising an option, picking an alternative, and they're doing it on the basis of what's available in that particular race at that particular time. A candidate with a 60 percent negative rating is usually a dead duck; but if that candidate's opponent has an 80 percent negative rating, it's a different story.

A campaign message can be expressed in a hundred different ways. It can be illustrated or symbolized using a variety of words and phrases. You can communicate it through slogans, signs, and speeches; you can deliver it via electronic media or the printed word. But no matter how it is conveyed, it must be clear, consistent, understandable, and relevant to the political choice at hand.

You may be wondering, OK, I know I need a campaign message, but how do I create one? Where do I find it? Is there a Book of Messages I can buy? Is there a software program I can feed data into that'll spit one out? Unfortunately, it's not that easy. If it were, every campaign would be an automated competition where the result would always be certain. Even though an effective campaign message can be described and dissected, developing it takes good instincts and solid judgment. That's where the science and the art of politics come together.

Often the words message and strategy are used interchangeably. They shouldn't be. They are two different things. A message answers the question: Why are you running? A strategy answers the question: How will you win? A campaign strategy includes a message and a means of delivering it; a campaign plan details how and when you will implement the strategy and at what financial cost.

The purpose of this article is to provide candidates, campaign managers, and political consultants a step-by-step guide to developing the right message. It's not a flawless formula, and it comes without a money back guarantee, but it's a valuable exercise that every campaign should go through. Even if your message is obvious, you should test it before you marry it. Here are the steps to follow:

Demographic profile. Get to know your constituency. Obtain numbers on voter group strength and remember that population, voter registration and voter turnout figures are three different things. Draw a simple statistical picture of the electorate by collecting data on partisanship, race, gender, age, employment, education, occupation, family status, home ownership, urban-rural, union membership, public employees, employment by industry, gun ownership, sexual orientation, religious groupings, special issue attachments, and traditional "Hatfield v. McCoy" rivalries

After you get the numbers, drive around your district, city, or state. Look at it. Get to know its communities, neighborhoods, and people. This will put a human face on the numbers.

Attitudinal profile. Take a hard look at voter attitudes in your constituency. The first step is to have an experienced pollster do a survey. A base or a benchmark poll can give you an overall reading of the political landscape, demographically and ideologically. What issues matter? What public figures are liked and disliked? Is the nation, state, or locality on the wrong or right track? What kind of candidates are they looking for and why? This type of survey should probe possible messages by using a variety of question techniques. If done properly, it's like mining gold. It's amazing what unexpected gems will pop out of a poll with a well-structured questionnaire.

Coalition profile. Divide your voters into politically useful categories that are simple to understand and meaningful to your candidacy. Answer this central question: What is the right combination that will get me a majority (or, where applicable, a plurality) of the vote on election day?

For example, if Candidate A is a liberal Democratic woman running for the state legislature against Candidate B, a conservative Republican male, and Candidate A's district (based on polling, past election results, and turnout history) is split 24 percent Democratic women, 21 percent Democratic men, 20 percent Republican women, 19 percent Republican men, 8 percent Independent men and 8 percent Independent women, her coalition profile may look something like this:

Coalition Profile

% of Each Group Candidate A Needs	Group's Share of the Electorate	Cumulative %Points
84% of Democratic Women	x 24% of the electorate =	20.16
70% of Democratic Men	x 21% of the electorate =	14.70
60% of Independent Women	x 8% of the electorate =	4.80
45% of Independent Men	x 8% of the electorate =	3.60
30% of Republican Women	x 20% of the electorate =	6.00
12% of Republican Men	x 19% of the electorate =	2.28

Cumulative Percentage Points = 51.54 (enough to win)

Coalition-building entails finding ways to bring together voter groups that often exhibit dissimilar political behavior. To get her magic 51 percent of the vote, Candidate A will have to build a coalition consisting largely of Democrats and women; to do that, she will need a message that primarily appeals to her Democratic base and secondarily attracts a sizable portion of women Republicans and Independents. Issues such as abortion, school vouchers, and capital punishment pose opportunities and dangers in this case since they are usually salient among voters she has targeted. If a survey of the district shows that 75 percent of the Democrats and 50 percent of the Republican women are pro-choice on abortion, then Candidate A may want to stress that issue. On the other hand, if Candidate A opposes the death penalty and candidate B supports it, and 55 percent of Democratic women and 80 percent of Republican women agree with Candidate B, this is clearly a perilous issue Candidate A should avoid. If Candidate B is smart, he will use it to drive a wedge between the groups Candidate A needs to cluster together in her winning coalition.

In building an ideal coalition profile, there may be more than one path to victory. If there is, test a few scenarios and go with the one that makes the most sense. Take the path of least resistance.

Your strengths. Make a list of your strengths as a candidate and as a prospective public official. Be objective. Ask friends and advisers, confidentially if necessary, and get an honest reading. Also use survey research for a measure. Always keep in mind the politics of your electorate, the temper of the times, voter partisanship and ideology, current hot issues, recent events that have shaped pertinent public perceptions, and the demographics of your constituency. Strengths may be personal, such as a reputation for honesty, a background of experience, a record of accomplishment, good people skills, and a pleasing personality; they may be ideological, such as having the politically right position on the most salient issues; and they may be strategic, such as geographic base, fundraising capacity, and interest group and party support.

Your weaknesses. Make a list of your weaknesses as a candidate and as a prospective public official. Again, be cruelly objective. Ask friends and advisers to contribute, confidentially if necessary. When doing this, also keep in mind the various factors that will likely influence public perceptions of your candidacy.

Opposition strengths and weaknesses. Make the same lists of strengths and weaknesses for each of your opponents or likely opponents. While it may be somewhat unpleasant to objectively identify opposition strengths, the most fun you'll have in this whole exercise comes when you get to list their weaknesses.

Lines of distinction. Study all of the lists carefully. Now, determine three things:

1. What "mirror opposite" strengths do I have that contrast directly with the weaknesses of my opposition?

The strongest campaign messages rest on "mirror opposite" strengths you have that play against parallel opposition weaknesses. For example, if you have an unblemished reputation for honesty and your opponent is publicly under criminal investigation for bribery and racketeering, you have the perfect "mirror opposite" on integrity, honesty and trust issues.

In 1992, Clinton's message centered on change, a perfect pitch to use against an incumbent whose party had been in office for 12 years when voters were looking for something different. Also, Clinton's image as a "people person" played well against Bush's image as an out-of-touch elitist, particularly when it was related to economic issues.

Contrast that to the effort to defeat Bush four years earlier. In 1988, voters did not want dramatic change. The economy was still doing well and many voters were afraid to change what they perceived to be successful Reagan-Bush economic and foreign policies. As a result, Dukakis could not make change stick as a message, a big problem for the out party. Because Dukakis was considered more of a technocrat than a populist, he also had trouble playing against Bush's personal weakness.

Something else to keep in mind: Often, a "mirror opposite" strength, while it sets up a good contrast with your opponent, is not big enough to make it your central message, although it may still be a very effective attack argument. A case in point: polls showed that Dan Quayle was a drag on Bush's ability to appeal to undecided voters and that Al Gore was a big plus across-the-board for Clinton. This was a "mirror opposite" strength for Clinton. Although it was a very important issue that worked to Clinton's benefit, it was not appropriate as the central campaign message. Clinton would have looked foolish campaigning on the theme, "Elect me and you'll get a better Vice President." Clearly, the distinctions that could be drawn on the "mirror opposite" economic change message were much more powerful and appropriate.

If you don't have "mirror opposite" strengths that contrast directly with weaknesses of your opponent, try to develop them over time or use "stand alone" strengths.

2. What major "stand alone" strengths do I have that my opposition lacks?

If you have no clear "mirror opposites," "stand alone" strengths become important as a substitute. They also form the basis of the positive side of your campaign.

An example of a "stand alone" strength would be if Candidate A has a great record of civic involvement (chaired charitable causes, volunteered for years in community service projects, etc.) while Candidate B has only a fair one. Even though this may not be a clean "mirror opposite" strength since Candidate B is not without some civic experience to point to, it's still a good "stand alone" strength that Candidate A can use to build a favorable case for his candidacy.

How do you know the difference between a "mirror opposite" strength and a "stand alone" strength? Try this variation of the last example: if Candidate A has a great record of civic involvement and Candidate B has no record and was also caught lying about it, a "mirror opposite" strength exists for Candidate A—a clean kill by anyone's estimation.

3. What "mirror opposite" or "stand alone" strengths does my opposition have, and what weaknesses do I have, that could become the basis of attacks against me?

This is the flip side of itemizing your strengths. Example: Candidate A is running for the city council and is only 23 years old with no governmental or business experience. Candidate B is 40 years old with eight years governmental and ten years business experience. In most elections, Candidate B would have two related "mirror opposite" strengths: age and experience.

Attacks against you, and attacks against your opponent, are not limited to "mirror opposite" strengths and weaknesses. You are subject to being attacked on any and all weak points you have, as is your opponent.

The difference between a candidate's "stand alone" weaknesses and his "mirror opposite" weaknesses from a public attack standpoint is that while "stand alone" weaknesses may make good attack material, they are probably not as effective as a central campaign message as are those that have a "mirror opposite" effect. Nevertheless, they still may become part of the mosaic to support your central message, although not the whole of it.

Be careful with your "stand alone" weaknesses, even minor ones. Your opponent may try to develop "stand alone" strengths into "mirror opposites" either through unanticipated events or by providing new information that may enlarge your weaknesses and magnify his strengths. Make sure you inoculate yourself before being attacked.

Craft The Message. It's now time to bring all this information together based on the lines of distinction discussed above and actually draft a message for your campaign. As a starting point, write down a sentence or short paragraph that summarizes the reason why the voters should elect you, keeping in mind your strengths, the opposition's weaknesses, and your points of inoculation. This is, in effect, your message.

Examine the strength and simplicity of these two well known samples of effective campaign message-making. In 1992, the winning Democratic message was:

> *Bill Clinton will bring change and an improved economy. He understands average people and their need for new hope. Bush-Quayle doesn't. That is why he will work for a middle class tax cut, expanded opportunity for the disadvantaged (working women, African Americans, gays, and the poor) and affordable health care for all.*

In 1984, the winning Republican message was:

> *Things are better now than they were four years ago because of Ronald Reagan's leadership. His policies have improved the economy, reduced inflation, cut taxes, curbed the growth of government, and strengthened the nation's military defenses. Let's not go back to Carter-Mondale.*

Your message, like that of Clinton's in 1992 and Reagan's in 1984, should contain an answer to basic questions: (a) Why do you want the job and what will you do with it? (b) Why are you better than the opposition for the job at this time? (c) What public policy issues support the need for your election?

Test the message. If you can answer "yes" to each of the following questions, then your message is probably on the right track:

Question 1: From a geographic, ethnic, partisan, social, and demographic perspective, will this message appeal to the groups necessary for my winning coalition?

This is critical. If your message offends one or more of the voter groups you need to coalesce around your candidacy, it's a loser. A poll is the key to answering this question.

Question 2: Does this message zero-in on both your strengths and your opposition's weaknesses? Does it take full advantage of mirror opposites, if you have any?

Go back through the lists you've made and recheck them.

Question 3: Does this message apply uniquely to you in this race (as opposed to being so generic that any other candidate could use the same message just as appropriately)?

Candidates who run on the basis of their general qualifications and experience when their opponents have comparable credentials is an example of a message that's so innocuous it doesn't grab.

Question 4: Is the message big enough? Is it something that hits home with voters, is it clear enough for them to understand?

Campaign strategist James Carville advised *Campaigns & Elections* readers that elections are won on "big" issues and "big" messages, things like war and peace, prosperity and depression, change versus the status quo, honest versus dishonest. He said "Political campaigns are music and the tuba will beat the clarinet every time. You've got to play big and loud over big issues, big things."

The earlier example of the 1992 vice presidential candidates was a good example of a contrasting "mirror opposite" strength that helped Clinton but was not "big" enough by itself to serve as the central message. Economic change was.

Question 5: Are you a credible messenger for this message?

Many campaigns devise the right message but their standard bearer has no credibility delivering it. When that happens, it's time to think about changing messages or getting out of the race. Often, right-message wrong-messenger candidates end up helping another candidate in the race who is in a better position to capitalize on public sentiment.

Question 6: Does the message help in some way to inoculate you on points where you are weak and subject to attack?

If Candidate A, who is running for sheriff, has no background in law enforcement, while Candidates B and C do, Candidate A may want to craft a message that attempts to turn his lack of experience into an asset. In this case, for example, if the last two sheriffs both had strong law enforcement experience when they were first elected but were forced to leave office in disgrace because of scandal, perhaps Candidate A could develop a message around the theme: *We've had enough corrupt insiders running our sheriff's office. We need new leadership and an outsider perspective on how to run an honest department.* It's a shot anyway.

Often inoculation can be done through the projection of vivid personal imagery. A very young candidate can wipe away a perception of being young-and-unprepared by demonstrating otherwise through mature carriage. A very old candidate can achieve a positive effect by projecting physical strength and vigor.

Franklin D. Roosevelt, who was severely crippled by polio, was unable to take even one unassisted step when he ran for President in 1932. The biggest criticism of him was that he was moving too fast, that he should slow down and give the country a chance to catch its breath. Ironic criticism of a paraplegic! FDR proved that a firmly established image of political mobility could go a long way toward eliminating what could have been an image of physical immobility. Whether he could have done that in modern times with news photographers capturing his every move is another question.

Nevertheless, Roosevelt was a master at the inoculation game and his career is a stunning example of how it can be played with success.

If you can answer these six questions with a certain "yes," then it is likely you have found a good message formulation. If you answered "no" to any of these questions, or have doubts, go back through all of the steps and do it over. Don't stop until you get it right.

If after trying again and again you still can't find the right message, you can always ask an objective person for help. Or, if you've already tried that option, you can always reconsider whether you should be a candidate for this office in this election. After all, if you can't convince yourself why you should win, how can you persuade the voters?

(*See worksheets for ancillary forms that relate to this article.*)

✓ What Not to Do in a Campaign

Here is a list of the most common mistakes made by aspiring politicians and their staffs. So, whatever your campaign role, here are 50 mistakes you should not make.

A Candidate Should Never:

1. Lie About Your Record.

We live in the Information Age. A candidate's every vote can be easily located in official journals or on computer. In addition, many political speeches are preserved on videotape and audio cassette. Before attempting to rewrite history, keep in mind that your opponent's staff probably possesses a thorough file on you. Any distortion may prompt a call to an enterprising reporter and destroy your credibility.

2. Manage Your Own Campaign.

Many good campaign managers have difficulty making the transition from the back room to the speaker's platform. By the same token, many good candidates do not make good campaign managers. A good candidate is one who allows the campaign manager to manage. Remember, one person cannot do two jobs at the same time—particularly when each job consumes 12 to 18 hours of each day.

3. Leave Fundraising to Others.

Unlike managing or scheduling, fundraising is a job where you must shoulder a significant part of the workload. A candidate not committed enough to ask supporters for money should not expect anyone else to do it for him.

4. Travel with a Large Entourage.

Even if you are not running as a populist, there is nothing that turns off voters more than a candidate who shows up with an entourage more befitting an oil-rich Arab potentate.

5. Fail to Articulate in 25 Words or Less Why You are Running.

If you can't do this, nothing else matters; your race will be over before it begins. To wit: the now-famous 1979 interview in which Ted Kennedy was unable to tell Roger Mudd why he was running for president.

6. Forget Your Family.

Win or lose, you will need them—and they will never forgive or forget your priorities. So be honest with them up front about the time commitments inherent in a political campaign.

7. Be Your Own Scheduler.

It is difficult—and politically unwise—for the candidate to decline a speaking invitation. So do not. Instead, let a staffer take the heat. Each campaign should have one person responsible for coordinating the candidate's schedule. When a supporter asks the candidate to attend an upcoming event, he or she should always be referred to the scheduler.

8. Attend a Sensitive Meeting Alone.

Traveling light does not mean flying solo. Whether you are in a court of law or the arena of politics, one person's word is as good as another's. The only way to prove your side of the story is to produce a witness.

9. Drive After Drinking.

Or, for that matter, talk after drinking. Any candidate who needs an explanation for this piece of advice does not deserve to win. This is yet another good reason not to travel alone. Besides being a witness at sensitive meeting, a traveling aide can fulfill the function of designated driver.

10. Try to be Someone you are not.

More than any specific issue voters can smell a phony a mile away. No one likes to be hustled, and any candidate who appears to be insincere or politically motivated will have a very short career.

A Campaign Manager Should Never:

11. Antagonize the Candidate's Spouse.

Whatever you do, under no circumstances should you irritate a spouse or an immediate family member. Regardless of gender, the spouse will almost certainly try to run the campaign. In so doing, he or she will inevitably distract the real campaign manager. If you want to keep your job, grin and bear it. The person sleeping with the candidate is more likely to have the candidate's ear.

12. Hire a Staff Without Clear Responsibilities.

Campaigns are crazy enough as is. Vague job descriptions not only waste time and resources, they spur turf warfare. You are much better off if your staff's competitive juices are being directed toward the opposing campaign rather than each other.

13. Leave Confidential Information on Your Desk.

Information is power, and campaign offices are full of people with less than altruistic agendas. Moles do not exist only in John Le Carre novels, and rival power centers are not the exclusive province of large multinational corporations. Each can be found in many campaign offices. Take no chances.

14. Put a Steering Committee Behind the Steering Wheel.

A Steering Committee is a good place for prominent people willing to donate their name and money to a campaign—but not much else. They should be paraded about for all to see; they should not be in charge of the campaign. Leave that to full-time professionals.

15. Worry about March Momentum in a November Election.

Starting early does not mean treating each day like Election Day. The early months are ideal for raising money, devising a strategy, setting vote targets, and building name identification. If you are making all the right moves early, your polls will show momentum later, even if they do not reflect it now. Such pacing will also go far to forestall candidate and staff preelection burnout.

16. Ignore the Inner Circle.

Every candidate has a circle of close friends whom he or she has known for years and whose opinions he respects. These people are trusted confidants and have only the candidate's best interests at heart. Even if they are not particularly astute, you must treat them with deference.

17. Keep the Candidate in the Dark.

A candidate does not need to know every detail of the campaign, but does need to have confidence that the campaign is functioning properly. Candidates do not like surprises. Big surprises—or lots of little ones—beget ex-campaign managers.

18. Share Your Doubts of Winning.

Campaign managers are motivators—and at times must be actors. The quickest way to insure defeat is to present a defeatist attitude to the staff.

19. Put Anything in Writing that You Would Fear Seeing on the Front of a Newspaper.

Letters, notes, and memos have a way of popping up in the strangest places at the strangest times. That is why confidential and politically sensitive information always should be verbalized, preferably face-to-face.

20. Give Consultants Too Much Leeway.

Like attorneys, consultants' time is their stock in trade. The final month of the campaign is not a good time to learn that your consultants are paid whether they win or lose.

A Fundraising Chairman Should Never:

21. Ask for Money Only Once.

Even the postman always rings twice; a fundraising chairman should call upon people four or five times. If a donor has not given you a flat-out "No," he or she ultimately may make a donation. This rule is particularly applicable to those who have already contributed. Your donors believe in and have invested in your candidate. That is why a contributor who has given once is far more likely to give in the future than someone who has not donated before.

22. Think Small.

The only thing worse than not asking enough people for money is to not ask people for enough money. It is far better to flatter people by asking them for too much than to insult them by asking for too little.

23. Take Rejection Personally.

People will say no. Sometimes even a lot of people will say no. But if love means never having to say you're sorry, fundraising means never feeling sorry for yourself. Expect to be turned down a lot. It comes with the territory.

24. Assume a Pledge is a Contribution.

People mean well, but when all is said and done there is usually more said than done. A fundraising chairman should not count money in the bank until it has actually been deposited.

25. Keep Sloppy Records.

Bad bookkeeping not only reduces your ability to raise money in the future, it can get you in trouble with the Federal Election Commission or the state election board. Any such incident is sure to embarrass the candidate.

26. Work for a Candidate Who Will Not Ask for Money.

A campaign involves a major commitment by many people—especially the candidate. Anyone not able and willing to make that kind of commitment, both in terms of time and money, should not be running—or you should not be working for him.

27. Worry About Your Batting Average.

Volume is the key to effective fundraising. That is why a fundraising chairman should never be reluctant to swing for the fences. Even if you strike out a lot, this is one instance where you are better off going three for ten than two for two.

28. Show Your Independence.

Contributors rarely donate money out of the goodness of their hearts They frequently expect something in return, even if that something is merely access. They see the fundraiser as a conduit between themselves and the candidate. A savvy fundraiser promotes that image by staying in close touch with the candidate.

29. Be Vague.

The more specific you are in making a request, the greater likelihood that someone will contribute. It is even better if you can tell people precisely how their money will be spent. Tell them you need X amount for a new TV spot, or Y amount for a GOTV drive.

A Press Secretary Should Never:

30. Leak to the Same Source Repeatedly.

The largest newspaper or media outlet should not receive every hot tip. Otherwise, the others will resent you for always giving the break to the big guy. Even if you save the biggest scoops for the biggest papers, toss a few morsels to the smaller sources every once in a while.

31. Go Over a Reporter's Head.

If you have a serious complaint, approach the reporter directly. If you have not complained much in the past and you really believe you have been wronged, you will earn points for expressing your displeasure directly to the reporter's face. Complaining to his or her boss will be seen as a direct assault on his job and pocketbook. Given reporters' pay scales, that is a mistake you do not want to make.

32. Be Afraid to Demand Access to the Candidate.

Reporters are cynical and quick to judge a press secretary's effectiveness. A press secretary kept out of the loop is useless, and few campaigns function as welfare centers.

33. Answer a Question When You Are Uncertain of the Answer.

Innocent mistakes can derail a campaign. You are better to let a deadline pass without a response than to have to correct a mistake in the next news cycle. But be sure you do respond.

34. Complain Repeatedly to Reporters About their Stories.

A premier rule of candidate-media relations is: Never argue with people who use ink by the barrel. You will quickly be reduced to background noise if you call a reporter every time you have a problem with a story. It also will prove counterproductive; just to show independence, the reporter probably will jab your candidate more.

35. Make Something Out of Nothing.

If you oversell a story, the press may buy it the first time but rarely a second and never a third. Then, when you really do have a significant story to promote, you will be ignored. A candidate who sees an empty press section at a major speech is likely to find a new press secretary.

36. Ignore Small Details and Personal Eccentricities.

Little details like what time an event starts and the exact location become magnified when a candidate has 13 events scheduled in a single day. Be sure you know precisely all of the details of a particular event—and make sure the traveling aide knows them, too. Also, keep in mind the candidate's personal preferences and eccentricities. Behind an unhappy candidate often lies an unemployed scheduler.

37. Force the Candidate to Backtrack Across the District.

Candidates find few things as frustrating as spending most of a day riding in a car when he or she could be outside pressing the flesh. Your job is to maximize the candidate's exposure—and minimize the amount of time wasted.

38. Commit to an October Event in May.

A campaign needs flexibility in the final three weeks before Election Day. Having to cancel scheduled events at the end of the campaign to provide this flexibility will unnecessarily anger a lot of people who are about to step into the polling booth.

A Researcher Should Never:

39. Overschedule Prior to a Debate.

The candidate must feel comfortable prior to a debate—or you risk a campaign-ending gaffe. An election can even turn on whether the candidate had time to shower and shave. Remember Richard Nixon's five o'clock shadow.

40. Schedule Early Mornings Following Late Nights.

A candidate is only human. He or she needs time to rest and unwind. At best, a tired candidate is uninspiring. At worst, he or she can make a costly mistake.

41. Make Verbal Commitments.

Misunderstandings between the campaign organization and committed or potential supporters regarding the candidate's time can be very unpleasant, and potentially harmful. The best way to protect the campaign is to put all arrangements in writing—in advance.

42. Leak An Attack.

The element of surprise is critical in politics. To maximize the success of an attack, you should do everything possible to catch your opponent off guard. The fewer people who know about your planned attack, the better.

43. Impersonate Someone Else.

There are many ways you can go about digging up information on your opponent. One way not to is to tell people that you are a reporter, government agent, or anything else. If the press ever finds out, and it probably will, the campaign would suffer a painful body blow.

44. Hurl Undocumented Charges.

Since both you and your opponent are public figures, he will not have much luck suing you if you slander him. But hurling accusations without proof has a way of turning the public against you. And that is the real jury you should be trying to impress.

45. Ignore Your Candidate's Vulnerabilities.

People in glass houses should not throw stones or other large missiles. Know your own candidate's weaknesses, so you know what attacks may arise—and can potentially backfire. This will also help you respond quickly and cleanly to any opposition attacks. You must make sure you know more about your candidate than your opponent does.

No One Should Ever:

46. Lie

When the lie blows up in your face—and it will—the candidate is not going to be the one to take the fall. Any attempt at damage control means you lose your job. If you refuse to lie, you still may be fired, but you will leave with your dignity—and future—intact. This is especially true of press secretaries, who once caught lying will quickly find they are of no value to the campaign—or any future campaign.

47. Forget to Say Thank You.

You do not need a Ph.D. in psychology to know people are more likely to respond positively if they feel appreciated. Campaigns are long and arduous, and staffers are invariably underpaid and overworked. An occasional "well done" and "thank you" goes a long way toward increasing productivity—and often compensate for an ill-timed temper tantrum.

48. Forget Who is the Ultimate Boss.

The quickest path to the employment line is to forget whose name is on the ballot. Only the voter can fire a candidate. But a candidate can easily fire a staffer—or a campaign manager.

49. Ignore Staff Meetings.

For a campaign to function at an optimal level, the staff must work as a team. Staff meetings not only allow you to exchange information, but reinforce the cooperative aspect of the campaign. They also allow you to remind everyone that the campaign is only big enough for one ego: the candidate's.

50. Break the Law.

It simply is not worth it. The press almost invariably finds out and, at best, your candidate is only mildly damaged. At worst, the campaign is completely derailed and you may never again work in a campaign.

✓ Joseph Napolitan's 100 Greatest Hints
Joseph Napolitan

Trade secrets from a respected pioneer of the political consulting industry:

1. Strategy is the single most important factor in a political campaign. This is the most important lesson I have learned in 30 years. The right strategy can survive a mediocre campaign, but even a brilliant campaign is likely to fall if the strategy is wrong. The strategy must be adapted to fit the campaign; you cannot adapt the campaign to fit the strategy. Also, this small but essential point: If you cannot write it down, you do not have a strategy.

2. There is no such thing as a bandwagon effect. For years, in countries all over the world, including the United States, campaign workers have told me, "People here like to be with a winner; they will vote for the candidate they think will win." Thereupon they proceed to release to the press poll reports showing their candidate ahead in the misguided expectation that this information will cause voters to line up behind their candidate.

If anything, I have found the reverse to be true: The supporters whose candidate is perceived as behind are motivated to work harder, while those of the candidate seen to be ahead tend to become overconfident and lazy.

Perhaps the most glaring example of this occurred in Venezuela in 1978 where the candidate of Accion Democratica, Luis Pinerua Ordaz, ran double-page newspaper ads for two weeks before the election with banner headlines reading: "The Election Is Over. Pinerua Has Won!"

Well, for Pinerua the election was over: He lost. But the most interesting statistic was this: The turnout in that election was 5 percent lower than in the 1973 election, and the drop was greatest in areas of normal AD strength. Apparently Adecos believed their leader, so they stayed home. A costly lesson.

3. Polls are essential, but do not be fooled by them. The only practical reason to take a political poll is to obtain information that will help you win the election. If the poll will not do that, you are better off spending your money elsewhere. Perhaps the least important information in a political poll is who is ahead at any given moment.

Polls are not infallible, especially in primaries, or when they are taken before the campaign actually begins. I will not run a campaign without adequate polling—but neither will I place total dependence on the polls. Nor will I make my polls public unless there is an unusual and extremely good reason for doing so.

4. Never underestimate the importance of a divided party. I worked on the presidential election in the Dominican Republic for Jacobo Majluta, president of the Senate and candidate of the PRD, the same party as the president, who was not seeking reelection. The party was badly split by a primary struggle in which Majluta defeated Jose Francisco Pena Gomez, mayor of Santo Domingo, friend and confidant of President Salvador Jorge Blanco.

After a shaky start, Majluta's campaign moved along nicely. I was confident we would win, but I was astonished when we lost to 78-year-old, legally blind Joaquin Balaguer. Our exit polls showed Majluta with 51 per cent of the vote; reportedly Balaguer's exit polls also showed Majluta with 51 per cent of the vote (this was a three-way race). In the end, we lost by a couple of points. Later we learned that the intraparty rift was so fierce that President Jorge Blanco himself voted against his own party's candidate for president, and many Pena Gomez supporters actively worked for Balaguer, the main opposition candidate.

Our surveys did not detect this phenomenon. We underestimated the damage caused by divisions in the party. And it cost us dearly.

5. Timing is critical. Using an issue too early—or too late—can nullify its impact. For a candidate who is not well known, an early media campaign might be essential. For a well-known candidate, early media might be wasteful.

If your opponent makes an easily refutable charge, sometimes it is better to let him repeat it several times, so that he will look silly when you counterattack. But sometimes it is essential to answer the charge immediately. It is difficult to teach timing. Much of it is instinctive. And in this era of computerized campaigns, it is nice to know that human judgment still plays a critical role in the campaign.

6. If something works, keep using it until it stops working. I have been involved in several campaigns in which our opponents ran television spots we knew were hurting us, and then they inexplicably pulled them off the air. After one of these campaigns, I asked a consultant to the opponent why this was done. He said they felt the spot had served its purpose, and they wanted to come on the air with new material. New is not necessarily better. Or, as they say, if it ain't broke, don't fix it.

7. Make sure the message is clear and understandable. Part of an overall strategy involves defining the right message or messages to be communicated to specific target groups, or the electorate as a whole. Whatever the message is, it should be clear and easily understood by everyone. The classic example is Ronald Reagan's message in the 1980 presidential campaign: "I will make

America strong and lower taxes." Nothing could be clearer—or more effective. If Jimmy Carter had a message in that campaign, no one has yet figured it out.

8. Never underestimate the intelligence of the voters, nor overestimate the amount of knowledge at their disposal. The electorate is not stupid. But often it does not have sufficient information at its disposal to make right (that is, favorable to your candidate) decisions. It is not their responsibility to go out and find this information; it is your responsibility to serve it up to them, on a silver platter if necessary.

If, at the end of a campaign, the voters still do not understand what your candidate is trying to tell them, it is the candidate's fault—not the voters'. No longer am I surprised at the sophistication shown by the voters in response to survey research questions, but I occasionally still am astonished by the lack of sophistication on the part of the candidate, and often that of his staff.

9. Negative attacks are better handled by third parties in paid media. This is not the place to discuss the merits or demerits, the morality or immorality, of negative attacks on an opponent. Personally, I follow a simple rule: The candidate's public record is fair game for attack, his private life is not.

But negative attacks are a fact of political life, and if you are going to use them, you might as well use them as effectively as you can. I prefer never to have my candidate attack his opponent in paid television or radio spots; I prefer always to have my candidate emerge as the "nice guy" on television.

When you feel an attack is justified, then let the negative message be carried by an announcer, or the copy in a print ad, or by someone other than the candidate.

10. Do not underestimate the power and penetration of radio. I have been singing this song for a long time, but some people do not want to tune in. Granted, television is the most emotional and persuasive of all the media—but radio is a close second and has several advantages over television: It is less expensive to produce; it can be produced quickly; it can be targeted more effectively than television; and it costs less to put on the air.

To me, one of the worst—and laziest—things you can do in a campaign is run the sound track of a television spot as a radio spot. This is as bad as running the same copy in a television ad and a print ad. They are different mediums. I have seen candidates spend $150,000 or more on television production in a campaign and then scream bloody murder when asked to approve a $25,000 budget for radio production.

Actually, there are more good television producers around than good radio producers, but just because someone can produce a decent television spot does not automatically mean he can produce effective radio. And they prove it all the time.

11. Do not underestimate the impact of an unpopular national administration. This is another one of those hidden obstacles, like trying to measure the impact of a divided party. I also believe this phenomenon is most important during presidential elections. Assuming the merits of the candidates are about equal, if you represent the party of an unpopular administration, you probably will lose. This is a condition to factor into your equation when you are trying to determine the attitudes of voters.

12. Perception is more important than reality. You do not have to be in this business very long before you learn this fact. If the voters think Candidate X is an honest man, he can steal the gold leaf off the statehouse dome and get away with it; if they think Candidate B is a crook, he can have four cardinals and 16 bishops attest to his honesty, and people will still think he is a crook.

The best living example of this (and maybe the best in all of history) is Ronald Reagan: He has American voters (a majority of them anyway) convinced he is protecting their money with a tight fist, while in reality the deficits his government has incurred are staggering almost beyond imagination.

And while Reagan is mortgaging the farm, he also is accusing Democrats of being the big spenders—and getting away with it. You take reality; I'll take perception any day.

13. Do not complicate the campaign. There are three simple steps to winning any campaign: (1) Decide what you are going to say. (2) Decide how you are going to say it. (3) Say it.

I have been in campaigns with so many committees, subcommittees, liaison committees, special-interest directors, colonels, captains, lieutenants and sublieutenants you have trouble finding directions to the men's room, never mind trying to receive a clear picture of what is going on.

Being a campaign manager or consultant in a major campaign is like being a professional football coach: You might know 1,000 different plays, but you can only use about 25 of them in any given game.

Campaign managers can waste money on many silly things—like expensive newsletters mailed mainly to supporters and campaign workers—only to wind up with insufficient funds to pay for an adequate media campaign. Everything should be as clear and uncomplicated as you can make it, from the table of organization to the graphics on the letterhead.

14. Protect home base first. If you have a strong base of support, protect that first, then go after other votes. It also is easier to increase the percentage of your vote in a favorable environment than to find an equal number of votes in a hostile environment. Do not take your base for granted.

15. Do not be afraid to invade opposition territory. This might seem to contradict the previous point, but read carefully: First you protect home base, then you invade opposition territory. I often run into candidates who will not speak before certain audiences because "they're all Republicans." (I'm sure Republican consultants run into the same problem with Republican candidates.)

I try to explain to my reluctant candidate why he should talk to those groups in very simple terms, something like this: "If you speak to 100 Democrats, and you have all their votes before you go in, all you can do, at best, is hold your own, and you might lose some. If you talk to 100 Republicans who start off being opposed to you, you can't lose any votes—and you just might gain some."

White candidates should go into black neighborhoods, black candidates should go into white neighborhoods; rich candidates should go into poor neighborhoods; city slickers should go down to the farm.

16. What you say in Peoria can be heard in Pasadena. Candidates sometimes have a peculiarly anachronistic idea that once they are away from their home turf they can say things they would not say at home. My favorite example of this occurred way back in 1962, when I was doing Endicott Peabody's campaign for governor against the incumbent Republican governor of Massachusetts, John Volpe.

Governor Volpe, a competent man who later went on to serve in the Nixon cabinet, made a speech in Portland, Oregon, in which he said he was opposed to the Medicare program proposed by President Kennedy. Not surprisingly, we heard about it in Boston. This was only a few days before the election. I churned out an instant brochure with this message: "Governor Volpe is opposed to President Kennedy's Medicare program. Endicott Peabody is in favor of it."

17. Try not to self-destruct. It is astonishing how often this simple rule is broken. Although I concede other factors were involved, I also am convinced that Walter Mondale lost whatever chance he might have had to win the U.S. presidency in 1984 in his acceptance speech at the Democratic National Convention when he announced that if he were elected he would raise taxes.

I cite Mondale only because the example is recent and glaring; candidates manage to shoot themselves in the foot with astonishing regularity.

18. Do not let your opponent have a free ride. Although I am not a great proponent of the negative campaign, neither can I be considered a "turn the other cheek" consultant. Too often I see, or work for, candidates who refuse to answer an opponent's charges, refuse to refute reckless accusations made against them, or do not want to "dignify" the opponent by replying to his remarks.

If your candidate has a solid lead, and you are confident your campaign plan is so well designed it can compensate for these charges, or if you frequently research the opponent's charges and find they are having no impact at all, then maybe, maybe, you can get away with letting your opponent have a free ride. But I'd advise against doing so.

The candidate does not have to refute each and every charge personally, but the campaign should do so. Otherwise you run the risk that the unrefuted statement, often repeated, will be perceived as the truth, and then you can be in real trouble. Also, you never should underestimate the cumulative damage such unanswered charges can cause.

19. Endorsements are fine if you use them properly. Popularity is not easily transferable. If the most popular political figure in the district (or in the state or in the country) endorses your candidate, this does not necessarily mean all his voters are going to vote for your candidate.

Used carefully and selectively, endorsements can be extremely helpful. Last year I was involved in a campaign where our opponent claimed my candidate was supported only by the political bosses. As a result, our first wave of television spots consisted of man-on-the-street interviews of average, ordinary people saying good things about my candidate.

If a candidate is thought to be an intellectual lightweight, find some heavy thinkers to endorse his candidacy and talk about his intelligence; if he is perceived to lack minority support, find some blacks and Hispanics or whatever the minority groups are in the district to endorse him in commercials.

I'm not much for the "celebrity endorsement," but sometimes testimonials can be given by nonpolitical people who might say, "I've never publicly endorsed a political candidate before, but let me tell you why in this election I'm supporting Joe Jones...."

20. Do not create exaggerated expectations—especially if you are likely to win. This is especially true in gubernatorial or presidential elections in which your candidate has a good chance of winning and hopes eventually to run for reelection. If you promise more than you can deliver, this will cost you at the next election. If the people forget what you have promised (and some of them are sure to remember), you can be certain your opponent next time around will remind them.

Better to be more modest and to set goals you have a reasonable chance of achieving. Also, sometimes promises are so exaggerated they simply do not ring true and can damage a candidate's credibility.

21. Take nothing for granted. This is critical advice, even if it is almost impossible to follow, because at times you simply must rely on the information provided by others in the campaign. In a recent presidential election, we were burned badly in the rural areas of a county, even though I had been assured everything was fine in those areas.

If you are suspicious that something might not be as it seems or as it should be, run an independent check. This might mean a flash poll using a different pollster in an area you have doubts about. If you are told money is no problem, be suspicious.

22. If you make a mistake, admit it and try something else. There are few perfect campaigns. Inevitably, mistakes occur. Usually, in a long campaign, a few mistakes won't hurt much—unless you compound them by repeating them.

In one campaign I was involved in, a television producer made several spots that generated a howl of protest from supporters of the candidate, who claimed they would withdraw their support if the spots continued to run. Faced with this, the producer became stubborn, said it would take awhile for the message of the spots to sink in, and urged they be run for at least two weeks. The campaign manager wisely decided to withdraw them immediately; supporters quieted down, and the candidate eventually won.

Earlier I suggested, "If it ain't broke, don't fix it." The opposite is true as well: "If it is broke, fix it." Everybody makes mistakes; the smart ones correct them.

23. The little things often are important. To reach people, you must relate to their level of understanding. For example, there was little complaint on the part of the American public about the country's bloated military budget, because few people could understood what the numbers meant. But when it was revealed the Air Force was paying $640 for a toilet seat or $125 for a hammer you could buy in a hardware store for five bucks, then people became aroused, because they could understand and relate to the situation in their own terms.

Sherman Adams, President Eisenhower's chief of staff, ran an effective White House and was one of the most powerful men in the government, but he was forced to resign, and the credibility of the presidency was damaged, because he accepted a vicuna coat from a Boston financier, a coat worth maybe $200 at the time.

The lesson here is do not always jump on the big things; the little one could prove to be much more important in turning the campaign.

24. Be leery of primary polls. Great advances have been made in political polling in the past 20 years, but one area that remains difficult to predict is the party primary. This holds true on all levels, from presidential primaries to local elections. One reason for this is the usually low turnout in the primary. Poll respondents may favor one candidate or another, but when only one in three or four turns out to vote, the results can be seriously skewed.

Even when several screening questions are asked to eliminate those less likely to vote, the actual voting returns often bear little resemblance to poll results. If your candidate is running ahead in the primary poll, do not assume you necessarily are going to win—and if you are running behind, do not be discouraged, because primaries produce strange results.

25. Recognize your own limitations. We are all better at some things than we are at others. No one I know in this business is equally talented in all phases of politics or campaigning. The best ones know what they do best and are not hesitant about bringing in experts in other fields.

Sometimes, individuals who are truly talented in one area, such as television production, put themselves and their candidates in big trouble by attempting to expand this expertise into areas in which they are much less effective. Pollsters are another group who fall into this trap: They often believe they are expert in designing campaign strategy just because they have obtained some interesting numbers in their poll. What's worse, campaigns, even on a high level, often make the mistake of confusing producers and pollsters and other specialists with strategists who have the ability to put all component parts of a campaign into place.

26. Don't panic over mistakes. They will happen. I never have been in a perfect campaign, and I doubt anyone else has. Mistakes will happen. Usually they are not serious; occasionally they are. The important thing is not to spend a lot of time crying about the mistake or criticizing the person who made it, but to decide how to handle it. In many cases, the best thing is merely to ignore it and forget about it.

Human feelings are important here, too. You do not want to ruin the morale of the campaign staff or unnecessarily embarrass or humiliate one of your good workers because of a mistake. If the same person keeps making the same kinds of mistakes, that's another matter, and you might have to fire him or her.

27. If you do not have to use negative campaigning, don't; if you do, make it sting. Like many consultants, I think there is too much negative campaigning these days, and the reasons are easy to understand: It is easier to move people to vote against someone than for someone. Nevertheless, although it might sound old fashioned, I think every candidate has an obligation to tell the people what he would do if he were elected and what solutions he has to their problems.

When you feel compelled to use negative campaigning, make it sting. If you are going to do it, do it right. Do not just rap someone on the knuckles, give him a good whack alongside the head. I prefer not to use negative campaigning if I do not have to, but I also prefer to win with negative campaigning than to lose without.

I do not subscribe to the concept of never mentioning your opponent by name. If you are going to call someone a son-of-a-bitch, leave no doubts in voters' minds about whom you mean.

I also believe negative attacks should be confined to a person's record and not to his personal habits—and never to his family. A candidate's record should be subjected to careful scrutiny and attack where warranted; the fact that his son has been arrested on drug charges or his wife is an alcoholic are, in my opinion, private family problems and not subjects for discussion in a campaign.

28. Dominate the dominant medium. Not long ago, I wandered into a bookstore, where I saw a book on how to run political campaigns. I looked in the appendix to see if my name was mentioned. When I checked the references to me, I found one that said, "Many campaign managers follow the advice of veteran political consultant Joe Napolitan to dominate the dominant medium."

Now I don't ever remember saying that, and I don't know where the authors of the book dug it up, but I think it's a hell of an idea. If it actually was mine, I'm sorry to have forgotten, and if it were someone else's, I hope he or she gets the credit due.

It makes such good sense. The dominant medium varies. In many campaigns, it is television. But in some it might be newspaper advertising or radio. In a contest for a primary nomination in an overwhelmingly Democratic congressional district in New York City, it would be direct mail. Whatever it is, concentrate your resources to make sure you achieve dominance, and chances are you will do well in the campaign.

29. Campaigns should be fun. Campaigning is an intense business, full of pressure and tension. But it also should be fun. If a campaign does not have its moments of joy and laughter or sheer insanity, then it can become boring and depressing.

There's nothing more debilitating than a dull campaign or a humorless candidate. I have worked for a few, and I do not want to do so again.

30. Establish your candidate's own credibility before you launch a negative campaign. No one has ever done this more effectively than Ronald Reagan in his 1980 campaign against Jimmy Carter. Today, all people remember about that election is that it was a Reagan landslide; but it didn't start out that way. Going into the campaign, voters had serious doubts about Reagan's political philosophy, and his potential to push the U.S. into war.

Wisely, Reagan spent the early months of his campaign easing those doubts and establishing his own credibility. Not until his campaign advisers were convinced that his own credibility was established did they launch a devastating negative campaign.

There is no doubt in my mind that negative campaign would have been much less effective if they had begun it earlier. There is a tendency today for candidates whose own positions are not known, whose own credibility has not been established, to go on the attack. My strong advice is to concentrate on the positives and establish your candidate's own credibility before making attacks on your opponent.

31. Do not confuse education with intelligence. There is a lot to be said for gut instincts and street smarts in political campaigns; it is not always the best educated people who are the most politically intelligent. Almost everywhere I have worked, I have encountered people with weak education credits and high intelligence.

The same is true of voters. Early in my career, I learned never to underestimate the intelligence of the voters nor overestimate the amount of information at their disposal. Providing them with the information is the campaign's responsibility; their intelligence will take over from there.

32. An election is like a one-day sale. This is what makes timing so crucial in a political campaign. If you are selling Fords or Toyotas, the customer can buy his car today, tomorrow, next week, or next year. But the product (candidate) in a campaign (sale) is available for only a few hours on one day.

You must gear your campaign to peak as close to Election Day as possible. Too often we have seen campaigns peak on Labor Day when the election is in November. From then on, it is downhill. It might be better to have a late peak than an early one; at least that way the campaign will be moving in the right direction on Election Day.

You have certain controls in the peaking process, such as media time buys and when to make major announcements, and although you might not be able to fine-tune the campaign to peak precisely when you wish, how effectively you manipulate the controls will determine how close you come to your ideal peak.

33. Differentiate between the essential and the nonessential. The wise candidate or leader learns early to distinguish between them, to make the essential decisions and take the essential actions himself and to leave the nonessentials to staff and others in his government.

The same guideline applies to consultants: Do not make a big thing of something that is not really important or essential, but if it is essential, utilize all your resources to achieve the objective.

34. They won't let you run in the general election unless you win the primary. It's just like baseball, where they won't let you play in the World Series unless you win the pennant. Yet how many times have we seen campaigns where the candidate thinks and talks of nothing but how he is going to beat his opponent in the general election, paying scant attention to his opponent in the primary?

In a classic case in Massachusetts, the incumbent governor, a Democrat, prepared television commercials and a whole panoply of other campaign materials to use against an incumbent Republican senator. His primary opponent was a mayor of a medium-sized city, and the decision was made to ignore the mayor in the primary, not to respond to any charge or attack.

All the governor's television commercials, signs, and bumperstickers went into the trash the morning after the primary, because the unheralded mayor had scored a smashing upset.

Advice for Candidates

35. The size of crowds bears little relationship to the vote. Another example from Venezuela: During one campaign, Accion Democratica held a rally in downtown Caracas. It was mobbed; more than 50,000 people turned out. Two days later, the Socialist Party, which never receives more than 5 percent of the vote, staged a rally on the same site with the same turnout.

In 1968, I was director of media for Vice President Hubert Humphrey in his campaign against Richard Nixon. One day Nixon toured Philadelphia; the crowds were enormous. Humphrey went through a few days later, the crowds were small. Humphrey won Philadelphia by 100,000 votes. The Republicans obviously did a better job in turning out the crowd, but at least in this case, not the vote.

36. Do not be hung up on slogans and logos. Too often a candidate or his advertising manager will be so hung up on a slogan or a logo that they will insist they be used in every television spot, every radio spot, every brochure, every print ad, and so forth. Use them where they work, and if they seem out of place, use something else or nothing at all.

37. Start early. You can never start planning your campaign too early. You can begin the campaign too soon; that's something else again. In my own experience, the best example I know of long planning period/short campaign was Mike Gravel's upset victory over Alaska Senator Ernest Gruening in the 1968 Democratic primary. We planned Gravel's campaign in December 1966; the execution of the campaign, pretty much according to what we had decided to do 18 months later, occurred during two weeks in August 1968.

By starting early, you have plenty of time to take and analyze polls, study your opponent and his likely moves in depth, design and discuss various possible strategies, select the best specialists to work on the campaign, and mentally prepare your candidate.

When you start late, it does not mean you have fewer things to do, but merely less time to do them.

38. Beware of easy solutions to complex problems. There are none. If the problem is complex, are the solution also must be complex. There are ways of providing simple explanations of proposed solutions, but anyone who comes up with a "simple" solution to crime, drugs, unemployment, inflation, housing, or a myriad of other complex problems clearly doesn't even understand the problem, never mind the solution.

39. Exude confidence—but never overconfidence. Personally, I prefer a low-key approach in this area: Express confidence that you will win, but say you expect a hard, tough campaign. This is especially true in a campaign where you are expected to win, start out strong in the polls, and then are lulled into a sense of false security and fail to do everything needed to ensure victory.

If anything, it is better to be less confident than too confident; it also will keep your staff working harder.

40. You need not oppose every position or statement by your opposition. Even the opposition is right sometimes, just as a stopped clock is right twice a day. By criticizing everything, you dilute the strength of your own criticism. I prefer to reduce the frequency of attacks, or counterattacks, but to make them really sting when you do use them.

41. A power base helps. It might not be absolutely essential to have a power base in a political campaign, but it sure helps. The base can be geographic (the candidate's home state, city, or county) or demographic (blacks, Hispanics, elderly, liberals, conservatives, whatever).

If you start with a power base, you have something to build on. If you do not, your first step is to create one, and that detracts from other things you can do. Any candidate who starts with a built-in power base has an advantage.

42. You are never going to please everyone. Candidates sometimes try to run campaigns by consensus; they think they can appeal to everyone, please everyone, without getting anyone angry. This just does not happen. Campaigns are a series of decisions, many of them easy, some of them difficult. Every time you make a difficult decision, some group of voters is not going to like it.

But if you do not make any decisions, or if you attempt to water down your positions so they become meaningless, no one is going to like it.

Advice for Consultants

43. Television spots showing large crowds are of little real value; they just make the candidate feel good. In one Latin American campaign, the advertising agency proudly showed me 22 spots they had produced for their candidate. At least 18 of them showed nothing but cheering crowds; not one of them showed the candidate talking to the people about what he would do for them if he were elected.

We made the necessary adjustments in that campaign, but this phenomenon exists, and it sometimes is difficult to persuade inexperienced campaign workers that such spots really do not help very much.

44. Every campaign is different; every campaign is the same. The object of any political campaign is to persuade voters to mark their "X" after one name instead of another. In every campaign, certain basics are similar if not identical. Every campaign contains the same essential ingredients: polls, strategy, message, advertising, organization, fund-raising.

But each campaign has its points of dissimilarity, and the approach and strategy must be defined and adapted to conform with existing elements. Just as generals often are accused of fighting the last war, we never should allow ourselves to "fight the last campaign." We must adjust our tactics to meet current needs.

45. You might be able to polish a candidate but you cannot really change him. I have seen candidates who have improved (and some who have gotten worse) in the course of campaigning, but

I have never been involved with a candidate who really changed very much. Sure, you can do some cosmetic things: Convince him to wear dark suits, cut his hair differently, change the color of his socks, buy more attractive eyeglasses, maybe even get him to be more prompt.

But almost all the time, you really just work with what you have, so you might as well adjust to this at the beginning of the campaign and adapt your campaign plan to fit your candidate.

46. Instill some sense of priority in your candidate. Rationally and logically, every candidate knows that just about every appearance he makes on television, especially in paid commercials purchased in prime time, will be seen by more voters than will see him in person during the entire course of the campaign. But virtually every candidate resists spending the time necessary to permit the best possible television production.

This is why it is so important to have the campaign scheduler someone who understands the importance of various activities, such as media production, and who will cancel a breakfast with 50 supporters so the candidate can have more time to prepare for television, or rehearse an important speech, or take a day's rest, or discuss critical strategy decisions.

47. Proceed cautiously in foreign elections. First, because you are a e foreigner, there will be natural skepticism about your ability or understanding of the problems. If you are an American, these problems usually are compounded.

A good friend of mine used to drive me to distraction in early discussions with presidential candidates in foreign countries. After one two-hour meeting, he was prepared to design the whole campaign, tell the locals what they were doing wrong, and give some very simple solutions to extremely complicated problems. Some of his analysis was right on the mark, but its effectiveness was dissipated by the speed with which he made his recommendations.

The first objective in dealing with candidates and their staffs in foreign countries is to win their confidence. Ideas they might reject if offered in the first meeting might well be accepted, or at least seriously considered, after they have developed some confidence in you. Proceed slowly and cautiously, even if you know right from the beginning what needs to be done.

48. Always let the campaign staff know you are not looking for their job. In my first meeting with the candidate's staff I give a little speech about my role in the campaign. I explain that I have no interest in being the governor's chief of staff or press secretary or head of the state lottery; all want to do is help win the election and go home.

I want them to look on me as a resource, a support system, not a threat. Usually this works, but not always; I know that in some campaigns some staff members, invariably those least secure about their own abilities, try to undercut my recommendations. Not much you can do about this; it's an occupational hazard.

But if you make the effort at the beginning to win the cooperation of the candidate's staff, and assure them your role ends on Election Day, then it's usually an easier campaign.

49. If your advice is not being accepted, quit. If your advice constantly is being overruled or ignored, you have two choices: Give in or get out. I always prefer to get out—not that it happens all that often, maybe three or four times in 30 years. Once I was retained as media consultant in a New York gubernatorial primary. One afternoon I had a cup of coffee with the representative of the advertising agency hired by the campaign that turned into a mutual complaint session. By the time we finished our second cup of coffee, we both agreed to quit.

In a situation like this, I usually tell the candidate and/or his campaign manager, "Look, you are telling people I am the media director in this campaign, but I really am not, because you are not accepting my recommendations. You are paying me money for advice you are not using, and I am spending my time working in a campaign where my advice obviously is not needed or wanted. Why don't we part company and stay friends?"

50. Settle your financial arrangements at the beginning. Better not to do a campaign than to do it and not be paid for it. You learn as you grow older. Early in my career, after meeting with the candidate and his team, I often would design what amounted to a whole campaign plan and submit it with my proposal to work for the candidate. Until I became smarter, they often would reject the proposal for whatever reason, and then use the campaign plan pretty much as I had written it. Now I will not write a plan until we have agreed on a contract.

There are certain expenses built into my fees. For example, first-class air fare. When you make 40 trips out of the country in a single year, as I do, it is not just a question of comfort, it is a question of survival.

Unless I know the candidate well or have worked for him before, I now insist on quarterly payments in advance. This is especially important overseas, where you essentially have no recourse if a candidate or party refuses to pay for your services.

I am perfectly willing to do campaigns for nothing or for a token fee, if the candidate is a good friend, or if it is a cause or candidate I really believe in and want to work for. But if we are talking about a business arrangement, it should be conducted on a businesslike basis—and that means being paid on schedule.

The surest way to avoid problems is to receive a chunk of money up front; at least that way you are not hurt too badly if the second payment never comes. This is even more important for television producers, who need to invest substantial amounts of money in production costs.

I must say that more than 90 percent of the political candidates I have worked for have paid me in full. A few did not, and their names are etched in my memory.

51. Research your candidate as thoroughly as you do your opponent. In almost every campaign, an individual or team is assigned to research the opponent's record, in the hope of uncovering things that can be used against him. In my campaigns, I insist we make the same effort researching our own candidate. If there is anything in the candidate's background or record we will need to defend in a campaign, I want to know it, sooner rather than later. Maybe the opponent's researchers never will find out about it; more likely they will. Better to be prepared.

I always meet privately with a new candidate to ask him if there is anything in his record that could prove embarrassing later in the campaign. Sometimes candidates tell you the truth; sometimes they do not.

My favorite story here concerns a southern candidate for governor, a free-wheeling bachelor. When I asked the question, this conversation ensued:

"Joe, do you know what they say about me down here?"
"No. What do they say?"
"They say I drink whiskey and chase women."
"Do you?"
"Of course I do."
How can you hate a guy like that?

52. Marginal improvements are important and often decisive. A fascinating book I strongly recommend is *Thinking in Time*, by Rich Neustadt and Ernest May. One of the points they make is that "marginal improvements are important." Although the authors are not referring to political campaigns, their advice is on target.

When you start a campaign with your candidate 30 or 40 points behind, there is no way you are going to make up this deficit in one gulp. You must chip away, make "marginal improvements," over a period of time. But even more important, most elections are decided by close margins, and if you make small improvements with eve group of voters, these will add up.

53. Know when to use bold strokes and when not to. There are times when a bold stroke is necessary to put some zip in your campaign. Usually, you can use a bold stroke if (1) your campaign is drifting and needs a spark; (2) you are in with the pack in a multi-candidate race and need to pull out of the pack; or (3) you are behind and conventional tactics are not moving the campaign.

By definition, a bold stroke can be dangerous and has the potential to backfire or be counterproductive. As a general rule, I recommend a bold stroke only when it appears nothing else will pull you out of a rut. Knowing when to use a bold stroke is as important as knowing how to use one.

54. Do not let your candidate think that just because he has said something once everyone has heard it. In the first place, to be a candidate, you must have a sizable ego. Part of that ego is the belief that because you make a statement or a speech, the whole state (county, world, universe) knows what you said and what your position is.

I once had the president of a Third World country tell me that his people could recite his speeches by heart, that they all listened to his talks on television, and that they all were familiar with his programs. "Fine," I said, "let's take a poll." The poll showed not many people the television programs; those who did usually had little idea of what the president was talking about, and they had no idea at all about what he was doing. We made some changes.

It is not only in the Third World that candidates or heads of state have these attitudes; they are prevalent wherever I have worked. If your candidate says something good or important, repeat it and repeat it until the message sinks in. Do not depend on a speech or news to carry important campaign messages; reinforce them with paid advertising.

55. Be prepared to produce media right to the end. In years gone by, it was common practice for a campaign to contract with a television producer to make a package of spots or longer programs. Often the finished package was delivered four or five weeks before the election. Not any more. Today, you must be prepared to e television, radio, and newspapers right up to election eve. You have the flexibility to capitalize on last-minute events and developments should be made with producer to be available right to d. If this is not possible, then an hour of studio time each day in the final week of the campaign for production, if needed.

56. Establish and maintain an immediate communications system. There are occasions in almost every campaign when you simply must reach the candidate, the campaign manager, the media director, the television producer, or the pollster in the campaign immediately. Unfortunately, these occasions usually occur at night, early Sunday morning, or in the middle of a holiday weekend.

One of the first projects in any campaign should to prepare a small directory of all the key people, with telephone numbers where they can be reached after hours, on weekends, or other inconvenient times. Naturally, distribution of this directory should be limited to those with a decision-making position in the campaign.

During the campaign, someone in the headquarters should know where everyone in the campaign can be reached. If a candidate is traveling, someone in the entourage should call "communications central" several times a day to report what is happening with the candidate and to find out what is going on at headquarters.

57. You do not have to love your candidate, but at least you should respect him. I have found it is possible to continue to work for a candidate you do not really like as long as you maintain some respect for him or her. If you neither like nor respect a candidate, then it is difficult to do your job properly. If you realize this at the beginning, it is not much of a problem: Just don't take the campaign. The difficulty comes when you start out having a decent relationship with the candidate, only to see it deteriorate during the course of the campaign. Then you have a tough decision to make: remain with the campaign and do the best you can, or quit.

58. Make sure your candidate knows why he is running and can answer the question: "Why should I vote for you instead of your opponent?" The classic example of this is Senator Edward M. Kennedy's fumbling the question, "Why do you want to be president?" put to him by Roger Mudd of CBS News in 1980. Kennedy might have lost the election right then and there.

Actually, it is astonishing how much difficulty many candidates have with this question. You would think that by the time they have decided to run, they would know the answer. Do not take this for granted. If the candidate does not answer the question to your satisfaction, work with him until he has a crisp, polished, sensible answer.

59. If your candidate has a difficult name, try to turn it to your advantage. Sure, it's nice to have candidates with names like Kennedy, Carter, or Reagan, but how about Ed Mezvinsky, Jim Scheuer, and Frank Licht? These were candidates I worked with, and all of them were elected—but not before we made special efforts to make sure voters knew how to pronounce their names.

In Mezvinsky's case, Tony Schwartz produced some classic (and frequently copied) television and radio spots poking fun at the name and deliberately mispronouncing it. The point of those ads was that even if people had difficulty with Ed Mezvinsky's name, they knew what he stood for.

In the case of Licht and Scheuer, we used rhyming: "Licht. Rhymes with teach." "Scheuer. Rhymes with lawyer."

Maybe I'm wrong, but I think people are hesitant to vote for candidates whose names they can't pronounce. How are they going to tell anyone who they voted for?

60. "Instant information creates involvement."—Marshall McLuhan. Politically, what this means is that the quicker you can deliver information about an event to the voters, the more impact it will have. Tony Schwartz is a master at instant production of radio spots to capitalize on fast-breaking news developments and linking his candidate (favorably) or opponent (unfavorably) to the news.

In a campaign last spring for an old friend seeking his eighth consecutive four-year term as district attorney, we took advantage of President Reagan's anti-drug campaign. Video Base International of New York, which produced the spots for the campaign, immediately dug out existing footage of my candidate, Matthew Ryan, in which he spoke strongly about his own anti-drug campaign. The VBI spot's narration began something like this: "Long before other candidates discovered the dangers of drug use, Matty Ryan had made it his No. 1 priority...." The spot worked and helped Ryan win.

The "instant information" formula works just as well, perhaps even better, in free media. We try to generate instant reaction to campaign developments what is news and usable by the press if issued immediately is old stuff and unusable if you let a day go by.

61. Learn where the real power lies. Sometimes the power positions are laid right out on the table of organization, but as often as not, the real power lies elsewhere. It could rest with the candidate's biggest financial supporters, with his wife or girlfriend, or with a trusted adviser, colleague, or associate.

This holds true for incumbents as well as for candidates. The intelligent consultant will quietly nose around until he finds out where the real power lies in a campaign or government and then will determine how he can utilize that power in the campaign. This also saves a lot of wasted effort dealing with people who do not really have the authority to make decisions.

Not all the wielders of real power are a bad influence; often they exercise their power cautiously, conservatively, and effectively. But it sure helps to know who holds it.

62. Analyze your losses. I think you can learn a lot more in a losing campaign than in one you win. For one thing, candidates (and consultants) seldom spend much time analyzing why they have won. They do not bother with postelection surveys and other tools available to them.

When you lose, you are much more likely to examine painstakingly all the decisions made in the campaign and the reasons for them, to reevaluate your strategy and decide where it went wrong, and to poll voters after the elections and see what you can learn about why they behaved as they did. Of course, if you keep losing, all the analysis in the world will not help much; then it is time to start looking for another career.

63. How a person intends to vote is more important than who he thinks is going to win. This is a point I have a great deal of difficulty conveying to candidates and inexperienced campaigners. I don't even know why pollsters ask the question about who the respondent thinks is going to win, because the results can be misleading and give the candidate a false sense of confidence.

I would always prefer to have a person say he or she plans to vote for my candidate but believes the opponent will win than have them say they are planning to vote for my opponent but believe my candidate will win.

64. Do not fool yourself or your candidate. It's okay to try to fool the opposition, or even the voters, but don't ever fool yourself or your candidate; this is a one-way ticket to disaster.

Candidates want to wait to take a poll until after some event that will give them a splash of publicity, so the poll results will be better. I would rather take a survey when the candidate is at the nadir of his popularity, so you get a true reading of opinion.

Last summer I was approached by representatives of a congressman to take a survey. The congressman had been office 32 years and was in his mid seventies. The only real issue in the campaign was his age. Yet the congressman's people knocked out every question in the survey pertaining to his age; they were worried they would "remind" voters how old the candidate was. This was ridiculous and demonstrated a lack of understanding of what polling is all about.

Candidates, of course, want to hear the optimistic analysis and prefer to ignore the pessimistic interpretation. Better they should know the truth.

65. Be persistent—but know when to back off. There is a difference between persistence and pigheadedness. If you feel something is important, do not accept a quick brush-off from the candidate, manager, or whomever you are working with. Put it in a different form, amplify it, answer their questions or arguments.

But if there appears to be no chance they will accept the idea, back off. It is possible the idea might not really be as good as you thought it was, or the candidate might have personal reasons that have nothing to do with its merits—but that he does not want to discuss with you or anyone else—for refusing to accept a suggestion.

66. Live to fight another day. Candidates and the "impassioned amateurs" I mentioned earlier often are willing to burn their bridges behind them in a campaign and do things that might have some short-range benefit but could have fearful long-range consequences. A consultant should be more rational. He lives on his reputations and win or lose, he must come out of that campaign with his reputation intact.

It also is worth noting that many candidates do not win the first time around, it often takes two or even three tries to be elected. I am as competitive or aggressive as anyone in the business, but there are lines I will not cross, because I know there is another day, another year, another campaign.

67. When you think you know it all, you don't. When I started out as a political consultant, I think I won my first 13 elections. Then I lost a gubernatorial primary, so I figured, "Well, I might lose to another Democrat, but I've never lost to a Republican." Then I lost to a Republican, and that theory was shot to hell.

When I was 35, I thought I knew all there was to know about campaigning and making people vote for your candidate. Now, more than 20 years later, I'm beginning to realize how little anybody really knows about what motivates voters to mark their "X" for one candidate or another.

Matt Reese and I were talking one day about a young consultant who had acquired a good reputation on the basis of winning several campaigns. I did not know the man, and I asked Matt, who did, how good he really was. "He's pretty good," said Matt, "but he'll be a lot better after he loses a couple of elections."

68. If you hear someone has said something nasty about you, do not overreact. It's inevitable, in this or any other business, that at some time someone is going to tell you one of your colleagues or competitors has said something nasty about you. Don't overreact. The person might not have made the statement, or the version you heard was taken out of context or unknowingly twisted. It might have been made in the heat of a campaign, in anger, in jest, or the person might have regretted it the moment he said it.

You can't have a thin skin and survive long in this business.

Now, on the other hand, if you really believe the statement was made, that it was made in malice, and you are hurt by it, then you can always observe the old political adage: Don't get mad get even.

69. Learn patience. This is especially true if you are working overseas, especially in places like Latin America or Africa. Sometimes it is difficult for American consultants, who have become accustomed to thinking that today's 4 o'clock meeting is going to take place at 4 o'clock today, to adjust.

I cannot count how many hours or days I have sat in hotel rooms or by hotel pools, waiting for a call from presidential palace. Now I come forearmed, with a stack of books, a box of cigars, and mentally prepared to wait.

70. Do not assume you have the contract until you have the check. Again, this probably is more pertinent to political consultants who work for foreign candidates, parties, or governments. And, of course, in other countries, if your contract or agreement is not honored, there is little you can do about it. I now require payment in advance, but still am stiffed now and then.

For those new to the business of overseas counseling, I strongly advise against any significant expenditure prior to receiving the initial payment This includes exploratory trips to discuss a contract with a prospective client; always ask for travel expenses to be paid up front. It is bad enough to have someone default on a fee, which represents time; it is much worse to have them renege on payments that also cover your own out-of-pocket expenses.

71. If your candidate wins, it's because of his charm, appeal, and powers of persuasion; if he loses, it's your fault. After managing a campaign that most political observers hailed as a sensational upset—and putting everything I had into it—I overheard the candidate tell a reporter that he really did not have a campaign manager, that he pretty much handled that himself. I did not say anything then, but later I remembered the old rule about not getting mad but getting even. I doubled the fee I had intended to charge him for the general election.

Few candidates will admit they lost because the voters did not care about them or their programs, or maybe they liked them well enough but just liked another candidate better.

72. Be tolerant. I already have said not to panic when a mistake occurs, but there are other times a consultant must learn to be tolerant—with the candidate, with the people in the campaign organization, with those with whom he has to work.

Those of us who have been in the business for a long time know that when we become involved with a new campaign, especially overseas, it sometimes feels as though we are reinventing the wheel each day. When you work in a different culture, a different environment, with less experienced people, it is easy to become exasperated. This does not do you or the campaign any good.

73. Maturity comes with age. In many I ways, I think I might have been a better consultant 15 or 20 years ago than I am today. In those days, I would argue and fight with my candidates and their staffs, pounding the desk, screaming and sulking. Now, I am more relaxed, more patient, more tolerant, and, I hope, more mature.

I also have come to realize that my function is to advise a candidate, not to pummel him into accepting my ideas. What I might have lost in pugnacity, I think I have gained in maturity, and I do not know any way to speed up this gestation period.

74. Do not take unnecessary risks. Again, this applies more to working overseas than it does in the United States, and maybe it is another function of age. But there are countries I will not work in, nor send anyone on my staff to work in. If you have any doubts, don't go. Campaigns are important but not that important.

75. Do not have too much sympathy for a candidate. Not many candidates are drafted. Most of them are candidates because they want to be, because they want the glory and power that the position they seek will give them. They are there of their own volition. As consultants, we have responsibilities to our candidates and to our campaigns. But the candidate also has certain responsibilities, and it is as important for him to fulfill his commitments to the campaign as it is for me to fulfill mine.

So do not waste time commiserating with candidates. If they were not willing to make the many sacrifices that being a candidate entails, they did not have to run.

Advice for Campaign Managers

76. Do not be afraid to bring in the real experts. The sense of insecurity that exists among campaign managers and advisers never should be underestimated. For some reason, this seems to be especially true in the Democratic party in the U.S.

In several recent presidential elections, the advisers and workers who helped obtain the nomination for a particular candidate blocked out talented specialists from working in the general election, some of whom had worked for other candidates in the primary, some of whom had not worked for any primary candidates.

It broke my heart in the 1984 presidential election to see all the talent on the sidelines not being used by the Democratic candidate—when he clearly needed all the help he could get. If you have access to the skills of a Tony Schwartz, or a Bob Squier, or a David Garth and you don't use them, you are making a mistake. Hire the best people you can find, and don't worry about whose feelings might be hurt.

77. Most campaigns do not know how to use consultants properly. This seems absurd, but it is true, and it is more true in foreign elections than it is in the U.S. Most candidates and their managers really have little idea about what a consultant does or should do. You must make this clear to them at the beginning, so their expectations are neither exaggerated nor unrealistic.

78. How much money you have to spend is not as important as how you spend it. Although no one will deny it is comforting to have all the money you need to conduct your campaign, it is not always the candidate with access to the largest amount of money who wins. There are many factors involved, of course, but certainly one of these is how effectively you spend the funds you have available.

It is easy to squander money in a political campaign—and many candidates do so. Occasionally, it is possible to drown an opponent in a sea of cash. But in most campaigns, assuming that each candidate has at least the minimum amount of money to mount a decent campaign, the likely winner is the one who spends his money best—or, put another way, succeeds in getting the biggest bangs for his bucks.

79. Running a campaign is not a democratic process. It is more like a military operation—at least if it is run right. All voices should not be equal in campaign discussions and decisions. A campaign should have experts and specialists in various areas. Their opinions should carry weight. If you need an operation, you should pay more attention to the surgeon's opinion than to that of the ambulance driver; if you need to get to the hospital in a hurry, then take the ambulance driver's advice.

The ultimate responsibility for making campaign decisions should rest with the campaign manager. If he wants to talk to the candidate about these decisions, fine. If he wants to accept a consensus from his staff, fine. But he certainly should not make his decisions on the basis of one-person, one-vote.

80. Make sure your candidate understands the issues. Those outside our business would consider this a simplistic statement; those in it know what I am talking about. Never mind the extreme cases, like the candidate for the U.S. Senate who once asked me, "What is this detente business, anyway?" Just consider the run-of-the-mill candidate who does not do his homework.

Last year, a Maryland television station embarrassed some senatorial candidates by asking them some simple questions on foreign and domestic policy. If it had been an examination in high school civics class, they all would have failed.

It is bad enough when the candidate is not informed about the other guy's issues; what is really bad is when he is not informed about his own issues. It happens.

81. Let your candidate talk to the people. In this era of "creative" television commercials, there is a tendency to make a whole package of spots in which the candidate never once talks directly to the people. This is a mistake. The people want to see and hear the candidate. Maybe he does not look like Robert Redford or speak like Ronald Reagan; they still want to see him, hear him, get a feel for him.

Those of us in the consulting business sometimes make the mistake of assuming we know more than the candidate. The longer I stay in the business, the more convinced I am that the eyeball-to-eyeball spot can be one of the most effective weapons in our arsenal.

82. Latch on to existing organizations. Creating an organization not only can be a formidable task, it can be expensive and difficult as well. Whenever possible, latch on to an existing organization, whether it happens to be a political party or special-interest support group.

Organizations that share the candidate's views on highly emotional subjects, such as abortion, gun control, or the nuclear freeze, can be of great organizational assistance to a campaign. At the very least, they can provide useful mailing lists; at best, they can provide bodies, experience, and money.

83. When you use new technologies, make sure you bring in specialists. It is not enough to buy or rent a couple of computers and hire a kid who has taken a course in computer programming and then believe you have "computerized" your campaign. If your campaign calls for any sort of sophisticated equipment or procedures, make certain you hire specialists who know how to operate that equipment or execute those procedures.

I have a degree of familiarity with how computers can be used effectively in political campaigns; it would never occur to me to try to run a computer operation, because I do not possess the required technical skills.

84. If your media materials do not work, throw them away no matter how much they cost. There is a tendency to think that if you have paid a lot of money for a television spot or a brochure, then it must be good. Often it is; sometimes it is not. And if you ever discover that a television or radio spot or print piece is not working, or, even worse, is counterproductive, then dump it immediately. At least you will save the cost of putting it on the air. If it really is bad, continuing to show it could damage your chances of winning the election.

Do not let the producer make this decision. A few producers are willing to admit that some of their materials might not be working very well; few will ever say, "This has turned out to be a bad spot; let's kill it."

Incidentally, I am not talking here about spots that have "burned out" because they have been shown a lot; this can happen to perfectly good materials that need to be replaced with new material. I am talking about material that is bad from the start, and should never be run, or material which, after being shown a few times, clearly is not working.

85. Restrain impassioned amateurs. A persistent problem for political professionals is the impassioned amateur—the person with enthusiasm but little experience—who does not have the knowledge to put the campaign in perspective. These people remind me of football fans who always want the coach to go for the first down when it is fourth down and a yard to go and cannot understand why the coach sends in the punting team.

On a volunteer level, these people usually are not much of a threat to the campaign, because they are not in decision-making capacities. When they become dangerous is if they hold important positions in the campaign, are large contributors who link their support to acceptance of their suggestions, and perhaps worst of all, when they are related to the candidate and in a position to influence his thinking.

86. Have a reason for what you do. Ask some tough questions of yourself about every step taken in a campaign:

- Why are we doing this?
- What will we get from it?
- What will happen if we don't do it?
- Is this the most effective way to use our money?

If you are working to a strategy, there should be a good reason—and if you are not working to a strategy, you are in trouble anyway.

87. Make sure you have good photographs of your candidate. This should be one of the simplest steps in a political campaign. In actuality, it always proves to be one of the most difficult. One of my first recommendations at the beginning of a campaign is to take good new photographs of the candidate in various situations, even if some good pictures already are available. I have found that you never have enough good photographs.

What often happens is the candidate will resist taking the time early in the campaign to have a good photographer spend sufficient hours with him to produce a good photo file, and then, in the crush of the campaign, when pictures are needed for brochures, signs, print ads, and a dozen other things, you are forced to use inferior photographs or grab some on the fly at the last minute.

Hire a top-flight still photographer. It is worth the cost. More people will see your candidate's picture than will ever see him in person.

88. Make sure your candidate gets some rest. It takes a big ego and a certain machismo for someone to be a candidate, and candidates often feel they must maintain their Superman image by forgoing rest and vacations. They act as though it is inhuman to admit they become tired and need rest.

This is a mistake. A tired candidate is an unreliable candidate, prone to error inclined to talk without thinking of the impact of his words, and certainly not looking his best. It is especially important for a candidate to take two or three days off going into the final month of a tough campaign. Even if he resists, insist that he take a rest. A candidate not at his best is a threat to the campaign.

89. Be careful in the selection of technicians. The campaign service industry is booming. Individuals and companies are available to sell you almost any kind of service you can conceive. But they are not all equally good; some, in fact, are so bad they can be counterproductive to your campaign.

One of the qualities an experienced consultant or manager brings to a campaign is the knowledge of who are the competent people in the technical area: computers, direct mail, production, telephone campaigns, and so forth. Obviously, in making their pitch, these technicians, will emphasize their successes and play down or ignore their failures. Check them out with other consultants, managers, or candidates know what questions to ask; take the time to call their references.

90. Preempt negatives. If there is something in your candidate's background that is certain to come out in the campaign, sometimes it is better to bring it up early and get it out of the way. I recommend this strategy only if you are virtually certain the opposition is aware of the fault and wit use it. And, of course, much depends on what it is.

I have found that voters will accept a candidate who drinks whiskey, has a physical handicap, or chases women, but except in rare instances, they reject candidates who use drugs, have been treated for mental disorders, or are homosexual.

If your candidate had problems with the law as a young man, then- you should try to use this in a positive way ("I know; I've been there") before your opponent slugs you late in the campaign by making the record public. If there is something on his record that sounds worse than it really is, then it should be explained before you are forced to go on the defensive.

91. Do not unilaterally talk about your I negatives if you do not have to. No candidate is perfect; every one has done or said things he wished he had not. Most of these are fairly harmless, and I don't think it's my responsibility as a consultant to show the candidate's warts: this is the responsibility of the press and his opponent.

I realize this point seems to contradict the previous one about preempting negatives, but it really does not. For example, if your candidate struggled through high school and barely managed to graduate from college, I do not think it is the campaign's responsibility to tell people that he might be a nice guy, but he's just not too smart. This is not the kind of issue the opposition can do much with, and there is no need for you to talk about it.

92. Do not distort your candidate's record; you're almost sure to be caught. In most cases, it is not the consultant who distorts a candidate's record, because most consultants are smarter than that. It is the candidate himself, and most of the time it is hard to figure out why. Candidates are constantly claiming they were graduated from Harvard University, when it turns out all they did was attend an occasional football game there, or saw combat in Vietnam, when what they really did was type reports on a supply ship 50 miles off the coast.

Why candidates persist in doing this is beyond me. I do not think the average voter much cares if the candidate went to Harvard or Appalachian State. Most of them didn't go to Harvard either. And, to me, "served in the Armed Forces during the Vietnam War" is sufficient, as well as accurate.

93. In a major campaign, always create a reaction unit. These go by various names. What they consist of is a small group of knowledgeable people in the campaign, with political sensitivity and experience, who meet regularly in the closing days or weeks of major campaign.

As a matter of personal preference, I like to have these meetings early in the morning and to limit the group to four for five members. The purpose is to analyze developments of the preceding day, to determine if any responses or other actions are needed, and to decide who should make the response.

Some of the time, perhaps most of the time, the best response is no response. But when a reaction is called for, it is important to have key people with decision-making responsibilities available.

94. Know what your opponent is up to. You do not have to be a political genius to realize the importance of monitoring your opponent's activities, but it always is surprising to learn how few campaigns do this on a systematic basis. You start with the record, if the opponent has held or run for office before, and try to find out who his advisers are and anything you can about their style. All public statements must be recorded and filed; all pieces of literature collected and reviewed. If possible, have someone attend his speeches and other public meetings. The better informed you are about you opposition, the easier it will be to win.

95. Your enemy's enemy is not necessarily your friend. It might be true in war, love, or high society, but it certainly is not true in politics. It could be true but, just as often as not, you might want to keep a fair distance from your enemy's enemy.

Often, these "enemies" are disenchanted or disgruntled former friends or supporters of your opponent. They might even have a legitimate complaint. But most of the time their hatred is passionate, clouds their thinking, and encourages them to provide you with a lot of "facts" that might be far from the truth. I advise extreme caution in dealing with your opponent's enemies, especially if they are people who once were close to him.

These observations hold primarily for individuals. There certainly are situations when a group, association, or even a whole social class is upset at an incumbent or frightened of a challenger and is willing to work hard for his defeat. This is a different situation, and usually these groups can be turned into assets.

96. Information is power, use it wisely. Intelligence is critical, especially if you have it before anyone else. Having information is one thing; using it effectively is something else. This is why I always cringe when I see a candidate spend $25,000 or $30,000 or more for a poll and then immediately announce the results. Knowing what the situation is, while your opponent might be in the dark, can be a great advantage. Any form of political intelligence can be useful. But like the raw data in a survey, it needs to be analyzed and used directly.

97. Learn how to count. Most people learn how to do this in kindergarten and then seem to forget when they are old enough to become involved in political campaigns. The ability to count is especially important when you are dealing with delegates in a convention. To have any real value, your estimates of strength must be based on a hard count. If the count is not hard, you are only fooling yourself and your candidate.

98. Just because something is different does not mean it is better. There is a compulsion in some campaigns to do "different" things. This is fine—if what you do differently is more successful than what you were doing. Often it is not.

Making changes just for the sake of making changes is, in my opinion, a waste of time, effort, and, probably, money. If what you are doing is working, stick with it. If you have used a specific technique in other campaigns and it works keep doing it until it stops working. If it becomes necessary to do something differently, make certain that what is different is an improvement.

99. Do not underestimate the importance of visual symbolism. Some candidates are said to have "presence" or "charisma." This often is due to how the candidate looks, dresses, and handles himself. A candidate does not need to be handsome to dress well and look good. I am suspicious if a candidate is sloppy in his personal dress and habits that he might be careless in other areas—such as looking after my tax money if he is elected.

And sometimes it is not a case of upgrading the candidate's clothes or style or use of symbols, but in downgrading them, as in the case of a candidate I once worked for in a southern state who drove a Rolls Royce. I suggested that if he really wanted to be elected, he would be better off driving a Chevrolet or a Ford, like most of his constituents.

100. Let the candidate's spouse take whatever role he or she wants. Most candidates are men, and most of them are married, and efforts almost always are made to push the candidate's wife to become involved in the campaign. Sometimes this works and sometimes it does not. I have seen wives of candidates who would make better candidates than their husbands. I also have seen wives who have been a disruptive force in the campaign and actually wound up doing their husbands more harm than good.

What I usually do in a campaign is take the candidate's wife to lunch privately, find out what she would like to do in a campaign, if anything, and then encourage her to do it. If she would prefer to sit the campaign out, fine; if she would prefer to accompany her husband, fine; if she would like to have her own schedule, fine. She need not be forced to do something she would be uncomfortable doing.

Once in a California gubernatorial campaign I had lunch with the candidate's wife early on. She was Mrs. Frosty personified when I met her. By the time we had finished lunch, she was completely relaxed and told me, "I had this idea you were going to want me to go out and make speeches and do things like that, and I was petrified. All I want to do is work quietly in headquarters." And that is what she did.

✓ Developing a Cogent Campaign Theme
Joel Bradshaw

Every October in even numbered years, voters are bombarded with hundreds of political messages from competing candidates. The messages are transmitted via commercials on television and radio, in broadcast and print news stories, over the telephone, and in the mail. All this attention has two basic purposes: to persuade people to vote and, more important, to entice them to vote for you.

In the midst of this numbing cacophony, undecided voters must make a decision. If your campaign is well conceived, well executed, intensely disciplined, and a little bit lucky, it will leave the voters with one, and only one, clear impression of you and the rationale for your election. Make no mistake, by Election Day the voters will have clear impressions of you and your opponent.

The question is: Will they have the one you intend or the one your opponent intends? The answer to this question lies in the campaign's ability to design a theme to unify its various messages and to stick to the theme throughout the campaign.

Simply put, a campaign theme is a statement of the rationale for your election. It should answer the question, "Why me now?" And because the other side of the question is whether your opponent should be elected, the theme also should contain an implied answer to the question, "Why not the other candidate now?"

Control the Debate

When you conduct a thematic campaign, you have a number of advantages:

1. By understanding the rationale for your own election and the defeat of your opponent, you can proceed to define the test by which you want voters to decide for whom to vote.

2. By establishing a clear contrast between you and your opponent, you define the choice you are asking voters to make.

3. If, as political strategist Michael Berman suggests, all campaigns are a series of unplanned reactions to unanticipated events, the theme provides a context in which to respond that permits the campaign to retain its consistency in responding to changing events.

4. Finally, a thematic campaign can be effective in communicating messages to different groups of voters, because the messages you transmit always exist within the context of the theme.

What this all adds up to is control of the debate during the campaign; this often is the elusive element that determines victory or defeat. It is critical for your campaign to determine its theme before you hit the Campaign trail. When you are asked the most obvious of all press questions, "Barclay, why are you running for govinor?" your response should be a statement of the campaign theme, and nothing else.

One need only remember Senator Edward Kennedy's entry into the 1980 residential campaign to understand how difficult can be the process of developing and closing on a theme and how important it is to do so before you announce your candidacy. In a nationally televised interview with Roger Mudd, then of CBS News, Senator Kennedy was asked, "Why are you running for president?" To the shock and dismay of his supporters everywhere, his answer was unspecific, unfocused, and filled with awkward and embarrassing pauses.

Now, we all know Kennedy had thought long and hard about running for president and, having made the decision, must have had a strategy in mind to win and some points he wanted to make about the rationale for his election. But absent the disciplined process of specific theme development, Kennedy mangled his response and left those watching with a view of a candidacy that was unfocused and unsure of itself. Voters received a clear impression of the candidate, but not the intended one.

Senator Kennedy is not alone. Dozens of major campaigns are conducted each cycle without ever closing on a theme. Many of them win, usually because the opponent also runs a themeless campaign. How, then, should you go about completing this difficult but important task?

First, remember that theme is a strategic not a tactical consideration. Developing a theme will provide a context for all your campaign messages. In contrast, defining specific messages, timing their delivery, and figuring out how and to whom to deliver them are tactical questions.

As in all key elements in campaign planning, you must begin with research about your electorate. Unlike the people who are active in politics, voters generally do not sit around thinking about government, politics, or the people involved in these fields. A public opinion study in the 1970s determined that the average American thought about politics and government fewer than five minutes a week. Although most people, if you ask them, will have opinions on matters of public concern, voters are subject to persuasion—if your campaign successfully can focus their attention.

Provide a Context

Voters' preliminary views about the country, their community, and the candidates provide you with a context to develop your theme. In any given electoral contest, voters will divide themselves into two groups relatively early. One group will have firm views on whom they will support; the second will have little interest and no firm views on the race. Those in the first group will divide again based on their choice of the candidates. Some will be for you, and some will be for your opponent.

You want to design your campaign theme to appeal to that amorphous group of uninteresteds and undecideds. Each year, candidates and political parties spend hundreds of thousands of dollars on research to identify and define these persuadable voters. The object of this research is to find the basis to persuade these voters to support one candidate. One finding appears over and over in this research: These persuadable voters make their selection primarily on the kind of people they think the two candidates are—and not on whether they agree with a candidate's stand on specific issues.

In the 1984 presidential election, public-opinion polls showed voters agreed with Walter Mondale's stand on most issues. Yet President Reagan was re-elected in a landslide. The deciding factor was one of personal image.

Define Your Image

One of the principal functions in designing your campaign's statement of its theme is to define your image for the persuadable voters. Three factors comprise this process:

Incumbency. This is by far the most important characteristic—and not just because incumbents tend to win most of the time. Incumbents have records in office, and these records have positive and negative aspects. Not only do the reform the basis of an incumbent's claim of experience and accomplishment, they also define the incumbent.

If an incumbent is in the race, the question before the voters is, "Should the incumbent be thrown out?" not "Should the challenger be elected?" It is axiomatic that challengers cannot defeat incumbents unless they can provide voters with credible reasons for defeating the incumbent. Consequently, it is inevitable that the incumbent's record will become the basis on which both sides try to prove their case. Incumbents and challengers alike, however, sometimes do not understand that the critical factor of incumbency how the incumbent's record plays terms of image and not in terms of isolated specifics. The question of incumbency, then, suggests a great deal more about your theme than the fact that there is a record to deal with.

If you are running against a two-term incumbent U.S. senator, you cannot stress experience as part of your theme. The senator clearly is more experienced than you are, and you will not convince voters to the contrary. If experience is the test that voters apply, the incumbent passes the test and wins the election.

On the other hand, if the rationale for your election is that now is time for change, the incumbent will face great difficulty convincing people that a vote for him is a vote for change, especially if he is a member of the majority party. If change becomes the test the voters apply, the incumbent fails the test and loses the election.

Style. How you look and act is the important factor in defining your image. In 1978, Colorado voters elected incumbent Governor Richard Lamm, a liberal Democrat, by a wide margin (60-40 percent). The same year, they elected William Armstrong, a conservative Republican, by a similarly wide margin over liberal Democratic incumbent Senator Floyd Haskell. In 1980, the same voters re-elected liberal Democratic incumbent Senator Gary Hart by a narrow margin over a moderate Republican.

Are these seemingly contradictory results really paradoxical? Not by a long shot. The three winners shared a common style. All were vigorous men in their forties, and although they had strong ideological convictions poles apart on the issues, they all portrayed a reasoned and pragmatic approach to specific policy questions. It was their style, not their substance, that the persuadable Colorado voters most readily identified with and that formed the basis of images voters chose between.

As cynical as it might sound, this primacy of style over ideology is of paramount concern in developing your theme. By listing all of your personal characteristics and those of your opponent, you can determine which characteristics to emphasize in developing your theme. The goal is to establish the greatest contrast of images between you and your opponent that work in your favor.

It is important to understand that what appear to be strengths or weaknesses very often are neither. They are simply characteristics. It is how the thematic debate in the campaign unfolds that turns these characteristics into positive or negative images of you and your opponent.

To illustrate, let's say a U.S. Senate race is between a 43-year-old, handsome, dynamic, articulate, energetic, vigorous, Republican member of Congress and a 63-year-old, bald, folksy, police hero, former Democratic governor, who is not a good public speaker. In this case, the Republican wants a theme that defines the test the voters apply as one of youth and vigor. The Democrat will run on a theme that stresses experience, maturity, stability, and personal warmth.

Both candidates will want to make the most of their strengths, minimize their weaknesses, and by contrasting these at every turn, attempt to weaken their opponent. By drawing attention to the contrasts, the Democrat wants the handsome, dynamic, articulate candidate to appear cold, glib, slick, and shallow. His objective is to select the personal characteristics he wants to stress in his theme, so he can project the image of his candidacy.

An additional consideration about image is your ideological positioning. Because your ideology is more important in determining your base of support than in moving persuadable voters, what is relevant in developing your theme is the degree to which you and your opponent are ideologically motivated. The voters on whom you will focus in developing your theme generally are not strongly ideological about politics. They are not likely to be persuaded to be for you on the strength of ideology; they are more likely to be persuaded to vote against you, if they feel you are too extreme in your views. It is not the nature of the ideology they are concerned with, but the strength of it in the image you project.

Political environment. It is here that political issues become part of the equation. The role that issues play in developing and executing your theme will form the basis on which voters will decide what kind of people they think you and your opponent are. To use a legal analogy, political issues are the evidence you will use to build a case for the voters; they are not the case itself. It is essential in running a thematic campaign first to determine the image you want to project and then to select the issues you will use to illustrate the image. You want to know which, if any, issues or problems are dominant in the voters' minds.

Obviously, you cannot convince people to support you if you are not talking about the major topics they care about. You want to identify issues about which voters feel strongly—including those with which your views conflict. If you have selected a viable image to project, your differences on these issues can be dealt with in a context that reinforces your theme. Naturally, you want to evaluate the position of your opponent on the issues as well as to ascertain that there will be sufficient evidence to suggest the contest set up by your theme.

Distill the Theme

At the conclusion of this process when you have evaluated the incumbency, your own and your opponent's personal characteristics, and the political environment—you are in a position to determine (1) a persuasive rationale for your election, (2) an image to project that is consistent with that rationale, and (3) the issues you will use and the way you will deal with them to bring your image to the forefront of the electorate.

When you have accomplished this, you will be able to formulate a brief statement that constitutes your theme, and you will be able to develop a slogan that sums up this theme in seven words or less. A slogan plays two important roles in a campaign. First, it helps voters remember what the campaign is projecting, and if it is used properly, it ties all the messages in the campaign around the theme. Second, the process of moving from the theme statement to a slogan helps the key actors in the campaign internalize the theme. This is immeasurably important in implementing the campaign.

It is difficult to create a theme and even more difficult to stick to it in absolutely every campaign communication. The greater the degree of internalization of the theme among everyone involved in the campaign, however, the more likely you are to achieve consistency. The purpose of the theme is to unify the campaign and to make it easier for voters to form a clear, positive image of you and your opponent in way that reinforces the rationale for your election.

In the sound and fury of all the campaigns confronting the voters, the thematic campaign has a better chance to penetrate with clarity.

✓ Spelling Out Your Strategy
Sharon Hargrave & Deby Snodgrass

Because top-of-the-ticket races routinely utilize and dominate most of the expert planning and proven planners, those who run for legislative or local offices often are left to their own devices—and mistakes.

It shouldn't be that way, and it is a mistake for a candidate for a state legislative office or county commission to believe the candidate can do it alone.

At a minimum, a volunteer campaign manager and steering committee are necessary for any campaign without professional help.

Once assembled, a "kitchen cabinet" and campaign manager should begin the strategic planning process. Like generals preparing for war, they should systematically evaluate the battlefield, armies, and firepower of the opposing sides.

A critical error often made during this time lies in the confusion of tactics and strategy. Of the two, strategy is the more permanent, as once the dynamics of the contest have been defined, dynamics do not change. The time and place of the contest and the candidates will remain the same. The art of strategy is in defining the variables correctly.

Tactics, on the other hand, are subject to change. As Sun Tzu, the Chinese philosopher of 2,500 years ago, so aptly put it, "just as water retains no shape, so in warfare there are no constant conditions.... All men can see the individual tactics necessary to conquer, but almost no one can see the strategy out of which total victory is evolved."

Strategy involves the over- or underestimation of an opponent or your own candidate. In developing your strategy for a downballot race, consider these factors:

The District: Review demographic data pertinent to the area, such as average age, household income, and racial diversity or homogeneity. This information can be obtained from census data, Chambers of Commerce, or public planning agencies.

Don't miss a large industrial complex because you don't know it is inside the district boundaries. Drive through the district to become familiar with its characteristics.

Voting History: Review voting patterns of the district by precinct to help define the partisan base vote in the area, as well as the number of swing voters and ticket-splitters.

For example, in State House District 26 of Oklahoma, precinct 1 is 18 percent Republican, 79.49 percent Democratic and 2.46 percent Independent. In the Reagan landslide of 1984, the president received 61 percent of the vote.

Two years later, Sen. Don Nickles (R-OK), the strongest Republican on the ticket in 1986, polled 46.6 percent of the vote. This voting history clearly establishes the fact that voters in this precinct do not vote party line, but are, by contrast, swing voters—giving their vote to the person, not the label. While a Republican will most likely lose this precinct, the swing voters here can help minimize the damage of the Democratic vote.

Previous election results by precinct can be obtained at the local election board.

Opposition Research: Detailed information about opponents—such as background, profession, and reputation—should be secured. If the race involves an incumbent, voting records, finance reports, past campaign literature, and newspaper clips should be obtained and carefully reviewed for potential vulnerabilities.

A classic example of utilizing an opponent's voting record is the Lux-Thorsness State Senate race in Washington State. Thorsness put out a mailing for Halloween that had a jack-o-lantern with the words "Lux's Taxes" carved on the front. Inside it read: "Gene Lux's tax votes are scary. So are his votes against tough anti-crime laws.... When our children go door to door this Halloween, we'll worry—because crime is up.... But the scary thing is that appointed-Sen. Gene Lux has been too busy trying to raise our taxes to do anything to help crack down on crime...."

This piece hit Lux on three major points—taxes, his poor voting record on crime, and the fact that he was appointed, not elected.

Researching your opponent's record if he or she is an incumbent—and stated positions if he is not—is critical to a well-developed and accurate strategic analysis. Spend as much time on this as it takes, and don't be afraid to go too far.

Check driving records for such things as drunk-driving incidents or criminal charges, and court records for lawsuits or bankruptcies. However, once obtained, be careful how you use this information—if mishandled, it can backfire on you.

The Candidate: Take time to carefully evaluate your own strengths and weaknesses. Define your base of power and identify groups who will or should support you. Shared experiences can include race, religion, college, occupation, or civic involvement. Region may also be an important factor, as in the Lahr race for State Representative in Illinois where Lahr said in his literature: "Guy Lahr believes it's time our State Representatives represented us, the people of southern Illinois, instead of some other part of the state."

The Environment: The mood of the voters is crucial to designing an effective campaign theme. You must ask: What are the voters thinking? How do they feel about the issues? What do they already know about you? About your opponent?

Without the benefit of a poll, these questions are extremely difficult to answer—at least with any objectivity. And unfortunately, candidates are often reluctant to spend the money to obtain the answers. But a campaign operating blindly is similar to a patient entering major surgery without an X-ray.

The Election: Examine closely the ramifications of the election schedule. In a special election, turnout may be the key, whereas in November of a presidential election year, persuasion may be a better tactic. Is the real contest in the primary or the general election?

Once the research phase has been completed, outline the winning coalition, identify motivational issues, define the campaign themes, and develop your messages.

The winning coalition is formed by evaluating what you learned in the initial research and deciding which groups should be targeted to help reach the needed 50 percent plus one vote.

Play from your strength. Where you are already strong, become stronger.

Where you are weak, learn your opponent's power base well enough to stay away. Don't make the mistake of activating your opponent's supporters.

In identifying motivational issues, define those that strike a contrast between the candidates—subjects on which the candidates decidedly do not agree and are important to the voters you need to win. Above all, avoid wasting time on issues that do not meet this criteria.

The act of defining the campaign theme can be more fun, and dangerous, than it first appears. Don't go with a knee-jerk reaction; think about it carefully.

Having developed your message and theme, outline some secondary messages. Each group targeted by the campaign may need a specific message crafted in order to activate its support, and press its hot buttons.

These messages may stress shared interests or may highlight motivational issues. Be careful that these secondary messages do not conflict with the central campaign themes.

If your strategy is not in writing, you don't have one. Refer to it, review it, change it as you receive more information.

Finally, have confidence in your strategy and prepare to develop your tactical plan. This will enable you to communicate your message to selected campaign audiences.

✓ Overcoming An Odd Name
David K. Neidert

Emotionally fragile children and political candidates have at least one thing in common: They are likely to suffer from having an odd name. Usually, children outgrow their vulnerability. But when politicians put their name on the line, they often find their schoolyard scars can affect their run for office.

Some political observers claim having Anglo-Saxon names secured the Illinois Democratic Party lieutenant governor and secretary of state nominations for two Lyndon LaRouche followers. After all, it is easy to see how an uninformed voter faced with the names Fairchild and Hart on one ticket and Sangmeister and Pucinski on another might vote for the candidates with "American sounding" names.

Of course, in some of our country's ethnic areas, such as the Polish wards of Chicago, an ethnic surname is a help, not a hindrance. Just ask some of the city's recent Democratic congressmen, William Lipinski, Frank Annunzio, and Dan Rostenkowski, all of whom represent districts where their names are assets, not liabilities.

Of our 40 presidents, only Dwight Eisenhower, Theodore and Franklin Roosevelt, and Martin van Buren have names that are identifiably non-English or Irish. Below the presidential level, candidates with ethnic surnames have met with electoral success, but many campaigns find they must make an effort to teach the voters how to pronounce the candidate's name.

When a candidate has an odd name, the problem usually falls to the media consultant to arrive at a creative solution. Republican media consultant Ian Weinschel says, "It's much easier to remember 'Johnson' or 'Smith' than it is to remember 'Zschau.' But a smart campaign will recognize this and work to overcome it." [Read the accompanying story to find out how Weinschel put together a creative campaign for California Senate candidate Ed Zschau.]

Some politicians simply duck the issue of unusual surnames. Representative Barbara Vucanovich (R–Nev.) (accent on the second syllable) spent her first campaign in 1982 spotlighting her endorsement by Senator Paul Laxalt and her credentials as a conservative Republican in winning first the primary and then the general election.

Her initial ad campaign was designed to make her credible as a candidate and to make her better known than her obscure opponents. No attempt was made to conduct an unusual media campaign because of her name, because no one thought it necessary.

Name Games

Other candidates, however, are forced to embrace such an approach. Salt Lake County (Utah) Commissioner Tom Shimizu (Shim-uh-zoo) faced the problem in 1982. Shimizu, appointed to the county commission in 1981 after the incumbent resigned, was seeking election for the first time even though he had the mantle of incumbency. Considered vulnerable at the beginning of the year, he ran a clever series of billboard ads asking, "What's a Shimizu?"

According to John Inch, Shimizu's top aide, the ads led to an avalanche of telephone calls to the local billboard firm from people who wanted to find out just what was a "Shimizu." The follow-up billboards answered, "He's your effective county commissioner." Shimizu won his election in a landslide and made himself credible enough to win the nomination for Congress this year.

Like Shimizu, other candidates and their advisers cannot resist the temptation to use the name in a clever fashion. Representative Bill Schuette (R-Mich.) (Shoo-tee) tried rhyme this year, using the slogan, "On Duty with Schuette." For his 1984 campaign, Schuette featured ads with a wing-tip shoe with the letter "T" painted on it to show voters how to pronounce his name.

Not everyone believes an unusual name harms a candidate. Thomas Barry, administrative assistant to Representative Robert Mrazek (D-N.Y.), thinks an unusual name might be an asset. "I don't think it presents a problem for the candidate," says Barry, who also served as Mrazek's 1982 campaign manager. "They're not concerned about the pronunciation. They're trying to use their name to promote themselves."

When Mrazek (Mur-ay-zek) first ran in 1982, he faced an incumbent with a national reputation and a name as unusual as his, John LeBoutillier (Leboot-lee-ay). LeBoutillier had spent his entire term as a highly partisan Republican, coming up with the irreverent rallying cry, "Repeal O'Neill."

Mrazek had served as a state legislator since 1975 and was well known in half of the district. Given financial help by an irate Tip O'Neill, he made Le Boutillier's personality the major issue in the campaign, saying the incumbent's "obnoxious behavior" made him ineffective. Mrazek's tactics led to a 10,000-vote victory.

Only this year, with a weak opponent, has Mrazek run radio commercials highlighting his unusual name. In the commercials, people are stopped and asked to pronounce his name. Several mutilate it before the commercial ends with a tag line, saying Bob Mrazek isn't concerned about how people pronounce his name but about the job does in Washington.

Gaining Credibility

In the Democratic primary for Baltimore's predominately black congressional district, Kweise Mfume (Ku-way-zee Em-fu-may) defeated several other prominent politicians, including the nephew of the highly popular retiring incumbent.

Mfume's name already was well known in the community, because he had a radio talk show and had been a highly visible and articulate member of the Baltimore City Council. Consequently, Mfume concentrated on issues separating himself from his opponents. The legal difficulties of the perceived front-runner, State Senator Clarence Mitchell III, also gave Mfume's candidacy a boost— as did his claims he would fight in Washington with the same tenacity he fought in Baltimore.

Mfume is the opposite of most candidates with unique names; he adopted the name "Kweise Mfume" as a tribute to his Afro-American heritage.

Two other candidates handled unusual surnames in different ways. When State Senator Arliss Sturgelewski (soft "g," accent on loo) announced her candidacy for the Alaska gubernatorial nomination, she not only had the problem of a name that was difficult to pronounce, but she also faced major opponents in the primary and general election.

In the primary, her opponent was former Governor Walter Hickel, a former U.S. secretary of the interior under President Nixon and a political institution in Alaska. Recognizing the two problems, Sturgelewski's strategist, Tony Payton, answered both in the same television commercial.

A gaggle of children ages four to five, tried gallantly to pronounce her name. None was successful; all mangled it. In the end, one tyke exclaimed, "Let's just call her Governor!"

The ad was an immediate hit, drawing favorable editorials in the Anchorage newspapers and giving the campaign an effective theme to use against Hickel. Her entire primary campaign focused around the "Let's Just Call Her Governor" theme. In an upset-filled Alaska primary (Governor William Shefield lost the Democratic nomination for reelection the same day), Sturgelewski defeated Hickel by a substantial margin.

Sturgelewski's approach is similar to one used by former Massachusetts Senator Paul Tsongas (D-Mass.) when he ran in 1978. Well known in his own district but unknown statewide, Tsongas (Song-us) ran a commercial in which a group of adults butcher his name, ending with a child looking at it and reading, "tickets."

Later in the campaign, when his statewide name identification had risen, a new commercial was released in which the same group of adults pronounce the name correctly, ending with the same child reading, "tickets." Tsongas won a crowded Democratic primary with 36 percent of the vote and defeated the incumbent 55 percent to 45 percent in the general election.

How Now, Ed Zschau?

Representative Ed Zschau faced a similar problem in California. Zschau's name is pronounced like the first syllable of "shower," to rhyme with "now" and "cow." In his earlier races for Congress, his name did not play that big of a role. When first elected in 1982, Zschau was unopposed in the

Republican primary; in his district this is tantamount to election. He subsequently won his 1984 race with ease.

But when he decided to run for the U.S. Senate, his name finally became a problem. Thirteen Republicans jumped into the race, including another member of Congress, a Los Angeles County supervisor, a prominent state senator, an equally prominent Los Angeles commentator, and a host of "minor" candidates.

Early on, Zschau decided on a heavy media campaign. Ron Smith, Zachau's campaign manager, proposed a series of commercials revolving around "the candidate with the funny name." Weinschel, the campaign's media consultant, rejected that approach, arguing that a series of cutesy ads would hamper Zschau's attempts to drive home his campaign message. He also thought Zschau needed to stress his ties to the high-technology industry and to present a senatorial image.

As a result, Weinschel designed a logo that became the campaign's trademark. A silver lightning bolt comes out of the upper right-hand corner of the television screen, diagonally crossing to the lower left. The bolt then spells the word "Z-S-C-H-A-U," floating to the right and stopping. Simultaneously, as if caused by the logo, the word "Zschau" whispers in a long electronically synthesized breath.

"There was some resistance until I showed them [the Zschau senior staff] exactly what I had in mind," says Weinschel. "Then they decided it was exactly what the campaign needed."

Perhaps more important, the logo taught people how to pronounce the name while also hearing substantive messages about the campaign. "We have reports of skateboarders cruising along, their hands to their mouths and whispering 'Zschau,'" says Weinschel. "When kids pick up on it, you know you've done something right." The voters noticed, too. Zschau, who started with 3 percent name recognition, easily won the Republican nomination with 37 percent of the vote.

Some Rules, Namely...

If a candidate's name is so unusual that some sort of accounting for it during the campaign is unavoidable, there are a few basic rules worth remembering:

- First, the image the candidate wants to create must be maintained. If the handling of an unusual name demeans the office the candidate is seeking, it will probably turn off voters in the process. Arliss Sturgelewski, by ending her commercial, "Let's Just Call Her Governor," conveyed a sense of competence in her races against an incumbent and a respected former governor. Likewise, Zschau's high-tech logo fit well with his high-tech image. Rather than detracting from his Silicon Valley roots, it reinforced them.
- Second, as Kweise Mfume demonstrated, a candidate will benefit if he can increase his name identification in the community before the campaign. Mfume's radio program coupled with his high profile on the Baltimore City Council made him a familiar figure long before he announced his candidacy for Congress.
- Finally, the more time the campaign spends directly tackling the name issue, the less time it has to develop its other themes. Zschau reinforced his name for the first and last three seconds of every commercial, allowing 24 seconds for other information. Mrazek ignored the name issue entirely in 1982, working instead to make his opponent the issue in the campaign, in effect turning the race into a Yes-No referendum on John LeBoutillier. If people didn't like LeBoutillier (and they did not), they would vote for Mrazek (and they did).

✓ Launching—and Deflecting—11th-Hour Attacks
Rich Galen

The World Series is over. The public finally has turned its attention to politics. And that 20 point lead you had in the July polls is now just a summer memory.

You tell the press you are not concerned; that you will continue to take the high road, focus on "the issues" and eschew "negative campaigning." However, you also decide it is time to gather your inner circle for a serious secret discussion. The topic: whether to turn your mother's picture to the wall and attack the opposition.

There are several factors—political and personal—to weigh before embarking on this course. To try to invoke voter sympathy, your opponent will accuse you of negative campaigning. As far as you are concerned, it is "comparative advertising." But the crucial judgment as to whether you are being justifiably comparative or excessively negative will come from the voters.

In a campaign, the voters' eyes behold what is happening through the lens of the media. If the paper thinks you are being negative, so will most voters.

The first problem is that negative ads are the subject of biennial media hand-wringing; there have been instances where press criticism of negative campaigning was so unrelenting that it turned the tide in favor of the candidate on the receiving end of the attacks. Of course, the columnists and reporters doing the complaining often are the same people who break doors down in trying to report the story being told by negative ads. That fact, however, somehow becomes buried in the background.

But you also are likely to encounter resistance to negative advertising from within your own camp, particularly among some of your more influential and well-endowed supporters. In general, these backers are business people who are not in the habit of saying bad things about important figures—at least publicly. For them, whether such negative tactics can win the election is a secondary concern. They are more concerned about whether association with these attacks will bring them a cold shoulder at next Thursday's Rotary Club luncheon.

That is not to minimize the unpleasantness negative campaigning can produce. Keep in mind that the other side also gets its turn at bat. When the Monday paper carries your charges against the opposition, everyone will think that your ads are terrific. But on Tuesday, when your opponent has launched charges of his own and his best friend has summoned you to a private meeting, negative campaigning will seem as much fun as sitting on the naughty bench in junior high school waiting to see the assistant principal.

There are virtually no hard-and-fast rules regarding if or when to launch an attack. However, the following factors need to be weighed:

- The Nature of the Constituency. Hard-knuckled politics long has been the norm in urbanized areas with highly mobile populations. On the other hand, you may want to be more careful in a district filled with fourth-generation residents who have gone to high school together. In such areas, highly negative campaigning often is regarded as the political equivalent of airing the family's dirty laundry.
- The Mood of the Electorate. While many voters will decry negative campaigning in the abstract, most political consultants believe the public has become more tolerant of this tactic over the last generation. But its effectiveness still can ebb and flow from year to year.

In 1980, when the voters were clearly in a "throw the rascals out" mood, four senior Democratic senators went down in defeat under sharp attacks from the National Conservative Political Action Committee. But in 1982, when NCPAC repeated its tactics, they badly backfired. Two NCPAC targets—Sens. Paul Sarbanes of Maryland and Daniel P. Moynihan of New York—used the attacks to collect both money and sympathy and went on to win reelection by landslides.

- The Identity of the Opposition. A first-time candidate largely unknown to the electorate often makes an easy target. The public is likely to be swayed by the first substantial information it receives about him—even if it is negative.

An 11th-hour attack on an incumbent is more difficult, presuming he has not wrapped his car around a tree while drunk nor been caught with his pants down during the closing weeks of the campaign. An incumbent has a record and a defined public persona; it usually takes months, not weeks, to poke holes in either of those.

Nonetheless, there are notable examples where incumbents have gone down in the homestretch. Take the 1980 race in New York for the Republican senatorial nomination between incumbent Jacob Javits and insurgent Alfonse D'Amato. Javits was a Senate titan with almost a quarter of a century of service in that body. But, when he announced for a fifth term at age 76, he acknowledged that he had a condition related to Lou Gehrig's Disease.

At first, D'Amato sought to attack Javits on the grounds that he was too liberal—and got nowhere. Then, in the closing weeks of the campaign, D'Amato's advisers decided to take the gloves off. They put a spot on the air referring to Javits' health problems, with the backdrop showing an unflattering picture of an aged Javits. The gap in the polls closed, and D'Amato won the nomination with 55 percent. While the ads were sharply criticized in the media, they succeeded with the voters because they simply repeated information already on the public record—and reinforced widespread doubts about Javits' health.

Obviously, if you are 21 points ahead with three weeks to go before Election Day, you should not waste time or money even mentioning the other candidate. Negative campaigning can backfire, and there are candidates who have launched preemptive strikes while comfortably ahead in the polls—only to see their leads evaporate.

On the other hand, if your race looks to be neck-and-neck heading into the stretch, you should consider going on the attack. In some cases, it may be wiser to avoid these tactics and concentrate your resources on a voter identification and GOTV program. But, in a close race, an attack strategy can help you to:

- Seize Control of the Debate. Your opponent already may be attacking you. Or he may be unveiling a series of initiatives that are gaining widespread media attention. In short, you have been put in the position of reacting to what your opponent says rather than setting the agenda yourself. Allowing yourself to be put on the defensive for long time is a good way to ensure that close race turns into a runaway—with you on the short end. A well-time attack can help you to regain the upper hand.
- Gain Attention in a Crowded Year. If you are running for state legislature you are competing for limited news hole and air time with contests for president, governor, senator and congressman—to say nothing of a host of other local offices and ballot initiatives. Given such diversions, the local newspaper and television station may have all be forgotten about you AND your opponent. A few negative salvos will convince a bored press corps to take notice

- Capitalize on an Opponent's Mistake. Again, Sen. Moynihan illustrate this point. In 1976, he was in a close race with then-Rep. Bella Abzug the Democratic senatorial nomination from New York. Abzug had tried moderate her fiery tone. But, about month before voters went to the poll she slipped—telling a reporter that she would not support Moynihan if he won the nomination.

Moynihan immediately jumped on her statement as evidence of the reemergence of the "old" Abzug incapable of being a team player. He then engineered a letter, signed by two-thirds of the Democratic county chairmen the state, criticizing Abzug's stance. The episode turned the momentum in the race in Moynihan's direction, and he went on to win both the primary and the general election.

Finally, if you are clearly behind in a race, you must make voters understand there are significant differences between you and your opponent. A tough "comparative" or "negative" spot—depending on your vantage point—could be your only chance of winning.

But remember that, in such attacks, voters expect the truth. The facts may be open to different interpretations—but they must be available upon request in a form the voters can understand.

For instance, your opponent is trying to blur his position on abortion in front of some audiences. Then you obtain a fundraising letter in which your opponent claims to favor abortion on demand. If being against abortion is an important element of your own campaign, you have a responsibility to present the contrast between your position and the oppositions. But be careful not to stretch the bounds of propriety in making such an attack.

Your opponent's letter may read: "Although there is a large segment of the community that favors abortion on demand in every instance, I do not. While there may be certain narrow circumstances when an abortion may be the only acceptable course of action, these should not be accepted as the norm." In that case, it is not permissible for you to say:

"My opponent recently sent out a fund-raising letter in which he said, and I quote, 'favors abortion on demand.' He did not want this letter to fall into your hands. And now you know why. He has been lying to you about his stand on abortion!"

Before you start chuckling, remember that this type of strained broadside occurs every year. Republicans often try to scare people with the abortion issue. And Democrats just as often will go to any length to get the elderly worked up about Social Security.

Now that you have decided to go on the attack, you need to decide where to deliver the attack—as well as selecting the deliverer. There are many times when the candidate himself should keep his distance from salvos being delivered in his behalf.

For example, a candidate has been given detailed information—with evidence—regarding his opponent's business dealings. For the candidate or his top aides to conduct a press briefing on this information would be unseemly; it would make them appear more preoccupied with digging up dirt than discussing the "issues" of the campaign.

So the state or county party chairman is recruited to release the derogatory information. Party chairmen are supposed to be political animals—and therefore less prone to criticism for playing hardball. The candidate who received the information gets the benefit while staying above the fray.

For the candidate, anything involving an opponent's performance in office—voting history, attendance record, number of junkets—provides a legitimate line of attack. However, if the opponent has a voting record that could be characterized as soft of crime, an attack will carry far more weight if it is delivered by the local chapter of the Patrolmen's Benevolent Association. A press conference showing a group of policemen in uniform is more likely to make the local five o'clock news than a harangue from the candidate himself.

A candidate who calls daily press conferences to deliver attacks will soon lose the media's attention. Such occasions should be reserved for when the candidate wants to throw down the gauntlet and deliver a sweeping broadside for the benefit of the evening news and the morning papers. Television advertising also can be used to deliver attacks designed for a large audience, although such commercials can be targeted to some degree. If you want to attack an opponent for voting against tax credits for day care, you may want to consider advertising during the afternoon soap operas—when a large number of viewers are women.

It is far easier to target specific groups using radio and mail. Because these media are less visible to the general public, you can be more irreverent—and nastier. When a voter is watching television, he or she is often focusing solely on the set. A radio can be playing while the listener performs other tasks. What may come across as overly nasty on television is more palatable on radio because of the listener's more limited degree of attention.

A classic example is the caustic radio commercial that helped to elect Republican John LeBoutillier of New York to Congress in 1980. The Democratic incumbent, Lester Wolff, often took round-the-world trips at taxpayer expense. So the LeBoutillier campaign produced a radio commercial with the sound of a jet repeatedly taking off, as a stewardess' voice intoned: "Next stop, Bangkok.... Next stop, Bombay.... Next stop, Istanbul."

The commercial went on to describe how many trips Wolff had taken and ended with a line emphasizing LeBoutillier's interest in the needs of the Long Island district: "John LeBoutillier. The only plane he'll be on is the shuttle between New York and Washington."

And what if you are on the receiving end of such attacks? Besides launching your own attacks to divert attention, your options include:

- Squelching the Charge. If the attack involves a serious charge of a personal nature, the candidate himself will have to respond; to wit, the recent controversy over Republican vice presidential candidate Dan Quayle's service in the National Guard. A major charge regarding the conduct of the campaign should be handled by the campaign manager, thereby insulating the candidate to some degree. Charges for which there is little evidence should be left to the press secretary. Letting the candidate respond simply will enhance the credibility of the accusation.
- Attacking the Attacks. Some candidates have raised doubts about an opponent's fitness for office by making an issue of the negative tone of the opponent's campaign. In the post-Watergate election of 1974, Democrat Bill Roy was closing in on Republican Sen. Bob Dole of Kansas by emphasizing Dole's closeness to Richard Nixon. Dole, who had never been implicated in any Watergate wrongdoing, cried smear—and began running a now-famous commercial showing mud being thrown at a picture of himself. The ad provoked a backlash against Roy's attacks and helped to save Dole's seat.
- Acting Contrite. The Charles Percy "I Got the Message" commercial of 1978 (see accompanying story) is perhaps the most famous example of this. But there are other variations, such as the New York mayoral race of a generation ago, when John Lindsay—beleaguered by garbage strikes, school strikes and unplowed streets—was in deep trouble. In his quest for re-election, his handlers came up with the slogan of "It's the Second Toughest Job in America." It was intended to acknowledge that Lindsay had made mistakes but to note that he had his hands full. And by elevating the stature of the New York mayoralty, it called into question whether

Lindsay's opponents—a colorless state senator and the bumbling city controller—were up to the job. Lindsay ended up winning reelection by almost 10 points.

Two hypothetical case studies illustrate some other tacks that can be taken to blunt a negative campaign:

Case One: "I did it, but it's not what you think."

"Ronald Republican voted to cut off aid to farmers!" blares the headline on the press release issued by his opponent—whom we'll call Donald Democrat. The press release, detailing how the Republican had voted to cut off aid to farmers whose cattle were dying from spoiled corn, is shrewdly delivered to the press just minutes before deadline. Ronald Republican's campaign is caught unaware, and his press secretary does not return a reporter's phone call until the next morning—after Donald Democrat's unrebutted charges have received major play in the press.

Yes, says Ronald Republican's spokesperson, his candidate did vote against a bill that contained a provision with aid for dairy farmers. But the bulk of the measure was designed to cut back on veterans' hospitals, and that's why his boss voted "No." In fact, adds the press secretary, Ronald Republican sponsored legislation later in the session to provide the same type of aid to dairy farmers, and the bill passed overwhelmingly. The attacker, Donald Democrat, now has two problems: He has allowed a minor act by his opponent to become a major campaign issue accruing to the benefit of Ronald Republican, and he has demonstrated that he does not know all of the facts.

Case Two: "Attack the source."

A group called Classroom Teachers for Better Education publicly blasts Ronald Republican for voting against borrowing money to pay for higher salaries for teachers. This could spell trouble for Ronald. No one favors worse education, and borrowing money to pay for better education does not sound like such a bad idea. Besides, Classroom Teachers for Better Education sounds like a legitimate group, and we all remember the awe we had for teachers.

A reporter calls Donald Democrat to learn more about this new group. "We are not acquainted with this organization, but we certainly agree with their positions," says Donald's press secretary. But, as it turns out, Ronald Republican's office has a bit more information: Classroom Teachers for Better Education is actually a front group for a highly controversial association of community activists. Donald Democrat must now defend his association with that association, and the original charge is lost forever.

The arts of attack and defense are both essential and respectable campaign techniques. A legitimate attack that has been thought through for its strategic value (how will it help us win?) and its tactical value (how will we accomplish this?) often is a necessary weapon in a campaign arsenal.

Now that you know the rules, here's wishing you happy hunting.

✓ Making a Name for Yourself
Beth Smith

In 1980, less than eighteen months after leaving his congressional staff job in Washington, D.C., the executive director of the New Mexico state Democratic Party, Bill Richardson, had an idea. He would run for Congress. Few people paid him much heed; he sought what many viewed as a worthless nomination for the right to be trounced by the First district's longtime Republican incumbent, Rep. Manuel Lujan.

But Richardson was persistent—and he had a gimmick. He loved to shake hands. Wherever he went, he introduced himself and shook hands with mothers, fathers, teenagers, even toddlers. Richardson shook, on average, 1,000 hands each day. At one point, he attempted to break the world's record for most hands shaken in a 24-hour period. He did not care whose hand he shook; he only cared how many.

Richardson's goal was to shake the hand of every district resident. The idea, he reasoned, might attract the media's attention and help him impress voters as hard-working, determined, and a man of the people.

Richardson never broke the record for shaking hands, and he ultimately was defeated by Lujan. But he nearly toppled the popular six-term incumbent and won the reputation of a hardworking campaigner.

When the state legislature created a new district in the northern part of the state, Richardson was ready. He announced his candidacy and cemented his image by adopting the slogan "Fighter for the North."

On Election Day, Richardson garnered 64 percent of the vote. He currently is completing his third term, the proud possessor of a safe seat.

Richardson's gimmick was unique, but his experience is common. All across the country, unknown political candidates are striving to find the particular set of notes which resonate with voters. If you are wealthy, you can overcome anonymity by spending thousands on television advertising; millionaire officeholders such as New Jersey Sen. Frank Lautenberg and Kentucky Gov. Wallace Wilkinson attest to the viability of this strategy. Even if your assets are more modest, you can overcome the "John Who?" syndrome by seizing earned media opportunities.

The Guiding Principle

For the candidate pursuing earned media, the guiding principle is the same: No matter whether you use words or symbols, make sure you say something about the personality or substance of your candidate. Getting attention is not an end in itself. It means for achieving a broader goal.

One way to create an image is to use political symbols. These help voters associate a name with the various ideas and feelings attached to a particular symbol. For example, if a voter sees a series of pictures of a candidate shaking hands every day, he or she will probably come to believe that this candidate is a hard worker. The voter will likely associate that candidate with all the virtues society bestows upon hard workers: honesty, earnestness, determination, and independence.

One candidate who did this successfully was Florida Sen. Bob Graham. Running for governor in a crowded Democratic field in 1978, Graham, then a little-known state legislator, held a series of "work days," in which he spent a day performing such salt-of-the-earth pursuits as pumping gas, milking cows, digging ditches, and loading crates. Through these efforts, the telegenic Graham was able to garner a disproportionate amount of media attention, finish second in the run-off primary, and eventually win the election.

But be forewarned: Use of symbols or gimmicks in and of themselves will not necessarily bring success. You must combine them with a successful message that speaks to voters' concerns. One candidate who failed to do this is Illinois Sen. Paul Simon, in his recent bid for the Democratic presidential nomination. Campaigning in the love caucuses, Simon received a great deal of coverage for always wearing a bow tie. His name identification and poll numbers quickly began to climb. The media was paying attention, and the voters were listening.

The problem was that nothing was being communicated. He wears a bow tie. So what? The tie might have symbolized independence. It might have symbolized a return to traditional values. Or it might have symbolized something else. But neither Simon nor his campaign staff effectively used the symbol to impart a message.

To avoid such misfires, you must answer four basic questions:

- What are we trying to say?
- Does it reinforce our message?
- Is the point being made clearly?
- Will voters react favorably to our message?

Appealing to the Audience

When pursuing earned media, you must consider three audiences: editors, reporters, and voters. Editors have finite resources at their disposal, and you must convince them your activity or event is worth their time. They will want to know what news value there is in your event. Are you saying anything different? And, particularly in the case of television news, is your event visually appealing?

Once you have persuaded the editor to send a reporter, you must persuade the reporter to convey your message to the voters. The first step is making certain that the reporter understands your message. You should determine how he or she will see an event. Will he or she view it only as a gimmick or ploy? Might the event inadvertently highlight any of the candidate's weaknesses? Might the reporter be distracted from your message?

Assuming you have answered these questions satisfactorily and the story plays in the press as you anticipated, you must consider whether the voters, after reading the newspaper or watching television, will react the way you want. Imagine yourself sitting in an easy chair after a long day's work, and reading or seeing the story. Is the image one that you find appealing? Consider what your polls have told you about voters' concerns, together with your knowledge about these people and their sensitivities. Now try to answer the bottom-line question: will most people be receptive to your message?

Choosing Your Tactics

Every election cycle brings new versions of time-worn favorites—and usually a few completely new ideas—for gaining media attention. There are, in general, six basic rules for garnering earned media:

Go for the Visual. Campaigns often call these "photo opportunities." The idea is to do something, anything, that is visually interesting. As Jack Pridgen, long-time press secretary to Sen.

Lawton Chiles (D-Fla.), puts it: "Creativity is far, far more important than money." Pridgen speaks from experience; his boss made an art form out of obtaining press for an unknown candidate.

In 1970, as an obscure state legislator, Chiles invented "The Walk," now one of the most popular media events. He spent 92 days literally walking across much of the state of Florida. The 1,003-mile walk was unprecedented in most people's view, and Chiles won tremendous press in every city and town he passed through. His walk proved so successful his name became etched in voters' minds as "Walkin' Lawton" Chiles. He went on to upset a favored Republican opponent to win the first of three terms in the U.S. Senate.

A visual event can even be as simple as wearing a particular hat or jacket. Democratic presidential hopeful Richard Gephardt, who until this year rarely had been spotted publicly in anything but a blue pinstripe suit, frequently donned a down parka and farmer's cap in his successful attempt to appeal to Iowa's beleaguered farmers.

Be Quotable. If your candidate or a staff member has a talent for "turning a phrase," use it; this can be a very powerful tool. The media loves to replay a line that is especially cute, witty, or barbed.

Tennessee Sen. Albert Gore succeeded on all three counts in a Democratic presidential debate. Criticized by Gephardt for advocating a foreign policy platform that "sounds more like Al Haig than Al Gore," the witty Gore retorted, "That line sounds more like Richard Nixon than Richard Gephardt." The crowd loved it; the media replayed it over and over.

Even if your candidate lacks the ability to turn a sharp phrase on a regular basis (and few are as skilled as Rev. Jesse Jackson in this respect), do not discount this device as a means of gaining attention. Even if you hit upon on a great line only once during a campaign, it could be the phrase that pays. (Remember how Walter Mondale stung Gary Hart in 1984 by asking "Where's the Beef?")

If you have a particularly strong phrase that you know will be gobbled up by the press, save it for a big event that will bc covered by television. If your line is especially time-sensitive, call a press conference and alert reporters you will have something significant to say. If for some reason you absolutely cannot get the candidate in front of the cameras, issue a press release saying simply: "Bob Jones, Democratic candidate for Congress, made the following statement...."

Find Your Target and Hit It Consistently. The media loves a fight. Attacks work especially well when they seem to reflect a previously unspoken sentiment. Keep in mind the target does not necessarily have to be your opponent. It can be an institution, idea, or problem.

Rep. Gephardt is a prime example. Little known at the outset of the 1988 Democratic presidential race, he attracted tremendous attention by attacking our country's trading partners—particularly Korea—for unfair trade practices. He used the trade issue to symbolize the larger issue of America regaining control of its economic destiny. By pitting himself against a distant enemy, Gephardt convinced people he stood with them.

Use an Attractive Package. This is the art of framing a routine story in such a way that the media finds it to be attractive. A candidate seeking to make economic development a key issue might start with a press conference and unveil a five (or six or seven) point plan with a catchy title to bring economic development to the district. The press conference can then become the kickoff to a three or four day tour across the district to highlight opportunities for economic development. Such a tour should include meetings with key leaders in business, academia, and government.

To achieve the visual element, you might stop at various locations which represent problems in each community, such as a homeless shelter or an unemployment line. You might also visit recent solutions, such as a new manufacturing facility or a strip of new small businesses. Each visual should relate to the proposals in the candidate's economic development plan. At each appearance, the candidate should reiterate the plan's major elements.

The success of this tactic depends on your ability to make the entire package so compelling that editors will send reporters to cover the trip. If you have a good relationship with local editors, pitch it to them. If you feel more comfortable talking to the paper's political reporter, you might be able to sell him or her on the idea. The reporter could then lobby the editor. When making your sales pitch, describe vividly—and accurately—what reporters can expect to see. Once a news organization has committed a reporter, even if it is only for one leg of the tour, you are virtually certain to receive some coverage.

Release New Information. This tactic is difficult for unknown candidates to use because they often lack access to newsworthy information. Incumbents have built-in advantages in obtaining new statistics, announcing new programs, responding to new proposals, and introducing new bills. Often, an incumbent wins attention simply by announcing an allotment of funds being made by another arm of the government. Just as often, he or she had nothing to do with procuring those funds, but still reaps the credit.

Challengers can do the same thing do so, you must develop your own sources of information think tanks are often excellent sources Nor research and new ideas, and usually are willing to share their findings. But beware: A candidate can do himself more harm than good if the information is questionable and cannot be proven quickly.

Even simple developments in your campaign, such as the release of a new poll, a new staff appointment, or a new endorsement, can win you coverage. But announcements of this sort should be made only after applying the Guiding Principle. If your candidate is positioning himself as a populist, you should not, for example, make a big splash about endorsements from established politicians.

Be Timely. Responding to new information is much easier than creating or obtaining new information. But timing is vital; your reaction to yesterday's news is meaningless. You must react to news almost the minute it breaks.

That means you must know when news breaks. Every campaign should have access to a news service. You can purchase or borrow services that are transmitted or received by computer. If you are on a tight budget, someone in the campaign may have a friend in a government office with access to the Associated Press wire or Nexis/Lexis (an electronic library with access to current news stories). If so, make sure you speak with that person first thing every morning to find out what is moving on the wire.

The importance of a timely response is difficult to overstate. If, for example, people in your district are concerned about toxic wastes, and you have made toxic waste cleanup a major issue, you must be prepared to make a statement on a moment s notice should you learn of a new study showing different levels of toxicity in nearby groundwater.

This way, you can immediately alert key staffers and discuss possible reactions. Do you hold a press conference at one of the testing sites, do you meet with families from a nearby neighborhood, or do you issue a strong statement urging specific action by involved officials? Whatever you decide, do it that day—in time for reporters to make their deadlines and in time for you to make the afternoon or evening news.

Take Advantage of VIP Visits. Very Important People are great for a campaign because they attract media attention and contributors. But keep in mind the Guiding Principle. What do these friends say about your candidate—and what do their friends say? Remember that especially in politics, a person is judged by the company he or she keeps. If, for example, you are running in a university district and you have the opportunity to bring in Sylvester Stallone, you may well decide that no news is better than some news.

Movie and television stars are not the only names that can attract attention to your campaign. Indeed, you may find your message is more clearly reinforced by association with famous people in other professions—athletes, clergymen, authors, artists, and business leaders.

Because your task is to gain media attention, you can be sure that bringing in a celebrity will provide you not only coverage but also good will. As jaded as they may be when it comes to politicians, political reporters can become as excited as anyone else about the arrival of a celebrity from the entertainment world.

Follow each of these rules closely and you quickly will find voters becoming increasingly aware of your name and your candidacy. Even if you do not shake 1,000 hands a day, you may still find yourself shaking hands with the majority leader of your state legislature—after he congratulates you on your victory in November.

✓ How to Insulate Your Attack Advertising From Viewer Backlash
Deno Seder

Attack advertising has acquired a bad reputation recently, and that's a shame. The central tenet of Democratic government is accountability to the public; questioning a candidate's record during an election campaign is the vehicle by which that accountability is delivered. Voters instinctively understand this crucial role, which is why they are often swayed by negative information.

Unfortunately, most attack ads aired in recent years are uncreative, mean-spirited, heavy-handed, tasteless, insulting or just plain stupid. Having watched them makes you feel as if you've just taken a bath in the Persian Gulf. They may impart information that will eventually wield influence in the voting booth, but most voters will be unimpressed, uninspired, unamused and resentful of the airwave pollution. Such advertising can easily be counterproductive; in a multi-candidate race it may even prove suicidal.

History strongly suggests that the most effective negative campaigns have been supported by a strong underpinning of humor, which appears to offer insulation from "shoot the messenger" backlash while leaving a lasting impression. Humor advocates cite several theories to bolster their case, many of them well documented:

Breaking Through the Clutter. The average TV viewer is now subjected to more than 2,500 commercials each month—more than 20 hours of sensory clutter. Ads that break through that morass and register have to be different in some meaningful way. Since most attack ads are dull and unimaginative, an element of humor can make an ad stand out. The humor is unexpected, and therefore helps distinguish the message from the flood of spots competing for the viewer's attention.

Triggering Recall and Acceptance. No quantitative studies have been published on the subject of audience reaction to humor in political attack ads but several such studies dealing with product advertising may be useful and pertinent. Last year, ASI Market Research discovered that humorous commercials had a 17 percent higher recall rate than those without a humorous content. In 1989, Video Storyboard Tests interviewer 25,000 viewers and found 58 percent rates funny spots more persuasive than serious ones.

Intellectual Appeal. Psychologist and advertising consultant Carol Moog offered this theory to the *New York Times:* "Humor gives people a way to vicariously express their aggression. It reaches them above the base consumer level. It appeals to their intellect, and makes them feel bright." Indeed, getting a joke can make one feel intellectually superior to those who may not have understood. Hence, sophisticated humor can be especially effective in well-exposed advertising, while a dumb gag might wear poorly, insult the viewer and cause its own backlash.

He Who Laughs Last

Other theories suggest laughter induces the flow of endorphins and other brain hormones, creating a sense of well-being or euphoria. "People like a good laugh," explains media guru Tony Schwartz when asked about the phenomenal success of his humorous attack ads.

One famous Schwartz creation originated the now-familiar "Pinocchio format," making the opponent's nose appear to grow as his statements are quoted. Another Schwartz masterpiece had no spoken copy whatever, just the words "Agnew for Vice President?" appearing on a TV screen while a man guffawed hysterically in the background.

Such "statements" can cripple the opposition, yet they leave the viewer with a pleasant feeling, not the bitter aftertaste that often accompanies sober attack ads. Instead of earning the resentment of the targeted audience for presenting a "downer," leaving them laughing creates a feeling of goodwill toward the sponsor, while actually accentuating the sting of the attack on the opponent. We all know that when Jay Leno or David Letterman start making jokes about a candidate, the effect can be devastating. If the public starts laughing at you, they're not taking you seriously, and that's a one-way ticket to political oblivion.

The Anatomy of a Comical Attack

In 1990, our firm was hired by the Louisiana Coalition, a bipartisan independent expenditure group formed to help defeat Republican state Rep. David Duke in his bid to unseat U.S. Sen. J. Bennett Johnston (D). There was nothing funny about Duke's background—which included parading around in a Nazi uniform and a stint as head of the Ku Klux Klan—but we felt it was so bizarre it would readily lend itself to satire and ridicule.

The humorous approach was especially valuable in this case due to the source of Duke's appeal. Louisiana has a long history of anti-Establishment politics, a tradition exacerbated in recent years due to the collapse of the state economy via depressed oil prices. The more the establishment attacked Duke as a dangerous man, the greater his popularity grew.

The only effective way to chip away at the white working class support that formed his base was to ridicule this extremist as an unstable whacko.

The creative vehicle we chose for communicating this message was at parody of the popular TV game show "Jeopardy!" which we dubbed "Jabberwocky!" A set was built, the show's host and contestants cast, and the 60second spot shot and edited—all in one week surrounding Memorial Day weekend. As on "Jeopardy!," the contestants chose a category, were given the answer and required to furnish the question.

Categories included Tax Cheats, Crazy Ideas, False Patriots, Good Buddies and Basement Booksellers. Corresponding answers were:

- He failed to file state income taxes from 1984 to 1987.
- He has advocated that America be divided into separate race of nations.
- He lied about serving his country and never spent a single day in the military.
- He hired ex-Nazis to work on his political campaigns.
- He says he's changed his ways, but last year he was caught selling Nazi books and tapes from the basement of his legislative office.

The answer to each of these questions was, of course, the same: "Who is David Duke?" The tag reiterated, with slightly different emphasis, "Just who IS David Duke?"

"Jabberwocky" worked beyond all expectations. In addition to exposure through paid media, it got extensive coverage in Louisiana and national media outlets. Duke was thrown on the defensive, and his momentum blunted. Instead of posting an anemic win that would have given cover and comfort to racists across America and stigmatized the state, Johnston was reelected handily by 11 points.

Follow-up

One word of caution: make sure your funny attack ad is funny. Show it to a cross section of disinterested people before you air it. Do they understand it? Do they get the message? Do they laugh or smile? Are they more inclined to vote against your opponent after viewing your momentary comedy?

If the answer is yes to all of these questions, run it. Call a press conference and have a screening. Hand out VHS cassettes of the ad, copies of its script and black and white stills taken from several of its frames. Chances are it will become a favorite campaign topic for the next several days.

Why is a humorous attack such a comparatively easy way to attract desirable attention? Voters and the media are starved for information about the candidates. They instinctively know that attack spots will be perhaps their best source of pertinent facts. The creative use of humor in these messages will make the assimilation of such necessary information a joy instead of a dreary burden. Campaigns are tedious enough; a little comic relief will carry a long way.

There's a saying about politicians in Louisiana that has currency elsewhere in the country, if less piquancy: "Lie, cheat, steal and the people will grant redemption. Bore them and you assure perdition."

✓ Linear Programming for Campaigns
John C. Blydenburgh

Linear programming is a widely-used, proven technique for allocating resources in business to maximize profits. Here, for the first time anywhere, is how to apply it to winning political campaigns so that you can target all-too-scarce resources of time, money and volunteers to achieve the greatest impact. What is most efficient for your campaign: door-to-door canvassing, telephoning, mailing? Radio, TV or space advertising? Which of these tactics or others should be used with more intensity and which with less ? What combination is the best?

The linear programming calculations required to make informed campaign resource decisions could have stymied you in the past. Not now. With the help of a microcomputer software package and this step-by-step guide you can rely on hard numbers and not guesswork to make your campaign not only efficient, but effective.

War is a practical metaphor for a political campaign. So, it should be of little surprise that linear programming, which came of age during World War II to aid in research for the U.S. Air Force, can be effectively applied in political campaign battles. Today linear programming is a valued operations research technique that is widely used in business and in the public sector to help in making resource allocation decisions. Political campaign managers should take advantage of this mathematical technique too in deciding how to make the most efficient use of the limited resources available for a campaign effort.

Fixed-Cost vs. Variable Activities

The general approach to political campaigning taken here is that it is useful to look at campaign activities in broad categories at the outset. First are the fixed-cost activities. These are one-time, one shot measures without which a campaign would not be a campaign. In some areas lawn signs are essential to a run for office, in other places bumper stickers are required, or billboards or ads in the local newspaper. Expenditures for these purposes represent fixed costs. A retainer for a campaign consultant and rent for a headquarters are other examples of fixed costs. Linear programming, a method for finding solutions to sets of simultaneous linear inequalities, is not helpful in allocating resources for fixed-cost activities.

The second category of campaign activities have a variable component. These are efforts which one can choose to make with greater intensity or less intensity, in a wider or narrower geographic area, or to contact more voters or fewer voters. Campaign communications techniques are prime examples of variable activities.

Within the variable category, there are two subcategories of campaign techniques. Each subcategory represents tactics which can be substituted for one another in the execution of campaign strategy. One subcategory includes campaign efforts which can be targeted: the campaign manager can decide which voters he or she wants to reach and which technique is best for reaching them. Examples of efforts which can be targeted are door-to-door canvassing, telephoning, and direct mailing. The other subcategory includes those mass media (or "shotgun") techniques which are much more difficult to target, such as the use of paid newspaper, radio and television advertising, or the pursuit of free media exposure. It is possible to control, to some degree, which voters are reached through such activities, but much less than with tactics in the first subcategory.

Linear programming is a helpful tool for making decisions about the allocation of resources to activities in both of the variable subcategories. It is perhaps most appropriately applied when deciding between different combinations of substitutable techniques in each of the variable subcategories. Although it is not necessary that techniques be substitutable in order to use linear programming, many campaigns can easily differentiate targeted from "shotgun" activities in deciding on a media budget or how to use volunteers.

Further, the method discussed below to quantify the effectiveness of campaign techniques requires direct comparisons between them, and this is easier to do if the techniques are substitutable. However, it is quite possible to model all variable techniques against all resources without regard to the substitutability of techniques. There is no technical reason why this cannot be done. The conclusion of this article further addresses this point, but recommends separate applications of linear programming to subsets of substitutable activities since such applications are more easily accommodated.

Identifying Campaign Goals

Linear programming requires that the user be able to explicitly identify an "objective function"—a clearly specified goal for the campaign. For the typical campaign manager, this goal is "to win." Linear programming can find a solution to the problem of how to make the best use of limited resources when "best" is defined in terms of making a contribution to winning.

The route to winning, of course, is perceived differently by different campaign managers. Some see campaigns as problems in mass communication, thus they maximize "communication" (through television advertising, etc.) and let the chips fall where they may. Others see campaigns in terms of cause and effect, where targeted contacts (phone calls, direct mail, etc.) cause voters to do one thing or another. These managers maximize "effect." Linear programming does not require a specific definition for the objective function. It only requires that the user be cognizant of an objective function. The beauty of the technique is that it helps the manager to use the best combination of resources and techniques to reach the goal critical to winning. The bad news is that it doesn't tell you if you're wrong about the relationship of your goal and winning.

The "classic" application of linear programming to a business problem is analogous to a situation faced by most campaign managers in a fairly complex campaign. Imagine a business which seeks only to maximize profit. It is capable of manufacturing at least two products (though linear programming is not limited to two variables); the products have different rates of profit; the products require different combinations of energy and labor to produce them, i.e., one requires more labor per unit of production and the other requires more energy per unit of production; the business has a fixed amount of energy and labor available. Linear programming is a technique for solving the problem of deciding, for a given level of resources, how much of each product to produce in order to maximize profit.

The analogy to political campaigning is straightforward. Profit is like the goal of the campaign (usually some variation on winning); the products are like campaign techniques (usually communication techniques); and energy and labor are like campaign resources. Typically campaign resources include money, volunteer labor and the candidate's time. Just about all other campaign resources can be acquired with these three.

Estimating Resources and Costs

The actual solution to linear programming problems for campaigns can be worked out with a microcomputer using programs readily available through any decent software supplier. But the calculations require that the user provide some crucial information. First is an estimate of the level of resources which will be available in the campaign, i.e., the constrained resources. Accepting my contention above about campaign resources, this means estimating the amounts of money, volunteer labor and candidate time which will be available in the campaign. Of course, early expectations about resources change through the campaign as a manager faces reality. This presents no problem, for one simply adjusts the model whenever any crucial information changes.

Other information which is needed is the per unit cost for each campaign technique, expressed in terms of constrained resources. For example, if the technique is door-to-door canvassing, how much money, volunteer labor and candidate time is required to produce each contact? This can be calculated by estimating the total amount of each resource needed to contact the target electorate, and dividing by the expected number of contacts. This should be done for each campaign technique. This yields an expression of the relationship between resources and the cost per contact (unit) for each technique.

As we will see, this expression will be in the form of one linear inequality for each resource. If there are three resources, and five campaign techniques under consideration, there should be three inequalities, each with five cost variables. Each inequality should be of this type: the total amount of a given resource is less than or equal to the per unit cost of technique one, plus the per unit cost of technique two, etc. through the five techniques. Again, if the estimate of costs is revised at any time during the campaign, the inequalities can be reformulated to take account of the new information.

Measuring Effectiveness

Finally, the campaign manager has to be able to quantify the relative effectiveness of each technique, that is, assign a number which is a valid measure of effectiveness. While we all have a sense of what is effective and where it is effective, quantification is no simple matter. However, applying an experimental method developed by Mosteller and Nogee to measure economic utility, a campaign manager's belief concerning the effectiveness of various techniques can be quantified with remarkable success. The numbers produced have no objective validity, but they do represent what the manager believes about the techniques under consideration in the context in which they are about to be applied. Though quantification is only in terms of the relative effectiveness of the techniques when comparing each to all others, the numbers which result are sufficient information to apply linear programming to solving resource allocation problems.

The procedure works like this. Suppose there are three campaign techniques available, door-to-door canvassing (D), telephone contact (T), and direct mail (M) (this procedure can be used for any number of campaign techniques). First, the manager ranks the three in order of effectiveness and without regard to costs. Suppose the ranking is as they are listed above, or D, T. M. Next consider the electorate to be contacted. Suppose 100 percent of the voters were contacted by telephone, the second most effective technique. Presumably that would have some positive effect, such as X percent more of the electorate will now vote for your candidate than would have had they not been phoned. Now, thinking of an exactly identical electorate, ask yourself "what percentage of the electorate would have to be contacted by a door-to-door canvass, the remainder being contacted by mail, to have exactly the same net positive effect (X percent)?"

Suppose, for the sake of illustration, that the answer is 60 percent, i.e., you believe that contacting 60 percent of the electorate by door-to-door canvass and 40 percent by mail will have exactly the same positive effect as contacting all of the electorate by telephone. The range of the scale (the highest and lowest values) does not matter because we are only measuring relative effectiveness. Thus we can assign a maximum value of 1.0 to the highest ranking technique and 0 to the lowest ranking technique. This enables a clever solution to the problem. We know that the effectiveness of telephoning on a given electorate equals .6 canvassing and .4 direct mail. Since $D = 1.0$ and $M = 0$, $T = .6(1.0) + .4(0)$, or $T = .6$. This provides a basis for quantifying the effectiveness of campaign techniques. (For more than three techniques, the same procedure is followed. The effectiveness of the second highest ranking technique through the penultimate is compared to the effectiveness of a mix of those ranked first and last, and values are assigned in the same way as with three variables.)

The numbers derived above cannot be used directly, because assigning a zero value to mail would mean that it would never be used, and the presumption is that we would not consider it in the model unless it was effective. This is easily remedied by a simple linear transformation of the derived scale. A reasonable transformation is to multiply each value by 5 and add 5. This transformation forces the range of the scale values to be between 5 and 10—a range probably close to most managers' sense of the effectiveness of each technique in terms of its ability to shift percentages of the vote. The values thus derived are D = 10.0, T = 8.0, and M = 5.0.

This transformation is technically feasible for two reasons. First, as measurement theorists point out, any linear transformation of a scale such as the one derived above is a valid scale itself. Second, the nature of the solution to the linear programming problem is such that it is relatively insensitive to small changes in the coefficients in the objective function. It is important to stress the word "relatively" here. The two-variable illustrations below should make this point clear.

A very brief methodological digression is in order for those who would object to the use of linear programming in this context because the relationship between level of campaign activity and effect" is not linear, that a saturation effect sets in eventually. This is, in theory, true, but in my own research (interviews with about 75 candidates and campaign managers, mostly for state legislative seats) campaign managers acknowledge the possibility of a saturation effect, but they feel it is virtually never reached in practice. Resources are just too scarce. Thus, granted that the relationship in question is more likely to be sigmoid than a straight line, most campaigns operate at the relatively linear middle region of the sigmoid. So, little damage is done by assuming linearity.

Deciding Among Four Techniques

Suppose a campaign is considering using four campaign techniques: door-to-door canvassing by the candidate (C); door-to-door-canvassing by volunteers (V); telephone solicitation (T); and direct mail (M). The objective function (O) is defined as the probability of winning. The objective function is expressed in general form as follows:

$$O = A1(C) + A2(V) + A3(T) + A4(M)$$

The "A" terms are the amount of each technique to be used, and it is these that linear programming is going to find for us given that we want to maximize O. The terms C, V, T and M are values derived from the Mosteller and Nogee experiment procedure quantifying the campaign manager's perception of the relative effectiveness of each technique. Suppose you go through the procedure and transformation and come up with values of 10.0, 9.0, 8.0, and 5.0, respectively. Then the specific form of the objective function would be:

$$O = A1(10.0) + A2(9.0) + A3(8.0) + A4(5.0)$$

Next is the problem of estimating the amount of each constrained resource available to the campaign. Suppose these values turn out to be 400 hours of candidate time; $5,000 in unrestricted cash; and 3,000 hours of volunteer labor.

Now estimates are needed for the cost per contact for each campaign technique, in terms of candidate time, money and hours of volunteer labor. Our hypothetical per contact costs have absolutely no basis in fact; they are for illustration only. Anyone applying linear programming should come up with her or his original estimates.

1. Candidate's time:
   $400 < .33(C) + .04(V) + .04(T) + .02(M)$
2. Money:
   $5,000 < .65(C) + .65(V) + .15(Tj + .80(M)$
3. Volunteer labor:
   $3,000 < .33(C) + .40(V) + .15(T) + .10(M)$

Common sense dictates additional constraints on the A terms: they cannot be less than zero nor more than the maximum feasible number of contacts for the setting of the application.

We now have all the information needed to find a solution (values for the A terms) to the linear programming problem. The nature of linear programming is such that before seeking the solution we already know that one of the A terms will be zero! This is because the number of non-zero terms in the objective function never exceeds the number of constrained resources. Since there are only three constrained resources, there only will be three campaign techniques with non-zero A terms recommended in the objective function. This is not obvious on the face of the problem, but it makes good intuitive sense and agrees with many campaign managers with whom I have spoken: campaigns with fewer resources should do fewer things at greater intensity.

Fine Tuning Your Model

An important additional consideration is the impact on voters arising from interaction effects of different campaign techniques. For example, phoning a voter before a direct-mail contact increases the chance that the mail will be read, thus increasing its effectiveness (one hopes). Treat interacting techniques as a single technique in addition to the two (or more) which make it up, with a total cost which is the sum of its parts.

Finally, there is the need to address the connection between the substitutability of techniques and the sample problem's identification of all campaign resources as reducing to only three: candidate time, money and volunteer labor. One might conclude that if the solution is right, then no campaign should ever engage in more than three campaign techniques (because there will never be more than three non-zero A terms in any objective function). I would maintain that this is true for any set of substitutable campaign techniques for which the assumptions of linear programming are met. Techniques which are substitutable, like those in the example, are performing the same function; those which are not part of a substitutable set are performing separate functions and should be treated separately, perhaps by running separate models. Thus each model for each set of substitutable techniques might recommend three techniques, leading to a total greater than three. Budgeting among subcategories (setting the constraints on resources) is the campaign manager's problem.

One element of substitutability has implications for the appropriate use of the model for particular campaign settings, defined perhaps by geographic areas or other means of identifying voters. It is perfectly feasible, and probably wise in many instances, to run a model for each setting. For example, cost functions and even effectiveness measures vary from setting to setting in heterogeneous electorates. Models can be employed based on any set of data. It is feasible to run a model for each setting. Although linear programming is as mute on budgeting among settings as it is on budgeting among sets of substitutable techniques, with a little more sophisticated mathematical modeling one can make a great deal of progress toward solving this problem, too.

The lesson here is that linear programming is only one of the many tools used by contemporary business decision makers which can be applied successfully to campaign decision making. And the efficient use of resources means the effective performance of a campaign's democratic function.

✓ Early TV Expenditures
David Welch

Three weeks from election day, in 1992, I called state Sen. Jim Greenwood and said, "I want to be the first one to address you by your new title, Congressman Greenwood."

Laid out in front of me, of course, were the results of our brushfire poll that showed a virtual dead heat between Democratic incumbent Peter Kostmayer at 40 percent and Greenwood at 29 percent. Just as importantly, Kostmayer's favorable-to-unfavorable ratio stood at barely 1:1. Perhaps even more significant was that Greenwood had pulled ahead of Kostmayer among working women by more than 10 points.

I told Greenwood that if the dollars were raised for a sustained effort, this campaign was his.

The problem was that there were no dollars. An that's because we took every dime we had, a total of $110, 000, and spent it on late September and early October television in the expensive Philadelphia market. It was a risky but crucial decision.

"The Spot," as we grew to call it, portrayed Kostmayer as seriously out of touch with such average daily concerns as paying taxes and bills and worrying about jobs. It showed a working mother tending to her kids in the morning, rushing off to her job, eating dinner with her family, paying bills with her husband, and putting her young daughter to bed.

After proclaiming that only Jim Greenwood understands her needs, she closed by saying: "I'm not sure Peter Kostmayer will ever get it." By going against the grain of 1992's conventional wisdom—which was to save money until the end in order to influence a late-deciding electorate—we took control of the agenda.

Our risk soon yielded a promising result. Suddenly, a campaign that had been down 20 points in June now took on renewed life. Volunteers came out of the woodwork, and we began raising money at a clip of $10,000 per day.

The sudden surge in fundraising enabled the campaign to execute its planned telephone-driven mail effort to the fullest extent and then go back on the air for the final 10 days.

The mail was essential because it zeroed in on Republicans and Independents who had been identified by issue and candidate preference during the quiet weeks of early summer. With the "Big Mo" on our side, two more key decisions loomed for the campaign. The first was whether to go positive or negative on television down the stretch. The second was what to do about Kostmayer's blistering attacks on Greenwood's Social Security position.

Although some in our camp wanted to continue driving the negatives on Kostmayer and put him away, we decided on a positive, upbeat, spot. It showed Jim Greenwood speaking to a rally of exuberant supporters and spending time with his family while the announcer read excerpts from the Philadelphia Inquirer's endorsement. Kostmayer's desperate pitch that Greenwood wanted to ruin Social Security—a damaging attack if believed by senior citizens—was answered by Greenwood's mother, Alice Greenwood. She wrote a highly personal letter to all seniors that brought shame on Kostmayer for stooping so low as to scare seniors. She saved her best line for the end: "Jim Greenwood will never vote to end Social Security. I'll make sure of it."

Kostmayer was also using radio to blast Greenwood on Social Security. We responded, dollar for dollar, with the same message we had used in the mail. Interestingly, this was the only radio we bought during the entire campaign.

Though I was the first to call Greenwood "Congressman" on Nov. 3, I won't be the last.

✓ Budgeting Campaigns
Ron Faucheux

1. Determine How Much Money is Available. The first step in determining your funding potential is to take a sheet of paper. Divide it into three columns. Label column one Sources, label column two Minimum, label column three Goal.

Under sources, list all your a potential fundraising sources, from Aunt Bessie to EMILY's List, from labor union PACs to personal loans, from the captains of industry to small donor supporters. Make sure you include the amount of money you will personally donate or loan to your own campaign. Of course, you need to make sure your sources and amounts are consistent with applicable state, federal, and local campaign finance laws.

For each source, fill in the "minimum" contribution you know you will get and the "goal" (or the maximum) you think you may be able to get and what you should ask for. Example: Aunt Bessie, though not extremely wealthy, is fairly well off and has always considered you one of her favorites. You know she's good for at least $500 and think if you plead and beg (which before it's over, you'll end up doing), you may be able to squeeze as much as $2,000 out of her in several increments. So, put $500 next to her name in the "minimum" column and $2,000 in the "goal" column.

Now, add up the "minimum" column. Take half of that number and that's what you probably can count on to raise from this list of sources. Don't be depressed if that figure is far short of your fundraising needs. If it looks like you're a winner, the numbers will increase. Also, if you run a well organized finance operation, you can increase the results. Remember, too, that this is your initial source list. During a campaign, you will identify many new sources, particularly if you're well organized and look like you have a chance at winning.

This exercise is a good way to force candidates into making a realistic analysis of how much money is out there. This is an essential first step to budgeting a campaign.

This is a critical part of the plan. It is always wise, and often depressing, to be honest with yourself when doing a budget. In politics, as in business, things usually cost more than you first think. Price increases, unanticipated problems, administrative overhead, crisis management, all of these things can easily make mince meat of a campaign budget.

2. Pick a Budgeting Approach and Stick to it. There are a lot of different approaches to budgeting. Some consultants suggest you do high, medium, and low budget scenarios, or ideal and barebones scenarios, depending on fund raising. You need to find the approach best geared to your needs. In any case, select one and use it throughout the campaign.

Perhaps a better suggestion is to do a single realistic winning budget based on what you need to win the race without any fat or luxuries in it. Even though it may be tough to ultimately achieve, it's still the goal that drives your entire fundraising strategy. You should focus on what you need to win, and constantly shoot for that. It's too easy to fall back on a barebones budget, but if it's inadequate to win the race, it can mislead you. Use a barebones budget only when you have reached a brick wall and know you won't have the money to fund your desired budget. When that happens, it's usually a bad sign but is not necessarily fatal. Often, your opponents will have the same problem.

You can also include various options (Option A includes three weeks of TV and radio, Option B includes two weeks of TV and radio, etc.) in your overall budget scenario. Initial budgets should be simply structured around line items and a timeline cash flow schedule. Even though we can talk about the details forever, for purposes of this guide we're suggesting a simple, quick, understandable approach that can be beefed up later with more information.

Budget line items should include every possible expenditure, generally centered on two major areas:

Communications and research—Television and radio time buys and production; newspaper space buys and production; direct mail, include printing, lists and labels, postage, mail shop, production and design for each piece, for mass mailings as well as smaller, targeted and in-house mail shop efforts; outdoor billboard space, production and printing; printing, design, typesetting, and pre-press for brochures, hand cards, tabloids, ballots, letterhead and envelopes, flyers, invitations, yard signs, posters, bumper stickers, body badges, buttons, volunteer cards; telephone banks (first determine if you're going to hire a professional firm or do it with volunteers, the later is often just as expensive and almost always less efficient than a professional phone system); media training and expert coaching for speeches, interviews, debates (a must for newcomers and experienced pole, alike); photography including photographer's fee, film and processing, make-up, and lighting; polling and research, including your first benchmark poll, follow-up surveys, tracking polls, focus groups and specific issue and opposition research activities.

Organizational—Staff salaries, expenses, insurance, taxes; headquarters rent, office supplies, equipment and furniture, daily postage, computer hardware, software, parking, decorations, petty cash, long distance, faxing, refreshments; consultant fees, retainers, salaries, expenses; travel, auto rentals, gasoline, air fare, cabs, buses, subways, hotels, meals, tips for the candidate and staff; legal, accounting, and other various fees (such as qualifying fees) and costs involving legal compliance and reporting; volunteer activities such as door-to-door canvassing, poll workers, rallies, and coffee parties (yes, make no mistake about it, even volunteer activities cost money); subsidies to political organizations to cover your share of campaigning (in some jurisdictions, there are legal restrictions on these activities, so watch out); gifts and donations, such as buying ads in high school football programs and tickets to charitable affairs; voter registration and special absentee programs (this may be part of your direct mail and phone bank line items); and last, but not least, election day GOTV programs (again, this may fall within your media line items).

3. Keep Your Options Open. You may want to build options into your campaign budget. For example, you may figure you need to provide an introductory "bio" spot which features the candidate's personal background and the other an attack spot against your opponent. However, if your opponent attacks you, you may need an answer spot, which would require adding the cost of producing and airing a third spot. That can be budgeted as an optional line item.

4. Remember: Timing is everything. Obviously a key part of strategy, message, and planning, timing is an integral part of the overall campaign. Timing is often the most difficult aspect of planning message communications and strategic implementation. It is also related to available money, which is why a cash-flow schedule is vital.

The timeline schedule should be broken into smaller and smaller time frames as you get closer to election day and spending activity increases. (See Budgeting forms in the worksheets.)

2

Campaign Technology: Computers, Database Management, and Voter Files

★ ★ ★

✓ Voter File Maintenance

Ren Babcock

Campaigns often do not understand their real audience. They spend a fortune on media trying to win support of people not registered, not likely to vote, or not living in their district, when instead they could be targeting their resources on those most likely to vote. The way to do this is through proper use of local voter files.

One reason a voter program is so helpful is it costs less and is more productive than a media campaign. Unfortunately, you need more people and more time to run a good voter file program than to buy newspaper, radio, and TV ads.

How the Voter File Works

Begin by obtaining a copy of your local voter file and putting it on computer. This file generally is kept by the county, but in some areas may be available from the state or your political party. In much of the country, the local board of elections supplies the county voter file—often on tape.

A voter file should include at least the name, address, party affiliation, age, race, sex, date of registration, and precinct of each registered voter. If you are lucky, it will also contain each person's voter history. If not, have it researched and entered. Then you can produce a list of frequent voters.

Once the complete voter file is assembled, start to narrow your universe. First, use voter history to isolate likely voters. Base your decision on prior elections for similar races; if you are running in a primary, turnout figures from general elections are of little relevance, and vice-versa. If there is a particularly salient issue which may affect turnout, take that into consideration.

After you have determined precisely which people are most likely to vote, try to identify favorable and undecided voters. You either can hire a computer company to match phone numbers to your file automatically or you can have volunteers look up the numbers in the phone book and enter them manually.

The next step is to establish a phone bank operation and send each confirmed telephone number to the phone bank. Call voters and solicit their opinions. Favorables can be put aside until election time draws near. Committed opponents should be crossed off your list. Undecideds and mildly unfavorables should be worked with a persuasion program.

The real advantage of a voter file program is that it makes it easier to identify your most persuadable voters. You can target your message based on any combination of race, sex, age, and geographic parameters, while making sure your direct mail program reaches a select group of voters with a specific message for the least money.

The success of your program can easily be monitored with follow up phone calls. If the program appears to be ineffective, adjust your messages and re-mail to your target groups. Or select new targets. Equally important, you can respond—and capitalize—on the remarks and actions of your opponent in a very short time.

As Election Day draws near, all undecideds and unfavorables should be re-identified by telephone. This information should provide an indication of how you are faring in the polls, as well as help you assess the type of GOTV program you run.

Choosing the Right Equipment

Most voter files are quite large; because they include the name of every registered voter, they are much bigger than the files of most campaigns. This may cause problems: although much depends on the number of fields per entry, a PC-AT cannot accommodate as many entries as some campaigns would prefer. If you use a PC, keep your file as small as possible.

The ideal computer for files over 25,000 would be a mini; this may mean farming out the work to a data services company. If you process files of over 10,000 records, you need at least a PC-AT or a 286 class computer.

Voter programs also require a great deal of printing. A high-speed printer is essential, because you must immediately follow up your phone calls with a persuasion mailer. Many campaigns farm out mailings to a local data processing firm. Should you fall behind, you should arrange to have a local firm to do your mailings from the data provided by your in-house computer.

Software is another major consideration. A good database manager like dBase III can easily handle most smaller voter programs. With dBase, you can import and export data easily, change, add, or delete fields, and sort/select without any programming.

You will need to break down the file by household, however, and this requires a program. If you must use an outside firm, try to find one that has worked with large name-and-address files. Be certain your contact understands exactly what you want, and stay close to the project. Make sure the programming charges are set before the program starts.

However you set up your household file, try to do all data entry in-house. This not only saves money, it gives you more control over the project and immediate feedback on your progress.

In summary, a good voter file program can be described in five steps:

- Buy or rent the best voter file available and put it up on computer;
- Isolate your likely voters;
- Learn their feelings about your candidate or issue;
- Test your message;
- Isolate and persuade your persuadable voters;
- Turn out your favorable voters.

Your budget will determine how extensive a program you can mount; a well-designed program could prove to be the best money you ever spent.

✓ Map-Based Data Management
Christopher Sachs

Just a few years ago, it was rare to find a political campaign that effectively utilized personal computers. These days, though, campaigns across the nation depend upon the capabilities of such programs as The Election Machine™ from Grass Roots Software, Winning Ticket™ from MARCOR, Inc., and Campaign Tracker™ from Ace Computer Solutions. These programs are text-based, as are the majority of PC and Mac campaign management systems, but they give the user the ability to sort and query on a voter database, to print mailing lists, and to organize the disparate elements of a political campaign into one cohesive view on the computer. Today, however, systems that go beyond simple list management functions are beginning to emerge in the political arena. These systems use geographical databases along with traditional voter lists and demographics to allow for more effective information analysis. One such system our company has produced is GeoVoter™, a Windows application developed by Map Applications, Inc.

What are the advantages of using a geography-based campaign management system over traditional text-based systems? There are many. The foremost advantage is in the system's ability to allow users to fully visualize campaign strategies. Imagine attempting to visualize and design a building without blueprints—only text descriptions of the site, lists of materials, and so on. The job would get done, but not in the most efficient manner, nor would it necessarily come out the way you had hoped. The use of blueprints (and now 3-D computer modeling) virtually guarantees that the building will be completed as initially envisioned.

This is exactly the kind of visual information a mapping system can give you. You can graphically see the state or district where the political battle is taking place. You can "click" on the map to display voter locations, voter attributes, media boundaries, street names, and more. Mapping your data is a much more powerful way to analyze list-based information because you can actually see the voters displayed on a map. In addition, voter icons can be color-coded to indicate crucial statistics or attributes, such as party affiliation, donations, position on an issue, and so on.

Imagine your voter list displayed in a snapshot with registered voters appearing as red icons, $1,000+ donors appearing as green icons, and independent voters appearing as gray icons on the map. With detailed information available on any voter or location at the click of a mouse button, you can see how you could quickly assess the details and get a real sense of the big picture. Using programs like GeoVoter, new lists of voters or voter attributes can be brought in to refresh the voter database throughout the campaign, on an almost daily basis if needed. Poll results can be searched and displayed, giving the campaign manager not only the latest information as soon as it is available, but also the ability to make sense of it quickly and to act on it immediately. Groups of formerly untargeted or loosely targeted voters can be collected into powerful new subsets of the voter list in any given area to give a candidate or an issue a new boost, possibly even the winning boost.

Another advantage of map-based systems has to do with the volatility of political boundaries. Redistricting produces new political lines that are often quite different from the boundaries used during the previous election. By tying voter data directly to a specific geographic location—that is, the latitude and longitude coordinate pair for the individual voter's house—you are assured that no matter which boundaries change from one election cycle to the next, your voter data is linked to a stable level of geography.

One other advantage: map-based systems, because of the very nature of graphically displaying data, require that the voter and list data used be virtually duplication and error-free. This is because such errors show up easily on a computer map (causing such phenomena as five "Tom Smith" icons, for example, to appear one on top of the other). Such errors or duplications may go unnoticed in a strictly text or list-based system, resulting in an increasingly ineffective effort by campaign personnel, and greater (and wasted) expense on mailings and phone solicitations. Incoming lists must be scrubbed free of address errors and duplicated records.

With the capabilities a map-based system offers campaign directors—the ability to visualize the campaign strategy as never before, through direct manipulation of the elements of a map, and with the capacity to print and plot the political landscape—it's hard to imagine a campaign in the not-too-distant future that is not waged, at least in part, on a computer map. An exciting new era for those of us involved in political campaigns is about to begin. Choose your weapons, as they say. Just make sure one of them exploits the incredible power of computer maps.

✓ Spotting Trends Through Databases

Roger Craver and Jeffrey Hallett

Issues and trends—the driving engine of politics—have always had a way of sneaking up on politicians in Washington, D.C. Usually, the Capital City is the last to know and, by nature of the legislative process, the last to act.

Few issues of lasting social or economic significance originate either in the White House or on Capitol Hill. Rather, as is the nature of democracy, they simmer deep in the grass roots, gather momentum "out there," and only after a fairly long period of gestation—sometimes years—do they become the object of national attention and concern.

Some of these issues and the movements that back them literally march their way into Washington and come roaring to the top of our national agenda; the suffrage movement, civil rights, women's rights, and the anti-war protests are examples.

Other issues gently simmer and bubble for years beyond Washington and then "suddenly" appear on the national legislative or political horizon because of catalytic events or the astute sense of political leaders who know an important new issue when they see one. Examples include the heightened concern for the environment, the nuclear weapons freeze, campaign-finance reform, the family-farm crisis, and issues relating to aging—Social Security, Medicare, and catastrophic health care.

Where To Spot A Trend

Fact is, no issue or trend "suddenly" appears out of the blue. Virtually every major issue can be spotted years before it is "discovered" by the national print media, the networks, and our political leaders. Issues invariably give off definable and detectable signals—if you know where to look.

Here are the places to watch:

- The "underground" press. Many specialized newsletters, magazines, and tabloids traffic in new ideas and are an accurate barometer of change. Readers of and contributors to such periodicals often are sophisticated leaders in their respective fields.
- The scholarly and business publications. Usually these periodicals spot trends and issues at least two years before they become "newsworthy" to the general and mass media.
- The local press. Perhaps most important of all, America's local daily newspapers are our most sensitive stethoscope when it comes to detecting the internal bubblings and gurglings of a national issue in the making.

By monitoring the changing amount and nature of the coverage being given to one issue and comparing this with the coverage being given to other issues, you readily can see the issue trends in America. This process is called trend analysis. It has been used since World War II by America's intelligence community, and it is being used increasingly by the commercial world to spot marketing trends and opportunities. It is just now beginning to find an application in politics.

Whether carried in a newspaper, magazine, technical journal, or over the airwaves, the stories that appear in the media are generated by events. More important, the stories the media cover must, by the very definition of "news," reflect something other than business as usual. They are reports of something new, different, controversial, or unusual.

A basic assumption of trend analysis is that, over time, what the news media report directly reflects those events, activities, or concerns that are of greatest importance to a specific community or interest group. In addition, the specialized and business press generally is a year or two ahead of the general-circulation press in discovering emerging issues.

While The Iron Is Hot

For several years, the direct-marketing firm of Craver, Mathews, Smith and Company has been working with Trend Response and Analysis Company to track emerging issues and, like an investor who charts the stock market, move when the moment seems appropriate.

In the course of our work, we have had our eye on a number of emerging issues. But before summarizing what we think are some of the top trends and issues to watch, a word about methodology.

The emergence of high-speed microcomputers and the existence of more than 3,500 electronic databases or "libraries" means people have a powerful new ability to monitor the ebb and flow of ideas and issues throughout our society. Technology now enables us to eschew the tedious tasks of reading through hundreds of thousands of publications, coding and clipping articles of interest, and filing the sundry scraps in a usable reference system.

Instead, we now have the ability to gain access to a multitude of online databases by using the common office microcomputer and modem. With this equipment, most anyone who has mastered the rudiments of modern office technology can scan and select pertinent information from commercially available databases and store whatever he or she wants in the personal computers memory.

Today's electronic databases contain nearly everything being written—from the most obscure special-interest magazine or technical newsletter to the world's major newspapers. The databases identify, code, and store the stories that appear in these publications. Anyone with an office microcomputer can command it to sift through and examine several million articles to determine the frequency with which an issue or subject has been mentioned over specific time and produce a graph that will depict the pattern, or trend, in minutes.

In addition, a set or Issues can be tracked through the media of choice to see how treatment and patterns of coverage differ. For example, the issue of pay equity for women may be examined in the national press, the business press, local newspapers, popular magazines, and selected women's magazines. By examining the frequency of coverage in the various media, you can formulate a fairly good idea of the importance of pay equity relative to other concerns as seen by these different media.

This sort of analysis is revealing. Not only does it provide measurable clues to which issues are about to emerge on the national scene, but it also provides the "vocabulary" and social context by which the issue is being discussed. For not only can the computer count the number of times a subject is covered, it also can be instructed to fetch a specific article and store it so it can be read.

In other words, if you want to speak to a local women's group about issues surrounding pay equity, such a system enables you to research the topic and understand the appropriate vocabulary. That way, your speech will not jar the ears of people sensitive to the issues.

Finally, this new form of issue or trend analysis enables you to conduct research in a manner that mirrors the speed with which issues emerge and change in today's climate. Traditional methods of analysis cannot keep up with a society where information now moves at the speed of light.

The most commonly used vendors of database services, sometimes called information utilities, are Dialogue, MeadData (which publishes Lexis/ Nexis), Bibliographic Retrieval Service (commonly called BRS), CompuServe, The Source, and Dow Jones Retrieval Service. There are many others.

Among them they provide electronic access to virtually every periodical published. The costs of these services range from $25-$125 per hour, plus the costs of your equipment and an annual subscription fee.

With this as background, here are some of the key issues that bear watching. They are coming up fast from the grass roots:

- The New Workers' "Revolution." Pay equity, like many other social-change issues, has been spearheaded by women. And any politician who dismisses it as "just a women's issue" deserves to be unpleasantly surprised. The trend line is clear. The issue of pay equity is closely aligned with a range of other workplace and job-related issues that are rapidly emerging.

The manifestations of this issue include equal pay for equal or comparable work, rapidly growing anger at the two-tier, dual-standard compensation schemes practiced by American business, the tragedy of massive layoffs, give-backs by union workers, and other sacrifices ostensibly aimed at "helping the company struggle through difficult times."

The media have focused their microscopes on seven-figure salaries for CEOs and golden-parachute schemes for management. As a result, the general public is becoming far more savvy in its ability to evaluate the "worth" of various compensation schemes and to challenge them.

The wise political leader will see this and begin to address voters on such issues of workplace democracy," tax incentives for companies that experiment with new compensation practices, and, of course, pay equity. Canada recently enacted sweeping new pay-equity laws. Similar legislation on the local and state level will not be long in coming to the U.S., budget crisis or no budget crisis.

- Workplace Privacy. The increased use of drug testing, the polygraph, and other forms of testing in private industry is creating a rising sense of unrest among blue-collar workers and middle managers. Many people believe companies are conducting such tests not to protect workers' health, but rather to make certain that their "human machinery" keeps on running with minimal maintenance costs.

The result: anger, resentment, and loss of productivity. Workplace privacy and related issues are of growing concern to those leaders who are prescient enough to worry both about the rights of the individual and the productivity of American industry.

- Family Issues. There is a group of related issues—day care, parental leave, elder leave—that are beginning to take off like a rocket. Coverage of these issues now is concentrated most heavily in the business press; employees are only beginning to deal with compensation issues beyond hourly pay or annual salaries.

These issues are beginning to be dealt with on a piecemeal basis in Washington, D.C. The politician who succeeds in weaving them together in the same way the voters perceive them to be interconnected will strike electoral gold.

- Emergence of the SuperIntelligent Voter. Behind the foregoing issue-specific trends is an information trend to which all leaders and their advisers need to be alert, and that is the increasing sophistication of voters. Thomas Jefferson's fondest hopes about the intelligence and common sense of the citizenry are taking on a new dimension. The trend is clear that we will soon no longer be a network-television society. In spite of the flash popularity of specific individuals and our habitual attention to the "major" news media, people increasingly are seeking information from more and more sources.

The local press, regional media outlets, and specialty publications are taking on added importance as sources of information. Consequently, those seeking to obtain attention or hold the loyalty of voters or other audiences will have to work harder to reach them. And to succeed they will have to treat them as the intelligent people they are—not as "those dummies out there."

- Dramatic Changes in National Priorities. The information revolution, a dispersion of power from Washington, D.C., throughout the country, and the increasing knowledge of Americans regarding the affairs of the nation, have forever altered the nature of federal-state politics and relationships.

When assessing the broad sweep of the many changes underway, there is strong support for a new emphasis on the political importance of governors and mayors. These are the officials who have been standing on the firing line as federal programs, support, and influence have eroded. These are the new managers and leaders who have been taking on the challenge of job creation, technological innovation, education reform, and recruitment of new industry from abroad. It is our governors and mayors who have been working most diligently and effectively to secure a better future for their state or city.

This year's list of presidential candidates already includes more than the usual number of "can do" governors, although several others have decided to sit out this race. They represent more than politics as usual. They are a mix of business person and politician.

What Will Voters Do?

The immediate political results of these emerging issues will be manifested in a greater willingness among politicians to try the "practical" or "common sense" approach. This has paid off in state and local governments where voters have demonstrated a willingness to fund new projects through higher taxes or bond issues and to contribute time and energy to special economic-development projects.

Voters will be far more understanding and supportive of those candidates willing to challenge the tried-and-true approaches of Washington, D.C. It is now more likely than not that issues today's politicians prefer to avoid are likely to be transformed into tomorrow's winning campaign slogans. Some of these include means testing for Social Security, higher taxes to meet clearly defined social needs, and far lower defense spending or "defense sharing" (splitting the costs of global defense with our allies).

Ultimately, the real change—the real shift in power—will be apparent when we see former U.S. presidents running for governor!

✓ Choosing the Right Campaign Software
Edward Segal

The selection of computer software may be one of the most important and far-reaching political decisions that a campaign manager will make during the course of an election.

Indeed, deciding which software to buy can be as critical to your campaign efforts as deciding which aides and consultants to hire. That's because it is possible to buy powerful and affordable computer programs that provide many of the same capabilities as bookkeepers, schedulers, volunteer coordinators, and researchers; or the services of pollsters, attorneys, fundraisers, printers, and mailing houses.

The good news is that there are literally dozens of computer programs on the market to choose from that can help increase the effectiveness of your campaign organization.

The software, also known as applications, includes word processing, spreadsheet, bookkeeping, graphics, desktop publishing and fully integrated systems.

This is also the bad news because, with so many different options to choose from, how will you possibly know which one is the best for your candidate? And how will you know whether to buy a no-frills, garden-variety application or a customized political software program that has been designed for use in campaign situations?

You won't. And you should be careful about basing your decisions solely on a software company's advertising claims or on the recommendations of someone who may know less about the subject than you do.

For campaign managers, the process of selecting software doesn't have to be any more difficult than interviewing someone who has applied for a top spot on your staff.

The challenge, however, is to ask "Sam or Sally Software" the same hard-hitting, penetrating questions you would of a job applicant who could play a major role in determining the success or failure of your campaign.

Your first step in the software decision making process should be to make a comprehensive list of every possible task that you think a computer program might be able to help you with on the campaign trail.

This may include: Drafting and printing reports, correspondence, and mass mailings. (With the right application, your campaign can personalize letters to hundreds or even thousands of potential contributors, voters, volunteers, and other supporters.

You can use databases to do research on campaign issues, as a source of ideas for news releases and position statements, keep track of the activities of your opponent, and make sure that you don't miss late breaking news that might affect the candidate and the campaign.

Creating customized databases of information about various aspects of the campaign, including the availability of volunteers to work in your headquarters; the speaking schedule of your candidate; the work of your staff; tracking the receipt of campaign contributions; creating, maintaining, and purging lists of supporters.

Sharing information among multiple campaign offices. By using special communications software and a modem (a device that enables your computer to send or receive information via the telephone), you can instantly send information such as work schedules, news releases, and survey results to workers in other campaigns or to staffs in branch headquarters offices.

Assembling campaign budgets, writing checks, tracking contributions, and expenses. Compiling reports or information about your campaign that may be required by secretaries of state, local election boards or the Federal Election Commission.

Designing, writing and producing newsletters about the views and activities of your candidate for distribution to targeted groups of supporters or potential contributors.

Preparing, conducting, and tabulating voter questionnaire and public opinion surveys.

After you have assessed and determined your software needs, then, like a politician about to decide how to vote on an important issue, make sure that you have all the facts you need, alternative courses of action, and consider the consequences of any software decision you make.

What To Do

Comparison shop. Compile a list of the major software packages on the market, and, just as you would evaluate the nutritional information on a box of cereal compare the strengths and weaknesses of the different applications.

Be an intelligent consumer. Ask questions, demand facts, and ask for proof of the software's claims.

Test drive the program before you buy it.

Ask to use or borrow a demonstration disk and an owner's manual so you can get a better sense of how easy or difficult the program will be for use in your campaign. Listen to the real experts.

Read magazines or newspapers that discuss or review the benefits or drawbacks of different kinds of software.

Once you buy the software, be sure to read the owner's manual, fill out the registration and warranty card, and save the purchase receipt. Keep this paperwork in a safe place in your campaign headquarters in case the software has to be returned or exchanged.

What Not To Do

Don't buy computers, printers, or other hardware unless you have decided which application you will use. If you buy the computer first, you may end up with hardware that can not run the software that you will want to use in your campaign. With campaign funds usually hard to come by, why waste them on what could become a glorified paperweight?

Don't be afraid to ask questions, no matter how dumb you think they might be.

Getting answers to your questions now will probably save you a lot of time, money, and even political embarrassment later.

Don't buy software with more features than you need.

Frank Tobe, of Below, Tobe & Associates in California, advises that "small campaigns, in a district of 10,000 voters or less—which is what most campaigns are—can get away" with using any word processing program. Above that level, it is time to think about specific software options suited to campaign uses.

Don't be surprised by how much you may have to spend in order to get the software you need.

Don't buy software that doesn't do what you want.

Don't waste your money on a fancy word processing program with limited "number crunching" capabilities when a dedicated spreadsheet program is really what you need.

Don't spend more than you have to. After you have decided which application to get, shop around for the best price, including calling both local computer stores and national discount software chains. But keep in mind that dedicated campaign packages are usually sold only directly from the manufacturer.

Don't feel you have an obligation to get a computer or software package in the first place.

Based on the office your candidate is seeking, and how much you want to spend, it might make more sense to hire a company or consultant to handle the campaign's word processing, financial, mailing or other computer-related needs.

The bottom line is: you don't have to be a software expert to effectively and authoritatively evaluate the value or usefulness of computer programs for your campaign.

You do, however, need to be a conscientious employer—and a thorough campaign manager.

✓ Winning Votes on the Information Super-Highway
Roger S. Conrad

It's two days before the city council is scheduled to vote on your client's plan for downtown development. You've spent months making your case to local leaders, the business community and the citizenry at large. In fact, all of the council members have at one time or another indicated they'll support your client's project, including the financing.

A well-planned grassroots lobbying blitz by a national environmental group—including a flood of phone calls and letters from around the country—seems to be giving several of the council members second thoughts. Worse, the local newspaper has added to the momentum to kill the deal by printing a number of articles questioning your client's financial dealings. It's critical that you do something now to turn the tide.

The solution: You organize a rally downtown to protest underdevelopment and to support your client's plan by communicating with your supporters over your campaign's on-line, computer bulletin board. You also contact citizen activists your campaign has identified using computer assisted or "predictive dialing" and urge them to attend as well. In addition, you ask them for permission to phone "patch" them in to offices of the council members to voice their support.

The result is an "earned" media event with a grass roots flavor that generates momentum for your plan's approval, as well as a barrage of favorable phone calls that at least partially balances out the negative effect of the environmental group's effort. As it turns out, it gives the wavering council members all the backbone they need to say yes.

Sound farfetched? What I've just described is something savvy campaigns around the country are doing every day with existing technology. In fact, many believe high-tech campaigning will ultimately revolutionize the business of politics, particularly once telephone and cable companies have completed their ambitious plans to wire America into a digitally-switched, fiber optics based "interactive network."

It's important to remember, however, that any technology, no matter how exciting, is just a tool. It doesn't relieve you of responsibility for making the right decisions or crafting the right substantive messages. And if used poorly, it could cost you irreplaceable votes and money. Below, we look at how successful campaigns are avoiding these pitfalls, and how they're using information highway technology that's already available and tested to boost success rates.

Interactive Systems

Much of the focus on the information highway has been on interactive communications systems, such as that being built by the year-old alliance between "Baby Bell" U.S. West and cable giant Time Warner. Bell Atlantic, Pacific Telesis and other phone and cable companies have also committed billions of dollars to construct interactive systems by the turn of the century.

Interactive systems are to be based on two relatively new telecommunications technologies: Digital switching and the use of fiber optic cable. Used together, these dramatically increase the speed and volume of data that can be shipped from one place to another making it possible for the same network to simultaneously provide everything from telephone and "500 channel" cable television entertainment service to home shopping and visual teleconferencing.

Many of the details of full service networks, however, are still very much in question. Most phone and cable company executives envision the television set becoming an interactive telecomputer. Andy Grove, CEO of computer chip maker Intel, believes the vastly more powerful personal computer will expand its role as the engine of future high-tech communications. Others see more of a mix, with homes owning a variety of appliances, each capable of sending and retrieving vast amounts of information. Finally, the Palo Alto Research Center—which correctly foresaw the rise of the personal computer—predicts that wireless or cellular networks will dominate.

Another question that's emerged is whether or not anyone will want to pay for these new services. In politics, the two-way contact that interactive communications offers holds great promise. But even the projects of the most firmly grounded people may ultimately prove to be pie-in-the-sky. For example, Doug Bailey, publisher of the successful daily, on-line political briefing "Hotline," and three other equally well-situated consultants, are planning to launch the American Political Channel, a futuristic system using "movies on demand" technology. If all goes as planned, viewers will someday be able to watch regular programming, as well as access videos on candidates and issues on demand. As of yet, however, the group has yet to launch its first broadcast.

Campaign consultant Scott Walker, who has worked for such Beltway mainstays as Senator Howard Metzenbaum (D-OH), believes ultimately federal and state legislators could be able to debate and vote on issues over interactive, audio/visual, tele-cable systems regardless of whether or not they're actually in the capital at the time. But even if technology permits this at some future date, few are likely to abandon Capitol Hill because of the networking and lobbying that goes on.

There are, however, three relatively new information super-highway technologies that are already being used by campaigns nationwide:

- Telephone technologies such as "Predictive Dialing," and related computer hardware and software. These now well-established techniques allow far faster voter contact than ever before by

automating dialing to eliminate extra motion by callers and by rapid, careful selection of prospects to call.
- Audio-Visual technologies, such as satellite transmission and narrowcasting of commercials on niche cable channels. These are limited in range now. But these innovations can speed up media production and provide lower cost alternatives to expensive broadcast advertising.
- On-Line computer technologies, including databases such as Lexis/Nexis and TimeNet, and the interactive forum/database "Internet." These have two major uses. First, they enable campaigns to do very focused issue and opposition research, to transmit their own messages within networks and to keep up with the media cycle in several locations simultaneously. Second, they're now being used by larger campaigns, political parties and PACs, to communicate with supporters far more quickly and cheaply than is possible using the mail or the telephone.

One caveat: These technologies are only as effective as how well they're used in each specific campaign.

The key is focus and cost. Don't try to adapt what you do just for the sake of having a flashy new technology at your disposal.

Predictive Dialing

Whether you're running a local candidate's campaign or advocating approval of a statewide initiative, "predictive dialing" can dramatically improve your results at a reasonable cost.

In layman's terms, predictive dialing is a computerized time management system for telephone banks. It involves special dialing equipment and software together with a live caller (unlike completely automated calling systems that play a prerecorded tape). With it, telephone bank operators have a computer screen and keyboard in front of them with a headset. Lists of names and phone numbers to be called are loaded into the system on tape or disk. When a phone number is dialed, the predictive dialing software can recognize and distinguish a live "hello," a busy signal, an answering machine, or the phone company saying the number is no longer in service. When a live "hello" occurs, the call is sent instantly to the first available operator who hears the "hello" in the headset as the name of the person being called appears on the screen.

Written into predictive dialing software are complex algorithmic programs that regulate and monitor the speed of dialing and the number of phones being answered so that people being called aren't forgotten on the line without a ready operator to handle the call. In effect, it predicts when someone will answer their phone and when a phone operator will be available to take the call.

There are two major advantages of predictive dialing over conventional phone banking. First is speed. The computer is capable of dialing dozens of numbers every minute. All busy signals, answering machines, disconnected lines and endless ringing is filtered out. Telemarketers are consequently free to concentrate exclusively on the task at hand: Asking the right questions and or delivering the right message. The result is a greatly increased number of calls per hour.

The second major advantage is targeting. Computers can instantly select only the numbers of the people who are members of a key demographic group or who answered yes to a specific question during an earlier phone call. The computer can also store dozens of pieces of information from questions asked to be used to select future calls.

Predictive dialing was first developed by large financial institutions for corporate proxy fights. But today, campaigns are using it in new ways. Mac Hansbrough of National Telecom Services, a telemarketing firm working for Democrats nationwide, identifies four major uses: Fundraising, polling, voter contact and mobilizing "grass roots" support for key legislative issues. "We can literally target any market we want, depending on the database," says Hansbrough, "and the potential savings in time and manpower are huge."

Predictive dialing's speed and targetability has induced more than a few state party organizations to use it for fund raising, including Republicans in Florida, Texas and most recently Wisconsin. R. J. Johnson, executive director of the Wisconsin Republican party, expects to use it to more than double his donor base from 1992.

Johnson has been able to cut the party's costs per communicator hour literally in half. That in turn has cut the average level of contributions needed to make telemarketing profitable to the $17 to $25 dollar range, dramatically increasing the party's ability to pursue donors, particularly when used in combination with direct mail.

According to Johnson, their productivity ratio will rise in coming years, as the percentage of calls shifts from simply cold calling partisans to renewing current donors, whose response rates will be much higher. Johnson is also using the information storage power of new software packages. This will help not only fundraising, but could be used down the road for voter identification and "get-out-the-vote" (GOTV) calls as the party's donor base becomes larger.

Wally Clinton, whose telemarketing business operates 300 telephones (many of which are equipped with predictive dialing), says that the new technology has "doubled our productivity." Clinton also points out that predictive dialing is most efficient when making a large volume of phone calls for political persuasion and mobilization but that a less expensive CATI (computer assisted telephone interviewing) system with "power dialers" is more economical and is better geared to doing fewer and longer calls that involve qualitative interviewing for public opinion surveys.

Many telemarketers use new phone technologies for voter identification. For example, suppose Candidate Smith is running for Senate and wants to focus his effort on undecided voters. First, the computer is fed a list of voters based on prior surveys and election data. As calls begin, interviewers ask voters who they supported in elections. Those who answer Smith's Republican opponent will be weeded out. They may be worth pursuing later, but not in this effort. Those who answer Smith, meanwhile, will be reminded to get out and vote. They may also be notated for a GOTV call or letter closer to the election.

Those who are undecided or who say no can then be wooed by a combination of direct mail and future phone calls.

Once the caller hangs up after any of the calls, a computer automatically enters the new information into the database. For those listed for a follow-up letter, names are sent via modem to the list vendor, who can then print a letter and envelope thanking the voter for listening and urging he or she to vote on election day for Smith. The letter, which is mailed that day, serves as a powerful reinforcer of the phone message.

Voter identification's power can be dramatically enhanced by combining it with "desktop mapping." According to Joe Pindell of Election Data Services, a voter's address or phone number allow attitudes to be automatically compared with demographic characteristics to aid in gauging the mood of particular groups.

Patch-Ins

John Davies of Santa Barbara-based Davies Communications, who manages campaigns for Republicans and business groups nationwide, says techniques such as predictive dialing can be particularly effective in grassroots lobbying when combined with the commonly used phoning technique of "patch ins." Strongest supporters of an issue—those who have been identified, educated and motivated—are selected from the database and phoned using the speed of computer-aided dialing. But rather than simply asked to call or write their congressman or county commissioner, supporters are requested to be patched-in or immediately connected to the office of the public official. The result is a motivated caller who feels strongly about an issue, something most public officials find very difficult to ignore.

For an issue in California, predictive dialing-located patch-ins helped Davies turn all negative vote before a county commission into a 5-0 victory for the proposal. Such a powerful tool, however, is in Davies' words "like a power torch. You can either build a bridge or cut off your hands." The principal danger, he says, is the risk of a backlash from too many phone calls in. "You want constant calls to build into a crescendo as the vote nears," he warns, "Too many calls at once look like astroturf, not grassroots." In one instance, for example, a Davies-orchestrated patch-in campaign resulted in a local government being paralyzed with too many calls. The upshot was a backlash against the callers.

One negative in using this new technology is the up front cost. Experts estimate that it can run upwards of $5,000 per phone for the necessary hardware and software to do predictive dialing. For a phone center with, for example 50 work stations, that involves a capital investment of over $250,000. In addition, it also requires sophisticated, well-trained administrative and supervisory personnel, which is why many campaigns prefer to hire professional phone firms as opposed to developing in-house "boiler rooms."

Will this technology ever cut the costs of political telemarketing? Perhaps, some suggest, in the long run when hardware and software costs decline and more people are familiar with them. In line with this, pollster Bill Hamilton believes these new technologies "may eventually bring down the price of public opinion polls" which use telephones extensively to interview scientifically selected samples. That would be good news for candidates who find it necessary to budget more and more for survey research. But for now, the costs of new technology often offset added efficiency, limiting cost-savings. Speed—no small factor in politics—is the big advantage, not cost.

If you choose to purchase equipment or services, be sure to shop around. Also figure out in advance what you want and be sure it's the most cost effective way of achieving it. When shopping for equipment, be sure you're not paying for more power than you need before you plunk down dollar one.

Channels of Influence

By far the most hyped feature of the information super-highway is the so-called "500 channel" network to be built by telephone and cable companies. Rather than actually provide 500 individual stations, this system (if built) will supposedly have the huge transmission capacity necessary for two-way audio/visual communication.

With channel compression—squeezing four, six or eight channels into one moving forward and the increased use of fiber optics, National Media, Inc. president Robin Roberts estimates that "within four years 40 percent of the country will have 500 channel capability. Roberts says he expects about

20 percent of channel capacity will be dedicated to pay-per-view and video-on-demand. The remaining 400 channels, he says, would be programmed specifically for even further political involvement. The potential inherent in a list is limited only by how it is cultivated and the imagination of the campaign.

Making It Work

While volumes can be written about how to get the best results from a telephone fundraising campaign, keep in mind that your object is not just to raise funds but to groom donors for future activism. With that in mind, it becomes important to be aware of the "people skills" that will motivate people to work for your campaign.

Be respectful of your donor base. Treat your donors as equals. They care enough about their country to get involved. That makes each one important to you. Treat them with intelligence and tailor your phone scripts accordingly. While you would never use the phrase "As you know" in a novel, it works wonders in a telephone script because it tells donors you think highly of them.

In addition, let your donors know that they are important. Thank them for their support and lavish praise on them. Telling them that they made a new TV spot or a newspaper ad possible lets them know they are an important part of the process. It generates enormous goodwill. Above all, don't be afraid to compliment them on their patriotism. Let them know they are doing their part for their country when they get involved.

Finally, do what you say you are going to do. In a time when political scandals are hiding around every corner, the last thing you want to do is reinforce ill feelings voters have toward politicians. If you're distributing Voter Guides, make sure they get a copy, and let them know how the distribution went.

The telephone is not some magic device that can bring in funds and volunteers quicker than Aladdin's lamp, nor is it a balm to cure all political ills. But when properly used, it is one of the most powerful campaigning tools available, in terms of money raised, goodwill generated, and volunteers recruited. All it takes for success is professionalism and attention to the details. It will make your efforts pay over and over again.

✓ The Permanent Campaign
Robert Blaemire

The concept of the Permanent Campaign is daunting to most elected officials but is, in truth, already a reality. Members of Congress find themselves raising money throughout their terms in office. Estimates range for $10,000 to $16,000 per week as the amount an average Representative or Senator must raise throughout his or her term to finance a typical campaign.

Traditionally, incumbents raise their campaign funds from large donors and PACs. However, this may change if current campaign finance proposals become law. Campaigns will be forced to raise money and build support in different ways. Even if reforms do not change the way funds are raised, the press is increasingly wary of the manner in which campaigns are financed.

It's easy to point out what is wrong with traditional campaigns and their funding. Solutions are not so easy but they do exist. Campaigns can solve these problems with time and creativity, which is only possible if a campaign is willing to write a plan, set a timetable and stick with it. Procrastinators need not apply. A good re-election plan requires early decisions and takes two-way interactive communication with voters.

How many times do we hear constituents say they only hear from their Congressman or Senator at election time? We tell our children not to cram for exams and to study throughout the year. Yet most incumbent officials wait to the last minute to organize a formal campaign.

The best approach recognizes campaigns as permanent affairs. By communicating continually with voters according to a written plan, much can be accomplished that not only makes the election season less difficult but allows the elected official to act more like a public servant and less like a candidate.

The Permanent Campaign does not require a campaign headquarters or full-time staff. It is designed to accomplish tasks that make reselection easier. These include:

- Raising money and building a large database of small donors.
- Adding information about I voter concerns to allow targeted contact with them.
- Eliminating from future communications the costs of reaching voters who are in opposition.

To start the Permanent Campaign, it is necessary to create a database that can be used for continuous direct mail communications. The essential element is response mail, for soliciting views and opinion as well as money or indication of support. By constantly adding response data to the database, future mail can be varied to a great extent, strengthening the bond being established between candidate and voter.

For those voters who are added to a donor database, their value over time is easier to demonstrate. The importance of the small donor will be enhanced, however, if Congress and state legislatures further limit individuals and PAC contributions. A large list of small donors is also a basis for continued fund raising in subsequent campaigns.

By building a database early and enhancing it regularly, candidates avoid the necessity of recreating the file prior to the campaign season. Their campaign communications can then be more selective with more varied messages; also, voters will grow accustomed to receiving mail from the candidate.

A well-executed program may not scare off all opponents, but it will create a foundation for a successful reelection campaign and send a message that the candidate is serious about keeping his or her job.

Fund Raising

The most appealing aspect of this plan is fund raising. Raising money through the mail takes time; messages must be tested among a variety of prospects. Once a donor is found, he or she needs to be sustained over time and continually upgraded.

But candidates should also recognize, unlike most national fund raising mail they have seen, there must be political value in direct mail for funds because the recipients are also their voters. Those who do not give will remain voters and, ultimately, it is their votes that win elections.

A fund raising database requires:

- The ability to segment the voter universe properly.
- Enhancements necessary for fund raising, such as modern cluster systems based on current census and individual data.

- Effective fund raising mail materials.
- Management of financial and donor information for legal reports and for sending appropriate "thank you's."

All of this can be handled without a permanent, full-time staff. It will require an efficient approval process of test and copy by the candidate so that a strict schedule of mailing can be followed.

An additional option is telemarketing. The same requirements exist: a good database, a fulfillment process for the money, efficient approval of script and so on.

Database Creation

Prior to raising money or soliciting views of the voters, a database has to exist. This can either be an existing voter file or one created from scratch. In some cases, alternative databases have to be considered because voter files are too expensive or difficult to obtain. There is, however, no place in America where an adequate database cannot be created.

It is critical to enhance files with data necessary for relevant communications. The extent of your ability to target segments of the voter universe will be a function of the amount of data available. That data may be voter history, ethnic identification, age, race, gender, income, and census-based cluster information. The more selective and precise your targets can be, the more your message can vary.

Segments have to be created on the file not only to test direct mail, but also to extrapolate the results on to the non-mailed universe. For instance, when a certain household type responds well to a mailing, further mailings would be mailed into households with the same profile. Each piece of information gained from one mailing will be used to make subsequent mailings more efficient.

Database Management

The database is a living thing. It changes over time with new information. Returned mail will result in deletions from the file. Antagonistic responses will result in the coding of those households so no mailings are sent there in the future.

The outcome of this process is the building of an excellent voter file in time for the election. The mailings during the campaign season would be done far more efficiently because of the updates on the file during the preceding period.

Data gained from response mail would include:

- Issue preferences.
- Candidate preferences.
- A willingness to volunteer time or to undertake certain tasks in the campaign.

Therefore, useful information would be continually added to the database and used in subsequent mail.

Cost

The cost of the entire Permanent Campaign process would include:

- Creation and maintenance of data base.
- A plan and schedule for implementing the Permanent Campaign.
- Design and writing of the mail.
- Production of mail.
- Caging, cashiering, and "thank you's" for donor mail.
- Providing appropriate legal compliance report information.
- A monthly retainer.

Every dollar spent in the non-election period is worth at least two spent during the campaign season.

As they build grass-roots support at a time when the competition is not active, candidates can get the attention of voters when they aren't competing with other campaigns. They can create a dialogue with voters that will not only help them win reselection but make them better elected officials as well.

An election is like a "one night stand" with the voters. The Permanent Campaign is more like a marriage.

✓ Voter Files as a Key Part of Voter Contact

Andy Downs

Voter files are tools, nothing more, nothing less. They are like the screwdriver that you wish you had when you open a "some assembly required" box at Christmas.

A good voter file alone won't win an election, but without a functional list, many other campaign tasks become inefficient or even worthless.

For example, if field canvassing is part of your plan, you have to know where voters live. If a phone bank voter-ID plan is part of the strategy, you have to have phone numbers to call. If your polling shows that you need to work with the 65-and-over crowd, how do you know which of the names on your database are in that classification? These kinds of targeting decisions, basic to a winning election campaign, require one simple tool: a voter file.

To communicate with the voter, the candidate needs at a minimum to know which constituent is a registered voter and where that registered voter lives. Beyond that, the more the candidate knows about the voter, the more persuasive and efficient the communication.

"Andy, great news," he starts. "I'm going to do it. The papers are filed. You are now talking to the next state senator from this district."

"You sound so confident," I reply.

"Are you kidding?" he continues.

"It's a done deal. I've got all those folks from my church. And I've got a hell of a big family. Then there's the country club, not to mention . . . ."

"But Jack," I interrupt. "How many of these folks actually live in the district? What about the other 99 percent of the voters? Aren't many of them accustomed to voting for the other party? Who are the voters that will support you?"

"Uh, good question," Jack stumbles. "Let me get back to you on that. I've got another call coming in."

From the very beginning, a campaign both uses files and creates files, without even thinking about it. It might help, however, if you do a bit more thinking about it—especially right up front. The idea is to have a strategy planned. Traditional precinct voter research using just the election return numbers gives information on partisan voting patterns, turnout, etc., so a campaign can target its efforts in those precincts where the campaign effort is most likely to produce a friendly vote.

But if Jack were to look beyond just the past election returns, and look at the voter files available for his district, he might find out that 50 percent of the frequent voters (those who voted in three of the last four elections) are over age 52. His younger voters tend to vote less regularly—but wait a minute—why did so many younger people vote in that one election a couple of years back? And, hey, look at this, if 60 percent of the voters under 35 all vote for the same guy, he is very likely to win. Now if only Jack could figure out why the young vote turned out in that one election.

Analyzing numbers from voter files alone isn't going to map out a campaign strategy—but it does provide you a good basis for preliminary research.

In Jack's case, he may want to look at a number of key factors:

Name: He has to make sure that it is spelled correctly and that it relates to a living, breathing voter who is registered in the jurisdiction in which he is running. Names of dead people or those who have moved out of the district are useless, unless the campaign plan has a section on intentional voter fraud.

Address: Jack needs a correct address in the district, and probably one with a carrier route and Zip-plus-four, if he is running any reasonably budgeted campaign. A street address is a must for any door-to-door targeting, including field canvassing, door knob-hangers and yard sign placements.

Householding: If Jack doesn't have the filed "householded,' grouping voters living at the same address, he ends up sending copier of the literature to several individual at the same location—a waste of money.

Telephone numbers: A functional number that actually belong to the voter described by name is basic element of a voter file. This may be the most-sought-after and least-understood option. Using phone banks for canvassing, persuasion, and get-out-the-vote efforts is very efficient, but only to a limited audience. Depending on the jurisdiction, 30 percent or more of the registered voters will likely have an unlisted telephone number.

Registration: If the jurisdiction has party registration, is the voter a "D," an "R." or something else? In those states that do not have partisan registration, skip on.

Voting History: This enhancement would detail which past elections struck the fancy of the voter enough to get him to go to the polls. Those that regularly vote will likely do so again, and should be persuaded to do so for you. Those who don't are unlikely to be moved by all but the precise, exactly correct pitch—weigh that option carefully, and against your resources.

Location: You absolutely must know in what county, congressional or legislative district, or precinct the voter is in to determine if he is yours.

Demographics: Gender, ethnic information, household income, home value, renter/homeowner information, size of household, years of education, and so on. These are all demographic enhancements that give you another cut at determining who is and who is not a good target for your campaign. Remember that most of this kind of information comes from the U.S. Census Bureau, which generates these reports based on information obtained in April 1990. When is that next election? Much of this Census information is aggregate. You know, for example, that voter Joe Smith lives in an area where 99 percent of the people are millionaires. Understand the demographic information, and whether it is statistical or actual.

Affiliations: To what special-interest groups or organizations does the voter belong? To which magazines does the voter subscribe? Overlaying voters who are Sierra Club members or Sierra magazine subscribers with your district may give you those individuals who would be appreciative of information on your environmental positions.

Assorted odds and ends: In what past campaigns has the voter been active, either as a contributor or a volunteer? What are the voter's issue hot buttons? This stuff comes from your home-built database and must be integrated with the other information you're collecting through the use of a professionally developed voter file.

"Andy, great news," Jack says, calling back two days later. "My brother-in-law is going to set me up with a computer and load it with the voter registration records from the state board of elections. This is one sweet deal!"

"Sounds good, Jack," I intone again. "But, Jack, I'm just curious—how are you going to clean up the list?"

"Whadya mean?"

"People die, Jack. They move. The clerk doesn't purge their names from the file. You need to get rid of the deadwood, say. "By the way, what are you going to do with the list then?"

"Target, Andy. I'm going to target the hell out of it," Jack replies. "We're going to zero in on those swing voters—hit 'em with smart bomb mailers and camp out on their doorsteps until they commit."

"How do you know who the swing voters are?" I ask, feigning innocence touched with sarcasm.

"You know, the folks in the precincts north and east of the city. Aren't those the tagged precincts?"

"Sure, but do your voter files tell you who is in what precinct?" I say.

"Uhhh, good question," Jack says. "Oops, the phone is ringing. Gotta get it. Call you back."

Keeping a list up to date is important. The usual means of cleaning a list is to match it against the National Change of Address (NCOA) file maintained by the U.S. Postal Service and against other "unmailable" lists maintained by national list vendors.

For small campaigns, you have to check the availability of these kinds of clean lists through the state or local political parties or a full-service political/advertising consulting firm. Odds are they will be running the stuff through one of the major list vendors.

It's not an expensive process—amounting to about $750 (equivalent to maybe 2,000 undeliverable pieces). Since the average rate of correction is four percent on a one-year-old file, you would need a minimum of 50,000 names to break even.

MC Squared Consulting, of Lexington, KY, for example, estimates they can clean up and enhance with telephone numbers and some demographic information, 15,000 name files for between $200 and $1,000.

"Andy, great news," says Jack, calling a few days later. "The files I have do include precincts. According to this counter thing, we've got 2,600 voters in the northeast precinct, 1,400 in the north precinct, and 2,000 in the—"

"Jack, oh Jack," I interrupt. "Don't those precincts have voter turnout numbers dangling somewhere around 25 percent, and don't you have a budget somewhere around nothing?"

"Yeah, that's why I want to use smart bomb mailers...."

"But Jack, which 25 percent of these folks voted?" I ask. "Which 1,000 of the 4,000 do you want to see at the polls?"

"Uhhh, voter history," Jack says, becoming pensive, if not peeved.

"I hear your phone ringing, Jack," I say. "See ya later."

If you are really lucky, your state file will have more information than expected, making enhancements cheaper or unnecessary.

At one extreme is Kentucky, where the files include precinct, date of registration, voter history, birth date, and party registration. It is as complete as you can get. But Kentucky is a rarity.

At the other extreme are the many states where files may not even be centrally maintained and where the local boards of election may be very difficult to deal with.

If the problem is not with the origination of the files, it is with their keepers. All too often computerized voter files maintained in-house aren't utilized to the fullest because the operator doesn't know how to use the software or because the brother-in-law who built the system knew nothing about campaigns.

If a campaign is going to go to the trouble of maintaining extensive in-house files, it should think out why way, way in advance.

It might be much easier just to call a supplier and say you want voters over the age of 52.

If you need walk sheets for frequent voting Republicans by street address—sorted by odd and even to ease the burden on the door knockers—you can order them from a supplier by precinct. No problem.

You want to flag (mark) the voters' files as they are identified so that by the time the GOTV effort rolls around, the campaign communicates only with the friends and good potential Friends.

"Andy, bad news." It's Jack, at the front door this time. "I lost—bad."

"Jack, I'm so sorry."

"I just don't understand . The campaign was so well planned. We needed those targeted voters, and we hit 'em with the smart bomb campaign mailers. We camped out on doorsteps." He sobs.

"Well, Jack, what did the smart bomb mailers say?" I ask.

"Here," he says, offering one. "Take a look. I didn't want to offend anyone."

It says: "Dear Occupant, Vote for Me."

"Is that all there is?" I ask, turning it over to look for the candidate's name—in vain.

Voter files are tools—nothing more, nothing less.

3

Public Opinion, Issues, and Opposition Research

★ ★ ★

✓ Strategic Polling
David Hill

Okay, now that you've got that expensive benchmark poll in hand—what's next? It's a question that frequently plagues political campaigns as they try to convert newly learned information into a plan for campaign strategy.

The use of polls is a widely misunderstood aspect of modern campaigning. Generally, campaigns start with a benchmark poll to understand the issues that are out there; then polls are used to focus on strategic adjustments to the campaign strategy.

Because of the proliferation of polls disseminated by news organizations, many people not only do not understand the benchmark poll, but also think that the regular private campaign polling is done exclusively to conduct trial-heat questions.

Good private polling is generally concerned with using polls to test campaign strategy. This is called strategic polling, and it is an essential ingredient in the development of a campaign's theme and message.

The most successful campaigns have a central theme that can be tested and fine-tuned to ensure clarity and appeal. While theme testing often uses focus groups or even less sophisticated qualitative testing, such as conversations with the proverbial man-on-the street, the most rigorous means of evaluating a potential theme is to subject it to a rigorous polling.

Strategic polling also can assist with targeting voters who must be singled out for special attention by a campaign. This targeting may take one of several forms. For example, a straightforward application is to identify those voters who will be most responsive to the campaign theme or message. Who are they? Where do they live? What kinds of media will reach them?

Campaigns may choose to target only those voters who are most likely to vote. Or, in a more sophisticated twist of strategy, a campaign may search for themes that actually decrease turnout. There is widespread belief that some voters who are cross-pressured by one or more competing themes in a campaign may respond simply by failing to vote. For example, if high-income voters are responding favorably to a "No New Taxes" theme advanced by a Republican campaign, a Democratic campaign can respond with a "Do the Right Thing" campaign. These competing themes may leave some wealthy voters confused about which party deserves their vote, thus decreasing their likelihood of voting.

Another strategic application of polling is to evaluate potential attack messages for use in the campaign. This can take the form of testing the relative effectiveness of various attacks that one might mount against an opponent, or test the efficacy of attacks that might be brought against a candidate.

One of the important differences between a strategic poll and a newspaper poll is the questionnaire design. While a newspaper poll will assiduously strive to avoid the use of any biasing questions, a strategic campaign poll may sometimes find it useful to write biased or one-sided questions to evaluate how effective a particular argument or point of view might be in prejudicing voters.

Private polling also will differ from newspaper polls in the degree of attention devoted to measuring intensity. While newspaper polling is typically satisfied with ascertaining simple ballot preference or issue approval-disapproval, the strategic private poll is significantly more concerned with nuance, scope, and depth of candidate or issue preference.

Private pollsters are keenly aware of the importance of intensity and the role that it plays in shaping predictable behavior as the result of opinion. For example, people who strongly disapprove of a candidate are much more likely to go out and vote for his opponent than are persons who simply favor a candidate.

First Build Superscale Ballot Questions

In a strategic analysis of ballot-preference variables, it is common practice to combine several ballot-related questions to build a "superscale1' of support for each candidate that runs from total support for Candidate A to total support for Candidate B. The midpoint of this scale is total indecision between A and B. One technique is to use several types of questions to assign a ballot scale score to each respondent.

Consultants will typically add one scale point for each answer that suggests solid, faithful support for a candidate. Thus, if a candidate is mentioned in the unaided ballot suggestion question, he gets a point; if his party is chosen in the unaided ballot he gets another; if he is thought to deserve re-election, another. The result is a ballot with varying degrees of ballot preference, not just a simple three-way division among A, B. and undecided, as in media polls. The scores will be collapsed into groups that indicate degree of preference.

A campaign can use these results to craft separate strategies or themes that attempt to reinforce supporters, cross-pressure opponents, and educate and woo undecided voters.

A campaign theme is much more than a simple slogan or batch of issue positions. One can have a slogan or have a position on two or three issues and still not have a theme.

Then Develop Themes To Outline Positions

The campaign theme is a statement that at once tells voters much about a candidate's position on a broad range of issues, about why the campaign is taking that point of view, and what the probable outcome in government underscoring that theme will be.

A key reason for having a theme is that it makes for efficient communication with voters. The theme may be short and simple but communicate a broad range of views. Even if only one issue is singled out for mention, a candidate is telling voters something about his broader value system. Polling provides valuable information about how voters infer issue positions a from campaign theme.

A campaign theme also will give voters some sense of where a candidate wants to take the city, state, or nation. In sales parlance, this is called selling the benefits rather than the product. Polling can be used to discover what voters would envision the perfect circumstance or situation The campaign then is predicated on explaining to voters how adopting specific set of issues and electing particular candidate create the ideal society voters described to the pollsters.

The key to using polls in then development is careful scrutiny of open-ended questions. One must search for recurring patterns of language, inference and linkage to understand how voters make associations among issues and ideas. A sophisticated statistical technique that requires computers—factor analysis—allows professional pollsters to scan through dozens of fixed-choice issue questions in search of patterns of answers.

A consultant can develop statistical estimates of the likelihood that a person who supports gun control also will support increased veterans, benefits or congressional salary increases. By identifying "factors," the task of theme development is simplified with the more subjective analysis of verbatim responses to open-ended items.

There are five or six broad political strategies that are employed in most campaigns. What differs is merely the tactics, and that is where polling comes into play. For example, the strategy of card stacking—the presentation of many apparent facts to bring either credit or discredit to a candidate—is effective if done correctly. The trick comes in knowing which are necessary to complete the task of crediting or discrediting the candidate. A proper poll can decide whether a given set of four or five facts, when presented in tandem, persuade someone to vote for or against a candidate.

Generally, strategy comes first. Your polling supports your strategy or helps to choose from two or three varieties of strategy. Campaign managers and consultants generally start the campaign planning process by using intuition and experience to choose one or two alternatives from the menu of major political strategies. The pollster then helps to choose the most appropriate strategy plus issues and tactics that will support the chosen strategy.

Potentially damaging labels can typically be found in a careful analysis of open-ended questions. For example, a follow-up question to a name ID item (Do you have a favorable or unfavorable impression of Sally Smith?) might ask about what the unfavorable respondent likes least about an individual. Computer programs designed for textual analysis—Persoft's IZE, Folio Corp.'s Folio Views, and Lotus' Agenda—can read a file of hundreds of these responses, looking for frequently used words or combinations of words that might constitute a label. Even the inexpensive grammar-checking programs that are so widely available—Reference Software Intl.'s Grammatik, and Que Software's RightWriter—can do simple word counts that can help in searches for labels.

Polling also is used to test third-party endorsers to find out whose testimonial would be most influential in determining or changing votes. The trick here is not to look for endorsers that influence your strongest supporters but to find endorsers that influence undecided voters or cross-pressure supporters of your opponent.

The public release of polling information can be viewed as an attempt to exploit the bandwagon strategy. Releasing a poll that shows you leading your opponent or closing the gap as you come from behind can be very influential in persuading voters to go with a winner.

Utilization of the glittering generality is often illustrated by attempts to tie a candidate to either good times or bad times. Almost every campaign must consider whether to call for continuity or change in government and leadership. Making this decision takes into consideration whether people think of the present time as especially good or bad. Evaluating the direction in which a campaign will lead the public toward change or perpetuation of the status quo, is an ideal application for polling.

Decide: Are You Pro-Change or Status Quo?

Another important consideration in developing the glittering generality strategy is to focus on identifying persons who are winners and losers under the status quo or a changed government. If one finds a strong pro-change orientation, things are seriously off on the wrong track, and one needs to understand what groups would be viewed as perpetuating those problems and the groups that would be winners if a pro-change orientation is adopted. Each strategy depends on understanding the financial situation of voters. Cross-tab analysis of issue positions and financial status are essential.

Another strategic direction—transfer—can benefit from the exploitation of existing, long-term schisms in the electorate. One of the more obvious of these is the natural competition of Republicans versus Democrats. Sometimes the mere mention of an opponent's party or one's own party preference will have strategic implications for good or bad. Note, for example, how few Democrats place that word on their billboards, bumper stickers, and other ads in much of the nation today.

Democrats realize from polling that their party name evokes images of profligate spending and higher taxes that don't help their chances. The technique here is to ask a generic ballot question—a question regarding whether the voter will vote for the Democrat or the Republican in the upcoming election. Typically, 50 percent to 60 percent of voters will answer this question, validating the importance of the transfer process through partisanship. Voters have a tendency to vote for the nominee of the party with which they identify, but it is important to understand which issues would reinforce or activate partisanship that might otherwise remain dormant in a campaign. Democrats frequently hope to move campaigns toward a debate on the need for compassionate programs, feeling that is a debate they can win. Republicans frequently try to steer campaigns toward economic issues, especially those related to taxes and economic development, two issues that naturally favor their point of view.

Beyond the most stereotypical positions associated with each party, it becomes trickier when one tries to identify positions in other areas that relate to inherent partisan competition. There has been considerable back and forth, for instance, with respect to which party would be best at keeping the United States out of war. While in some circumstances the Republicans are viewed as more internationalist and more likely to intervene, there has been a time when Republicans were more isolationist and laissez faire in their attitudes toward foreign policy.

Beyond the obvious division surrounding partisanship, other active or latent divisions in the electorate can be successfully exploited in campaigns with clever polling. Even within the category of urban versus rural there are specialized flavors that might become a linchpin of strategy. In one Midwestern state, my firm found that people who reside in small towns have a unique, particular agenda that sets them apart from either urban or rural/farm residents. There are also important interactions among the primary political variables that must be analyzed. These are especially important to Republicans who are attempting to assemble a winning coalition that includes conservative Democrats, a voter group essential to GOP wins in most Sun Belt states.

The trick is to construct an interaction variable that also includes race. The bivariate category of "conservative Democrat" can often include black voters that describe themselves as "conservative" that will almost never vote for the GOP candidate even when the Democrat is a flaming liberal.

You should create a stand-alone category of "white conservative Democrat" to get a fair estimate of the Democratic vote a GOP candidate may attract. The result of this exercise might be a segmented vote goal for each political target group.

The importance of developing a broad based theme in a campaign cannot be over emphasized. George Wallace ran a campaign for president with the slogan "Stand Up for America." It was an effective slogan, but it alone did not communicate Wallace's key theme. The theme of his campaign was to make winners out of a white underclass that felt oppressed by a coalition of the well-to-do power elite and welfare recipients who jointly benefited from government largess without working and who were tolerant of dissidents whose anti-war and civil rights demonstrations threatened an orderly society.

The Dukakis campaign, in sharp contrast, never seemed to develop a coherent straightforward theme. One controversial campaign commercial haplessly tried to portray political consultants who were planning the Bush campaign as the enemy, to no good effect. Voters were not threatened by political consultants conniving to shape their patron's image. While people don't care for manipulative campaigns and consultants, it is not a factor in shaping voters' ultimate candidate preference, or at least it ranks well behind candidate images, issue preferences, and a half dozen other variables.

Whenever a theme is selected and agreed upon, polling can help in the selection of issues and campaign tactics that complement execution of the theme. If the theme is pro-change, it is important that polling be used to identify several important issues that voters see as the best illustrations of the need for change. If voters feel that economic calamity is due to foreign competition, it is important that a poll identifies the most salient examples of excessive or unfair foreign competition, examples that people feel most intense about.

There may be different alternatives to evaluating a pro-change agenda in dealing with foreign competition. Do people prefer to deal with the problem by simply stopping foreign imports (such as when John Connally said the Japanese could park their cars on the docks in Yokohama) or should the problem be dealt with by less extreme action, such as limiting imports or the ownership of land in this country? Might there be less stringent requirements, such as requiring that foreign land and property purchases be documented so that the information would be available to the public?

When testing these protectionist themes, an important technique for assessing their vote potential is to identify categories of voters that might respond to them. Cross-tabs with "sector dependency" variables are especially helpful.

Another consideration in shaping the theme and issues of a campaign is the relationship that those themes and issues have to a given candidate. If a campaign is built on a theme that speaks to income redistribution, it makes most sense to have someone who seems sympathetic to that point of view. An individual whose reputation is that of a major industrialist who has built a fortune off cheap labor without significant regard for employee benefits might have difficulty convincing voters that he could be sympathetic to the underclass.

Polling is used to understand not only what themes are acceptable and what issues support those themes, but also whether a given candidate can carry out those themes. Sometimes the question may not be so much whether John Doe can execute this theme and issues agenda but whether a person who has his or her profile can.

Voters Pick Candidates By Political Affiliation

Voters may not know John Doe, but if John Doe is a Republican and businessman, they may draw conclusions about whether he could be an appropriate promoter of a given theme or issue. Because of these linkages, polling may often benefit from testing generic descriptions of a candidate as opposed to the actual candidate himself.

Sometimes it is best to ask vote directly whether they would be more or less likely to vote for a candidate who ran on each of several slogans. Sometimes, too, it is important to ask voters what they think a certain slogan means. Working through one illustration we have already discussed, for example, if one were to test George Wallace's slogan "Stand Up For America," we would ask voters: "What do you think George Wallace meant when he said, 'Stand Up for America?" or, "Tell me one or to things that would be involved in standing up for America?" or, "What would be one or two things that George Wallace would do if elected president?"

In asking questions such as these we could see whether a slogan is producing results that in voters' minds a generally consistent with the goals o the campaign. It is particularly important to prevent an opponent from exploiting an inarticulate statement of goals.

If we find that "Stand Up for America" was not perceived as a clear pro-change message, then our opponent could simply suggest that "Stand Up for America" is a pleasant patriotic slogan, but that what the country really needs is fundamental change, possibly taking away some of our vote.

If "Stand Up for America" was not perceived as having economic implications, our opponent could exploit that fact and we would not be maximizing the benefit of our chosen theme of class struggle. Another polling application involves helping to decide how the theme should be imparted to the voters. Do they listen to news-talk radio, easy listening, classical, or country music radio? Only in drive-time or all day long? Do they read newspapers? What television shows do they watch? Do they receive cable and view cable channels such as CNN?

Many of these questions can be answered directly by polls or by matching poll demographic results with media ratings, such as those published by Neilson and Arbitron. If a poll shows problems with 18 to 34 year old females, then we can place spots on radio stations and in television programs that skew toward younger women.

Sometimes it might be even more efficient to ask in the poll about specific media usage. Then we might discover that women who are 18 to 34 years old and who listen to country and western radio are the crux of the problem. This might reduce the need to place greater protection to people and its two major themes are protecting senior citizens on fixed incomes from economic difficulties and protecting young people from crime, one frequently will use polling to extract the best or most effective spokesperson.

Would it be better to have a young mother talking about having enough police to protect her children from crime as they return home from school, or to have a police captain speaking about the same issue? Would it be best to have a senior citizen or a person who is a named officer in a group such as AARP making the recommendation? This issue frequently arises concerning environmental groups. Even if one assumes that one wants to have an environmental group make an endorsement, there are so many different flavors and varying degrees of credibility to environmental groups that one always has to check to see what works.

Public release of a poll can sometimes have a strategic impact on a campaign. The word that one is making progress can energize workers and cause donors to match their previous contributions. Favorable polls also can make party committees and PACs pay attention to your campaign in a cluttered electoral environment. But a poll released can backfire on strategy if it shows you to be too far ahead, causing your donors to feel no contributions are necessary and voters to feel less motivated to vote on election day.

A poll should be released whenever a candidate shows significant progress so as to be close enough to the front-runner to overtake him, or actually to be the front-runner in a close race. Releasing polls showing a candidate behind is a tricky business. If one has made enormous progress, say doubling your support from 14 percent to 28 percent, that may seem like an outstanding accomplishment that one wants to share with the political elite. But 28 percent, despite doubling previous support, still amounts to barely one of four voters.

Newspapers Love Horse Race Polls

Releasing a poll through the campaign alone often does not have the credibility of getting the poll published in a newspaper. In contemplating the public release of a poll, one should consider what makes the poll newsworthy and increases its chance of getting into the papers and influencing public opinion. Among these factors are sample size, degree of competition and whether the results are surprisingly at variance with expectation.

With respect to sample size, newspapers have varying degrees of expectation. For some state or local surveys, samples as small as 250 to 300 may get reported by the newspapers as a credible campaign poll. In statewide races, reporters expect a minimum sample size of 500 or more.

Newspapers have a greater tendency to publish polls that seem at once consistent with expectation but slightly at variance, thus getting greater newsworthiness. If everyone thinks you're behind your opponent by a 2-to-1 margin, but you show you're behind only 1 1/2-to-1, that poll may have some credibility and get published. If everyone thinks you're ahead 2-to-1 and your poll confirms that, the poll may be perceived as having little news value. If the general impression is that you're behind 2-to-1, and you want to release a poll showing yourself leading, chances are that the newspaper will consider the poll self-serving, perhaps even rigged, and be reluctant to print it.

As a rule, newspapers are more likely to publish a poll in a race where there is a very strong sense of a horse race. A consideration in getting media acceptance of private campaign polls is the general veneer of professionalism communicated with the released poll. A poll release should be clear about the poll's methodology, the sample size and sampling error, the dates on which the poll was conducted, and the wording of any relevant questions. By providing these kinds of details, one is communicating a professionalism that increases the willingness of the newspaper to pass along the information. By preparing a professional release that communicates all this information, albeit while still spinning the results in a way that is more favorable to your candidacy, the campaign significantly increases the likelihood that it will convince an editor to publish the results of its poll in a news article.

✓ Getting the Most Out of Your Benchmark Poll
Ed Goeas and Brian C. Tringali

Nobody can anticipate every twist in the campaign trail, but an accurate benchmark survey built on sound, ongoing research helps you to plan effectively, respond to crises and solve problems.

Benchmarks show you the lay of the political land on various issues and the overall political environment. But more often than not, these crucial surveys are done without any attention to the goals of the campaign. That's a mistake.

To create an effective benchmark, think about what you want from a survey before you go into the field.

In your first survey, you should look at an incumbent's vulnerabilities. If you're an incumbent, this is the time to check on job approval among voters. Also test voters' opinions on issues or specific themes that might be used later in the campaign.

Once you establish survey goals, design a survey. A good questionnaire walks a respondent through a conversation.

When constructed properly, the interview flows naturally and you gain a maximum amount of information.

Get a feel for open-ended issues and find out what the most important problem is in the local community.

Bring your survey down to the local level whenever possible.

Step By Step

Sample the ballot generically. Ask "If the election were held tomorrow, would you vote Republican or Democrat?" for whatever office you are testing. Your candidate must poll better than that generic ballot to win.

Always ask general approval questions before asking push questions (questions that give additional information about a candidate to test people's reactions). Don't ask a respondent if they know a candidate has a DWI conviction before you ask them their overall opinion of the candidate.

Test for name ID. And when you do, make sure you have four favorable responses to every one unfavorable. A ratio of three-to-one is still OK; if you drop as low as two to one, you have serious concerns. A one-to-one ratio is extremely hard to beat, but there are exceptions like Sen. Jesse Helms (R-SC), who has won with a one-to-one margin.

Check for interest in the election; do people even intend to vote? Remember that older and better educated people vote more. If you have them on your side, you're doing well.

Then, do a ballot test. Ask "Would you vote for the Republican candidate A or the Democratic candidate B?" Rotate your ballot; ask Republican first and Democrat second, then switch to Democrat first, Republican second.

Test from the top of the ticket. Ask respondents who they like for president, then Senate, then House and down to local officials. This will help you gauge how your candidate fits into the roster the voter sees when he walks into a voting booth.

Ask hard and soft re-elect questions. A hard re-elect question would be "Would you vote for candidate A no matter who runs against him?" A soft re-elect question is "Would you vote for candidate A or do you think someone else can do better?" Anyone who answers "yes" to the hard re-elect question is probably with you no matter what. Anyone who answers "someone else should have a chance. . ." on the soft re-elect question will never vote for you. Concentrate your efforts on the voters that aren't in either camp.

Finally, check for who has the momentum. Before the demographic questions, ask who your respondent thinks is going to win. Undecided voters are most likely to vote for the perceived winner.

When the results come back, make sure they match your understanding of the district, state, or region surveyed. The demographic answers should reflect what you already know to be true about an area. If you're surveying an urban area and 50 percent of your respondents are college graduates you're only talking to the cream of the crop and your survey is missing a portion of the electorate. Be skeptical.

Or, if you know from past elections to expect one-third of your support from a certain county, and a survey comes back showing only one-quarter of your support comes from there, something is wrong with your sample.

Getting Off the Bench

To fully understand the puzzle, you need to delve into subgroups of the electorate, Republicans, older people, pro-choice activists. Analysis should compare data about various subgroups against the whole sample. As you examine each subgroup, look for variance, a percentage by which a subgroup deviates from the whole sample. Any variation of five percent or more in either direction is a sign of more or less support from a subgroup. Establish a support ceiling with each subgroup of the electorate and work towards that goal. Look for groups that traditionally support your type of candidacy but where you are underperforming. Target them to build support.

Stick To Your Best Issues

Finally, look at the answers to the issue questions in the survey. These answers will help you develop campaign themes.

Don't ask a bunch of issue questions if you're not prepared to act on those issues.

If you don't have the money to produce and air cable TV ads, don't ask questions about how many homes are wired for cable in the district you're running in. Don't ask religious affiliation questions if you're not doing any religious targeting.

More importantly, don't waste time and money on issues that will not affect how you run your campaign. Don't ask opinions about the B-2 bomber if you and your opponent share the same stance.

Issues are only important if they show contrast between candidates.

✓ 10 Myths About Political Polling
Robert G. Meadow and Heidi von Szeliski

Let's de-bunk misconceptions about survey research in political campaigns:

1. "I know my constituents, so I don't need a poll."

Legislative districts are large. No matter how involved you are with the community, it is possible to know only a small fraction of the constituents. Many candidates and public officials keep in touch with their friends, neighbors, business associates, supporters and community activists as well as the small number of people who make their positions known through letters or phone calls. But the opinions of these individuals are often quite different from those less involved and less interested in politics—in other words, the very people who make up the bulk of the district.

Failing to understand that the people with whom you are in touch are often not representative of the district at large can seriously jeopardize a campaign. A poll is conducted with a random sample of likely voters, not just those activists or those with whom you are in contact.

2. "I don't need a poll to tell me what to think or what to do."

In a representative democracy, candidates and public officials are elected to reflect the views of the people they represent. The best way to find out those views is to have a reliable measure of public opinion—a poll.

Pollsters do not tell a public official or candidate what their positions should be on the issues, or how they should respond to public policy questions. A pollster's job is not to tell a candidate what to think. But a responsive and responsible public official must know the range of opinions within his or her district. A good poll can provide that information.

A pollster will not try to change your opinions based on the results of a poll, but you want to modify your vocabulary or emphasize different points as a result of a poll. A public opinion survey can guide a campaign with necessary information, such as what issues to emphasize, as well as provide the strategy to communicate the reasons behind positions and decisions in such a way that more support for your views might be generated.

3. "As soon as I hire a pollster, I'll never see him or her again."

A pollster should be committed to the campaign, and have experience in election and public policy polling, not market research. The pollster should be attentive to the campaign, working on only a limited number of campaigns at once. Think about it. If a pollster is working on seven U.S. Senate races, three gubernatorial campaigns, 16 congressional races and a dozen state legislative races during the same election cycle, how much attention do you think your campaign will receive? Expect the attention of the principals of the firm selected, not junior analysts who have limited experience and no involvement with this particular campaign.

While you need to benefit from the experience of your pollster, expect the race to be viewed as distinct from others. A poll should be custom-designed for your district, not some off-the-shelf questionnaire used in countless other races.

4. "I already have a consultant—I don't need another one to play with numbers."

The pollster, as a member of your strategy team, should be the keeper of the message. The pollster should play an ongoing role to make sure the message is on track and on target at all times. All voter communication should convey a consistent message, so the pollster should be available to review speeches, direct mail, television and radio advertisements, and other campaign messages. Of course, the pollster is not the campaign manager, nor is the pollster the speech writer, or the direct mail, or television specialist.

5. "A poll costs a lot of money. I'd rather spend my money on other things."

Most campaigns budget about 5 percent to 10 percent of the overall campaign budget for research. The costs of a research program are based on the size and scope of the campaign, and there are two key variables—the length of the questionnaire and the number of people interviewed (sample size). A typical benchmark poll contains about 75 response items, and usually takes about 20 minutes to complete. For a high-quality, professional public opinion survey, expect to pay anywhere from $12,000 to $17,000 for a sample size of 400. Shorter, follow-up polls, taken midway through a campaign, are less expensive. Overnight tracking polls taken for fine-tuning near the conclusion of a campaign, cost even less.

6. "All I want to know is what portion of the vote I am getting."

Too many people think that polling is just about the trial heat question: "If the election were held today, for whom would you vote?" Everyone could wait until election day to find that out. A poll should be designed to develop a strategy, to find the winning arguments for the campaign, its strengths and weaknesses, as well as the strengths and potential vulnerabilities of your opponent.

A poll should be conducted early, before the campaign begins in earnest, so that the message, the announcement speech, and early walking brochures are all guided by the poll results. It is better to have the message designed right the first time, than to spend the rest of the campaign correcting it. Perhaps most importantly, a poll will be able to tell which messages are right for which voting constituencies, such as women, seniors or those in a particular geographic area.

7. "Let's use campaign volunteers to take the poll."

Volunteers are a precious resource and they must be used most effectively—to persuade voters that the candidate should be elected. Comprehensive interviewing requires trained interviewers skilled in administering the questionnaires and who maintain their neutrality. Supportive volunteers may tend to overstate the case by wanting to give you the information they think you want to hear. They may argue with those supporting the opponent because, as volunteers, they want to convert all voters to your side. This is why they should be used for persuasion calling, voter identification, and phone banking.

The accuracy of the data collected by volunteers cannot be, and should not be, guaranteed. Donors who must consider the viability of your campaign simply do not trust volunteer polls; they depend on the reputation of the polling firm. Some campaigns that attempt to use volunteers find that the interviewing process (which should take three to four days) can take up to six weeks because of scheduling difficulties. Volunteers often "burn-out" when interviewing, and are then not available to the campaign during the critical get-out-the-vote phase of the campaign.

8. "Polling is a luxury I really can't afford."

You can't afford not to poll. First, if the message is wrong, or given to the wrong people, you limit the chances of success. Second, because in large districts a candidate cannot communicate with all voters, there is a need to know which voting groups need special attention, and which voters do not need as much attention, either because you will always have their support or never have their support, no matter what. A comprehensive benchmark poll that analyzes voting groups and the messages to which they respond will save money in the long run by enabling the use of a voter communication budget most effectively.

9. "All polling firms are alike."

No, they are not. In fact, they vary widely along a number of dimensions. Some polling firms are commercial market research firms that dabble in politics, do not have the experience, and simply do not understand political polling. Other firms are political polling specialists, but are retained by so many campaigns at once, that the principals of the firm simply cannot give the attention to each campaign that it requires. Some firms simply throw a book of computer printouts at the campaign or give a one-shot oral briefing and do not provide any written strategic analysis or campaign recommendations. And some firms charge additional fees for a written report, while some charge monthly retainers for ongoing consultation. They move on to the next campaign and they are not heard from again.

The very best firms do several things. First, they take on only the number of campaigns in which they can provide the level of attention the campaign requires. Second, they give campaigns full, comprehensive, written reports that serve as the basis for the strategic plan. These reports look at each question, and each demographic group so that the messages for each group are clearly identified. Third, they remain part of the campaign strategy team, and are available to the campaign through election day and beyond.

10. "Pollsters just give candidates the information they want to hear."

Good pollsters do not. The campaign team needs to understand the political landscape, not stroke the candidate's ego. If a pollster "cooks the numbers," or asks biased questions, a candidate has the wrong pollster. Remember, the purpose of a poll is to provide the candidate with accurate information to hone the message and communicate with the voters. The one place a candidate cannot tolerate "yes" people is when hiring a pollster. A pollster who is known for fabricating or manipulating data will have no credibility with a fundraising base.

✓ Using Tracking Polls
Allan Rivlin and Lisa Grove

It's only human nature, and there is no use fighting human nature. Whenever we have tracking numbers coming out of the field, the campaign manager can be counted on to call 10 minutes before the numbers are ready—about 7:30 in the morning—and ask, "Who's ahead?"

Everyone knows the real value of tracking polls is not in the head-to-head horse race numbers, but it is impossible not to look first at the if-the-election-were-held-today-how-would-you-vote question. By the time a tracking program is in place, the election is just a few weeks away, and naturally, everyone's interested in who's ahead.

But now the real work begins as we turn to the question at hand: How do the data in the survey help us make the few remaining decisions? There must be only a few remaining decisions at this point in the campaign for a tracking program to be warranted. If there are no decisions left to make, there is no reason to divert resources from the media budget for more research. If there are more than a small number of remaining decisions about the campaign's central message this close to the election, you don't need a tracking survey—you need a miracle.

Tracking the Elusive Message

Coming just weeks or even days before an election, the tracking survey offers the last chance to adjust the campaign's message to the voters. Whether an issue has been left undecided by design or because earlier research results were open to more than one interpretation or even because the dynamics of the race have changed, final decisions must be made when the results of the tracking survey are in.

There are three primary functions of a tracking survey. First, to assess the impact of the campaign's previous communications efforts. Second, to assess the impact of the opposition's campaign on votes' views. Third, to make the final decisions about the campaign message and audience in the crucial closing days.

An Overall Research Program

You can't talk about a tracking poll without explaining how it fits into an entire research program. Tracking surveys are the last phase of a research program that, ideally, included focus groups, a benchmark survey, and media testing.

The focus groups helped us generate ideas and design questions for the benchmark survey. The benchmark survey focused our attention on a small number of positive messages about our candidate, points of comparison with the other candidate, and occasionally, outright political attacks.

These potential messages were passed on to the campaign and its media consultant, who created several new spots.

The spots were tested to tell us which ads do the best job of achieving specific objectives, such as telling the candidate's story, convincing voters the candidate is tough on the crime issue, setting out a distinction in the candidates' economic positions, or letting voters know our opponent's real priorities.

The tracking program will be used to make decisions about which media markets to hit and how many times to air which ads in the final days of the campaign. In addition to the campaign's paid advertising, the results of the tracking survey will have some influence on the emphasis the candidate places on various issues in his or her speeches, statements to the press, and debate appearances.

Tracking Survey or Tracking Program

Campaigns can spend any where from $8,000 for a single tracking survey in a state legislative race to $18,000 for a congressional race to $300,000, or more, for continuous six to eight weeks of nightly tracking for a major statewide race.

The simplest kind of tracking is a single survey of 400 voters spread over two or three nights of calling. This gives the campaign one more snapshot of public opinion roughly two or three weeks before the election. Well-funded campaigns will set up a more elaborate tracking program with calls every night for two to six weeks to give the campaign a moving picture of public opinion.

One common tracking program involves 150 completed interviews per night for 15 nights, starting about two and a half weeks before the election and continuing until the Thursday before the election. Adding three consecutive nights of calling together gives a rolling sample of 450 interviews. On Wednesday, for example, we would be looking at results collected on Sunday, Monday, and Tuesday nights. On Thursday, we drop Sunday's results and add in Wednesday's numbers. The combination of three nights of results gives us a statistically valid and continuously up-to-date picture of changing opinion.

Of course, it is nearly impossible not to spend time worrying over the statistically insignificant results of the 150 interviews form the most recent night of calling. If we have dropped two points among last night's sample, it is hard to believe we are really headed in the right direction, even though the sampling error for 150 interviews is plus or minus eight percentage points.

What to Ask

The questionnaire for a tracking poll will be very short, usually about five to 10 minutes in length. Even if the survey is 15 minutes, that is not enough time to assess voters' attitudes toward the mortgage-interest deduction, unless this happens to be the issue prior research has determined to be the campaign's central issue. Tracking questionnaires generally include the standard favorability, job performance, and vote questions. So we know who said what, we include at the end of the survey a limited number of demographic questions such as age, education level, and party affiliation. However, it is the "internals" that provide us with the most useful data.

The benchmark survey was used to identify a small number of key issues and perceptions upon which the election will turn. The short tracking survey will only have room to follow up on these key questions, to gauge how much they have changed since the benchmark. This will give the campaign the answer to two strategic questions: "Is our message cutting through and moving voters?" and "Have we neutralized our opponent's message?"

Decades of research in attitude formation shows that voters generally do not make decisions to move away from one candidate and move directly to the opposition. Voters first change their attitudes toward the candidates, then they usually move into the undecided column before making a switch. Therefore, the much more interesting numbers are gained form the survey items that relate directly to the contents of the ads both sides have been airing.

Tracking surveys provide a unique opportunity to measure the impact of the ads on vote choice (which explains why the call from the media consultant rarely trails the campaign manager's call by more than five minutes).

If we have set ourselves a goal of using the candidate's record on education to demonstrate that the candidate cares about families and children, then we will want to look for increases in how well words and phrases like "cares about people like me" and "is working to improve education" describe our candidate. Likewise, we may look for increases in characteristics like "represents the special interests" or decreases in "shares my values" for our opponent when airing an ad that gives information about his or her record.

When airing "informational" ads about an opponent, there is often a point of diminishing returns when an attack is no longer cutting through or, worse, is having a backlash effect on the campaign. Knowing when to make the switch from positive to negative (or vice versa) is critical in the closing days of a campaign. So we often look at how phrases such as "is being too negative in his/her campaign" describe our candidate.

We used this technique in the last election cycle to help give us the margin of victory we needed in a close statewide race. Candidate "Smith" had a lot of information to share with voters about opponent "Jones'" record. However, we were concerned voters might think Smith was running a negative campaign, even if the media team was careful to make the ads as informational as possible. So, in the nightly tracking program we monitored agreement with the statement, "Smith is being too negative in his campaign."

As the chart demonstrates, the Oct. 28 tracking results showed Jones' vote falling below Smith's vote and agreement that "Smith is being too negative" rising above Jones' vote for the first time. These results indicated that the informational message had an impact, but now it threatened to create a backlash. We immediately switched entirely back to our positive message.

In other words, when the proportion of voters who agreed with the statement rose above a critical level—and other tracking data convinced us that the information had its impact—we switched back to our positive message.

In a race where our tracking results showed the lead changing hands several times in the weeks before the election, we managed to be in the lead on election day—the only survey that really mattered.

✓ Using Calculus to Interpret Tracking Polls
John McLaughlin

Sooner or later you hear about an election that defied the polls and went against the odds. Often the reason for that so-called upset can more accurately be attributed to a misreading of the technical data provided in a poll. An artful analysis by a pollster who understands the dynamics of the electorate can take raw data and turn it into valuable information.

However, there may be a different, more scientific way to look at public opinion. What if polls that reflect public opinion do not move in a logically straight line that gives a snapshot in time that can be set up on a graph? Who said public opinion moves in a straight line, anyway? Instead, what if public opinion moves along a curve and can be plotted on a graph using calculus? After all, isn't public opinion the result of the communication of information that may accelerate and drop off in different proportions than a straight line could show?

Technically, in calculus, the geometrical interpretation of the derivative of a function is the slope of a tangent line to the graph of a function at a point.

As a simple product of a mathematical equation, the slope is important to the straight-line graph because it is the slope that lets you know whether you are moving in a positive or negative direction and the rate at which the movement is occurring.

Look at a hypothetical race where candidate Jones leads candidate Smith in tracking polls taken Tuesday, Thursday and Saturday immediately preceding an Election Day.

In the first face-off, Jones has a commanding 33 point lead—48 percent to 15 percent. In the second poll, Jones inches up to the magical 50 percent mark with Smith at 18 percent—a 32 point gap. But on Saturday, the poll shows Jones at 48 percent and Smith gaining a healthy 10 points to 28 percent. The common projection is that Jones—with a 20 point lead—will still win.

Wrong, at least in some cases.

When mapped out in a linear, straight-line fashion, using the two most recent polls, there is a closing of the gap at a rate of five points per day, not enough to overcome the Jones lead by election time, just three days ahead.

Using this algebraic linear method to plot the election results, Jones would still lead 45 percent to 43 percent on Election Day—with a significant percentage of undecided voters. But if public opinion is plotted on a curve, the results are different—with equal confidence in the projection.

What if public opinion moves with a greater degree of velocity resulting from the amount of advertising and new information, particularly electronic information, communicated by Smith in the days before the election? Instead of using algebra, using calculus would set up a slope that does not feature a fixed value that is constant, but rather a slope whose value changes over time to reflect the velocity in the speed of communication of information and its effect.

Solving the equation to predict the Election Day results now shows Smith beating Jones by a 56 percent to 37.5 percent margin—a significantly different result.Using calculus to find the derivative of a function for various points in time would show when a function is increasing, decreasing or at a critical point. More important, this analysis takes into account the instantaneous rate of change with which public opinion is more likely to move and therefore is better able to predict an outcome in a volatile political race.

A pollster using just a little more science can consider other interpretations of standard polling data and eliminate some of the mystery of a volatile political race. Pollsters should understand that public opinion rarely fits a simple, straight line. It's a different theory, but in this age of demassified, electronic media, a seemingly better theory to predict public opinion chances.

✓ Piggy-Back Polling
Q. Whitfield Ayres

Accurate polling data and analysis have become a critical part of a modern political campaign. As a general rule, a campaign should expect to spend from 5 to 10 percent of its budget on survey research. Using that guideline, a $1 million campaign will be able to afford a substantial amount of sophisticated research.

A $50,000 campaign, on the other hand, will not be able to afford so much as one good poll. Are there ways for low-budget campaigns to have the benefit of professional polling data?

The answer is yes, but only under the right circumstances. The beginning of wisdom about polling in low-budget campaigns is the recognition that a bad poll is worse than no poll at all. At some point a campaign worker who does not understand the methodology of polling will want to grab a telephone book and start making calls. Tell him to stuff envelopes instead.

The numbers produced by an ad hoc poll will be worse than useless and they will cause you to spend your already limited resources in precisely the wrong way.

Try and find someone who understands polling methodology and who wants to help your campaign on the faculty of a local college or university.

To produce reliable numbers, he or she must have access to a number of telephone lines, adequate computer hardware, and quality statistical analysis software. They must also be willing to generate the sample, train the interviewers, supervise the calling process, write the computer program, and analyze the data.

Needless to say, you are not very likely to find someone who is knowledgeable about statistics and willing to invest that amount of time and effort for one poll and no pay at all.

The most likely source for professional polling is an established survey research organization. But those organizations are not affordable for low-budget campaigns. At least if they are acting alone, the costs are prohibitive.

The way around the cost of polling is to piggy-back a question or two onto a survey conducted by a better funded candidate. Another option is to join with other candidates to fund one poll with the costs split evenly. For these approaches to work smoothly, the other candidate (or candidates) should:

- be from the same political party
- be running for different offices
- have the same constituency.

These approaches can work for statewide campaigns where there are a number of contested offices. A gubernatorial candidate, for example, may be willing to allow a candidate for secretary of state to add a question to his or her poll, or candidates for county commissioner and county treasurer may jointly conduct polls.

The total cost for one professional poll can range from about $8,000 to more than $40,000 depending on the size of the sample, the length of the questionnaire, and the reputation of the polling firm. The cost of piggy-backing will run from $500 to $1,000 per question and will decline as the number of questions increases.

If you can afford only two or three questions, in most cases you will want to ask about name identification (heard of favorably, heard of unfavorably, heard of with no opinion, never heard of). You will want to ask this question about both you and your opponents. Part of the decision about what to ask, in addition to that, is linked to the stage of the campaign you are in. A pollster will help you select the most useful question.

Two important issues need to be resolved before committing any funding for a piggy-back or jointly funded poll:

- Will the other candidates funding the poll have access to your numbers?
- Will the other candidates be allowed to release the entire poll, including the data on your race, to the press or other campaigns?

Once these issues are resolved with the other candidate or candidates, you need to ensure that the pollster not only understands those agreements, but also has the strength to live up to them under pressure.

One of the other candidates piggy-backing questions on a poll may see you as a long-term rival and may pressure the pollster for the numbers for the race in violation of your agreement. You must be satisfied in your mind that the pollster has integrity and will resist that pressure.

The piggy-backing or jointly funded options are less desirable when no other candidates—other than direct competitors—have the same constituency. This is normally the case in races for the U.S. House of Representatives, except where a state has only one congressional district. Piggy-backing a question on a poll conducted by a better-funded candidate with a different constituency may still be possible, but the arrangements become more complicated.

The key problem is sample size.

If you are running in one of only two congressional districts in the state, you can piggy-back questions on a statewide poll of 600 voters and still end up with 300 respondents for your district. That is on the low end of an acceptable sample size. But if you are running in one of six congressional districts in a state, and the poll still includes only 600 voters, you would likely have a sample size of only about 100 individuals—too small to do you any good.

This problem can be overcome by over-sampling within your district to obtain a reasonable sample size. This procedure will, however, substantially increase your portion of the polling cost. If you are faced with this situation, talk to the pollster to determine whether the piggy-backing and over-sampling technique will save you sufficient money over a fully funded poll to make it worthwhile. If you are running a low-budget campaign and are fortunate enough to have other candidates to work with who meet these criteria, then by all means take advantage of it.

But when you are not in a position to obtain professional polling, you are better off trying to win your race totally without polling data. Your instincts are a better guide to developing your message and spending your resources than an amateur poll.

✓ Tips For Women Candidates: Questionnaire Development
Beth S. Schapiro

In 1978, Virginia Shapard ran for Congress in a suburban/rural district in Georgia. A popular and effective state senator, she faced a male opponent in the runoff. A major issue used against her was that she needed to stay home and tend to her husband and two young children.

In 1990, Ann Richards ran for governor of Texas. A popular state treasurer, she faced a male opponent in the general election. A major charge against her was that she was not tough enough to make the hard decisions required of a governor.

Are these just annoying remarks coming from an opponent, or did these perceptions reflect widespread voter sentiment? The candidates' polling data held the key.

Polling is particularly important for female candidates because this kind of research can help uncover perceptions, attitudes, and candidate expectations that might be rooted in gender. Despite societal changes and the growing number of women in public office, voters still perceive male and female candidates differently. Some of these perceptions can work to the advantage of female candidates, while others can be detrimental. A good campaign will be aware of those differences and will develop its strategic plan accordingly.

Situations where being a woman has a positive impact include:

A race where the voters are looking to send a message. A recent study commissioned by EMILY's List, the National Women's Political Caucus, and the Women's Campaign Fund concludes that the voters see female candidates as populist outsiders who can effect change and who can make government work for ordinary people.

An election in which honesty and ethics are important. Voters generally assume that female candidates, are honest and have integrity, unless proven otherwise.

A race focused on domestic issues. Voters are more likely to associate women with education, health issues, and other traditionally female interests.

Still, there are an equal number of important situations where gender could present a negative impact.

These include the following:

A woman running for a seat that has never been held by a woman before. Having always elected men to that seat, the voters are more likely to be aware of the woman's gender before they focus on her qualifications.

A district that does not have a tradition of women holding public office. If there are few or no women in public office at any level, then gender is likely to take on an increased significance in the minds of the voters.

An electorate with more traditional attitudes toward women in general. A female candidate may face heightened awareness about gender among some older and rural voters, particularly in parts of the South.

So where do you incorporate gender in the research design? The basic research components and the quantity of research do not change significantly. You will still conduct a benchmark poll and possibly focus groups. You will still need to conduct follow-up and tracking polls during the campaign to test the themes and the media.

If gender looks like it will become a major issue, you must know how to combat perceptions that could cost you votes. Gender questions asked in focus groups and polls educate the campaign staff about the impact of gender from the outset. The initial focus groups and benchmark poll will test for its impact.

When developing questions for the survey, be aware of some of the traditional differences in perceptions and expectations of women candidates.

The differences are rooted in sex role stereotyping. The first difference is the women's role in the family. The voting public pays more attention to a female candidate's family status than a man's family status. Married women are expected to have the support of their husbands.

Mothers of children, especially young children, face close scrutiny about what happens to the kids if Mom is elected to office. The higher the level of office and the farther away from home, the more import these issues are.

The second difference is the set of perceptions that revolve around character traits. Women running for Congress are more likely to need to prove their toughness on defense, foreign affairs, and crime. Women running for executive office such as governor or mayor often need to prove their strength and ability to lead.

Finally, women need to prove their knowledge on such issues as defense and foreign affairs, as well as on budgetary matters. Never mind that the woman candidate in a race is an accountant and worked on Capitol Hill as a senior legislative assistant to a prominent senator on the Armed Services Committee for 10 years. The male opponent—who may have spent the Vietnam War years in Canada, for example—might still be assumed to have these strengths. One way to get at gender-based distinctions is to use a split sample methodology for some of the questions. Almost all of the questions asked every respondent will be identical. But, on a very small number of questions, half of the sample will be asked the question one way, while the other half will be asked questions in a way that is designed to provide critical input about a woman candidate.

For instance, a common question involves a choice between two hypothetical candidates. It might read: "I am going to read brief descriptions of two candidates for Congress." After reading the two descriptions, respondents are asked whether they prefer Candidate A or Candidate B and to explain their answer.

To test for the impact of gender, use the word "woman" and add female pronouns to the Candidate A description when it is asked of half of the sample. For the other half, use the word "man" and male pronouns. The wording for the description of Candidate B must remain the same for all respondents. The follow-up question asking why the respondent made that choice also remains the same. Compare the answers.

There are two places to look to determine if gender is an issue: first, examine the percentage of voters who choose each candidate in both samples, and see if support for a male Candidate A is higher than, lower than, or the same as for a female Candidate A. If the numbers are higher or lower, than you can safely assume that gender is an issue.

Second, analyze the answers to the follow-up question. There may be respondents who tell you openly that they will not support a candidate because she is a woman, or there may be more subtle reasons based in gender. When analyzing these kinds of questions, look at the answers through three progressively smaller lenses.

First, look at responses from the entire sample. Does gender seem to emerge as a consideration? If so, around what issues, characteristics, or candidates? Regardless of whether gender surfaces anywhere within the entire sample, the second lens is that of broad demographic groups. Analyze each question by sex, race, age, religion, income, education, party identification, location, and any other variable that might differentiate among subsamples of the overall population. Look especially for differences between men and women.

The third, and most discrete level, is within subgroups of the broad demographic groups. Break each sex down into categories by age, in come, and other variables that might be important in your race. Study these results.

Identify the specific groups of voters who are likely to react to the fact that the candidate is female. Determine just what it is about gender that has an impact.

The data analysis should enable you to understand who is likely to support a female candidate and why, as well as who will not. Being a woman does have an impact on the voters, but it is certainly not the only factor that voters look at. The candidate must still be credible.But gender factors need to be merged into your overall campaign strategy taking into account strengths and weaknesses. Hopefully, this will result in an election-day victory.

✓ How to Create a Flexible Last-Minute Tracking Program
Michael LaVelle and John McLaughlin

In the final weeks of a campaign you face a slew of curveballs. Last-minute tracking polls can help you adjust your stance and avoid getting beaned.

One of the most dramatic examples of how critical a tracking program can be occurred in 1987. Many Republican incumbents who polled prior to October assumed they were safe, and chose not to use tracking polls. When the stock market collapsed, and economic pessimism took hold, voter opinion turned sharply against them.

Those who were not tracking were effectively blind sided. On the other hand, candidates who were tracking saw trouble coming and made adjustments. GOP incumbents who ordinarily would have run positive, low-key campaigns, realized they had to go on the offensive and attack their opponents, particularly on economic issues including taxes and wasteful government spending.

The lesson: Even bare-bones tracking can alert you to trouble or signal opportunity if you know what to look for.

The Right Track

The intensity of your tracking is limited only by your budget. Every campaign would love to conduct a comprehensive, 1,000-sample daily survey. But the cost of that level of frequency and sample size is too great for many to bear.

The appropriate number of interviews and the proper time interval between them for a local race, within a single media market, is about 200 interviews every third day. A well-financed, statewide contest involving multiple-media markets should consider 300 interviews every other day.

The 200-interview tracking program using about 10 questions can be designed and implemented for approximately $10 to $12 per completed interview. Thus, 200 interviews every third day over a 30-day period cost $20,000 to $24,000. This includes interviewing, data processing, transmission of results, analysis, and telephone consultations. A relatively large tracking program say 30 questions— might work out to $20 per completed interview.

If you have to make a choice between the number of interviews and the frequency of interviews, cut the frequency. Small sample sizes produce erratic results.

The size of the sample will directly affect the program's margin of error. For example, if only 150 interviews are conducted per cluster, the tracking program may be inadequate, especially for statewide races with large media markets. The overall accuracy of a single survey of 150 is +/- 8 percent 95 times out of 100. The results will come within +/- 6.7 percent only 90 times out of 100.

You can see how a small sample size can cause an unsophisticated poll watcher to jump to conclusions based on sampling error. To minimize overreactions, tracking data is often presented as a "moving average" among three or four of the most recent interviews. This flattens the peaks and valleys caused by sampling error.

The time interval between interviewing clusters should be constant so each round of data processing is comparable. It is better to schedule interviewing every other evening, or every third evening, as opposed to several days on and several days off.

The Fast Track

A basic tracking questionnaire might include:

- A voter likelihood/screening question.
- A favorable/unfavorable rating for each candidate.
- A ballot test.
- An open-ended "why vote for" question.
- A few background questions about the respondent such as his or her ideology, party enrollment, age, gender, geographical area, etc.

Tracking polls help your advertising message adapt to shifting perceptions, so also ask questions related to the themes of your advertising and your opponent's advertising.

Finally, in close races, tracking enables a campaign to keep an eye on the all-important undecided vote. There is some preliminary data which suggest that the percentage undecided in late tracking polls in a given locality is inversely related to the turnout in that locality. In other words, turnout will be lower in areas where tracking polls indicate there is a relatively high percentage of undecideds. This is very useful information for targeted turnout drives.

This year voters seem to be growing more independent, and fast-breaking national and international news stories are likely to exert significant influences on election outcomes. While tracking data certainly cannot guarantee victory, it does give a campaign the most up-to-date and reliable information modern survey methods can provide.

It is up to the campaign to make the most use of this information, converting it into effective techniques, creative tactics, and a winning strategy.

✓ Group Process Techniques and Campaign Planning
Murray Fishel

Focus groups are the hottest thing going in political campaigning today. Cheaper than polling, and often more revealing, sessions with small groups of people are being used to develop and test slogans, commercials, issues, images and more.

However, focus groups are only one small group technique for generating critical strategic information. Nominal Group Technique, Idea Writing and Structured Brainstorming are three other methods for running small group meetings. Here's how to apply these information-generating techniques in campaign planning sessions for races at the state and local level.

In recent years the use of small group process techniques to improve strategic decision making has grown dramatically. In politics the best known of these techniques is the focus group. Pollsters and media specialists are increasingly using sessions with small groups of people to assist them in making the qualitative decisions that are always involved in political campaigns. In particular, the feedback received from focus groups enables these campaign professionals to make better strategic judgments about slogans, radio and television commercials, advertising layouts, colors and photographs.

I have experimented with three small group techniques in political campaigns for races ranging from city council elections to statewide efforts. In each of these contests, the techniques were utilized to facilitate the planning process for the entire campaign. They have been used from four to 16 months before an election to generate critical strategic information at costs ranging from $1,000 to $4,000; detailed campaign plans are then prepared from the information collected. The cost of a single focus group can run as high as that for this entire planning process.

The three approaches employed in these group sessions are Nominal Group Technique, Idea Writing and Structured Brainstorming; the latter is a method which is virtually identical to that used in focus groups. All three techniques have their origins in research to improve organizational decision making and are being used regularly in business and government.

Each small group approach is described, along with its strengths and weaknesses. Then a list of questions is provided for each of four meetings to address: 1) candidate/opponent strengths and weaknesses, and major issues; 2) campaign media and the message; 3) organization; and 4) fundraising. Finally, the specific method and procedures will be matched to each question to permit you to understand exactly how small group process techniques are applied in an actual campaign. The techniques and sessions outlined below have been used effectively in the campaign planning process not only by me, but also by students from Kent State's graduate program in Political Campaign Management.

Nominal Group Technique

Nominal Group Technique (NGT) was pioneered by Delbecq, Van de Van and Gustafson. Its purpose is to structure a small group of six to 12 knowledgeable and action-oriented people. This method works best for any subject that involves list generation, e.g. a candidate's personal, professional and political strengths and weaknesses.

After a brief introduction to the process, a series of stimulus questions are given to which participants respond in writing on paper provided by a "facilitator." They are urged to work quickly, quietly and independently of one another. This silent generation of ideas constitutes the first of four stages in the conduct of the NGT meeting. Step 2 involves the round-robin recording of these ideas by the facilitator on a large pad of newsprint on an easel in front of the group. Each person contributes one idea at a time. When an idea is raised which duplicates one on an individual's list, he or she is urged to draw a line through it. Participants are instructed to pass when all of their ideas have been listed before the group. Step 3 involves the clarification and combining of similar ideas; no ideas are combined if one person disagrees. And finally, step 4 of the NGT involves voting. Though votes are not taken on all questions, voting, where appropriate, permits the facilitator and leadership to have a clear sense of group ideas, and to ascertain whether or not there is a consensus.

In political campaigns, the NGT has a variety of applications. Since it is best used as a list generator, NGT is most helpful in producing information on the following topics: candidate strengths and weaknesses; opponent strengths and weaknesses; issues; messages; appropriate environments for TV commercials; fundraising events; media events; polling questions; potential volunteer leaders; finance committee members, and the like.

There are several important benefits associated with NGT. First, it provides enormous amounts of information to outside consultants or local staff. Second, this information is generated very quickly. (My experience is that 50 percent of time spent on planning meetings is eliminated.) Third, since the facilitator utilizes a pad of newsprint, the campaign has a detailed and easily accessible summary of group ideas without the need of a secretary. Fourth, the process reduces the disparities between verbal and non-verbal participants, ameliorating problems frequently encountered in political meetings. Fifth, since the outside consultant is the facilitator of the session, rather than an active participant, NGT reduces resentment toward the "outsider." Finally, and perhaps most importantly, NGT contributes to team-building in the campaign. Participants are pleased both with the amount of work the group has completed and the quality of the effort. Individuals realize that others besides themselves really can have good ideas and information which may help the candidate to win. The process contributes to the development of group ownership of the campaign; the campaign becomes our campaign for Smith, not simply Smith's campaign for governor.

NGT is not without its limitations, however. The process cannot work without the commitment of the candidate and participants to "play by the rules." The facilitator is defenseless against a group that will not follow the structuring guidelines. She/he must remain neutral in the sessions or the meeting will no longer be Smith's group which is meeting to give its best collective judgment to the candidate. Second, NGT will devolve into chaos without a trained facilitator, not unlike any other meeting in which there is no effective moderator. Third, the process requires that participants be task-oriented and informed about politics in the district. If the plan given to the candidate is to be good, the information on which it is partially based must also be substantial. Fourth, NGT is a qualitative research process which means that the information is subjective. NGT is not a quantitative method, despite the use of occasional votes. On the other hand, data developed through the process can be tested quantitatively by polling, should a campaign have sufficient resources. One must guard against the seductive power of NGT; the information is still just judgments—but judgments informed by the collective intellect of the group.

Idea Writing

A second small group process technique is Idea Writing (IW). This technique is particularly useful for tasks that involve creative work. It is frequently used after lists are generated with NGT.

IW is used with a group of four to 12 task-oriented people, at least some of whom have creative backgrounds (artists, publicists, writers, etc.). Again the process is led by a trained facilitator.

IW normally involves five stages. First, the group is divided into sub-groups of three or four people. The group as a whole is then provided a stimulus question to which each individual responds. Each person has a folded legal sheet of paper on which his responses are recorded on the left-hand side. During the writing process, participants are urged to work quickly, quietly and independently of one another. After five to seven minutes, sub-group members begin to exchange their sheets with others within their designated sub-group. The team members place their evaluations on the right-hand side of the folded sheet; individuals may say that their team-member's idea is wonderful, terrible or improvable. If they suggest the latter, they write how they believe the idea can be strengthened. After each sub-group member has evaluated the sheets from others in his/her group, each team is instructed to meet in order to synthesize the best of the group's ideas. Instructions are given for each of the sub-groups to return with three or four of the team's best ideas. As the teams consider their ideas, a captain is appointed with the responsibility of summarizing the best ideas on a large pad of newsprint. After 30-45 minutes, all of the sub-groups are reassembled together and the team captains summarize the best of their team's ideas.

In political campaigns, IW has a variety of applications. It is used to explore ways in which candidate weaknesses can be controlled or neutralized during the campaign. Second, it can assist in the conceptualization of radio and television commercials. Third, it helps in the production of creative media events. Fourth, IW facilitates the development of slogans and messages. Fifth, the process can aid in the conceptualization of print materials and layouts. And finally, IW can assist in the development of creative fundraising events.

There are three major strengths associated with IW. It is a technique which helps to tap the diverse creative talents of a small group. Also, IW produces a more comprehensive, sophisticated and organized product than NGT, and it permits group members to evaluate and synthesize their own ideas.

Like NGT, IW has some weaknesses as well. Because the technique demands creative writing, participants must be able both to write and work creatively in a small group. Not all individuals are comfortable with this setting. Moreover, since ideas are evaluated by sub-group members, individuals must be able to withstand the criticism which may be directed toward their contributions. In addition the composition of the group must be heterogeneous to avoid another potential limitation on IW results. Too many like-minded participants are likely to produce "group-think," a phenomenon which by definition limits the potential for creative problem solving. Finally, the failure to follow up on the recommendations and solutions emerging from the process is likely to cause the creative energies stimulated by the group meeting to dissipate, thereby negating one of its major contributions.

Structured Brainstorming

The final small group process to be discussed is Structured Brainstorming (SB). This technique, as noted earlier, is virtually identical to a focus group. The major difference is that a focus group is composed of persons who are consciously selected to help the campaign solve a problem. The Structured Brainstorming session is held with those who attend planning sessions. (The composition of the groups will be explained shortly. It is sufficient now to know that focus groups pay particular people—women, labor union members, etc.—to help a campaign deal with a particular problem, while the SB session occurs with a campaign planning group.)

SB is a "piggyback" technique. It is used after IW or NGT, either to enrich the information provided, or to try to promote consensus within the group. It is this quality which makes it so similar to the focus group. Basically, the group facilitator must get the group to provide as much detailed information as possible. For example, after a list of professional qualifications is generated through NGT, the facilitator may ask for the group to call out specific details associated with one career activity. The process is continued until a detailed "map" is provided with dates, names, experiences, etc. Similarly, after the IW has produced three slogans from each of the four sub-groups, the facilitator may employ SB as a tool to help move the group to consensus on a single slogan. In general, SB is the tool which is best used to embellish NGT facts and to arrive at consensus on creative ideas.

SB has three primary strengths. First, the technique produces rich amounts of specific information on topics such as candidate professional strengths. Second, SB promotes team-building, through the development of consensus on many important topics and the sense among group members that they have contributed equally to the generation of useful campaign information. Finally SB helps specific campaign staff to perform their tasks with greater ease. For instance, a research person can work directly off the actual information generated during the sessions on candidate professional strengths to research the candidate's record. Similarly, a hand-card can often be written directly from the information produced in an SB follow-up session.

Problems arise when consensus is not, reached during the meeting. This may cause frustration in the group. A trained facilitator is absolutely essential with SB since some form of closure will still be necessary. Judgment and experience will be critical to move the group to this closure.

Four basic planning sessions

What follows is an outline of four planning sessions, along with specific guidelines to give a candidate to facilitate the selection of good task oriented teams. The actual questions used in the small group meetings are also listed.

I. Candidate/Opponent Strengths and Weaknesses; Critical Issues
Time: Six hours. Composition: Ideally, this session will include the candidate, campaign manager and others who know the candidate personally and/or professionally. All participants should be conversant with the district's politics. Size: Six to 12 participants. The questions:
1. List two reasons why X should run for Congress.
2. List two reasons why X should not run for Congress.
3. List three positive adjectives which you believe best describe X as a person.
4. List three positive experiences which you believe provide X the background to be a good public official.
5. List three political advantages X has in the race for Congress.
6. List three personal. attributes which will detract from X's chances of success.
7. List other problems reducing X's chances of winning.
8. Are there skeletons in X's closet which, if known, will undermine X's chances of winning.
9. Given X's perceived weaknesses, write single statements which you believe will permit the campaign to neutralize the weakness or convert it into a strength.
10. List three or four issues on which you believe the incumbent (or X) is vulnerable.
11. List three issues which you believe are likely to emerge as the focal point of the 1986 race for Congress.
12. Let's agree verbally on the major contenders in the race for Congress in 1986.
13. List two major advantages and disadvantages that X has against each.

Not all of the questions listed above need to be asked for every race. Obviously, the first and second are used when your candidate is opposing an incumbent. Similarly, others may be omitted according to local circumstances.

II. Media and Message
Time: Three to four hours. Composition: Ideally, participants will include the candidate, manager and two or three carry-overs from the candidate session. The balance of participants should have creative backgrounds. Painters, journalists, public relations staff, musicians, etc. are some of the people who may be most helpful here. Size: Four to 12 participants. The questions:

1. Given the summaries provided from the work sessions on candidate/issues, and given what we believe to be X's major strengths and Y's primary weaknesses, write what you believe X's slogan should be.
2. Given this slogan (or basic idea for one), list two or three recurrent themes which you believe X should stress.
3. List three or four media events which X can execute to reinforce the slogan and themes through the free media.
4. List three or four creative radio spots to reinforce the slogan.
5. Here's a list of TV production methods and their appropriate descriptions. List two or three which will best capture X's strengths.
6. List two or three settings in which we can best capture X's strengths for TV commercials.

III. Campaign Organization and Direct Voter Contacts
Time: Three hours. Composition: Ideally, this session should include the candidate, manager, field director, plus others who have had organizing experience. People who are good with details are often excellent here. Size: Six to 12. The questions:
   1. Door-to-door work (walk-n-talks, literature drops, etc.) are high-quality contacts; there are n precincts in the district. What kinds of contacts can the X campaign realistically execute?
   2. How many volunteers can we realistically recruit, given your past experiences in the district?
   3. Base consider the following organizational chart that is being passed out. Let's see if we can reach a consensus on what the organization of X's campaign should be.
   4. Note that the organizational chart has a series of tasks at least some of which require central control and direction. Others may require decentralization in execution and/or control. How should the X campaign divide these responsibilities?
   5. Write the names of any individuals who might play a leadership role next to that role on the chart.
   6. Write the names of individuals who will volunteer for X's campaign on the paper provided.

IV. Fundraising
Time: Three hours. Composition: Ideally, this session will include the candidate, manager, finance chair and others who are experienced in raising money. Individuals who know where a community's money is located and have experience raising money are particularly good here, e.g.; bankers, United Way staff, etc. Size: Four to 12.
The questions:
   1. Research shows that X needs to raise n dollars to be competitive in the race for Congress. For planning purposes, let's agree verbally on what we should target as a large donation from an individual or PAC. And, what should we target for an intermediate donation? A small donation?
   2. In the top rung of the triangle provided place the total number of PACs and individual contributors from whom we can raise the large donation. Do the same now for the number of intermediate and small contributors in the next two rungs on the pyramid.
   3. There are three basic methods of raising money: face-to-face solicitation, events and direct mail. In the Table provided, place the percentage of total dollars the candidate must

raise from face-to-face solicitation. Then, in the space marked special events, indicate the percentage of net dollars to be raised from events (net dollars = dollars after costs are subtracted). Finally, in the space marked direct mail, place the percentage of total dollars we should raise from this method.
4. On the time line provided, place the percent of dollars X should raise on a monthly basis between now and Election Day.
5. On the sheet headed CREATIVE EVENTS write as many creative events as you can in the next five minutes. Place the ticket price you believe should be charged for each of the events listed. Also, place the amount of net dollars which you believe can be raised by that event.
6. Look at the finance organizational chart that is now being distributed. Does the group want to modify it?
7. List the names of two or three people who you believe would be good finance chairpersons on the sheet provided.
8. List the names of persons who you believe would be good finance committee members.
9. Finally, on the sheet provided, write the names of people who you believe can coordinate a fundraising event.... Run the direct-mail program.... Organize special group fundraisers. Identify the skill of each person next to the name.

The total time required to run the four small group sessions with the questions presented above varies. The shortest time for the sessions has been 12 hours. The longest the meetings have taken is 16 hours. Notably, the time spent will increase dramatically when the facilitator is not skilled.

Table 1 provides a guide for you to better understand how each of the questions are handled in the sessions. The first column indicates the session and questions, consistent with the numbering system set forth in the preceding discussions of the sessions. The second column identifies the technique (abbreviations used) that is appropriate. The third column indicates whether or not votes are taken.

Follow-up

After the sessions are completed, a local person is trained to write up the summaries from the lists and notations recorded on the large pads of newsprint. No information is excluded. Remember, the primary purpose of the sessions is to generate helpful information both for the overall campaign strategist and the staff, and to permit the strategist to use as much good information as possible in formulating a detailed campaign plan. In addition, the sessions tend to produce a cohesive team consciousness by stimulating contributions from a variety of people, both individually and collectively. Consequently, the exclusion of any data can detract from the gains made in the planning sessions.

After the summaries are completed they are mailed to the facilitator/strategist; I have received summaries as long as 30-40 pages. The overall campaign plan will utilize the information in the summaries where appropriate, and state reasons why some of the ideas have been excluded. When the plan is completed, the facilitator/strategist can return to the district to go over it with the campaign staff. Disagreements are then resolved—one way or another. The end result is a relatively detailed plan of action which permits the local staff to focus on its execution, and avoid being waylaid by planning itself.

✓ A Guide For The Focus Group Observer
Christopher J. Herbert

What reforms do people really want in health care? Why do voters oppose a sales tax for new roads? How can homeowners be convinced to allow a new real estate development adjacent to their neighborhood?

On any given weeknight in America, from Atlanta, Georgia, to Yakima, Washington, hundreds of focus groups are being conducted to gauge the tastes, preferences, and inclinations of the American public. Although most focus groups concentrate on consumer marketing, they have also made their mark in the world of political research. Not only do they help elect candidates, they also play an important role in the passage and defeat of ballot propositions.

To an increasing extent, focus groups are being used whenever public opinion has an important bearing on how an issue is resolved. Although focus group findings can't yield statistical projections in the manner of quantitative survey research, they are powerful tools nonetheless. Most research techniques do not allow you to watch the information gathering process in action. While you learn results and what they mean, the techniques of collecting the research data are hidden.

The art of the focus group is born of the skill of asking questions. Unlike quantitative research, however, qualitative research techniques allow far greater flexibility in what questions are asked and how they are structured. Just remember that the art of asking questions should not be confined to the moderator querying respondents.

Planning Questions

Good focus group observers regularly ask themselves questions as well:

- What are the broad issues I would like to cover during the course of the discussion? (Pick ten or so issues.)
- What specific questions would I like to have answered as a result of these focus groups? (Pick five or so questions.)
- What do I already know about the issue under consideration?
- What facts are under discussions (Don't guide the focus group and try to anticipate their likely responses.)
- What does the body language of listeners in the group say about a respondent?

Mirror, Mirror

Often a one-way mirror separates a focus group observer from the respondents. This can be an effective visual barrier, provided you keep certain guidelines in mind. Respondents are usually quick to determine that a one-way mirror is present; it's a good idea for the moderators to tell respondents about the mirror, the audio taping, and the fact that they will probably be observed at some point during the discussion. The following actions will negate the one-way nature of the mirror:

- Getting too close to the mirror. People or objects closer than 12 to 18 inches can sometimes be seen faintly.

- Lighting cigarettes, smoking, or otherwise using a point source of light behind the mirror (at any distance). You won't be seen, but the source of light will, reminding respondents that someone is back there.
- Turning on the lights in the viewing room. If you want to be sure you are detected, this is the way to do at! Keep in mind, any light from behind the mirror is a problem, even from adjacent rooms or from a door opened to the outside.

While it can provide a good visual barrier, the one-way mirror is less effective in masking sound. When the group is active, very quiet talking is permissible in the viewing room. But when the focus group respondents are not making noise, the viewing room should be quiet, too. Even if the respondents are carrying on a lively discussion, they are likely to hear any loud noise from behind the mirror: coughing, laughter, exclamations of delight (or horror).

The best rule: If you want to talk, particularly for an extended period, do so outside the viewing area. Not only, will this help keep respondents from hearing anything, but it's also considerate to those who may be listening intently to the discussion.

Another important element of good observation is understanding what function the moderator serves in the process. Before the focus group takes place, the moderator will need to develop a questionnaire that must be followed very closely.

✓ How to Conduct a $10,000 Focus Group for Less Than a Grand
Scott Walker

Your poll reveals the perfect attack opportunity. Or does it? Will the voters perceive your comparison campaign as too negative? Your poll under-represented recent retirees. Do you have to conduct another survey to analyze this crucial group?

The pollster says you're on the winning side of the abortion issue. But how important is it to the voters?

Unless you're running a congressional or statewide campaign, your staff and volunteers are probably being facetious when they answer these questions by saying, "If we had $10,000, we could do a couple of focus groups." Here's good news: you can get valuable information from a focus group for less than $1,000.

A focus group, or a focused group interview, is a technique that brings together eight to 12 selected respondents with a facilitator to observe the attitudes, values, and language that voters use to discuss a select set of issues. To be of value, a focus group must answer questions for your campaign.

The strengths of a focus group are different from those of a poll. A focus group will not tell you whether a position is mostly favored or mostly opposed by the electorate. A focus group will tell you how voters approach issues, how much thinking they have done about issues, how deeply they care about different issues, what wording resonates best when taking a stand on an issue, and how willing the voters are to accept and believe more information on a topic.

By knowing these things, you can select and design messages to persuade and secure voters.

Plan, Plan, Plan

There are several elements to planning and conducting focus groups:

- Where do you do this? What equipment is needed?
- Whom do you want and how do your find them? Once you find them, how do you persuade them to attend?
- Once you have the people you want in the place where you want to do this, what do you want to ask them?
- How do you ensure a productive, free-floating yet focused discussion?

In order for your campaign leaders to have confidence in the results of a focus group, they must have as large a role as possible in planning the sessions. Begin planning four weeks in advance. By involving more people in the planning stages, you will increase the chance of getting answers you can use.

Since your campaign will consider focus groups as a tool to answer questions, the first thing to examine is the construction of the questions. You may already know where the uncertainties lie, or, if you have analyzed the results of a recent poll, you may be brimming with follow-up questions you wish you had asked. Write these questions down.

Invite your trusted advisers to a question-generation session. No question should be rejected out of hand. Ask your advisers these questions:

- "What answers would be most helpful in creating our literature?"
- "What answers would be most helpful in designing our mail?"
- "What questions will lead to those answers?"

By the time this planning session is finished, you will have at least 30 questions. If necessary, rewrite the questions to ensure that they are open-ended.

During a 90-minute focus group, the chosen facilitator might have time to ask just 12 to 15 questions. Choosing the most important questions, and arranging them in the proper order, is crucial. This is why the set of questions to be asked is called a question path. The wrong ordering can influence participants or give them clues about the answers you want to hear.

A few rules guide the general structure of the question path. First, questions should always proceed from the general to the specific. In this way, the question "In what area could local government be doing a better job?" would come early; "How would you evaluate the job being done by the Country Board of Supervisors?" might be in the middle, and "What do you know or think about County Supervisor Smith?" would come late in the session. You should always determine whether the participants view an issue as a problem before asking them to evaluate solutions.

The study of public policy gives us a systematic way to assess issues and problems. Voters are blissfully unaware of the details of policy theory, but these same details will help you discover winning issues.

From Policy to Politics

There are seven numbered stages of public policy development:

1. Problem recognition: You know that the trash is never picked up on schedule. Do the voters perceive this as a problem? You better find out before unveiling your strategy for improving trash collection.
2. Problem definition: Is the lateness of trash collection perceived as the real problem, or are people more concerned about the animals that knock over trash cans at the curb? The answer will tell you whether your focus should be the timeliness of trash collection or the need to beef up the animal control department.
3. Option generation: What ideas can your participants come up with to solve the now-defined problem?
4. Option evaluation: What factors will the voters use to judge your plans and promises? What kinds of information do they find believable and useful?
5. Option selection: From a range of possible solutions do the participants gravitate toward the same solutions you would endorse? If not, why not? What specific arguments or information would make your idea more attractive to the voters?
6. Implementation: Would the participants feel comfortable with a promise of quick action? Should the plan be introduced all at once, or in steps?
7. Evaluation: How do the participants judge the policies already in place? How would your candidate's effectiveness be judged? Having read this summary of the public policy process, think of other questions that you would like to ask.

Working with your chosen facilitator, go back to the notes that you made to record the questions in the first place. Copy each question on a 3"-by-5" card. In the upper right corner of each card, place the number 1 through 7 that corresponds to the public policy process outlined above.

The question "What is the biggest problem facing Our town?" would be a problem-recognition question, and you would put a "1" on the card. The question "How would you know if Country Commissioner Smith was doing a good job?" would get a "7."

Once you have all the questions rated, ignore these numbers, as these ratings should not affect the next step of the operation. Look at each question again, and ask yourself: "How specific is this question?" In the upper left-hand corner of each card, place a rating between one and five. In this case, a "one" represents a very general question with a "five" representing a very specific question.

The question about the biggest problems facing Our town would rate a "one," while the question about "County Commissioner Smith" doing a good job might rate a "four" or "five." If you intend to follow a question with a more specific question, such as, "When you see that County Commissioner Smith usually votes against the other four commissioners, how does that make you feel?," then the original question would rate a "four" and the follow-up question would rate a "five." The ratings are just a judgment call, and they can all be revised later.

Do not fall into the trap of assuming that specific questions will also score low on the public policy process scale. Once each question is rated on each measure, lay the cards on a grid. Make seven horizontal rows representing the seven categories of public policy; and make five columns representing the five rating categories you could give on the basis of specificity.

You may not have a question to put in every cell and your distribution may be lumpy. But you now have a way to decide which questions are more likely to contribute to a smooth-flowing and productive focus group.

Your question path should begin with the upper-left corner of the grid (those with a "1" and "one" rating) and proceed on a diagonal to the bottom right.

If any of the questions carry a policy process rank and specificity rank that differ by more than one point, discard it outright. If any of the discarded questions sound like real winners, reword it so it would likely fit in the diagonal path.

Remember, time is limited. By following this diagonal you will ask the most general questions about things that you are least able to capitalize on, and ask the most specific questions about the things that are the most effective in campaign communications.By the end of your focus group session, when your group is at its most talkative, you are likely to get statements that can be used verbatim. While these statements cannot be attributed, they may be used in your literature or paid media.

Decide in advance how much time you will allot to each question. You should also decide which questions you want everyone to answer directly, as opposed to those that you can afford to throw open to see where an interchange takes you.

Asking everyone to respond to the first couple of questions gets people involved and used to talking. If, in the last 20 minutes of the session, there are still some participants who are not participating, ask everyone to respond to your last couple of questions. This will give every member of the group a chance to contribute the quintessential phrase that will move the masses.

Sweat the Details

In the rehearsal stage, start with a welcoming speech and thank the participants for coming. Reassure them they will be compensated (at the end of the session) for their time and trouble.

You should remind the participants that you are not selling anything and that the session is being taped for the benefit of the client. For that reason, you address each other by first name only. Introduce your assistant (this person must not be the candidate or the candidate's spouse) and explain that this person is taking notes just in case the tape doesn't come out.

During the focus group, you want to encourage disagreement. Tell the participants that you value all opinions, and you want everyone to speak up, especially when they disagree with something that has been said.

You don't want to disclose the client but you want to help the participants stay on track. Get them started by going around the table and ask each person to tell the group their first name and something about themselves. It is best not to ask them to reveal something too specific, like how long they've lived in the area, as these things can create status in the group and perceptions of status can result in one participant deferring to another's opinion.

When you ask subsequent questions, always make it clear whether you want an answer from each participant, or whether you're throwing the floor open to general discussion. Be sure you're only asking one question at a time. If a question for general discussion draws no response, press for comments. Say something like, "How does that question make you feel?" After the first few questions, patterns will begin to emerge. Some participants will jump to answer the questions. Others will speak only if you ask them directly (i.e., "What do you think about that, Greg?"). Yet others will speak only when no one else does, out of fear of contradicting or interrupting others. A good facilitator can get all participants to comment on the important questions in the last 30 to 45 minutes. When the time is up, thank the group again and distribute their promised reimbursement. Cash is customary, and plain white envelopes help to keep the sponsor anonymous.

If extra people showed up beyond your set number (and you will generally ask more people to come than show up because there will always be no-shows), the assistant should take them aside, thank them, pay them, and send them off. Don't use more than a dozen people, and don't seat anyone after the session has started.

Keep two cautions in mind:

First, it is safer to do more than one focus group. Weird results or responses that are not representative of a larger universe are not common, but if the one exception occurs on your watch, you could be headed for a blunder. It's better to be safe than sorry.

Second, there is no substitute for experience. If you believe that your problems are so subtle, complex, and pivotal that only the best intelligence will suffice, hire a pro to run the focus group. The $10,000 that you would otherwise spend sending the wrong message may seem like a bargain afterwards.

✓ Ad Testing in the Electronic Age
Allan Rivlin, Lisa Grove, Mark Mellman, Ed Lazarus, and Steve Hopkins

Electronic advertising testing proved to be so indispensable in the '92 cycle that we predict everyone will be using it. The following scenario gives you an idea of how it works.

Some 60 specially screened, hardworking American swing voters sit in the conference room of the Holiday Inn in Pasadena, CA. Each participant has a pad of paper, a pencil, and a small, handheld dial resembling the one used to adjust an electric blanket.

After a few welcoming remarks, the moderator asks a series of demographic and attitudinal questions. The participants dial their responses. Then the show begins.

Participants see several political advertisements. Some of the ads are for Bill Clinton and George Bush, others are for Barbara Boxer and Bruce Herschensohn, the candidates for the California U.S. Senate long seat.

At the start of each spot the participants are instructed to set their dials to 50. When the spot begins, they are told to dial toward 100 if they are feeling more favorable to the candidate being advertised or toward zero if they are feeling less favorable.

The dials are hooked up to a computer. The computer records the position of each dial, once every second. As the dials change, the research team instantly sees the results for the group as a whole, as well as for several predefined subgroups. When Boxer says, "It's time to take care of our own," the lines and arrows shoot upward. When Bush says, "They look inward, we look forward," the lines are flat. We began using electronic ad testing in limited contexts during the '88 campaign cycle. By the '90 cycle, we were using it for several of our clients and answering calls from other firms who were interested in experimenting with the technique. In this cycle, we tested the media for most of our statewide campaigns and statewide referenda campaigns and to improve the AFL-CIO direct mail program.

We still conduct focus groups at the beginning of our involvement in most campaigns, but now we seldom use traditional focus groups to evaluate a campaign's media.

For about the same cost as a series of focus groups, electronic ad testing offers far more information—from 60 respondents—in half the time. Participants respond to the material individually with their own dials so there is very little "group think" effect. Top line results are available instantly, allowing the creative team to start making a few editing changes in a spot the next morning and have a more effective message on the air the next day.

The second-by-second evaluations allow us to improve rather than just rate each spot. In some cases, particularly effective images can be taken from relatively weak spots and reworked as the center of a stronger, more engaging piece. Conversely, ad testing can pinpoint any minor changes needed to correct an otherwise strong spot. For example, one testimonial spot tested especially low for believability. Why, participants asked in a discussion later, were they supposed to believe a bunch of actors? The creative team decided to insert each person's name and home town on the screen. (They really were local residents and not actors.) The problem was solved.

Testing the opinions of the campaign and the consultants against the reactions of real swing voters is well worth the effort and expense. In one case, the campaign manager in a tough Senate race was on the verge of firing his media consultants because he had such low regard for the quality of the spots they had produced. However, the spots tested very well and, after undergoing some small changes, were instrumental in what turned out to be a landslide re-election victory.

Among the lessons learned from media testing in the '92 cycle: Voters responded poorly to flowery descriptions of the candidate using words like "respected", "hard-working" and "integrity." What they responded to very well were more concrete examples of the candidate's accomplishments on their behalf. Similarly, voters did not respond well to negatively loaded descriptions of the opponent, though apparently substantive and well-documented attacks on an opponent's record were highly effective.

Advertising testing offers more information from more people in less time than the traditional research methods it replaces. With the airwaves getting more expensive and crowded in each successive election, there is an ever-growing need to make every half-minute count by putting up media that is as engaging and persuasive as possible. For these reasons, there is little doubt that many more spots will be tested in the '94 and '96 cycles than ever before.

✓ Effective Opposition Research
Rich Galen

Opposition research, in the modern political campaign, is the process of finding out as much about your opponent as your opponent probably knows about you.

It is easier to do opposition research against a long-term incumbent than it is against a relative newcomer. An incumbent has cast votes, filed forms, made statements, and sponsored legislation. A newcomer has performed few of these tasks, so it takes more work to ferret out the facts.

The problem most campaigns have with opposition research is they spend too much time looking for the big knockout punch—the one piece of information which will be so damaging that the opposition will simply crumple in the dust.

That almost never happens. Gary Hart's presidential campaign did not collapse because one night the candidate fell upon a bed of Rice. It fell apart because of years of accumulated reports of sexual misconduct. Joe Biden's presidential campaign did not fail because one speech was borrowed.

It collapsed under the weight of small inaccuracies, distortions, exaggerations, and borrowed speeches.

In most cases, the best you can hope for when compiling opposition research is a fact which will cause the opposition to lose a day from its campaign plan to answer a charge brought by you or a supporter. One day lost in early May, when there are some 180 days left in the campaign, is not a big deal. But one day lost in late October might prove critical for a candidate in a tight race.

Where to Find the Information

The first step in researching your opponent is to examine the public record. The local newspaper is a readily available public source. No matter what office you seek, there is a newspaper which covers the post. If you are running for city council in a rural town, the paper of record may be a weekly. If you are running in a large district, there will be many more newspapers to look through. Stay away from radio and television stations, however; they generally do not have the facilities to permit historical research.

If the local newspaper does not have a readily available morgue, your local public library or a nearby college library is a good secondary source. After you have clipped all the stories about your opponent and filed them into some meaningful categories, your next step is talking with the old timers.

Old timers are not necessarily old chronologically. They are the people who have been involved in the political process for the longest time. They know where the bodies are buried. And they generally will tell you. Be sure to read the newspapers first, however, so you have some basis in reality when they start spinning their yarns.

It also is useful to have read the clips so you can ask some specific question about the rumors and scandals which f made it into print. You may have to d o some legwork to reach the bottom of these little mysteries. It probably will be worth it.

Never Lie

There are few knockout punches in opposition research. A lie on a resume is one of them. Early in the campaign you should somehow obtain a copy of your opponent's resume. A resume is entirely controlled by the subject-author. People assume the candidate has provided the information which appears on the resume. They also assume it is accurate.

It had better be. A lie on a resume is often fatal to a campaign. In 1982 a former New York congressman named Bruce Caputo planned to run for the United States Senate. His resume claimed he had served as a uniformed officer in the Pentagon. In fact, he had worked in the Pentagon as a civilian employee. No amount of explaining could overcome the error. The campaign ended.

When checking an opponent's resume, call each of the colleges and universities listed and find out whether the opponent ever went there, and whether he or she graduated. Find out what kind of degree he or she received. Was it in music? Art history?

Also check the section on awards and civic achievements. Did he really receive the Outstanding Jaycee of the Year award, or was he only a finalist? Was she really the winner of the Americanism In Action essay contest run by the local American Legion, or was she merely an entrant?

Play Detective

To find out what kind of person your opponent really is, you need to play detective. Start by calling your opponent's former employers to learn about your opponent's work habits. Was he or she ever fired? If so, for what? Excessive absenteeism? Insubordination? Theft? Make sure that it was not for a good reason, such as standing up for the rights of a female co-worker who was being sexually harassed by the boss.

Even if your opponent left a job with good recommendations, check to see that he or she really held the position cited on the resume. Did he or she overstate—even just a little bit—his importance to the organization? We all have a tendency to do that on our own resumes. But most of us are not running for public office.

Minor vandalism charges, like shooting mail boxes on country roads while in high school, will not cause your opponent to fold up his tent and return to his previous line of employment. This is not to say you should condone such activity. But absent a pattern of continuing crimes, it will not make much difference today.

On the other hand, charges such as drunk driving, prostitution, solicitation, and spouse-beating are valid areas for public discussion. But beware: Such volatile charges often backfire. You must be very careful to whom you tell the story—and how you tell it.

Running Against an Incumbent

Ferreting out information about an opponent who has served in public office may lead you to distant places. First, there are what political consultant Bill McInturff calls the Seven Deadly Sins of Incumbency:

Casting bad votes or missing votes. Whatever office you seek, you should learn how your opponent voted on the most controversial issues. It is not always easy to discern what a particular vote means, or what a particular piece of legislation does. A congressman once remarked during debate on the floor of the House that the titles of bills and the titles of Marx Brothers movies were identical: Neither had anything to do with the content that followed.

All votes will be noted in the official journal of the legislative body involved. The votes your opponent missed are fair game. Most people will accept an attendance record of at least 85 percent. Anything worse is, again, a proper subject for public inquiry.

Taking trips at taxpayers' expense. Taxpayer-sponsored junkets must be reported somewhere. It may be in the city auditor's office, or it may be with the secretary of the Senate in Washington. Some travel is necessary and a worthy use of your hard-earned tax dollars. But how many trips to foreign locations are necessary for a member of the House Agriculture Committee? How many times does a Minnesota state senator need to go to Los Angeles?

Voting for his or her own pay raise. Most people cannot give themselves raises. Many people cannot even ask for raises. They must wait either until someone else negotiates a new contract which covers them or until they are granted a cost-of-living adjustment. When elected officials raise their own salaries, it looks like hell—especially members of Congress. Just make sure your opponent did not support the pay raise because he or she is the sole support of two aged parents—both of whom are confined to a nursing home.

Voting for new or higher taxes. No elected official wants to be known as the person who raised your taxes. Everyone knows how much waste exists in government because they have read about the military's $1,300 toilet seats. Everyone believes government does not work as well as it should because everyone has had to wait in a line to renew his or her driver's license or register their home or automobile.

Wasting more money, or raising the salaries of public employees who are surly and unresponsive, is a bitter pill for many taxpayers to swallow. There may well be good and decent people who serve as public employees, but they never seem to wait on me when I stand in a government line. And they are not the ones running for public office.

Not living in the district. State laws regarding residency differ, but common sense dictates that any member of Congress must live at least part-time in the Washington, D.C. area. If your opponent has taken up permanent residency in the state or nation's capital, you may be able to hang him or her on it.

A nice visual is the hotel where your opponent stays when he comes "home" or, better yet, a picture of the post office box which is his legal residence. Conversely, a cute picture of his Victorian home in the expensive Virginia suburbs of Washington—perhaps with his wife's Mercedes parked in the drive way—makes a lovely postcard to your opponent's constituents.

Rep. Denny Smith (R-Ore.) used this tactic with considerable success in ousting House Ways and Means Chairman Al Ullman in 1980. A Smith TV spot contrasted Ullman's Oregon residence—he moved from one post office box to the next—with the three homes in the metropolitan D.C. area which the congressman owned. Once the ads hit the air, Ullman was politically dead.

Becoming involved in a scandal. Unfortunately, public scandals for elected officials are hard to come by. Legislative bodies, like physicians, tend to protect their own. Congress has an annoying habit of exempting itself from many of the laws it imposes on other government agencies and private entities. No sex discrimination regulations, no health and safety rules, no nothing.

When a member does do something so awful that Congress cannot ignore it, the most frequent penalty usually handed out is the "censure." This calls for the offending legislator to stand before the presiding officer and watch him wave his finger and say, in effect, "You are hereby censured." That is it. The guy walks right from there to lunch in the members' dining room.

On a rare occasion, as in the current case of Rep. Mario Biaggi (D-N.Y.), a felony conviction will spur the House Ethics Committee to recommend removal of a member. But this carries with it the peculiar odor of regicide, and might lead the masses to believe incumbents should, once in a while, be thrown out in favor of someone new.

Repeating any of the above. A standard responses to any of the seven deadly sins is: "I did it. I'm sorry. I'll never do it again." Proving that he or she has done it again can have a salutatory effect on your campaign. Look again at the Hart and Biden examples: It was not so much the triggering event which caused their campaigns to go under; it was the accumulated weighty repeated errors in judgment.

Money Does Not Fall From the Sky

Every incumbent raises money. It does not just fall from the sky; it comes from somewhere or someone. In most jurisdictions, every candidate must report the source and amount of each contribution. Incumbents often receive a stipend, or honorarium, for addressing a convention or association. All honoraria and gifts also must be reported.

For most members of Congress, a typical honorarium is approximately $2,500. Often, the honorarium donor has an interest in a particular piece of legislation. Obtain a list of your opponent's speaking engagements and compare it with a list of his or her committee assignments and related votes. There may well be at least the appearance of impropriety.

Many candidates for state and local office, and all candidates for federal office, must file regular reports detailing both their income and expenditures. These are public documents, and they are fair game for public scrutiny.

You should not hesitate to inform the media which business, labor, or ideological groups are bankrolling your opponent. But do not solicit funds from people listed on your opponent's financial disclosure reports; that is illegal.

Triple-Check Your Facts

The saddest words in politics are not "what might have been." The saddest words are "Oops, I guess I should have checked that." Before launching an attack on your opponent, triple-check every charge you make. Small errors in fact—for whatever reason—will do far more to damage your campaign than the original attack could ever have done to your opponent's.

A recent congressional candidate in Connecticut had a terrific attack set up against his opponent. His opposition research showed that the incumbent had missed every vote held by a particular subcommittee during the previous Congress. Unfortunately, when the ad was produced, the graphics people did not have quite enough room for the word "subcommittee." So they omitted the prefix "sub."

Naturally, the incumbent produced a record of the votes cast at the full committee. The issue went from the incumbent's performance on the subcommittee to the challenger's attention to the truth. Before you launch an attack based upon your research, make sure your people have asked enough questions. If your opponent's attendance record is bad, check to see if there is a justifiable reason. There are not many, but if it was because his 1 year-old daughter was undergoing chemotherapy for leukemia and the opponent was spending nights at her bedside, you will be burned.

One other note: Be careful how you collect the information. In his 1986 campaign, Wisconsin Senate candidate Ed Garvey hired a private detective—who subsequently posed as a reporter—to investigate his opponent, incumbent Sen. Robert Kasten (R-Wis.). When word of the incident leaked, reporters were irate; the incident cost the senator far more than he ever could have gotten in return.

Do Unto Yourself

Your opponent will not stand by idly as you do all this research. In all likelihood, he will be busy compiling an opposition report on you just as you are doing on him. The best way to protect yourself against a blind-side attack is to have an opposition research report prepared on yourself. If you are an incumbent, examine the public record for votes, statements, attendance, and contributions with a critical eye.

If you are a challenger, look carefully at your resume and ask the kind of questions you would not want the opposition to ask. If you do not do this, you run the risk of fighting a defensive action day after day. Heed this advice and you will be ready to respond to attacks quickly, cleanly, and cogently.

Having a reasonable, believable response is often enough to blunt an attack. Many campaigns will throw a jab. Most campaigns lack the confidence to follow with a right cross. By doing your homework, you can stop the jab and start landing your own punches.

✓ Challenging Your Competitor's Weaknesses
Terry Cooper

If you're challenging an incumbent, or running for an open seat in competition with someone better known or more experienced than you, the odds are that you're going to lose—unless, that is, you have skillfully used opposition research.

Opposition research is exactly that—information that can be used as leverage to enhance communications of a message by specifically attacking an opponent's weakest points. It is an essential ingredient to an underdog campaign.

Opposition research has taken on an increasingly important place in campaigning because of voter inertia—the tendency of the vast majority of the electorate to reelect the incumbent or vote for the better-known candidate unless someone gives them a good reason to do otherwise.

Quality opposition research uncovers those reasons, if they exist. Good opposition research also provides the facts upon which sound decisions can be made about almost every topic that influences the success or failure of a campaign.

Joseph Gaylord, then executive director of the National Republican Congressional Committee, made the point in a monograph called "Flying Upside Down: 88 Truism To Help Guide Challenger Campaigns." Gaylord said it was essential to research the opponent" and to do it as early as possible because it becomes the basis for intelligent decision-making in such areas as issue and theme development; scheduling and targeting; publicity and advertising; fundraising and field organization."

Many campaign managers naively budget thousands of dollars for media, hoping to deliver an interesting and convincing message, while spending next to nothing on the opposition research that helps tell them what the message should be.Even when the campaign's creditors are about to disconnect the telephones and evict you from the headquarters, persevere on opposition research.

Opposition research is not negative campaigning. That aspect of the modern campaign has to do with the choices you make in communicating a message to others. Opposition research, again, is simply knowing where the other guy stands vis-a-vis your positions—and hitting him at his weak points.

Understand Your Own Candidate First

Second, opposition research is governed by the consultants' idiosyncrasies more than a set group of events such as those that might guide polling or targeting. Make sure that the person you hire not only knows what style of opposition research he is going to use, but also trusts it deeply.

It may seem like a basic point, but you first need to understand your own candidate before you can research your opponent. You don't want to spend time researching any issue on which the two candidates essentially agree, which your candidate simply won't discuss, or which your candidate can't use. As a consultant, you need to learn the candidate's biography, including such personal items as service record, marital history, medical history, criminal, and traffic record, past use of drugs and general financial holdings. You need to learn what issues your candidate wants to campaign on, even though you may later tell him to change. You also need to know what he wants to avoid.

Opposition research entails knowing your own political following and going out of your way to show the broad group of voters that may be undecided that they do not fully know your opponents' following. Too often campaigns have gone right over the voters heads by focusing on national or international issues that interest only political insiders, rather than their constituencies.

One of the biggest dangers in having amateurs do opposition research is that they tend to be precisely the political and policy junkies that are most likely to be blinded by the bigger, mega-issues instead of those that hit closest to home. Make sure that your researchers, before they bury themselves in books, are personally involved in ascertaining local voters' sentiments and are going to be guided by those sentiments.

The tried-and-true tool for assessing sentiment is survey research—polling. If you can afford both good opposition research and a good poll, you're solid; but if not, you can attain some of your opposition research goals by other means.

Where to Find Your Information

Here's where to look:

- Published data: Voting records, business records, and census reports are a cornucopia of useful information. Does your district have a high proportion of home renters? Maybe landlord-tenant laws are significant. Do you have a large percentage of senior citizens? If so, seniors' issues I could be important. The census reports also cover each jurisdiction's educational attainment, income, occupation, and racial heritage. All are valuable, basic pieces of information.
- State governments: City and county crime statistics give you a read on the safety in the areas of your district. The state employment service compiles data on unemployment and employment from which you can deduce whether the number of jobs in your district is growing or shrinking. The state department of education collects reams of data about school systems, including results on standard proficiency examinations. The state department of health can tell you about such subjects as child immunization rates, low birth-weight, and teen pregnancy rates. The folks at the state finance department probably dissect each city and county budget showing where they get their money and how they spend it.
- The Local Media: Every so often, you'll find that a local newspaper or radio or television station has done a poll of local sentiment. Whether or not the methodology was pure or the results have a 95 percent level of confidence, the findings can be extremely enlightening. In any event, the local newspapers and broadcast media report on the local happenings and those happenings can translate into issues and themes.
- Conversations with Informed Citizens: Talk with five or 10 knowledgeable local people. They may be party officials, local officeholders, former campaign managers, reporters, editors, or "leading citizens" such as the head of the chamber of commerce or the retail merchants' association. Ask them what's on people's minds that a candidate for the office involved ought to be addressing and what the perfect incumbent would have done to represent his constituents during his last term in office. With this information in hand, there are two important questions to consider:

- What do the voters who should vote for you, but have been voting for the opponent, give as their reasons for voting for him?
- What do even the opponent's strongest supporters among "your" voters admit are his weak points?

On the first question, the opponent's strengths need to be assessed. The most devastating criticism a campaign can level against an opponent is a documented, persuasive attack on the opponents perceived strengths. If you can take away the opponent's strong points, he'll collapse like a house of cards. But make sure your arguments are credible as well as factual. You can attack an opponent's strengths with facts, but if the public doesn't find your argument credible, you gain no ground.

On the second issue, you have to sense whether there are any major, disqualifying weaknesses to focus on. If your candidate is an officeholder or is otherwise well known to the voters, you'll want to ask those same questions about your own candidate. If the opponents campaign is well organized, it's going to be researching your candidate's record—and you certainly don't want to get blindsided.

When you've finished gathering information about the district, the voters, and how the voters perceive your candidate and the opponent, organize what you've learned into a paper that you can circulate to other key people in the campaign. You should try to rank-order voters concerns and, whenever possible, indicate whether an identified problem is getting better, staying the same or getting worse. That document will be a partial list of the criteria on which you measure your opponent's performance. It will also be a partial list of the criteria against which you measure your candidate's performance.

Now it's time to plan research angles or avenues of inquiry. And it's a good idea to write them down. Identify every subject that would be an actual voter concern and ask yourself: "How would I establish whether the opponent has a good or bad record on that issue?"

Ask, 'How Can I Find Serious Weaknesses?'

Review the opponent's strengths and ask, "How would I determine whether he's truly good or bad on that?" Consider the opponent's weaknesses, and ask: "How can I find out just how serious that weakness is?"

Let me take an example. Let's say the newspapers repeatedly refer to the opponent as being attentive and responsive to his constituents, and voter after voter you've talked to lists "good constituent services" as a great strength. Are there any chinks in that armor?

First you have to define more specifically which constituent services the opponent performs well. Suppose he answers mail quickly, conducts frequent town meetings, and seems to attend every graduation, wedding, parade, and wake in the district. All well and good, but what other constituent services are there and how well has he performed them? For example, are all needed focal road improvements being made promptly? Put together a list of local needs and ask what he's doing about them.

This process, planning avenues of inquiry, is the most important and most challenging aspect of opposition research. It demands creativity. The time you spend thinking up lines of inquiry may be the key to your candidate's election.

The fact-finding process in which you learn about the voters and their sentiments, and the thinking process in which you plan your avenues of inquiry, will give you a variety of topics on which to focus as you go about researching your opponent's record. But there are other signposts to follow. You need to examine not only what the opponent did but what he didn't do. Did he choose not to serve on the legislative committees that deal with the issues most important to the voters?

Contrast Campaign Promises with Deeds

Even though crime was an enormous problem in the district, did he fail to sponsor or co-sponsor any of the major anti-crime initiatives? Inaction can be deadlier than misguided action. If your opponent was only recently elected, compare and contrast his campaign promises with his accomplishments.

Look for flip-flops and contradictory votes on the same issue. Keep in mind that not every reversal of voting is a flip-flop because the facts may have changed. A cost-of-living raise for state employees may be too little in times of budget surpluses, but way too much during a period of budget deficits.

Look for patterns, too. One bad vote, one missed vote, one outrageous statement during a debate, one misrepresentation of one's voting record, can be all the material your campaign needs for a hard-hitting radio spot or a point in a subsequent debate. A pattern of problems raises the broader question of whether the opponent's judgment is unacceptably flawed.

You also need to look for possible juxtapositions. One state legislator voted against exempting human food from the sales tax but had sponsored legislation to exempt rabbit food, creating a good target. One current candidate, a state senator representing a densely populated suburban district with youth sports occupying every park and ice rink, voted to exempt farmers from tort liability but opposed exempting volunteer coaches and officials from tort liability to players and spectators. Such juxtaposition illustrates a candidate's bad judgment.

Let these ideas guide your search through an opponent's record. Go through every aspect of an opponent's record with a fine-toothed comb and with an open mind. Most of the time when you actually do the research, you'll find at least one important fact you weren't even looking for and can use effectively.

Elected Officials Often Say Dumb Things

A corollary is this: Never underestimate the ability of elected officials to say and do incredible and dumb things. Can you imagine a law allowing state government to foreclose on the homes of deceased Medicaid recipients to recoup Medicaid payments? Two states have such laws. Someone voted for them. Can you picture voting against requiring school systems to condition high-school graduation on proof of functional literacy? In 1982, 128 members of the U.S. House voted against such a measure.

After conducting the basic research, organize it and reduce it to a usable form. That means start early, finish early. The good researchers will ask other professionals in the campaign what is important to them. Different campaigns want their reports in different ways. One dyslexic candidate wanted a report on audio cassettes to listen to the information on a car tape deck. Some media consultants want the information reduced to one page while some campaign managers want every gory detail.

These reports should be terse, readable, and persuasive. If there are technical terms, it should be explained in layman's language—be it parliamentary procedure or subject matter. The reports should be scrupulously accurate. You may have done the research, but your candidate gets the blame—and is raked over the coals—for your errors.

Opposition research can be fun, gratifying, useful, and decisive. It can prove the rationale for your candidate running, and the reason for voters to reject your opponent. But it can't make a silk purse out of a sow's ear.

If your opponent has a good record, no amount of opposition research will defeat him. At best, you'll uncover a few minor dereliction's, not nearly enough to change the results. Understand that. Where the results of your research are meager and the odds against winning are long, there can arise a temptation to fudge a little. Never give in. Falsification or misrepresentation of the data, if discovered, would not only doom your candidate, but damage him personally, even though he may have never known.

If you're managing an opposition research project, realize that even the best researchers lose now and then. Resign yourself to some loses, and keep your principles.

✓ Researching the Records
Bob Norris

Researching a political opponent is one of the most daunting challenges facing a campaign. It's also a great deal of fun. Sure, finecombing your way through a tangle of bureaucratic documents is boring. So is panning for gold—until you hit the mother of all mother lodes.

Research is a tool to get the truth to the voters about the records of all the candidates. It provides you with the hard evidence you need to show how your agenda and your abilities compare with your opponent's. If you really are the better candidate, if your opponent really is misrepresenting herself or abusing her position, then you have an obligation to set the record straight.

Voters will not do this research themselves. Even reporters rarely take the time to do more than restate the official version of events drafted by press secretaries. You cannot expect the voters to know intuitively that your candidate is superior, nor can you expect reporters to do much more than report. So you better have the facts at your disposal if you want to trash the other side.

There are a lot of areas apart from legislative records that should be part of your research project. But roll-call votes, bill sponsorships, effectiveness in getting the right bills passed, and attendance all say a lot about whether or not a representative is doing the job for which she was elected.

A "yea" or "nay" vote is incontrovertible evidence of how a legislator feels about important issues and how she is likely to act in the future. When cross-referenced to other data—such as campaign contributions and personal finances—it becomes even more significant.

What are these records? How should they be interpreted? Following is a brief checklist:

Votes

Roll-call votes are the most direct evidence of what a legislator is doing. This is her job. How can you find out if she is really representing the views of the district?

Use the journal indexes and vote databases. If your opponent is a member of the U.S. Congress, these resources are plentiful and easy to use. I suggest starting with the Congressional Record, Legislate, CQ's Washington Alert, NEXIS, Congressional Quarterly, and, best of all, the Democratic Study Group's bipartisan vote books. If you are researching a state legislator, these resources are scarcer and more difficult to understand. Most of the official journals of state legislative bodies do have subject indexes, but most of these limit their reporting to shorthand minutes of proceedings rather than verbatim coverage of debate. Often this is simply a report of the title of the bill or the motion or the amendment followed by a list of how the members voted. You will need to find another way to figure out what was really going on.

Some states have other official publications that report on legislative activities. Such a book might be a year-end digest with additional indexes, or a party publication. But even these can lack the detail you need to understand what the political and policy considerations were. For this you might have to work backwards.

Check newspaper indexes for stories covering the legislature. Find stories on issues that will be important in this campaign and then use the journal indexes to track down when the roll-call votes took place.

Although much of a legislative battle consists of procedural and parliamentary maneuvers, these esoteric activities rarely move voters one way or the other—it is the simple, easily explained data that proves most effective.

Does the member's sponsorships really affect the needs of the district? Has she succeeded in turning her public policy ideas into successful legislation, or have her bills languished in committee? And, when you can find them, the clean votes on sexy issues that can be easily explained and are difficult to refute can be invaluable.

Even when you find one good vote that illustrates your theme well, avoid jumping to the conclusion that you've found the "silver bullet." You must be prepared for your opponent's response. Look at all related votes through out a legislator's career, and do not give her the opportunity to respond with a long list of votes on the same issue that makes your attack seem petty.

Beware, too, of questioning votes that your opponent cast along with credible legislators. In the special '89 election to fill Dick Cheney's seat, Democrat John Vinich made the mistake of failing to anticipate that his use of a vote dealing with crime would offend the Democratic governor—who signed the bill—and many of his Democratic colleagues—who voted the same way as his Republican opponent. Several days of bad press later, it was too late to take it back.

Some Other Angles

Carefully examine votes where the legislator is in an extreme minority These votes, if on an important issue are contrary to the feelings of the voters become a powerful symbol that this legislator may be seriously out of step.

It wasn't long after I started doing research that I noticed that there is a core of incumbent Republicans who vote against everything. These Libertarian, anti-government attitudes appeal to many voters who are fed up with government, but their consistent no-votes make it easy to illustrate how they are actually voting against real laws and programs that help people in the district. A vote against passage of the transportation appropriations bill is really vote against rebuilding the bridge that your voters must use every day to get work. A vote against funding for the Department of Education is really a vote to shut down the Head Start program on which the children in your town depend. Look at what other analysts are saying.

The best sources are scorecards from respected public interest groups. Make sure your own findings on particular issues are shared with influential groups concerned about this issue before charging forward with an attack yourself. Environmental Action's listing of Arlan Stangeland as one of the "dirty dozen" in 1988 was far more effective than the same charge from his opponent. The legitimate interest groups can rarely be manipulated, but if they are presented with solid evidence of perceived wrongdoing, they will usually act.

Attendance

Is a representative earning her taxpayer-financed paycheck? One of the best ways to answer the question is by assessing whether or not she is on the job, doing what she was elected to do: make decisions. The clearest measure of this is how often a representative is missing during roll-call votes.

How do you interpret this figure? In the U.S. House of Representatives, a voting attendance record of less than 90 percent is very rare. If you find that your opponent's attendance is only 85 percent, you've got something. Yet, if you say—"Mary Smith has a terrible attendance record. It's only 85 percent"—the voters will think you're stretching things. Put it in context.

Look at the attendance records of the members from the general geographic area or the entire state and say, "Mary Smith has the worst attendance record of our entire delegation" or "the worst record of any representative or "She is in the bottom 5 percent of the Assembly."

Look also at the list of specific missed votes. Even with an attendance record of 90 percent, a legislator would have missed many votes, dealing with millions or billions of dollars. This is even more powerful if you can show that the legislator was off collecting campaign contributions at a $1,000-a-plate fundraiser or getting an honorarium from the oil industry at a seminar in Puerto Rico when an important environmental vote was considered on the floor.

Joe Slade White's 'Godzilla" commercial aimed at Don Young's frequent missed votes is a good example of using this issue. An airplane is sitting on a runway while water is sprayed over the plane. The announcer stated that when Young was asked where he was when he missed an important vote, he had claimed his plane was grounded. In the closing scene, as a toy dinosaur attacks the plane, the announcer asks, "I wonder what his excuse will be next time?"

Sponsorships and Co-sponsorships

A legislator's real priorities can be illustrated by the types of bills she chooses to sponsor and co-sponsor. Legislators and their staffs are asked every day to add their names to countless bills on a wide variety of topics. They tend to do so for many reasons, and these decisions may not be subject to close scrutiny by the member.

It's easy to co-sponsor a bill you think won't go anywhere if the chief sponsor is an ally or friend, or if the bill summary captures the eye of a press secretary who sees the possibility of a good press release, or if a constituent or contributor advocates the bill. It can be one of the easiest areas for a legislator to err, yet how can that legislator deny she really didn't believe in the goals of a bill she allowed her name to be on?

On the other hand, the fact that a member neglects to co-sponsor a bill seen as improving the lot of voters also raises questions about her priorities. If she is spending a lot of time working on commemorative bills such as "National Dairy Goat Awareness Week" (I'm not [making this up) and neglects to co-sponsor—or, better yet, even opposes—a bill to help the local textile industry, you have the evidence needed to illustrate her priorities in a simple and understandable manner.

Looking at sponsorships not only gives you a picture of her priorities, but by calculating her success in getting these bills enacted, you can illustrate her competence on the job. In a 1988 commercial used by California state Sen. Gary K. Hart, who was running against incumbent Robert

Lagomarsino, an elementary school class was asked the results of their assignment: to report on bills their congressman had turned into law. To a shocked classroom, one child responded that he couldn't find any—not one. "I guess Congressman Lagomarsino didn't do his homework" was the conclusion.

Committee and Subcommittee Records

This is where the real work in most legislatures gets done, but the examination of these records requires even more attention to detail and a closer analysis. The techniques are the same as examining floor proceedings, but the dangers are magnified.

Many committees maintain sloppy records; others make a concerted attempt, in a bipartisan manner, to protect all their members from criticism for what goes on in committee hearings and mark-ups. These records are public; you have a right to them. But you have to be especially careful to ensure that you'll get the needed backup from knowledgeable insiders if they are asked by a reporter or anyone else to verify your statements.

In one race we painstakingly proved that a certain Republican incumbent rarely participated in his committee activities. Yet when a majority committee staffer was asked to comment on the charge, he told the press this could not be proven since the committee keeps no attendance records.

We could prove it, and we did. But we were forced to spend valuable time and energy arguing the facts instead of the substance of the charge.

Follow the Money Trail

One point needs to be reiterated: It would be a mistake to confine research on incumbent legislators to an examination of only their record as legislators.

Whom a candidate takes money from, what financial investments she has, what sort of career she had prior to running for office—all these reflect on a candidate's character and ability, and thus should be examined to determine her real commitment and dedication to public service.

All these data must be integrated into the findings of your legislative research and lead to a credible and defensible description of the candidate. You're looking for the symbols that describe the candidate in a manner that can be used to deliver the simple and credible message that drives a winning campaign.

When the research is done, remember the most important rules:

1. Double-check everything down to the dates and roll-call numbers of votes.
2. Check everything again.
3. Be credible. Ask yourself what an interest group, a reporter, a staff person, or anyone with some knowledge of the bill might say when asked about it.
4. Don't get esoteric. Know how to deliver the message in a short, understandable way and how to put it into context for the area you're running in and the voters in your district.
5. There is never any reason for a researcher to distort or exaggerate the facts. Your media consultants and your pollsters and your speech writers might well be justified in emphasizing different issues or rephrasing your interpretation as events unfold—but you need to have your initial report as a reliable source of solid facts. Everyone on the campaign must be confident that they are not basing their decisions and action on the wishful thinking of the researcher.

✓ Running Your Op Research Through a Two-Minute Drill
Joseph Rodota

In a perfect world, a campaign manager spends Labor Day perusing the artfully written, carefully documented analysis of the opposition and prepares the final advertising and free media strategy.

Perhaps a few quick questions are passed to the research team: Is it possible to update the total cost of new programs our opponent has proposed? Are there any more flip-flops? Responses are provided quickly, by fax.

I have yet to meet that campaign manager.

Despite the increasingly long lead times in opposition research, Labor Day will find you with many stones left unturned in the quest to explain and categorize the record of a political opponent. You'll have no rest until the last questionnaire has been answered, the last debate has been held, and the last television commercial has been released.

What should you do in the final three weeks? It depends.

The Marathon's Last Mile

Let's first consider a hypothetical campaign that planned ahead. We'll call it Change for Congress.

As early as January of this year, Change's campaign strategy team received and reviewed a detailed fact book that synthesized months of research into the public record of the opposition, incumbent Congressman Chester "Check" Bounce.

Using the Congressional Record, Bounce's every utterance was captured, every bill sponsored or co-sponsored was found, and every fee hike or tax increase was exposed.

The National Taxpayers Union analysis of Bounce's franking privilege was thoroughly checked, as were back issues of ACLU newsletters. Meanwhile, Bounce's performance at the House Bank was stitched together through newspaper accounts and other sources.

Thus compiled, the fact book, at about 50 pages, neatly set out the case for giving Bounce the bounce.

During the last three weeks, you should be providing your campaign, Change for Congress, the following information and services.

1. A detailed analysis of any campaign literature put out by the Bounce campaign. These analyses should be produced and distributed internally on a regular basis to alert senior staff of any blatant misrepresentations.
2. An analysis of Bounce's television spots within hours of their release. During the closing days of Bruce Herschensohn's primary campaign for U.S. Senate in California this year, the text of one of his opponent's commercials was released at noon, two hours in advance of a scheduled press conference by the opponent, Tom Campbell.
Fifteen minutes before the conference, however, Herschensohn's critique of the spot had already been faxed to approximately 100 reporters. Herschensohn's criticisms were reported—and confirmed as fact—in nearly every published analysis of Campbell's commercials.
3. Review everything produced by your own campaign for factual accuracy.

4. Assist in debate preparation. Sequester yourself with a stand-in for the opponent and train him to do a credible impersonation of Bounce defending his record in mock debates with your candidate.
5. Contribute ideas and theories based on what has been found and what has been used to date. You know better than anyone what arrows remain in the quiver.

The 100-Meter Dash

Let's turn to a campaign that's a little behind the power curve.

With just few weeks to go, you know virtually nothing about the challenger. You have to build a file within 72 hours, using everything in the public domain without wasting a single minute. Politely put, you're between a rock and a hard place. Your task is quite a challenge, but it can be done.

What used to take four weeks to complete can often be done in four days, thanks to the wide availability of online databases and card catalogues, faxes, laser printing, and Federal Express. This is no time to write the definitive biography of your opponent or confirm that he's paid his Rotary Club dues on time. Your task is to come up with four or five items that can be used in the last debate or in the final advertising blitz.

At this point, you are looking for a needle that will burst your opponent's balloon. In just a few days, a crash research project can reasonably obtain the following information:

- Your opponent's personal financial disclosure statement.
- Lawsuits filed by or against your opponent.
- Confirmation that your opponent bothered to vote in recent elections.
- News articles mentioning your opponent. (Available from one of the major online vendors).
- Securities and Exchange Commission filings of any company in which your opponent has invested or served as a director or top executive.
- Local news stories, if they have been maintained by a local librarian or if the local paper has a morgue file that is available to the public.

Whether you stay in-house or use a hired gun, one word of caution: Your opposition researchers should never ever wander off the reservation and embarrass the campaign.

In the closing weeks, a stray research call can be exploited by the Opposition. Inexperienced in-house researchers are the ones most likely to self-detonate and should be supervised closely. (It is also a good idea to keep an eye on overzealous volunteers). In the political world, no good deed—or bad researcher—goes unpunished.

✓ Researching Your Own Candidacy
Rochelle S. Dornatt

There are three reasons candidates should research themselves before a campaign:

1. The dumbest people in the world are those who believe they're smarter than their opponents.
2. Never assume your constituents know or understand who you are or what you do.
3. Always assume your opponent does.

Candidate research is an integral and fundamental element of any campaign framework, but many campaigns think of it only in terms of the opposition. Good candidate research creates a complete picture of your record, too, so you can compare it to your opponent's.

Don't risk building your campaign strategy in a vacuum. Start your research early, and concentrate on strengths and weaknesses.

Incumbents enjoy a lot of campaign advantages, hut they are especially vulnerable to good opposition research. Whereas a challenger, especially a first-timer, may have to defend his private record more than his limited public one, an incumbent runs with the extra burden of public accountability. Voters judge how well they were represented.

A classic example of a candidate who would have benefited from knowing his own record a little better came during the 1984 U.S. Senate race in Texas. During the Democratic primary campaign state Sen. Lloyd Doggett, at a public debate, accused one of his opponents, former Rep. Bob Krueger of having voted for federal monies to assassinate unfriendly dictators. Krueger vociferously denied the charge and dared—nay! defied!—Doggett to prove it. Doggett then read chapter and verse of the date, bill number, and roll call vote wherein Krueger had, in fact, voted for CIA undercover operations to remove certain troublesome dictators. Krueger, caught unaware, could not respond and had no defense. Doggett carried the debate.

Get To the Source

Research can he used to support any facet of a campaign:

Strategic: to develop the strategy of the campaign or predict what a candidate might do in a given situation.

Offense: to erode the strength of an opponent or to persuade the undecided voters in your favor.

Defense: to inoculate the candidate, to fuel counterattacks, or to know what issues of your opponent's not to attack because of your own poor record on that issue.

A thorough understanding of the demographics of the state or district in which you are running—the playing field—is an important first step for developing campaign strategy, identifying issues, and targeting your message to specific voting blocs. Because population shifts between elections, assumptions that held in previous years may no longer apply in your district, don't just study recent events. Learn the area's history, too.

The bulk of research about your district can he done with Census Bureau reports on file at your local library. Other sources to tap include the Bureau of Labor Statistics, the Consolidated Federal Funds Report, and the city/county clerk for party and voter registration.

Next, comb your own record, especially your legislative history. You must know how what you've done looks—good or bad—to both voters and the press, so you can be prepared to promote or defend your actions.

A legislative record provides the most ammunition and the best defense in virtually any campaign. With database services such as Legi-Slate and Washington Alert, sifting through legislative history does not have to be exhausting, just exhaustive. These computerized systems let you conduct vote research, statement research, and hill research from your desk.

A logical way to organize a vote analysis is to categorize by issue each vote you made and record your position. Record the arguments for and against that vote. Look carefully at procedural votes, too, which at a glance appear noncontroversial, but may hide deeper meaning.

If you are a first-time challenger, you may not have a legislative history to defend, hut that won't stop your opponent from trying to project your record in business and the community into some unflattering hypothetical scenarios. Meet with your accountant, your attorney, community, and religious leaders with whom you are affiliated and dig through all your accomplishments and failures with them.

One volatile area found in the backgrounds of both challengers and incumbents is finances. Money will always he a contentious topic in campaigns. Each candidate should know exactly the status of his or her investments, tax returns, salaries (earned and unearned), dividend and interest income, and, of course, contributions.

The first place to look for financial information is the clerks office of the legislative body in which you serve. All honoraria, travel reimbursements, gifts, and other income will be recorded there. For federal campaigns, the FEC is your best source. And don't overlook franking accounts.

Information gathered throughout the research process will accumulate quickly into reams of facts. Though it is important to have the details for clarification and verification, you must synthesize the information into manageable messages. Whether your methods are electronic or manual, categorize and subcategorize, then memorize.

The bottom line of any research activity is to he prepared. Research gives you the material you need to defend yourself, as well as giving you the information you need to disarm and diminish your opponent. Campaign research undertaken early means a well prepared base for later campaign action.

✓ Using Exit Poll Pools
Philip Porado

Is there any reason for campaigns to be excited about the upcoming national test of the new Voter Research Service? Excited may be overstating it, but interest is growing as election day nears.

Although the VRS exit polls won't affect this year's elections, assessments of their performance will surely have an impact on future elections. So come November 6th, while the pundits decide whether the coordinated effort produced more consistent and comprehensive details about voting in 1990, political pros will be trying to glean useful tidbits about polling technology that will help 1991 and '92 clients. But first, the industry, like the media outlets that subscribe to the service, will have to pay.

When the four major news networks—ABC, CBS, CNN, and NBC—decided to pool their resources to collect election-night vote counts and exit polling information, they knew it would save them money. But it also created a salable commodity: data.

"We decided to make the data available to any newspaper, radio station, or television station who wants to buy it," says Warren Mitofsky, executive director of VRS, the New York based operation in charge of gathering exit polling data that the four networks will use to prepare election night projections. CBS is the paymaster on the VRS project, covering all the bills and being reimbursed by the other three members of the pool. Mitofsky ran the CBS News Election and Survey Unit for 23 years before signing with VRS.

VRS is offering two types of service—basic and enhanced—to its subscribers. The two services differ in the amount of demographic data provided, the speed with which the data are updated, and the ability of the data feed to interface with other computers within a news operation.

Users of either the basic or enhanced service will be able to log onto the VRS mainframe computer in Syracus, NJ, and call up states to which they subscribe. Candidate and party votes counts are available on a statewide, county, or precinct basis.

In addition to numbers, basic service subscribers will get "garden-variety demographic data like sex, age group, and race," according to VRS director Richard Silverman, also a CBS vet, who spent 20 years with the network's survey unit before moving over to VRS. "Users of the enhanced service will get extra demographic data," Silverman adds, "stuff like which issues are most important to Republicans or Democrats, and why people voted the way they did."

Consider the Sources

VRS is collecting election data from three sources. First it pulls raw vote counts for every state, broken down on a countywide basis, from the News Election Service, a pool sponsored by the major television networks, some large newspapers and the wire services. NES uses civic groups to collect vote counts from captains in all 150,000 voting precincts nationwide.

NES processes data and feeds it to pool members, including VRS. But NES data gets processed too slowly for VRS clients to take advantage of during prime broadcast time. So VRS is training its own surveyors to collect data from 3,000 sample precincts. With this data, Mitofsky says, VRS can make accurate projections ready in time for 8 p.m. and 9 p.m. newscasts.

The final source for VRS data will be onsite interviews employees of Radnor, PA-based Chilton Corp. "They'll be at 1,400 polling places asking people their age, sex, gender, party affiliation. that will allow us to show how Warren Mitofsky groups within the U.S. are voting," says Mitofsky.

Field operations will remain, for the most part, low-tech, according to Silverman. The Chilton pollsters and the vote counters from NES will not rely on high-tech gadgetry to send polling data to VRS's mainframe. Instead, pollsters will phone their results into operators sitting at keypunch terminals.

"We tested a variety of hand-held computers," says Mitofsky. "But we found they weren't reliable."

One concession to technology will be the 3,000 VRS field operatives who will enter their data into the mainframe via touch-tone telephones.

Mitofsky is confident that all the elements of his service will work smoothly on Election Night. VRS was tested this year covering the Illinois primary for two stations and the California primary for six stations. Illinois ran smoothly, but there was a minor problem with California. "NES wasn't operating in California, so we had to go to the California Secretary of State's office for our vote-return data," says Mitofsky. "Their computer was down part of the night, which gave us a hard time calling close races."

Absentee ballots, which have caused problems in past elections, will be compensated for. VRS's computer is equipped with a series of models that allow it to adjust its projections for areas with high absentee turnout. "Those areas have been identified from voting histories, and are worked into the program that makes the predictions," Mitofsky says. "That, combined with the fact that we call every county in advance to see how many absentee ballots have been mailed, allows us to run a computer model that can predict absentee results."

Dialing For Data

Subscribers can dial into the mainframe and use data any time during election night, but the basic plan requires users to hang up and call in again for updates.

As part of its fee, VRS provides a piece of software that translates straight ASCII code into a cross-tabulated format of election results. The software will be preprogrammed to receive data only for the states the user pays for. Basic service costs $1,000 for a small market—the size of Augusta, ME—and $4,000 for a market like New York City.

Enhanced service is updated continuously onscreen without redialing. New numbers pop into place on the crosstabs as election results are processed by the mainframe.

A bonus of the enhanced service is that it will interface with newsroom text systems. "Wire services use a standard code structure which any newsroom computer system can talk to," says Silverman. "So we use it."

Enhanced service data can be incorporated into a variety of television character generators and even the systems that generate on-air charts and graphs. "Character readers like Chyron can be programmed to take data in from VRS and continuously update themselves until the moment they are fed out on to the air," says Silverman.

Buying the Numbers

VRS's enhanced service will sell for $10,000 in a market the size of Los Angeles—$5,000 for cities like Amarillo, TX. Sounds like it could turn quite a profit, but that's not the idea, according to Mitofsky. "This is not a money-making proposition," he says. "If we thought we'd make a profit, we'd lower the rates until we were only taking in enough money to break even."

An interesting wrinkle to the pricing structure is that every TV station, even network-owned and operated stations, has to pay for VRS service.

"If you're WCBS in New York, and you want exit poll data to prepare a segment of your newscast on election results in the five boroughs, you have to pay," Mitofsky says.

Mitofsky says he expects a subscriber list to be locked up by early October. "A lot of stations are taking the basic service this year because it's not a presidential year," says Silverman. "Stations that have automated on-air graphics systems are using the enhanced service this year as a practice run for '92."

So how can campaigns get their hands on VRS data?

Mitofsky takes a flippant view of this, describing a cloak-and-dagger network of elections past when campaign managers called inside sources at the networks for data.

"They used to have to get someone to leak data from ABC, CBS, and NBC so that they could compare the polls and see how their guy was doing," Mitofsky says. "Now all three [networks] will have the same data, so we've cut down their workload."

Under the current marketing structure, there are no provisions to sell VRS data to campaigns. "We're set up to sell to media outlets only," says Mitofsky. But if campaign managers or consultants approached VRS for data, Mitofsky says he would treat them like any other customer.

All this, however, assumes consultants would want the information in the first place. Denver-based consultant Rick Ridder says, "We call the networks mostly out of curiosity." Ridder says exit polling data could be used to reallocate get-out-the-vote resources, but only if you know "one hell of a lot about the sample, and you decide it's a sample you can trust."

Otto Bos, manager of Pete Wilson's California gubernatorial campaign, goes even further. "Having a tracking poll before the election is a higher priority if you want to adjust your campaign and win," says Bos. "By the time people go to the polls, you're not on TV, you can't alter your mail program so unless you're talking about putting human billboards on the freeways, the program's pretty much set."

Bos and Ridder concede that exit poll data would come in handy to examine a candidate's performance after a primary. "But out of a general, it's not much good except for postelection studies," says Bos.

"Exit polling data is a valuable tool to figure out how your campaign worked," Ridder adds. "But it's not much good to you on Election Day, because you'll find out how you did in 12 hours anyway."

4

Targeting and Demographics

★ ★ ★

✓ Targeting Your Message
Robert Blaemire

Political campaigns are often characterized by a couple of pieces of conventional wisdom. One is that you pick cherries where the cherries are and another is that every campaign wastes 50 percent of its money but can never figure out which 50 percent.

Both of these sentiments are appropriate introductions to discussions of targeting.

Campaign assets are always severely restricted—there is only one candidate, the calendar always shrinks, and money is always hard to come by. These are reasons why a campaign needs to place a high priority on taking advantage of the multiplier effect of professional targeting in directing a message that appeals to those most likely to respond favorably.

The essence of winning elections is persuasion, and not every person is affected equally by a persuasion technique. As campaign resources begin to diminish, it becomes increasingly important to make sure those resources are directed at voters who hold the greatest likelihood of being persuaded to vote for you.

While it is easy to understand why a campaign must target voters, the methods of doing so are esoteric. Campaigns spend their resources according to judgments that are influenced by how voters performed in the past. As a result, the more information we know about previous voter performance and attitudes, the better we can make assumptions about the future behavior of those voters or voter segments.

We want to be able to make educated judgments about every expenditure we make; expenditures not only of money, but of all campaign resources.

Campaign resources are limited, and the manner in which they are allocated should always be a function of intelligent decision-making. Targeting is one piece of the decision-making process.

Where should the TV time be purchased? How many gross rating points should you buy and in which markets? Where should field operations begin to prioritize their efforts within their geographical jurisdictions? Which types of voters need direct mail for persuasion? Which need GOTV mail?

These and other resource allocation questions are common to campaigns. You cannot run your TV ads on all channels in every market constantly. Your organizers cannot organize everyone. You cannot mail all households in the state or district repeatedly. At its basic level, targeting is the vehicle for allocating resources and providing information aimed at persuading voters. Your targeting options include individual, household, group and geographic. Each of these options has different strengths and weaknesses for various campaign programs.

All are imperfect. If our objective is to predict behavior, what we know about the voter or about the voter's previous performance is essential. Then, picking the correct method of targeting is critical.

Individual Targeting

The most important targeting method is individual targeting. The more we know about individual voters, the better we can communicate with them. The better the communication, the better our chances at persuasion. And, the better the persuasion, the greater our likelihood of success.

If we can compile information on an individual that either provides a profile of the voter or of the voter's tendencies based on past actions, we can design programs to get that voter to perform in a certain way.

Lists of registered voters are the best possible resource for communicating to individuals whose profiles or previous performance make them targets. Unfortunately, many jurisdictions do not have this kind of information readily available and, far too often, the information available is not computerized.

The more available this information is, the easier it is to formulate and transmit messages, apportion volunteer efforts, purchase radio and TV time, send direct mail, make phone calls and direct other campaign resources.

To use individual targeting, you need an enhanced voter file. While, as with any list, it may be old when it arrives at your headquarters, it is a tool that can be updated and coded to make it useful to the development of voter contact programs.

Household Targeting

Spending campaign resources wisely means getting the most bang for your buck. Ranking individual targets by household helps make sure you maximize your impact. Sending mail, for instance, to multiple-person households where more than one person fits your targeting scheme means that you have a better chance of receiving more votes than if you send the letter to a single individual. Having appropriate household profiles and accurate household capabilities means that phone, walk and mail programs can be implemented with a greater sense of efficiency and economy.

The best database for household targeting is a voter file that is householded. In the absence of a quality voter file, there are a variety of large list brokers who manage wide-coverage household files with valuable demographic data.

Each has strengths and weaknesses that may not be immediately apparent. Those mostly compiled from the phone file, for instance, are not always good for direct mail.

Group Targeting

Membership organizations are a form of group targeting that can often be helpful as a tool for disseminating your message. Appeals made to groups are usually based on issues that have wide agreement among the membership, whereby appeals to individuals and households may be made more on the basis of that person's or household's perceived self-interest. A campaign can appeal to either the members of the group or its leadership for support.

Lists that make up interest groups arrive from a variety of sources, including the membership lists of some of the organizations themselves. When a campaign has a variety of types of lists available, they should be merged into overall targets for each campaign program.

However, it is sometimes preferable to let the leadership speak on behalf of your candidate in direct communication with its members. It certainly sounds less egotistical when the group's leader makes claims about a candidate than when the candidate makes them shout himself.

Geographic Targeting

The oldest professional form of targeting is by precinct. In other words, by using previous precinct-level performance you can predict future performance. Beware: precinct boundaries are occasionally re-drawn, upsetting the basis of these calculations, and you must be aware of where precincts are affected by a re-mapping.

As a substitute for individualized targeting, precinct-based targeting has to be seen as aggregate and therefore not as precise. Sometimes, however, individual data is not available and precinct targeting becomes critical.

The main problem with precinct targeting is that using it often means that messages are sent to weak voters or opponents in good precincts while missing good voters or supporters who live in bad precincts. Since a vote is a vote is a vote, where a person lives is just not that important.

There are many ways to use the information provided in a precinct targeting plan. Determining the appropriate use is a function of the particular campaign task. For instance, if your constituency swings back and forth from Democratic to Republican, using the degree a precinct swings from one election to another is a way to prioritize precincts. If GOTV is your greatest priority, turnout percentages are particularly relevant.

If precinct targeting is your sole means of targeting, you might select all voter households by precinct for direct mail. If, on the other hand, precinct targeting is used for some tasks in the campaign but not as your sole means of targeting, you might use it as a means of prioritizing literature drops, bumper-sticker days, house parties or other geographically-based programs. Precinct targeting should be used with the proper perspective, understanding the value of the information while understanding its limitations.

Certain assumptions are built into precinct targeting that involve selecting data from a specific previous campaign. Which race was used for the "Baseline Democratic Vote," for instance, is an important ingredient in drawing conclusions. Campaigns should make sure they understand what assumptions are built into the calculations and the factors that went into these assumptions. Precinct targeting is best used for ranking areas for walk programs, for volunteer efforts and in combination with individual targeting.

Combining precinct with individualized targeting can be powerful, for example, in the South, where Democratic registration is disproportionately high but Republicans are elected in certain types of elections. Selecting a voter who is a Democrat yet lives in a precinct that votes Republican may mean that the same voter falls into the Bad Dems category. Bad Dems would be described as Democrats who perform as Republicans and are usually the type of voter that Democrats must persuade in order to win.

Simply stated, a precinct that votes 100 percent Republican and has 100 percent Democratic registration is a 100 percent Bad Dems precinct. All Democrats can be placed on a spectrum of good to bad in this respect, and targeting takes over. But targeting is really the easy part of the campaign—a means to an end. Persuasion is the real goal.

Precinct targeting lists are compiled with publicly available election returns at the precinct level. Some simple calculations may be made on a spreadsheet to provide targeting characteristics. More complicated assessments may require specialized software. These calculations appended to precincts on a voter file allow for every kind of targeting. The precinct data used in combination with voter data allows the campaign to rank people by "Democratic-ness," for instance.

When discussing geography, it is important to define the terms. The concept of targeting demands that we aim toward the greatest degree of specificity when allocating our campaign resources. In other words, individual targeting is said to be the best form of targeting because that level is as specific as you can get. The other, less specific, end of the spectrum would be the entire state or district—100 percent of the geographic universe. Looking at the district as a targeted universe is not, however, targeting. Segregating the state or district into counties narrows our focus some.

Slicing those counties into precincts is more specific—and targeted—still. Narrowing our focus to census block groups, which will be smaller still after the 1990 census data is released, is even more specific and targeted. In other words, we know that we cannot hit our targets with a shotgun, but need a rifle instead. The rifle can hit a specific, small target without causing extraneous damage. The shotgun approach incurs risks the campaign may not be able to afford.

Another type of geographic targeting to consider is census-based targeting. Using census information may miss various political, geographic and individual characteristics, but it offers the ability to predict household behavior on a basis of lifestyle.

Cluster Targeting

A final type of geographic targeting is called geodemographic targeting. It uses compiled census information to come up with a profile of individuals. Some political campaigns have used it effectively since the late 1970s by incorporating census data with voter information to cluster people by lifestyle and geography. The lifestyles have been discerned by several items of census information, such as buying patterns, television viewership and other consumer habits and trends.

A valuable use of cluster data is for buying radio and TV time, specifically when a campaign poll is cluster identified and can be married to Arbitron data, allowing time to be purchased on programs listened to or watched by various cluster groups.

Another valuable combination of data is to cluster encode a voter file, allowing you to slice and dice the cluster group based on political information and performance. All of this is consistent with the theory that the more you know about your voters, the better you can communicate with them.

No campaign has unlimited resources—it is necessary to find ways to spend them wisely. Understanding the data resources available about an election jurisdiction will illuminate how you can target, and how you cannot. The more information available, the more precise your targeting.

To phrase it as an analogy, consider the problem of hitting a target with an arrow. First you have to know if the arrow can reach the target at the distance of the target from the weapon. In addition, knowing which forest the target is in is not enough; you have to know the tree to which it is attached. The thing to remember is that near misses do not count in target practice or in politics.

✓ The Key to Effective Targeting
Mark Gersh

The Watergate scandal of 1973-74 helped the Democrats ride a wave of anti-Republican sentiment to score major gains all across the country. In the 1974 congressional elections, many long-time Republican incumbents went down to defeat at the hands of young, upstart Democratic liberals. One of these outspoken liberals was a working-class minister by the name of Bob Edgar.

Campaigning as an anti-war, anti-Nixon Democrat, Edgar unseated a Republican veteran in Pennsylvania's Seventh congressional district. Located in the affluent Philadelphia suburbs of Delaware County, the Seventh district had been one of the most rock-ribbed Republican districts in the country. Yet Edgar quickly proceeded to compile one of the most liberal voting records in the nation.

Perhaps more surprising, Edgar managed to win reelection five times, always by narrow margins, including twice amidst landslide victories by Ronald Reagan. When Edgar vacated his House seat in 1986, he did so voluntarily; he ran (unsuccessfully) for the U.S. Senate.

How did the liberal Edgar manage to survive for so long in such a Republican district? The answer, in a word, is targeting. Edgar identified and courted those towns and precincts with the greatest concentration of swing voters—areas whose voting histories indicated residents to be especially persuadable. By focusing intensively on such areas, Edgar attracted many voters who normally would have voted Republican.

Unfortunately, a targeting program is not a panacea for a weak candidate. Elections generally are won by good candidates, with the help of strategically planned media, strong field organization, judicious polling—and, often, a bit of luck. The only time a targeting program can impact an election is when there is a tight race between two formidable nominees.

Targeting provides important clues about your strengths and weaknesses in various portions of the district. Targeting can point out your soft spots and help you devise a strategy to counter any weakness. Indeed, by beginning a targeting program early, you may be able to recognize your opponent's vulnerabilities first and exploit them to your advantage.

During a campaign's initial phases, the targeting program begins with staffers gathering basic—and often essential—information.

Start with Basic Data

The Edgar example is instructive but hardly unique. Targeting is neither science nor art (it probably falls somewhere between the two); for the most part, its practice does not require the hiring of a battle-scarred political consultant. In politics, information is power—and much of the power necessary for a successful targeting program can be found at the county clerk's office or the local election board.

Elements such as voter registration lists, Census Bureau tracts, and polling data all can help you construct a detailed electoral and demographic analysis of key constituencies. You can use this profile, in turn, to ascertain where to allocate scarce resources and to determine which appeals will impact the greatest number of persuadable voters.

Electoral Data. The first piece of information any campaign must examine is recent electoral data. Because targeting begins at the precinct level, start by developing a precinct-by-precinct breakdown of previous election results for a wide array of contests.

Your list should begin with returns from the last three races for the office you are seeking. Then add results of recent presidential, senatorial, and gubernatorial contests, as well as other significant statewide races. Finally, you should examine any salient local races and ideologically-based referenda involving your area.

This exercise allows you to separate highly partisan precincts from the more independent ones. In Edgar's campaign, he was able to identify strong Democratic precincts which he could count on for support, in addition to staunch Republican precincts where he had little chance to make inroads. By doing so, he was able to isolate the areas ripe for targeted voter appeals.

For the candidate running in 1988, elections dating back to 1980 or 1982 may have some relevance. You will do better, however, to concentrate on obtaining more recent results. Keep in mind that precinct boundaries in many localities are frequently altered. If massive boundary changes are making your job more difficult, concentrate exclusively on the two most recent elections.

Demographic Data. This information offers invaluable insights into the racial, ethnic, and socioeconomic characteristics of your potential constituents. To locate the relevant data, begin with the census.

During the last census period, several states participated in a federally-sponsored exercise designed to correlate precincts with census boundary units. Consequently, in some areas staffers can facilitate targeting by meshing demo graphic information with political data.

Besides race and ethnicity, available demographic data should provide basic information such as age, occupation, income, and education level, as well as specific details such as the heating/air conditioning capability of an individual's home. In states where precinct and census boundaries are not correlated, you still may be able to isolate census data for a given precinct.

Edgar's races also illustrate a campaign's ability to use demographic data to identify pockets of opportunity not readily apparent from electoral analyses. His stands on issues such as the environment and campaign finance reform, for example, resonated with high-income, well-educated GOP white collar voters. Edgar's staff studied the demographic data, discovered the areas in which such voters were concentrated, and mailed specifically targeted appeals to these voters.

Remember, census information now available was collected in 1979-80; its relevance depends in part on the stability of your district's population. Also, be aware that voter mobility has increased sharply in recent years, thereby complicating efforts to develop accurate targeting data.

A Simple Yet Sophisticated Program

Voter Files. If the bad news is voters are moving more often, the good news—thanks to the computer age—is the currentness and quality of voter registration files has improved markedly during the past five years. Take advantage of this by matching precinct lists with voter registration files.

This step is crucial, particularly in states which do not require registration by party. In these states, located primarily in the South and Midwest, you still can discern party affiliation by tracking the number of times a voter has participated in the Democratic or Republican primary.

Edgar's extensive targeting program illustrates the advantages of this matching process. By combining precinct targeting with individual voter history, he was able to isolate swing precincts and households containing likely voters.

From the voter files, Edgar's staff learned which households had consistent records of participation. This is especially important in off-year elections, when many voters drawn to presidential races tend to stay home. From this list, Edgar's campaign isolated likely voters for door-to-door canvassing and direct mail.

Polling. In the early stages of most statewide and congressional races, candidates frequently underwrite a bench mark poll to learn more about various districts and regions. Candidates seeking lower-level offices will often choose the less expensive option of designing a poll in-house. In either case, you can increase the sophistication of your targeting program by merging the polling results with the data already gleaned from past elections, demographic information, and voter files.

While polls conducted by professionals often yield more useful information, they may not be worth the money to a candidate seeking local office. For polling purposes, many counties and cities are too small to qualify as an acceptable geographical sub-group.

Keep in mind, however, a professional poll of a broader geographic area incorporating your district will include a detailed demographic breakdown. This information can be used to check the demographic data collected through census tracts, and helps mitigate the problem of outdated census information.

Geographical Analysis. A candidate can waste large amounts of time shuttling between targets of opportunity located at different ends of a sprawling district or a large congested city. To avoid this problem, determine the location and accessibility of persuadable precincts. If several important precincts are adjacent or readily accessible to each other, a candidate can save travel time and maximize the time he or she spends meeting with voters.

Nonpolitical Overlays. You can significantly improve the quality of your targeting data by relying on seemingly non-political information such as driver's licenses and housing files which contain the age of many voters. Housing files in particular can help identify large pockets of senior citizen votes.

A Formula for Success

Before you start turning out the vote in targeted precincts, your campaign must know how many overall votes it needs to win. By combining information on party performance and ticketsplitting tendencies, you can establish vote goals for each precinct, ward, and township. These goals will enable you to recognize problems quickly and adjust strategies accordingly.

In 1984, for example, Edgar captured approximately 90 percent of swing voters, a level few candidates achieve. His targeting research established early on that he would need to achieve this high a figure in order to win. With this in mind, his campaign set specific precinct-by-precinct goals. As these goals were met in September and October through the identification of new supporters, Edgar's people redirected their resources to problem areas.

You can establish these goals by developing a "Persuasion Index" and "Persuasion Percents." At this point you may need to bring in an experienced consultant. Computing these indices involves a complicated series of mathematical calculations, the elements of which are weighted differently depending on the nature of the race he Persuasion Index is a numerical estimate of ticket-splitting voters at the precinct, town, or ward level. It is determined by combining current voter registration figures, actual voter turnout in previous elections, and voters' past volatility. The index will help you determine where the candidate should spend his or her time and where the campaign should concentrate its limited financial resources.

The Persuasion Percent measures the percentage of persuadable voters in a given district. It is a calculation based on such factors as past candidate showings and party loyalty. It is designed especially for voter contact activities aimed at individual households.

If, for example, a small town only has 200 voters, it may not be time-effective for a candidate to campaign there when he or she could be meeting with more voters in a nearby city. If that same town has a Persuasion Percent figure of 20, however, that translates to 40 persuadable voters—and suddenly makes voter contact efforts in the small town worthwhile.

The best ticket-splitting precincts have Persuasion Percents of 30 to 35. Even this score means a majority of voters in these precincts still are staunch partisans. This is why you need to gather additional information from voter files, polling data, and phone banks before implementing expensive direct mail programs. Otherwise, you run the risk of wasting effort and money on voters already supporting you or unlikely to be converted.

In Edgar's case, the district-wide Persuasion Percent was 15. In 44 precincts, the percent was at least 20. Edgar targeted these precincts most heavily, and in roughly a quarter of those precincts, he ran more than 20 points ahead of Walter Mondale in 1984. In fact, in every single one of those precincts, Edgar ran at least 17 percent above the national Democratic ticket.

Applying the Information

Successful, cost-effective campaigns are the ones which plan ahead, set realistic goals, work hard, and maximize scarce resources, particularly time, money, and volunteers. You can use the Persuasion Index and the Persuasion Percent to help maximize these important resources and guide decisions on candidate appearances and voter contact efforts. Five areas where they can help include:

Scheduling. Initially, candidates must allocate much of their time to areas with the greatest concentration of persuadable voters. In the closing days of a campaign, prime GOTV targets are added to the equation. When using targeting data, the general rule says schedule a candidate in all precincts containing one percent or more of the persuadable voters in a given district.

To assist in scheduling, targeting studies should include a breakdown of persuadable voters at different levels. A computerized targeting base allows you to present data at several geographical levels simultaneously. This is important because voter contact and GOTV decisions are made on a precinct-by-precinct basis, while scheduling is done at the township level.

If, for example, a certain county has 10 percent of the total number of persuadable voters, it makes a major difference in scheduling—and many other campaign activities—whether those voters are spread throughout five townships or concentrated in two precincts within a single township.

Voter Contact. Targeting alone cannot provide the basis for determining which voters should be canvassed and which should receive direct mail. But, when employed in conjunction with polling data, it can help a campaign decide where to concentrate its resources.

Polling data may, for instance, suggest a weakness—or indicate an opportunity—with an important demographic group. If your campaign has already merged precinct boundaries with census data, you will know precisely where that group is concentrated.

In Edgar's 1984 race, polling data indicated Mondale was very unpopular in the district. More telling, the data signaled problems for Edgar among traditionally Democratic blue collar voters. If these people were going to pull the lever for Reagan, Edgar would have to convince them—

quickly—not to vote a straight ticket. Edgar's targeting program alerted him to this, and he immediately began stressing the issues of primary importance to these crucial voters.

Media Planning. No campaign can target its media advertising to a single precinct. Consequently, the number of persuadable voters in a given television market is a critical factor in planning media buys. When dealing with more localized media such as newspapers and radio, it helps to know the number of potentially persuadable voters in a given city or town. If swing voters are concentrated in a couple of towns, the local radio station or newspaper may merit increased advertising and greater attention from the candidate.

Targeting takes on particular importance when a candidate competes in a district comprising a relatively small portion of a large media market. During his 12 years in the House, Edgar competed in a district which bordered the Philadelphia media market. Because television advertising in that market is prohibitively expensive for a congressional candidate, especially when most of the viewers do not even live in Delaware County, Edgar eschewed paid TV. Instead, he relied on targeted direct mail and various voter contact techniques.

Fundraising. Precincts and demographic groups that reflect a homogeneity of upper-income, well-educated voters with clear partisan loyalties are potential fundraising targets. In certain instances, direct mail fundraising can help subsidize voter contact activities. In these few cases, even if a direct mail fundraising appeal returns only 25 1 cents on the dollar, it still may persuade undecided voters—and thus prove to be money well-spent.

Get-Out-the-Vote. Besides identifying swing voters and ticket-splitters, targeting data can help you pinpoint areas containing highly partisan voters in areas with variable turnout levels. The emphasis should shift to these areas in a campaign's final stages. With the help of targeting data, GOTV programs can quickly be focused on the most promising precincts. Edgar spent much of his time seeking support from Republican voters in swing districts. During the final two weeks of the campaign, however, he concentrated on GOTV in the precincts most supportive of him. Within Pennsylvania's Seventh district, there are 25 precincts boasting an average Democratic vote of at least 60 percent; these precincts were the principal targets for Edgar's GOTV campaign. Without careful targeting, Edgar might have turned out loyal Republicans who might otherwise have stayed home.

Keep in mind that the same partisan loyalty information used for GOTV efforts late in a campaign can facilitate voter registration earlier on. Ethnic and racial statistics can help you craft a registration strategy aimed at particular demographic groups with long-standing party loyalties.

Although proper targeting requires a great deal of work, Edgar's repeated wins—and especially his 1984 victory—prove the worth of such a program. On Election Day, Mondale lost Pennsylvania's seventh district by a 62-38 margin. But Edgar ran better than 12 percent ahead of the national ticket and eked out a 412-vote victory.

More telling, some 63,000 voters split their tickets in support of both Reagan and Edgar. Without an intense targeting program, this outspoken liberal Democrat would have been buried in the Reagan landslide. Instead, he won another return-trip ticket to Washington.

✓ Targeting Voters Without Boosting Your Negatives
Wayne C. Johnson

Few parts of the campaign manual have been so thoroughly rewritten over the last five years as the theory of targeting. Traditional strategies have been—is debunked too strong a word?

In many ways, learning the new systems is easier for the novice than the seasoned professional. I am reminded of a conversation with California consultant Tim Macy in 1980 after we had beaten a string of "old guard" pros by utilizing a new (at the time) approach to campaigns.

I was feeling pretty cocky when Tim said, "These guys were the best. They just stopped learning. Remember that in about 20 years when it happens to us."

Macro-targeting

Macro-targeting represents the traditional model, which itself was largely a product of traditional survey techniques. We attempted to define the particular by sampling the universal.

The fatal flaw of macro-targeting is that it presumes the arbitrary categories selected for cross-tabulation are meaningful. We bought into this methodology even though most of us realize that how we ask a question determines, to a great extent, the aggregate answer.

For example, far fewer respondents answer "yes" when asked, "Do you believe abortion should be legal in all cases?" than when you ask, "Do you believe abortion should be legal for purposes of sex or gender selection?"

How can we have any confidence in answers that are so malleable? Traditional survey doctrine suggests we should seek to frame questions in the most neutral way possible. Unfortunately, neutrality isn't the point at all. The reason we get such radically different percentage responses is because very few people have the identical view of any Issue.

Every issue is really a basket of issues. Choice vs. abortion vs. gender selection vs. legality vs. morality vs. privacy vs. parental consent vs. father's rights vs. rape/incest exceptions, ad infinitum. We'll look at micro-targeting's answer in a moment, but for now, let's examine how we tried to deal with the imprecision of demographic targeting and why it so often failed.

A. Efficacy of positive data—From the first surveys, we learned things like "62 percent of the voters favor taxing the wealthy." So, wunderkinds that we are, consultants would send a mailing to all the voters telling them that the wealthy need to pay more taxes.

The problem was that the positive data (read: majority position) was as likely to be a lukewarm opinion as a strongly held opinion. In this case, the wealthy mail recipient was far more likely to react than the middle-income person receiving the same mailing. We soon found that it was possible to mail on 70 percent-plus issues and still lose in a landslide. Why? Because we were unable to properly evaluate the relative importance of the positive and negative messages. The positives came and went while the negatives accumulated. While taking only "popular" positions, we managed to offend over the course of a campaign, collectively, 51 percent of the voters.

B. Enhanced Demographic Targeting—From this dilemma came the first attempts at "screening" the message to "target" subsets of the universe. After chasing "clusters," "pips," psychographic overlays, and a variety of other targeting tools, we found that none seemed to be better predictors of voter behavior than partisanship. Why? Partisanship was a self-identifier. The individual voter had filtered the messages of the political culture and chosen a label, usually "Republican" or "Democrat."

We began to ask what the value of targeting was if none of the tools produced a predictive index higher than party registration? That's where the commercial marketers opened a door which we almost missed....

Microtargeting

Our problem was that we had all been told that there was an election on the first Tuesday after the first Monday in November. That turned out to be wrong. In every race, there were hundreds, even thousands of elections going on, simultaneously. Every individual voter was weighing a completely different set of variables and making decision. As often as not, we weren't even addressing the issues the individual voter thought were important. One voter was voting for environmentalist candidate Jones, while his neighbor was voting for Democrat Jones, etc.

Commercial marketers learned the lesson long ago that few products can retain 51 percent-plus dominance of a consumer market. A stroll down the lane at your local supermarket clearly illustrates the phenomenon.

There was once corn and wheat. Corn came in flakes. Wheat came shredded in little biscuits. (We Republicans were the wholesome little biscuits and, of course, you Democrats were the flakes.) Then some marketing whiz wondered if people who like the taste of wheat might not prefer the texture of flakes. Soon, there were bran flakes and corn chex. Before long, cereal marketers were adding sugar, then raisins. Then, taking sugar out. Then nuts and berries, added to cereals shaped like turtles and honeycombs.

Okay, here's the part where it gets interesting.

Three major manufacturers are making almost all the brands, apparently competing against themselves. In reality, they are competing within market subgroups against their competitors' products in those sub-groups, not against themselves at all. Seriously, is a 45-year-old going to trade that box of Grape-Nuts for a box of sugar-coated Ninja Turtles? Lesson for us? Pretty simple, really. The same consumers who buy cereal, vote. And they vote for and against, or choose not to vote at all, for reasons as complex and varied as their other consumer choices.

We must begin to recognize that the submarket of "environmentalists who want lower taxes," for instance, is holding an election on election day and if we don't know which issue weighs more in the decision-making process, the environmentalist may lose this subgroup of voters to the tax-cutter, or vice versa. There are also environmentalists who are pro-life, pro-lifers who are anti-death penalty, tax-cutters who are pro-choice AND pro-death penalty, etc., etc.

In other words, every voter is weighing multiple variables in coming to a buying—or voting—decision. These variables have a different weight to every individual voter, creating literally millions of permutations within a universe of voters as small as 500 people. (Thanks to consultant John Feliz and pollster Val Smith of META Information for getting this through my head.)

How do we deal with voters who refuse to prioritize issues according to our issues grid? Very simple. Stop thinking of voters as parts of groups and start thinking of voters as individuals. In other words, the ultimate micro-target is a completely individual treatment of each individual voter.

Forget the "direct mail is for targeting, television is for broad-based messaging" dichotomy. The political television spot of the future will be individually designed for each individual viewer household. It will be computer-assembled from a databank of sound and visual images tailor-designed to the individual voter, delivered by cable. The problem is not that we are technologically ignorant, but that what I am talking about requires looking at voters completely differently. I haven't done a district-wide mailer in eight years. Why? Unless they're puffballs full of mindless blather, they do more long-term harm than short-term good.

Does that mean that all demographic data is meaningless? No, but it does mean that we have the ability to use it far more effectively if we learn how to eliminate the unintended collateral damage that so often results from group-based targeting.

It is not a question of dividing down to the smallest subgroup, but rather building subgroups from the individual up. This requires direct individual voter input. The more advanced campaigns use walkers and phones to collect data, not to simply parrot messages.

For the local legislative or congressional candidate, the starting point is obvious: you must have the list of eligible voters on computer, with the ability to "flag" or code individual voters. As you collect voter-specific information about individual voters, flag the individual voter record.

Your precinct walkers need to ask questions about how voters feel about specific issues. That data gets keyed. Your phone banks ask questions about issues. The responses get keyed. We are already making direct contact with actual voters. Why shouldn't we be collecting data in the process?

Generally, you are looking for strongly-held opinions not shared by a majority of voters, or certainly not shared as intensely by a majority of voters. I would much rather have the names, addresses, and phone numbers of 800 people who are adamantly opposed to gun control than a list of 5,000 who casually support it.

If your candidate supports building a bridge and 35 percent of the voters strongly agree, while 40 percent strongly disagree, with the rest comatose, who in their right mind would mail or phone a "build the bridge" message to an individual voter without first knowing which side he was on? How do we find out? Why not ask him? Clearly, this requires a much greater portion of campaign budgets to be spent in building the database, perhaps as much as 40 percent. The pay-off is that your voter-contact money builds positives and stops building negatives. In an election, the latter is often far more important than the former.

A side benefit of voter-specific microtargeting is that a manpower-intensive campaign with a minicomputer can match superior financial resources. Home-based phoners and walkers can collect a massive database on individual voter preferences, attitudes, etc., which can then be appended to the voter file. For a small, underfunded local race, an even simpler "grid" can be developed by working directly with index cards. Print as much information on each card as you have, including voter name, address, phone, and party registration.

Include a "grid" of alpha and numeric characters. When your phoners reach a voter, record identification questions by circling the appropriate characters. You can then "sort down" the voters using the grid. Assume you have four basic ID questions, A, B. C, and D. Based upon the answer to each question, you may have several "branch" questions. This is really just basic polling technique.

For example: "Have you heard about the city incorporation measure?" Those who answer "YES" are asked follow-up questions. Those who answer "NO" are given an information message, before reverting to the questionnaire.

For example: B. "Do you favor or oppose the incorporation measure?" "FAVOR" and "OPPOSE" are indicated by circling "B-1" or "B-2."

You have now divided the electorate into six groups: those who already knew about the measure and favor it, those who knew about it and oppose it those who did not know about it and now favor it and those who did not know about it and now oppose it, plus the two undecided groups.

Ask the supporters, "Which of the following four reasons would you say are important to your decision: 1) incorporation will save tax dollars; 2) incorporation will provide better police and fire protection; 3) incorporation will stop uncontrolled growth, or 4) incorporation will help us deal better with traffic-congestion problems?

Opponents of the measure would be asked questions that you have determined are the most likely arguments to win back opponents to your cause.

On a congressional race level, you would usually try to computerize your phone banks, so that each response that is keyed online immediately prompts the next appropriate question. You then have the data already sorted for variable messaging to the defined subgroups.

In a campaign in 1991, individual voter-specific data found its way back into our GOTV phone scripts and lasered onto individual door hangers. That meant each targeted voter found a personally-tailored message on their door election morning. If we're doing less, we're dinosaurs headed for the tax pits.

And whatever you do, don't make the mistake of copying the big campaigns. By far, the worst expenditures of resources are usually those made by state parties and presidential campaigns. Why? Because everything has to make it through a committee of people who have been out of the trenches for a few years. And in this business, that's a lifetime.

✓ 11th Hour Targeting
Matthew Dowd

Targeting? Who wants to think about numbers and demographics and swing voters with less than a month to go before election day? The answer is, you should have thought about targeting long before now.

If you haven't, resource and time constraints will likely prevent you from doing much at this point in the game. At any rate, you probably have been running the campaign by the seat of your pants anyway, so you may as well continue to do so and hope you win on election day. But there is a better way.

First, a few basic points about targeting in general. Basic targeting should include overall estimated turnout, turnout goals, vote goals for your candidate, and estimated base votes for your opponent. The targeting also should include breakdowns by media market, county or parish, and precinct, as well as absentee/early vote goals and estimates.

The overwhelming majority of campaigns spend most of their resources in the last few weeks of the race. In many campaigns, 75 to 80 percent of all available campaign dollars are spent in the last month. That means every decision you make in the "end game" takes on added importance.

If done properly, targeting provides you with a road map and a very valuable tool for the final days of the race.

Comparing Tracking Polls with Targeting

Tracking polls will give you a good indication of how the race is progressing. Comparing the polling numbers, using the demographic and geographic categories, to the targeting data will tell you how close you are to your original estimates and goal levels—estimates of what you'll need to win on election day.

Those comparisons will also determine what resources need to be used to shore up areas where you are not performing at levels necessary to win. Those resources include, among others: the media buy, direct mail, phone banks, field operation, and free media, which includes candidate and surrogate travel.

For instance, if the polling shows you are not performing as well as you need to among women, then shift your television radio buy to programs with heavy female viewership. You might also want to alter the spot's message in some way that will appeal more to women or utilize a female announcer in the spot.

In Bob Bullock's 1990 race for lieutenant governor of Texas, the tracking polls in the last three weeks showed we were not at the levels among women that were necessary to win. We made a decision to put a female announcer in the last spot and add an education message on the TV media and direct mail. The race was won with a little more than 51 percent of the vote, and Lt. Gov. Bullock carried the women's vote.

You may also want to adjust resources based on what the poll tells you about geographic elements in the race. For example, by comparing the polling to the targeting, the numbers may show that you are underperforming in a certain area or county. If so, the campaign could shift phone banks or have the candidate do some free media hits in the troubled area.

The polling should provide you with some indication of what the turnout might be throughout the district or state. Again, with targeting in hand, the campaign might consider shifting resources to help enhance turnout. Near the end of the campaign, these resources would likely include phone banks, block walks, or radio/television advertising directly aimed at increasing enthusiasm among the base voters.

In addition to your own polling, there will be other polls available from third-party sources to gauge how the campaign is doing. Newspapers and television stations may be doing polls toward the end of the race. Other campaigns will be conducting polls that may include your race, or provide you with useful information regarding how the ticket is doing or what turnout will be like.

Again, only by comparing the polls to your targeting will you be able to tell if your numbers are where they need to be to achieve victory.

Comparing Absentee Voting with Targeting

Your initial targeting will have given you goals for absentee/early voting in various areas and precincts for your campaign. By monitoring the actual voting—not whom people are voting for, obviously, but how many votes have been cast—the campaign can gauge whether goals are being met. There are bound to be areas that are underperforming, and the campaign should use this information in determining where to shift its resources.

Early or absentee voting can also tell how well or how poorly your opponent is doing. There will be areas or precincts that comprise your opponent's base (your weakest areas), and by watching the early voting results you can tell how well the opposition is doing.

Normally, early voting can be examined on a day-to-day basis, so you can continually make adjustments in your campaign. You can see if the decisions you've made in the last days are actually working, and then adjust the plan as needed.

Election Day

In a close race, election day activities could provide the margin of victory. For example, your initial targeting will tell you how many votes you need in various areas and precincts. This is especially true for your base vote; you will need a certain turnout in your base in order to win.

On election day, it is essential to have people checking key polling places at various times to give you an indication of how your candidate is performing with respect to preset turnout goals. These poll checkers can call in the numbers to a central location, and then actual vote turnout levels can be compared to estimates from your initial targeting.

In those areas where the campaign is underperforming, the election day phone banks and block walkers can be shifted to held increase turnout.

For example, in Bob Lanier's 1991 race for mayor of Houston, we noticed on election day that certain precincts were below our target level. Phone banks were shifted accordingly, and we were able to bring turnout up to the necessary level. It is amazing what 100 phone callers can do to turnout in nine or 10 precincts in a matter of hours. (I guess we shouldn't wonder why so many pew pie have unlisted numbers.)

It is usually best to check the key polls at least twice on election day—once in midmorning and once in the early afternoon. You need not cover all polls with watchers, but you should have people checking the key ones based on your initial targeting. Remember: concentrate on your base areas first, where turnout matters the most.

The candidate or campaign surrogates also can be used to target areas that are underperforming. Sending the candidate into these areas can help generate enthusiasm and increase turnout.

Election Night

The polls have closed, and you think there is nothing else to do—especially with targeting—except wait for returns and go to the party. If you have your targeting prepared with needed vote levels by county or precinct, you'll know early on election night whether you won or lost. Obviously, it's better if you can get your hands on an exit poll, but most campaigns will not have this luxury.

On election night there ought to be key precincts to watch for initial returns so you'll know if you are going to win, are about to be crushed, or if it'll be a long night before anyone knows who won. This kind of information reduces the already high stress level on election night—especially for your candidate. My best advice: The earlier you know, the better. And that's why targeting is so important.

✓ Ticket Splitting: Dead or Alive?
James T. Kitchens and Larry Powell

Hunting ticket splitters is like hunting unicorns—everybody knows what one looks like, but nobody ever sees one.

And, like the unicorn, ticket splitters may be hard to find because they don't exist. Ticket splitting, it turns out, is simply a behavior, not a demographic creature.

That conclusion is supported by numerous studies, and it has important implications for political campaign strategies, such as:

- The number of potential ticket splitters has been consistently and dramatically underestimated.
- Ticket splitting is a common voting behavior, but the voters don't fit a popular demographic profile.
- And ticket splitting could be a self-fulfilling prophecy created as a by-product of campaign communications.

To test these ideas, we analyzed voting data from the last midterm election in Florida, a state with a record of electing both Democrats and Republicans to statewide office.

Florida also has a diverse cultural and ethnic population. If ticket splitting occurred more prominently in one area than others, the results could be extended to other electorates across the nation with similar populations.

Further, in 1988, the Florida Democratic Party commissioned a study of ticket splitting—using traditional methodology—that attempted to project ticket splitting in 1990. Using data from the results of the 1990 election allowed a comparison between actual ticket splitting and the projection.

We began the analysis by reviewing the conventional wisdom on the mythical ticket splitter, a body of literature starting with the 1972 book, "The Ticket Splitter" by Walter deVries and Lance Tarrance. DeVries and Tarrance viewed ticket splitters as voters with specific demographic and personality traits—suburban, white-collar workers looking for problem-solving candidates.

That stereotype suffered serious damage when Republicans started appealing to rural Democrats in the South.

Other studies have indicated ticket splitting is not limited to those voters with weak attitudes. A study by Dorothy Nesbit concluded that even well-informed party loyalists might cross party lines.

Nesbit's research is important because it focused on the role of messages—rather than demographics—in defining ticket splitting behavior. She noted that partisanship could be weakened by issues, ideologies, and appeals to moral standards. Her findings implied ticket splitting could occur with nearly 50 percent of the voters.

Still, political strategists usually ignore the campaign implications of such research, falling for the self-fulfilling prophecy that only certain people—electoral unicorns, if you will—are ticket splitters.

They are targeted for campaign communications, but that only fuels the self-fulfilling prophecy. By increasing communication with those voters, their ticket-splitting behavior is increased.

Success supports the contention that these were prime ticket splitters, but what if their reactions were due more to technical communication skills than their ticket-splitting susceptibility? Perhaps many potential ticket splitters have been missed simply because campaigns have not targeted them.

The extent to which ticket splitters can be underestimated has been demonstrated. In 1990, a study conducted for the Florida Democratic Party, using 1988 election results, projected 500,000 ticket splitters for the 1990 elections.

When the final results were analyzed from the 1990 election, it was found that there were more than 900,000 ticket splitters. At least one-third of the voters appeared willing to consider candidates from the other party.

In the past, those additional ticket splitters were not identified due to weaknesses in the standard methodology.

In the 1990 Florida elections, this approach dictates comparing results from Secretary of State and Commissioner of Education races. In those races, Republican Secretary of State Jim Smith defeated Democrat Jim Minter 59-41 percent, and Democratic Education Commissioner Betty Castor defeated Republican Claude Kirk 66-34 percent.

The standard county-by-county analysis of those races provided an estimate of 865,209 split tickets, a number exceeding the previous estimates of 500,000 from 1988 data. More importantly, even this estimate was conservative.

In many cases, the Smith/Castor comparison did not represent the most ticket splitting in a county. The traditional analysis produced the highest ticket-splitting estimate in only 25 of 67 counties, or 37 percent. In more than 60 percent of the counties, ticket splitting in other races exceeded the estimates from the Smith/Castor comparison.

With the multiple campaign analysis by county, 902,889 split tickets were found, an increase of 4.4 percent. Some differences were dramatic. Initially, only 16,089 split tickets were identified in Leon County. The multiple analysis raised the count to 21,175—a 32 percent increase—in the treasurer's campaign. Washington County showed an even larger statistical increase of 71 percent (from 982 to 1,676 in the Comptroller's race).

Further analysis indicated some of these estimates were still low. Precinct data on four counties (Bay, Brevard, Gulf, and Palm Beach) were randomly pulled and the multiple analysis at the precinct level was repeated. Three of the counties had precinct-level ticket-splitting frequencies that exceeded their maximum estimate.

The combined effect was a 4.2 percent increase in the maximum estimate for the four counties. If that trend holds statewide, the 900,000-plus number underestimated total ticket splitting by more than 36,000 voters (36,339), meaning nearly 940,000 voters split tickets in Florida's 1990 elections.

These results have several implications. First, ticket splitting is more prevalent than previously thought. In Florida, more than 400,000 potential ticket splitters were overlooked by traditional studies—a sign that campaigns may be underestimating the number of persuadable voters in the electorate.

Second, ticket splitters are not a stable group of swing voters who control elections. Quite the contrary, different people split tickets in different races.

In Florida, they are geographically diverse. Republican Tom Gallagher won the treasurer's race by 500,000 votes with a high rate of ticket splitting (29 percent) from the Jacksonville media market. However, Democrat Lawton Chiles won the governor's race by 460,000 votes with a ticket-splitting rate of only 13 percent in Jacksonville. Instead, his ticket-splitting support was stronger in the Tampa (20 percent) and Miami (19 percent) media markets.

Third, some ticket splitters skip elections, causing a drop-off in some races. More than 3,530,000 voters marked ballots in the governor's race, with more than 600,000 Republicans splitting to the Democratic candidate.

Only 3,370,000 voted in the race for commissioner of agriculture, a turnout of 160,000 fewer voters. The Democrat won by a 360,000 vote margin with 528,336 ticket splitters. But this was still 80,000 fewer split tickets than in the governor's race.

And fourth, ticket splitting varied significantly from campaign to campaign. The 1988 study reported a ticket-splitting rate in south Florida (the Miami area) of only 5 percent; in 1990, the same area had a ticket-splitting rate of 21 percent. Conversely, the 1988 study reported nearly 180,000 ticket splitters in the Florida Panhandle. Our 1990 study found only 89,000.

The contention that ticket splitting occurs on a much broader basis than suggested by traditional studies. As many as one-third of Florida's voters are potentially persuadable.

The Persuadables

These voters are not distinct demographic creatures, but people whose behavior changes from one election to the next. It might be more accurate to call them "Persuadables"—people willing to vote for candidates rather than parties.

What activates their behavior, it seems, is campaign communications. When candidates communicated with voters, ticket splitting increased regardless of whether the voters fit demographic profiles of a ticket splitter.

In some instances, partisan ties were overriden by a candidate with a strong message. In the race for commissioner of agriculture, for example, Bob Crawford campaigned on consumer concerns about importing fruit from nations with lax standards on pesticides.

Commissioner of Education Betty Castor (a Democrat) picked up strong support from Republican women. Treasurer Tom Gallagher (a Republican) got votes from Democrats after it was revealed his opponent had bounced personal checks. And all of the candidates attracted additional ticket splitters from their home county.

Each factor had the potential to loosen a partisan anchor, thus giving voters a reason to support a candidate from another party. Such findings should prompt a re-evaluation of past assumptions. Ticket splitting is a behavior, not a personality trait, and it is a by-product of communication. In other words, it may be time to stop hunting unicorns and to start reaching larger numbers of persuadable voters.

✓ Electoral Targeting, Part I: Do-it-Yourself
Murray Fishel

Targeting is a political campaign technique I designed to maximize the efficient use of scarce resources—people, time and money. In politics, two kinds of targeting exist: demographic and electoral. Demographic targeting generates population characteristics within election districts and is particularly helpful in determining which areas in the district may be receptive to specific campaign messages.

Why Electoral Targeting?

This article focuses exclusively on electoral targeting. Furthermore, it assumes the targeting will be done around the dining room table by six volunteers with six hand calculators, six small pizzas and four six packs of beer.

Electoral targeting helps a campaign understand the historical voting patterns within an election district. Some areas regularly have larger turnouts than others; others regularly support Republican candidates; still others typically support Democratic candidates. Determining which voting tendencies are in each area is a researchable question. Campaigns can actually compare the relative importance of each area to every other area in the election district. Table 1 helps to show the logic of electoral targeting. Knowing the voting patterns of each electoral subdivision as they relate to the above categories is of critical importance to the campaign. Research will show some to be very significant, while still others may be totally insignificant to our campaign. And, that, ultimately, is the purpose of electoral targeting.

Table 1
Logic of Targeting

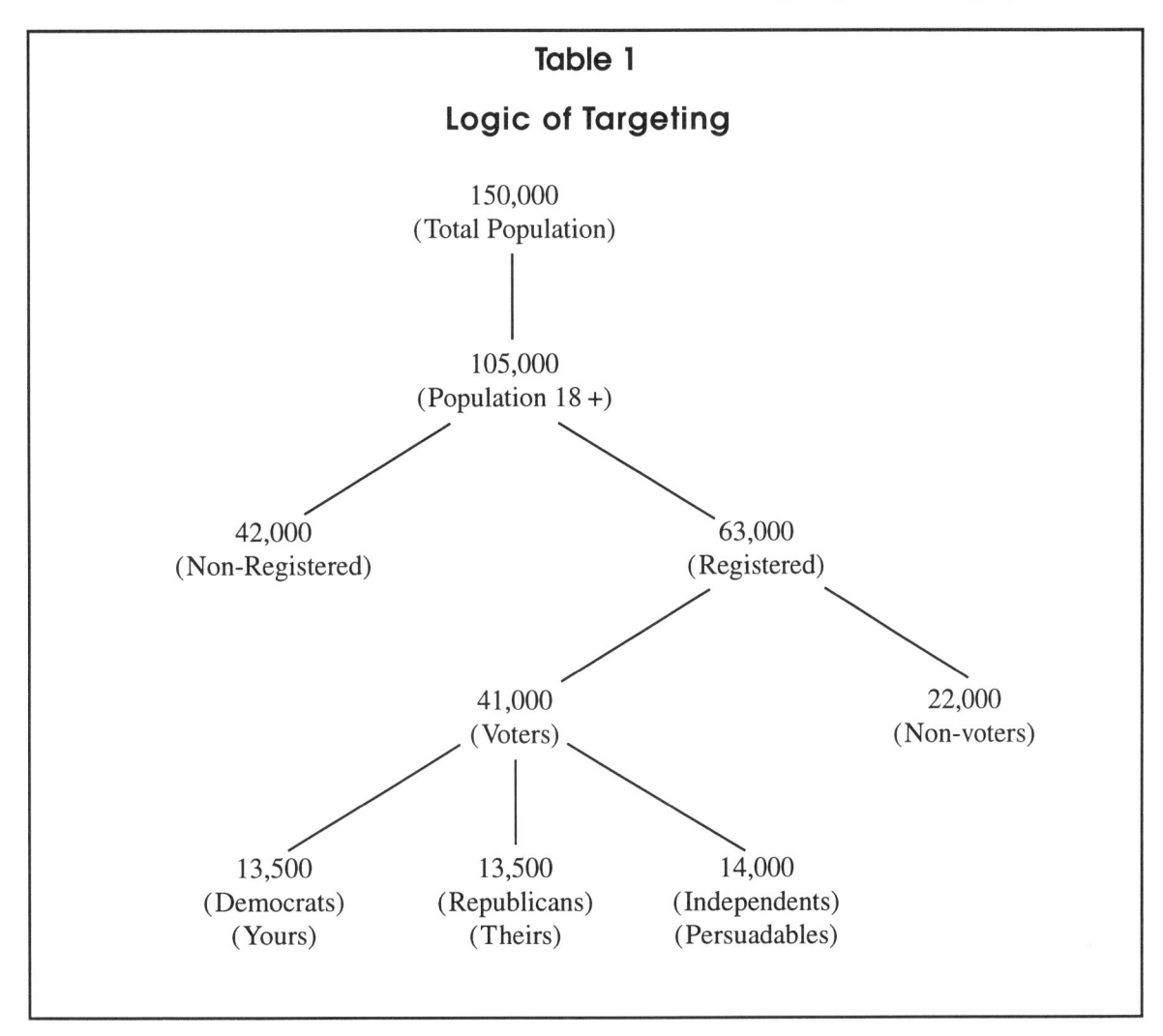

```
                    150,000
              (Total Population)
                       |
                    105,000
               (Population 18 +)
                   /         \
            42,000            63,000
        (Non-Registered)    (Registered)
                            /        \
                      41,000          22,000
                     (Voters)      (Non-voters)
                   /    |    \
            13,500   13,500   14,000
          (Democrats)(Republicans)(Independents)
            (Yours)   (Theirs)  (Persuadables)
```

Information generated by electoral research has a variety of potential applications to a political campaign. It can aid us to schedule candidate and volunteer time wisely; similarly, it can help determine areas for literature distribution, direct mail, telephoning, yard sign placement, voter registration, and get-out-the-vote activities.

This particular article outlines and describes the electoral process in general. Part II will detail the data analysis and evaluation aspects of targeting. Electoral targeting is a process with five basic stages: planning, field work, data development, data processing, and data analysis. Each stage requires campaign leaders to address specific issues.

Planning

Planning for targeting demands that the following questions be answered:

What should my unit of analysis be? In election districts with a total population under 300,000 the unit should be the precinct (or whatever the lowest election reporting unit is called in your area).

Should I use primary or general election data? Use only the data for the election in which your candidate is immediately involved—primary data for primary elections and general election data for general elections.

What races should be included in the data base? Three approaches should be considered both for primary and general election targeting. Each will be discussed in order of importance.

- Ideal targeting includes three races—a high visibility, a low visibility and a representative race. The high visibility race is the one in which turnout tends to be the highest. Typically, these races involve executive offices, President, Governor, and/or Mayor. A low visibility election is one which produced the district's lowest vote total. Often, low turnout elections are for county, state legislative or certain municipal elections, such as Clerk of Courts or City Solicitor. The representative race involves an election identical to that sought by your candidate.
Thus, the representative race for a county commissioner candidate is a prior commissioner election.
- Practical targeting is the second possible approach. Such targeting will use at least two races—high visibility and representative.
- Short-cut targeting, the third potential approach, involves the use of the representative race for the last comparable contested election.

However, information should be collected only for contested elections. Landslide elections should be excluded from consideration.

What time frame should be studied? Like in the response to the third question, there are three possible approaches—ideal, practical and shortcut. Ideal targeting uses three election years, practical targeting two election years, and short-cut targeting a single year. Use odd numbered years for targeting comparable elections; use even numbered years for elections therein.

How do I decide whether to undertake ideal, practical or short-cut targeting? Two considerations affect the selection of the targeting approach: First, the time available to do the work; and, second, the amount of redistricting that has occurred in the district.

Since targeting can be done very early, often two years before an election, campaigns should strive to complete the ideal targeting program—at least three races in each of three years. However, many campaigns start the research process late. While this is unfortunate, such a campaign is wise to use the practical targeting scheme, rather than none at all. Short-cut targeting is ill advised, except when time is very short and a representative race is available.

Redistricting always complicates targeting—only data from unchanged precincts are reliable. Often, when redistricting occurs, a combination of ideal and/or practical and short-cut targeting can be employed. For unchanged precincts ideal targeting should be used; for altered precincts one can use practical and/or short-cut targeting. Ultimately, there is no magic formula for the campaign in the selection of the appropriate approach. Good local judgment is always required. Two principles may help guide you: "More is better" and "anything systematic is better than anything random." (There are many variations possible to increase the reliability of the data base, especially after redistricting. One could use three or four races from two years or three races from one year or two races from two years, etc.)

For summary purposes, let's assume you are targeting a state legislative race for 1984. An ideal targeting approach might include the following races in the following years:

1982 Governor (high visibility)
County Auditor (low visibility)
State Representative (representative)

1980 President (high visibility)
County Treasurer (low visibility)
State Representative (representative)

1978 Governor (high visibility)
County Auditor (low visibility)
State Representative (representative)

The data base for the practical targeting exercise might be:

1982 Governor
State Representative

1980 President
State Representative

And, the short-cut approach would rely on information from the contested race for state representative in 1982.

What measures should be used to understand voting behavior in an election district? As a rule, more measures permit a campaign greater flexibility, thereby facilitating the rational targeting of activities. A brief list of common measures is provided in Table 2. For all targeting work precinct registration figures should also be collected, preferably by partisan identification. (Actual calculations for each of the measures will be demonstrated in Part II.)

Table 2
Targeting Measures

A. Partisan Primary Measures

1. *Average partisan turnout.* This figure shows the average number of partisans voting in each precinct in the primary election.
2. *Percent of effort index.* This figure shows the percent partisan contribution of each precinct to the total partisan district vote.
3. *Efficiency index.* This index measures the relationship between average partisan precinct turnout and partisan precinct registration.
4. *Fall-off* shows the difference between the number of partisans voting in the high and low visibility elections in the precinct.

B. Partisan General Measures

1. *Average party turnout.* See A.1 above.
2. *Average party strength.* This variable shows the average *percent* partisan vote in each precinct.
3. *Average fall-off.* See A.4 above.
4. *Percent of effort index.* See A.2 above.
5. *Efficiency index.* See A.3 above.
6. *Average swing vote.* This measure shows the percent of precinct partisans who abandon their party affiliation—that is, who ticket-split. (Typically, swing voting is a high visibility race phenomenon; for example, a Democrat votes for a Republican candidate for President, but reverts to other Democratic candidates lower on the ballot.)

C. Partisan General Measures

1. *Average turnout.* This figure shows the average number of registered voters in the precinct likely to vote.
2. *Percent of effort index.* This variable indicates the percent contribution of each precinct to the total vote cast in the district.
3. *Efficiency index.* This index measures the relationship between average turnout and total precinct registration.
4. *Average fall-off.* This variable shows the difference between the total votes cast in the precinct between the high and low visibility races.

Field Work

How do I start field work? First, explicit worksheets must be developed for the data collection process. In developing these worksheets you must select which approach to targeting you will use—ideal, practical or short-cut. Having made that decision, one basic data worksheet is developed for each of the races. Table 3 and 4 are examples of worksheets for primary and general elections, respectively. Note the forms already include precinct names, the election year, and column headings. Multiple column ledger sheets are easily adapted for the construction of the basic data worksheet.

Where do I find the election results? Election data are available at the County Board of Elections (or comparable office in your city or state). In collecting the information two options are available: to copy the data at the Board or to secure copies which can then be used at home. The latter is preferable.

Table 3
Basic Data Worksheet

Year_____
Office_____

Precinct	Jones[1]	Brown	Gray	Total[2]
F City 1				
2				
3				
4				
5				
6				
7				
8				
9				
10				
G Twp 1				
2				
3				
4				
Totals				

Total Vote[3] _____

[1] Enter the vote received by Jones on the precinct line under her name. Do the same for Brown and Gray.

[2] The total vote is obtained for the precinct by adding the votes of Jones, Brown, and Gray.

[3] The total office vote is obtained by adding the precinct totals for each precinct.

How can I insure that the volunteers will collect the data properly? The questions is partially answered through the proper construction of the basic data worksheets. The rest of the answer involves common sense: accompany the volunteers to the Board and, at the outset, supervise them in entering the data in the appropriate cells on the worksheets. This is extremely important. Any mistake in recording information will affect both the data processing and analysis phases of the targeting process. Incorrect precinct voting information is dangerous to the campaign.

A caveat to campaign leaders is appropriate here. Copying numbers all day is neither glamorous nor exciting work. It is downright boring. Consequently, it may be hard to keep volunteer spirits high. Three suggestions may help: explain both the rationale and importance of targeting to the volunteers; subdivide the work between several volunteers; and, involve these volunteers in later phases of the process.

Table 4
Basic Data Worksheet

Year_____

Office_____   Vote Cast_____   General_____

	Reagan (Repub)[3] # %	Carter (Dem) # %	Anderson (Indep) # %	Other # %	Total[2]
F City 1					
2					
3					
4					
5					
6					
7					
8					
9					
10					
G Twp 1					
2					
3					
4					
Totals					

Total Vote[3] _____

[1] Enter the number of votes received by the Republican candidate, Reagan, on the precinct line under Reagan #. Do the same for the Democrat candidate, Carter, the Independent candidate, Anderson, etc.

[2] The total vote for the precinct is obtained by adding the votes received by Carter, Reagan, Anderson and Other.

[3] To obtain the Republican % for the precinct, divide the precinct Reagan vote by the precinct total and multiply by 100. To obtain the Democrat % for a precinct, divide the precinct Carter vote by the precinct total and multiply by 100. Repeat the same procedure for Anderson and Other.

What next? After worksheet construction and volunteer training, the information must be entered onto the Worksheet. Each candidate's precinct vote is placed in the appropriate place on the worksheet.

Data Development

Data development involves the creation of summary tables for each of the variables included in the targeting exercise. Tables 5 and 6 show such tables for one primary and one general election variable, Average Democratic Turnout and Average Swing Vote respectively.

This process is essentially a transitional phase which involves moving information from the basic data worksheets to the summary tables.

Table 5
Variable 1: Average Democratic Turnout
Primary Election

Precinct	'80 Pres Total[1]	'80 Stat Rep Total	'82 Gov Total	'82 Stat Rep Total	Grand Precinct Sum[2]	Average Dem Turnout[3]
F City 1						
2						
3						
4						
5						
6						
7						
8						
9						
10						
G Twp 1						
2						
3						
4						

[1] The figure in this column is taken from Basic Data Worksheet, President, 1980 Primary, for each precinct. Similarly, the precinct total vote for each of the other three races will be taken from the respective Basic Data Worksheets.

[2] The grand precinct sum is obtained by adding the precinct total for each of the four races included: '80 Dem Pres + '80 Dem State Rep + '82 Dem Gov + '82 Dem State Rep = Grand Precinct Sum.

[3] Average Dem Turnout is obtained by dividing the Grand Precinct Sum by the number of races included, in this case, 4.

Table 6

Variable 1: Swing Vote
General Election

Precinct	'80 Dem Pres %[1]	'80 Stat Rep Dem %[2]	Swing Vote '80[3]	'82 Gov Dem %	'82 Stat Rep Dem %	Swing Vote '82	Total Swing[4]	Average Swing Vote[5]
F City 1								
2								
3								
4								
5								
6								
7								
8								
9								
10								
G Twp 1								
2								
3								
4								

[1] The % Dem figure here is obtained from the Basic Data Worksheet for the office of President for the Precinct.

[2] The % Dem figure here is obtained from the Basic Data Worksheet for the office of State Representative for the precinct.

[3] The swing vote is the difference between % Dem Pres and % Dem State Rep. (Ignore signs of + or − .)

[4] Total swing is obtained by adding the precinct swing vote in 1980 and 1982. (Ignore signs.)

[5] Average swing vote for the precinct is obtained by dividing total swing vote by the number of years included, in this case 2.

Data Processing

In this phase of electoral research calculations are made for each of the measures. Calculations will be made with the use of hand calculators with memory, and the operators skills required include addition, subtraction, multiplication, and division. Each of the calculations for the measures listed earlier will be shown in Part II.

Data Analysis

There are two basic approaches to the analysis of targeting information: to develop a "pick" variable or to create a composite index. A "pick" variable is simply one measure which is stance, in a general election and in a swing voting then used for a specific campaign activity. For instance, in a general election and in a swing voting district (45-55 percent partisan), candidate time might be targeted on the basis of the swing vote variable; volunteer time in the same district might be assigned by using the partisan strength measure.

The basic assumption here is to maximize the likelihood of securing both swing and partisan voters. Fall-off vote is often used as a "pick" variable for get-out-the-vote activities; high partisan strength precincts may be targeted for direct mail, telephoning, and door-to-door work.

When utilizing the "pick" variable approach, all precincts are simply rank-ordered on each variable from most to least significant. Campaign work can then be assigned in a rational way, consistent with available volunteers, time, and resources.

The second targeting approach is to develop a composite index of important variables. This process is more tedious; however, it permits a campaign to create a single, new measure which itself summarizes all of the variables considered important by the campaign leaders. A composite index can be created by following the instruction in Table 7. The election district is now targeted. It is targeted on a rational basis, consistent with the campaign's goal of attracting the votes needed for victory. Part II will demonstrate this process.

Table 7
Creating a Composite Index

1. Select the important measures and conduct all preliminary activities noted earlier in this article by performing the calculations.

2. Rank-order the values (not precinct names) for each of the measures.

3. Divide the ranked list for each of the measures into quartiles (four relative equal groupings). Assign the first Quartile (most significant) four points, the second quartile (significant) three points, the third quartile (marginal) two points, and the fourth quartile (insignificant) zero points.

4. Weigh the variables to reflect their overall importance to *your* campaign, increasing the point values for the quartile rankings of the more important district measures by a factor of two or three.

5. Return to a list of the precincts with the *original* calculations for each of the measures. Locate the precinct's score on the measure and place the precinct name on the rank-ordered list.

6. Create a summary table with column headings for each of the included measures.

7. Place each precinct's point scores on the table.

8. Total the precinct scores.

9. Rank-order the final point totals.

10. Create the new composite index, quartiled in the same way as noted earlier. Quartile 1 will include the most significant precincts, quartile 2 will include the most significant precincts, quartile 3 will include the marginal precincts, and quartile 4 will include the insignificant precincts.

Electoral Targeting II: Analyzing the Data
Murray Fishel

So far, we have described electoral targeting in general—outlining how historical voting patterns are charted so that campaign resources can be allocated in a rational manner to abstract the votes needed for victory. This article is more explicit, teaching you how to analyze electoral data and use this information in your campaign.

The following assumptions have been made: 1) the targeting will be done by volunteers with hand calculators; 2) a practical targeting approach is needed—the candidate is a Democrat running for state representative so that a high visibility and representative race will be examined in each of two years; and 3) the field work and data development stages of the process have been completed. (See Fishel, Part I, Spring, 1983.)

Section I of this article targets a primary election with the "pick" variable approach. Section II targets a general election by creating a composite index. (Fishel 1983, pp. 18-19.) A nonpartisan election is not addressed specifically because the calculations are all similar to those demonstrated in targeting for partisan races.

Section I: Partisan Primary Election Targeting

The database for this targeting exercise is presented in Tables 8–12. Table 8 gives the partisan registration figures for the district, while Tables 9–12 represent the Basic Data Worksheets for each of the four races included in the exercise: President 1980, state representative 1980, governor 1982 and state representative 1982.

Table 8
District Registration

Precinct	Rep	Dems	Ind	Total
F City 1	153	225	80	458
2	101	158	131	390
3	90	95	70	255
4	60	106	102	268
5	43	87	50	180
6	72	119	88	279
7	75	106	91	272
8	109	127	47	283
9	103	165	50	318
10	40	157	89	286
G Twp 1	60	219	92	371
2	61	120	70	251
3	53	110	56	219
4	95	110	115	320
Totals	1115	1904	1131	4150

Table 9
Basic Data Worksheet
Primary

Year: 1980 Office: President (Dem)

Precinct	1 Kennedy[1]	2 Carter	3 Total[2]
F City 1	82	80	
2	51	54	162
3	30	31	105
4	21	32	61
5	29	29	53
6	32	46	58
7	37	43	78
8	52	68	80
9	36	30	120
10	17	43	66
G Twp 1	40	55	60
2	51	51	95
3	42	64	102
4	31	36	106
Totals	551	662	67

Total Vote[3]..........1213

[1] Enter the vote received by Kennedy on the precinct line under his name. Do the same for Carter.

[2] The total vote is obtained for the precinct by adding the votes of Kennedy and Carter.

[3] The total office vote is obtained by adding the precinct totals for each precinct.

Step 1 is to calculate the total vote cast in each precinct for each of the races. Identical calculations are made for each precinct in each of the four races. (See Table 9) Examples:

F City 1 82 (Kennedy) + 80 (Carter) =162   F City 2 51 + 54 = 105

Step 2 is to determine the total office vote for each of the four races. That figure is obtained by adding the precinct totals. For instance, the total office vote for the 1980 presidential primary is derived by adding the figures in Column 3, Table 9.

$$162 + 105 + 61 \ldots = 1213.$$

Identical calculations are completed for the other three races, yielding the following totals: state representative 1980, 1055; governor 1982, 1246; state representative 1982, 1055.

Step 3 involves determining the grand district sum (GDS) for the four races. Thus,

$$GDS = 1213 + 1055 + 1246 + 1055 \quad GDS = 4569$$

On completion of these three initial calculations the information can be transferred from the Basic Data Worksheets to the summary tables. Targeting will be based on four measures: average Democratic turnout, percent of effort index, efficiency index and fall-off.

Table 10
Basic Data Worksheet
Primary
Year: 1980   Office: State Rep (Dem)

	1	2	3
Precinct	Jones	Brown	Total
F City 1	28	114	
2	27	69	142
3	14	36	96
4	9	30	50
5	17	27	39
6	11	62	44
7	18	51	73
8	36	73	69
9	14	46	109
10	18	38	60
G Twp 1	27	54	56
2	32	59	81
3	24	69	91
4	19	33	93
Totals	294	761	52

Total Vote 1055

Table 11
Basic Data Worksheet
Primary
Year: 1982   Office: Governor (Dem)

	1	2	3
Precinct	Vitale	Prince	Total
F City 1	74	78	152
2	50	51	101
3	35	33	68
4	41	14	55
5	32	30	62
6	46	40	86
7	39	38	77
8	71	50	121
9	43	30	73
10	45	27	72
G Twp 1	59	40	99
2	40	61	101
3	46	60	106
4	36	37	73
Totals	657	589	

Total Vote 1246

Table 12
Basic Data Worksheet
Primary
Year: 1982   Office: State Rep (Dem)

Precinct	Jones	Brown	Gray	Total
F City 1	24	52	66	142
2	25	39	35	99
3	10	17	6	33
4	10	25	13	48
5	10	19	16	45
6	13	22	22	57
7	11	14	25	50
8	17	44	35	96
9	18	29	38	85
10	13	18	36	67
G Twp 1	12	22	29	63
2	29	44	40	113
3	17	30	48	95
4	10	17	35	62
Totals	219	392	444	

Total Vote 1055

Measuring Average Democratic Turnout

There are two steps in calculating the average Democratic turnout. First, the grand precinct sum (GPS) needs to be determined. This figure is obtained by adding each precinct's total vote for each of the four races. (See Table 13, Column 5.) Examples:

$$\begin{array}{ccccccc} & \text{Pres} & & \text{Repr} & \text{Gov} & \text{Repr} & \text{GPS} \\ \text{F City 1} & 162 & + & 142 & + 152 & + 142 & = 598 \\ \text{F City 2} & 105 & + & 96 & + 101 & + 99 & = 401 \end{array}$$

Second, the average Democratic turnout is tabulated by dividing the grand precinct sum by the number of races included, in this case by 4. Table 13, Column 6 shows the end result of this process.

Table 13
Basic Data Worksheet
Primary

Precinct		1 '80 President Total[1]	2 '80 State Rep Total	3 '82 Gov Total	4 '82 State Rep Total	5 Grand Precinct Sum[2]	6 Average Dem Turnout[3]	7 Rank-ordered precincts
F City	1	162	142	152	142	598	150	150
	2	105	96	101	99	401	100	112
	3	61	50	68	33	212	53	102
	4	53	39	55	48	195	49	100,100
	5	58	44	62	45	209	52	85
	6	78	73	86	57	294	74	74
	7	80	69	77	50	276	69	71
	8	120	109	121	96	446	112	69
	9	66	60	73	85	284	71	64,64
	10	60	56	72	67	255	64	53
G Twp	1	95	81	99	63	338	85	52
	2	102	91	101	113	407	102	49
	3	106	93	106	95	400	100	
	4	67	52	73	62	254	64	

[1] The figure in this column is taken from Basic Data Worksheet, President, 1980 Primary, for each precinct. Similarly, the precinct total vote for each of the other three races will be taken from the respective Basic Data Worksheets.

[2] The grand precinct sum is obtained by adding the precinct total for each of the four races included: '80 Dem Pres + '80 Dem State Rep + '82 Dem Gov + '82 Dem State Rep = Grand Precinct Sum.

[3] Average Dem Turnout is obtained by dividing the Grand Precinct Sum by the number of races included, in this case, 4.

Examples:

F City 1 598 (GPS)

F City 2 401

4

4 (# of races)

= 149.5 (rourtd .5 + UP) = 150

= 100.2 (drop .4 or less) = 100

After obtaining these averages, the precincts are rank-ordered from most significant to least significant (listed in Table 13, Column 7).

Average party turnout is a critical measure in partisan primaries. A cursory glance at Table 13 shows F City 1 with an average of 150 Democratic voters, a figure nearly three times greater than F City 4—average of 49—and nearly twice as large as F City 6's average of 74 votes.

In targeting campaign resources one could logically expend three times the effort—people, time and money—in F City 1 than in F City 4. Indeed, if average partisan turnout was the single measure used in targeting, that would have to be the conclusion. It would then guide all candidate walks, volunteer walks, literature drops, telephoning, direct mail, yard sign placements, etc. On the other hand, one must be careful to avoid single variable targeting. Other measures can permit the campaign to expend its resources more effectively.

Measuring Percent of Effort Index

To calculate the percent of effort index, the grand precinct sum is divided by the grand district sum. Examples from Table 14:

Table 14
Percent of Effort Index

Precinct	Grand Precinct Sum	Grand District Sum	Percent of Effort	Rank-ordered precincts
F City 1	598	4569	13	13
2	401	4569	9	10
3	212	4569	5	9,9,9
4	195	4569	4	7
5	209	4569	5	6,6,6,6,6
6	294	4569	6	5,5
7	276	4569	6	4
8	446	4569	10	
9	284	4569	6	
10	255	4569	6	
G Twp 1	338	4569	7	
2	407	4569	9	
3	400	4569	9	
4	254	4569	6	

$$\text{F City 1} \frac{598 \text{ (GPS)}}{4569 \text{ (GDS)}} = .13 \times 100 = 13\%$$

$$\text{F City 2 } \frac{401}{4569} = .09 \times 100 = 9\%$$

The results of the calculations for the district are shown in the last column in Table 14 along with the rank-ordering of the precincts.

The percent of effort index is often an early measure, providing the campaign with a quick and rough view of the district's electoral behavior. The measure is particularly useful as a tool in helping to allocate candidate time in the campaign. Indeed, a formula can be developed for candidate scheduling. For instance,

$$\frac{60 \text{ campaign days for the candidate}}{600 \text{ total campaign hours}} \text{ 10 hours per day for campaigning}$$

Hence,

$$\text{F City 1 } 600 \times 13\% = 78 \text{ hours}$$

$$\text{F City 2 } 600 \times 9\% = 54 \text{ hours}$$

Remember, however, campaigns need to be careful. Candidates should spend little of their time in low turnout areas—even volunteer time might be restricted here—because some votes are going to come from these precincts anyway. If one excludes the candidate from such areas, that means more time can be devoted to high effort areas. And, that requires an adjustment of the percent of effort figures.

Measuring Efficiency Index

To determine the efficiency index the average Democratic precinct turnout is divided by the precinct's total Democratic registration. (See Table 15) Examples:

$$\text{F City 1 } \frac{150 \text{ (Avg - Dem Turnout)}}{225 \text{ (Dem Registration)}} = 67 \times 100 = 67\%$$

$$\text{F City 2 } \frac{100}{158} = .63 \times 100 = 63\%$$

The results of the process are shown in Column 3 of Table 15, along with the rank ordered precincts.

The efficiency index is an extremely important measure. It shows the actual performance of Democratic voters in the precinct. In effect, the measure indicates the probability of Democrats casting ballots in the primary.

Using Table 15 examples, G Twp 3 is the most important precinct in the district, with 91 percent of the eligible Democrats voting on Election Day! If the campaign relied on average Democratic turnout or percent of effort measures, this extremely salient information would have been obscured. F City 1 would have been considered the district's most important precinct.

Table 15
Efficiency Index

Precinct	1 Average Dem Turnout	2 Total Dem Regn.	3 Efficency Index %	4 Rank-ordered precincts
F City 1	150	225	67	91
2	100	158	63	88
3	53	95	56	85
4	49	106	46	67
5	52	87	60	65
6	74	119	62	63
7	69	106	65	62
8	112	127	88	60
9	71	165	43	58
10	64	157	41	56
G Twp 1	85	219	39	46
2	102	120	85	43
3	100	110	91	41
4	64	110	58	39

The efficiency index can be used to allocate candidate time. Think of it, for every 100 registered Democrats reached by the candidate, he or she is contacting 91 probable voters. How's that for efficiency? The index is also helpful in deciding the sequence of precincts to be contacted through telephoning and direct mail. Since these activities can be costly both in dollars and/or volunteer time, every effort must be made to maximize their efficient use and impact.

When considering the relative importance of average Democratic turnout or the efficiency index as targeted measures, be guided by the following:

- Average Democratic turnout is best used to allocate volunteer time in literature drops, walk and talks and coffees.
- The efficiency index is most relevant for allocating candidate time, direct mail and telephoning.
- Depending on available resources, always start at the top of the rank-ordered list of precincts and proceed as far as your resources will permit.

Measuring Fall-Off

The fall-off vote is the difference between the number of partisans voting in the high and low visibility elections. It is primarily a measure of potential partisan turnout and is secured by subtracting the precinct total vote for state representative from its presidential total vote in 1980 and the state representative race from the governor's race in 1982—that yields total fall-off. The average is calculated by dividing total fall-off by the number of election years included, in this case 2.

In determining fall-off, the raw information is simply transferred from the summary table for average Democratic turnout (Table 13.). Examples:

	'82 Total					
	Pres Total	Rep Total	Fall off	Gov Total	Rep Total	Fall off	Fall off
F City 1	162	-142	20	152	-142	10	30
F City 2	105	-96	9	100	-99	1	10

Now, the 1980 and 1982 fall-off votes can be entered onto Table 16. The average is achieved by dividing the total precinct fall-off by the number of years included, in this case by 2. The results of that process and rank-ordered precincts are displayed in Table 16, columns 3 and 4.

Fall-off vote is most helpful in targeting get-out-the-vote (GOTV) activities and, sometimes, Election Day activities. Obviously, those areas with the greatest fall-off can be targeted for the most extensive GOTV work.

Table 16
Fall-Off Vote

Precinct	1 Fall-Off 1980	2 Fall-Off 1982	3 Total Fall-Off	4 Average Fall-Off	5 Rank-ordered precincts
F City 1	20	10	30	15	25
2	9	2	11	6	23
3	11	35	46	23	19
4	14	7	21	11	18
5	14	17	31	16	17
6	5	29	34	17	16
7	11	27	38	19	15
8	11	25	36	18	13
9	6	−12	6	3	12
10	4	5	9	4	11
G Twp 1	14	36	50	25	6
2	11	−12	−1	−1	5
3	13	11	24	12	3
4	15	11	26	13	-1

Section II: General Election Targeting

In the preceding section the targeting approach was presented in the form of "pick" variables—tabulations for each precinct on each measure were made, rank-ordered and then used to target specific campaign activities. In this section the district will be targeted on the basis of a composite index. Five measures will be used: average Democratic turnout, average Democratic strength, average fall-off, the efficiency index and swing vote. (The percent of effort index is omitted.)

Field work has produced the four basic data worksheets displayed in Tables 17-20 respectively.

The total precinct vote needs to be determined for all candidates. (A suggestion here. Never do the calculations on the original Basic Data Worksheets. Always make copies first, safely storing the originals.) The precinct's total is obtained by adding the first four columns on Table 17. The total is then placed in the respective space in the table. Identical tabulations are then made for each precinct in each of the four races.

Table 17
Basic Data Worksheet
General

Year: 1980 **Office: President**

Vote Cast[1]

Precinct		Reagan (Repub) #	%[3]	Carter (Dem) #	%	Anderson (Indep) #	%	Other #	%	Total[2]
F City	1	187		191	48	19		2		399
	2	123		120	44	28		2		273
	3	91		69	38	19		2		181
	4	56		73	48	16		6		151
	5	61		68	49	7		3		139
	6	55		89	55	15		4		163
	7	83		83	47	8		3		177
	8	170		130	40	22		5		327
	9	143		82	33	20		4		249
	10	151		71	29	21		2		245
G Twp	1	221		79	24	28		2		330
	2	186		132	38	30		3		351
	3	165		96	35	14		0		275
	4	131		65	30	17		1		214
Total		1823		1348		264		39		

Total Vote..........3474

[1] Enter the number of votes received by the Republican candidate, Reagan, on the precinct line under reagan #. Do the same for the Democrat candidate, Carter, the Independent candidate, Anderson, etc.

[2] The total vote for the precinct is obtained by adding the votes received by Carter, Reagan, Anderson and Other.

[3] To obtain the Republican % for the precinct, divide the precinct Reagan vote by the precinct total and multiply by 100. To obtain the Democrat % for a precinct, divide the precinct Carter vote by the precinct total and multiply by 100. Repeat the same procedure for Anderson and Other.

Next, the total office vote for each of the four races is derived by adding the precinct totals for each of the races. Example: See the total column in Table 17, 399 + 273 + 181. . . = 3474. Similar routines are conducted for the other three races, yielding the following totals: Table 18 state representative 1980 – 3210; Table 19 governor 1982 – 2616; and Table 20 state representative 1982 – 2539.

Following that the percent each Democratic candidate received in each precinct in each of the four races is tabulated by dividing the number of Democratic votes cast in each precinct by that precinct's total vote. (See Table 17) Examples:

$$F \text{ City } 1 \ 191 = .48 \times 100 = 48\% \ 399$$
$$F \text{ City } 2 \ 120 = .44 \times 100 = 44\% \ 273$$

The percentages are then placed in Table 17 under the column heading %. Identical calculations are then completed for each precinct in each of the four races. (They are completed for you and are located in the appropriate columns on each of the Basic Data Worksheets.)

Having completed the three preliminary steps, the balance of the data processing and development phases of the targeting exercise can now be undertaken. Summary tables with appropriate column headings have already been created. Specific information from the Basic Data Worksheets can be transferred to the appropriate summary table.

Table 18
Basic Data Worksheet
General

Year: 1980 Office: State Rep

Vote Cast

Precinct	#	Densell (Rep) #	%	Brown (Dem) #	%	Total
F City	1	102	269	73	371	
	2	106	146	58	252	
	3	102	66	39	168	
	4	54	80	60	134	
	5	64	59	48	123	
	6	81	66	45	147	
	7	54	113	68	167	
	8	188	106	36	294	
	9	148	87	37	235	
	10	159	68	30	227	
G Twp	1	152	160	51	312	
	2	150	173	54	323	
	3	149	104	41	253	
	4	125	79	39	204	
Totals		1634		1576		

Total Vote 1055

Table 19
Basic Data Worksheet: General

Year: 1982 Office: State Rep.

Vote Cast

Precinct		Johns (Repub) #	%	Vitale (Dem) #	%	Other #	%	Total
F City	1	136		186	57	4		326
	2	81		111	56	6		198
	3	58		57	47	6		121
	4	47		44	47	3		94
	5	39		46	52	3		88
	6	46		82	61	7		135
	7	66		73	52	2		141
	8	128		122	48	4		254
	9	106		89	44	6		201
	10	111		80	40	7		198
G Twp	1	152		79	34	2		233
	2	151		133	47	2		286
	3	94		92	47	8		194
	4	77		70	48	0		147
Total		1292		1264		60		

Total Vote 2616

Table 20
Basic Data Worksheet: General

Year: 1982 Office: Governor

Vote Cast

Precinct		Blue (Repub) #	%	Vitale (Dem) #	%	Total
F City	1	136		186	57	326
	2	81		111	56	198
	3	58		57	47	121
	4	47		44	47	94
	5	39		46	52	88
	6	46		82	61	135
	7	66		73	52	141
	8	128		122	48	254
	9	106		89	44	201
	10	111		80	40	198
G Twp	1	152		79	34	233
	2	151		133	47	286
	3	94		92	47	194
	4	77		70	48	147
Total		1292		1264		

Total Vote 2616

Average Democratic Party Turnout

Average Democratic turnout is determined by adding each Democratic candidate's vote in each of the four races, creating the grand precinct sum. (See Table 21, Column 5) The GPS is then divided by the number of races included, in this case by 4 —'80 President, '80 State Representative, '82 Governor and '82 State Representative. Column 5 in Table 21 shows the result of this process. Examples:

$$\frac{\text{F City 1 } 827 \text{ (GPS)}}{4 \text{ (\# of races)}}$$

$$\frac{\text{F City 2 } 497}{4} = \frac{124}{207}$$

After obtaining the averages, the precincts are rank-ordered on the bottom left-hand side of the Table. They are then divided into quartiles, with the top quartile representing the most significant precincts, etc. The quartiles are noted to the right of the numbers. (Since there are 14 precincts it is impossible to have equal quartiles. My suggestion here is to divide the quartiles as follows: Q1–4 precincts; Q2–4 precincts; Q3–3 precincts; and, Q4–3 precincts. The simple principle here is that it is better to overcampaign than undercampaign in potentially significant areas. A second caveat is in order to deal with ties. Wherever ties occur, break the tie by increasing the size of the more important quartile. Decrease the size of the next adjoining quartile accordingly. For instance, in Table 21 two precincts tie with an average party turnout of 63.

They are included in quartile 3, leaving only one precinct in quartile 4.

Each quartile is then assigned a point value reflecting its relative importance. The following guide is offered:

Quartile	Description	Points
I	Most Significant	4
II	Significant	3
III	Marginal	2
IV	Insignificant	0

The points are then placed on the table to the right of the brackets. (See Table 21) The factor-loading information on the bottom right of the Table will be discussed shortly.

Table 21
Average Party Turnout
(Democratic Party)

Precinct		1 '80 President Total	2 '80 State Rep Total	3 '82 Governor Total	4 '82 State Rep Total	5 Grand Precinct Sum	6 Average Democratic Turnout
F City	1	191	269	186	181	827	207
	2	120	146	111	120	497	124
	3	69	66	57	58	250	63
	4	73	80	44	55	252	63
	5	68	59	46	69	242	61
	6	89	66	82	84	321	80
	7	83	113	73	60	329	82
	8	130	106	122	126	484	121
	9	82	87	89	107	365	91
	10	71	68	80	88	307	77
G Twp	1	79	160	79	97	415	104
	2	132	173	133	151	589	147
	3	96	104	92	100	392	98
	4	65	79	70	75	289	72

Rank-ordered precincts and quartiles

207 147 124 121	4
104 98 91 82	3
80 77 72 63 63	2
61	0

A factor loaded of 2

Precinct	Factor Points
F City 1	8
2	8
3	4
4	4
5	0
6	4
7	6
8	8
9	6
10	4
G Twp 1	6
2	8
3	6
4	4

Average Democratic Party Strength

Average Democratic strength represents the average percentage of Democratic votes received by the four candidates in each precinct. To make the calculation, take the appropriate percent of Democratic votes from each of the Basic Data Worksheets and enter them on the summary table. (See Table 22) Then add the four percentages, creating a grand percentage total for each precinct. Finally, divide the grand percentage total by the number of races included, in this case by 4. The result in Table 22 displays the results of this process.

Table 22
Average Party Strength (%)
(Democratic Party)

Precinct		1 '80 President Partisan %	2 '80 State Rep Partisan %	3 '82 Governor Partisan %	4 '82 State Rep Partisan %	5 Grand Percentage Total	6 Average Party Strength
F City	1	48	73	57	56	234	59%
	2	44	58	56	62	220	55%
	3	38	39	47	46	170	43%
	4	48	60	47	57	212	53%
	5	49	48	52	72	221	55%
	6	55	45	61	63	224	56%
	7	47	68	52	59	226	57%
	8	40	36	48	51	175	44%
	9	33	37	44	54	168	42%
	10	29	30	40	48	147	37%
G Twp	1	24	51	34	41	150	38%
	2	38	54	47	59	198	50%
	3	35	41	47	51	174	44%
	4	30	39	48	50	167	42%

Rank-ordered precincts and quartiles

59, 57, 56, 55 ⎫ 4

53, 50, 44, 44 ⎫ 3

43, 42, 42 ⎫ 2

38, 37 ⎫ 0

A factor loaded of 3

Precinct	Points
F City 1	12
2	12
3	6
4	9
5	12
6	12
7	12
8	9
9	6
10	0
G Twp 1	0
2	9
3	9
4	6

Examples:

$$\text{F City 1} \quad \frac{48 + 73 + 57 + 56}{4} = \frac{234}{4} = .59 \times 100 = 59\%$$

$$\text{F City 2} \quad 44 + 58 + 56 + 62 = 220 = .55 \times 100 = 55\%$$

After completing the process the precincts are rank-ordered, quartiled and assigned points, as noted on the bottom of Table 22.

Average Democratic Fall-Off

We have seen that fall-off normally measures how many fewer people vote in low visibility elections compared to races for higher office. Thus, the total number of precinct voters casting ballots for president is generally greater than the total number voting for state representative. However, that figure is not a partisan measure.

When partisan fall-off is analyzed, one often discovers a "fall-up" vote, meaning more partisans cast ballots for the lower visibility party candidate. This phenomenon can be an important measure, since it shows precincts with a disposition to vote for a party's candidate for lower office. Since this exercise is for a state representative candidate, potential fall-up voting is of considerable importance. Fallup votes are noted on Table 23 by the minus (-) sign preceding the total fall-off votes.

Average fall-off is obtained by adding the '80 and '82 fall-off votes cast and then dividing by the number of years included in the data base, in this case by 2. The finished results of the process are located in the last of column of Table 23. Examples:

	1980 FO		1982 FO	Total FO	Average FO
F City 1	−78	+	5	−73	−37
F City 2	−26	+	−9	−35	−18

After determining the fall-off, the precincts are rank-ordered, quartiled and assigned points, as noted at the bottom of Table 23.

Table 23
Average Fall-Off Vote
(Democratic Party)

Precinct		'80 Pres. (Dem) Votes Cast	'80 State Rep Dem. Votes	'80 Fall-Off Votes Cast	'82 Gov. (Dem) Votes Cast	'82 State Rep Dem. Votes	'82 Fall-Off Vote	Average Fall-Off
F City	1	191	269	−78	186	181	5	−37
	2	120	146	−26	111	120	− 9	−18
	3	69	66	3	57	58	− 1	1
	4	73	80	− 7	44	55	−11	− 9
	5	68	59	9	46	69	−23	− 7
	6	89	66	23	82	84	− 2	11
	7	83	113	−30	73	60	13	− 9
	8	130	106	24	122	126	− 4	10
	9	82	87	− 5	89	107	−18	−12
	10	71	68	3	80	88	− 8	− 3
G Twp	1	79	160	−81	79	97	−18	−50
	2	132	173	−41	133	151	−18	−30
	3	96	104	− 8	92	100	− 8	− 8
	4	65	79	−14	70	75	− 5	−10

Fall-Off

−50 ⎤
−37 ⎥ 4
−30 ⎥
−18 ⎦

−12 ⎤
−10 ⎥ 3
− 9 ⎥
− 9 ⎦

− 8 ⎤
− 7 ⎥ 2
− 3 ⎥
  1 ⎦

 10 ⎤ 0
 11 ⎦

A factor of 1

Precinct	Points
F City 1	4
2	4
3	2
4	3
5	2
6	0
7	3
8	0
9	3
10	2
G Twp 1	4
2	4
3	2
4	3

Efficiency Index

As noted in the section about primary targeting, the efficiency index measures a precinct's performance in voting. The same index is determined for general elections. However, here we must also measure the performance of Independent voters because of the heightened importance of their votes to the outcome of elections. Opposition voters should be ignored and their registration figures are therefore omitted in this calculation.

Table 24, Column 2 includes the total Democratic and Independent registration, as presented in Table 8. The general election efficiency index is obtained by dividing the average Democratic turnout by the total Democrat and Independent registration. The end result is shown in Table 24, Column 3. Examples:

F City 1 207 = .68 X 100 = 68%305
F City 2 124 = .43 X 100 = 43%289

After the indices are determined the precincts are rank-ordered, quartiled and assigned points, as noted at the bottom of Table 24.

Table 24
Efficiency Index

Precinct		1 Average Party Turnout	2 Dem + Ind Regist.	3 Efficiency Index
F City	1	207	305	68
	2	124	289	43
	3	63	165	38
	4	63	208	30
	5	61	137	45
	6	80	207	39
	7	82	197	42
	8	121	174	70
	9	91	215	42
	10	77	246	31
G Twp	1	104	311	33
	2	147	190	77
	3	98	166	59
	4	72	225	32

Rank-ordered precincts and Quartiles

			A factor of 2	
			Precinct	Points
77 ⎤				
70 ⎥ 4				
68 ⎥				
59 ⎦			F City 1	8
			2	6
			3	4
45 ⎤			4	0
43 ⎥ 3			5	6
43,43 ⎦			6	4
			7	6
39 ⎤			8	8
38 ⎥ 2			9	6
33 ⎦			10	0
			G Twp 1	4
32 ⎤			2	8
31 ⎥ 0			3	8
30 ⎦			4	0

(When employing the efficiency index to allocate candidate time, telephone calls and direct mail in general elections, no contacts should be made with Republicans. Such contacts are likely to stimulate their oppositional voting behavior. Walking lists, calls and envelopes should be completed for Democrats and Independents exclusively. This will again permit us to maximize the impact of our contacts.)

Swing Vote

Swing voting means partisans abandon their partisanship—that is, they ticket-split. It is an increasingly significant phenomenon in general elections and at the same time, it tends to occur at the top of the ticket. Thus, a Democrat may vote for a Republican for president, governor or mayor, but revert to Democrats for state representative, county auditor and city council. Because the numbers of swing voters are rising, general election targeting must evaluate their importance. The swing vote is the percent difference between high and low visibility candidates of the same party. Table 25 shows the percent received by the Democratic candidates for each of the four races in each of the precincts and their respective swing votes for each year in the precincts. The average swing vote is obtained by dividing the precinct's total swing vote by the number of years included, in this case by 2. Examples:

	1980 SV	1982 SV	Total SV	Avg SV
F City 1	−25	+1	= 26	+213
F City 2	−14	+ (−6) = 20		+210

(Signs [+ or −] are ignored when calculating the swing vote. We are interested in the percentage of voters who show shifting party allegiances. It doesn't matter at what level individuals abandon their party. What is significant is they abandoned it in the first place.)

After the swing vote for each precinct is determined, the precincts are rank-ordered, quartiled and assigned points.

Table 25
Average Swing Vote

Precinct		'80 President (Dem) %	'80 State Rep (Dem) %	'80 Swing Vote %	'82 Governor (Dem) %	'82 State Rep (Dem) %	'82 Swing Vote %	Total Swing Vote	Average Swing Vote
F City	1	48	73	−25	57	56	1	26	13%
	2	44	58	−14	56	62	− 6	20	10%
	3	38	39	− 1	47	46	1	2	1%
	4	48	60	−12	47	57	−10	22	11%
	5	49	48	1	52	72	−20	21	11%
	6	55	45	10	61	63	− 2	12	6%
	7	47	68	−21	52	59	− 7	28	14%
	8	40	36	4	48	51	− 3	7	4%
	9	33	37	− 4	44	54	−10	14	7%
	10	29	30	− 1	40	48	− 8	9	5%
G Twp	1	24	51	−27	34	41	− 7	34	17%
	2	38	54	−16	47	59	−12	28	14%
	3	35	41	− 6	47	51	− 4	10	5%
	4	30	39	− 9	48	50	− 2	11	6%

Rank-ordered precincts and quartiles

17 ⎤
14 ⎥ 4
14 ⎥
13 ⎦

11 ⎤
11 ⎥ 3
10 ⎥
7 ⎦

6 ⎤
6 ⎥ 2
5 ⎦

4 ⎤ 0
1 ⎦

A factor loaded of 3

Precinct	Points
F City 1	12
2	9
3	0
4	9
5	9
6	6
7	12
8	0
9	9
10	6
G Twp 1	12
2	12
3	6
4	6

The Composite Index

This index permits us to create a single, new summary table which itself reflects all measures included in the targeting program. To calculate it, each variable in the targeting exercise must be weighted. Clearly, not all measures are equally important.

Guidelines for Weighting Measures

1. Percent figures are more reliable than whole numbers.
2. Average party strength is the most important measure when your party is the dominant party in the district. (You can win with a "normal" vote.)
3. Average swing vote is the most important measure when the opposition party is the most dominant party in the district. (You can't win with the "normal" partisan vote.)
4. Average party turnout is always important to get the "regulars" to the polls. But, it is not as significant as percent measures.
5. The efficiency index is always important, especially in allocating direct mail and telephone resources.

Scaling the Variables

In assigning weights to specific targeting variables, the goal is to create a point scale for comparison of points between precincts. The specific variable weighting or factor loading is less important than building dispersion into the index. The end result must be an index which reflects the relative importance of precincts according to divergent variable values.

The variables used in this general election targeting exercise were: average party turnout, average party strength, fall-off, efficiency index and swing vote.

Weighting begins by establishing a common numerical base for all the variables. That base is consistent with the rank-ordered quartiles completed for each of the five measures. Hence, the common numerical base is as follows:

Quartile	Points	Description
I	4	Very Significant
II	3	Significant
III	2	Marginal
IV	0	Insignificant

The key weighting judgments need to be made—that is to determine the factor loadings for each of the variables. The factor loadings for this exercise are 3, 3, 2, 2 and 1 as presented in Table 26.

All that I have done is to multiply the quartile points by a factor loading value. For instance, a factor loading of 2 increases the points earned by precincts in the top quartile from 4 to 8. Similarly, a factor loading of 3 increases precinct points in the first quartile from 4 to 12.

Table 26
Factor Loadings

Measure	Loading	Q1	Q2	Q3	Q4
Average party turnout	2	8	6	4	0
Average party strength	3	12	9	6	0
Fall-off	1	4	3	2	0
Efficiency index	2	8	6	4	0
Swing vote	3	12	9	6	0

Quartile Points span Q1–Q4.

Explanation of Factor Loadings

Swing vote and average party strength are weighted equally and most heavily. Both were assigned a loading of 3. That judgment was reached by looking at the overall district partisan vote. Table 27 provides the information required for this calculation, all of which is taken from the Basic Data Worksheets.

Table 27
Grand District Sum and Grand District Democratic Sum Totals

Race	Grand District Sum	Grand District Democratic Sum
President, 1980	3474	1348
State Rep., 1980	3210	1576
Governor, 1982	2616	1264
State Rep. 1982	2539	1371
Totals	**11,839**	**5,559**

The Democratic percent for the district is determined as follows:

$$\frac{5{,}559 \text{ (GDDS)}}{11{,}839 \text{ (GDS)}} = .47 \times 100 = 47\%$$

The district is generally a swing area.

Given the basic competitiveness of the district, my judgment is that the campaign must do well both in the high Democratic strength areas and the swing precincts. Each of these variables therefore received a factor loading of 3.

A factor loading of 2 was assigned both to average Democratic turnout and the efficiency index. The logic here is simple: the campaign must get both Democrats and Independents in key precincts to the polls. That will require extra work in certain precincts.

Finally, a factor loading of 1 was assigned to falloff. Given the extensive fall-up voting in this particular district, the measure loses some of its saliency. The campaign can't learn which areas are likely to produce higher turnout as the information currently stands.

New precinct point totals

Return now to Tables 21–25. On the bottom right hand side of those Tables you will note both the factor loading and a rank-ordered list of the precincts with their new point totals for that variable.

The Summary Table

A summary table can now be created which will present a combined listing of each precinct's total points in the exercise. The factor points for each district are taken from Tables 21–25 respectively and placed on the summary table. That information is presented in Table 28. The total points column of Table 28 shows what each precinct earned on the five variables—and are rank-ordered at the right column.

Table 28
Summary Table of Measures

Precinct		Average Party Turnout	Average Party Strength	Average Fall-Off Vote	Efficiency Index	Average Swing Vote	Total Points	Rank-ordered precincts
F City	1	8	12	4	8	12	44	44
	2	8	12	4	6	9	39	41
	3	4	6	2	4	0	16	39,39
	4	4	9	3	0	9	25	31
	5	0	12	2	6	9	29	30
	6	4	12	0	4	6	26	29
	7	6	12	3	6	12	39	26,26
	8	8	9	0	8	0	25	25,25
	9	6	6	3	6	9	30	19
	10	4	0	2	0	6	12	16
G Twp	1	6	0	4	4	12	26	12
	2	8	9	4	8	12	41	
	3	6	9	2	8	6	31	
	4	4	6	3	0	6	19	

The Final Composite Index

Table 29 now identifies those precincts which are most important to our Democratic candidate. Note that they have been quartiled and identified by key words. The candidate now has a single measure reflecting five key district voting measures, to determine where people, time and money will do the most good for his or her campaign. Pick variables are still available should there be a need to determine how and where a particular campaign resource should be utilized.

Table 29
Final Composite Index

Precinct	Total Points	Descriptive Terms
F City 1	44	Most Significant
G Twp 2	41	
F City 2	39	
F City 7	39	
G Twp 3	31	Significant
F City 9	30	
F City 5	29	
G Twp 1	26	
F City 6	26	
F City 4	25	Marginal
F City 8	25	
G Twp 4	19	Insignificant
F City 3	16	
F City 10	12	

5

Fundraising: Strategies and Techniques

★ ★ ★

✓ Planting the Money Tree

An early priority of any campaign is establishing a fundraising organization. You start by drafting a finance plan and budget, then go out and recruit your heavy hitters. The key is knowing who to ask—and what to ask for.

Whether you are running for the United States Senate or your state legislature, you need money, and you need a plan to raise it. In short, you need a fundraising plan that spells out on paper how much money you will require for the campaign, when you will require it, and where and how you intend to raise it.

Okay, so fundraising is not your favorite aspect of campaigning. You think other people should take care of the money so you can concentrate on the issues. You believe that the unions (or big business, take your pick) love you, so money will not be a problem.

You do not mind calling people, but you cannot be expected to ask for money. Besides, you reason, you do not need to raise money, Somebody Else is Doing It For You.

What you really believe, then, is fundraising is your highest priority—right after everything else in the campaign. Stop kidding yourself.

Nothing is more effective in creating a realistic campaign strategy than knowing you need X number of dollars by a specific date. Otherwise, you will have to cut some campaign activities.

Writing a fundraising plan will help you to set priorities and to identify cash flow and budgeting problems, which in turn can help prevent major headaches down the road. It also will help you build support for your campaign by bringing you closer to voters—and major donors.

The first time I had to write a fundraising plan, I thought it was a complete waste of time. I was convinced writing a plan for something as fluid as fundraising, in something as fluid as a campaign, was pointless. After all, I reasoned, the thing would be out of date within a month.

I was wrong. What you are writing is not a bible to be taken literally but a general path to guide you.

The Key Questions

You need to raise most of your campaign money months before Election Day, so do not waste time stating the obvious. Go to the meat of a fundraising plan. A good one answers these questions:

How much money can we raise? Campaigns typically have three fundraising goals—the absolute bottom line, the middle ground, and the dream. The absolute bottom line should be just that: the bare-bones minimum you need to win this race. The middle ground should be your most realistic fundraising assessment, the dream plan is the amount you will raise only if everything goes right.

Among the three, stress the realistic assessment, and, if you must err, do it on the conservative side. It always is easier to devise new ways of spending additional money than to devise new ways to raise more money. If your figures show you are scraping bottom, double check to see if you have underestimated any potential sources of income. If your figures prove right, you need to have a serious talk with your campaign manager.

If your plan calls for raising enough money to finance the dream budget, and you are sure you have not been overly optimistic, that is terrific. You should, however, urge your campaign manager to be cautious in spending until the plan has proven itself.

When do we need it? A fundraising plan that targets the bulk of its activities for September and October plays havoc with a campaign budget that requires paying vendors and buying radio time in August. The closer you get to the election, the easier it is to raise money. But you will never get to that point unless you tap into a rich vein early on. Keep in mind that early money and late money (assuming the campaign is going well) typically flow into a campaign but that you have to force a trickle midway through.

Above all, make sure your fundraising plan will work, not just look pretty next to the campaign plan and the budget. If your campaign strategy calls for spending $100,000 by August 1, but you do not think it is possible to raise that amount by then, reassess your fundraising efforts. If you think you can raise only $75,000, reschedule expenditures based on that figure rather than falling $25,000 short. If you raise the additional $25,000, consider it a bonus. The campaign will manage to spend it.

How are you going to raise it? This is the key to the fundraising plan. Your first step: Identify possible sources of money. This seems obvious, but you would be surprised how many candidates never go through their Rolodex and pull names. You need to be creative in developing a resource list; tapping your friends, business associates, and various issue groups will give you plenty of opportunities.

Tell Them What You Want

Once you determine likely sources for your campaign coffer, roll up your sleeves and go after them. The most effective fundraising pitch comes directly from the candidate. And the best way to attract early money into the campaign is to contact friends, relatives, and business associates and ask for a contribution. Have a specific dollar amount in mind, and encourage people to make one large contribution. Do not parcel them out over the course of the campaign.

Avoid the common mistake of asking for too little. Start at the top and work down. If you only ask for $25 few people will say, "Oh no, please let me give you $100." If you start by asking for

$100, you can always work down to $25—and you are more likely to get a contribution somewhere in between.

Target and recruit major donors—people who can write big checks and raise an even larger amount among friends and associates. The major donor network works a bit like Amway. Major Donor A, for example, contributes $500 and agrees to raise $2,500. In the process, he introduces you to Mr. or Ms. Potential, who also agrees to become a major donor. Over time, with a lot of nurturing, you will build a fundraising network.

Because of personal financial assets as well as contacts, major donors are a critical component of the fundraising plan. Make sure the large donors named to your business council or finance steering committee understand you are counting on them and the financial commitment they have made to the campaign. This is not the place for "name only" types.

Have a Party

In addition to developing a major donor network, a plethora of activities exist for raising money. These include meet-the-candidate house parties, special events, receptions, and dinners. The key to their success is keeping the overhead down. House parties, for instance, should be virtually cost-free. Try to schedule three or four house parties in one evening.

Consider fundraising outside the district, perhaps through a regional campaign committee. Do you know someone in a nearby city who has the ability to raise a substantial amount of money and who is willing to host an event for you? Are any of your party's incumbents willing to host an event for you in his or her district?

PACs and special interest groups can be a significant source of revenue for any campaign. You should work them from the beginning, include them in campaign activities and keep them abreast of your progress. It takes more than a call to get a good contribution: you must sell yourself and your candidacy. One of the biggest mistakes is to take the PAC and/or special interest community for granted.

Another way to obtain large contributions is to feature celebrities at fundraising events. You do not have to have Paul Newman to draw financial supporters—although most candidates would jump at the chance. Think who will help increase the draw with specific target groups. The chairman of the House Finance Committee may not be a big draw for the general public, but a local banker who has been sitting out the campaign may pay to have lunch with him.

Be Precise

Assigning projected dollar amounts to each type of fundraising activity is the hardest part of writing the plan. Naturally, the more information you have, the more accurate your numbers will be. Some of the basics:

- Discuss your goals for direct solicitation with your campaign manager, your spouse and other people whom you trust. Ask your major donors how much they will commit to raising and how many new people they can recruit.
- Break down your district into the smallest territories that make sense—precincts and counties, for example. Find out who the leaders are in each area. Ask them how much candidates have raised in the past and who raised it for them. Discern whether other campaigns will dry up the money, and whether your opponent is so strong that you should not expect much.

- For out-of-district fundraising, consider the costs involved in traveling. Ask how much money your candidate can raise. Then contact someone else from the area and see whether that amount is realistic.
- Consider the cost of celebrities. Do they require an honorarium? Who pays their airfare? Do they require a suite?
- Call people in the PAC and special interest community to find out how they view your race. Is it important to them? Do they truly believe you can win?

When you have answered these questions, you are ready to guesstimate. I use conservative numbers; high on the expenses, low on the income. If, for example, an event will cost between $300 and $500, use the $500 figure.

Structure and Explain Your Plan

Your plan should include a narrative that explains what you are going to do and how you are going to do it. As with any plan, there should be an introduction and conclusion.

The most significant part is the summary. I always include two summaries—one that details the fundraising scenario by region and type of event and that lays out the plan on a month-by-month basis.

A final tip: When you are speaking with leaders of various groups, tell them how much you want to raise from their community or membership. They will feel more a part of your campaign if you emphasize how important a responsibility they have in keeping your campaign rolling.

Your campaign also will benefit from knowing the big picture, including the broad range of fundraising activities and opportunities. It will give them a more realistic and positive perception of how the campaign is to be financed.

Writing the plan helps you focus on what your campaign needs to by each particular date. The payoff is a body of information that will help to shape your campaign strategy, give you a better grasp of where to raise money and how best to spend it, and provide some assurance that you will not be spending beyond your means. Your plan will help you avoid the mistakes that result in losing elections.

✓ Why You Shouldn't Rely on National Money
Norman Kurz

Having raised money for two upset winners who bucked conventional wisdom—U.S. Sen. Paul Wellstone of Minnesota in 1990 and U.S. Sen. Joe Lieberman of Connecticut in 1988—I see a number of lessons in the way they approached fundraising that should be instructive.

Both Lieberman and Wellstone paid attention to basic fundraising and political tenets. Each built a statewide base, attracting in-state contributors who were resolicited and who helped create grassroots support that later translated into an effective field operation. Skilled use of free media as part of their overall media strategy proved critical in the end.

By contrast, it's also clear that other Senate challengers who were presumed strong enough to mount close races fell short because they misplaced their priorities. They misallocated their resources on hopelessly futile attempts at national fundraising.

First, challengers must construct and operate within a sensible budget that recognizes the difficulty of raising money in a context where few others believe they can win. A lot of candidates make the mistake of putting the media cart before the fundraising horse. They're advised they'll need so many millions to run so much media and then justify that amount of media with bogus numbers showing how much they'll raise from all the people who said they would help. Of course, the promise of help is just about the worst thing a candidate can hear unless it's immediately followed with specifics nailing down how much help and when it will arrive.

Wellstone never deluded himself into thinking he would raise several million dollars. Even though he could have raised more than he did from out-of-state individuals, he made a fundamental decision early on that it was neither worth it nor essential to win if it came at the cost of forsaking campaign time in Minnesota.

On the other hand, in one of our other 1990 campaigns, former Louisville Mayor Harvey Sloane's run to unseat Kentucky Sen. Mitch McConnell (at one time viewed as the Democrats' best opportunity for a pickup), began with the premise that Sloane should raise as much as $5 million.

Yet even with the earliest start of any 1990 challenger, there was no chance he could raise enough in Kentucky and among political action committees to get close to that figure. So he was saddled with the burden of marketing himself around the country.

Concentrate on the Basics

The foremost imperative is for challengers to put in place a thorough and comprehensive in-state political fundraising apparatus, and continually to enhance those operations as much as possible. I stress both political and fundraising efforts because a strong network provides both types of support.

Few candidates find the cities and towns in the states as glamorous as the prospect of plucking the wallets of stars in Hollywood or financiers in New York. Of course, what most challengers fail to remember is that national givers have sitting senators flattering them regularly, and the contributors have little room on their plates for anyone else.

Instead, challengers should spend more time figuring out how to squeeze every penny out of their own states, using an array of fundraising programs targeted at various income levels. For example, while Wellstone liked nothing more than campaigning in the cafes of small towns across Minnesota and soliciting small dollar donors in labor halls, Sloane preferred working both coasts, usually to little effect.

This is not to argue that challengers should forgo national fundraising. It's an important and often indispensable part of their overall finance operation. The point is for most challengers to understand that, unless they're running against the likes of a Jesse Helms, they usually stand at the rear of the line of priorities for out-of-state contributors.

Wellstone came to understand that if he every hoped to convince out-of-state and PAC contributors to participate, he first would have to demonstrate viability at home. As the consummate outsider, Wellstone had no hope of matching or even remotely approaching U.S. Sen. Rudy Boschwitz's $70 million. He understood he needed to reach a threshold of at least $1 million (by election day he'd raised nearly $1.3 million) to do TV, but his focus from the outset was to supplement a low-budget campaign with high-intensity grassroots organizing.

The relationship between low-budget donors and grassroots is often underestimated by large statewide campaigns, generally for no good reason. For example, in contrast to Wellstone's concentration on the grassroots, Boschwitz's unsuccessful 1984 Democratic opponent, Joan Growe, banked everything on media and actually cut her campaign's field organization in the final weeks. It's a course of action that was absolutely unthinkable for Wellstone, who had full-time field staff in all eight congressional districts and recruited 4,000 volunteers who worked the state as if his race was for the town council.

In the Sloane case, there was particular irony in his low commitment to an intense grassroots field operation. One of the campaign's major selling points to out-of-site contributors was the fact that Kentucky Democrats have a voter registration advantage of about 5 to 2. Sloane pounded that theme to demonstrate winnability—"we don't need any Republicans so long as we get our voters out to the polls"—but then failed to mobilize an effective outreach to those Democratic voters. Instead, he relied on the state-coordinated campaign, which was not enough.

Notwithstanding their best efforts, virtually all Senate challengers end up being especially disappointed with the reception they get from the Washington political community. They all assume a certain segment of PAC and individual money simply will flow into their coffers. It is a major shock to candidates who have enthusiastic supporters at home that movers and shakers in the capital do not share the same enthusiasm.

The most galling aspect of this discovery is that this attitude is even held by the PACs with whom they are ideologically compatible. Candidates expect these groups to be more passionate and bolder than the business PACs and thus more sympathetic to challengers. But, lobbyists for arms control, civil rights, pro-choice, and similar interests are just as conservative in their decision-making when it comes to making political contributions. (Nothing made Wellstone more angry than to be told by one such progressive PAC—which admittedly loved his politics and opposed Boschwitz vehemently—that it could not contribute because of "fiduciary responsibility" to its own members).

The truth is that Washington is probably the most cynical town in the United States; it loves front-runners and winners. Only two things seem to count: good polling numbers and, to a lesser extent, the bottom line of the quarterly FEC report.

Having said all that, it's also obvious that every candidate and each campaign is unique: few strategies scan be copied successfully by dropping them intact into the political culture and dynamic at work in a different state in a different year. The useful lesson is that the common thread binding candidates who execute shocking upsets is that they do not rely on big money.

Most states are a lot more like Minnesota and Kentucky than the few mega-states where there really may not be any alternative to raising huge sums of money to finance heavy media. Thus, an overall strategy in which well-timed and well-conceived media is but one component of an overall $1-to-2 million budget has a chance to succeed.

Even in the 1990s, it is possible to win a campaign at any level through the old-fashioned verities of detailed attention to local politics. Build networks of donors and grassroots operatives who can get out the vote and pay for it.

✓ Fine-Tune Your Party Fundraising
Al Mitchler

Despite a slow economy, or thanks to it, 1991 and beyond will be banner years for political fundraising if tactics and technologies adjust smoothly to shifting political priorities and donor demographics.

A New York ad agency would call the primary political fundraising strategy of the 1990s niche marketing. Because the great issue areas that welded fundraising networks together for the past 14 years have evaporated or are on the wane, political pros are faced with soliciting smaller, more highly defined clusters of potential donors. No longer can we prospect on a single issue such as arms control, drugs, taxes, or abortion, then throw those givers into a single monthly pot and treat them loosely as a single membership organization.

Now, while continuing to prospect on single-mirror issue areas, donors are segmented in separate files, each targeted with boutique-design mailings. (All of those copywriters I threw out of work when the commies surrendered can now be rehired).

Soon, the strength of a fundraising organization will not be weighed by how many thousands of donors there are on a small-donor file, but by how many different donor files can be managed. Each file will be attuned to an issue, a personality, or some other such specific type of information vehicle.

In other words, the good old days of the anti-communist letter or the blame-the-extremist-liberal-Democrat letter are gone. We are nearing the point in fundraising where we must carry on a very specific dialogue with givers.

He or she will no longer be satisfied with the emotional hyperbole of the past. At the National Republican Senatorial Committee, for example, we may end up with 20 different active files of anywhere between 5,000 and 20,000 individual donors, each of whom is motivated by a different monthly copy platform.

Personal Pitches

Computers made personalized direct marketing—the illusion of personal correspondence—viable. But more than half a generation has passed since we first started using mass direct marketing, and few donors are still fooled when they get a "general" letter mailed specifically to them. Only by constructing programs and letters to meet their needs will we have continued success with them.

To accomplish that is not as hard as it sounds. You probably receive plenty of checks wrapped in letters full of advice and political preferences. Instead of ignoring those comments, load them into your data bases and reference them back to the donor. In some cases, you may even have to write—heaven forbid—individual notes to acknowledge specific comments or donors. It is all part of a common sense strategy to return to the "personalized" flavor fundraising mail which worked so well a decade ago.

In addition to using mailboxes to forge a new relationship with donors, direct marketers need to provide real people for donors to contact. The growing use of toll-free 800- and charge-per-call 900- telephone numbers reflects fundraising's sensitivity to this need as well as a smart application of technology to building fundraising strategies.

Donor Demographics Have Changed

Once you have the tactics down, there is one more little hurdle to successful fundraising in the 1990s: The donors who traditionally have supported all direct-market fundraising in the U.S. are slowly fading away.

Those who came out of the Depression, fought World War II, and believed in mother, God, and country are no longer the bulk of our audience. We face a new generation who do not know the ideal world of Ozzie and Harriet. They were raised on All in the Family and M.A.S.H. This generation of political supporters knows America is not always right politically, that there are two sides to every issue, and that war is not always victorious.

Perhaps the change is for the better, provided the fundraising successes of the '80s can be adapted to the realities of the '90s.

✓ Wheedle A Fortune: A PAC Fundraising Plan
Kristine E. Heine and Richard F. Mann

Money is to a political candidate what air is to a deep-sea diver. If there is not a steady supply, the result invariably is fatal.

If you plan to run a mid-level or high-level campaign this year or next, your fundraising plans must be in place very soon. And if one part of that plan calls for you to approach political action committees for funds, this article will help you begin that process.

Basically, three funding sources are available to most candidates: political action committees, political parties, and individual contributors.

Political party committee contribution limits depend on the office you seek, the population of your state, and other factors. These basic contributions limitations do not apply to "bundled" contributions from PACs, independent expenditures, or other wrinkles in election law.

Despite the controversy over the influence of PACs, they are only the second largest source of campaign funds; individuals remain the primary source. Not only do citizens provide the majority of the money for candidates, but their support often is essential if you hope to obtain PAC donations as a secondary source.

Start Planning Now

Your challenge in obtaining money from either of these sources calls for you to devise a fundraising plan and to implement it. For incumbents, fundraising is a continual process. For challengers, the quest for money must begin the day they decide to run for office.

Even before seeking campaign funds, you should develop a plan that incorporates your objectives, such as gaining name recognition, obtaining support from various constituencies, overcoming biases and opposition, and developing a supportable platform. Next, determine what tactics will achieve these objectives and how much this strategy will cost. Finally, you and your advisors must balance the price of each tactic with its potential benefit, set priorities, and develop alternative plans if monetary goals cannot be met.

For example, can flyers distributed door to door take the place of billboards? If you cannot afford prime-time television advertisements, should you place fewer spots or drop your plans for television altogether? These sorts of considerations will force you to reevaluate your strategic plan throughout the campaign.

Selection of a finance committee is the next step. Ideally, the committee chair should have good contacts in the community and be well respected. Committee members should represent major constituent interests, such as. small business, industry, unions, farmers, attorneys, doctors, realtors, teachers, bankers, and developers. Each committee member must make a financial as well as a personal commitment to your campaign. Says Suzann Hammelman, chairman of Hammelman

Associates, a Washington, D.C., fundraising firm, "It is difficult to ask others to give when you haven't done so yourself."

Of course, your members also must be willing to work. Each member should be assigned a fundraising goal and the committee should meet regularly to review its progress.

To establish a base of steady income for the campaign apparatus, some candidates set up an annual dues-paying organization. For example, the members of Senator Rudy Boschwitz's (R-Minn.) Washington Club are committed to paying $250 annually for four years. Formed after the election from a list of large contributors, the organization expects each member to recruit 20 others. The club operates in a businesslike manner, with annual meetings at which the senator reports on his special achievements and goals for the coming year.

Boschwitz also solicits donations apart from the club. According to Richard G. Nelson, Boschwitz's finance director, 29,000 individuals contributed to the senator last election, and campaign strategists hope to double the number before his re-election bid.

Generally, campaigns raise money through a combination of special events and mail solicitations. Names of potential donors may be obtained from political parties, voter-registration lists, your own business and social contacts, your finance-committee members, contributors to your previous campaigns, and direct-mail houses.

Money Attracts Money

Developing a strong "house list" of potential contributors, calling unproductive names, then determining the most effective means to solicit the remainder throughout the campaign takes time. This is perhaps the major reason the fundraising process must begin early. Another is that PACs begin their own process of deciding whom to contribute to shortly after each election. It is critical, therefore, to lock in PAC dollars quickly. A third reason for beginning your fundraising process early is that large, initial war chests can frighten potential challengers from entering a race.

Your campaign must pay attention to certain details, such as providing contribution cards and business-reply envelopes at coffees, rallies, and other appearances and making sure that all contributors receive a thank-you note and periodic newsletters or mailgram updates on your campaign. It also means identifying, stalking, and bagging big contributors.

Some candidates steer clear of PAC contributions altogether, thus forcing them to devise creative means of raising funds from individuals. For example, Representative Jim Leach (R-Iowa) raises all of his funds from individuals and places a $500 cap and an Iowa residency requirement on contributors. With average contributions of $20 to $25, Leach raised more than $180,000 for one re-election effort.

The Leach campaign organizes many inexpensive events, such as $5 chili suppers, pig roasts, and spaghetti dinners, to expand their donor base and build electoral support. The 30-50 Iowans who attend each event have an opportunity to talk with the congressman. Leach's finance committee also conducts direct-mail campaigns, "high dollar" events—$25 to $35 cocktail parties—and a yearly dinner at the Leaches' Iowa home. In addition, the congressman maintains high visibility throughout his district, appearing in parades, at county fairs, and at schools.

If you would rather seek a balanced mix of individual and PAC contributions, you can follow a fundraising rule of thumb that no more than 25 percent of your contributions may come from PACs; a higher percentage indicates a lack of support at home. However, PACs are an important source of large dollar contributions, so think carefully before you eschew them.

During the most recent campaign, PACs gave approximately 80 percent of their money to incumbents. If you are not an incumbent, you quickly must become acquainted with various influential groups in your state and the rest of the country, learn how to utilize national direct-mail solicitations, and identify and introduce yourself to managers of the nation's 4 PACs, most of which are headquartered in Washington, D.C.

To accomplish this, Representative David Price (D-N.C.), who defeated an incumbent, held a number of $25-$50 fundraisers throughout his state. Professional fundraisers also organized events for him with PACs in Washington and New York. Most of Price's PAC money came from unions and special-interest groups, such as the Sierra Club, Voters for Choice, and the Committee for a Sane Nuclear Policy.

Never having held office, Price lacked a legislative record on which to solicit contributions. As a result, to woo funds he relied on his reputation as the state Democratic party chairman and a university professor.

Endorsements Help

For challengers as well as incumbents winning the endorsement of political organizations in your state is a major factor in obtaining financial backing. Local endorsements are preferable, because they not only will make monetary commitments, but also often will encourage their members to become involved in the campaign.

Before you start soliciting a PAC, learn as much as possible about it. For instance, does it have facilities in your state or district? What are its criteria for giving? Who in the PAC decides which candidates receive money?

One-on-one meetings work best when seeking money from PACs, but if you lack the time or funds to organize such meetings, telephone calls and written solicitations can prove fruitful.

Some fundraisers ask people within the Washington, D.C., PAC community to host small functions where some of the sponsor's colleagues can spend several hours talking with the candidate, to become better acquainted with his or her views and personality. (Of course, the cost of such fundraisers, if underwritten by an individual PAC, must be counted as an in-kind contribution and included in the donor's contribution limitation.) Others organize successful fundraising dinners with the New York financial community, for example, where members of a Senate committee appear as guests on behalf of their colleague and attract contributors to the event.

Most PACs have finite financial resources and restrictions on the time they can spend examining the records of potential recipients. You can improve your prospects for obtaining money by targeting PACs whose interests coincide with yours and by providing as much relevant information as possible about yourself when soliciting funds. Be sure to include interest-group ratings, a synopsis of your legislative record, and a list of your committee assignments. (For non-incumbents, list the committees to which you aspire.) For example, only three days after the 1986 election, Senator Donald Riegle (D-Mich.), facing reelection in 1988, issued fundraiser invitations highlighting the four committees on which he will serve in the 100th Congress.

Experienced candidates keep track of how much PACs can afford to contribute and are willing to accept whatever amount each can donate. As an example, the American Pharmaceutical Association PAC recently was invited to a congressman's fundraiser. Although the PAC had reached its contribution ceiling and could not pay the full price, the incumbent's financial manager urged PAC officers to be present at the event. As a result, the member received a partial donation, rather than nothing from the PAC, and earned the association's goodwill.

One reason incumbents receive most of the money is because PACs know them best. Either the PAC's lobbyists have worked with the incumbent, or the PAC is able to judge the incumbent's record. But challengers can find ways to tap the same sources of funds. For example, the Hotel and Restaurant Association PAC will consider giving to challengers who are recommended by local union representatives or by members of Congress.

Another way to tap in to the PAC circle is to encourage your friends and supporters to contact their own business or union PACs to solicit funds for you. Ask members of your congressional delegation to host a Washington, D.C. breakfast where you can meet PAC representatives.

In addition, be sure to respond to organizations' questionnaires; these help PACs become acquainted with new candidates and introduce incumbents to newly formed PACs.

Because a candidate's campaign staff and strategy often are determining factors in obtaining PAC financing, your campaign manager and finance committee leaders should be certain to identify and meet important PAC directors early in the campaign, armed with knowledge of how to make the best impression.

Some groups, such as the Business Industry PAC (BIPAC), are influenced by a candidate's need for money, competitiveness, and non incumbency. Recipients of BIPAC funds also must prove they have the support of their local business community, measured in terms of individual and PAC contributions from hometown organizations. In addition, recipients of BIPAC dollars must demonstrate their plan for winning election.

Political parties' qualifications for recipients of campaign contributions are similar to those of PACs. For instance, the Democratic Congressional Campaign Committee requires candidates to have viability, a good campaign organization, and a successful fundraising record.

In the final analysis, you are the key to successful fundraising. The most sophisticated fundraising strategies are for naught if you are not attractive to campaign workers, the electorate, and financial supporters. Be prepared to spend up to 80 percent of your time scouting out funds in the early stages of your campaign. You will find those individuals who make a monetary commitment also become involved—and they vote for you as well.

✓ Ollie, Inc.: How Oliver North Raised Over $20 Million
John Persinos

Oliver North has worn several hats over his remarkable career: Marine Lieutenant Colonel, decorated Vietnam veteran, National Security Council aide, U.S. Senate candidate, conservative cause celebrity, and talk radio host. It was Iran-Contra that made him a household name, but these days his greatest claim to fame is his prowess as a direct mail fundraiser.

In his failed bid to unseat U.S. Sen. Chuck Robb (D-Va.) in November, North raised $20.3 million in a single year through direct mail solicitations, major donors, telemarketing, and fundraising events. About $16 million of that amount was from direct mail alone, making North the top political direct mail fundraiser in the country in 1994 (excluding Michael Huffington's personal check writing in California). North also can boast the biggest direct mail haul for a statewide campaign in political history.

In addition to sheer dollars raised, North's effort was distinguished by its nationwide scope and its grassroots breadth. North received contributions from all 50 states; the top five were Virginia, Florida, California, New York and Texas. "High population was the major reason that those states really panned out for us," says Ted Lupberger, who administered North's fundraising data base.

As a candidate, North had unusual national appeal. When called to testify before Congress in 1987 about his role in the Iran-Contra scandal, North portrayed himself as a scapegoat for the Reagan administration and a victim of the liberal media—a put-upon, medal-bedecked family man and military hero. Although convicted in a jury trial on several charges, notably aiding and abetting the obstruction of Congress, his convictions were overturned on appeal and his image among conservatives is that of a latter-day Dreyfus. North has remained a rallying point for true believers, positioning himself as a power broker for populist conservatives in the future.

"It was a crusade, a cause," says Tim Carpenter, North's former campaign manager. "It was the critical press coverage, which made North look like an underdog, and the emotion of the candidate that helped drive the direct mail."

North retains legal ownership of all donor lists, which means he now has a direct mail machine that he can kick into gear at any time. "There were two goals involved here—obtaining the actual money and obtaining the donor names," says Mark Merritt, former press secretary and deputy manager for North. "Those names can be rented or mailed to for a long time."

North also retains the ability to quickly raise large amounts of money. This will become even more important as campaign reform legislation limits the size of allowable contributions. The capping of donations necessitates a broader donor base—the sort of base that direct mail delivers. "We had a lot of true believers who sent $2 or $3 contributions," Carpenter says.

North's strategy of raising smaller donations from a larger number of people not only filled his campaign war chest, but expanded his volunteer base. North started his direct mail campaign with lists of target demographic groups that agree with him on key issues—anti-gun control, pro-life, school prayer, strong defense, anti-gay, and the like. He also utilized lists of supporters that he had compiled over the years, as a speaker on the rubber chicken circuit. One notable list derived from the "North Defense Trust," a fundraising effort from 1986 to 1992 that raised $20 million to pay for North's Iran-Contra legal bills.

North rented newer lists from obvious sources, such as the National Rifle Association and conservative religious groups, but he also tested scores of non-ideological lists as well. "Sometimes, we'd just pull a registered voters list and test 5,000 names, if we saw that a high number of people in that geographical area had contributed already," Carpenter says.

Never Stop Asking

"We never stopped asking, we never stopped prospecting," Carpenter says. "And we always asked in different ways. But all appeals had to be cleared and stand on their own merit."

Overall, the North campaign raised $20.3 million from a total of 275,000 contributors; about 245,000 of those donors were direct mail givers. That makes North's list of donors the largest ever compiled in politics. Many contributors gave two or more times. The average contribution was $28.11, across the board. More than 13 million fundraising letters were mailed, from September 1993 to November 1994.

A team of direct mail vendors took part in the mail effort, for a total fundraising cost of $11 million. Those vendors included Eberle Associates, Vienna, Virginia; Right Concepts, Chantilly, Va.; American Target Advertising, headed by direct mail legend Richard Viguerie, in Fairfax, Va.; Direct Mail Communications (DMC), Forest, Va.; Squire & Hartfield, Oakton, Va.; and Richard Norman Co., Reston, Va. Each firm applied its own specialty to the process. Most campaigns don't use more than one firm for direct mail; North preferred several vendors whose activities were coordinated according to their particular strengths.

"I urge campaigns to start thinking about using a team of direct mail vendors, the way we did, instead of just relying on a single vendor," Carpenter says. "It brings the spirit of creativity and free enterprise to a political campaign. I think a regular vendor who a candidate goes to over and over again can sometimes take a client for granted and get complacent." Merritt adds another practical point: "Ollie's sheer direct mail volume was too much for any single mail house to handle by itself."

Viguerie brought an historical point of view to the campaign. In the early 1970s, when national candidates with intense ideological followings began prospecting for money, it was specialized list brokers like Viguerie who showed the way. For North, Viguerie provided lists of dedicated conservative voters that he only makes available to his own special clients.

Richard Norman is another conservative activist, with an increasing reputation in political circles for creative flair and good instincts. "Norman had the ability to sit down with Colonel North, and in 24 hours put together a package that reflected the colonel's personality and principles," Carpenter says. David Tyson, president of Right Concepts, focused on creative copy writing; Bruce Eberle's strength was the logistics of getting the mail out; DMC's strength was conservative religious fundraising and their access to those types of lists; and Squire & Hartfield provided experience in commercial fundraising, for a corporate sensibility in package creation.

The entire team together, Norman says, was greater than the sum of its parts. "We had an open door policy," Norman explains. "Anyone who was a Republican who believed in conservative causes was welcomed aboard."

The North for Senate Campaign also raised $200,000 from political action committee (PAC) contributions; $545,000 from the Republican party; $2 million from telemarketing; $1.8 million from special campaign events; and $500,000 from personal calls made by North himself to key contacts in his Rolodex.

The latter tactic is always effective, but it's often overlooked or ignored by candidates who feel uncomfortable putting the squeeze on associates and friends. "Candidates are notorious for not wanting to be the person to ask for money," Norman says. "North felt no such inhibitions."

Life in the Bunker

The worst fundraising week, March 11-18, was when North's opponent in the Republican primary, former Office of Management and Budget director James Miller, released a Ronald Reagan letter that was critical of North. Among other things, the letter suggested that the former Marine was a liar. "It made national news and undermined North's credibility," Carpenter remembers.

At the time, the campaign had more than 1.4 million pieces of prospect mail going across America. The campaign lost money that week. "It was a tough week, but serving in that campaign was like being in a bunker all the time," Merritt remembers. "You knew you were going to get hit again and again; you just never knew by whom."

During the best fundraising week, August 27-Sept. 2, the campaign raked in $1.5 million. Historically, campaigns have avoided the month of August for direct mail because it's a time when people are distracted by vacations and the like. North's managers thought differently. "We were riding the Republican tide nationwide," Carpenter says. "We could feel a surge—and we could see it." Merritt says polling in the final weeks showed North moving up, slowly but surely, until he was virtually dead even with Robb. "Some polls actually showed us ahead of Robb," he says. "The end of the race called for more paid media, which meant more direct mail." When it came to choosing a mailing list, North's operatives knew that it wasn't sufficient to merely pick people with common interests. North crafted a message that grabbed potential donors and stirred a cause, motivating contributors to open their checkbooks. "People wanted to be part of the cause," Lupberger says.

North's direct mail packages were designed to be "interactional" for people who are predisposed to give or have already done so. North turned the recipients of his mail into armchair activists. Importantly, North made the package carry the same general theme of the campaign. Every piece of mail had the look and feel of the candidate; every piece was also graced with simple campaign logos and letterhead design.

"North signed 75 of the 79 different letters that we sent out," Carpenter says. "Four weren't signed by him: One was signed by his wife, one by Bob Dole, one by Phil Gramm, and one by me. Out of the group, mine did the worst. Direct mail needs a personal touch. A common mistake is to send out direct mail solicitation letters that are signed by unknown staffers. That tells prospective donors that the candidate doesn't care enough to write himself. But North put his heart and soul into each letter."

When it came to repeated dunning of proven givers, North didn't need to tell the reader why he or she should support the campaign, since they were already proven supporters. North explained the need for another contribution—for example, to buy more television and radio spots. It was an interactive resolicitation that provided a sense of participation; created urgency; and reinforced a bond between the candidate and the donor. Here's an excerpt from one of North's most effective solicitation letters. It makes an urgent appeal and starts with a compelling "grabber" lead sentence:

Like any good solicitation letter, this appeal uses short, punchy paragraphs throughout. The opening stresses the importance of the election and grabs attention. The rest of the letter sets up the stark ideological choice; asks for help to defeat a common enemy; stresses the need for money; and establishes dollar amount donation parameters. Important points are underscored and suggested dollar amounts are restated near the end.

"We made sure that each need stood on its own," Carpenter says. "It had to be clear and specific. Donors don't like to send money for amorphous 'campaign overhead.' They're afraid their money will be wasted. A candidate's request must be focused and specific—such as, say, a minister asking the congregation for money for missionary work in Africa."

The best performing mail appeal was a letter by U.S. Sen. Phil Gramm that said: "The National Republican Senatorial Committee will match your contribution with coordinated expenditure...." For every dollar that was contributed to the campaign from that mail piece, the Republican party was committed to matching it. "Donors were attracted by the idea of getting a big bang for the buck," Carpenter says.

Carpenter points out that nationwide radio and television appeals for money did not work. "One theory is that the demographics weren't right," Carpenter says. "I think we put those spots on TV where the viewership was younger and they weren't used to giving to a candidate."

These TV spots, with 1-800 numbers, were tested in Arkansas and Texas, and flopped as money-raisers. "The results were so bad, we canned these spots immediately," Norman says.

On the other hand, telemarketing always netted additional money and never failed to boost direct mail reply. "In fact, each time we followed up mail with phones, the response on the mail was higher than normal," Norman says. The campaign's outbound, telemarketing overlay, he says, increased money raised from the direct mail packages by about 15 percent.

The campaign coupled telephones and mail twice, in September and October, when the race with Robb was hottest. During that period, the campaign was mailing once a week to the entire contributor file. Thus, during those 60 days, proven contributors were getting a piece of mail every week and a telephone call once a month. The campaign raised $1.4 million in those two months, for a cost of $400,000.

Scarlet Letter

The campaign spent every penny that it raised; indeed, it ended with a deficit of about $600,000. It's important to remember that no campaign devotes all of its money to campaigning; for example, $11 million of the money that North raised was devoted to fundraising overhead.

"Unlike California Senate candidate Michael Huffington, North didn't have his own money to spend," says Jeb Spencer, a Republican fundraiser and vice president of the Conservative Television Network. "He had to go to the bread-and-butter givers, the low-dollar folks. It requires a large over-

---

Dear Friend and Supporter,

There are only 26 days left until Election Day. And right now, victory or defeat depends on my ability to:

1. Flood the TV and radio airwaves with campaign ads;
2. Launch the largest "get-out-the-vote" campaign of all time to guarantee that every Virginia conservative goes to the polls.

My friend, as I write you this urgent letter, I am neck-and-neck with my liberal opponent Chuck Robb in the polls. But there is no longer any question that this race is going to go down to the wire.

And in all honesty, my ability to win depends greatly on whether or not you will rush my campaign an emergency donation of $15, $20, $25, $50, $100 or more—today. Please, my friend, I know you have already done more than your fair share on my behalf....

---

head expense to reach these people and build a house file that you can mail to again. If you want a good mail package, you have to spend at least 60 cents to get a piece of mail into a potential donor's hands. On average, about 2 percent will respond. North raised more than $20 million, but he didn't spend it all on pure campaigning."

In the end, North's superb fundraising operation could not get him a seat in the Senate. North lost the bitterly contested race to Robb, 45.6 percent to 43 percent, with 11.4 percent for independent candidate Marshall Coleman.

Despite the fervor and generosity of his supporters, North could not overcome the Iran-Contra stigma that alienated many moderates and even conservatives. It certainly didn't help when Virginia's venerable Republican senator, John Warner, refused to endorse North and convinced Coleman, one-time Attorney General and gubernatorial candidate in Virginia, to mount an independent candidacy. For North, his involvement in trading arms for hostages was a Scarlet Letter that no solicitation letter could erase.

However, North's accomplishment goes beyond raising $20 million in a single year. He also put in place a dedicated citizens' army that's ready to answer the next Call to Arms. He made a lot of new friends, and he intends to keep them by continually enriching his data base. One way North keeps supporters active and interested is through his nationally syndicated call-in radio show.

"Oliver North will continue to be a force in American grassroots politics for a very long time," Merritt says. "His appeal continues across the country and remains widespread. The future of fundraising is with small donors; that's Ollie's great strength."

While North wasn't a winner, there's no doubt that he remains a player.

✓ The Secret of My Success: Candidate Fundraising

How much do candidates loathe the chore of raising money? "Most candidates would rather embalm cadavers than raise money," says Larry Purpuro, NRCC communications director.

The rising tension between political candidates and their fundraisers is one of the great untold stories of Campaign '92. It used to be that candidates viewed their financial advisers and fundraisers with trust, reverence, and gratitude. Now, they are viewed with irritation, suspicion, and hostility.

How does a fundraiser cope with such attitudes? "One of the greatest challenges for any campaign manager or adviser is to convince the candidate, who would rather be out shaking hands and having fun with people, that raising money is indeed one of his or her prime roles," says Linda Hennessee, veteran fundraiser and administrative assistant to Rep. Jim Bacchus (D-FL). According to Purpuro, one of the modern campaign fundraiser's most important tasks is to convince candidates that their ability to raise money is the truest measure of their commitment to their own campaign.

"We tell them, you are asking [for money] not for the man, but for the campaign," says Purpuro. When congressional candidates come to Hennessee and ask for her help, she says the first thing she tells them is that they're going to have to raise money. "They all say they'll do it—but they all lie. Here are some strategies to use with reluctant candidates.

1. Include the candidate in identifying key prospects.

"We pick his brains for all his own acquaintances and knowledge base," says Mark Rodgers, who supervised fundraising for Republican Rep. Rick Santorum's successful campaign to oust a seven-term Democrat incumbent in suburban Pittsburgh in 1990.

"It's a cooperative process," says Rodgers. "We put people he knows together with those we know. For each of the 100 key donors we developed a specific strategy, and then it was just a matter of following it through."

Hennessee works in concentric circles outward from the candidate, starting with the candidate's family and close friends. Then she builds outward to members of the candidate's profession, high school and college classmates, fellow church members, neighborhood and activist groups, corporate boards, and, finally, any person or group deeply opposed to the opponent's stand on a particular issue.

Steve Linder, a veteran Republican fundraiser in Lansing, MI, advises his challenger clients to start with a "Can't Say No" list of family, business associates, groups who chafe under regulations the opponent strongly supports, and people who simply loathe the incumbent.

2. Insist the challenger candidate contribute to the campaign.

"If you don't give your own money, how can you expect someone else to give you money?" asks Sheryl Wooley, who managed the successful '88 campaign of Rep. Porter Goss (R-FL).

There is no rule regarding how much a candidate should contribute, either in dollar amounts or as a percentage of the campaign budget. Linder thinks, however, that challengers should contribute on a sliding scale based on their financial ability.

3. Find a venue that works.

While no candidate is enthusiastic about begging for cash, certain approaches mitigate the stress and discomfort.

Hennessee points to a recent Roll Call listing of '92's largest congressional campaign expenditures in which her boss ranked eighth out of some 1,500 candidates in the "mobile phone" category.

"When you have a district where you have a lot of driving, I found it was always a good idea to give him a call list while he was in the car," explains Hennessee, adding that Bacchus seems less resistant to making calls when he's out of the office and, therefore, wouldn't otherwise be doing anything "really productive."

4. Set aside fund raising time on the candidate's schedule.

Budget your candidate's time to include almost daily fundraising.

The key is getting control of the schedule either directly or through the campaign manager and simply refusing to schedule him for anything but telephone time. Of course, that is easier said than done.

There's a political side to a campaign and a fundraising side. When the latter encroaches on the former on an almost daily basis, it can produce unwelcome strains within the operation.

Wooley recalls giving Goss a list of names to call. "The next day he would come back and [tell me] he just never had time to call. So we scheduled calling time in the evening. I would dial the phone and while he was talking to one person, I would dial another person."

5. The phone is king.

Sure, fundraising events, where the candidate can sprinkle a few remarks on patrons like a benediction, are helpful. But, according to Meyers, such events are the "flourishes" to a productive fundraising campaign.

Personal appearances by candidates aren't nearly enough by themselves to get the job done. "If we set up a meeting with 10 major donors, it's nice to know that [the candidate] can make a good pitch and raise the money," says Meyers. "But the phone is really the mechanism that does the job for you on a consistent, day-to-day basis."

If the candidate wastes too much time playing telephone tag, have an aide call in advance to set up a time when the candidate can expect to reach his prospective donor.

The key is to find the best time of day to make the call and to determine whether you should call the donor at home or at the office. Top fundraisers insist it's almost always the office, but the time of day is in dispute.

Linder, for instance, finds late afternoons perfect because his clients often find prospects still hard at work in their offices after secretaries and other aides who would otherwise screen the calls have left for home. Often, the boss answers the phone.

Hennessee says she finds mornings best, but, in any event, "avoid Friday afternoon like the plague."

Some candidates have achieved legendary reputations as fundraisers without producing a dime from phone time.

Purpuro cites Cary Edwards, a former New Jersey attorney general who was the first of seven Republican candidates to max out at the state-imposed ceiling of $1.2 million in the '89 primary race for governor. The real fundraising dynamo behind the scenes in Edwards' campaign was his wife, Lynn, who, along with her husband's staff, did a masterful job of pushing all the right finance buttons—including the touch-tone dial.

Edwards himself, though, did not make a single call in which he asked for money, recalls Purpuro, who worked on the campaign. Edwards was heavily into denial—denying, that is, that he wasn't pulling his weight in fundraising phone time.

"We locked him in a room with eight people, dialed the phone and handed him the receiver," says Purpuro. "He swore for the first and only time I ever heard him." After 10 minutes with the donor, Edward hung up—without ever once asking for a contribution.

"We gave up at that point," says Purpuro. "We realized he'd never be able to do it." Edwards lost the primary by a close margin to Rep. Jim Courter.

The final irony: Republicans in the New Jersey Assembly, awed by the ex-AG's alleged prowess as a fundraiser, made him finance chairman of their successful effort to recapture control of the state legislature.

6. Give the candidate a script, or at least detailed notes.

Meyers, like many fundraisers, provides his clients written instructions—a script, actually—of what to say on the phone to prospective donors.

Wooley explains why many candidates need to have what to ask written out for them. "A lot of people who could be very good fundraisers could do it for somebody else," she says, "but they have great difficulty doing it for themselves."

Have a staff member scribble a few key facts—spouse's name, number of kids, where the candidate last saw the potential contributor—in the margin of the candidate's script to give the solicitation a personal touch.

7. Make the candidate say the G-word.

The Edwards experience underscores the difficulty of getting candidates to reel in their catch once they hook a donor on the line. "The second problem with most candidates is when you get them on the phone, they don't know how to ask someone to give," says Hennessee. "You have to almost literally dance around the room and remind them of why they're on the phone. It's agonizing."

Nobody likes rejection, least of all politicians. "Candidates have big egos," Meyers points out. "They don't like to hear people say 'No.' " Wooley has her own way of dealing with the stammering and stuttering of otherwise eloquent speakers when it comes time for one of her clients to make a closing pitch at a fundraising event.

"Porter [Goss] would always say, 'I really hope that I can count on your support.' That was about as close as he could get," says Wooley. "So I would be the one who would jump up and chime in with, 'Yes, we want their support, but we want their money, too.' "

On the phone, of course, Goss' difficulty in going for the close was more difficult to deal with. "I wouldn't take the phone away from him, but I'd be yelling 'Money!' in the background. Then some of the people [Goss had called] would he followed up with later [by staff.]

8. Turn up the pressure.

"Rick [Santorum] needs to feel he has a reason to call, beyond just calling to say 'I need your money,'" says Rodgers. "There needs to be a sense of urgency to require the cold calling to take place. When he felt he had good news to share, he'd say, 'This can be won, but I need to buy three more spots during the Pirates game."

There are dozens of other ploys, such as allusions to the candidate's rapidly escalating status in the polls or citing a specific amount that's needed for last minute media buys to reach undecided voters.

Linder encourages his clients to tell donors that the campaign will have to shut down its phone bank if it doesn't raise a certain amount the night of the call.

Ask donors who have maxed out and can't contribute any more to pitch the candidate to five of their friends. Just make sure you don't flout campaign finance laws by pressuring the supporter to launder the cash through family members or domestic help.

9. Beware the candidate who shows an unbridled interest in fundraising.

Jeff Taylor, NRCC's director of incumbent services, tells an illuminating tale about managing the '88 Florida congressional campaign of retired Gen. James Dozier, one of Porter Goss' four primary opponents.

Dozier, a former tank battalion commander in Vietnam who won a Silver Star, was a genuine warrior-hero. In addition to his combat exploits, he had been kidnapped and held hostage by the Red Brigade before being rescued by the Italian police in 1981. Politics, however, was another matter—and this was the general's first try at elective office. Taylor picks up the story:

"The general ran into a Pfister, a member of a very wealthy family that manufactures faucets and other bathroom accessories. The general told me that Pfister told him, 'General, I think you've got the right stuff and I'd like to see you sitting in Congress.'

"I said, 'General, this is great. First we hit him up for a thousand bucks and then we hit him up for a 'Rolodex' letter to a 1,000 of his wealthiest friends. There's no end to what we can get out of this.'

"The general, however, seemed determined to take this project on himself. He said, 'Well, Jeff, I want to cultivate him. Let me take charge of this one.'

"I'm the idiot campaign manager. What do I know? I said, 'OK, he's your project.'

"By the end of the campaign, Pfister had given us a grand total of a hundred bucks. Great cultivation! That tells you how hard it is sometimes to get these guys to raise money."

Dozier, by the way, finished third in the primary, with 19 percent of the vote.

The Dozier saga may have been frustrating, but at least it wasn't criminal. In a California Republican congressional primary four years ago a frazzled preface favorite—a hospital official short of cash and in danger of losing—panicked and wrote a $150,000 check to his campaign out of hospital funds. The ensuing scandal hit the newspapers five days before the election. The candidate, who lost, wound up checking into a mental facility before the votes were even cast.

The final question: Are there any candidates out there who genuinely like fundraising?

"Bill Paxon (R-NY)" says Rodgers. "He's an animal. You never see him without his phone."

But that's another story.

✓ Pushing the Envelope: Direct Mail Fundraising
John Persinos

So you think direct mail fundraising is only for well-known national candidates? Think again. An increasing number of state and local campaigns are using direct mail to raise big bucks.

Direct mail is a political alchemy by which even obscure candidates can transform lists into gold. Technological wizardry is cutting costs and making it possible to segment lists with great precision. Meanwhile, more lists are available than ever before.

In the early '70s, national candidates with intense ideological followings began shaking the mail money tree. Both George Wallace and George McGovern used it effectively in 1972 to amass millions. Specialized consultants and list brokers, such as Richard Viguerie and Morris Dees, showed the way. Following in their footsteps have been other national celebrities, such as Jesse Helms, Pat Robertson, Ted Kennedy, and Oliver North. In recent years, both national parties and a diverse array of pro-choice, Christian Right, environmental, feminist, and business groups have relied heavily upon direct mail fundraising.

"Many of the direct-mail techniques that work for big-name national candidates can also work for smaller, local ones," says Tim Roper, president of Odell, Roper & Simms, direct marketers in Falls Church, Virginia. "The obstacle for small campaigns used to be a lack of economies of scale, but technology has brought the costs down."

Historically, unknown challengers for state and local offices rarely raised money through the mail. But now, lower-profile candidates can adapt the same tactics used by the Jesse Helmses and Ted Kennedys to their own political situations. The "nichifying" of mailing lists—a trend that parallels the segmentation of the national media in general—is a major trend that's empowering these smaller campaigns.

The key is targeting an identifiable potential donor base, a group of individuals who can be easily motivated based on a specific philosophical pitch. These situations illustrate the point:

- District Councilman Smith helped defeat a controversial rezoning request outside his district that was strongly opposed by environmentalists. He can target several thousand voters spread across town who were the most intensely opposed to the rezoning issue. Smith may not be able to ask these emotionally charged non-voters for votes, but why shouldn't he ask them for money?
- State Representative Jones is a champion of plaintiff rights. When she runs for re-election, she will get the customary $1,000 check from the state trial lawyers PAC. But she needs more than that. Her best approach: use mail to directly solicit additional contributions by reaching personal injury attorneys all across her state. Her message transcends her district's borders and impacts a large potential donor base that can be cultivated through issue agreement and repetitive contact.
- Citizen Brown is running for lieutenant governor of a small state, a largely ceremonial and powerless office that attracts few natural contributors. Brown is a real estate broker. There are 12,000 realtors in his state and another 3,000 contractors and developers. Brown, who is a strong supporter of real estate issues, should package his pitch and turn it into a statewide crusade, using mail as the message carrier. "Don't you think there should be at least one statewide elected official who makes property rights and economic growth his fight?" he could ask these 15,000 individuals who will assuredly answer "Yes!" He can then ask for not just votes and volunteers, but also for money.

In these examples, not one of the hypothetical candidates—Smith, Jones or Brown—are celebrities running for national office. But each has found a clearly identifiable potential donor base with available mailing lists that is susceptible to broad-based, mail-intensive fundraising.

Less is More

Another compelling reason to turn to direct mail is the looming prospect of campaign finance regulation. Regardless of how reform legislation in Congress eventually pans out, the overarching trend at the federal, state and local levels is to lower caps on contributions. The capping of donations necessitates a broader donor base, and direct mail is the key—even in smaller races that don't now use the mail to raise funds. In addition, the more changes there are in the regulation of campaign finance, the more professionalized fundraising becomes. Direct mail, with all of its sophisticated targeting permutations, is part of that professionalization.

"The doors to traditional sources of campaign cash could soon slam shut," warns Roger Craver, a Democratic consultant. "That makes direct mail a timely option. That's especially true if reform establishes a threshold of small gifts to qualify for public matching funds."

Raising smaller donations from a larger number of people not only fills your coffers but also expands your volunteer base. As an increasing number of candidates scrounge for dollars, direct mail is becoming a fundraising weapon of necessity.

Fundraisers report that campaign money is especially tight this year, due to a bumper crop of candidates. PAC donations are stretched to the limit. The situation will only intensify if Congress passes legislation that further curbs PAC giving. Meanwhile, state and local campaign rules are mirroring the federal trend toward contribution limits. The increasing solution to finding smaller contributions from more contributors: direct mail.

Charles Pruitt, co-managing director of A.B. Data in Milwaukee, says that mail is a bargain when compared to the cost of other media. "It's hard to quantify, but direct mail is cheaper," he says. "Besides, broadcast media don't have the virtues of direct mail in delivering a targeted message to a targeted constituency."

Keep in mind, though, that your costs depend on your specific tactics. Your first issue is to decide who you want to reach. For example, you might want to start with membership lists of organizations with which you're sympatico. Or you may initially target demographic groups that you agree with on key issues—seniors, farmers, feminists and the like.

The Medium is The Message

In recent years, purveyors of direct mail political fundraising have applied new technologies and created new techniques to maximize efficiency and results. Two good examples are the integrated use of mail and telephone follow-up programs as well as the mailing of VHS videos as part of the solicitation package.

Liz Welsh of the Clinton Group recommends integrating the telephone into any direct mail campaign you devise. "We've found that coupling the telephone with mail often doubles our response rate," she says. Stephen Clouse, a Republican consultant based in Milwaukee, prefers to make the initial contact over the phone and follow it up with a direct mail piece.

Clouse is a big believer in using videos with direct mail. Notably, he used videos as a fundraising tool in last year's special state senate races in Wisconsin. When Democratic state senators (notably

Sen. Russ Feingold, D-Wis.) were elevated to Congress, a slew of ambitious local Republicans were desperate to raise money and step into their empty shoes.

Political videos first appeared in the early 1980s. Direct marketers initially feared that they would replace direct mail, but Clouse points out that videos don't replace mail—they enhance it.

"Video communication is a powerful tool because it mixes sight and sound together to create feelings and mood," he says. "But if you're going to sell a viewer on a candidate or issue, you can't just give them general information and hope they will respond. You must tell them exactly what you want them to do and then give them a way to respond."

He says that the cost to duplicate videocassettes for mail campaigns is as affordable as a four-color direct mail piece. On average, a campaign video can be duplicated, packaged and sent for under $2.00 per list name.

While the cost is down, the perceived value remains high. Potential donors and voters will be more inclined to pop it into the VCR and retain it for multiple viewings. "Few people will take a video and toss it in the garbage like 'junk mail,'" he says. In addition, more than 80 percent of all households have VCRs.

Clouse cautions that it's not enough to simply mail the videos. "If you do, fewer than 20 percent will ever be played," he says. "The video must be part of an overall strategy of set-up and follow-through. It has to also include a letter and accompanying literature which states the pitch, presents the need and conveys the issues. You have to tell them what the problem is and clarify what you want them to do about it."

Clouse says his typical response rate for video direct mail packages has been 15 percent, adding that this rate is even better than it seems because it involves high dollar donors that give $500 and up. He says the corresponding direct mail response without videos would probably be 1 to 5 percent. The highest percentage rate he ever achieved was 28.5 percent, for the candidates in the special senate elections that were held in Wisconsin two months after the 1992 election.

"Everyone said donors were tapped out, but we mailed them anyway," he recounts. "Not only that, but 65 percent of the people to whom we mailed were not current donors. They were prospects."

A common failure, he says, is to merely enclose the video in a videocassette box. "You have to integrate video with the best principles of direct mail and telemarketing."

Clouse refers with pride to one of his most successful direct mail clients, Republican Peggy Rosenzweig. Previously a member of the Wisconsin assembly, Rosenzweig raised money to capture her state senate seat by using mail with videos.

"We decided to magnify her personality because she's a naturally attractive, energetic and articulate person," he says. "We sent a video that showed her interacting with voters and colleagues. It was a way to give people a lasting and favorable impression about someone who was relatively unknown. In the accompanying letter, we asked people to look at the video."

The Personal Touch

In all cases, it's imperative to develop a highly personalized letter/package. "For the folks you know, you should be as highly personalized as possible," Roper says. "The ideal candidate will write personal notes and stick 'em in the envelope—a handwritten P.S. at least. Try to rely on the strength of the candidate's own personality, and less on rhetoric. Cross off the surname and have the candidate scribble 'Dear Joe,' or whatever."

Pruitt says that personalization and verisimilitude make the difference. Technological advances are making greater personalization possible, a trend that in turn has been fueling the direct marketing business. Pruitt says his firm uses 'in-line' laser printing that enables it to personalize multiple pieces of a package with the recipient's name. But there's a caveat to using the latest technology.

"Smart, sophisticated and informed people are receiving this mail, so don't get too enamored of high-tech gimmicks," Pruitt warns. "The most effective technique is to create a personalized piece that's tailored to the candidate's own particular style. Your job is to stand out from the rest of the junk mail and get people to open the envelope and write a check."

This advice is especially apt for local candidates. "Glossy, ad agency style pieces within the package can backfire," attests Welsh. "It sends the message, even if it's subliminal, that 'Hey, they don't need my money.'" Pruitt agrees. He advises smaller, local candidates "to stick to a two-color, printed-at-the-shop-next-door look."

Republican direct mail consultant Lee Miller likes to use touchy-feely motivators in low-budget, small campaigns. His classics include the handwritten Wife Letter that begins: "Let's talk woman to woman."

Clouse offers this advice in drafting the pitch letter. "In your first three or four paragraphs, you must capture the reader's interest by appealing to his or her emotions. 'You-oriented' rather than 'Me-oriented' letters work best."

After the opening, he suggests these steps: Let the reader know why you are writing—i.e., to ask for help; make your case by explaining the reason why the reader should support your candidate; document your need by explaining why you need money; and establish urgency by showing why you need the money now.

Grab Their Attention

The package must be an attention-grabber, especially for candidates who lack name recognition. The most effective mail pieces, say experts, are oversized packages—not only "9 X 12s" but some the size of a desk blotter pad. Jumbo packages are typically perforated along the edges, making them easy to tear open, with a teaser message emblazoned on the outside of the envelope. Inside are the pitch letter, the response card, a business reply envelope and myriad inserts.

Jumbo packages boost response because they stand out from the clutter in the mailbox. Another reason for their efficacy: Large packages have larger type and are easier to read by older people, who tend to be big contributors.

Other "grabber" techniques include sending not just video but audio cassette tapes as well. Pruitt cites the audio tape he used to solicit donations for the campaign of Sen. Joseph Biden (D-Del.) for the Democratic presidential nomination. The tape presented excerpts from Biden's best speeches (presumably those he wrote himself), concluding with an appeal for support. In addition to standing out, the package conveyed Biden's message and oratorical skills.

Pruitt points to his work for Sen. Daniel Patrick Moynihan (D-N.Y.) as another example of effective teaser copy. A package his agency created for the Senator was mailed in a solid black window envelope, with a drawing in white of a hand gun on the front of the envelope and these words in large red type: "In Hell's Kitchen, there was one thing we all knew. Never kill a cop." Another recent Moynihan package says on the envelope: "Guns don't kill people. BULLETS DO." Both packages use tough talk to convey a message attractive to Moynihan's natural constituency—New York liberals.

Here's an envelope teaser that A.B. Data developed for the Democratic Senatorial Campaign Committee:

Q: What are the five most frightening words in American politics today?
A: United States Senator Oliver North.

Once reserved for the big boys, this kind of strategy is now being mimicked by lower-level candidates around the country. It's especially common for unknown candidates to adopt the mantle of anti-establishment maverick.

Take a look at the direct mail letter on page 21. The opening "grabber" is laced with superlatives: "This letter is one of the most important I have ever written, and one of the most difficult. It is also the biggest favor that I have ever had to ask of my family, friends and supporters."

The letter is being mailed out this summer by Buena Park City, California Councilwoman Donna Chessen to potential donors throughout Orange County, in her bid to unseat state Senator Rob Hurtt (R-Garden Grove) in the Fall. Sen. Hurtt is a businessman, conservative Republican, evangelical Christian and now—thanks to Chessen's direct mail campaign—an evil poster boy for the local Democratic fundraising machine.

We've "deconstructed" Chessen's letter to reveal the strategy behind its composition—a strategy that the new right has been using since the '70s. Just as Republicans in California for years black-balled competitors by associating them with Tom Hayden and Jane Fonda, now liberal Democrats like Chessen are turning the direct mail tables by portraying Hurtt as an extremist.

"Unknown, underfunded challengers can raise a lot of money by going negative and focusing on how bad the other guy is," says Robert Kaplan, the Democratic consultant behind Chessen's direct mail campaign. "The pitch with Chessen is to oppose Hurtt, not so much to support her. He's perceived in the community as being very anti-gay and anti-woman, so we've targeted our mail to gay and feminist mailing lists." So far, he says, the response rate has exceeded 15 percent, considered extremely high in the industry.

In Massachusetts, state Senator David Locke takes the same road. Locke raises considerable money for his own campaigns and for local Republicans by demonizing the Democratic Senate President, Billy Bulger.

"Direct mail is a great vehicle by which smaller candidates can portray themselves as underdogs," says Locke's Philadelphia-based direct mail consultant, Stephen Meyers. "But it has to be done right."

Meyer's techniques are blunt. Here's an excerpt from a high-response letter that he crafted for Locke: "Bill Bulger is a career politician who cares more about his own personal power than about the needs of the people of Massachusetts. He is a perfect example of the kind of politician people all across the country are rejecting... The choice is clear. Do you want more of the same backroom politics with Bill Bulger running the Senate like his own personal fiefdom? Or would you rather see a Republican majority with me as Senate president?"

Meyer successfully used the same "buck the system" approach for another obscure local Republican in Massachusetts, state Sen. Jane Swift. In her case, the campaign set up a press conference and then he tied the letter to her statements.

Swift's fundraising letter states, in part: "I've enclosed a copy of a newspaper article about my campaign kickoff two weeks ago. I told the large crowd of supporters that I would continue being an independent voice working for them in Boston... As your state Senator, I haven't been afraid to make waves. I've gone up against the legislative leadership, the special interests...."

Bob Bullock, Democratic Lieutenant Governor of Texas, took a similar approach, by inserting a flattering news clip from the Texas Monthly with a fundraising letter he sent out in February. It's an especially effective tactic for unknowns. First you stage an event to generate press coverage; then you use the news clips in your mailings to prove that you're a "player" with credibility.

Is It Working?

One of the most difficult decisions candidates must face before pulling the trigger on an expensive direct mail fundraising effort is whether it will be cost effective. Most consultants agree that a good candidate with the right message targeted to the right mailing lists can generate money. The question is: will it generate enough money to pay for the mailings? The answer to this enigma is test marketing, where you take your total potential donor base (the universe) and randomly select out of it a smaller number to prospect. If it works on the smaller sample, it will probably work on the entire universe. If it doesn't work, save your money.

This is a critical issue for campaigns. If the average cost of a direct mail piece is 40 cents and your universe contains 50,000 names, one mailing will cost $20,000 and a follow-up at or near $20,000, for a total of about $40,000. So, if at least 1,000 contributions averaging $40 aren't generated, or 500 averaging $80, or 2,000 averaging $20, then it's a loser. That's why it may make sense to test only 5,000 names. A $4,000 bust is a lot easier to survive than one 10 times as large.

Another factor is repetitive giving. A donor list that costs as much to create as it produces may not seem like a good idea, but if it becomes the basis for additional, repetitive giving over a long period of time, it may still be worth its weight in gold. That's the key to many of the ideologically oriented lists used by Richard Viguerie, the Christian Right, EMILY's list, abortion groups, and national and state party campaign committees. As Roper puts it: "When I'm prospecting, my goal is to break even. If I spend ten grand and get back ten grand, I'm happy because I've generated names."

In many state and local races where the potential donor universe is particularly tiny in numbers (i.e. 500 physicians, 300 union leaders, 400 minority contractors, etc.), testing the list may be a waste of time.

Motivating the Troops

When it comes to choosing a mailing list, it's not enough to pick people with common interests. The candidate—especially a challenger who isn't well-known—must craft a message that grabs potential donors and stirs a cause. Contributors have to be motivated to give.

In 1992, in the traditional Democratic stronghold of south Texas, an Hispanic Republican and political novice named Henry Bonilla mounted an insurgency, largely funded by direct mail, to evict Democratic U.S. Rep. Albert Bustamante. His "underdog" message was targeted to Democrats who were fed up with the scandal-tarred incumbent. Before Bonilla, it would have been highly improbable for a Republican to run for office south of San Antonio. Now several Republicans, both Anglo and Hispanic, are running for county office and using direct mail to raise money.

Karl Rove, a Republican mail consultant in Texas, says the sort of "guerrilla mail" war waged by Bonilla depends on "the right list, with the right message, at the right time. Targeting proven donors isn't enough—they must be motivated by the specific candidate."

Bonilla's experience showed that to motivate, a candidate doesn't have to take an overtly ideological stand. It's possible for non-ideological candidates and campaigns to use direct mail within the limits of their local districts.

When congressional districts were last redrawn, Bustamante's became a convoluted, sprawling 58,000 square-mile behemoth with numerous media markets. His purpose was to use redistricting as a sort of incumbency protection plan, by making it prohibitively expensive for an unknown challenger to buy enough media.

"Bonilla couldn't have won without direct mail fundraising," says Jim Lunz, Bonilla's adviser in 1992. "But in our mail packages, we used a fairly straightforward 'Time for a Change' theme. We used registered voter lists and lists of registered Republican primary voters. The latter group is a particularly motivated bunch, because the district has been historically Democratic."

Lunz is now crafting the same strategy for two unknown Hispanic Republicans who are running for the Texas legislature in the Fall: Fernando Cantu, who's running for state senator from Laredo, and Pete Nieto, who's running for state representative from Uvalde. "When it comes to reaching voters in some of these small rural towns, direct mail is my most cost-effective alternative," Lunz says.

Hit 'em Again

Roper says it's a good idea to create an "interactional" mail package for people who are predisposed to give or have already done so. "Don't just ask for money," says Roper. "Make them armchair activists. Ask them to sign petitions to get on the ballot, or ask them to attend a fundraiser. Send them a membership card to your campaign—people love to get a piece of plastic with their names on it. Most importantly, make the package carry the same general theme of the campaign. It has to have the look and feel of the candidate."

When it comes to repeated dunning of proven givers, a candidate doesn't need to tell the reader why he or she should support the campaign—they're already supporters. He or she must explain why to send another contribution. Resolicitations must be especially interactional. You must establish need; provide a sense of participation through questionnaires and the like; create urgency; and reinforce a bond between the candidate and the donor.

Improvements in the look of the package such as better paper will pay bigger dividends in resolicitation mail. Consider putting together a more expensive package, particularly if it's going to high-dollar donors. The ideal look: As if the candidate pulled the letterhead from his or her desk drawer and typed it. Make the letter from the candidate, not the campaign.

Brad O'Leary, a radio talk show host and political consultant, offers advice that's seemingly counterintuitive. He says to aggressively resolicit during the final two weeks of the campaign. "Candidates don't understand why you should resolicit when the coffers are already full, but the fact is that voters like to give during the hottest part of the battle," he says.

✓ Organizing Fundraising Events

Jill Gowan Bauman

Everyone knows that special events are one way to raise money. In the political arena, where maximizing the return on all fundraising efforts is imperative, campaign strategy and resources determine what kind of events to hold and when to schedule them.

Although it may be less expensive to schedule small, "high donor" events at personal residences which are coordinated by campaign staff but paid for by the host (or hosts), they may require too much of the candidate's time.

Large fundraising events can generate a large amount of gross funds as well as create a press opportunity and require comparatively little of the candidate's time. But large events can be risky because they cost the campaign money, require considerable staff and volunteer time and, if poorly executed, can result in low profits and even public embarrassment for the candidate.

However, if planned well, large events can result in high profits and great exposure for the candidate. Here are a few rules-of-the-road for planning and coordinating a trouble-free and profitable large special event for local, state, and federal candidates:

- Start early and plan ahead. Make sure your date does not coincide with another fundraising event, an important community event or with a holiday.
- Find a location that is accessible to the majority of your contributors. Make sure it has plenty of parking.
- Set your host levels and ticket price to maximize income without discouraging targeted donors. Remember, it is easier to sell by the table than to sell single tickets.
- Your special guests should add excitement (not cost!) to the program.
- Analyze your donors and create target lists for hosts and guests.
- Create a comprehensive event timeline so everyone's efforts can be coordinated.

The Budget

- Keep your event simple. With the exception of the highest-priced functions, donors do not want their dollars going to elaborate invitations, fancy flowers or filet mignon.
- Be creative. Use inexpensive, reusable decorations; consider a "preset" meal so the speeches will not be interrupted by waiters.
- Prepare a preliminary budget that enables the campaign to plan its allocation of financial resources to the event. Get estimates for such costs as invitation printing and mailing, parking, catering, audio/visual equipment, entertainment and decorations.
- Update this budget as variable costs, such as postage and food, are finalized.

The Host Committee

- Build the host committee early to give them plenty of time to pre-sell their commitments. Your host committee will determine the overall success of the event.
- Secure host commitments by sending a personalized letter from the candidate describing the event and requesting specific sales pledges, followed by calls from either the candidate or the campaign finance chair.

- Remember some hosts will fail to meet their goals, so get as many commitments as possible and assign someone full time to monitor and support their sale efforts.

The Invitation

- The invitation should impress—it is a cheap advertisement—without being too glitzy or expensive.
- List all information about the event, including the entire host committee. You may wish to include, as a thank you, major donors who are not working on the particular event.
- Proof the copy several times. Incorrect information will confuse your donors and your most important supporters will not appreciate misspellings of their names!

The Mailing

- Deliver invitations to your hosts before dropping the general mailing to give them a head start on fulfilling their commitments.
- Write hosts' names on the response cards, which allows your staff to track host sales and do accurate follow-up.
- Get as many invitation lists as possible from your hosts so any duplicate names can be removed from the general mailing list.
- Prepare a general mailing phone list that your volunteers can use to call as many people as possible to encourage their attendance.

Publicity

- Help the press do their job by informing and inviting them.
- Reserve a press room at the venue for interviews and schedule as time allows.
- Brief all guest speakers to prevent any surprises at the event.

Seating

- Seating is every event's nightmare. Have a good tracking system in place so you know who is assigned to a host, who needs preferential treatment and who is alone. You can use index cards, a spreadsheet, or a computerized event manger.
- Pre-group tables. Use a large diagram of the room and Post-its to assign hosts. Finalize the seating plan with campaign leaders who know the players and the relative importance of each participant.
- For a dinner, use seating cards. Name tags with table numbers are fine for luncheons and breakfasts.

✓ Eight Cardinal Rules of Writing Fundraising Letters
Mal Warwick

1. Use "I" and "you"(but mostly "you").

In fact, "you" should be the word you use most frequently in your fundraising letters. Your appeal is a letter from one individual to another individual. You aren't writing a press release, a position paper or a brochure.

Rudolf Flesch's studies on readability supply the fundamental reason the words "you" and "I" are important: they provide "human interest." Stories anecdotes and common names (and capitalized words in general) have some of the same effect—but the most powerful way to engage the reader is by appealing directly to him or her: use the word "you."

For example, in one fundraising letter, see how the author uses these powerful personal pronouns to establish intimacy:

You Are a Dream Catcher.
I peeked in on some of the younger kids who were already asleep.
You protect our children from nightmares. You save them from poverty, illiteracy and despair.
I hope you'll keep this card to bring good dreams to yourself and your family.

A singular salutation should be used even if the letter is addressed to a married couple. (Only one person at a time reads a letter!) Abolish the plural "you" from your vocabulary (as in "Dear Friends," for example). Try to avoid the royal "we," too; it smacks of condescension and will detract from the personal character of your appeal.

Use of the singular will require that you stick to a single letter signer. You'll cause yourself two problems by using more than one signer:

a. You won't be able to enliven your letter with the personal details and emotional asides that might come naturally in a letter from one person to another.
b. With multiple signers, you'll sacrifice "suspension of disbelief," to wit: your reader's willingness to accept that your letter is actually a personal, one-to-one appeal.

Think about it: how am I to believe that two or three busy people who don't live together or work in the same office have collaborated in writing a fundraising letter to me? Which one of them typed the letter? (Or was it really someone else?) Did they both actually sign it? These are not questions you want your readers to be asking!

When to break Rule Number 1: You may write a letter in the first-person plural if—but only if there's a very special reason to do so. For example, if the letter is to be signed by a married couple or your organization's two venerable co-founders or a famous Republican and a famous Democrat. Even in such exceptional cases, however, I advise you to craft the letter as though it were written by only one of the two signers, in much the same manner as one of those annual family letters that arrive by the bushel every December. Something like this:

Howard and I had a terrific time at the yak farm, but the same can't be said for the yaks. (Yea you guessed it: the kids were up to their old tricks!)

2. **Appeal on the basis of benefits, not needs.**

Donors give money because they get something in return (if only good feelings). To tap their generosity, describe what they'll receive in return for their money-such benefits as better government or attention to important issues or larger causes served. (Remember: most donors read your letters in the privacy of their own homes. They don't have to admit their own mixed motives to anyone—not even themselves.)

When to break Rule Number 2: If you're sending a genuine emergency appeal, you'd be a fool not to write about your campaign needs and graphically so! But if it isn't a real emergency—and you're really in trouble if you habitually cry wolf then write about benefits, not needs. In the long run, you'll raise a lot more money that way.

3. **Ask for money, not for "support."**

Almost always, the purpose of a fundraising letter is to ask for financial help. Be sure you do so—clearly, explicitly and repeatedly. The "Ask" (pardon my jargon) shouldn't be an afterthought, tacked onto the end of a letter: it's your reason for writing.

Repeat the "Ask" several times in the body of the letter as well as on the reply device. It may even be appropriate to lead your letter with the Ask.

The Ask should appear at least twice in the letter and twice again on the reply device. The request for funds should be clear and explicit.

When to break Rule Number 3: Many direct mail packages are structured not as appeals for funds but as invitations to join a membership organization. Others feature surveys or other donor involvement devices. In these cases, de-emphasize the financial commitment, and highlight membership benefits—or stress the impact of completing the survey or mailing the postcards you've enclosed.

4. **Write a package, not a letter.**

Your fundraising letter is the single most important element in the mailing package; no fundraising appeal is complete without a letter. But it's only one of several items which must fit smoothly together and work as a whole. At a minimum, your package will probably include an outer (or carrier) envelope, a reply envelope and a reply device in addition to the letter.

Think about how each of these components will help persuade donors to send money now. Make sure the same themes, symbols, colors and typefaces are used on all elements so the package is as memorable and accessible as possible. And be certain every element in the package relates directly to the Big Idea or Marketing Concept. Packages may contain not only a letter, but a reply device, a photo or brochure, a reply envelope and perhaps other pertinent information.

Now re-examine your components. You should have:

a. A Big Idea, emphasized on every component of the package except perhaps the nearly test-free reply envelope.
b. The "subtext" (or underlying theme) of gift giving is explicit almost everywhere and implicit everywhere else.

When to break Rule Number 4: Sometimes it pays to spend a little extra money on a package insert that doesn't directly relate to the Marketing Concept. For example, a gift offer might be presented on a "buckslip"—an insert specially designed to highlight the premium—but the offer might not appear anywhere else in the package (with the possible exception of the reply device).

5. Write in clear language.

Use compact, powerful words and short, punchy sentences. Favor words that convey emotions over those that communicate thoughts. Avoid complex phrases or big words. Minimize your use of adjectives and adverbs. Don't use abbreviations or acronyms; spell out names even if their repetition looks a little silly to you. Repeat (and underline) key words and phrases. Use simple, unadorned language, free of pretense.

When to break Rule Number 5: A letter that could have been written by a 12-year-old might not look right bearing the signature of a U.S. senator, so follow this rule judiciously. (But don't make the mistake of confusing big words, complex sentences, and complicated thoughts with intelligent communication: the most literate fundraising letter is clear and straightforward.)

6. Format your letter for easy reading.

Be conscious of the white space around your copy; the eye needs rest. Indent every paragraph. Avoid paragraphs more than seven lines long, but vary the size of your paragraphs. Use bullets and indented paragraphs. In long letters, try subheads that are centered and underlined. Underline sparingly but consistently throughout your letter—enough to call attention to key words and phrases (especially those that highlight the benefits to the reader), but not so much as to distract the eye from your message.

When to break Rule Number 6: Don't mechanically follow this rule. Some special formats, such as telegrams or handwritten notes, have formatting rules of their own. Remember that you want the reader to believe—or at least to act as though he or she believes—that you've sent her or him a telegram, a handwritten note or a personal letter.

7. Give your readers a reason to send money NOW.

Creating a sense of urgency is one of your biggest copywriting challenges. Try to find a genuine reason why contributions are needed right away: for example, a deadline for buying tied to a theme or an approaching election date. Or tie your fund request to a budgetary deadline so you can argue why "funds are needed within the next 15 days." There is always a reason to send a contribution now. And the argument for the urgency of your appeal bears repeating—ideally, not just in the text of your letter, but also in a P.S. and on the reply device.

When to break Rule Number 7: Be careful about fixed deadlines if you're mailing via bulk rate. (Instead of giving a date, use a phrase like "within the next two weeks.") Don't belabor the same arguments for urgency, lest your credibility suffer. And try not to depend on deadlines based on actual dates in large-scale mailings to acquire new donors: the value to those letters will almost always be greater if you can continue to use the same letter over and over again.

8. Write as long a letter as you need to make the case for your offer.

Not everyone will read every word you write, but some recipients will do so, no matter how long your letter. Others will scan your copy for the information that interests them the most. To be certain you push their hot buttons, use every strong argument you can devise for your readers to send you money now. And to spell out every argument may mean writing a very long letter; it may also mean repeating what you've written to the same donors many times in the past.

Don't worry about boring your reader by restating your case: research repeatedly reveals that even the most active donors remember very little about candidates or organizations they support.

✓ Scripting a Political Banquet
Ron Faucheux

Countless banquets are held throughout the nation featuring political speakers. They may be luncheons or dinners, candidate fundraisers, nonpartisan testimonials, professional, civic, or charitable functions

With this much rubber-chicken being consumed on the hot-air circuit, one would think banquets of this type would run like clockwork. Unfortunately, many don't. Often, they're dreadful bores that drag on for hours. But it doesn't have to be that way. This article attempts to explain how to organize a political banquet, keeping in mind everybody's needs, schedules, and sensitivities. The following are tips to follow:

Open with a Pre-banquet reception. Before many luncheons and dinners, receptions are often held to give the audience time to arrive and mingle. Pre-luncheon receptions may be as short as 30 minutes (remember, people are usually busy during the work day) and should never exceed one hour. Pre-dinner receptions average one hour, but if it's a formal event with special festivities—such as a meet-and-greet with celebrity guests and live music—then the reception could last for up to two hours. A pre-luncheon reception need not include food and liquor, but may. A pre-dinner reception would usually include light hors d'oeuvres, but may not if the occasion is informal and the admission tab is small (say, $35 or less).

If the centerpiece of your reception is a big-name personality, you may want a two hour reception to give you ?cusp ion? in case of a late arrival.

Time it tight. There's no reason why political banquets have to last forever. Slow-moving banquets are excruciating not only for the audience but also for the guest speaker, who often has other things to do. Only a carefully scheduled program, with everything coordinated in advance, will make sure the pace moves along at the right speed.

Take care of all internal organizational business—if there is any—during the meal. Don't stretch out the entire program to handle housekeeping matters, wasting everybody's time.

Coordinate program and food service scheduling. At the banquet itself, make sure the facility or catering service hosting the luncheon or dinner is thoroughly briefed on your scheduling needs. If you want salads or appetizers on the table when guests are seated, make that clear in advance. Get the timing nailed-down when the various courses of the meal are served and tables are to be cleared. Often, caterers and facility staffs will follow a timing plan far different than what you desire. Communicate with all of the supervisory staff serving your event, and not just the management or sales people who may not even be there during the event itself.

Provide adequate, specific information to speaker. Give the guest speaker every possible detail that may help him or her, including: (a) a road map if the site is difficult to find or the guest is not familiar with the area; (b) precise information about the location, address, room name, and phone numbers; (c) explanation of the program's format; (d) length of speech; (e) the possibility of a question and answer session; (f) press coverage; (g) availability of a podium, audio/visuals, microphones, stage area, and special lighting; (h) phone numbers; (i) the exact time when he or she will be needed.

Guest speakers tend to be busy people. If they're active candidates for office or public officials, their schedules may be packed with overlapping appointments. A guest speaker, for example, may be the keynoter at two or three banquets or meetings in roughly the same two or three hour time-span. Detail the schedule of events for your guests so they can pinpoint when to arrive and when to leave. Don't demand a guest speaker show up at the opening of your pre-banquet reception and then stay for the entire banquet. Let them know, within a reasonable window, when they will be introduced. Even though guest speakers, should be invited to all of the events and festivities surrounding banquets, don't expect them to attend them all.

Be careful when providing location information, particularly if it involves a chain hotel. Many cities have plenty of Hiltons, Holiday Inns, Sheratons, and Marriotts, and all of their names are similar: the Airport Marriott, the Downtown Marriott, the East Downtown Marriott, the Downtown Airport Marriott East, etc. If you tell your speaker the banquet will be held at "Washington's Capitol Hilton," you need to be mindful that Washington has both a "Capitol Hilton" and a "Washington Hilton." Specificity about the distinction is vital.

Another matter: parking. Especially if the banquet is held in a busy downtown area, provide for parking of the guest speaker's car, or at least information as to the best place to park. An irritated, sweaty, hurried speaker, who just spent 30 minutes circling the block, may not only be late but may also fall short in performance.

Get pertinent information from the speaker in advance. First, ask if the speaker has special dietary needs. If the banquet features a fixed menu, as most will, let the speaker know what's on the menu in advance and offer substitutions if needed. That may be a good thing to do for other guests, too. Remember:

There are as many ways to cook chicken as Forrest Gump's friend Bubba had ways to cook shrimp! Try to come up with a menu that is appetizing and safe. Don't feed people too much or too little. Don't serve overly spicy or exotic foods that may disagree. Broiled or baked fish and chicken are so often used because they are safe. Boring, maybe, but safe. You can always zest up an entree with a snappy salad, appetizer, or dessert when budget matters.

Second, determine if the speaker will bring a guest at the time the invitation is extended. If you want the speaker to bring a guest, say so; if you can't accommodate a guest, or too many guests, say that upfront, too.

Third, obtain from the speaker biographical material to be used in an introduction. The next section sharpens the point why this is important.

Fourth, find out if the speaker needs any audio-visual equipment, such as a walk-around microphone, an overhead or slide projector, a VCR and monitor, or an easel.

Fifth, ask if the speaker has handouts to distribute. If the speaker is selling something, you may want to be specific about what he or she can and can't distribute. Also, if the speaker is discussing highly technical matters that need graphic support, you may want to suggest handouts as a way to save time. There's no reason to recite facts and figures that are better communicated in print.

Sixth, obtain all possible emergency phone numbers to call if the speaker is late. Having an office phone number won't suffice if it's for an eight o'clock dinner and the office is closed. Get car, phone and beeper numbers, if the speaker has them. Also, find out, if possible, where the speaker is scheduled to be before your banquet. If you know that he or she is attending a Chamber of Commerce meeting at the town library, it gives you a point of contact if there's an unexpected delay or potential scheduling snafu.

Properly introduce the guest speaker. Not having a prepared introduction can be a cause of embarrassment, especially if you're rushed into asking the speaker on the way to the podium to give you some quick points that you may or may not remember to mention.

As a rule, introductions of speakers should not exceed one minute. If the speaker is famous, you may want to dispense with obvious biographical material ("Bill Clinton, married with one child, was elected Attorney General of Arkansas in . . .") and, instead, focus on qualitative statements ("This President has made significant strides in opening our nation to the realities and opportunities of the global marketplace . . . .")

Introductions of speakers who may not be household names should highlight current position and occupation, educational background, major claims to fame, authorship of books and major studies, and a short explanation as to why this speaker is well qualified to discuss the topic at hand. Avoid negative or embarrassing personal information or anecdotes. Don't mention the speaker's age (unless it's relevant) and don't discuss the speaker's marital status (you never know if someone has recently separated or divorced, or has just been engaged).

There's nothing worse than imparting incorrect information in an introduction. To say the speaker is a United States Representative when he is, in fact, a United States Senator, is a faux pas of great magnitude. To guess-out-loud that the speaker is a graduate of Ohio State at Columbus, when she's really a proud alum of Ohio University at Athens, is a no no.

If the speaker brings along a spouse, he or she should be introduced for a round of welcoming applause. If the speaker brings along staff, you should ask the speaker if the staff members in attendance should be introduced. In many cases, they are not. Never, ever introduce someone to "say a few words" without advance warning and permission.

Make sure there's speech topic congruity. Nothing will anger speakers more than finding out right before their presentations that they are supposed to talk about something other than what they were led to believe. Be specific well in advance about subject matter. If you want a local state legislator to talk about school reform, and not his or her potential gubernatorial candidacy, clarify that point.

Direct the speaker to the head table. Usually, it's a good idea to have a head table to provide focus to the program. Depending upon the room, though, it's not always a necessity to have a head table that's elevated or set apart. In a less formal setting, the head table may simply be a centrally located table just like the others.

As soon as the guest speaker arrives, make sure someone is assigned to walk him or her to a pre-assigned seat. Speakers shouldn't have to wander around, looking at place cards or guessing where to seat.

The speaker should also be seated next to the master of ceremonies so it's easy to communicate between them.

Give the speaker a five-minute warning. Five minutes before the speaker is to be introduced, the master of ceremonies should notify the speaker. This gives the speaker time to make a rest room exit, gobble the last bite of dessert, or review notes.

Don't ever surprise the speaker with a sudden, unexpected introduction or public request. Always give them advance warning.

Make sure everything works. There are many annoying things in the world—watching a bunch of non-mechanical klutzes trying to find a microphone's on/off switch is one of the worse.

Do careful microphone checks before (a) the banquet begins and (b) the presentations commence. If repairs or adjustments are needed, they should be made when the audience is not focusing on the podium. Inspect the volume. You want everyone in the room to hear without straining.

Always make sure there's a microphone/lighting/audio-visual person available to unscrew problems upon a moment's notice. Whether it's playing a tape on a VCR, using a slide projector, or turning the lights up or down, have someone there who knows how to handle the situation. Fumbling around with switches, plugs, tapes, and wires during a presentation is not only boring but goofy looking.

If you have to turn lights off to accommodate slide shows or overhead projectors, make sure when the speaker is finished with them that the lights go back on. Some speakers may keep you in the dark, but they shouldn't be asked to speak in the dark.

Protect against bothersome noises. It is very distracting when there are outside noises heard during the presentation. These nuisances can come from many sources: loud waiters and busboys, a raucous function occurring in an adjoining room, piped-in music, or street sounds. Try to make sure you select a room for your dinner not prone to these intrusions. The best way to kill a good speech is to ask someone to deliver it over the racket of extraneous clatter. So don't.

Find out about press needs and sign-in lists. Before you open your banquet to press coverage, you may want to discuss the matter with the guest speaker. If the speaker intends to make a major announcement at the banquet or is in the middle of a major controversy that is attracting unusual press attention, special handling may be required. In the case of presidential candidates and major national celebrities, an entire press operation may need to be set up.

In most cases, speakers will appreciate it if you at least notify the press. Nevertheless, let them know what you intend to do in this department before you do it.

Some speakers, particularly candidates, may want to obtain a list of audience names and addresses to send follow-up correspondence. You should decide if this is possible before the event, determine how you will handle sign-in sheets, and discuss coordination. For various reasons, some groups won't hand over such a list to a guest. How you handle it is up to you.

Be careful with raffles and gifts. Before you announce that a distinguished guest will select raffle winners, ask first. Many politicians don't like to draw names in contests—they fear that while they may make one person happy, they'll displease the rest.

It is customary to give a guest speaker a small gift. There are a number of considerations here. First, if the speaker is a public official, there may be a prohibition against receiving gifts over a certain value. Second, don't give a gift that is overly pricey or personal, even if it's legal. A local bar association that gives a state judge a $7,000 Rolex watch would be a bit much. Third, don't give a gift that is large or awkward to carry. Lugging off an elaborate flower arrangement or an over-sized framed picture can be an uncomfortable experience, especially if it's done with hundreds of pairs of eyes on you. The best gifts are usually small office accessories costing under $25.

If you give your guest a hat or article of clothing, don't publicly ask that it be worn. It may be embarrassing, particularly if there are newspaper and TV cameras around. One can recall the stark terror on the face of John Kennedy every time an eager MC handed him a Stetson or some type of ethnic headgear. If the speaker doesn't put it on, don't make an issue of it, let him or her off the hook gently.

✓ Victory in Defeat? Retiring Campaign Debts
Ann Stone

Everyone in the business of politics has faced the dreaded day after the election with a stack of bills totaled at one end of the table and a woefully slight checkbook at the other. Depending on how you look at that table, the sight can either discourage or inspire you.

It inspires me. I believe there is virtually no campaign debt that can't be retired quickly, and that, with a little creative direct response, the post-election fundraising can draw better than the pre-election mail.

I can't promise that the following suggested approaches are all adaptable to your candidate's situation, but they illustrate that there are numerous options to consider for retiring your campaign's debt.

The Victory Letter—Accompanied, of course, by copies of the vendor bills. Try a telegram style that mixes the thrill of victory with the pesky agony of outstanding bills.

The Follow-up Telegram—After the win, send this telegram to inform supporters of the pending threat of vendor lawsuits. I remember one campaign where the treasurer was so upset by the telegram, he called personally to offer a contribution.

Former Candidate Hosts TV Show with Would-be Constituents—I once had a candidate who had a cable TV show during which he hosted a special "Grassroots Sound Off." He invited his donors/supporters to be guests on it, and enclosed tickets to the show in a debt retirement letter. Even though he lost his race, the mailing won big.

The Am-I-Being-Too-Personal?-Letter—The losing candidate sends a very chatty personal letter that tells his supporters how much they meant to him. He says now that the campaign's over, he feels he knows his supporters well enough to call them by their first names. If they think that's a good idea, they just have to let him know on the enclosed reply memo.

The Wits' End Letter—This one's a real winner—probably because it was born out of total frustration! I inherited a Senate debt that was two years old. They had tried everything, and nothing worked, so we went with a direct approach. We wrote donors and told them we were at our wits' end. We didn't want them to have to give any more, but we still had this tremendous debt. Did they know of any other ways we could eliminate it?

The response was overwhelming. They offered to give as often as they could, and we turned their suggestions into a second letter in which we asked people to vote on the ideas that were submitted. The "more letters" option won hands down.

Never underestimate the loyalty and generosity of your donors. Be creative, be personal, and don't be afraid to ask.

✓ Psychology of Silence: Psyching Out Donors
Robert L. Kaplan

There is an art to asking for a political contribution. It is far more complex than raising a few dollars for a church raffle or a worthy charity.

Successful fundraising will come as a direct result of the willingness of the fundraiser to deliver a hardhitting, practical and philosophical pitch to convince donors that they are making a good decision.

Before making these personal appeals, develop an agenda that focuses on the decisions you want the donor to make.

Your tactics are designed to convince the donor that the question is not so much whether to give, but how much.

In the pitch, you must build a case for your campaign that provides a compelling reason for someone to open his checkbook. On initiative campaigns, it might be a pocketbook issue; supporters of candidates might he approached on the basis of access or philosophical alignment.

Whatever the approach, it must be presented clearly and precisely. You must give prospects an "opportunity" to join with the campaign in a common cause.

Make the donors feel good about themselves in their effort to shape a better community. At its core, a successful fundraising philosophy is based on asking, asking again and asking one more time.

The most important single element of the solicitation is how much to ask for. Choose a number that is 10 percent to 25 percent in excess of what your research shows contributors should donate. Once you state your number, keep silent until they respond.

The biggest fundraising sin is to say to someone: "Can you please contribute $100 or whatever you can afford." This gives the potential donors an out that allows them to cut below the mark.

A successful solicitation requires you to pass along information that shows the campaign's or candidate's needs and how they match those of the prospect.

Part of your approach must be to discuss what the impact of their contribution will be. For example, you could say: "Our polls show that if we get our message out, we win. Getting our message out will require us to do X pieces of mail at Y cost. Can we count on you for Z dollars to pay for part of that mailing?"

After the request is stated, stop cold. Do not babble. Do not be offended or afraid of the silence. Make your request known and stop. Period. It is the prospective donor's turn to speak.

Use the silence to your advantage. Observe your prospect's movements to ensure you do not project any similar discomfort, and you will be seen as a much stronger person.

While the silence continues, your mind will race with thoughts like: "What happens if he tells me to go take a flying leap?" or "How long should I wait for him to respond, 30 seconds, a minute...." Face-to-face fundraising is an art, not a science. The point is, you must concentrate on giving the prospect time to respond and deal with the urges that make you believe two minutes have passed when in reality it has been just 15 seconds.

If you are then faced with a series of objections or denials, don't be deterred.

Anyone who is as blunt as to say "no" flatly should be asked why. Listen to their comments, respond to their objections and ask again for the number that you initially targeted.

Don't cut the request.

If you're told no a second time, then you should appear to be the compromiser—lowering the target and reaffirming the need for the prospect to support the cause or candidate.

Handling objections should promote the solicitation process. You should never attack the prospect.

But be ready so you cannot be put on the defensive.

Anticipate the objections so you can address them in your presentation.

Be honest in your response to questions and objections.

When presenting a comparison of your candidate and the opponent, be fair in that comparison. This is no time for rhetoric.

And be a good listener. You're not there trying to badger a prospect, but to interpret and respond to their objections with forceful counter arguments.

Never interrupt a prospect. The prospect listened to you, and now it is your turn to listen to them. Be patient.

If you do not listen, the objections will take on a greater degree of importance in the prospective donor's mind. In listening to the objection, understand two elements—what the objection is and why it is being voiced. There may be two different answers.

Respond first to the most important objections. Weaker objections will often go away if they are ignored as more important objections are ameliorated. Objections can also be differences of opinion. Differences of opinion create the need for different tactics. It is not necessary to have a debate about which opinion is right or wrong, but to acknowledge they are different.

Respect this difference of opinion and do not let it stand in the way of a successful solicitation.

Throughout the dialogue, look for the points of common ground. It is your goal to raise money: To do so requires the maximum amount of communication about shared beliefs.

For example, if a particular contribution capability is a critical objection shows a difference of opinion that contains a fact that is shared, use it to your advantage.

Say something like, "While that may be true, let's look at the 10 other things we agree upon," starting with the shared point.

In the end, return the conversation to the issues you agree upon and to the subject at hand—raising money for the shared common cause or candidate. Then repeat your request for a contribution. People have little motivation to make contributions when things are going well. It is only when threatened with some imminent pain—be it real or political—that donors respond. In looking for the right kinds of themes that should be prominent on the mind of the prospect, make sure the donor has been for the campaign's success. And remember, conflict creates results.

Theme and message are a part of your overall fundraising plan—and they are vital to your success.

The plan serves as the road map to your destination and enhances the motivation and positive attitudes necessary for successful fundraising.

With the plan worked out and the pitch delivered, keep in mind that the donor prospect is highly unlikely to offer more than he is asked for. Therefore, rating the prospect's aspect of successful fundraising. You will always cringe when a prospective donor quickly says "okay" to a request for $100, making you feel that $150 may have been possible.

You may think it is possible to say, "Boy, you agreed so fast, I think maybe I asked for too little. How about increasing to $150?" Forget it. It doesn't work that way.

The fundraising process makes you more of a negotiator than a simple fundraiser.

Realize that generally fundraisers fail 98 percent of the time. That statistic is one reason why many campaigners dislike fundraising. It gives them the feeling that they are not good at it.

If the pitch or negotiation is successful, you've got one last problem: collecting the money. Compared to collecting checks, gaining commitments may be the easier part of the fundraising process.

As with all aspects of the solicitation, you want to remove as many excuses for the donor as possible. Instead of having a donor say, "I'll send you a check next week," or "I'm sorry, my bookkeeper is out today," simply give them a choice as to when the check could be obtained. One good option: "Let me give you my Federal Express number. I need your check tomorrow."

While there is an additional cost to these pitches, you are much better off having the check in your hands and the campaign moving along than doing countless call-backs and reminders.

✓ Tapping the Local Till: Small Scale Strategies
Bill Wachob

Successful fundraisers never forget the basics:

1. It's easy to raise money from known donors. Work at the margins to bring in new donors.
2. The entire universe is your pool. Don't just solicit cash from the usual suspects.
3. Know your audience. Don't try to sell a raffle ticket to a $1,000 prospective donor.

If you can grasp these guidelines, just add some creativity and start entertaining the money right out of donors' pockets. Here are a few fun project ideas to get you rolling.

Do the Newsletter One Better

One-time contributions in the $5 to $10 range may not seem like much, but what if hundreds of them came in the mail every month, and all you had to do to inspire them was make an initial solicitation and send out a monthly letter or campaign newsletter?

For little or no effort—and practically no cost—you can raise thousands of dollars a month throughout the course of the campaign. That goes a long way toward paying the rent and keeping the phones hooked up for most campaigns.

That's what my mother and sisters did for my Pennsylvania congressional campaign in 1986. They solicited $5, $10, and $15 monthly contributions from people who wanted to give but couldn't afford the $50-a-plate dinners we hosted.

Putting together a program that would attract low donors was easy. Keeping them in our stable was just a matter of discipline.

We produced a simple one-page flier and return envelope and began passing them out at every campaign event.

Before we knew it, we had a few hundred monthly donors we could count on. Then we put their names in a database, and every month a volunteer would write a letter from me filled with "confidential campaign information" and dates of upcoming campaign events.

The update was mailed in a standard campaign envelope with a return envelope inside for contributions.

The project was completely volunteer driven, the cost was minimal, and the $2,000 a month it raised was a steady source of income that covered our phones, supplies, and rent.

Art for Politics' Sake

If you're running a campaign in a college town, try an art auction/wine and cheese reception to pull in professors and other nontraditional givers.

Find some local artists to donate some of their pieces and who can persuade other artists to do the same. These folks also should be able to find a place to hold the event.

This doesn't have to be a university-only event; others can and should be invited. You can charge a modest ticket price—between $5 and $20—to cover any overhead and have a local auctioneer handle the event.

The idea for this event came from some local artists who worked on my campaign as volunteers. They became interested in the fundraising process and decided they could solicit their contemporaries to support the campaign.

But they needed a less political premise to attract them.

Once they decided on the art auction, the event took off. One group was put in charge of soliciting works of art. They asked their artist friends, who asked their artist friends, and so on.

A second group was in charge of logistics. One volunteer knew a local gallery owner and persuaded him to donate space in exchange for having his gallery name appear on the invitations. Together, they worked up an invitation list.

They mailed to professors, artists, partisan political groups, and known supporters. In the end we had more than 60 works for auction everything from hand-crafted pottery to some fine paintings.

The event netted more than $15,000 in one night, and having the artist volunteers handle the entire thing meant very little time and effort was expended by the campaign staff.

Overhead was kept down by persuading a local winery and a local cheese merchant to donate refreshments in exchange for free ads in the auction program.

That's kosher for local races, but it may not work where you live. Some states allow corporate contributions for non-federal elections; others don't, so know the law before you proceed.

For federal elections, business contributions are forbidden. So if you persuade a local businessman to donate goods or services to your campaign, make sure it appears on your FEC disclosure forms as a personal contribution from the business owner.

Garage Barrage

If works of art won't go over in your area, try auctioning off household appliances and odds and ends at a garage sale-style event.

Get started by putting a volunteer in charge of soliciting stuff from local business supporters. You'll be surprised by the quality of the items you can collect.

Our campaign was given some 100 items including new lamps and carpeting from a furniture store, dinner-for-two coupons from a restaurant, and an oil change from the local garage.

The auction itself was generously hosted by a local restaurateur whom we even persuaded to provide a buffet table and drinks.

He set the ticket price at $5, and we ended up inviting about 200 local supporters. Some 125 attended. With virtually no campaign staff time or cost and with a nominal ticket price, the auction raked in $10,000.

In Any Event

Whether you are publishing a newsletter or running a fundraising event, involve everyone on the campaign in a way that makes sense for them and makes money for you. In other words, lay out as little actual cash as possible and have fun.

Obviously, events and monthly donor clubs won't fund your entire campaign, but they will make significant additions to the kitty. They also get more people involved in fundraising.

The golden rule is: ask, ask, and ask again. But, before you start sifting through the likely donors for easy money, make new donors and non-traditional givers an important component of your overall fundraising program. All it takes is some imagination and energy.

✓ Plan To Strike Gold: Set up a Motivated Finance Committee
John Bennett

Any campaign that hopes to raise adequate funds—no matter what office the candidate seeks—must recruit a great many individuals to the fundraising process. Without a solid organization dedicated to this cause, the campaign never will attain its goal.

For such a plan to succeed, everyone involved in the fundraising process must understand exactly what is expected of him or her. Specific quotas and deadlines must be assigned to everyone—from the finance chair right down to individual workers. Otherwise, no one will feel accountable, and the funds will not materialize.

The benefits of a wide and deep finance organization will become readily apparent, not only by the volume of money flowing into the campaign coffers, but also by the timely manner in which it arrives. A strong fundraising presence not only sends a clear signal to opinion leaders that your campaign intends to win, but it serves to attract key people to the campaign.

One way to keep your network of fundraisers informed of their progress and motivated to fulfill their commitment is to set up a personal "account" on computer. North Carolina Governor James Hunt's 1984 Senate campaign set up such a system that generated a monthly printout with the fundraiser's name, amount raised to date, and commitment outstanding.

Without a strong and deep finance organization, the fundraising structure described here simply will not succeed. If the groundwork is done properly, and the organization is assembled in time, fundraising activities will run like clockwork.

Campaign Finance Director

The finance director is the most important person in your campaign, other than the candidate and the campaign manager. If the director fails to raise the necessary funds the campaign will falter. The following characteristics most often are found in good fundraisers:

1. Commitment. Commitment is the most important characteristic of a finance director. This person must be willing to work 14-hour days, every day throughout the campaign, demonstrating unflinching commitment and dedication. The director is charged with raising adequate money to run the campaign, after all, a task requiring a tremendous amount of personal attention, and a strong sense of self-direction.

2. **Aggressiveness.** The finance director not only must be willing and eager to ask others for funds but should demand the same ability of others.
3. **Management Ability.** A good fundraiser must be able to delegate responsibility and know how to maximize the abilities and talents of the finance-office staff. The finance director should have good relations with subordinates but at the same time should command their respect.
4. **Maturity.** A mature individual who is just as comfortable talking with a wealthy developer as with a farmer will be successful. Someone who is uncomfortable around people of varying social and financial standing will not be able to meet the campaign's fundraising goals.
5. **Credibility.** The finance director must have credibility. This is crucial to raising funds. The director should be perceived as enjoying a close relationship with and as having constant access to the candidate. (In the Hunt senatorial campaign, most people with whom I came into contact in North Carolina expected I would go to Washington, D.C., with Hunt and would be their "ear" in D.C.)

Creating A Finance Board

Most campaigns create finance committees that cater more to egos than to fundraising. These committees, for the most part, are honorary and not productive. They seldom meet, and their role in the campaign is nebulous. Any campaign making such a mistake pays for it, whether they realize it or not.

I clearly understand the politics of catering to the egos of supporters, but I strongly recommend that this kind of stroking be left up to the political division of the campaign, not the fundraising arm.

Given the Herculean task the finance board should be assigned, never worry about having too many members on file. Rather, worry about having too few. A basic tenet of fundraising states that the more people responsible for fundraising, the less each will be asked to raise—and the greater will be their prospects for success.

Each finance board member, however, should be asked to raise a large amount of money. Their personal and family contributions and the donations of those they solicit should count toward their quota.

The composition of the finance board should be based on one consideration—the ability to raise the amount requested. Do not be an "equal opportunity appointer"; leave that to the political division. By appointing persons who obviously are not heavy-hitters, the board's attractiveness and its abilities will be diluted.

In addition to the error of appointing unproductive members to such a board, many campaigns only ask the "big boys" who have a long track record of raising political funds to join the board. There are dozens of people looking for a way to become involved in politics who know how to play the big-stakes game—often and better. Always solicit outside the regular arena. For example, look for young executives in the chambers of commerce of the larger cities and ask members of the finance board for names of people in their communities who might be receptive.

I have found that many people in their thirties and forties want to make a name for themselves. Give them a chance to serve on the "big board," and enable them to meet the candidate and other campaign principals periodically, and you might find these people will perform better than many of their elder colleagues. In addition, many people understand that serving on a finance board can be good for their own business.

Understanding why people might want to serve in this role is key to putting together a successful, strong board. These men and women are, for the most part, very well-to-do and enjoy a tremendous degree of independence. Nevertheless, you can offer them some enticing rewards, including personal access to the candidate. Having a personal association with and access to the future lawmaker seems to be the primary reason people contribute heavily to a candidate. It is a powerful lure.

Less often, you will find people who become financially involved simply because of what they hope to receive in return—favorable legislation. These few people hover around every campaign, and their expectations never should come as a surprise. Gladly accept their support and money, but only if it can be done without obligation. Their goals are the most obvious and easiest to address.

Who Are Potential Members?

For some people, a primary reason for serving on the board is to gain access to business leaders. The finance board should be a prestigious group of business leaders from around your community or state, and the campaign should market it as such to attract other members. These potential members are likely to be found among the following groups:

- All contributors of $1,000 or more to all of your party's candidates in the past six years. Big givers enjoy associating with other big givers. Generally, anyone who can give $1,000 can raise or give $10,000, if the appeal is right. Lists of such people are easily obtainable. Do not exclude donors to your previous opponents. They might be looking for an open door into a leadership position with the campaign.
I have found some of the best board members are from losing campaigns, and they greatly appreciate the opportunity to become involved in a winning effort.
- Major governmental board and commission members. These people surely know the benefits of being involved in government and politics. They are perfect candidates for membership. Locate lists of those persons who served or currently are serving on major boards and local or state commissions.
- Business and civic leaders. These men and women, regardless of candidate preference or party affiliation, understand the benefits of covering their political bases. Consequently, they are prime candidates for membership. Having these well-known names on the finance board lends status and credibility to the effort.
- Young entrepreneurs. Successful young people who have money either through inheritance or initiative are an excellent asset to a campaign. Generally, these members attract new sources of funding. They are most energetic and willing to fulfill their quota obligation.

How To Solicit Members

The finance director should solicit help from high-level campaign staff members to compile a list of people to recruit. Once this process is complete, the campaign principals must decide the best way to approach each person. This should take only a few days. Every day wasted is a day your opponents might be making that first call.

Before approaching any potential member, the solicitor should have a "sales" pitch firmly in mind. Regardless of how the approach is made (either one-on-one or in a group) an impression should be created that the campaign has a strong organization and intends to win. Very few solicitors work at doing this; they simply start a conversation with a potential donor or go into a meeting of high-dollar givers shooting from the hip. I suggest the following approach:

The people targeted for membership on the finance board are, by and large, business oriented. They deal in business-like terms. A clear-cut plan with a bottom line makes a strong impression on them. As a general rule, they never have seen a campaign prospectus; if presented with one, they likely will be impressed and will think seriously about becoming associated with a campaign with well-defined goals.

The finance director, after meeting with the campaign accountant and the computer operator, should develop a page campaign prospectus that addresses the key issues and costs of the campaign. The first page of the prospectus should be a personalized letter from the candidate thanking that prospective board member for his or her interest in the campaign. It should point out four or five major campaign themes, but concentrate on the that of business and economic development :

A second personalized letter from the finance board chair should follow, a outlining the contents of the prospectus. This letter serves to give the contents credibility—just as an accountant's signature gives credibility to an annual report.

The remainder of the prospectus should be broken down into the following sections:

- Polling Data. Choose numbers from polling data that show the candidate to X be strong and viable with high positives and low negatives.
- Media Costs. Expect everything in this prospectus to fall into the hands of your opponents or the media within 24 hours. For this reason, do not include sensitive information. Nevertheless, the overall cost estimate of the media buy may be included. An estimate on the high side will indicate to the opposition that the campaign is serious and in the race for the long haul.
- Campaign fundraising schedule. The schedule should include the methods and expected revenues from efforts such as phone banking, direct mail, fundraising events (both small and large), and so forth. List these as occurring during a certain season of the year, rather than a certain month, so you do not give too much detail to outsiders.
- Budget. This should be a capsule version of the costs anticipated by the campaign in the different categories. For the desired effect, have it printed on an accounting ledger sheet, and let it serve as the financial summary of the prospectus.

The campaign-finance prospectus should show potential finance board members how the candidate is going to win. It plays to their business sense. It looks like an investment prospectus with goals, timetables, flow charts, budgets, and returns for investors. Finally, it plays to their egos, because it is packaged individually—much as a company packages a plan for its senior board members—with their names on the front cover, in an attractive binder, with personalized letters, and so forth. By presenting the campaign finance plan in this way, potential board members are more likely to agree to serve and to give their best efforts.

Arrange regular meetings for the finance-board members. At these meetings, the campaign pollster, media consultant, campaign manager, finance chair, and candidate should give a presentation designed to reinforce the feeling that the campaign is being run professionally and intends to win.

Finance Committee

In the case of a statewide campaign, a finance committee, in addition to a finance board, should be established for those individuals who commit smaller amounts to the campaign's efforts. Perquisites, similar to those offered to the finance board, should be available for members of the committee, and members should be worked in a fashion similar to the board. They need not receive the same degree of attention, however. This committee will allow the campaign to develop and maintain a large base of high-dollar givers who cannot raise the $10,000 required for membership on the finance board but who want to be on the "inside."

County Finance Organization

No group involved in fundraising will prove to be more important over the campaign cycle than the county finance chairs—again, especially in a statewide campaign. These people ultimately are responsible for implementing the many programs and carrying out the multitude of requests emanating from campaign headquarters. They are responsible for raising funds to meet the county quotas—an essential element of ensuring a well-financed campaign. The county finance chairs should be named as early in your campaign as possible, so that fundraising can begin immediately.

Because of the demands placed on the county finance chairs, steer toward nonprofessionals and young people. Although the campaign will solicit professionals, many of these people—especially attorneys cannot be relied on to spend the necessary amount of time fundraising. Attorneys, as a rule, are over committed and enjoy the exposure more than the work. Young people who want to make a name for themselves and become involved in politics are good candidates. The position of county finance chair carries an air of prestige that can be attractive to an up-and-coming individual. Young people are likely to put in longer hours and approach their tasks with more creativity than older adults.

You do not necessarily need someone with great community stature for this post. When selecting a county finance chair, you want an individual who will take the fundraising plan, follow it carefully, and make it work. The statewide campaign will provide the tools that a county finance chair will need to succeed.

Because these positions are so important, many candidates will want to make the contact personally—by telephone to people in smaller counties, in person to large ones. (Many other candidates hate this task.) Prepare a prospectus for the county finance chairs in much the same manner you did for the state finance board. Include in the package their county's quota, timetable for raising the funds, assistance available from headquarters, and so forth. Organizing the county finance structure is critical to the success of this plan and to achieving your aim of raising adequate funds for the campaign.

Delegating responsibilities to as many people as possible has clear advantages. It provides the headquarters staff with a greater list of persons to call upon, and it helps ensure that the job is completed on time. In addition to naming a county finance chair, consider recruiting a county finance committee. Such a body is most needed in the larger counties and can greatly assist the county finance chair meet the county's quota. Each of these committee members should be given a personal quota, and they should be expected to meet it.

Shouldering the Burden

Creating the finance structure outlined here can remove a tremendous burden from the campaign staff and the candidate. Putting this structure in place early not only allows the campaign to implement fundraising programs locally, but also sends a message to your opposition that your campaign has its forces in place and has secured support from the movers and shakers in each community.

The key to success for this entire system is the finance director. The director must wield a great deal of influence in the campaign, be involved in all decision making, and enjoy a reputation as the candidate's right hand. Otherwise, the finance network will not respond when the finance director calls. To donors, giving money to this individual should feel like giving it directly to the candidate.

Building a strong finance board and (if the campaign is a large one) finance committees, is critical to the success of the high-dollar fundraising programs. Without these committees to call on for support throughout the campaign, it will become difficult to organize large-ticket fundraisers and call on other potential high-dollar contributors. In the early stages of your campaign, developing this group of influential and visible supporters greatly enhances both the campaign coffers and the political image of the effort. Therefore, it should be given top priority.

Consider the finance team to be a big family. These people work best when they feel appreciated. Always keep in mind that they are putting in many volunteer hours, taking on great responsibility, and coping with serious pressures. To make their work easier, the campaign must have the sensitivity to keep these people working and feeling good about their efforts.

✓ Direct Mail Resolicitation
Mal Warwick

A smart donor renewal system can easily be undermined when you pay too much attention to the fundraising ratio—the cost of each dollar raised.

Let's say your candidate initially tells you it is unacceptable to pay 38 cents for every dollar raised by your donor resolicitation direct mail. She insists you drive the ratio below 30 cents.

That's easy to accomplish. Here's all you have to do.

- Reduce the frequency of resolicitations. This will improve the response rate on each mailing to your donors.
- Stop mailing to less recent and less generous donors. This will raise both the average gift and the response rate.
- Mail cheaper packages. The result may be to slightly lower both the average gift and the rate of response—but it's also likely that you'll raise more proportionally for every dollar spent. In the example illustrated here, this combination of choices is projected to raise the response rate from six percent to eight—33 percent higher than under the 38-cent-per-dollar program. The cost of the direct mail donor resolicitation program for the year will accordingly drop from $128,000 to just $50,000.

The upshot of these changes Is that your fundraising ratio will drop from 38 cents to 26 cents, an improvement that will please your candidate.

That is until you start explaining the disadvantages. In this case, overemphasis on efficiency in your donor renewal system would be counterproductive because:

- Your net revenue will drop by $66,000, or nearly 32 percent.
- Your donor list will shrink by several thousand individuals. By mailing 100,000 few resolicitation packages, you won't just be cutting costs. You will also be missing thousands of opportunities to gain new donors, and to bring lapsed donors back into the fold. If you or your candidate is shortsighted, she will pay the price. Remember, your donors are your friends and supporters; you owe it to them to keep in touch, regularly.

✓ Secrets of Political Fundraising
Jill Barad

You raise the money when you ASK for it. Spontaneous, unsolicited, significant contributions are rare. No one sends in money without being asked.

Campaigns cost money—lots of money. Without it, any discussion of a political campaign is merely academic. You can be the best candidate in the world, but without the money to deliver your message, no one will ever know it.

The first question a candidate must ask before he or she undertakes a race is "How much will it cost?" The second question: "Can that amount be raised?" And the third: "Where and how are we going to get it?"

Of all the reasons campaigns don't raise as many dollars as they could, none is more important than the fact that most people hate to ask other people for money face to face. Almost every fundraising device I ever heard of (direct mail, coffees, etc.) was invented to ease the agony of asking for money. Making phone calls for money is part of the candidate's job description: they are the best man or woman for the job. It should be understood by everyone in the campaign that fundraising has a high priority in the candidate's schedule, and the candidate should be actively involved in recruiting the finance committee.

Planning a Budget

The campaign budget must be a realistic compromise between doing everything you think might be needed and the actual amount of money that can be raised. The budget will reflect the various elements of your strategy:

- paid advertising
- precinct organization
- staff
- voter mail

You will need seed money for brochures, headquarters rental, contribution envelopes, phones, letterhead and the first payment to consultants.

Early money should come from large donors, from face to face meetings or by telephone. Members of your inner circle, your closest friends and supporters, should give you as much as they can. After all, if they don't support you, who will? Getting your inner circle together and practicing asking them for money—"testing the waters"—is one way to assess your overall chances.

Organizing the Finance Committee

Key members of your inner circle may become the initial members of your Finance Committee. The Chair should have stature in the community—someone who has direct access to those from whom money will be solicited. It would be helpful for them to be wealthy and have influence with other rich people. He or she should have political or financial clout. The Chair should believe in the candidate, and be able to convince others. He should be able to speak and make a "pitch" at a fundraiser.

The Committee needs the credibility of well-known names—persons with professional standing or visibility in the community, political influence, outreach to organizations and community, geographical diversity, and the ability and willingness to contribute money and to solicit others. Committee members should meet at least every two weeks and share experiences, determining which approach worked and which didn't.

Solicitation Checklist for Finance Committee Members:

1. Know as much about the campaign as possible.
2. Make your own contribution first and make it as generous as you can.
3. Know your prospective donor. Make use of the best conditions possible for asking.
4. See the giver in person if possible.
5. Ask for a definite amount and tell them for what specific purpose their contribution will be used. Confide how much you are giving and how important the race is to you.

Developing the "Pitch"

Developing the candidate's reasons for running will build a foundation for all solicitations used by the campaign.

The candidate should write out these reasons on one sheet of paper, making the most persuasive and compelling arguments possible. Make it as tight, short and succinct as possible.

Be sure to mention the financial goal of the campaign; you may also want to list the campaign Chair and committee members, and important endorsements.

Developing Your Prospects

You must start a campaign with a solid list of prospects. You may have a wonderful candidate, but who is going to support you? Most campaigns don't have to worry about finding constituencies—they are already built in:

- members of the candidate's church or temple PTA, League of Women Voters
- alumni of a candidate's alma mater
- business associates of the candidate and finance committee members
- clubs, organizations, professional societies

Incumbents have built-in prospects from major donors, friends, potential contributors, special interests, lobbyists and constituents.

Identifying Your Giving Constituency

The candidate should sit down with a large yellow pad and write down names of everyone they know:

- INDIVIDUALS (This applies to candidate and spouse.)
- friends, relatives
- professional organizations, clubs
- college class, law school
- church and temple members
- business clients and associates
- partisan clubs
- social clubs
- homeowner groups

This is the chance for them to list all those people who ever said they'd be a great candidate, or should run for office. Have the candidate go through all their business cards, Rolodex, Christmas card list, etc.

- GROUPS (that give to political campaigns)
- PACs
- organizations
- businesses
- women's groups
- labor unions

Three important questions:

1. Who doesn't like the incumbent? (Has the incumbent made enemies?)
2. Who has an economic interest in the office?
3. Who likes the candidate?

After developing this basic list of prospects, have the Finance Committee members use these techniques to build their own lists in a group brainstorming session. You will then have your list of prospects.

Rate Your Prospects

The process of rating prospects is very important. It will help you target and tailor your solicitations and show the prospect you have given careful thought to their role in the campaign. Rating your prospects will help you determine your campaign goal.

Determine with your finance committee:

1. Your potential givers
2. How much each should give. (Go over the list of prospective contributors one by one. Assign a dollar amount to each.) How wealthy are they? How close are they to you on your issue? What is their economic interest? How much do they give to similar candidates or issues?

3. Who will ask whom? What members of your committee can influence the giver? Peer relationships are critical in fundraising. The right person asking can get significantly more money. Before the finance committee members can ask others, they must give first, and at a substantial level.
4. When?

Figure out the best conditions possible for asking. It is important to identify each donor and to understand the profile of that donor. This means not only assessing their giving potential but how the donor expects to be treated. Does the donor require stroking or being taken out to lunch? See the contributor in person if possible. The asking can be done over breakfast, lunch, or in private meetings in his/her office.

Closing the Deal

1. ASK for the contribution and ask for a specific amount. You don't have to be brilliant—just be honest, open, and direct. No cute ploys, no innuendoes, no hints, no beating around the bush. And above all, don't feel intimidated or guilty about asking someone for money. You will raise money when you ask for it-preferably face to face.
2. Now—WAIT. Don't fidget, don't apologize, don't make small talk or jokes and don't soften the request or negotiate.
3. Say, "Thank you for your contribution" or "thank you for your time. May I contact you later in the campaign?"
4. Ask for suggestions for other contributors.

Thank You and Re-Solicitation

The candidate should personally write the donor to thank him for his time and help. A ways go back to the donors later in the campaign. Re-solicit donors several times prior to election day, preferably once every 6 to 8 weeks.

The most likely donor is someone who has already given. The goal should be that each donor gives twice.

What to Expect from a Professional Fundraiser

One of the least understood roles in a campaign is that of a professional fundraiser. All too often candidates assume the fundraiser will come with his or her list of prospects and proceed to call them to ask for money for the campaign.

Sorry. A professional fundraiser is not a "Golden Goose," but the person who creates the climate so the money can be raised. They should plan the strategy that fits you and your campaign, help you find your prospects and help you learn to become an effective fundraiser.

A professional fundraiser won't ask your prospects for money or guarantee results. They will charge you a fixed fee (usually with an up front payment since most of the work is done at the beginning of a campaign) and will not work on commission.

6

Scheduling, Campaign Administration, and Post-Election

★ ★ ★

✓ The 16 Rules for Effective Scheduling
Colleen Maguire

Whether you win or lose, when you conduct your Monday-morning quarterbacking of your election campaign, do not overlook the role of your scheduling operation. Remember when the candidate failed to appear for a campaign rally? How about when headquarters sent the candidate to an airport without identifying the airline or flight number? Or when the candidate showed up at one high school when he should have been at another?

If you won, these stories might, be humorous now, even if they were not too funny to the candidate or others involved at the time. If you lost, these incidents might be why you lost. They are common examples of scheduling problems, and they can mean the margin of victory. Without a doubt, a good scheduling operation definitely is needed to win and often is at fault if you lose. Unfortunately, time is a key element that cannot be replaced.

When you set up your next campaign, be sure to consider the following rules for your scheduling operation:

Rule 1: Only the scheduler does the scheduling. Like the point guard on a basketball team, the scheduler sets the pace of the campaign. With people from inside and outside the campaign requesting the candidate's time, one person must be designated to make sense of the confusion. Fact is, those with whom the campaign ordinarily deals view campaigns that employ a scheduler as more professional than those that do not.

In practice, the scheduler bears responsibility for the candidate's perception of the campaign. If the candidate continually is sent to events where few people show up, the candidate might begin to doubt the judgment of the campaign staff as well as his chances of winning. Inevitably, this causes the candidate to want to take a greater role in scheduling—something that only will subtract from the time he can devote to campaigning.

Here is a mantra the candidate must memorize and use whenever someone asks for an appointment:

"I am not sure of my schedule; please call my scheduler."

This simple phrase will prevent many migraines, and everyone will feel comfortable knowing the candidate did not commit to the Twelfth Annual Porkerfest that only ten people attend each year.

This mantra is important for the campaign staff to memorize, too. In one campaign I worked on, the press secretary had scheduled a one-on-one interview with the political writer of the area's major newspaper. At the same time, the finance director had scheduled a meeting with a major contributor. Neither had checked with me beforehand, and I was left to limit the damage. I determined that alienating the reporter would harm the campaign, and luckily, the major donor was amenable to a rescheduled meeting. From that point on, that infamous phrase rolled easily off staff members' tongues.

The lesson here is that neither the candidate nor the campaign staff should have to say that awful word: No! Leave it to the scheduler to wear the black hat. As such, each time the campaign must turn down an invitation, the scheduler should sign the rejection letter. In this way, the candidate never is perceived as not caring about a group or an event. The most popular reason for declining an invitation is "due to a conflict in the candidate's schedule." All acceptance letters should be signed by the candidate.

Rule 2: Know how the candidate likes to campaign. How can you send a candidate out for a 16 hour day of pounding the pavement and pressing the flesh if he lacks the stamina to do so? I worked with a candidate who needed a one-hour nap in the afternoon; if I blocked out that hour, I knew I could have a strong candidate until 10 p.m. Without the nap, the candidate would be done around 8 p.m.

In addition, be acutely aware of the candidate's strengths and weaknesses. If the candidate is an uninspiring speaker, make sure he gives only brief comments at an event. Also important: Know if the candidate will eat in the car between campaign stops and is willing to change clothes in the car. Finally, be especially conscious of the candidate's "protected" time—vacations or special dates, such as birthdays and anniversaries. Don't fudge on these times or the candidate's family will be unhappy.

Rule 3: Know all there is to know about the event the candidate is scheduled to attend. One way you can expect the unexpected is to design and photocopy your own form that the candidate or an aide can refer to for every campaign event. Such a form should include the following information:

- The date, time, and location of the event.
- The type of event (reception, dinner, or rally, for example).
- The number of people expected to attend.
- The requirements of the candidate (long speech, short remarks, informal introduction, for example).
- What type of clothing should the candidate wear?
- Should the candidate's spouse attend the event?
- Who sent the invitation?
- Will other dignitaries or candidates attend?
- Is the event open to the press?
- Which reporters are attending? Print? Radio? Television?
- On what date was the invitation received?

Rule 4: Know the electoral district or state well enough to get from here to there. Obviously, the scheduler must know the geographics of the area and the drive times between campaign stops. If you have given the candidate improper directions or have miscalculated distances, the candidate surely will speak up in no uncertain terms.

Airports are another concern: Know how late the airports are open and how long it takes to walk from the parking lot to the gate. Also, the runway length of certain airfields will determine whether certain planes are allowed to land or take off.

Rule 5: Do not schedule any event more than two weeks ahead of time. Because political campaign schedules must remain flexible, and because the campaign season is extremely volatile, scheduling any event too long in advance leaves the campaign open to the possibility of having to cancel. Exceptions to this rule are debates and fund-raisers, which must be scheduled with adequate lead time.

Rule 6: Do not have a desk for the candidate at campaign headquarters. Absolutely not. The candidate should be out campaigning.

Rule 7: Do not put a calendar of activity on the wall for all to see. You want to attract spies?

Rule 8: Each request for the candidate's time must be in writing. The exception, of course, is a request from the candidate's spouse or family. This rule protects the candidate as well as whoever extends the invitation. Consider all requests at a weekly scheduling meeting, which itself must be scheduled into the candidate's time. I find these meetings are best conducted on Monday afternoons. This way, the scheduler is able to mail the proper correspondence early in the week and to have the schedule for the following week fairly well complete by Thursday.

Anyone who needs the candidate's time should attend these Monday meetings so that everyone understands and accepts the upcoming schedule. Not everyone needs to receive a copy of the schedule, however. Early on, a decision should be made on who in the campaign absolutely must receive a detailed copy. Everyone else should receive a less detailed, or "clean," copy that has only locations, times, and telephone contact numbers on it.

Rule 9: Don't be afraid of the word "detail." There is no such word as "overload" in the scheduler's vocabulary. When an invitation comes in, find out as much information as possible about a specific event. If campaign staff members or the candidate are unfamiliar with the facilities in which the event is to be held, start asking questions. Unless everything seems fairly straightforward, be prepared to send someone ahead to check out the arrangements. If you do not know the exact location of an event, ask for directions and include them on the detailed schedule.

Be sure to include telephone numbers for each campaign stop. Nothing is more frustrating for a traveling aide than to know the candidate will be late and to be without a telephone number to notify the organizers of the upcoming event. The organizers will be much more sympathetic if they receive a call—and they will be able to hold the crowd—than if the candidate shows up 45 minutes late with no explanation. Nothing looks worse on the news than having the candidate appear at an event where once there were 200 people and now there are only 20.

Rule 10: Publish a press schedule. A press schedule is nothing more than a clean copy of the schedule that is updated every morning. The process of informing reporters of the candidate's schedule depends on the rapport between the press secretary and the press. Delivering the most up-to-date schedule and making sure the candidate shows up on time is crucial to receiving the press coverage every campaign craves. Your candidate's appearances are not the only press-worthy events of the day although you would like to think that is the case. Being known as a campaign that holds true to the schedule will increase your chances of receiving news coverage.

During a campaign in 1983, the candidate for whom I worked appeared at all scheduled stops, while the opponent often did not show or came very late. One reporter told me my candidate was predictable and therefore easier to cover.

The press need not know all the appointments a candidate has, but it does need to know when and where a big event is scheduled. If you are conscious of reporters' deadlines and provide them with necessary information, the campaign is much more likely to receive fair treatment. Reporters do not have to subscribe to the candidate's views, but they must be able to believe the candidate will show.

Rule 11: Establish a press theme for the day. The campaign's strategy team (the candidate, campaign manager, press secretary, scheduler, and whoever else is involved) should agree on the message the campaign wants to discuss each day. Do not confuse the press by talking about too many issues at once.

For example, if the schedule calls for the candidate to stop at a factory gate and talk about unemployment, then the rest of the day should be spent hammering home that theme at subsequent stops. Talk about toxic waste or agriculture another day.

Rule 12: Know your coalitions, and maintain good relations with members. Although it is important to notify the press, it is equally important to notify the area's elected officials and party leaders when the candidate plans to attend an event in their backyard. This notification may be by telephone or letter, although I prefer the written acknowledgment if there is time, because I have proof if someone says he was not notified.

Rule 13: Be an active scheduler, rather than a reactive scheduler. Every candidate receives invitations to appear at political events, but what about those blocks of empty time on the long-range schedule? Other possibilities exist if the scheduler is aggressive, has done all the homework, and always is looking for appearance opportunities. Nothing is wrong with asking an organization's officers if your candidate can appear at their next meeting. You never will know if the organization welcomes such appearances until you ask.

But where to begin? Initially, look at the standard meeting groups: the Lions Club, the Chamber of Commerce, the Optimists Club, the Rotary Club, and so forth. These civic groups have established weekly and/or monthly meetings. If you know your candidate will be in a certain town for a Monday-morning meeting, perhaps the Lions in the adjacent town will allow your candidate to address its regular Monday luncheon. Compile a list of meeting places, times, and the respective presidents of the groups. Community calendars can work for you in a similar fashion.

Another source is the local political party's calendar of events. In most cases, the candidate automatically will be notified or invited of special party-sponsored events, but just in case, this might be an option at some point.

Perhaps the best method for reaching a large number of people in a short period of time is to stop at the local shopping mall. Be sure, however, to check out the mall's regulations regarding political activity. Each mall has its own rules, and nothing is more embarrassing than to have your candidate escorted from the mall by uniformed security men. The list of opportunities for impromptu stops is virtually endless; factory gates and door-to-door canvassing are tried-and-true methods of meeting voters.

To fill other open time slots, ask the campaign press secretary to set up appointments with reporters and editors at local newspaper offices and radio and television stations. Let the press secretary help you do your job by doing all the contact work for this.

Rule 14: Work with the scheduling operations of other political campaigns. Occasions might arise in which you will learn that a candidate on your party's ticket cannot attend a certain event. Staying in touch with other campaign schedulers might enable you to fit such a stop into the candidate's schedule. When working on a statewide campaign in 1981, I developed a good rapport with other statewide candidates' schedulers. Each week, we notified one another of the events we could not attend in hopes that one of the other candidates might be able to fit into their schedule. Such cooperation kept party regulars happy, because at least one candidate was able to attend most every event.

Rule 15: Prepare a briefing sheet for each event. A concise briefing sheet for each event allows the candidate to read about the event en route and to keep the information fresh. Determine who is to be responsible for briefing sheets in various situations. Preparing a briefing for press drop-in is the responsibility of the press secretary, and preparing one for a major-donor meeting is the responsibility of the finance director. Make it clear to everyone that the briefing sheet is due on the Friday prior to the upcoming week of campaigning. This way, the candidate's schedule and all the briefings can be in good order before the weekend.

The briefing sheet should contain the following information: the name of the person who sent the invitation; the time, location, and type of event; expected crowd size; whether other dignitaries are expected to attend; and the last time the candidate visited the area Most important, be sure to induce what is expected of the candidate length and topic of speech, questions that might arise from reporters or from the audience (as well as possible answers), whether the candidate will be introduced or only will work the crowd.

Other information that will better prepare the candidate includes a list of elected and party officials and other key people who might be in attendance.

If the campaign employs an advance person, be sure to let this person know what to expect as well. The advance person must check to see that everyone involved in an event knows and understands the timing (who goes where and when), whether the microphones are in place and working, where the candidate enters and exits, and so forth.

Be sure to file all briefing sheets because they contain vital information, I have found they come in handy.

Rule 16: Debrief the candidate and the traveling aide after each event. For future reference, the scheduler must find out about the crowd size and response, how the candidate's travel arrangements worked out, and whether the press covered the event. This information will be useful in determining if the candidate should go back to a specific area or event. Just a warning though: Sometimes it can be difficult for the candidate to sit still long enough for a debriefing.

Rule 17: Be sure follow-up letters are mailed promptly. These letters are important, but they may be fairly perfunctory. ("It was good to meet you at the Lake County Lincoln Day Dinner," and so forth.) In addition to being a sign of politeness, the letters add to your record and are simply another opportunity to communicate with voters. In the case of an incumbent's campaign, however, another opportunity presents itself: "If I can be of any assistance, please do not hesitate to contact my office." A challenger should plug the upbeat nature of the campaign: "With help from people like you, we will win in November."

The campaign scheduler's life is not simple during the campaign season. Along the way, you undoubtedly will make some friends—and some enemies. But by following the foregoing rules, your campaign is bound to be well organized, and that is nothing but good news for your candidate.

✓ The Art of Campaign Scheduling
Carol Hess

Campaign scheduling is one of the most critical and challenging jobs in politics. After the candidate and the campaign manager, the scheduler should have greater responsibilities and more awareness of what's happening than anyone else in the campaign. It is his job to hold the campaign together by serving as a communications link to individuals and groups in the candidate's constituency and between the divisions of the organization. A good scheduler will recognize that the candidate's time is a campaign's most important resource, and will follow a scheduling strategy that eliminates wasted motion. Here's a road map to that straight and level campaign trail.

All successful candidates must allocate time to raise money, appear before community interest groups and meet both the general public and individual voters. How to combine these activities in a rational manner is the job of the scheduler. And many factors affect the juggling that is necessary to put together a daily schedule which moves the campaign toward its objectives. Some of the variables are:

- whether the candidate is campaigning full or part-time
- the size and makeup of the district
- the energy level of the candidate
- his or her family obligations
- whether the race is a primary or a general election

If you are starting from scratch, don't panic! Scheduling begins slowly, but it becomes easier as you reach out into the community. One contact leads to another, that one to two others and so on.

First, lists should be secured which include the names and addresses of party leaders, elected officials, representatives of community organizations, clergy and other VIPs. The candidate should be present in the early stages of research to provide his input on the people you have identified and additional contacts. Key members of the candidate's campaign staff—the campaign manager, media and public relations consultant, treasurer, fundraiser, volunteer coordinator and research coordinator—should be consulted also. Once you have a good base of contacts and know how to reach them, you're well on the way. But there are a number of campaign scheduling rules that should never be broken and some tips that can make the first-time scheduler's life much easier.

Organization and Details Win

The politics of a campaign can be learned, but if the scheduler is not organized and attentive to details, the campaign can collapse. Get a file box, or preferably a computer, to keep names, phone numbers and other pertinent information at your fingertips; most of the campaign software packages on the market today have a scheduling function to maintain critical information. It's a valuable feature. Any contact, any name that is mentioned, should become a card or a computer file entry. Here are some rules to follow in building your core scheduling file of contacts and events.

Always add a phone number to a contact's name.

There are always snags in a schedule—people don't show, events get altered and other last minute changes take place—which require someone to get in touch with a contact. Nothing in a campaign is accomplished in a leisurely manner; everything is almost always an emergency and having contacts and phone numbers in place will save hours of aggravation.

When entering data into a computer, attention to phone numbers and other contact-specific information can save a great deal of time during the course of a campaign. The scheduler should develop a series of codes (for escorts, organization contacts, VIPs, etc.) which can be used to identify each person in the scheduler's file and which should be entered at the same time as other critical data.

A regular print-out of all volunteers that a campaign enlists can be mined for new contacts to input and tag as well. The scheduler should make every effort to facilitate the communication of such information between different divisions of a campaign organization.

All messages, scraps of paper and other information about events must be forwarded to the scheduler.

The candidate must be cautioned not to be his own scheduler. All invitations must automatically get passed on to the scheduler. Invariably, the candidate will meet friendly supporters who will offer event and contact information. As the campaign progresses, there is too much information for a candidate to retain or follow up on. Missing an important event because the candidate or a key staff person forgot to tell the scheduler is a serious lapse in organization. Be militant with the candidate and the staff about reporting events and contacts to you.

Track all scheduling information in a loose-leaf notebook or a monthly file with daily tabs. Whether you use a computer or not, you need a hard copy of all requests for appearances by the candidate for daily schedule plans. Simple questions can be answered more efficiently by referring to a hard copy of the schedule than by accessing a computer program. And, it often happens that when you want access to the computer, someone else is inputting. Finally, computer breakdown will not result in campaign breakdown when you have a hard copy of critical scheduling information.

Develop a form to take down scheduling information. Most campaign-oriented scheduling software incorporates the same basic data in on-screen formats and in printouts. Even if you use a computer, you need a form like the sample by the phone and in your scheduling file. Try to get as much of the required information the first time a contact is made.

You must also subscribe to all of the local papers right from the start. This is a worthwhile investment to generate a full range of scheduling options. As soon as possible, the campaign or the scheduler should find volunteers to clip the papers. However, it is the scheduler who should do the actual scanning of the local "rag" and circle the events to be clipped. Do not leave the job of clipping to first-time volunteers who do not know what to look for. The clippings should be pasted onto the daily sheet so that the scheduler can enter events on a master sheet or into the computer file.

Another way to learn about events and develop contacts is to establish relationships with friendly schedulers for other campaigns and with staff for incumbent officeholders. There should be five or six people with whom the scheduler maintains regular communication—that means a call at least once a week. Where the county or regional party operation is alive and well, one of those calls should be to the party office. This is an excellent way to coordinate appearances by your candidate with popular candidates for other offices.

You must always prepare a file copy of all campaign schedules and other schedule-related memos.

Communication is the vital ingredient of all successful campaign operations and the scheduler must make particular efforts to be prepared for the all-too-common occurrence of schedules getting lost and misplaced in the myriads of paper a campaign generates. But this is not the only reason for keeping detailed file copies. Once the contacts have been made, they can be utilized by the candidate once in office or in future races; the scheduling agendas can be the basis for his activities as well in the years after the campaign.

The candidate, the candidate's family, the campaign office and the campaign manager should all have copies of the schedule. The escort or driver should have a copy too in another color or in a special folder; this will eliminate the burst of panic when the candidate is on the road and cannot locate the instructions for the next event.

Prepare the schedules on a daily and weekly basis, allowing for some flexibility and input from the candidate and the campaign manager. Ideally, the daily schedule should be ready the night before. At some point in the campaign, the candidate will have to delegate all of the decisions about his waking hours to the scheduler. To assuage the candidate's fears that the best possible schedule has been prepared, set aside space on the bottom of the daily calendar for FYI (For Your Information) notes. Include other events taking place and who is covering them for the campaign. It sometimes happens (only to the other candidates, of course) that it rains and events are cancelled. The FYI notes provide last minute options to the candidate. (This brings up another scheduling nightmare, not adequately covered in most software programs on the market, how to incorporate the alternate or the "rain-date" schedule.)

The scheduler should have worked out with the campaign manager several alternate plans for rain and other major calamities that leave unforeseen hours for candidate activities. These hours might be utilized for such efforts as door-to-door work in apartment houses, or fundraising and VIP phone calls.

Remember: confirm events whenever possible, especially if the candidate is going to speak. Follow-up is critical, but the scheduler shouldn't have to call four times on a particular event. If the candidate misses an event, arrives outrageously late (everyone accepts slightly late) or cancels at the last minute, it creates a negative impression about the campaign—that it is not organized or "doesn't care about us." The outside perceptions of the campaign are a vital aspect of winning. And the competence of the scheduler plays an important role in creating the right impression. Only he or she should make scheduling arrangements. There is truth to the old adage "too many cooks spoil the brew." Too many schedulers tarnish the campaign image as events and "commitments" get tangled.

Once events have transpired, the daily schedule should be reviewed by the campaign manager, the candidate and the scheduler to work out problems, assess needs and capitalize on what is effective. In this regard, the scheduler should serve as an escort for the candidate several times during the course of the campaign to get a sense of what's happening in the field and whether or not the flow of information on events and contacts is working as smoothly as possible.

Ideal Qualities

Peristance, tolerance and unflappability are ideal qualities. Getting escorts for events and arranging for contacts at functions are major scheduling chores, even if a candidate has a full-time driver. Determining who are the best contacts, where to meet them and at what time, often requires many phone calls.

If a candidate is going door-to-door, it is good politics and advisable to inform the local district or precinct leader of the candidate's presence in the neighborhood; it may be important and effective to have the district captain or another local figure join the candidate. He or she should not go to an event unaccompanied. Where possible, escorts should reflect the type of event the candidate is attending. For example, at an ethnic affair, it is only smart politics to have someone from the event introduce and escort the candidate around. When attending a luncheon sponsored by a woman's group, it is foolish for a male candidate to be escorted only by male assistants. The candidate's escorts should blend into the crowd, wherever possible. They can be more effective when not drawing unnecessary attention away from the candidate.

Making arrangements for escorts and events often takes as long as the few hours spent in a particular neighborhood or at a community function. Last-minute cancellations and changes are daily occurrences and cannot frustrate or caus'e the scheduler to lose his or her cool. One scheduler I worked with took each event so personally that after having spent her time to set up and confirm a particular function, she took personal umbrage at having to cancel. She felt that her word and reputation were on the line when she promised that the candidate would show. Every effort should be made to keep to a schedule, but in the hurly-burly of a campaign no plan is inviolate. To guard against potential negative fallout from missing an event, the scheduler should maintain a list of last-minute campaign stand-ins, whether they are relatives or active campaign workers.

It is crucial that the scheduler always be on the lookout for "visibility" opportunities for the candidate. At the local level, candidates have a finite number of people and events and often have more time to get out and "press the flesh." Events providing local candidate exposure might include: a midday fashion show in a local department store or high school football games. Bowling alleys, movie lines, outside bazaars and fairs are good places to meet voters. But the scheduler must be particularly attentive to events the press might cover.

Pitfalls to Avoid

People in general, and politicos in particular, like to gossip. But politicians hold grudges and have long memories; the scheduler is a friendly ear and it may be important to listen, but definitely not to participate. Never tell stories or pass on gossip or you risk undermining a positive atmosphere for the campaign and positive image for the candidate.

The scheduler is a key voice and ear to the outside world. She is always asking people for favors—whether it is to walk with the candidate, meet him at 6 A.M. at a train station or squeeze him into a program as soon as he walks into a crowded ballroom. A cheerful voice goes a long way. Conversely, when people are vying for the candidate's time, a friendly "no" may still be a "no," but it is couched in a different hue. I have known schedulers who were so protective of their candidates that they actually built a wall around them, and the perception of inaccessibility, abruptness and coldness of the scheduler, rubbed off onto the candidate.

The scheduler also may find himself in the middle of family tiffs. Even with the most supportive spouse, there are always disagreements. Politics is a seven-day-a-week, 24-hour-a-day obsession, but don't lose sight of the fact that a candidate has a personal life.

Parameters for dealing with family members should be set up early in the campaign. Careful thought must be given to how much time needs to be spent at home and when. It is important to provide the spouse with a schedule, too, so that when his or her presence is required, he or she has sufficient notice and has planned for it. Regular communication is important so that the spouse feels as much a part of campaign as possible, and schedulers should recognize that they are a critical link between the campaign organization and the candidate's family.

Very often the spouse will be an active part of the campaign and have a schedule of his or her own. This should be prepared by another individual under the supervision of the chief scheduler. The failure to inform a spouse about campaign schedules can quickly lead to a situation in which the spouse is not supportive, or worse, demonstrates downright hostility toward everyone in the campaign and engages regularly in verbal battles with the candidate and staff.

Commitment and Teamwork

In addition to preparing candidate family members' schedules, there are a host of other scheduling-related jobs that need to be filled in a campaign. These include that of newspaper clipper (previously discussed), and a full-time assistant who is fully apprised of each step in the scheduling process to help make contact calls and to take over when the scheduler is not available.

A targeting scheduler is another full-time position, when the candidate intends to do a lot of door-to-door campaigning. The regular scheduler does not have the time to prepare the candidate's walking schedule and should only note time, place and escort in the daily schedule log. In addition to mapping out the district, determining logical walking routes, finding escorts and selecting the areas and types of people to be visited (all homes, all Democrats, etc.), the targeting scheduler has to provide accurate directions and special memoranda on who is being visited and why. If the determination is made that it is important to visit senior citizen centers, for example, gathering the lists, prioritizing the importance of each center and providing contacts and telephone numbers of contacts should be the targeting scheduler's job. Only when all of this information has been collected should the scheduler enter the picture and make the final arrangements.

Another position in the scheduling department is that of a weekend team scheduler. Once the campaign is in gear (in the summer and the fall), there will be or should be other teams of volunteers distributing literature, attending events as surrogates and advancing the candidate. For a local-level race many of these activities take place on weekends when volunteers are available. The weekend calendar must be coordinated with the scheduler, but its preparation, implementation and the collection of names of volunteers should be another person's responsibilities.

It is important that one person have overall responsibility for the scheduling team's functions. Scheduling is an ongoing learning process and continuity is an essential ingredient. There can be considerable turnover in campaigns, but it should be apparent from this article that no one should accept the position of head scheduler unless they are fully committed to a candidate or his goals, and to seeing a campaign through to its conclusion.

You can't be a scheduler if you can devote only a few hours a week on the same day each week. Events are always changing. The unexpected happens. Candidate and staff have to know who to call to get results. The scheduler must be on call so anyone within the campaign can advise him of new opportunities for the candidate or of any breakdown in scheduling plans. A full-time commitment enhances communication within a campaign and fosters an awareness of what's taking place in a community, while lapses in scheduling organization and follow-through can be disastrous for the campaign effort.

But accepting general scheduling responsibilities, brings rewards. The scheduler is always in the know about every event and the candidate's activities. The candidate comes to rely on the scheduler as his right hand throughout the campaign, and will unquestionably notice a smooth operation running on schedule without last-minute hitches. If the candidate is elected, the scheduler is clearly in line for an important administrative post. Because committed and organized schedulers are worth their weight in gold.

✓ Essentials for Campaign Headquarters

The nature of politics dictates a campaign should pay a lot for some things and not a lot for others. That's why campaign offices are not judged on their looks: it's what's inside that counts.

Don't pay a lot for space. In fact, if it doesn't violate finance laws, have office space donated. Even if you have to pay market rates, try to get a month-to-month lease.

If you sign a lease, be sure you can break it once the campaign ends, especially if you lose.

The same goes for furniture. If you can't get it free, get it cheap. The office primarily will be used to store paper and phones, so most of the office account should be spent on those resources.

Phones

Lease your phones, don't buy them. If you win an office, the government will provide a phone. If you lose you won't want to talk to anybody anyway.

You still need a long-distance service, so keep it cheap. Consider leasing an 800 WATS line for a statewide or national race. It's no secret that people are more likely to phone you if they don't have to pay for the call. And look into setting up 900-lines for fundraising. Because the law is still being written on this aspect of campaign finance, consult your attorney and secretary of state or election office before contracting with a 900 service. Also, don't overlook the cost of "dedicated" phone lines for your PC modems and faxes.

PCs and Other Equipment

PCs. Copiers. Faxes. Their importance in a modern campaign can not be underestimated. All can be borrowed or leased, but there are variables in features and financing that you will want to consider. Will the PC handle your database needs? What about graphics for flyers and newsletters? Do you need a special printer? Can the copier reduce and enlarge? What kind of volume does it handle? Can you fax press releases to more than one news organization at a time?

Shop around for service agreements, also. If something breaks, you want it replaced or repaired immediately, not "when the part comes in." After all, no campaign wants to get caught with it's PC down.

✓ Setting Up Headquarters
Rick Ridder

"Why is it Democrats seem to feel that orange crates make the best campaign furniture?"
—Matt Reese, 1982

There is a deep-rooted belief among Democrats that the more dilapidated, scummy, and ill-heated a campaign headquarters is, the greater the righteousness of the campaign. No true campaign could have both the people's and the campaign staffs interests at heart.

As a result, the decor of campaign headquarters gains mythic qualities in Democratic campaigns. Never has a winning campaign had a headquarters that was clean, comfortable and furnished with more than pre-World War II overstock.

Indeed, some partisans have claimed that the reason a campaign lost was because it wasted its money on nice headquarters. This meant the losing campaign staff was working in an environment that would likely have been shut down by OSHA and only maybe had functional desks and chairs.

With this in mind, after 23 years of field organizing, here are the worst campaign headquarters I have encountered.

Richard Lamm for Governor of Colorado—1982: From the outside, it looked perfectly reasonable. There were windows, a square lawn and plenty of parking. Inside were desks and chairs bought from a closeout sale of a nonprofit organization terminated by Reaganomics.

Then it rained.

Every afternoon the staff prepared for the inevitable afternoon thunderstorrns. Typewriters and computers were covered files were put away, and a bucket brigade was formed to place wastepaper baskets at strategic locations. Some days, we didn't catch all the water, and the office was blessed with the squish of saturated carpeting and the aroma of rotting flooring.

Naturally, this building was considered to be such a prime example of a quality headquarters that it was used not only by a Democratic U.S. Senate campaign in 1984, but again by a gubernatorial campaign in 1986.

The Liberal Democrats headquarters, at various locations in England, in 1989 through 1991: Foreign political parties are not necessarily any better than the domestic variety.

The first was in the town of Northumberland, Yorkshire. It featured particular maladies of space and heat—having neither. More campaign staff were crammed into a smaller space than in the Apollo spacecraft. The single action of an individual moving his or her chair created a chain reaction of bodily contortions by other workers.

The lack of working space was compounded by the overcoats, which were required inside as well as outside. It was February, and northern England was more than cold. If there was central heating, no one could find it. Where there were space heaters, there were so many workers that finding your way to a desk was impossible. The entire experience taught me why the Brits serve their beer warm.

Eugene McCarthy for President, Chicago, IL—1968: It was my first political campaign. During the Democratic National Convention, the McCarthy campaign's duplicating and stuffing operation was located in a coat closet of the Grand Ballroom of the mezzanine level of the Conrad Hilton Hotel. During the course of the convention, the battle between the Yippies and the Chicago Police Department raged not more than —yards from the hotel's entrance.

As part of its arsenal, the police used a healthy dose of tear gas, which became subject to Chicago's fickle winds. The tear gas would slowly waft up to the mezzanine level where it promptly settled—for days it seemed. The duplicating room staff, donning ski goggles, wet bandannas, and many other methods to minimize the effects, looked like something from a bad science fiction movie.

George McGovern for President, Billings, MT—1972: Sometimes in a campaign all one really wants is to get a good bed. That wasn't the problem in Billings, where the headquarters was situated at Joe's Waterbed outlet.

Work was difficult because the entire campaign staff was operating out of seats on waterbeds. If that wasn't bad enough, when it came time to go to sleep, Joe showed me to a model bed in the display window.

Gary Hart for President, Washington, DC—1984: It was unique. It was a second floor walkup with one window and that was in the entrance way. Innumerable shelves housed only a few empty movie reels, and there were three rows of seven theater seats bolted to the center of the volunteer area.

Upon moving in, it took little time for the campaign research department to focus on the history of the building. Within a week, the truth was known. Its previous incarnation was as a kiddie-porn shop. But it wasn't only the building's heritage that accounted for the ambiance.

By January, the campaign had run out of money to pay the heating bill. Unless a heating oil supplier could be conned into providing heat without an up-front payment, the office was chilly until 3 p.m. daily. At that time, the movie theater below the office switched on its heat for the afternoon show.

The good news was that within the hour, heat had risen. The bad news was that the electrical system in the building was so bad that turning it on created an electrical surge that froze the computer equipment.

The volatility of the computer was only a part of the office equipment problem. The other part was rarely did the campaign have the same copier for more than a week.

What became know as the "copier de jour" syndrome was the result of the campaign's inability to pay for a copier, so the campaign "demoed" various brands for a week at a time before the distributors caught on that there was never an intention of renting the device.

After a few weeks all distributors in the Baltimore/Washington area had . . . .

[Editors note: At this point, the fax machine from Mr. Ridder's current campaign headquarters failed, and all communication was suspended—indefinitely.]

✓ How to Protect Your Campaign from Danger and Dirty Tricks
Troy King

The world is witnessing increased political terrorism, such as the bombing of the World Trade Center in New York, the assassination of Mexican presidential candidate Luis Donaldo Colosio in Mexico, the attempted assault on Prince Charles in Australia, and the failed plot against former President George Bush in Kuwait by Iraqi assassins.

It's always an appropriate time to assess the ability of your campaign to respond to security or safety emergencies.

Every campaign has one common ingredient: maximum public exposure. Security and safety are really just additional ingredients in the campaign's enormous array of logistics and responsibilities, but they can also be matters of life or death.

On the Road Again

Transporting the candidate from one appearance to another is among the most dangerous situations a campaign faces, especially in larger, more congested cities. Assuming that small or large motorcades or caravans may, at some point, be a part of your candidate's itinerary, the campaign manager should utilize only drivers who can demonstrate a safe and reliable driving record.

Motorcade routes should be driven prior to the candidate's actual transportation. Unexpected road construction, rush hour congestion, roads susceptible to adverse weather conditions or traffic accidents can destroy a campaign schedule if the candidate isn't able to reach his or her destination. In addition, an alternate motorcade route should be considered in the event of all unforeseen occurrence or obstruction.

The primary vehicle for the candidate, whether it's a car, bus or van, should be assigned to one of the staff members whose sole responsibility is its maintenance. This person should make sure that the vehicle contains, at all times, a mobile telephone, a first aid kit and emergency road equipment.

In the event that the campaign is traveling from one city to another, whether by car or plane, one member of the staff should also be assigned the duty of securing the candidate's luggage—at all times. Airports present special problems for security in large campaigns. A member of the staff should make contact with the airline customer service representative and the airport police prior to the candidate's arrival. Both organizations can provide invaluable assistance in getting your candidate through the airport and on board the right airplane.

Prior to the arrival of your candidate at a planned event, the campaign manager or a designated advance person should personally meet with the host committee and examine the program schedule. The advance person should especially note where the candidate will be seated in respect to emergency exits; secure a location for a "holding room" (with a telephone); obtain a name list of greeting line participants and fellow platform speakers; and know where the rest room is located. Consideration should be given to the arrival point of the candidate and to the candidate's walking route to the speaker's platform.

In addition, it makes sense to send a campaign staffer to the event in advance of the candidate. If at all possible, that person should be equipped with a cellular telephone or hand-held radar for communication with the candidate's car. This is not only a security precaution for "early warning" information but it is also helpful to the host committee for crowd organization.

Planning for the event should take into consideration crowd size, speech topic and any expected demonstrations. For security at publicized events, your best bet is to hire experienced off-duty police officers. These professionals can assist you in determining the number of security personnel needed to adequately provide a safe environment for the candidate and guests.

Spy vs. Spy

Volunteers are essential to the operation of a campaign headquarters. Nevertheless, persons with ulterior motives can sometimes infiltrate a campaign to commit sabotage. Volunteers and hired office personnel should be screened as closely as possible; at the very least, obtain their names, addresses, driver's license numbers and Social Security numbers for your permanent files.

Here's more advice for fostering greater campaign security:

- Campaign headquarters will occasionally receive crank or obscene calls, veiled or overt death threats, as well as correspondence to the same effect. These matters should not be dismissed or taken lightly. Procedures must be implemented by the campaign manager for the recording of the calls and the preservation of any threatening written material. The campaign manager's contact at the local police department (usually the criminal intelligence division) should be alerted immediately. If the candidate is federally protected, notify the nearest U.S. Secret Service office.
- Package and letter bombs have become a dangerous tool of terrorist groups and the mentally disturbed. Initial consultation with the local police department concerning the identification

and handling of such items should be accomplished prior to the opening of campaign headquarters.
- Occasionally, the campaign office will be visited by persons who, although apparently harmless, are deranged or are simply looking for "hand-outs." Again, the police department can advise you on a procedure for handling these situations.
- Hot button issues such as abortion are increasing the occurrence of demonstrations not only at site events, but at campaign headquarters. To provide for the safety of your personnel and the security of your office, a security plan should be in place that has met the legal guidelines set forth by local law enforcement authorities. Discussions with the local police department can also provide you with intelligence about any particular group that has demonstrated public violence concerning sensitive issues with which your candidate is involved.

✓ Keeping the Steering Committee on Course
Cathy Allen

We've seen the evidence before: A cadre of politicos files into somebody's living room. The beleaguered campaign manager tries to answer 30 questions; 29 ask why something is not being done. The candidate wants to talk about recent bad press. The retired school board member starts telling stories of how things were when he ran 10 years ago, and everyone else wants to discuss rumors they've heard recently about the opposition.

You guessed it: This must be a campaign steering committee meeting in midtown America.

Steering committees can be roughly defined as a campaign board of directors, a small group of intelligent human beings from various backgrounds who are supposed to be a reality check on the campaign. However, frequently they are ill-conceived, disorganized, inconsistently run and composed of people the candidate doesn't want to hire.

With the increasing trend toward more professionalized campaigns, the whole idea of steering committees is changing. Today's progressive campaign has a steering committee of activists who represent a range of constituents a candidate is hoping to reach with the campaign message. There should be no more than 12 members (special guests can help with particular problems) and it should not meet more than semi-monthly.

Important Hint: A steering committee is not supposed to be a human checklist of things the campaign should do. Rather, it is a reflection of how the campaign message is getting through to the target voters.

Family members are best left off the committee; they will have plenty of access in other ways. In addition, the steering committee should have a few political pros and at least one or two devil's advocates who can question the basic campaign strategy plan.

Next Hint: Beware of the professional steering committee member, the local pot who has been on dozens of steering committees but does not actually lift a finger to do work. You want great minds, but avoid thinkers who are not doers. In fact, the best steering committees are those whose members will put up yard signs, help raise money, show up at important volunteer events, and even take time off in the last weeks of the campaign to roll up their sleeves to put the candidate over the top.

Each steering committee must have a written agenda, preferably prepared by the campaign manager. The agenda needs to reflect the key areas included in the campaign plan. For example, the steering committee should not be debating whether or not to buy balloons for local parades. Instead, it sets the overall budget guidelines and budget allocations for big ticket items like the paid media, staffing, field organization and implementation, fundraising and polling.

Other candidates' strategies—and how they are working or cutting into your support—are properly reviewed by a steering committee. How the candidate responds to a challenge or a tough question also needs to be on any meeting agenda.

Remember that the steering committee is an objective team for conventional wisdom and advice to the candidate.

Warn members not to individually tell the staff, manager, the consultants or even the candidate what to do: they should offer a good list of options from which the candidate and the manager can choose.

Steering committees are stabilizing influences during the most confusing and intense phases of the campaign. Use them to help keep the campaign balanced, with focus on the big strategy picture.

As the strategy of a campaign becomes the responsibility of professional consultants who often are from out of town, steering committees are valuable gauges of local rules. For example, the way things are done in upstate New York may not be appropriate for central Washington state.

At its worst, the steering committee is a tense struggle for power with many members trying to prove how much they know and how much the campaign does not.

However, when it operates best, it is a great sounding board for the campaign manager, the consultants, and the candidate.

Final hint: Choose your members wisely.

✓ Hiring Your Media Consultant
Karl Struble

I got into the media business ten years ago for one simple reason—I thought I could improve its quality. In race after race, I saw political advertising that completely missed its intended target and felt most campaigns were poorly served by condescending media consultants.

Over the last decade, the industry has improved: the ads have become more sophisticated, and the consultants more sensitive to client needs. Unfortunately, campaigns continue to utilize a primitive process when choosing a consultant. They do little in-depth research on the firms they are considering and allow the consultants to control the interview during face-to-face presentations. Simply put, most campaigns are bad consumers.

Think about it. Choosing a media consultant might be the most important decision a high profile campaign will make. Half or more of its resources will be entrusted to that one firm, as television becomes the primary medium by which it communicates with the public.

Why is such an important selection process allowed to be so haphazard and superficial? I suspect it stems from the fact campaigns and candidates are often intimidated by media consultants. We're celebrated "wizards" who earn "big bucks" conjuring up "media magic." And we're usually damn good salesmen with forceful personalities—slicksters with "an attitude." Most campaigns want to believe they're hiring the "baddest dude" on the block—part witch doctor, part hit man—but an honest look at any consultant will expose foibles, blindspots and deficiencies.

To demystify the industry, you must first stop believing everything a consultant tells you. Treat the process as if it were an opposition research project. You can count on us to detail our strengths, but its's up to you to sketch in our weaknesses.

To that end, here are a few basic guidelines that will help you separate fact from hype:

1. Background Check.

Ask consultants for a full list of clients for the last two election cycles (including phone numbers for the candidate or campaign manager). The list should be comprehensive, including winners and losers in both general and primary elections. Call every listed person and ask a battery of questions: Did they get what they paid for? Was the advice sound, the work on time and on budget? Were the ads effective, the principals accessible? Would they hire the firm again? Losers are a particularly useful sources of information, but their comments need to be taken skeptically. Consultants often get slammed when the losing candidate deserves the blame, but if a pattern emerges—buyer beware.

2. Quality Control.

Ask the consultants to provide all the ads produced for both a winning and losing campaign of your choice, enabling you to judge for yourself what the average quality of a firm's work might be—beyond the "greatest hits" they may put on their demo reel. Check with the campaigns in question to make sure the consultant didn't delete some of the "dog" ads. If you detect such shenanigans, drop the firm from your list; as a rule, consultants who deceive you before they're hired will deceive you after they're hired.

3. Headlines From Hell.

Look into the press coverage consultants have received. The last thing you need is for your consultant to become an issue in your race. In an age of ad reviews by the press, check to see if a consultant has a history of inaccurate or controversial commercials. The easiest way to conduct this search is to go to the library and pull articles about the firm or the media produced for their campaigns.

4. Time Is Money.

A vitally important, but often overlooked, component of a media campaign is the expertise of the time buyer. A beautifully produced, high-impact ad will be of limited effectiveness if it is not targeted to the right audience or aired at the lowest possible price. All time buyers are not created equal; they do not have the same skills, experience or research data. One campaign may succeed in purchasing time for ten to 50 percent below what the the competition has contracted for; that alone can make the difference between winning and losing.

5. The Moses Syndrome.

Watch out for prophets with stone tablets.

Some consultants are notoriously arrogant and inflexible. How can you avoid hiring a tyrant? Seek out the appraisals of other political professionals on a few salient points: What has been the consultant's reputation for working with campaigns? When meeting with the candidate and top staff, does the consultant ask informed questions and listen intently to the answers, or do they sit there and pontificate?

Trust your instincts about your ability to interact with such people. While this relationship isn't a marriage, it's not much different. Pick someone you can live with.

6. Summer Love.

Make sure the consultant will be with you all the way and has your success at the top of their agenda. Again, it's a question of reputation; check the references.

Many consultants will restrain themselves from pushing to the hilt for a client if they feel it might injure their own contacts within the industry or the political power structure. There are wonderfully creative mavens who consistently fade in the stretch; they may spread their resources too thin or just abandon you for a more promising campaign. It's easy to look like a genius in July. You need a consultant who will stand by you when the going gets rough in October.

7. Star Attractions.

Whether or not their lofty reputations are deserved, consultant "superstars" do lend a degree of marketability to the campaigns they service. Having a well-known consultant aboard will help you loosen the purse-strings of some PACs and the national party committees, but not as much as is often theorized. Typically such shops run a high volume business where the principal's contribution will be minimal. Assess the tradeoffs and judge for yourself if signing a star quality firm is worth the price—in dollars and sense.

8. How Much?

Fees come in every conceivable size and configuration and are usually flexible—so haggle. Some consultants require an up-front retainer or creative fee, while others prefer to be paid on a month-by-month basis. Try to negotitate a payment schedule to fit your campaign's cash flow and reporting requirements. Like most ad agencies, consultants make their serious money on media buy commissions. If your total buy will be substantial, ask them to commit to a smaller cut after the flight of dollars reaches the stratosphere. Get a good price, but don't go looking for a rock-bottom line. You get what you pay for—so you ought to pay for a media consultant who knows how to win.

9. The Eternal Questions.

Don't be afraid to resolve the all-important details: Who in the firm will be responsible for the race? Who will script the ads, oversee the shoots and supervise the editing? How many statewide, Congressional, or other races will the firm handle? What is the average production cost for one TV spot? Does the firm mark up production costs or expenses? Will they defer some of their fee or time commission in the form of a winner's bonus?

If you let these points slide, you're stuck with what the consultant wants to give you at any given mornent. Don't accept vague generalities. Demand hard answers and firm commitments. Make consultants write it in blood—or, at least, put it in the contract. It's the only way to guarantee you'll get what you require.

So do your homework! Better to be a stickler at the start, than a loser on Election Day. The right media consultant for your race isn't necessarily the one with the most press clips or the biggest ego. Look for the firm that best fits YOUR needs and personality, answers YOUR tough questions to YOUR satisfaction, and will not shrink from serving YOUR interests in all circumstances.

After all, WHOSE CAMPAIGN IS IT?

✓ Understanding Media Fee Structures
Maura Keefe

When Campaigns & Elections magazine decided to conduct a media fee survey, we knew we had our work cut out for us. Disbursement reports filed with the Federal Elections Commission are anything but precise in their descriptions, due to extremely vague regulations. Interviews with the principals are usually even less enlightening: Trade secrets are closely guarded in the political field, and none so dearly as the billing practices of media consultants.

Democratic TV guru Michael Shannon laughed aloud when asked if attribution for his figures could be made, both by firm and specific client: "I don't mind helping you," he allowed, "but I don't want to drop my drawers in front of everybody." Lord knows, no one would want to see that. Stonewalling consultants and cryptic FEC reports aside, a few fascinating facts have come to light.

Media consultants have four main sources of income: creative fees and/or retainer installments; commissions from media buys; production expense mark-ups and bonuses (usually for winning). Rarely, however, will a media firm charge a client from all these directions at once, but the absence of one element may indicate the padding of another. For instance, if the media buying for a campaign is assigned independently of the media consultant, the consultant will receive no commission and will likely charge a larger creative fee to compensate. Here's a rundown of the five major elements of media consultant charges, with an accounting of how and when they are used:

Creative Fees. A flat, one-time charge levied up-front (though often payable in installments). A number of consultants rely solely on this method for their entire compensation. "If some dumb bastard is going to hire me in August after he's all but lost his campaign," moans one such practitioner, "I'm sure as hell not going to charge him less than the guy who signed on when he should have."

Retainers. An agreed-upon consistent amount, payable at regular time intervals for as long as the consultant serves the campaign; the closest equivalent to a salary arrangement.

Time-Buy Commissions. A percentage of every campaign dollar that is spent buying time on radio and TV stations. Well-established media consultants usually have in-house buyers and may insist that they be assigned the task, thus coopting what is usually regarded as the most lucrative end of the business.

A fifteen percent agency commission is automatically built into station rate cards, but it does not apply to political ads. Station reps now invariably interpret FCC rules as requiring them to sell at 85 percent of the card rate to any authorized representative of the campaign, whether or not they are part of a recognized agency.

Because of this unusual leverage enjoyed by campaigns, consultants will commonly knock two or three points from the standard 15 percent commission, if they are allowed to control the buying. They may then subcontract with an independent buyer, who will usually require four or five percent. If the campaign contracts directly with the independent, the rate may be six or seven percent.

Volume discounts are commonly offered with all types of buying arrangements, but usually only for campaigns with a media budget in seven figures.

Production Mark-Ups. A percentage of all expenses incurred in the production of media advertising (film crews, edit suite rentals, talent fees, etc.). Not many consultants will admit to using this form of compensation, perhaps because it is the hardest to track. By denying the existence of a markup, a media maven can keep his other fees high and create more subsurface padding room via this column on the ledger.

Bonuses. A common contract feature among smaller, less-established firms and their odds against clients. Typically, such campaigns have trouble raising money; they can spare little before the election, but will be shoveling the stuff after they win. The arrangement thus becomes something of a Faustian bargain, with a heavy incentive feature for the investing consultant. Those who regard themselves as good handicappers of political horseflesh will be tempted by such a scheme, which can pay off handsomely in the cash-starved off-year.

The subtle differences between these fees can make media billing something of a shell game, and here the hand is loathe to educate the eye about its slides and sleights. Cards pasted to their vests, a few consultants were willing to shed a glimpse of light on this darkest mystery of the campaign industry.

The question which caused the greatest consternation among these reticent respondents was: "What commission percentage was charged in that campaign?" The usual pat answer was "We don't disclose that information." Of the twenty advisors we queried, half reported they did not do the buying and took no commission. Only four were willing to disclose their commission percentage, just one of whom admitted to charging less than the commercial standard of 15 percent. Another consultant deftly evaded the commission query with a quick quip: "Everybody's telling you they charged 15 percent, right? Well, if you believe that, I've got some real estate to sell you."

We also asked our respondents if they charged clients a creative fee, a retainer or both. No one distinguished between the two charges. As GOP maestro Stuart Stevens put it: "In my mind creative fees and retainers are the same thing. The only reason consultants like charging 'creative fees' is that it implies they're being creative."

Whatever its name, this consultant's fee was paid in all but one case—Russo/Marsh's effort for successful congressional challenger "Duke" Cunningham (R-CA), because it was a "shoe-string campaign" according to partner Sal Russo. He claimed any money made from this client came from a small mark-up on shooting and editing charges. "Only three or four thousand dollars came through our books on that one. It wasn't a typical situation," Russo explained.

Why do certain lucky campaigns get cut such sweet deals? Usually there are hidden motives to such acts of generosity. Perhaps the national committee is pressuring the firm to take on a promising-but-poor campaign gratis, in exchange for some work down the road or along a parallel avenue. Or maybe the consultant is receiving oblique compensation from another source—the state party, a PAC, or a political power. Such arrangements may violate the spirit of certain election laws, but are elusive to pinning down and probably legal.

There are, of course, less tangible reasons for mounting a low-budget longshot. If a consultant feels the candidate is underrated, he may figure on the good publicity attendant with a surprise showing. If the candidate wins, he's probably a lock for future business and a dynamite referral.

This is not to say that the consultant with a heart of gold doesn't exist. Occasionally, a cut-rate deal for a cash-poor Quixote may result from genuine personal admiration and/or dedication to a political agenda. Imagine that.

✓ Avoiding Last-Minute Legal Hassles
Philip R. Recht

All the other articles are telling you how to win. That's important. This article just might keep you out of court. Or prison. That's more important.

The last three weeks of a campaign pose a variety of legal risks and challenges. Campaigns perceived to be ahead are flooded with last-minute contributions that strain record-keeping systems and heighten the risk of reporting errors. Campaigns on the wane struggle to find the resources to reverse the tide.

Both sides trade attacks as the air and ground wars mount. Libel, defamaion, disclaimer, and equal opportunity laws are implicated; lawsuits often arise.

Election day itself may bring polling place breakdowns, over-zealous last-minute voter persuasion or interference activities, and delays and irregularities in the ballot count. Legal intervention—ranging from friendly chats with election officials to lawsuits seeking orders restraining illegal conduct or expanding voting hours—is often required.

Campaigns must be prepared to effectively handle these eventualities.

Fine-Tune Your Record Keeping System

During the last three weeks, federal campaigns have two major reporting obligations.

First, they must file periodic reports that itemize contributions received and expenditures made. In the days immediately preceding the election, campaigns must file daily "late-contribution" reports listing all contributions of $1,000 or more—including those from the candidate—received during the prior 48 hours.

State and local campaigns may face similar or even stricter requirements. California candidates, for example, must file late-contribution reports within 24 hours of receipt of contributions of $1,000 or more.

Failure to follow these rules exposes a campaign to significant fines or penalties—up to $10,000 or twice the amount of the contributions involved for violations of federal law; up to $2,000 or the amount of the contributions involved for violations of California law.

Willful violations have resulted in criminal prosecutions. The candidate, campaign treasurer, and campaign committee can be held legally responsible for any violations of federal and state campaign finance laws.

A well-organized recordkeeping system is the key to avoiding these problems. Take the time right now to check your system for leaks. Make sure your recordkeeping includes all necessary component parts—including separate histories for individual contributors, daily contribution and expenditure logs, and separate files for inkind and questionable contributions.

Equally important, all fundraisers and other persons handling contributions must understand the need to:

1. obtain the requisite contributor information (i.e., name, address, date, and amount for contributions of $50 or more, and occupation and employer for those in excess of $200);
2. check contributions for possible violations of contribution limitations and restrictions, and
3. immediately turn over all checks to campaign accountants.

Remember: Late-contribution reports are due 48, and sometimes 24, hours after receipt of the contribution by any campaign agent. If fundraisers sit on checks, the deadline will be missed. Additionally, make sure there is sufficient accounting staff to log in all contributions on a daily basis and keep up with late-contribution reporting obligations. Where your staff is short, hire more help. With fines running $2,000 or more per violation, the extra expense will be worth it.

Review All Ads and Mailers for Compliance with Defamation and Notice Laws

A candidate commits defamation and may be sued for damages—including punitive damages—when a candidate knowingly or recklessly makes a false factual statement that accuses the opponent of a crime, tends to injure the opponent in his or her profession, or exposes the opponent to ridicule and shame. Granted, such lawsuits are infrequently brought, as even the most victimized opponents shy away from the expense and negative publicity perceived to accompany such lawsuits. Moreover, constitutional prohibitions against "prior restraints" make it virtually impossible to obtain orders enjoining further distribution of the defamatory material.

Thus, little in the way of actual relief can be achieved before election day.

However, enough defamation suits are filed each year (with the filing typically accompanied by a press conference in which the defamed candidate accuses the opponent of sleazy tactics) to justify the precaution of running all questionable ads, direct mail, and speeches by campaign counsel.

Along this line, federal election laws, federal communication laws, and many state laws require political ads to carry appropriate sponsorship identification and authorization notices. Broadcast outlets increasingly are aware of these rules and often will not carry ads that do not have appropriate notices. To avoid embarrassment, time, and expense in recutting ads—and possible fines for violations—review all ads for appropriate notices. If you suspect your opponent is in violation of defamation or notice laws, immediately contact campaign counsel to review the materials in questions and your options.

Monitor Media for Equal Time Opportunities

Though the FCC repealed the "Fairness Doctrine" in 1987, the notion that candidates are to be afforded equal media opportunities is not dead.

In fact, the "Equal Opportunities Doctrine" generally mandates that a candidate have the same opportunity as his or her opponent to appear on broadcast media and cable TV, with certain exceptions for newscasts, regularly scheduled news interview programs, and the like. The "Zapple Doctrine" requires the same with respect to a candidate's spokesperson and supporters.

The "personal attack rule" requires broadcasters to advise a candidate, and provide the candidate with an opportunity for rebuttal, whenever the candidate's honesty, character, or integrity is attacked during a discussion of public issues by a person not formally associated with the opponent's campaign.

Otherwise, radio and TV stations must afford candidates reasonable free access or the opportunity to buy reasonable amounts of advertising time.

Other than the personal attack rule, these doctrines are not self-executing. To be in position to assert your rights, assign volunteers to monitor and tape those programs (e.g., news, public affairs broadcasts, talk shows) that are most likely to present rebuttal or equal time opportunities, and consult with an FCC specialist whenever such potential opportunities appear.

Establish an Election Day Compliance Program

Election day poses a host of potential operational problems. Polls may open late, voting machines may break down, registered voters may be turned away from the polls, unqualified persons may be allowed to vote or obtain assistance, poll watchers may engage in improper partisan activities, and your opponent's supporters may engage in improper electioneering and intimidation within the polling area.

Such problems—all of which are governed by state law—can be resolved through friendly conversations with on-site election officials or, particularly in the case of improper intimidation efforts, calls to the local police. Sometimes, however, court intervention is necessary, especially when an order is sought extending polling hours.

Train workers in the key voting entitlement and polling place rules of your state. Place workers at the polls with instructions to resolve problems through friendly persuasion of on-site election officials. When problems persist, workers should contact the campaign manager or counsel.

In the meantime, counsel should prepare for the possibility of court intervention by drafting court papers concerning anticipated problems and determine which court or judge will handle, and what procedures will govern, those problems that may arise.

Observe the Count and Preserve Your Options for a Challenge

Stories are legion of delays in election night tallies; worse yet, of miscounts and alteration or destruction of ballots and absentee ballot applications—all of which are necessary to reconstruct the true results.

Particularly in close races, it is crucial to guard against fraud in the count and to take the necessary steps to preserve the campaign's right and ability to challenge the election results.

To do so, familiarize yourself with the applicable rules—again, state law governs this area—concerning the time, place, and manner of vote counting, as well as the steps and deadlines that must be taken and met to challenge precinct results and absentee ballots.

On election eve, station observers at all significant locations with instructions to assert the campaign's rights whenever an irregularity appears. Observers should be instructed to take detailed notes of all such incidents so as to assist the campaign in the inevitable day-after analysis of its options.

✓ Post-Election Duties
Maren Hesla

Standing in your headquarters, looking at the pile of beer bottles in one corner, the overflowing trash cans, and the bedraggled strands of crepe paper, you know that finally it's all over. You won. You lost. In some ways it doesn't matter, because in either case there is still a long list of things that need to be done.

Win or lose, election day doesn't mean the campaign's completely over. Don't make the mistake of thinking that your defeat (or your victory) has freed you from obligations. Loose ends left untied will inevitably trip you up.

"Why bother?" you ask. If you're confident that you'll never run for office, raise a family, do business, or otherwise participate in the community in which you ran, then you don't need to worry about post-election responsibilities. But most of us have a real life we're returning to, or further political ambitions. In either circumstance it's critical that we take a few simple steps to close up shop.

FEC Reports

Your most important obligation is a legal one. If you ran in a federal election, don't forget that last FEC report. You're required to file a post-general election report—days after the general election. According to Scott Moxley at the FEC, the maximum fine for failure to file is $5,000. The maximum fine for a knowing and willful violation is $10,000. Local and state laws vary, but almost all states require some sort of closing report.

Debt Organization

Next on the must-do list is developing a plan to deal with your debts. Sit down with your accountant and prepare a list of all outstanding accounts. Friends and supporters might be willing to forgive your debt. Others will be willing to settle for a smaller amount than you actually owe. Remember that individuals are still limited by the maximum contribution laws. Make sure that any debt "forgiveness" complies with election rules.

You must contact each and every person and vendor to whom you owe money to determine the minimum amount of money she requires. Don't make assumptions.

After you've totaled all your obligations, work with your creditors to determine a schedule of payments.

If you owe your media consultant $1,000 in last-minute production expenses, she'd much rather arrange a $100-per-month payment for 10 months then have you disappear into the woodwork.

The key point is to communicate with people. Let them know you're aware of your financial obligations and that you intend to fulfill them.

Fundraising

I won't sugarcoat it: the most difficult type of fundraising is debt retirement for someone who lost. Conversely, it can be a positive joy to retire the debt of a winner. There's something perversely delightful in asking for $1,000 from someone who wouldn't return your calls last week.

If you've organized your debt, then you know how much money you need, and when you need it. In some instances, the easiest thing to do is get a loan, pay off all your debts, and then owe just one bank. The danger in this plan is that the interest payments can mount quickly. Whatever your approach, have a fundraising plan to meet your payments in a timely manner.

Keep in mind that elections end just as the holiday season is beginning. Fundraising in November and December can be difficult. Your primary targets are your contributors who never gave the maximum. Don't overlook contributors who have maxed out but whose spouses never contributed. The bottom line is that you need a written plan with timelines for various activities (mailings, appreciation dinners, one-on-one solicitation) that will bring in enough money for you to meet your obligations.

Utilities and Final Bills

In addition to the pre-election debt, you're going to have some final bills rolling—phone, electric, etc. Make sure these bills have a way of getting to you (see forwarding address, below) and don't forget to budget for them, keeping in mind the monies already paid if a deposit was required. Also, don't forget to disconnect all the appropriate utilities.

Thank-you Notes

They're not just for weddings anymore. Taking the time to send out a short letter to your contributors, volunteers, supporters, and even your staff will reassure everyone that their effort was worthwhile, whether or not it was successful.

Many folks will want to know about your plans for the future. A thank-you note can lay the groundwork for your next run for office or establish that you're returning to private practice. One pleasant letter goes a long way toward fostering the goodwill that you'll need if you want to ask people for their help in the future.

Thank-you notes are just as important for winners as losers. The last rap you need is "now that she's elected, she's forgotten about all us little people." One good letter can put that fear to rest. Inevitably there will be some discussion within the campaign on whether or not to include a fundraising pitch in the thank-you notes. Call me a slave to Miss Manners, but I strongly favor a letter of appreciation with no requests for contributions.

If you did your job correctly, these people were probably solicited relentlessly for the last three months. Give 'em a break! And on the pragmatic side, you might be able to get more out of them if they have received a letter that reminds them why they supported you in the first place.

List Collection

In the final weeks of the campaign phone lists, yard sign lists, volunteer lists, and donor lists all got farmed out to a multitude of people when your lines at the office were so clogged that no one could call in or out.

Get those lists back—especially the donor lists. If you're ever going to run for office again, those lists are your most important asset. If you're one of the fortunate campaigns that kept everything on computer, it's not a question of retrieval as much as cleanup. Ask your resident computer jockey to print out a final copy of all your different lists, and make sure you've saved everything on clearly labeled disks.

Follow Up on Your Buy

Your media buyer should compare the time that was bought with what stations actually aired. In some cases there's a discrepancy and you may be owed money. Most firms do this automatically. If you bought your own media or used a firm that doesn't ordinarily buy political ads, you need to follow up and ensure that this gets done.

Forwarding Address

You'd be amazed by how many campaigns fail to leave a forwarding address with the post office. The forwarding address can be the candidate's home or a post office box. What's important is to make sure people can continue to reach you after you've closed your office.

Loaned Items

The trusty coffee maker. The old but adequate Xerox machine. Many such items are loaned to a campaign. It's your responsibility to return them to the proper owner. Usually you can sell anything the campaign bought that can't be stored or will be obsolete by the next election.

Yard Signs

Many communities have a local ordinance that specifies how long after the election yard signs can stay up. While most of your supporters will take care of the signs themselves, others, especially seniors, need your assistance. Give someone the specific task of cleaning up yard signs. You may even want to implement a yard sign recycling program.

Analysis Weekend

An analysis weekend can be your most productive post-election activity. November or December, while everyone's memory is still fresh, is the best time to review your campaign. What worked well? What failed? Where did we exceed our expectations? Where did we fall short? Why?

This is a useful experience for winners as well as losers. If you plan to run again, this is a wonderful start to your coalition building. Ask members of the labor community to come in and talk about whether you utilized their assets. Ask your fundraising committee to discuss your financial goals. Everyone will have an opinion. It's important to give people a forum in which to share those thoughts. You'll probably harvest a number of useful ideas for the next campaign.

A post-election analysis should be organized with a specific agenda, questions, and goals. Don't trade war stories; take a critical look at your efforts with an eye toward improving the results. Right now you may be dreaming about a month on the beach in a pina colada-induced haze, beginning November 4. But take time in those dreams for a little practical activity, and you'll end 1992 with a jump on 1994.

✓ How to Knock Down Your Campaign Structure
Alexander B. Thomson

Perhaps the most tedious job faced by an electioneer is the closing down of a campaign. The excitement and adrenaline that carried to you through months on the trail and 18-hour days leading up to the election are gone. The only tasks remaining are mundane—paying bills, filing reports, and moving equipment and documents.

Though "close-down" is anti-climactic, this final phase of the campaign can be extremely important. Poorly executed, it could lose thousands of dollars and condemn campaign principals to a myriad of legal and financial problems.

To avoid such transitional problems, a campaign manager should use the following set of simple guidelines:

Secure Equipment

Two weeks before Election Day, the campaign "mop-up" team should re-confirm the location of all campaign equipment, securing any part of it that will not be used in the closing days of the effort.

Also prior to the election the "close-down coordinator" should schedule the pick up of all other rented equipment for the day after the election.

Although you may need one or two items for a short post-election period, try to have all equipment returned as soon as possible. Even though it may be paid for through the end of the month, resist the temptation to keep it unless the item is actually needed in closing operations. The more quickly equipment is returned, the faster you can address other tasks. Particular care should be taken in securing the phone system. Any experienced campaign manager will tell you that telephones have a way of disappearing after an election.

As Judgment Day nears, many of the campaign's phones can be consolidated for GOTV use in a central location. When the staff moves to the victory celebration on election night, collect and secure all phones in the headquarters. Any cellular phones, beepers, fax machines, and similar equipment should be locked away as well. These assets alone may account for several thousand dollars which can be used to pay off the debt and properly close down the campaign.

Pre-arrange with the phone company to disconnect most of your telephone service the morning after the election. The well-timed cutoff of services will hasten the return of your phone line deposits and can save a campaign hundreds (maybe thousands) of dollars in service and extraneous long distance charges. The lines can be shut off as soon as the move to a wrap-up office is accomplished.

Document Retention

The campaign's financial and administrative records may prove to be vitally important. Lists and documents should be moved at regular intervals to a secure location; a well-documented inventory should be kept by the custodian of this repository. It would also be wise to provide receipts to each local office manager who turns over items for safekeeping.

Headquarters

When signing a headquarters lease, be sure it covers a brief post-election period for closing operations. Two or three days should be all that is needed to shut down a "field" office. Your central headquarters should take a couple weeks to shut down. Your "close-down office" should be established and functioning before the election, serving as the repository for all records and equipment no longer necessary for immediate operations. Access to this office should be tightly controlled to avoid the loss of these valuable and important items.

This is not a momentary enterprise: small campaigns will need to maintain their closedown office until roughly three months past the election; the same phase may extend more than a year for a major federal campaign. A place to store all financial records will be needed for three years.

Vendor/Debts

Contact all your vendors and suppliers immediately after the election to request a final invoice. Inform them of the location of your close down office and provide them with an honest opinion regarding when they will get paid. Most vendors know that it will take time to clear any outstanding balance at the end of a campaign. Keeping them informed of your efforts to clear the debt makes for better working relationships. Discuss and arrange payment schedules if that is realistic.

FEC/SEB Reports

The Federal Election Commission (FEC) and most state election boards (SEBs) require the full disclosure of all campaign debts. Fundraising to retire debts usually must conform to the contribution limits and other regulations which applied during the campaign. A federal campaign cannot formally "go out of business" while it still has debt. Detailed procedures apply to debt settlement and must be followed to the letter. During the period that debt is being paid off, regular FEB/SEB reports must be filed, disclosing income and expenses. The candidate or even campaign officials may well be held liable for some campaign debts [see sidebar]. Any sale of equipment, donation of supplies, income from list rental or transfer of assets (to a new committee or the party) must also be disclosed.

Promptly file a forwarding address (that of the close-down office) with your local post office as soon as your central HQ closes. If you had a number of field offices, you should file a change of address for each location. This move will speed delivery of late contributions as well as bills and invoices.

Taxes and other Reports

Most serious campaigns for mid-level office and above pay at least a few staffers; they will be required to file both final-quarter and year-end statements and payments for federal payroll taxes. Final payments into state unemployment funds and other required state taxes must also be made in a timely fashion.

The campaign must prepare and provide a W-2 Wage statement for each employee who was paid more than $250 by the campaign in a calendar quarter. These statements reflect federal, state, and FICA taxes withheld as well as any other state requirements. Consultants receive a similar document—Form 1099—which reports all fees over $600 paid to them by the campaign.

These documents can be prepared immediately following final payroll, and must be submitted no later than January 31. If payroll continues into the next year, another set of tax filings will be required for that year as well. Some campaigns are required to file an IRS tax form 1120 POL which taxes a campaign on its interest and unrelated income. That form is due by the 15th day of the third month following the end of the year, but extensions are available.

Many states require monthly or quarterly filings as long as wages are being paid. Other state requirements may include an annual franchise tax, organizational officer disclosure, or permit to occupy offices. Although compliance with these requirements can be a nuisance, it is important to remember that constituents deal with similar paperwork burdens; much negative publicity and ill will can be created by the mismanagement of a campaign's business affairs.

✓ Surviving Transition Travails
Mark Siegel

The glow of victory is a rush. It is also short lived. Almost as soon as the keg runs dry at the victory party, you must begin the transition from campaign to public office. Converting your electoral apparatus into a legislative/administrative support team is a daunting task. Hundreds of important decisions must be made in an extremely short amount of time. In order to hit the ground running and make a positive impression on the press and your new colleagues and constituents, your transition planning must be flawless and well-timed.

The following is a step-by-step guide to make your ascension to power as successful as possible.

Step I: Choosing A Chief-of-Staff

The choice of a top lieutenant is the most important decision faced by a newly elected politician. The CS (or AA—for Administrative Assistant) will be responsible for the smooth operation of the legislative/executive office and will advise the new office holder in his/her official decisions. This position demands complete trust and is often filled by the longtime aide or friend who ran the campaign do not, however, however, feel obligated to give this position to your campaign manager: your political success relies on the professionalism and competence of your CS/AA. Choose the best available.

Once this position has been filled, the next CS/AA should immediately be installed near the seat of government. In the case of congressional AA, he will actually be provided with a temporary cubby hole in the foyer of the Rayburn Office Building several weeks before his boss is sworn in.

Having a representative in the capital or city hall lobbying on your behalf is invaluable—especially in the days before a new government is installed, when there is much jockeying for committee selections, office space, and staff.

Step II: Retiring The Campaign Debt

You do not want to bring financial baggage into your new office. Since you have won, the task of retiring your campaign debt should not be difficult. Those who supported you in the past will surely follow up on their successful investment, and you can now expect political action committees and interested individuals who may have been on the "wrong side" of the campaign to do their penance. Assisting with debt retirement efforts gives them an immediate means of making amends.

Step III: Hiring A Staff

Every new congressman is allowed to hire 16 full-time and two part-time administrative staffers on a payroll exceeding a half-million dollars; other public offices are given similarly structured allowances for support personnel. If you are an elected representative, you'll want to divide your staff between your district and the seat of government. Rural districts may require multiple small district offices. The more urban the district, the smaller the local staff required for a thorough constituent service apparatus. Don't hire your full complement of staffers immediately; reserve a few positions until you get feedback about where you need the most manpower.

According to Earl Bender, a Democratic campaign consultant who has helped organize many congressional offices, "hire at least someone—a former AA, legislative director, or office manager who knows where things are, how to get office supplies, where a bill goes after it's introduced, how to deal with legislative counsel, which direction the bathroom is in." Reinventing the wheel will not serve your (or your constituents') political interests.

After you get your committee assignments, recruit committee staff members with the necessary public policy expertise. Concentrate on those with knowledge of the internal workings of the legislative body and your committee. Strong preference should be given to a competent staffer from your own area, as well as your own party.

Most governments have a clearinghouse for employment information that can be a helpful conduit of talent, but they may be legally restricted from providing sensitive partisan information. Some partisan groups keep a talent bank with a fuller picture of information and should be your first stop for resumes. Not that resumes will be hard to come by; you'll be deluged with them.

Step IV: Lobbying For Committee Assignment

The fate of your political career may hinge on committee assignments. Clearly notify your legislative body's steering committee of your committee preferences. Contact your party leadership as well as the individual members of the steering committee to enlist their support for your choices (hopefully you will have had the good judgment to make some preliminary contacts here during the campaign). Have the dean of your local delegation working on your side.

As a freshman, you will want assignments that give you instant visibility and credibility. Foreign Affairs or Judiciary are intellectually stimulating, but rarely do they bring the bacon home to your district. Cross pollinate your district's needs with your intellectual preferences.

Step V: Establishing Press Operations

Consider keeping your campaign press secretary in the district office, where your public relations effort will be focused. A legislative assistant in the capital office can act as supplementary press secretary. Regardless of your decision, make sure that you have at least one communications expert within your staff. Ensure that this person has extensive press experience in the capital.

Step VI: Setting Up A Constituent Service System

People assume you're in office from the moment your elected. Starting in early November, you will receive bagfuls of mail dealing with policy issues and casework. Acknowledge receipt of the mail, and indicate that a substantive response will follow as soon as possible after you are sworn in. Establish a mail tracking system, perhaps under the direction or advice of a direct mail consultant. Most of your constituents will interact with you exclusively through the mail; the form, content, style, and speed of your response will shape their perceptions of your competence.

Step VII: Coordinating With Your Predecessor

Same-party replacements usually present few transitional obstacles, but a smooth transfer of power can be difficult if you are dealing with an incumbent whose butt you've just kicked. Have your AA glean as much information from the outgoing staff as possible, and begin working with them—at least on the constituent caseload—prior to your swearing-in. Maintaining an amiable relationship with the previous officeholder and their staff can reap enormous benefits in the form of bequeathed equipment, databases and inside tips.

Step VIII: Making The Most of Orientation Events

The administration committees of Congress and many legislatures conduct training sessions and publish manuals for new members and their AAs. Harvard University (Cambridge, MA) also conducts a valuable training seminar for new congressmen in the month following each biennial election. Take full advantage of these resources. The sessions are instructive, and early interaction with the members of your freshman class can give you a head start in the politics of the chamber. Good friends make useful colleagues.

Step IX: Getting A Jump On The Office Space Scramble

As a freshman, you'll be at the back of the line for office space assignments. Inspect the available options and rank your preferences; there is a drawing for office space and you won't have much time for such decisions once the process begins. Occupying the best available space is more important than it may seem. Reality often follows perception in politics, and you'll need to make a good impression from the very beginning. Visitors from the district will swarm your office at your swearing-in; if the office looks smooth and functioning, constituents and the press will presume you've hit the ground running and forget suspicions that you may be in over your head.

Step XX: Launching The Re-Election Effort

You're still a candidate and still running. Don't close down your campaign office entirely; leave it staffed for a few months, possibly indefinitely. Fundraising in particular must begin immediately, whether you have incurred a debt or not. But the best re-election campaign tactic is establishing a good reputation in office, and the first weeks of your first term will be critical to this task. Well-executed constituency service is the key to consolidating, expanding and intensifying your electoral base; good press relations from the outset could generate substantial and positive press coverage for years. Always give constituents—especially influential supports—access to the decision making process, but without guarantees of outcome. Remember, while no vote is devoid of political impact, good policy and good politics need not be mutually exclusive.

✓ Four Reasons to Retain Your Campaign Staff After You Win
Robert W. Doyle

The thrill and emotion of the victory party soon gives way to the reality of assuming office. All of a sudden, you, the candidate, are the public official-elect.

The voters of your city, county, district, or state have placed their confidence in your ability to lead. Sure, you and your campaign staff ran a remarkably organized and effective campaign. But, who will you now turn to as your right hand?

Often, the answer to that question is: your campaign staff. Perhaps the most serious challenge that faces incumbents from the county sheriff to the congressperson-elect is selecting the right staff to organize a newly won office. Former campaign staffers offer these four key advantages as transition and administration staffers:

1. Campaign staff know you and understand your agenda.

You and your campaign staffers have slaved together and built a mutual understanding and respect. Campaign staffers are familiar with the way you like to do business. They know what makes you tick. They know your family and the demands of your not-so-public life. They understand your idiosyncrasies and have become expert in lifting your spirit. The same people who wrote last-minute campaign ads and press releases at 3 a.m. are the ones who know you, and more importantly your political agenda, best.

Too often the glowing promises that candidates make during the campaign become lost in the administration. Naysayers and bureaucrats dismiss your ideas because "that is just not the way it is done." Academics and opponents have other ideas that sound less risky now that you are in office. As the incumbent, you are less likely to be bold and make the major changes that sounded good from your former perspective as an outsider.

Campaign staffers have a way to cut through these problems. They are the ones that preached your campaign gospel. They are the most loyal to your message and they feel a personal stake in its realization. Their continued involvement in the process will ensure strong support and constant awareness of the political agenda upon which you were elected.

2. Campaign staff know your district and its people.

Your campaign staff has memorized the precinct maps of your district. They know which streets are boundaries for each precinct, and they know which areas have high party performance. Further, they know the Rotary Club president, the Chamber of Commerce Chair, and the administrator of the local senior center. Simply, they know your district, and the movers and shakers. Most likely, they have accompanied you to speaking engagements throughout the district, and talked to community leaders more than once about your candidacy.

Campaign staffers also know the kind of people you represent. They fielded the calls in your campaign headquarters from citizens who complained about your position on taxes. They maintained constant contact with the 75 volunteers who got-out-the-vote for your campaign. And, they read the local letters to the editor, knocked on voters' doors, and talked with literally hundreds of local voters.

3. Campaign staff can provide political input and advice.

Throughout the course of your incumbency, former campaign staffers have a unique perspective: that of political advisor. Since the root of their interest was the campaign and its political impact, they evaluate every issue for its political significance. Their help and advice can be invaluable. Their insight could help you avoid a potentially damaging local issue, or accomplish something that made up a major portion of your campaign platform. They are a constant "political conscience" that offers daily reminders of the promises of the campaign. They can help keep you on track.

Campaign staffers also tend to be more "people oriented." They are familiar with dealing with citizens and finding out answers and diffusing problems. Campaign staffers are less likely to get bogged down in day to day administrative details. They will understand the overall objective, and help you to stay the course of your campaign commitments. They are prepared to drum up grassroots support in the community for your initiatives, and they know how to organize and prepare public relations campaigns for specific proposals.

4. Campaign staff are loyal and dependable.

You largely entrusted your political and personal reputation to the actions and discretion of your campaign staff. As they join you in office, campaign staff retain that remarkable sense of loyalty and mission. Chances are they got involved in government with you, and will leave the office when you do. You and your staff have been through the fires of the campaign and learned to depend on each other's ability and coolness under fire. With former campaign staffers at your side, you can count on them to watch your back, support your every move, and remain loyal to you and your agenda. Staffers who are retained or are recruited from other fields share that sense of personal loyalty. In a sense, you and your campaign staff climbed the mountain together and share those same feelings of accomplishment and joy.

To achieve success in office, incumbents must be true to the spirit of their campaign. Former campaign staffers offer a remarkable resource to new incumbents: loyalty to the political agenda, proven ability under fire, and personal knowledge of your constituency.

Entry-level turnkey systems for a California Assembly office—a package that includes hardware, software, and a cleaned-up voter file—start in the $26,000 range, irrespective of the vendor, according to Mike Shulem, president of Data Plus Imagination. His Monarch Constituent Services, which dominates the California Assembly, is among systems priced in that range.

On the high end, ATEC's products, including hardware, can range anywhere from $15,000 for three to four users of its correspondence management application, and up to $500,000 for a system that handles appointments, scheduling, constituent management, and spreadsheets for up to 100 users.

7

Direct Mail: Strategies and Techniques

★ ★ ★

✓ How To Move Votes Through the Mail
Dave Gold and Tony Marsh

With broadcast TV rates spinning out of sight, the superior targeting qualities of cable and persuasion mail appear to be shifting the typical metro area races, where broadcasts are prohibitively wasteful of hard campaign's message mix. Mail has become a particularly attractive alternative as census information can now be evenly laid over political subdivisions through new mapping software. It has always been the medium of choice for lower-ballot and metro areqa races, where broadcasts are prohibitively wasteful of hard-earned campaign dollars.

To catch up on the latest advances in message mail, we invited over two of the nation's most successful and experienced practitioners: **Tony Marsh** (Russo, Marsh + Associates; Sacramento, CA), and **Dave Gold** (Gold Communications; Austin, TX).

Q: When can persuasion mail be as effective as TV in delivering the message?

Gold: It's the principal vehicle for delivering the message for lower ballot races, where TV is often prohibitively expensive and inefficient. But for statewides, it can still play a vital supporting role in general message delivery, beyond its targeting function. For example, in the Jim Hunt [1992 North Carolina gubernatorial] campaign we used persuasion mail to reinforce the message being delivered by TV to the key persuadable voters. So we came in, targeted a statewide group who we believed to be among the key swing voters in the gubernatorial campaign, and did a series of three mailers aimed at reinforcing the basic message that was on TV: [opponent] Jim Gardner's bad business record. We were able to keep reinforcing that hammer by presenting the detailed documentation behind what was being presented on TV, removing the skepticism of the voter—"close the sale," in a sense. They would say, "Well I guess it must be true what they're saying on TV. Look here at all the documents behind it." A call-back poll done after the election found that Gardner's negatives were significantly higher in the households that had received the mail.

Q: Mail seems to be the most popular message medium for coordinated campaigns. How do the dynamics of your "cordcam" efforts vary from the work you do for candidates?

Gold: In terms of our experiences, there are two different kinds of coordinated campaigns, one of which is the multi-candidate operation, such as the Florida state House program we participated in that handled over thirty races.... They provided individual campaigns with the services of a major direct-mail consultant, a general consultant, posters, and even postage at times.... What you end up doing in the multiple races is handling issues in great detail, in contrast to statewide coordinated campaigns which are more focused on GOTV....

Marsh: In this last election, we did the Oregon state House candidates—about 15 of them.... We were able to set some common themes statewide that played through all of the mail programs. Survey research showed that [Democrat Gov.] Barbara Roberts' tax-hike proposals were extremely impacting. We were able to turn the whole economic issue into a tax issue and pretty much maintain a consistent theme and style throughout most of the targeted state House races. Consequently, Republicans in Oregon did pretty well at the state legislative level.

Another example was in 1982, when we did the George Deukmejian campaign for governor of California. Because of the direct mail piece at the end of that—the GOTV absentee ballot piece—Deukmejian won by something less than one percent of the vote. He actually lost at the polls on Election Day, but because he carried the absentees so substantially, he won the election. So in terms of GOTV and that sort of thing, coordinated mail programs between party organizations and candidates can be terribly beneficial.

Gold: Where you are talking about legislative races, coordinated campaigning can make a much higher level of professional services available to individual campaigns. If the state party is hiring a pollster, he or she can do work for multiple races at a much cheaper rate than if each candidate went out and hired their own pollster. And so it is in mail; you can achieve economies of scale through commonality of themes, as well as reinforce each other's campaign.... We handled mail for the last year's targeted state Senate races in Connecticut, where—at the outset—they thought the Democrats were going to pay dearly for having been the ones who carried [Independent Gov. Lowell] Weicker's sales tax—the first in state history. And we found, through good survey research, that people were upset about that but realized that it was inevitable. They were more in favor of repairing the tax than repealing it; they thought it was badly designed. So we were able to mitigate the effect of that one issue and won enough races to maintain control of the Senate. If everybody had gone off on their own, they wouldn't have been able to do the necessary research and deliver the cohesive message that is necessary to register with the voters.

Q: What about the non-party slate card? It's a form of a coordinated campaign that has come to dominate Democratic politics in California. Will it catch on elsewhere?

Marsh: Evangelical Christians are starting to use it pretty extensively, and other groups have found out about it. But now there are so many competitive ones in California, they're starting to lose their impact.

Q: Are Republicans are using them now too?

Gold: Everybody's using them: special interest groups are using them, the NRA is using them—everybody.

Marsh: The environmental card, the pro-choice card, the fundamental Christian card.

Q: The slate card was one of the keys to the success of California's Berman/Waxman machine. It seems they lost their punch in the last election.

Marsh: To some extent. The Berman/Waxman operation was second to none for a long time when it came to list segmentation and the whole technology of the targeting process using various media, but principally direct mail. As others are now catching up, they are losing their edge.

Gold: I've always felt that slate-cards have a great deal more impact on ballot propositions and lower-ballot races than races at the top of the ballot. And particularly if you're going into the state of California: they have this huge, long ballot. If you get a slatecard from people you trust that says "here are all these propositions that you don't want to have to bother to research; here's a safe way of voting," that can be a powerful influence. When it comes to a ballot question that people have any awareness, they're not going to pay attention to the slate card; but it's a way of feeling safe about voting on stuff that they're not aware of.

Marsh: But if every Tom, Dick, and Harry started dropping slate cards on those obscure campaigns, chances are pretty good you'd be a little more confused and you'd have to look toward other sources.

Q: It sounds like there is a difference between the way you would pitch a referenda direct mail persuasion campaign versus the candidate persuasion campaign. What are some of those key differences, apart from referenda campaigns being more issue-oriented?

Marsh: Persuasion mail does some things better than anything else. whether it is an initiative or a candidate campaign. Its extreme targetability makes it particularly effective for initiative campaigns. As you develop your coalition base for any given position. you have to deliver an appropriate message for each persuadable group one they will respond to. Persuasion mail can do that better than anything else.

Gold: It is also more effective on the attack than in presenting positive messages.... Television is a passive medium... it washes over the voter, and some of its message may end up sticking. Mail is an active medium; it has to engage voters and make them want to pay attention to it. It's easier to do that with negative material.

Q: Do you have to hit them between the eyes?

Gold: Yes, starting with attention-grabbing graphics. But even if it's got a good hook you have to maintain their interest and it's just far tougher to do that with a positive message about an issue or political figure.

Marsh: You're right, television is a cool medium... people don't have to participate to get the message. In direct mail, you've got to open something and read it and get actively involved in it; it's a very hot medium. I mean, you're gonna get a message out of there if you get involved in it. Our challenge is getting people involves in it once it gets into their mailbox.

Gold: Even if you can get people involved, you may not get them to read every word of the piece, so design it to be scanned as well as read. Have headlines and subheads, some junk quotes, outlines to photos where the eye is more likely to go. That will allow them to scan it and get the largest part of the message that you want delivered.... If you've managed to hook them and get them actually to scan it with some attention, then you've had a major impact. It's easier to do that on the attack. People always say, "I hate negative campaigning," but what they're thinking is "tell me more."

Q: Okay, television IS a cool, personal, intimate medium and it seemed—in the last cycle—to have more of a double edge when used for negative messages; it provided more potential for backlash. You have to be more careful with negative TV today the news media is going to come down on you more readily that they used to. Since mail is a hotter medium, can't it get away with a harsher attack? Doesn't that mean we're going to see attack carried more and more by mail?

Gold: I'm not so sure that you can get away with harsher attack with mail; you have to have the documentation. But because you can provide more documentation in the mail than in a thirty second TV spot, I think you can be more powerful on the attack via mail. But I still contend it is most effective is when it's working in sync with what you are doing on television.

Marsh: Because mail is a hot medium, it is a low-backlash medium. Television is a high-backlash medium. You can't put a message on television about being pro-life or about school busing or anything like that without creating a great deal of clamor and reaction in the community. If you can pick a list of pro-life voters and mail them a piece of mail talking about being pro-life, the backlash is going to be much less.

Q: Then it's a combination of the sensory differences in the media and the fact that you can more carefully target with mail?

Gold: While you want to focus the broad public attention on a broad message, you may have an important sub-message—say, the issue of choice. So you may want to keep your TV focused on your broad message—say the economy—but still hit a substantial sub-set of voters with a pro-choice message.

Marsh: I see so many campaigns that hire a television consultant, a direct mail consultant, a radio consultant and a newspaper advertising consultant—and the consultants never talk to one another, other than maybe once every two weeks on a conference call. The candidate ends up with 17 advertising campaigns, each with its own message.... They'd be better advised to flesh out their basic thematic approach, making sure that all the media reinforce it by dovetailing with one another, each doing what it does best.

Q: What are some of the changing conditions and technologies that have recently affected the role of persuasion mail?

Marsh: Something really exciting is happening with computer technology and our ability to target messages in political campaigns: We are slowly building a household-by-household, voter-specific list of people that gives us tremendous knowledge about each household. Things like: their propensity to vote, what issues concern them, what magazines they subscribe to, what kind of refrigerators they own.... Some of these characteristics obviously carry more political implications than others, but unexpected correlations can arise if you do attitudinal research extensive survey research with lots of demographic crosstabs. If you overlay attitudinal responses onto seemingly non-predictive information that is available on the list—things like what kind of car people own, how many weapons are in the household, whether they have a fishing license—you all of a sudden start seeing some correlations that can enable you to target on an extremely refined basis. That's really important, given the fact that the cost of mail—both postage and production—has gone up so substantially in the last six, seven years.

Q: So while costs are accelerating, the technology is helping you keep up in terms of effectiveness.

Gold: Yes. The ability to target one narrowly allows you to remain cost-effective, not only in the face of rising costs, but also the evermore crowded mailbox.... There you're competing not so much with political opponents but with catalogues—Sears, Sharper Image and Victoria's Secret.

Marsh: In California, New Jersey and other heavily urbanized areas, it's getting to the point where during the last two or three weeks of the election cycle, you can expect to find anywhere from three to six pieces of political mail in your mailbox The graphics have to be punchier, the copy more powerful, the photographs more stunning if it's going to be opened and read.

Gold: And while voter file information is becoming more and more precise, the quality varies tremendously from state to state; and so the applications of persuasion mail as a medium vary considerably from state to state.

Marsh: That's right. And it can be terribly expensive to build this file and add all the bells and whistles that are currently available out there. And once it's built, somebody has to take on the task of maintaining it, which can also be a terribly expensive proposition.

Gold: It's not an individual candidate that's going to maintain that kind of voter file. It's a job for a state party or a vendor one or the other.

Marsh: One of the reasons we do legislative races is because they allow us a great flexibility in experimentation that we wouldn't otherwise have. We just did a legislative race where we actually started with the basic voter list provided by the state of California, then hired people to call every household. For households we couldn't call, we hired people to go canvass with a questionnaire of 17 or so questions on everything from issues to demographics. Then we took that list and matched it against all kinds of commercially available files—various subscription things and census information.... We actually got this thing to a point where we knew, pretty precisely, who was going to vote, whether they were a potential absentee voter, and the kinds of issues and concerns they were going to base their vote on. Having said that, I estimate that it would cost somewhere in the neighborhood of 10 to 12 million dollars to duplicate that list effort statewide in California.

Gold: And in California you start out with a far superior voter file than found in most states.

Marsh: And California has a very mobile population; the file goes out of date at the rate of about 20 percent a year. So, yes, you start out with a terrific file, but the cost of maintaining it once you get it going—is far higher than some place like Ohio.

Q: Is it possible to deliver a direct-mail piece that's effective for both persuasion and fundraising?

Gold: You might be able to do that early on in a primary kind of situation. Potential donors are people who are interested in politics; if you're in a multiple-candidate primary field and mailing to hard-core Democratic activists, you might be able to squeeze some money out of it without compromising your persuasive message.... But it would require [a carrier] envelope with lots of information inside, along with a return envelope—all the kinds of things that are required to have any response rate in fundraising. Those people... are the exact opposite end of the spectrum from persuadable voters in the general election—those who are the least political of people who actually do vote... and who are your typical persuasion targets—at least in the general election. The idea of going to them and asking for money is a complete waste of time.

Marsh: I think there is one situation in which it can work, and even then the fundraising potential is marginal. When I did Randy Cunningham's campaign in San Diego against [then-congressman] Jim Bates in the '90 cycle, we knew we would have only about $150,000-$200,000 for the general election in a district that was only 35 percent Republican. We had to find ourselves 30,000-50,000 Democrat voters that shared some characteristic in common with Cunningham: pro-lifers or evangelicals or motorcyclists or Navy veterans.... One reason or another, they had to have some common bond with Randy Cunningham. We did find 65,000 Democratic names eventually, put those all on a computer in the office, and then started pumping out persuasion mail segmented to their interest. And we always put a little tag in there about money. "If you care about your motorcycle off-road riding rights, vote for Duke Cunningham—and send us a check for ten dollars.".... It wasn't so much a program that paid for itself, but it allowed us to add a couple or three pieces of persuasion mail to various groups we couldn't have otherwise afforded....

Gold: These were self-mailers?

Marsh: No, most of them were in envelopes.

Q: You generally don't use a carrier envelope in persuasion mail, do you?

Gold: And that's why visibility is a tradeoff. If it wasn't in an envelope with a return envelope, your odds of getting any money back would have plummeted.

Marsh: I disagree with part of that.... I use carrier envelopes a lot in persuasion mail.... The rule depends on what circumstances the campaign faces. You can expand an issue in a more credible way with a letter from a third party than you can in a graphic piece. In a graphic piece, you can footnote everything and show the documents you are taking things from to provide more believability. But generally speaking, if somebody gets a big, glossy, graphic piece in the mail, they assume it came from the opposing campaign. If they get a letter from the National Taxpayers Association, then you can kind of sneak up on them and say, "This should concern you because we're taxpayers like you and here's why we don't like so-and-so."

Gold: I'm not saying never put something in an envelope for persuasion mail purposes, but I think it is the exception to the rule. More often than not, when I want to present a letter, I do it in a self-mailer—maybe even an oversized post-card.

Marsh: As I mentioned earlier, I try to dovetail different media for message reinforcement. I pick a plot-line for my campaign and send out a graphic piece to introduce it. Say, "Joe Democrat is for raising taxes; therefore, you shouldn't vote for him." List all the tax increases he's voted for or supports in the graphic piece. Then, follow up three or four days later with a letter from the Taxpayers and Homeowners Association that says, "We're outraged that Joe Democrat supports all these tax increases." That way, you enhance credibility and reinforce the message....

Gold: If you have a really good third-party source that is strong enough to get people inside the envelope, then you have the exception to the rule that I would agree with you on. But probably more often than not it's an envelope that simply is not going to get opened.

Marsh: It depends on the envelope. If it has printed indicia, a slapped-on label and all that other nonsense, it's probably not going to going to get opened. If it's hand-addressed and has a live stamp and a return address that makes sense to people, then chances are very good that they're going to open it.

Gold: I once saw a persuasion piece that was absolutely brilliant in an envelope, for [Texas Sen.] Phil Gramm in 1984. We would have beaten up on him with his awful record of voting against seniors.... We had all the documentation in the world, but he responded with his mother on television talking about how Phil would never treat her or any other senior that way. They followed that TV spot with a hand-written letter from Miz Gramm—handwritten... it looked like it came from an old lady and glowed with references about what a wonderful son Phil was.... It was a very powerful and effective piece of follow-up persuasion mail in an envelope.

Q: There is no way of settling the argument, is there? Persuasion can't be tested practicably, whereas with fund raising you sample a list, you try a package, and you get a very definite return back.

Gold: That's the fundamental difference between direct marketing and all other advertising. Direct marketing—whether it's fundraising or some cheese in the mail or whatever—can directly measure the response and accurately tell you what you're going to do. With all other advertising... it's very difficult to measure the actual effectiveness of what does and doesn't work. There have been some studies of what people do and don't read... we've done some studies with focus groups—

Q: There is often a wide gap between how people say they react, and how they in fact react.

Marsh: Exactly.... I think it's insane that we spend billions of dollars every election cycle on a form of media that nobody's ever tested, which is persuasion mail. I don't understand why the Republican party... [doesn't] pick a couple of districts, segment them into ten or—different geographical regions and run different kinds of mail programs in each of those regions, with nightly tracking on the impact of that mail.

Gold: You can make the same case—to a certain degree—about all advertising.

Marsh: But in a political campaign, if you are doing nightly tracking and you're changing your tracking instructions on television every day or two days or three days—you can see how people are shifting around; you can tell what's working during the course of the campaign.... The problem with the persuasion mail is you're going to do seven pieces during the course of that statewide campaign.... With television, you can go in and tinker with the spot; if something's not working, you can pull it back, edit it and get it back on the air the next day. With persuasion mail, once you've dropped it in the mailbox, it's gone. It's unlikely you're going to fine-tune the same piece and send it out again.

✓ Targeted Direct Mail
Richard Schlackman and Michael Hoffman

Persuasion direct mail is only as good as the names you choose to mail to. Your award winning brochure is worthless if it isn't delivering the right message to the right people. How can you make that match?

Polling and past election results are vital to the identification of your vote-optimum audience. Once you establish that, it's time to turn to your voter file—the computer file of registered voters in your district—for the demographic information that will provide your telescopic gunsight. The more voter file information you have available, the more strategically and accurately you can target your mail pieces.

Finding the Target

Polling is helpful on two levels. In the macro sense, it will tell you if you need to concentrate on a precise direct mail campaign—where local concerns and interest groups determine your target audience—or a more general media campaign which addresses broad national concerns. Is your electorate more interested in getting the roads fixed than cutting the federal budget deficit? Do people want your candidate to save jobs at the local steel mill or do they want a new national industrial policy?

This year the polls showed a more dramatic tilt toward the larger national concerns than ever before. Consequently where in previous election years we would have concentrated on sending different mail pieces to different local interest and target groups—this cycle we sent more pieces about national issues to a broadly segmented target audience.

On the micro level, polling will tell you which demographic groups of people are moved to vote for a candidate based on specific stands on specific issues, certain candidate attributes, or particular points in his/her record. For example, if you ask a question about abortion rights, proper polling will not only tell you who the pro-choice voters are, but provide crosstabs that show you which demographic group of voters is influenced by particular aspects of a pro-choice message.

Another information set that can help you target is past election results. A good report on returns will tell you the voting history of the district on a precinct-by-precinct basis. On the Democratic side, the National Committee for an Effective Congress (NCEC) produces the best such reports. Using a variety of elections, NCEC ranks precincts by their propensity to vote Democratic, by the percentage of the total who are registered Democrats, and—most importantly—by persuadability. Persuadable precincts are comprised of swing voters who may go Democratic then shift to the Republicans in another. Such variable segments are less tied to a political party and are more likely to be moved by campaign messages.

Your election report will let you know where to concentrate your resources. In precincts that have historically gone your way, you can concentrate on your get-out-the-vote (GOTV) effort and save your persuasion tactics for elsewhere. You can also ignore those precincts that always vote for the other party: no matter what you tell them they won't vote for you; any activity in that quarter will only kick over an anthill. Save your resources for persuadables and your own people.

While polling information comes from a random sample, and election results come from precinct information, your voter files will take your targeting to the most basic level—individual names and addresses.

Zeroing In

Once you have used polling and voter behavior to plan your strategy and tactics for direct mail, you need a system to get it delivered. The quality of your voter file will determine whether you can meet your targeting goals. Voter file information originates primarily from counties, and while some provide detailed information on a computer format, others have name and addresses on typed sheets or in the actual voter log books. If you plan to do detailed targeting with your voter file you will need a competent computer voter file vendor to handle the information gathering and processing.

A good voter file will include numerous identifying characteristics: Name, address, date of birth, date of registration, phone number, ethnicity, party affiliation, voting history and carrier route coding (to save money on postage). Some voter lists have less information, others can be enhanced to this full complement by companies who possess alternate listings, such as motor vehicle licenses and registration.

The key to successful demographic targeting is not only in having this data, but the ability to manipulate it. The best tool for this manipulation is a count book, or cross-count profile. A count book is when you take your voter file information and create a series of ranges to group voters together. For example, if you have date of birth on file you can include a list of age ranges that look like this:

	Voters	%	Households	%
UNDER 25	28,968	8.9%	24,941	12.6%
25-34	59,921	18.5%	48,540	24.6%
35-44	66,966	20.7%	52,356	26.6%
45-49	26,653	8.2%	22,660	11.5%
50-54	19,823	6.1%	17,262	8.7%
55-64	32,360	9.9%	27,345	13.2%
65 and over	49,554	15.3%	39,569	20.1%

... or any range that you think will be most useful. Note that the number of households from voters is usually reduced by about 25 percent. This is important from a budgetary standpoint since you only mail one piece per household.

If party affiliation is available in your state, you can break down the information not just about the individual voter, but also about that voter's household. Party information in a voter file may look like this:

Democrat
Republican
Independent
Pure Independent
Pure Democrat
Pure Republican
Democrat or Independent
Republican or Independent

So if you need Independents to win your election, it may be easier to influence an Independent who lives with a Democrat than an Independent who lives with a Republican. Your count book will let you know who they are.

But a count book goes one step further. After defining these ranges and giving you totals, it cross-references all of this information. Therefore, we not only know how many Independents live with Republicans, we know how many 55 and older Independents live with Republicans.

In a recent congressional election, we took the count book idea one step further. We added our election data to the voter file through the count book. All it involved was creating a series of count book flags based on a predefined set of precincts. In the count book we had a flag called "Persuadable Precincts." All we did was take that group of precincts marked persuadable by NCEC and define them on our count book. So not only could we tell who were the 55 and older Independents who live with Republicans, but we knew which ones lived in persuadable areas.

Bombs Away

Once you have your targets and you are comfortable with your voter file, you need to put it all together. Let's continue that abortion rights example:

We know that to win this election our liberal-Democrat candidate needs a big turnout from his party base, plus a majority of Independents in his vote column—along with some Republicans. Polling indicates that we can use the abortion rights issue combined with many other messages—to accomplish these goals.

We decide to send only one piece about abortion rights as OUI budget is tight, and we know the economy is a more important issue to the voters. The message of this abortion drop is, "The government doesn't belong in the bedroom." The goal again is to move pro-choice Independents and Republicans and simultaneously energize a major portion of our Democratic base. Our targets for this piece are the following:

All Independent Women
Independent Men Under 55
Republican Women under 55 who live in high Democratic precincts or who live in a mixed Republican/Democratic household
Jewish Republican men in high Democratic precincts
Democratic women who live in a mixed Democratic/Republican household
Republican men under 55 who live in mixed Democratic/Republican households.

We know from polling and intuition that Independent women will likely be moved with a pro-choice message. We also know that older Independent men are not pro-choice in this instance. We assume Republican women who are surrounded by Democrats, either in neighborhood or household, are more likely to be pro-choice. Jews are overwhelmingly pro-choice, whether Democrats or Republicans, so we may be able to move some Republican men from this group to our side. Democratic women who live with Republicans are more vulnerable to Republican messages, so we took this opportunity to shore up our base.

A Republican man whose wife is a Democrat is ripe for our antigovernment pro-choice message. We could have added more groups to these targets including: Republican women who live alone and

Democratic men in high Republican precincts. How deep your targeting goes will probably be determined by your budget. You'll run out of money before you run out of groups to target.

The key to successful persuasion mail targeting is in having lots of information available and in putting together the strategy and tactics to utilize it. The better your voter file is—and the better the computer vendor who manipulates it—the more precisely you can target your mail. With the help of polling and election results, you can target the people you need to win and send them the messages that will move them to your side.

✓ Blending Media with Mail
Ross Bates

What do you do if you are a Puerto Rican woman who is one of four Latino challengers in a congressional primary against an Anglo incumbent with 10 times more money?

What do you do if you are an African-American Democrat running in a state House district that is more than 70 percent Republican and has long been controlled by a Republican machine?

The answer for Congresswoman-elect Nydia Velazquez of New York and Representative-elect Thaddeus Kirkland of Pennsylvania was in brewing up a new type of communications mix. Their communications program blended a strong traditional field and ethnic-media program with a modern persuasion mail campaign that tapped into the voter anger of 1992. This created a winning mixture that beat the odds and produced election day victories.

A Different Use for Persuasion Mail

Usually, television or radio communicates the general message, persuasion programs target more specific versions of the same message, and the field program is run in coordination with the targets of the mail program.

But these campaigns were different. Because of the size of the media markets—New York City for Velazquez and Philadelphia for Kirkland—mail was by far the most efficient means of communication.

In both campaigns we crafted a strong persuasion message that appealed to the whole electorate. Electronic media and field programs were highly targeted to fortify our base of ethnic voters while persuasion mail set out the general message.

In both campaigns, we tapped into the mood of anger at "politics as usual." In both campaigns, the targeted messages of the field and electronic media carried the opposition to "politics as usual" one step further to tap into voters' desire for empowerment. Our persuasion mail message was the same, however, no matter if the voter was white, African-American, or Latino.

Nydia Velazquez: Beats the Conventional Wisdom

New York's congressional reapportionment created a new Latino seat centered in Brooklyn. But soon after the final lines were announced, Congressman Stephen Solarz changed the political equation by jumping into the race.

The conventional wisdom said the Latino candidates would split the vote, leaving Solarz able to use his $2-million campaign war chest to win enough non-Latino and Latino votes to survive the primary. Fortunately, we had a poll by Bill Johnson of Johnson Survey Research which showed that the conventional wisdom was wrong. Solarz' opponents were not four interchangeable Spanish surnames. In fact, Velazquez had a high name recognition and high positives among Brooklyn Latinos, whereas Solarz had high negatives and potential negatives throughout the electorate.

The mail program blended positive and negative messages that appealed to all aspects of the potential primary universe. The primary universe was of different ethnicities tied together by a strong liberal ideology, a tendency to view problems on a local level, and an antipathy to politics as usual. Therefore, we used a unified message instead of running separate mail campaigns to Latinos and Anglos: Velazquez was not just the best Latino candidate, she was the candidate who best represented the concerns of all members of the community.

It wasn't enough to just attack Solarz for bounced checks, pay raises, and the usual anti-Congress complaints. Those issues were used as proof that he did not understand the problems of the neighborhoods.

One mailer showed a picture of the Capitol with the headline, "Congressman Solarz' House is Not in Our Neighborhood." Another mailer featured some people from the community saying, "Congressman Solarz, you picked the wrong neighborhood." This contrast worked equally well for all segments of the district. The field program was extremely successful in targeting the Latino and African-American communities of Brooklyn, Queens, and the lower east side of Manhattan. The effort culminated in a successful election day GOTV program led by Local 1199's volunteers.

There was also a strong effort in the free and paid Latino media, led by Wilda Rodriguez with the assistance of Frank Robles. Velazquez won the election with a strong showing in her base among Brooklyn Latinos and enough votes in the other geographic and ethnicity groups to provide a comfortable margin.

Thaddeus Kirkland Beats the Republican Machine

Delaware County, PA, has one of the few old-style political machines left in the country. The Republican Party has a seemingly iron lock on patronage, politics, and policy. As a result, the city of Chester, a poor, mostly African-American community, has a Republican registration of more than 50 percent.

When an opening occurred in the 159th House District, including Chester and some white townships with even higher Republican registration, the machine put up John Taylor, a reliable Anglo politician in his 70s who had served in a variety of local government and law enforcement positions.

If the task confronting the campaign of Democratic candidate Thaddeus Kirkland, an African-American community activist, wasn't difficult enough, there was also the question of Kirkland's past, which included a conviction several years earlier for cocaine possession. Although Kirkland had kicked the habit and was speaking out at youth forums throughout the area against drug abuse, a campaign for a convicted drug seller against a retired sheriff in a 70 percent Republican district did not seem promising, to say the least. Once again, we did not differentiate our mail program. We targeted both black and white voters with a message of change. We showed Kirkland as someone from the community who had overcome the dangers of the streets and was now committed to making a difference.

Our positive mailers illustrated how Kirkland was a force for change and a source of community pride. Our negative and comparative mailers hit on the need for change and on Taylor's comfort with the status quo.

At the same time, an extensive field campaign was hitting the streets. Focusing mostly on the African-American community, the campaign registered 1,400 new voters and went door-to-door to 8,000 of the 20,000 households in the district. There was also a strong program of radio advertising on African-American stations, with ads produced by Hank Sheinkopf stressing an empowerment theme. We also produced a mailer highlighting the fact that Dr. Martin Luther King had attended a seminary in Chester to urge community residents to "keep his dream alive."

The result was an unprecedented groundswell of support. But because of the "stealth" nature of mail and field, the other side never caught on until it was too late. The result was an overwhelming victory for Kirkland, with tremendous margins in the African-American community and 25 to 30 percent of the white vote, more than any local African-American candidate had ever received.

✓ How to Personalize Direct Mail
Wayne C. Johnson

Political advertisers should recognize that direct mailers are also direct marketers. The almost obsessive attention to the measurement and analysis of response data that characterizes direct marketing has a parallel application in measuring political advertising.

Direct mail fundraisers are well aware of the phenomenon of "package fatigue." (This occurs when a particular mail package or genre of mail packages contaminates the universe into which it is mailed and thereby alters response patterns. The usual effect of this phenomenon necessitates a reformulation of the "offer.")

Yet while many political professionals attempt to analyze the efficacy of message, few attempt a systematic analysis of the messenger.

We analyzed a number of heavily contested California primary races to determine if there were any similarities among the most effective issues or types of communication vehicles that drove those issues home. There were.

Direct marketers tend to think in terms of cycles. A fundraising package can be resurrected a year or even several years after it has run its course. The recycling of Life cereal's "Let Mikey try it" commercial is an obvious example of an idea whose time had come and gone, and then come again.

So it was in California, where many of the victors dusted off several campaign techniques that voters hadn't seen in a few years. In particular, tabloid newsletters and the "spouse letter." Almost without fail, campaigns seemed to profit greatly from these seemingly nonpolitical mailings. The spouse (or daughter or mother or other family member) letter worked irrespective of the party, ideology, or orientation of the candidate employing the tactic. In some cases, tracking showed jumps of as much as 15 to 20 points following the delivery of one of those letters.

There seemed to be a premium placed upon those mail pieces that appeared personal as opposed to political. Slick brochures, in some cases, had a contrary effect to what was intended, marking the sender as "the politician," although that's conclusionary and the purpose of this type of analysis is to focus not on the "why" but the "what." Nevertheless, it did happen and it was measurable. Another vehicle that was particularly effective was one of the oldest forms of political mail, the tabloid.

Tabs that most resembled small hometown newspapers seemed to be the most effective. Many campaigns were using the tabloid because they didn't have the budget to print more traditional political mailings. Not only were the tabloids able to address a number of issues, but in many cases they cost only one-third of what coated stock campaign brochures cost.

The tabs we produced had every appearance of a small town newspaper, including letters to the editor, editorials, and editorial cartoons. (I still have a stack of change-of-address cards mailed in by recipients who had moved but didn't want to miss the next issue.)

So effective was the tab that in the only race we lost in 1992, the opponent produced an exact duplicate of our tab and "withdrew" the paper's endorsement of our candidate just days before the election. (Nice shot, Rich Schlackman of Campaign Performance Group). To enhance credibility, candidates needed to go the extra mile in 1992. Annette Pombo, wife of newly elected Congressman Richard Pombo, added the Pombo's home telephone number to the handwritten letter she sent to voters.

Not surprisingly, she spent a week answering hundreds upon hundreds of calls. Equally unsurprising, more than half of the callers just wanted to see who would really answer. Who really answered was either Richard or Annette.

There were more votes in the households of those who called the Pombos' home than in our margin of victory on election night. See what kind of delivery vehicles are working. Recognize "package fatigue." Pay as much attention to what is working as you do to why it is working. (The former is often measurable by objective criteria, while the latter is more likely an exercise in speculative self-delusion). And don't hold back on anything that will make your voter contact more believable. For the '90s, credibility is the name of the game.

✓ Direct Mail Fundraising Roundtable: The Pros Speak

Here, together for the first time, are some of the top political direct mail experts in the United States: Ed Burnett (Ed Burnett Consultants), Sandy Clark (The Fidler Group), Roger Craver (Craver, Mathews, Smith and Co.), Morris Dees (Craver, Mathews, Smith and Co.), Joe Hartman (independent fundraiser), Richard Viguerie (The Viguerie Company), and Guy Yolton (Yolton Advertising, Inc.). Having conducted political direct mail successfully for campaigns at all levels over many years, these seven experts were invited by *Campaigns & Elections* to tell us the secrets of their success. And they did, as their transcript attests.

C&E: The idea of this roundtable is to have an instructional session for our readers—to get all of you who constantly deal with direct mail together to discuss direct mail specifically as a political fundraising tool. There are many other uses for direct mail in the political process: recruiting and stimulating volunteers, issue development, opinion molding, getting-out-the-vote, laying groundwork for your future campaigns—and so on—but we would like to focus today on political fundraising by direct mail. We'd like to start out with a definition of direct mail. What does the term mean?

Yolton: Direct mail is pretty much what the name implies. It's reaching customers or prospects directly by mail, composing, putting together mailing pieces or mailing packages, putting postage on them and getting them mailed out to people or institutions you have reason to believe will respond positively to your appeal.

Burnett: Direct mail is just one form of what we call "direct response" retail. In retail marketing, you're trying to get a direct response—a sale—by any means—mail is one of those means.

C&E: Is it true that most American households are flooded each week with direct mail pieces of all kinds, that most of it is thrown away without being opened or read, and that this competition for the recipient's attention negatively affects the impact of direct mail for political fundraising?

Dees: Mailboxes have been flooded since Sears, Roebuck sent out their first catalog and people started shopping by mail. Effective direct response pieces work because they are effective—the number you put in the mail is irrelevant.

Craver: I think one of the great misunderstandings about direct mail is that there is some limited size pie out there that gets carved up in just so many ways. That simply isn't the case. There are enough meaningful causes and issues out there that lend themselves to direct mail treatment.

Yolton: I have seen actual statistics compiled by the U.S. Postal Service and supported by the Direct Mail Marketing Association (DMMA) and others that indicate how many pieces of "advertising mail" the average householder receives in a week's time or day's time, etc., and it comes out to be much less than what you described as a "flood." A flood is in the mind of the floodee, so to speak.

C&E: I think the survey you're mentioning showed that the average household receives some 13 pieces of direct mail per week.

Burnett: Not quite. The correct answer is in the "Household-to-Household Mail Flow Study" published in the Direct Mail Marketing Association magazine, from a survey made by the University of Michigan. (I wrote the article so I know about it.) It shows that the average household receives 15 pieces of every kind of mail per week. As such I take exception to this word "flood." The average person is actually very eager to get mail—in fact, all the surveys ever made in this business have indicated that the average householder is very eager to receive the mail, and in farm/rural areas, they actually lean on the mailbox waiting for the mail to be delivered. It's no flood.

Hartman: Don't you think that the members of the particular group who receive political fundraising mail get more than the average? It's a more affluent group, it's a more interested group, and the 15 pieces per week might not be applicable to the market or group we are focusing on here today.

Clark: That's probably true. By and large, the richer buyers are what we call "buyers for the moment." (That's my vernacular.) People have tended to buy better and faster over the last 25 years that I've been in direct mail. When I first came into this business we were happy to get a two dollar order and pull two percent; today we're selling $10-$20 items and pulling five percent. So it's a real dollars per-thousands evolution. I'd second Ed's objection to the word flood. I think that direct mail is a nonconfrontory form of selling/marketing that allows an individual to deal with you on his terms, not yours.

Dees: I think we have too narrow a definition of direct mail to start with: mailing out letters. Direct mail in political fundraising is used not just to get new donors, but to go after the donors you already have, whether you got them through direct mail, television ads, newspaper ads, cocktail parties, or whatever. Most of Senator Kennedy's donors do not come from direct mail, yet we're using direct mail to chase them down again after we have them. And secondly, direct mail serves many other purposes than just raising money. First of all, you can get a hundred thousand donors and break even—and that's a big success because you've gotten a hundred thousand people you can now write to ask them to go to caucuses and get other people out to vote. If you placed an ad on television, or a commercial, you get nothing but the ad on television. But when you spend the direct mail dollar you end up getting individuals who can continue to help you because you can resolicit. And when you send out direct mail, you're sending out an advertising piece that tells about your candidate in depth. And even if you pull a two percent money response, 98 percent of the people got the letter, and most of them probably read the letter or portions of it. So fundraising direct mail serves more purposes than just fundraising—it raises consciousness as well.

C&E: It is said that direct mail can be directed to specific individuals or audiences with greater control than any other media. I don't think that anybody would question that statement. Is that true in comparison to the telephone? How is direct mail more personal than a telephone call to request funds?

Craver: The telephone is a far more intrusive instrument. You have an initial negative reaction to overcome. Telephone, even though it's one person speaking to another, is not as personal a medium as direct mail. You can't develop a train of thought in as organized a way by telephone as you can by direct mail. We've done a lot of testing of telephone and have found it to be fairly ineffective in most of the standard applications that mail is used for.

Dees: But on the other hand, telephone is excellent for following up on donors that have already given—especially the donors who have given an average of, say, $25 or more.

Hartman: And this control is important. I remember when a president was coming to our Capitol during a gubernatorial election. We had only five or six days notice. Well, we got out 12,000 letters in very quick order. Now to call that many people on the telephone would be impossible. But you have control there—you can act quicker by mail than you can by telephone under those circumstances.

C&E: Direct mail is said to be a "flexible" medium in terms of time requirements and message transmitted. Is this really so, relative to, for example, television, the telephone, radio, etc.? Are message formats and direct mail packages easily and economically changed? For example, if you sent out a direct mail package and you discovered that people were responding to a particular aspect of that copy and you wanted to emphasize that a bit more in your next drop, can you do that easily, economically, relative to changing the format of other media?

Burnett: Well, I'm sure there will be lots of comments on this one! Basically what you're really talking about here is passing a test and then ruling out certain options. In the campaign for Eisenhower, they made ten tests and found that "I am going to Korea" outputted the others by six or seven to one, so they stopped using the other nine. It's pretty obvious that they learned, and learned fast to make that change.

Viguerie: You have to be flexible in your format to be successful. It's well known that people do not remember your copy. You think you've written some great prose that is going to be remembered throughout history, but people don't remember the copy. What they remember are the graphics. So when you think that a package has run its course, and you won't be successful with it in the future—if you don't do anything but change the graphics, you will find that many times you'll have a very successful package again. Just change the color, change the type face, put some different graphics in there and you'll see your returns pick right back up.

Craver: To illustrate that—everyone remembers Morris Dees' six-page letters for George McGovern. But I'm not sure anyone remembers what they said.

Dees: We changed the size of the envelope, we put different color corner cards on because we were mailing millions of pieces and often to the same people [Editor's note: a "corner card" is the return address on the "carrier" or mailing envelope.]

Viguerie: And sometimes don't even put corner cards at all—sneak up on them. Force them to open it before they know who's writing to them.

Dees: No, I always put on corner cards.

Clark: Political fundraising mail, as a rule, is the poorest user of graphics in the entire spectrum of direct mail. You rarely see a picture, you rarely see more than a second color, you rarely see different sizes. Rarely different shapes, rarely token devices that are now standard in the rest of the industry. When you talk graphics I think you should define it better—it's every physical and visual variable of the package—not just type.

Dees: I once got a piece of mail that said, up top, "Cornelia Wallace." Inside was a Christmas card and it said: "All you have to do is sign this Christmas card and give George the thing that he wants the most and that is to let him know that he'll have no financial worries in this election." (Laughs all around) "And I'm enclosing a Christmas card and all you have to do is put your check in there and he'll be so happy." Well that was a very, very successful mailing. Mr. Viguerie's company did that one, and I'd say a Christmas card is good graphics.

Clark: But it's a device—not graphics.

Dees: It had Jesus on the front cover.

C&E: It's important, clearly, to get professional help with your direct mail effort. If somebody decides to run for the U.S. House or Senate, or even lower level offices, do they need to seek professional help in organizing their direct mail campaign? Couldn't somebody who's already working on their campaign put together a direct mail program for them?

Dees: My feeling is this: you've got to have an individual who has had considerable experience in making people respond by some kind of distinct medium, whether it's direct mail, television, radio, newspaper. You need somebody who understands the numbers. Somebody who's worked selling gifts through the mail. You've got to have an experienced direct mail individual. Otherwise the tuition you'll pay just to learn the direct mail business will be too high. The time you'll waste will be too valuable. Unfortunately, there aren't too many people around who head up their own mail order marketing firm who are willing to volunteer their time for political candidates. Therefore, the professional direct mail consultant is very important. I get two, three calls a week, and I refer them to everybody who is sitting right here at the table—at least most of them.

Viguerie: I appreciate your honesty. Listen, Morris gave me one of my biggest clients, George Wallace.

Dees: I love George, but the love isn't that deep. I love Cornelia more. I just think the little fee that's paid to agencies is well worth it. I got a call yesterday from 60 Minutes. The lady will be calling you up, I forgot her name now, but I gave her your two fellas' names. (Dees points to Viguerie and Craver.) Somebody wrote a letter to 60 Minutes and said that the fundraising companies get the first million dollars raised, and that they tell the candidate: "Since you get the matching million, you keep the match, I'll keep the first million." And direct mail fundraisers have gotten a black eye because what people don't realize is fundraising companies probably get 15 dollars per thousand mailed, which is far below an advertising agency's 15 percent commission, and then the other goes to cost. The consultants have to overcome this false impression that they raise the money to benefit themselves.

Hartman: This is part of the entire picture of federal campaigns which must become more professional. Years ago we all can remember when we had hundreds of capable women who would do these things for us, perform these functions of the campaign for us. Today, that person has a full-time job. And in campaigns we're finding there are difficulties in getting competent volunteers to do the work. We're finding that it's easier to hire professionals than to do it ourselves. The only way elections can be run now is to use more and more professional help. And you're seeing that in every election.

Burnett: I can't argue with the need for professionalism. But there is one critical aspect of the five parts that make up direct mail. They are: copy, package, offer, timing, and the lists. It's the list. If I had my druthers, I'd rather have a good list and poor copy than good copy and a poor list. Therefore, the local person can, with a little bit of help and the knowledge of where to get the right list, do very well in this business. He can do better than he ever dreamed if he knows anything about the list business. That's the key to this.

Viguerie: One reason why direct mail has somewhat of a "country cousin" image in politics is because of the lack of available professionals. I have a friend who was involved at a high level in George Bush's first congressional campaign in 1966, and he said, "Richard, you know, you make your living in direct mail, you think it's great and wonderful—I wouldn't give you a nickel for it, because we used it for George Bush and it was a bomb, just a disaster. But regular television was beautiful, we went to New York and hired two of the best professionals we could get and they put together some fabulous television and it elected Bush.

But direct mail—we used it and it was just a bomb." And I said, "Bill, that's very interesting, I know who did your television and radio, but I'm curious who did your direct mail?" And with a very straight face he said, "Well, we had a couple of women volunteers do it." And he doesn't understand why to this day his direct mail didn't work. And that is very common in politics and political campaigns. They wouldn't dream of having a volunteer, or the candidate's next door neighbor's best friend who doesn't have a job, do their television for them. When they spend $300,000 on television they want professionals. But they think nothing of using a volunteer to do their direct mail and wonder why it isn't effective.

Dees: Let me interject something here. There are many sharp women in this field that you should have invited for this panel. Patricia Segal, who was director of direct mail over at the DNC [Democratic National Committee] and is now doing Carter's direct mail and doing a superb job; and Daphne Dwyer, who works for Stewart Mott and Mott Enterprises, has done a great deal of political fundraising. I think both of them could have contributed significantly to your panel. Both of them are very sharp, and I'm sure there are many others.

Clark: I'd like to second one thing that Richard said about using professionals, because this is not limited to the fundraising business. I was in the offices of a magazine publisher the other day, who resides in the same building as Ed Burnett, and he's trying to rejuvenate the magazine. And they were committing three test packages, in October, through the mail, written by their editors. Now, I said to them, as I will say to you, I've been involved in probably ten million dollars worth of copy testing in the last 20 years, and in that period of time only one editor's package has ever worked. I said: "So you're going to commit three test packages, your entire copy test, to an editor's package. I think you need a pro in there. I don't care which pro you hire, there are many of them." And they looked at me like I was coming from another world. There's a lot of mistrust. People don't trust us, Richard. They think they can do it better themselves.

Viguerie: Yes, for some strange reason direct mail has a different image in their minds than other forms of advertising. They learn to read and write in the first grade; they know where the post office sells stamps; they know how to buy envelopes—what's the big deal about direct mail? But they wouldn't dream of not using professionals in every other aspect of their business, whether it's in the legal, accounting, or whatever. But in direct mail—what's the big deal, I know how to read and write, and how to buy stamps.

C&E: What role should direct mail fundraising play relative to other types of fundraising—benefits, telethons, cocktail-party fundraisers, dinners, etc. What variables do you weigh when you decide what portion of your fundraising or what proportion of your campaign budget you're going to spend on direct mail?

Viguerie: A brief answer. There are many factors. One of them is the candidate. I was involved in two campaigns for president this year. Now one, Phil Crane, running two years before the election with one percent support out there, relatively unknown, you budget maybe in an advertising way 95% on direct mail. You can't afford to go out and raise that much money through telethons, telephone, cocktail parties, and big dinners. But if you're John Connally then maybe it's the reverse with receptions, dinners—this type of thing.

Yolton: A typical example is the last time Chuck Percy ran for reelection. We were asked to do a direct mail fundraising campaign for him, which we did on a limited budget. But all of the work, and the effort and creative activity that went to put that campaign in the works, of course, was mainly directed to an Illinois group of people. The money we raised by direct mail didn't amount to diddlysquat compared to what he raised with two fundraising dinners in Chicago. In that case, did he need direct mail? Well, he wanted it as part of the total mix but he recognized that it wasn't going to be as important to his campaign and his fundraising as these other ways of doing it.

Craver: In my experience, the principal factors that tend to remain constant are these: the time that the campaign has to explore and exploit direct mail and the constituency it represents. If the candidate has an apparently middle-of-the-road position on the issue(s), that doesn't generate much passion on either side, probably direct mail isn't going to play as important a role in his campaign as the other forms of fundraising. Certainly if they don't have enough time to explore and exploit a direct mail campaign then it can be disastrous. That's probably the biggest single error campaigns make in using direct mail—they simply don't commit the 18-24 months necessary to let the ball of string run out the way it should.

Hartman: Don't you think it depends on the size of the campaign?

Craver: Yes

C&E: Do local level campaigns use direct mail?

Craver: Some do. Last time around Joe Fisher over in Northern Virginia used it very effectively. I haven't done much congressional mail so I really don't have much experience.

Viguerie: I would say that a fair number use it, but I don't know that I would really call it direct mail. It's taking a brochure that the candidate's wife put together and putting it in an envelope. And I don't really call that direct mail.

Yolton: And you always print it in red, white, and blue. A picture of the candidate and his family in red, white and blue. (Laughs)

Clark: Actually, in Darien [Connecticut], we've got a couple of candidates for whom we've done classic direct mail. It's not been fundraising so much as getting-out-the-vote kind of mail. But you can use mail on a very small scale. I think you do depend on the good offices of somebody who knows what they're doing rather than the proverbial housewife, but if you follow some of the larger successful patterns, it can help at the local level. Particularly for the guy who isn't terribly well known.

Viguerie: I feel strongly that the lower the office in terms of visibility—Congress, the state legislature, local and city offices—direct mail's importance in the overall picture increases. Direct mail can be devastatingly effective in the lower offices because you're competing and you can't afford, of course, to go on television and in the newspapers that are distributed over several hundred square miles. You just want to focus in on a few square miles. And direct mail could be, in terms of your advertising, anywhere from 90-100 percent of your budget. And it can be devastatingly effective.

Burnett: Richard, you've published some data showing what percentage of the people that are able to get the primes and go to work in direct mail, how they come out in the elections. Would you like to talk about that for a minute?

Viguerie: Ed, I'm not sure I follow you. I publish very little information. We've got a bunch of con artists sitting around here (Laughter)

Dees: Who's talking about a bad reputation? (Laughter)

Burnett: I think you said that given the lists in direct mail, the man that uses it compared to the man that doesn't will win X percent of the votes.

Viguerie: Oh I see. Yes, I recall saying that a number of times, but that is just something off the top of my head. I feel that, everything else being equal, at a lower level, a direct mail campaign conducted by a professional should prevail over a campaign that doesn't have one, somewhere in the area of 90 percent of the time. Because in most all areas of campaigns—again if the situations are relatively equal—you're going to be offsetting each other. Each campaign is going to have a pretty knowledgeable campaign manager, they're going to have intelligent billboards, bumper stickers, volunteers, radio/television ads—all that's going to be offsetting each other. The one thing, campaign after campaign that we're involved in, that we don't find the opposition doing, is intelligent direct mail. It's a rare campaign that we're involved in when we have an opponent that is also conducting an intelligent direct mail campaign.

Craver: And one of the difficulties there is that direct mail is viewed principally as a fundraising medium and not as the overall advertising medium it should be.

Clark: No communication that gets opened does just one thing. It's doing two, three, four, five things. If you write a communication just to get 50 bucks, you're kidding yourself. You're leaving an impression in somebody's mind about that candidate. Whether they give you the 50 bucks or not is almost academic.

C&E: Apparently it's a cardinal rule of direct mail fundraising that you only want to do one job at a time. So if your primary objective with a letter or package is to raise funds, you don't want to, for example, with the same letter, try to get people to sign up as volunteers, conduct an opinion survey, promote a straight party voting ticket, etc. Now, if that's the case, if you're only supposed to go after one thing at a time how can a campaign afford to send out all the different mailings for all the different things?

Craver: I don't think that is necessarily the case. Getting the reader to participate in a public opinion poll or getting him to volunteer may reinforce the capacity to raise money. There isn't any hard and fast rule that says you can only ask the reader to do one thing at a time. There's a hard and fast rule not to confuse the reader. But their participation will enhance their giving.

Yolton: There's that famous political disaster where one of the big list compilers sold the Republican National Committee and the Democratic National Committee on a joint fundraising effort, signed by Adlai Stevenson and Dwight Eisenhower. It was close to being the biggest bomb of all time!

Viguerie: A PAC, when they do a mailing, is trying to cover the waterfront in candidates: give us money and we will give it to half a dozen, a dozen, or whatever number of candidates, in your best interest. And that is a lot more difficult money to raise than when you're focusing in on one specific person. It is easier to do one thing in a mailing than a number of things. Traditionally you'll find it easier to raise money for one person than for a dozen.

C&E: How do you coordinate your direct mail activity with other media programs?

Dees: In McGovern's and also Wallace's campaign, they had 30 minute programs talking about Vietnam or blocking the school house door or whatever, and at the end of it there was a fundraising pitch for X dollars. It might not have paid for the radio or TV time but it brought donors into the overall pool. Right now we have a five-minute spot for Senator Kennedy that we're going to run, with a fundraising pitch at the end of it. And we might pay for 20-30% of our total overall cost and that's valuable too. We ran the Georgetown Speech—we copied it and ran it in several media markets—and every place we ran it, it more than paid for the cost of the television. We were getting across the Georgetown Speech and the fundraising pitch was paying for it. As a general rule, it's hard to make television pitches for fundraising work, and to pay for the television time. But if you're going to run a television pitch and you've got time to put a nice message at the end of it, put it on.

Burnett: Would it have paid to mail that speech then?

Dees: Yes, that's what Senator Kennedy did. That's like his Manifesto in the second phase of his campaign. It sets forth his positions very well. And we're mailing that and it is in fact bringing us at least two dollars for every one dollar spent and maybe even better.

Viguerie: There are a number of things that can be done to coordinate the various media that you're using and are not usually done. There are a lot of sophisticated things that can be done, too, but a lot of things that are not all that sophisticated—just kind of basic—that you seldom see being done. For instance, you know usually mouths ahead of time (if not a year) when the candidate is going to announce his national campaign. And when you announce your campaign for president, or for the Senate or whatever, the media covering that is significant.

We did it for Crane. We mailed heavily at the time of his announcement. And the difference between the direct mail response in those next seven days, and three or four weeks later was significant. It was a two or three to one difference. You must get your direct mail to arrive at the time of the big media hype. Many magazines are friendly. You know that magazine X or Y is going to write a favorable article. They're going to put your candidate on the cover. You ought to be planning to rent that magazine's subscriber list and have a mailing go out to them at the same time the issue will be arriving. And when you're going to have a big, national paid TV advertisement for 30 minutes or so, you ought to have direct mail arriving the same time. You expect to win a primary next week and you expect a big media hype from that, then you ought to have direct mail arriving at the time of your expected victory.

Clark: It seems to me that direct mail is written with one theme, and advertising/television with another. There's rarely any bridge between the two, there's rarely any similarity. And, to echo a point Ed made earlier—that many of the themes are tested in the mail and as one guy said to me about his campaign television: "Boy we've really got a Pepsi Cola kind of television commercial." And I said, "Well, you don't have Pepsi Cola kind of fundraising. They don't fit together well."

Dees: Direct mail is me writing you a personal letter. Television is saying something to the masses, like a newspaper ad. And a Pepsi Cola-type ad might sell the candidate well, but it takes a totally different psychological approach to get a person to part with their dollars. The themes of both have got to be the same or you wouldn't be selling your people on television, nor would you be selling them in the mail. When you say themes, your theme might not be "Stand Up for America" or whatever it is, but the issues that you're dealing with have almost got to be singular or you won't be successful. The theme is the same but the approach is different. Kennedy's theme for both direct mail and television are very similar, but his television pitch is made for a different kind of audience.

Viguerie: Television is a sort of shotgun approach. And direct mail is more the rifle approach. When you're going to a list of people you know something very specific about: they are for or against gun control, for or against increased expenditures in the national defense budget, whatever—you want to be speaking primarily to that one specific issue. But beyond that I feel the question is valid—there is not enough coordination between the direct mail and the overall effort. And I primarily would fault the hierarchy of the campaign, because, again, in most campaigns—not all, but the vast majority of them—direct mail is sort of a country cousin.

Dees: An individual, to get elected, usually shouldn't use the same theme they publicly run on, for their direct mail (at least for cold prospects). Direct mail only works on those people that have a pretty strong left or right ideological bent, and that's not the kind of theme that usually will get you elected. The letters for George McGovern may scream out: "We must stop the war. We must do this, that or the other." They're going to a very narrow segment of the population. I found them played up in the press very little and I don't think that hurt us very much. Even though the candidate might not want to sign the letter because he says he'll get some pressure, it can be effective as the rifle approach. But on the other hand, his television is trying to reach a much broader group of people. He doesn't want to turn too many of them off.

Yolton: You get money from your friends, but hopefully you get votes from the whole spectrum.

Dees: That's a good statement.

Yolton: Something that potentially can confuse people is this question of ability to test with political direct mail. Richard's mentioned the fact that you have these chances to coordinate the various media with direct mail. You do a certain amount of flying by the seat of your pants in putting together your direct mail package in political direct mail. Unlike traditional direct mail and mail order operations that Time/Life and others conduct, where they test everything three to six months ahead of any roll-out of mailings, you simply don't have that advantage with political direct mail. The timing is much stricter. And it might be an interesting thing to talk about that, because it seems to me that that's where true professionalism needs to cover the floor. You simply don't have the time to test and you better have people creating your political direct mail that have experience, and have the ability to quickly respond to whatever the current political situation is if it might help you raise money or provide some other positive response.

Craver: There's no question about it. When it comes to political direct mail the "high trapeze" part of the act involves the judgements you have to make without doing a lot of tests. You simply can't test a lot of this stuff—you don't have time. Morris has a letter out this morning to the Kennedy people for what he did last night in Pennsylvania. That had to be done three days before Pennsylvania. You have to make some judgements and you have to go with it. John Anderson is going to announce an independent candidacy tomorrow. I don't know what he's going to say, but we have to be in the mail with two million pieces tonight!

Viguerie: And something else that these gentlemen aren't saying is that one of the reasons that you see so little good political direct mail is that most of these people work for agencies, but you're not able to delegate much of the creative work. When you win a primary one day and you want to get in the mail in 24 hours, you don't ask someone who's had a couple of years of experience to go out and raise you a lot of money. You invest a lot of money in a mailing. It's got to be right the first time. There's no—"Well, we've-made-a-slight-error-here,-we'll-correct-it-next-month" type of thing. It's got to be letter-perfect the first time. And you don't delegate that type of thing. There's just a few people that have that type of talent and experience.

Burnett: Can you use television to test theme concepts, much the way we use the telephone to test a theme to find out if an American Management Association Seminar will go or not?

Dees: You can use television to test what the next television commercial will do, but you can't use television to tell you what direct mail will do.

Clark: But isn't there a lot of market research done before you start some of these campaigns? Don't you have some ideas of the strengths and weaknesses of the candidates What is the public's perception of your candidate? What is the public's perception of his strengths and weaknesses?

Dees: There are polls being done by your pollsters, naturally.

Clark: Well, it seems to me there's an awful lot of political direct mail being done where one just writes a letter and doesn't really know what the public feels.

Yolton: Well, it comes from experience with having done a certain amount of political direct mail to a certain constituency. It's not a whole lot different than if you are selling subscriptions to an outdoor magazine, you're going to hit the adventure types. Richard knows pretty much what he can say to the conservative audience, just as Morris and Roger know what they can say to their people. For instance, Roger wrote one letter overnight! You're not only denied the opportunity to test in many cases, you're even denied the opportunity to get the client's approval of what it is you're putting in the mail—because he's not around to read it!

Clark: But he didn't shoot with a rifle. Mailing two million pieces—that is not a rifle!

Dees: That is a rifle. That's the smallest barrel rifle I know of in direct mail: two million pieces. I think the best way I've heard it put is: Get the Mail Out the Door. I was raised on a farm, and me and my daddy were up on top of a tin roof one time nailing nails. If you've ever nailed nails in tin, you know you have to tap on it to get it through first because you might hit your thumbnail. I was sitting up there tapping away like that and Daddy said, "Hell, go on and hit the nail, you may bend a few." That's the way it is with direct mail. I think it's much better to get the stuff out the door. And I can tell you this: if there's seven people sitting around trying a lawsuit, there would be seven good ways to try the lawsuit if they are all good lawyers. And I can tell you there are five or six good direct mail people around this table and all of us would have a different approach on how to write the Anderson letter, and all of them might do equally well. I think you make a mistake in trying to wait too long. Get the stuff out, because direct mail can be used in every political campaign that's in existence. At least going back to the donors you already have. You simply can write them a letter quicker than you can talk to them on the phone, go get them, shake their hands, give them corn beef or, whatever. I don't care if you don't have 500 donors or 1000 donors. I did a campaign for Donald Stewart [former] United States Senator from Alabama. And Donald Stewart called me up and he said, "You know, Morris, I need some help, I haven't got any money." He had 1,200 donors. So we got a letter out to all 1,200 donors, quick, and that raised him, I think, $40,000, and it was enough to get him on the move. But my goal in any kind of fundraising, whether it's direct mail that's raising money for the Southern Poverty Law Center, or for any organization, the National Rifle Association—whoever, is to get names of people who've already given to you in a pool as quick as you can. Because everytime you write these people a letter, you will get back anywhere from five to 30 dollars for each one dollar you spend. And you can write this special group as frequently as every three weeks without causing any problem.

Viguerie: We're raising money for a congressman's re-election campaign and he has a national reputation. So we're not going to just conservative lists. There are several million conservative contributors out there. We're looking for the people who have identified themselves as being seriously concerned about high taxes and big spending by Congress. And we write them a letter targeted to that issue. Other people have identified themselves as being very concerned about national defense.

Dees: You can't run the *Newsweek* subscriber list and raise money for a political campaign. I just don't believe that's possible. You have to target.

Yolton: Getting back to what Morris said about getting mail out—years ago at McGrawHill I learned an axiom I've quoted many times. I guess its translatable into an Alabama accent (Laughs all around): if you don't get something out, you won't get anything back... you've got to get it out. It may not be perfect, but do it anyway.

Viguerie: Of all the sins that are committed by people who have some knowledge of direct mail and political campaigns is this vacillation: is this brochure better than that one; is this color better than that; what should I do here; should I put this in the package or should I do this—just do it! Get it out. Wish it on your competition that they will test nonessentials, unimportant things. Just push the mail out the door. And don't worry about the quality. So you could have taken an extra six days and gotten it done perhaps a little better. Better to slap a label on it and get it out in 24 hours. Make it happen, do something.

C&E: Is that the only difference between direct mail at the presidential level, the statewide level and the local level—you have more money to play with, and you can test, and try some different graphics, etc.? How would you say it differs other than that?

Dees: No, on the contrary. I would say in political campaigns at the national level you don't have the money to play around with, generally. In George McGovern's campaign, which was the flushest I've ever worked on, we still didn't have any money to play around with anything. I've never been in any campaign that the money wasn't spent before you ever got it in.

Viguerie: I see political direct mail fundraising as sort of like seed corn. You go out, put some money together, you make some test mailings, and some good money comes in. And now you know which lists to follow up on, you put together a big campaign and the television man comes along, or the pollster, and grabs your money, and spends it on something else, and he's eaten the seed corn.

Dees: We call it seed peanuts. You make a good point though that I think anybody who is going to be reading this roundtable ought to understand. Direct mail is an investment unlike any other in a political campaign. You get a return on it. In McGovern's campaign, we got rather hard-nosed about it. I opened a bank account that only I could sign on. I wouldn't even let our treasurer sign on it. So when the money came in, it went into that bank account immediately and I had the chance to pay my suppliers first. So we got first call on the money we raised and were able then to pay the postage for the next upcoming mailing. And then what was left we gave the campaign, and that caused a lot of gnashing of teeth. Now we are doing this in Kennedy's campaign. We set up a special bank account, we did our direct mail and when the money came back it went into that account. They couldn't put it in any other account because I made everybody sign an agreement that they wouldn't do it.

Viguerie: I knew I was going to learn something today. Thank you, Morris.

Dees: I did it for the benefit of getting results. But the ad agency that was helping us was extremely appreciative of this approach.

C&E: Let's move on to specifics now. First of all, lists. Mr. Burnett has said that the weakest part of many direct mail programs is the list, because they are taken for granted. How does a campaign make sure it is using good, productive lists for fundraising? How does a brand new campaign start a list? What are other sources of lists useful to political fundraisers?

Craver: As Morris indicated, the mailing lists of people with affinity interests—particularly people who have given money to interests that are similar to those of your candidate—represent the best mailing lists. Now, any candidate should be able to, if he or she has a stand on the issues—a stand other than right up the middle of the road—should be able to locate at least some mailing lists. If you're a candidate in the middle of the road who doesn't have a strong stand on any issues, then, in my experience, direct mail isn't going to work for you. In terms of compiling lists, or building a list from nothing without going to a list broker, I think a candidate who does this is preparing to leap off a bridge. Obviously, the best list a candidate can build is one with people who have already given him money for other offices or perhaps names from organizations whose letters he's signed. George McGovern signed a tremendous amount of liberal mail before he ran for president. So he had access to those lists. Obviously, even a candidate's Christmas card list, if it's a small campaign, is a beneficial list. But for the big national campaigns, or even the congressional campaigns, we begin with donors to affinity issues. And once we use these donor lists, then we get into the lists that tend to traffic in similar issues.

Hartman: I've run one congressional and one gubernatorial election in Connecticut. We went back and picked up names from the governor's last campaign, the last senate campaign, the latest congressional campaigns. Then we took the 18 most populous towns in the state and these represent 50% of the state's population. We just took those lists and put them in the computer. Those were lists of proven donors to these campaigns. Those lists were punched in to the computer in three ways. They were put in alphabetically, they were put in by zip code, and they were put in by descending order of amount given to the campaigns. So we'd get into our office in the morning and if we really needed money, and we always did, we would go down the list from the top and call the top givers who hadn't been hit yet.

And I must say that initially, my biggest help in this effort was an occasional telephone call to a guy I was told was a professional fundraiser named Morris Dees, and charged me up every time I called him. But it worked, and we continued in that vein in Connecticut. Now we might be absolutely wrong, and I'm sure there are many other ways of doing it. The older I get the more I realize there is more than one way of doing something right.

Burnett: Why did you leave out the rest of the state?

Hartman: Because there just wasn't the manpower available. We should have done it if we could have but there wasn't the manpower available. And we used that list for other purposes, for instance, cocktail parties. If we give a cocktail party, we knew by taking our zip code list whom we should invite and we went to those people and asked them if they had five friends they could invite. Well then the organization invited those other people.

Craver: So, you used certain criteria to qualify these people, one of the principal criteria being that they had given to other political candidates. I remember when we started Common Cause, there weren't many liberal lists. There were a lot of charitable lists, but not a lot of liberal, social action lists. And I remember going to the Library of Congress and looking through literally hundreds of magazines, reading them, figuring what kind of person would subscribe to them so I could rent their subscriber list. It was the only way I could think of to widen that list market.

Burnett: You're talking now about what we call the psychographics of the list, as opposed to the demographics: it's the life style—what they do, what they buy, what they will pay for, what magazines they will subscribe to. And that really is the key when you go into the outside world. There is an acronym for what Guy was talking about earlier, which in computer language is NINO—Not In, Not Out. Joe, I'm surprised you didn't put all the names on computer in the Connecticut campaign you mentioned because then you could have at least mailed them instead of just stopping them altogether.

Hartman: It was for the same reason that someone just spoke, Morris, I guess, on the seed corn. In the beginning of the campaign we sat down with the political people and they said: "We have $3,000 to raise all your money and we want a million and a half!" And they even wanted to use that $3,000 for other purposes than just raising more money, too!

Yolton: Well, it seems obvious that if you get a good voter registration list that represents the political persuasion of your candidate that you must have a wonderful mailing list. Isn't that true, Roger?

Craver: Absolutely wrong. (Laughs all around).

Yolton: I baited you!

Craver: Voter registration lists are seldom good sources for fundraising of any kind, particularly direct mail.

Yolton: Practically never!

Burnett: Even if they're primes, that is, people who vote in the primaries?

Dees: I've got some experience in that area to share with the readers. In 1972, McGovern won the California primary. The modern way to do it is to go out and get people to do your canvassing. You get the ones, the twos, the threes, and the fours. The ones are the people who say they are definitely going to vote for you before the election; the twos are leaning your way, the threes are leaning away from you, and the fours are opposed to you.

    Well, after the California primary, we had 450,000 ones or people who definitely said they were going to vote for us. And the campaign managers wanted to mail the ones a fundraising appeal: "We've won California in a big way," etc. And we also needed the money for the convention or something else, I don't know what it was for, but we had a good reason to want money. And we wrote the ones a letter. I suggested they test 5,000 randomly picked, and they were so positive it would work that one individual even put up all the money. And he lost all of his money. We didn't even get back the postage!

Viguerie: Direct mail is simple. I don't know why people make such a big deal out of it. I say this partly tongue-in-cheek, of course, but it's not as difficult as people make it out to be. If you want to do fundraising, you go to fundraising lists. You go to voter lists if you want votes. But why would you use a voter list if you want money? It just doesn't make sense to do it that way.

Dees: There's something else to it. My background is really in business. My first national fundraising letter was for George McGovern. Up till then my fundraising had been just a minor little nothing back home. My experience was in business. Now, this tale has been often told but I think it might help explain something about fundraising to the readers.

Sears, Roebuck or some company, says Sears, was interested in selling suitcases by mail. So they decided to get lists from a company like Fuller Brush who had traveling salesmen—people who had just gotten a job and all needed a suitcase. They had to have a suitcase because they had to travel, and if they didn't have one they could sure use one. And they took these lists and developed a terrific offer for suitcases: special bargain suitcase, etc. And they took a thousand of those people who had just gotten a job with Fuller Brush Co. as traveling salesmen—high prospects, you'd think, for suitcases. And then they took a list of just 1,000 regular mail-order buyers—people who had bought something in the mail. And the people who supposedly needed suitcases flopped, and the others outputted them ten to one. And what it's saying is this: first of all, people have to have a propensity to do something by mail. Obviously, you must be saying in your mind—well where do you get people who are mail-oriented to start with. They filter in one way or another. They come in through some type thing: they subscribe to a magazine because they get interested in water skiing, so then they've bought something by mail. But there's some individuals who simply just will not do anything by mail. And that's a characteristic about them. They're not used to writing something out, putting it in an envelope, sending it, and hoping to get something back later. That's the separating characteristic right there.

Viguerie: What we're talking about here is not mail order buyers—we're talking about political direct mail contributors. You answered the question correctly, but let's not lose sight of the fact that here we're talking about people who will give to a candidate through the mail, you're talking about a very, very small portion. We have millions of people who will give to a conservative cause, but maybe less than ten percent of them will give to a candidate.

Craver: Yes, on the liberal side this year: Kennedy, Anderson, and the big national liberal senatorial races, McGovern, Bayh, these people—maybe a total of 350,000 people will give money in these 1980 races.

Burnett: How much prospecting has to be done to get the names of the 350,000?

Craver: Oh, probably 30 to 40 million pieces.

Burnett: Less than one percent.

Craver: Yes, till it all settles down.

Burnett: You're explaining one more factor in psychographics. The one that gives, psychographically is different from people who won't give. The person who responds by mail is different from the person who doesn't respond by mail. So you have to be very careful where you go for your lists.

Dees: The calls that I get, right off the bat they'll say, "Well, all the teachers in Arkansas have endorsed me and I can get a list of all the teachers." And I say: First of all, I don't think you can raise money in Arkansas on mass appeal because you don't have enough potential lists out there." And they say: "Oh but I got the lists, don't worry about that." Well, just because you've got a list of all the teachers doesn't mean anything. Now there's a more liberal teacher group called—Mr. Shanker runs it—I don't know the name.

C&E: American Federation of Teachers.

Dees: Now that one has about 300,000 teachers, and that's not the NEA [National Education Association] which is more a middle-of-the-road group. Well, back when McGovern was running, Shanker endorsed him, and we got a letter written by a teacher who had gone over to Vietnam and gotten both legs shot off or something like that. I can't really remember but we got as strong a pitch as we could come up with; we sent it with a personal note on the bottom from Shanker saying "We endorse this whole thing," and it was not successful. And it just goes to show you, with the hottest cause, the hottest letter, and everything else, just because you mail a list of teachers doesn't mean you'll raise any money from teachers.

Burnett: Note that he's talking about another methodology: which is third-party endorsement. This can also be used in fundraising, but obviously doesn't work as well on one group as another.

Viguerie: Well, I'm not so sure. We don't know. If he had tested with and without the third party endorsement, then maybe we'd know.

Dees: I did, because I was running 50,000. I mailed the standard McGovern letter to them.

Viguerie: Which worked better?

Dees: I don't remember. When we get hot into a campaign after we know a package works, I don't even keep up with it. It might be good for Herb's history book but I could care less. [Editor's Note: Herbert Alexander writes a quadrennial analysis of presidential campaign finance.] All I know is whether it's working or note. But we do keep good statistics on most of our results.

C&E: So you don't duplicate things that have worked before and mail again on that same theme?

Dees: Sure, that's about all you do.

Viguerie: Senate candidate X over here calls us and wants us to do the 90-day wonder thing— maybe only a 30-day wonder type of thing. The election's in 30 days and he wants you to perform 22 miracles for him. In which case we just go to the files and pull a letter that we wrote last year or whenever.

C&E: It is said that in no advertising medium does copy play a more important role than in direct mail. Why is that so? And what role does copy play?

Yolton: As we said, direct mail is the personal medium. The whole theory and strategy of developing a direct mail piece is to write copy that is a "from me to you" message. Because direct mail arrives in people's mail box and it is their personal mail box, the closer you can come to writing copy that conveys that personal message, the better chance you have of getting a favorable reception, and a favorable response to your direct mail. So, certainly copy is more important in direct mail perhaps than anything else—space advertising, beautiful pictures, several pages of ads at once well-chosen things can get attention, but not necessarily the kind of direct response that you want.

C&E: What are key elements of good copy? What role do such things as believability, order, conversational/personal tone, direct, action oriented phraseology, proof of statements, etc., play?

Yolton: Well, all of those things are probably more important in direct mail than they are in other forms of advertising because you are asking people to perform an act of faith, in that you are asking them to respond sight unseen, and you say something is going to happen as a result of their responding but how do they know? They have to have some faith that that something is going to happen, that the dollars they are donating to your candidate are really going to be used in order to further the candidate's election potential. So that some nice neat things like believeability build some kind of order into your copy so it's easy for people to understand, and you use a conversational/personal tone because it is a personal message. All of those are just part of the art form of writing direct mail copy. It is a "personal" type of skill.

C&E: What are the relative merits of short vs. longer copy? The trend now seems to be to longer letters—even five to seven pages. Why?

Yolton: All that matters is what works. And if you have a long story to tell and an educational job to do, and you're trying to instill a sense of involvement and support, you probably can't do it with three paragraphs, not in prospecting you can't. What works best is what determines how long your letter or copy is.

C&E: How do you know what works best? How do you know what is going to work best in sending out a letter? You might send out two to three pages of superb copy....

Yolton: Morris and Roger are the ones that are writing long letters and I would have to assume that it comes from their positive experiences in the past. Morris claims he doesn't do any testing, but at least he has a gut feeling.

Dees: I think of myself as a copy-writer first. Nobody invented long letters for political fundraising. I'm sure they were used before we used them for McGovern—we just got credit for using them.

The long letters that we decided to write for George McGovern were based on Time/Life's program. They'd been writing four, five, and sixpage letters that sold books for years. People had, in the past, not looked at political fundraising as merchandising a product or trying to sell something. And so, I got the Humphrey/Muskie letters that were sent out in the past in 1972, pre-'72, right in that era. And basically they said: "My name is Hubert Humphrey and I'm running for president, or my name is Edmund Muskie and I'm running for president, and maybe a couple or three paragraphs—I stand for the good of the country, that kind of approach, and please send me a contribution. Well, what we then did was apply the techniques that had been used successfully selling books by direct mail. You've got to tell a good, solid, selling story.

Now with Ted Kennedy this time we used a letter, six pages long. And I was really nervous about it because I felt: Well, everybody knows who Ted Kennedy is, and we ought to just write a short letter, a one page letter. And I was flying back from Miami on the plane and I jotted out a one page letter, and called Roger and said: "Roger, we've got to test a one-page letter, we're not taking anything for granted." We tested a one-page vs. a six-page, and the six-page beat it. And we also did this for Anderson this time. We tested the long versus the short. If you've got a donor that's already given to you, I think it'd be unwise to write much more than one page—two at the most. But when you're going out to a new donor, prospecting in this volatile market you're talking about, then it may take a lot more than just a one-page. It may take a brochure, or something else. The point that I want to make on copy, especially with respect to going bade to your own donors, is that direct mail should be fun. It should involve people. I subscribe to the theory that adults are really just kids playing in a big treehouse. When you were a little kid you'd clip the coupon off the back of the cereal box and send off for the Captain Midnight ring—right? Well, I think we are all still motivated by the same kind of exciting things. You should involve your donors and make them feel they're going to get something back.

Our last Kennedy mailing offered an engraved inaugural announcement to be sent in January.

And our response was just tremendous. And there was a little note that came from me, as finance director, on a separate little slip that said: Memo to John Doe from Morris Dees, Finance Director, and I said: "Please help me raise this money for Sen. Kennedy." Then three or four little paragraphs and the last one offered an engraved announcement. We also sent posters of a Jamie Wyeth painting. Anybody who sent in $25 or more, got a 24 X 36-inch Jamie Wyeth poster. And we had a little label in our package that said: "Mailing Label for Poster" and we had a color picture of the poster in there. And it was something they could take out, put back in, send back. It was tactile involvement.

Clark: That's mass marketing: "What am I getting out of it?"

Dees: It isn't just getting something out of it. The most successful program I've ever been a part of was a mailing for George McGovern which cost $25,000 and took in over a million dollars. We sent everybody perforated cards saying: "Here are four checks and fill out these four checks and one's dated for each month—August, September . . . etc.

Viguerie: That's not mass marketing. He's still marketing to his audience—he's not mailing yet to cold prospects—he's mailing to his previous buyers.

Dees: But then in order to do that we sent them a little pen that said "FMBM" on it: For McGovern Before Miami, with a little label that said: "Contents Jewelry," so they could even see it coming back to them. It made them feel important. I'd like to ask you a question, Dick. How do long letters work in prospecting for conservative causes?

Viguerie: Morris, people make too much out of direct mail now. Like I said earlier, it's not all that big a deal. It's relatively simple. If you want to ask a stranger for a favor, you've got to talk more than if you want to ask a friend. What's the big deal. When you're prospecting you're talking to strangers. If it's January 1971, you can't write a successful one page letter for George McGovern. But if it's October of 1972 and you're writing to your friends, all you need is one page. So, it's just not that difficult. When you're writing to somebody for the first time, they know nothing about the campaign, maybe they've never heard of the candidate, they don't know what your needs are, the media isn't hyping the campaign—it takes a lot of copy. If you were in a retail marketing environment, you wouldn't dream of restricting your salesmen to only eight seconds, or even 60 seconds. It doesn't make any sense. So why would you try to do it in direct mail fundraising?

Clark: At one point, I got to spend a lot of Time, Inc. money in copy-testing direct mail. We tested size, format, number of letters and so forth. Generally, we found that the more you spend on direct mail in pure cost-per-thousand, the more you will get back. So, if you wanted to take a four-page vs. a six-page letter, a six-page letter will generate more response than a four-page letter. A six-page letter with a brochure generated more response than a six-page letter without a brochure.

Burnett: There must be a stopping point.

Clark: There is obviously a mythical stopping point, but in broad terms the more we spent the more we got back. I didn't say cost efficiently—I'll get to that in a minute. But I think this is particularly true in prospecting. You're offering new customers, new buyers, new prospects—you have to be prepared to spend more money than you think you need to in order to get them in the door. Once they're in the door, you can do a lot more with them. By and large, you don't spend down the first time. Spend up. It's a sound investment! When anyone starts to write a fundraising letter, they should ask themselves: "Why should the guy receiving this letter do what I want him to do? And when they finish writing the letter they ought to read it and say, "Did I talk him into doing it? Did I answer that question?" And if you didn't, throw the letter out and start again. Too much mail from every area: publishers, fundraisers, etc. never comes up with a valid reason as to why I should reach in my pocket and come up with ten dollars.

Burnett: It's your only salesman. But, I'd like to have you talk about cost-efficiency, Sandy, because we're talking to a group where usually there are very modest budgets. They can't afford such things as: "Pick up this and put it in a slot." Let's see if we can't help them. If you were a small operation, a local campaign for instance, what would you tell people to do about their direct mail?

Clark: In most cases I think that some visual representation of who your candidate is, is essential—a picture of the guy. In fact we did exactly that for a guy running for the local board of selectmen in Connecticut. His wife took the pictures. We had about 2,000 printed and we had them at the dump, in the schools, so everybody saw our candidate good ole Bob So and So. He won by a landslide. We had him talking about the critical problems in the town in the brochure. We wrote a letter that went at them real hard about why we thought the town was going to hell in a handbasket if we didn't elect this great guy. I think that's important. The brochure can be very simple, it can be black and white.

Burnett: What were the rest of the factors?

Clark: We had a response card and we had a telephone number. I think absolutely essential is a telephone number. If anybody ever does any direct mail without a telephone number and they get mad because they get no responses, they are loony as hell. And what do you do when they call on the phone, and they pledge their ten bucks, what do you do? You sell them a yellow pennant and you get another pledge and then you sell them another pennant, etc. On the local level, a little town of six thousand families, this is entirely possible because we did it.

Dees: I think you have to be very careful with placement of phone numbers on your return cards. A novice in direct mail will want to do several things—get volunteers, get phone numbers, etc. The thrust of a direct mail fundraising should be solely to get money. There shouldn't be any mention in the package of a phone number and something about volunteering because the person can easily say: "Well, I'll at least volunteer now. I'll give next time." On your return card have a place way down below where you have them list information like phone number, whether they want to volunteer, etc. But it's got to be in small print, way at the bottom and definitely not in the letter.

Viguerie: Let me just say one thing about volunteering and phone numbers in fundraising. You've got to keep in mind what your objective is. If you're going out to raise big bucks, locally, not going out of state or anything, but in your geographical area, in your Congressional area, Senate area, you could depress returns by talking very much at all about volunteering in the campaign, phone numbers, etc. Because in the type of society we have now, people like to do the easiest thing: "I'll send $25, but whatever you do, don't call me on the phone, don't knock on my front door." And we know in direct mail that if you say: "We'll mail you something," as opposed to if they think you might knock on their door, you're going to get a lot more returns. They mail money if you say you're going to mail something. So, be careful about giving the person the impression that by sending his or her $25 contribution in they will open themselves up to a lot of calls asking them to participate in the campaign. Most just don't want that involvement.

Dees: There's a way to do it. First of all, in a small block you give them the chance to put a check: "I'd like to volunteer to help in the campaign." This is small, way down there below the money pitch. And then down below that it says: address, phone number, etc., and it appears that you need the phone number only because they volunteered to help in the campaign. Nobody will give you their phone number unless they've already decided to volunteer. It's part of the total picture, it's not separate—give me your phone number.

Clark: And further on the cost-benefit ratio, in prospecting in the mass audience, the difference between cash-up-front offers vs. charge orders is significant—three times the response with charge orders. Yet most of the prospecting mail that I've seen is all cash-up-front offers. Why not take advantage of credit cards?

Viguerie: I believe that offering the use of credit cards depresses most direct mail fundraising returns for some reason.

Clark: How about your own billing operation, where you can actually upgrade them through your billing series as all the publications do.

Viguerie: We all upgrade, of course. Ask them to give twice what they gave previously.

Clark: Subscribe to Time today and then watch the first three bills. See what they try to sell you. They make money on their billings.

Burnett: Dick, did you say that offering the chance to use a credit card over the phone reduces response?

Viguerie: In all the tests I've seen in fundraising. Yes.

Craver: Same here. The only exception to that has been with the National Organization for Women. Women, at least activist women, appear to use their credit cards differently than women do for other causes.

Burnett: Isn't the world changing now a little bit. Maybe credit cards are more used?

Craver: We test this stuff every couple months, every year.

C&E: Let's talk about the package for a minute. How do you choose such things as type face, ink color, paper weight and color, carrier envelope style—all these things?

Viguerie: Let me just make one general comment. Again, we can talk, all of us here, till suppertime tomorrow about the different ways to approach it. As I've said before, it's very simple. Seriously! In writing somebody cold, write as if you're writing to a friend asking them for some help. So, if you're writing a letter to a friend, what would you say? What would your letter look like, what would the typeface look liked Just write that letter and use the type of reasoning consistent with the economic situation you have in the campaign as to what you would do if you were writing to a friend. If you're writing to somebody who can give you a thousand dollars and you know this person, or he's previously helped a candidate similar to yours, you don't put a photograph on the outside of a carrier envelope. Because you just don't write letters like that. So just do it very simply. What would you normally do in the course of your everyday correspondence? This should be the guiding rule.

Dees: I have a comment concerning copy. I've been in both the business world and the fundraising world. My first inclination after getting into fundraising was, well, let's have a window envelope with something showing through. In fact I did that for an organization called the National Coalition to Ban Handguns. We had a window and through it showed a decal that you could stick on your car. And probably everybody in the room got one of those because we mailed millions of them.

Viguerie: I didn't... but then I guess I wouldn't be on your list, Morris. (Laughter)

Dees: That was using a slightly different package. It didn't come from John Smith, Candidate for President. It came from an organization—National Coalition to Ban Handguns—and I believe Archibald Cox's name was stuck above the label. But the label had a teaser line which said: "Do you have the courage to put this sticker on your windshield?" And so they knew. And people loved it. Have you ever picked up those little stickers that stick and unstick and you peel the back and forth? You've done that—stick it back, stick it back. I think it's got a sexual connotation to it. The people just wanted to get their hands in there and see if that thing really did stick and unstick. And that became a very successful thing. But when it comes to fundraising, when you're asking for money it's the personal touch. I've seen exhaustive tests done by many organizations, where they used the Time/Life package, the envelope that has pictures on it, all kinds of things. And it seems that the more personal, direct approach: the #10 envelope or the Monarch size—the smaller envelope—tend to work better with a plain simple corner card or with no corner card. And we've tested all those unique, business size envelopes.

But there are no rules and I think that's the rule. Because sweepstakes work very well in fundraising, they're now being used quite a bit. Just as long as you let it be known that the prizes were donated by some good friend who wants to help. Just so long as you can give logical, rational reasons for what you do. I think McGovern's direct mail was unique in terms of package and style and design. But for the traditional direct mail package use that personal letter and you'll come out a lot better. It's called "sneaking up on people with believability." Probably one of the most effective direct mail letters I ever sent out was one that was a "My dear friend," and it was from a candidate. But inside the package was a letter that was sent to the candidate by somebody on yellow legal paper and it was handwritten in ink. We had called the person up and asked their permission to use it and it said: "You know, I think your candidacy is the thing that is going to save this nation. And it's going to rescue us from the problems that are facing us and for future generations to come, etc., etc. And I'm an old age pensioner and I don't have much money, and I'm sending you this five dollars that I really don't have, I borrowed, blah, blah."

And then it was signed. And you could just see tears dripping off the bottom of the page. We reproduced that letter exactly as it was, and stuck it in the package. And then we attached a little P.S.: "Enclosed is a letter I received yesterday morning that really made me stop and realize that my running for Senator from Arizona really is important. And I wanted to share that letter with you." Now that's the kind of little touch you put in there that is just more effective than any window envelope.

Clark: It's called the pub letter, which virtually every magazine in the business uses.

Viguerie: It's not exactly a pub letter, it's different. A pub letter is a reinforcing kind of thing from the management of the establishment.

Dees: The very word you use—pub letter—publisher's letter which to the uninitiated is a letter included with an offer of the *Time/Life* series of books on Animals and Nature or whatever and there's a letter from the Publisher saying: Before you decide not to order these books, please read the enclosed letter. And it says: you may not really believe we are going to give you a free book, etc., but it truly is free. I'm Hedley Donovan, publisher of this big company, and I'm telling you its free, you get it, you keep it. Now, in Kennedy's latest fundraising mail this time, we used a pub letter. But what it said was, before you decide on your contribution to Senator Kennedy, please read the enclosed. And it is a little thing, and you open it up and on the inside, it said—I forgot the exact wording—but it was from me as Finance Director, and it got around to saying that for anyone who gives a contribution of $50 or more they'll get a medallion that can have historic value. Kennedy means history, touch of history and all that. And our average contribution was around $34.95/$35.00 which is considerably higher than anything I've ever gotten in fundraising before. And the number of $50 contributions wanting the medallion was way up there. So that is the way to take a personal letter and put something in it that is commercial.

Viguerie: Something else commercial you did there was not to ask do you want to buy this or don't you—in other words, do you want to give or not. It was how much do you want to give? The assumption is already that they're going to give. It's do you want to give $25 or $50—you assume they're going to give something.

Dees: That's right, Dick. We've learned that the average contribution for many causes, be it political or whatever, is: $17-$18, something like that. This is something we've learned. I don't know what it would be with your people, Dick, $12, $15, whatever. But then you try to do things which make the letter very personal. For example: "I'm launching my campaign next week, and our first effort will be fundraising for a television drive in New Hampshire. Our budget for New Hampshire television is $250,000, and I'm asking 10,000 people to give me an average of $25 each. Naturally I understand that some people will give slightly more than that and a few may not be able to give that much. But if I get an average of $25 each, only 10,000 people will have to contribute and we'll have our media money." That's doing two things. It's fixing a figure in their mind and people are very susceptible to suggestions of what amount to give. Secondly, its telling them that their contribution will make a difference. If you got a letter from President Carter saying: Send me ten dollars and help retire the national debt. Well, that would be like throwing a cup of water in the river to make it rise. And people won't believe that their ten dollars will do much to bring down the national debt, which we attribute mainly to Republicans and Nixon and the Conservatives. (Laughs all around.)

Viguerie: Maybe 40-50 years ago, Morris, you could sell that to the American public but not today! Morris, I might add something to your television budget example. The point I want to make is that you should always use specifics. It's $249,325 or $251,000. Be specific. Don't use figures that look like you just reached up and pulled them out of thin air.

Dees: Put a little budget in there.

Viguerie: It shouldn't come out to an even figure like $1,000 or $500,000. Billboards don't cost $100, they cost $92.35 or $102.40.

Yolton: Another strategy to achieve this is to explain that you have to equip your headquarters. A chair costs so much, and your telephone bill for a half a month is so much, and so forth. Give people a lot of specifics, and you don't do it in $15 and $20, etc. You do it in $17.95. Make them feel that they're actually buying a chair or actually financing the telephone bill for a month or a half-month.

C&E: At what point do supplementary or emergency appeals for funds become counterproductive? How many pieces can a proven donor be sent before he/she gets turned off? How many pieces should a prospect receive without contributing before being written off? At what point should you write them off?

Craver: On the question of how to go after your existing donors, I find it hard to see how you can overuse them if you have legitimate needs. After all, they became a part of the enterprise and you have an obligation to keep them apprised of how you're doing. And then the political angle. In Mo Udall's presidential campaign, toward the end, we mailed them once a week, and every primary he lost he raised more money. In Anderson's program, we're doing it about every 18 days now, and it will probably increase in frequency.

Clark: You keep mailing a customer or prospect file until it's cheaper to go to Ed Burnett and buy new lists at $50-$60 per thousand. That's your cut off.

Viguerie: Amen. Direct mail is simple. You quit mailing a list when it no longer achieves your goal. And if your goal is to break even, you quit mailing when it no longer breaks even. It is not a difficult thing.

Burnett: There are two kinds of lists, those that work and those that don't.

Viguerie: But keep in mind what your goals are. Overall, if a program achieves its goals, don't quit mailing.

Craver: The difficulty people who—don't do much direct mail get into is that they let irrelevant factors enter into the decisionmaking process instead of making it a matter of simple economics. Suddenly such questions as good taste, the tone, dignity, and the opinion of the candidate's wife, and Lord knows what else enters into it. The point is, if a package is working on a list you keep mailing it until it stops working.

Viguerie: I couldn't agree more, Roger. I think it's important to go back to something at the very beginning of the roundtable. Morris and others commented that we must remember that what we are engaged in is direct mail advertising. This is an advertising medium. And it's not only fundraising, it's also promoting and advertising the candidate. And if somebody gets a couple of letters in their mailbox a week from the candidate they may object, but if they see two Ford

Motor Company ads the same day on television they don't think anything about it. They might see six ads per day for Coca Cola—they don't think anything about it. But most people don't make the transition that direct mail is advertising mail.

Burnett: I get worried about some of the readers that we are addressing here. They are smaller fry than some of these national campaigns we are talking about. I'd like to make it clear that they've got to learn early in the game to test those things that are significant. You don't test color of the envelopes, and you don't test whether you sign it with this man's name or another man's name, and you don't test whether or not the letterhead should be printed in blue or in black. You do test the list, you do test the appeal, you do perhaps, if you have time, test the package. But you don't spend time and effort on those things which are fruitless and will not make a significant difference.

C&E: If each one of you could come up with just one bit of advice for the smaller campaign people, not the big national candidates who can afford to hire experts like you. What one piece of advice would you give to local candidates on conducting direct mail programs?

Craver: The greatest sin that I've seen is a failure to ask for money. My piece of advice is that if you've written that letter and gone through all that motion specifically ask someone or tell them what you have in mind and give them a suggested figure to send. And I would back that up with the advice Guy Yolton gave me when I first got into this business ten years ago, when he was helping us with Common Cause, and that is: mailing something is better than mailing nothing.

Viguerie: The advice I would give to campaigns, at any level, that are interested in using direct mail is you need to start early. Of all the sins in political direct mail I think perhaps the greatest is starting too late. I don't care how great you are in business, if you've got ten percent as much time to work with as your opponent, he's going to run circles around you. You've just got to start early. If you start a year before the election with a direct mail campaign, you're not starting early—that's late. You should start your direct mail at least two years before.

Burnett: How would you use those two years, Dick?

Viguerie: Ed, it depends on the campaign of course, and what your objectives are, but basically if you've got two years, find a professional. You really need a professional. There are unfortunately just a limited number of people who make their living full time in political direct mail. But almost every community has somebody who has a good, working knowledge of direct mail or advertising. I don't think I could offer better advice then to start early and get a direct mail pro involved.

Clark: Too many letters come to my house folded so I don't know what I'm getting. Don't! If you're doing mailings do it so it starts, "Dear Mr. Clark." I'm reading the letter from the moment it comes out of the envelope. I guess the only thing I would add which probably dovetails off Dick's a little bit: don't spend too little money on mail. I realize in political campaigns there's never enough money. But don't spend too little. Don't try to make $1,000 do the work of $5,000 because you're going to do it wrong. So it's important to be realistic.

Burnett: I have two bits of advice. Number one, do not get into this trap of making a continuous series of one experiment and then say: Ah hah! It did or it did not work. Number two, people spend a great deal of time on the best graphics, the best copy, the best package, the best appearance, and then they send out the errand boy to fetch the mailing list. And the mailing list is the thing which affects the returns the most. Therefore, if you find someone that knows something about the list business in your area, and knows something about the kinds of people who are going to respond to different appeals, and knows something about demographics and psychographics, latch on to him. Because he can be helpful to you.

Yolton: I might offer something that's akin to what Roger said: Don't beat around the bush about what it is you're after. There's always the temptation, I think, when the candidate or candidate's associates get into the business of putting together the direct mail campaign's program, they want to talk a whole lot about the philosophy of the campaign, the positions of the candidate, and a lot of things like that. They can go on for paragraphs writing one of those essays. When you do that you may lose your audience. The person who receives your letter is going to say to himself: "Why am I getting this message, at this time, on this subject? What's in it for me?" Answer that quickly. Get to the point early and then support it.

Hartman: I'll go part way with Mr. Viguerie. You can't be an amateur in this game anymore. But I think it's wrong to go to someone who does just plain advertising—a nice person in town who does advertising—and then ask them to do your political campaign. I think that's very much like going into an electronics shop to have your automobile engine fixed. If you're going to spend the money you should spend the money with someone who has done political direct mail and knows something about it. I'm not so sure that one is entirely applicable to the other. And I would spend the money, if you're going to do it, to get the proper professional guidance.

Viguerie: There are probably ten good political direct mail experts in the country. And there are probably 4,000 people running for Congress alone.

Hartman: The advice you get from someone who is not experienced in the direct mail field, even though they may be experienced in advertising, is sometimes more negative than positive.

Clark: Joe, if you're in Des Moines, Iowa, and you're running for a state seat, your choice is a housewife, your wife, or yourself, or the local guy in town who does some advertising, I'd pick that guy in a flash because he has a sense of writing and communication skills. And I think that's the point. You can't get a direct-mail pro in every single situation, in every single election. But I've had good friends who are not direct mail copywriters per se who have done campaigns for people that were winners. They made some mistakes, but they were a lot better than picking somebody off F and 14th Streets out here to do the campaign.

Yolton: Getting something out is better than getting nosing out.

Craver: There are just hundreds and hundreds of campaigns that don't have the money or the expertise. I get calls all the time from managers of congressional races and lower that have never done direct mail and want to try it. They have to go for whatever they can get nearby, and they don't have the money or time to afford to use these scarce direct mail experts. I always tell them that one of the things they should do is that when they get the blue line of their copy, give it to somebody else and say: find the mistake.

Viguerie: Because I promise you there's one in there!

Burnett: Can we talk about what it costs to buy some of these experts we've been discussing?

Viguerie: Let me just say that it really depends on the level of the campaign. If you're running for U.S. Senate that's one thing. But if you're running for the state legislature, you're not going to be able to afford one of the well-known, national professionals. But you might be able to establish a relationship with them where you can call him once a month or so.

Hartman: That's exactly what I was talking about. You can get guidance. If you can't get day-to-day operation, at least get guidance.

Viguerie: Exactly. I have people who want to hire me to advise them on a state senate campaign. I'd love to in many cases but I just can't. But sometimes I can help over the phone. But send us something, maybe we'll critique it over the phone, but we can't afford to take them on as full-fledged clients.

Clark: I don't think there's any one of us (and particularly the agencies) who aren't at this moment carrying somebody along for free. It has to be. It's the nature of the business.

Hartman: Let's be a little more specific. Must all candidates—for example running for the U.S. House—should they or should they not have professional supervision over their direct mail?

Viguerie: Without question they should. But some campaigns need direct mail more than others. If you're running for Congress in the New York City area, Los Angeles, or Chicago, direct mail might be 80 percent of your advertising budget. You can't afford to go on T.V. Say you're running in a primary. You're in only one of 12 congressional districts served by the mass media where you only want to talk to registered Democrats or registered Republicans. You want to talk to maybe four percent of the people that television reaches there. So direct mail is the only thing that makes any economic sense.

Hartman: That's so true. In western Connecticut there is simply no such thing as political advertising for anyone because it's wasteful. Same for Northern New Jersey because you have to be able to afford one of the New York stations. So direct mail becomes even more important there than it does to a candidate in New York City.

Craver: If I had to put together a survival kit for a congressional candidate who couldn't hire an agency I would: (1) tell him to find a list broker who has done political work of the ideology that he deals with, because all lists are not the same. That is, pick a list broker on the right or left of the aisle who works with candidates on the right or left of the aisle. Secondly, get on Richard Viguerie's mailing list and read the stuff—or ours or Guy's—the causes that are in the mail all the time and study them. Because this stuff is tested. The tuition, as Sandy puts it, is millions and millions of dollars. And it has already been spent to learn what works, so follow it.

Hartman: I'm wondering if the ball isn't in the experts court. If you people are really doing your job, wouldn't you have in your organization a setup for presidential candidates, a set-up for—say—senatorial candidates, and one for congressional candidates?

Viguerie: I've thought about that so many times and tried. Where it breaks down in our operation, and maybe Roger can add his thoughts to this, but where it breaks down in our effort is in the fundraising. If they just came to us and said: here is a budget, whether it's $10,000 or $100,000, and use this intelligently for direct mail to help get the candidate elected. We can do that, we can develop boiler plate copy, and everything can work. We take it off the shelf, take a state senate campaign's program that's worked successfully off the shelf. But 99.9% of the campaigns, in fact 100% for me, but I say 99.9 because somewhere there must be somebody who doesn't want us to raise their money but does want us to use direct mail to get them votes. Most take our voter direct mail programs, quite frankly, because we force it on them. Because we know how to use direct mail to help them get elected. But really the vast majority of the campaigns want us to raise money only. They want money to spend on television. I say: "Hey, if you want us to help you get elected, you're going to spend your money in ways that we think are most effective in helping you get elected." If only three percent of the audience is going to see them on television, I'm not going to bust my rear end and have my people stay up late Sunday nights or get up early Saturday mornings to have them waste the money.

Craver: The thing that is difficult for lay people who don't get involved too much is that whether you're doing it for a state legislator or the President of the United States, the time, the thought processes, are the same. And my idea of hell is to do any more political business than we now do—which is about 20 times more than I would like to do. It is the most unpleasant way to make a living that man has ever invented.

Viguerie: I know how to simplify my life. I know how to enjoy life. I know how to play golf two or three times a week and spend more time with my family, but I have made a conscious decision not to. Because, like Roger and Morris and Guy, we believe strongly in certain things. And we want to make the sacrifice in this area to help the people get elected that we believe in. Because with our experience, we could all of us make a lot more money by not getting involved in political campaigns. If you have a client that's been with you eight to ten years, and you're mailing seven, eight, nine million letters a year for him, and then this guy comes along, who's running for Congress, and he wants you to mail 12,000 here and 14,000 there, and maybe he mails 100,000 over three months—who's easier to work with? And the staying up late at night, and getting up early in the morning for a guy that's going to be with you for three months at most and mail 100,000 letters if you're lucky—it's madness!

Yolton: As Richard says, they all start too late. You're immediately thrown into a crisis atmosphere. Additionally, you're dealing with prima donnas. If you had to deal only with the candidate that would be fine, but it's all these underlings who are surrogate prima donnas that you must deal with. You tear your shop up, and give everybody in your company a nervous breakdown, and on the day after election clay, suddenly you don't even have a client!

C&E: Thank you very much gentlemen. A fantastic session. You all are to be congratulated on your sincerity, frankness and candor.

✓ Using Postcards to Overcome Mailbox Clutter
Michael Vallante

With any piece of direct mail, there are two challenges: first, cutting through the clutter of the mailbox; and, second, getting people's attention.

In New Jersey's 1991 state legislative elections, we sought to overcome these problems with what we labeled "Postcards Over the Edge."

The postcards allowed Republican candidates to hit a single issue that survey research had shown would move voters away from incumbents and into the Republican column. The loud colors and unique size of the postcards, 6 inches by 9 inches, meant that it stood out in the clutter of the politically saturated mailbox of the voter.

This size, combined with the fact it was printed on postcard stock paper, kept the production cost in the 12-cent to 14-cent range. In those cases where the quantity went up, the production price dropped below that level to near a dime. These savings meant that we had the capacity to mail twice as much without increasing the budget.

Postcards provided a package for the voter that stood out in the mailbox. The postcards featured nothing for the voter to open or follow, and the message was communicated in 30 seconds or less.

Now that we had a direct-mail piece that stood out in the mailbox, the next challenge was to come up with a design that would capture the interest of the voter.

We used a photo on the front that caught people's eye and evoked an emotional response (laughter, anger, curiosity). The photo not only had to capture people's attention, it had to begin to lay the groundwork for the presentation of the issue and message. The copy on the front had to be short and punchy and serve as a reinforcement to the photo.

On the back, there was usually another photo and more text, continuing the story. We believed that the copy had to be underlined, or in bold or in italics for those who would want to get the message quickly.

In writing copy, it is important to remember that this type of mail doesn't allow you the time to introduce an issue—only to capitalize on an existing issue that the voter already cares about. The purpose of this kind of direct-mail piece is to make people aware of your opponent's stand on an issue, not explain your own candidate's position.

In one postcard, we had a picture of the incumbent with a smile on his face and his feet on the desk. The look on his face said it all: "I'm having a great time and I'm getting away with it." The copy we used was "Greetings from Trenton" to make it look like a tourist postcard from the incumbent.

The back was a hand-written message in the first person. It factually stated what the incumbent had voted for in Trenton (especially for Florio's tax increases). We had the incumbent's signature in type so that there could be no legal arguments about forging his name.

In another postcard, we used a trick photo of a New Jersey Turnpike toll station with a "For Sale" sign affixed. The copy read: "Trick or Treat." It was done in bright orange and dropped to hit on Halloween.

The back panel was an actual photo of our three Democratic opponents, taken from their own brochure. The copy explained how they had pulled a trick by selling the New Jersey Turnpike and how the trick had cost the state its AAA bond rating. In both of these cases, we had a mail piece that stood out in the mailbox, hit an issue that was of principal concern to the people, and presented in such a way that it attracted voter attention.

Postcards are good for attack campaigns, but are only effective if they focus on a single issue that the voter is already aware of. The job of the mail piece is to ride an emotional feeling that already exists with the voters. Each postcard was an individual effort. None of the postcards in different races was tied to each other.

Postcards are not good for positives. They don't provide the style, the quality, or the space to introduce your candidate or present positions positively.

✓ Cost Effective Voter Contact
Robert Blaemire

Shopping for political products and services should be no different than shopping in the mall. To get your money's worth, you must be an educated consumer.

Most campaigns now recognize that they must have the ability to generate personalized voter contact, whether in person, by phone or through direct mail. The primary tool enabling that voter contact is a voter file. However, achieving a successful and cost-effective voter contact campaign requires a sophisticated voter file of high quality, managed by a knowledgeable computer vendor.

With apologies to David Letterman, a fellow Hoosier, here's a "Top Ten List" of questions any candidate, manager or consultant should ask when looking for a voter file for an upcoming campaign.

1. How old is the data?

It's obvious that dead people don't vote—at least in most parts of the country. Trying to contact them only wastes precious resources; the same is true for people who have moved away. At the same time, you are unable to contact voters who have registered since the list was compiled. So, the older the list, the greater the likelihood that you are attempting to contact voters who are out of your reach.

2. What are the purge practices that have governed the maintenance of this database?

If the state has a purge law, you need to know what it is and whether or not it is enforced. If it is, do the voter files reflect that enforcement? We have one file from a state with no purge law and, as a result, have done our own purging by eliminating those names who have failed to vote in four successive elections after the date of registration.

3. Is voter history on the voter file or can it be appended?

The ability to select for contact those voters who vote frequently is critical to any campaign. Knowing whether and when voters cast their ballots is so critical that all campaigns should do what they can to get voter history data onto their files.

4. Has the file been improved with NCOA?

The National Change of Address computer program improves lists enormously and the costs are well worth it. All address changes over the previous 36 months are available to match to your voter file and most vendors can also identify addresses known to be undeliverable. The potential savings far outweigh the costs, which is easy to demonstrate to any campaign.

5. What data is available on the file or can be appended by the vendor?

In addition to accurate names and addresses, campaigns need to have as much personal information as possible to target voters effectively and efficiently. The most important data are age, race, gender, party and voter history. If any of these items are not available on the acquired databases, your vendor should discuss the ability to obtain that information. Also useful are census items, such as income and educational levels, which can be appended to any database.

6. What legal or contractual restrictions exist when using the file?

Knowing this in advance of using a database can avoid costly and troublesome problems down the road. If you assume you are going to be able to use a file continuously, find out up front. If there are ways you may not use a database, such as fundraising, for instance, you should know that in advance. What are the political and technical experiences of the vendor? The nuances and demands of each race are unique; campaigns are better served by having a vendor who can adapt to the specific campaign environment. Beware of inexperienced vendors!

7. How flexible is the vendor in the products and services it offers?

It's important to know that the vendor is available when you need him or her. It's also important to have a vendor who can produce products as you need them. Many vendors have a "take it or leave it" attitude as far as their products are concerned. While there are limits to a vendor's ability to customize products, the vendor must be able to produce materials as they are needed. Decide what you want and make sure the vendor can provide it. Many vendors, for instance, will provide mailing labels but will not offer full service printing and mailing.

8. Are the vendor's products priced competitively and fairly?

Comparing prices is always important but also make sure you fully understand the pricing. Does the price list explain all of the potential charges? Are there volume discounts? Are you charged differently for complicated orders? Do the selections you make each have an additional cost, like pizza toppings?

9. What is the management and ethical reputation of the vendor?

If you think the reputation of the vendor isn't important, there's some Florida swamp land I'd like to sell you.

8

Telephone Direct Contact: Strategies and Techniques

★ ★ ★

✓ You Make the Call
Read deButts

The two-story building is shoddy looking: paint is chipping off its sides, windows are broken out. In a stained nylon chair in the lobby—which is really just a hallway—you sit back and try to imagine what a "phone" room will look like.

Fifteen minutes pass, and a man bolts through two green, heavy metal swinging doors. He's wearing a flammable polyester suit and thrusts out his hand. "Welcome to Speak EZ Telemarketing," he smiles, and you catch the glimmer of a shiny metal tooth. "We're glad you're here."

You follow him up a dark, rancid stairway and your shoes stick to the steps. You wonder what chemical grime could cause such a glue-like substance. A single naked light bulb flickers in the hallway. You reach for the railing, and your hand sticks. At the top of the stairs, you huddle through a corridor into an open room. You hear the hum of voices and the occasional slam of a receiver.

The room is jammed with tables in a space no bigger than your living room. Telephone wires hang at shoulder height, and the floor is littered with paper. In the center, like a prison guard, sits a supervisor on his perch overlooking the callers. The lighting is so dim you can barely see. Some callers are shuffling paper and carrying on conversations while others are manually dialing 10-digit numbers on rotary-dial telephones.

A few seconds pass—you feel like getting sick. Shiny Tooth notices the alarmed look on your face and starts blathering about how much people like working at Speak EZ.

"They can't get enough," he blurts, "telemarketing is the most rewarding job in America . . . here, you make a call." He grabs a telephone from mid air and thrusts the receiver in your face. You scream, horrified that you'll have to call your third grade teacher and try to sell her a new pair of nylons. Light pours in, you hear your dog, Mario, barking in the backyard, and you awake in a cold sweat.

Thank god, it was only a dream . . . or was it? Phone banks may have, until recently, looked like the one in your dream, but in the last five years the industry has entered the next generation.

317

Technological breakthroughs in automatic dialing systems and ergonomic work spaces have propelled the industry toward the 21st century. If you're thinking of hiring a phone bank to help you get elected, here are a few things you should know.

Identifying voter sentiment using direct telephone contact is as critical to the campaign as having a good candidate: telephones can present an accurate picture of the electorate. By using telephones to randomly survey voters, a political research firm can further define a campaign message and track the effectiveness of media campaigns and mail blitzes.

With an ever-changing electorate, telephones can play a crucial role in keeping a campaign on track. They can also be tightly controlled, thus allowing a campaign team to expand or contract the targeted voter list based on availability and election day turnout needs. In addition to measuring voter sentiment, telephone contact can also directly affect election results by identifying key segments of the voting population. These contacts encourage voters to turn out on election day, which is why you need to begin the vendor-search process early.

Typically, a campaign will want to line up a phone bank at least 10 months before election day, even though voter identification work may not start for several months.

Let's look at a hypothetical race for Federation senator, with Capt. James T. Kirk planning his race for office. Jim Kirk may use a combination of voter-contact techniques—ID, advocacy, and advocacy ID calls—to identify, reach out, and cajole voters to cast a ballot for him.

First, Kirk's pollster must identify the important issues so that Kirk knows what he must say to voters to get elected. Although Kirk was once a Star Fleet captain, tough times and staff cutbacks have left him with a tight budget.

Let's see how he works through his voter-contact program. Kirk's loyal campaign manager, Mr. Spock, learned a tough lesson in his last campaign. He contracted a telemarketing shop that specialized in fundraising and sales instead of a firm that understood campaign voter contact. Consequently, the voters told Spock that they would support his candidate even though they had no interest in voting.

Spock realized that he needed to locate an operation that could handle voter identification and persuasion programs without using heavy-sell techniques. This time Spock's logic pays off. Here are his notes on proper vendor selection.

Begin by creating a short list of suppliers who meet these criteria: have a large capacity for automated calling; a long political resume; is cordial to your party; a reputation for quality; and the ability to produce mailing labels.

Spock talked with other candidates running for office, checked advertisements, and called current office holders to unearth which firms were used for their telephone work.

The first task was to put the telephone specifications in writing and outline how long you expect each calling program to last. Attach a sample script so the vendor can estimate the length of an average call and ask him or her how you might improve the script.

Be clear about what you expect from a potential supplier and get it in writing. State that you need the calls completed by July 31 and that accompanying mailing labels will need to be produced by August 2.

Explain that you will want several sets of labels for each identified response group so you can conduct follow-up mailings. Phone bankers are thrilled to get specifications in writing; they are accustomed to responding to verbal requests.

If phone bank location isn't critical to your campaign, consider contracting with a vendor in a state where there's a good labor pool and little local accent (unless an accent is desirable). Large telemarketing operations are often based in areas where accent-free voices are plentiful.

Once you've narrowed the field, run through a checklist to make sure you've factored in all the costs and are certain of what you're buying.

Key Questions

Here are a few questions you may want answered:

Is the vendor automated? If your supplier tells you he's "automated," ask him how he defines automation. Does he use computer-assisted calling, personal computers, or speed dialing capabilities? Most phone banks use some automation. Advanced firms use predictive dialing machines linked to a larger computer capable of managing phone lists—these firms tend to be efficient in high volume/shortcall duration voter contact programs. Don't be shy: ask each vendor to explain how its system works in layman's terms.

How long does the caller training last? Is caller training extra? If you need special training to ensure your project is understood by each caller, tell your supplier and ask if it will cost extra. Most firms allot a specific amount of time for training.

What other type of work does the vendor do? Firms specializing in direct sales may not have the trained staff to do voter contact. The transition from a market-research to political-persuasion trained staff is especially difficult since research interviewers must be completely unbiased.

In what format should the phone numbers and addresses be supplied? Is magnetic tape formatting extra? If your voter file is on tape, make sure it is in the preferred format. If not, find out how much it will cost to convert it.

Does the phone bank use a quality long-distance carrier? Some heavily discounted carriers route outbound calls through relay stations hundreds of miles from the most direct route. This can result in periodic static on the lines, occasional disconnected calls, and an echo effect.

Can the firm produce labels in a postal pre-sort? Some automated shops can produce labels for mailings from the same central computer that managed the calls. Check to see what your vendor's capabilities are.

What type and frequency of reports should you expect? You'll need to monitor the project daily. Tell the vendor you expect daily reports, ask for their standard summary, and be sure it is adequate. If not, draw up what you'd like to see and send it to the vendor.

What is the capacity? Capacity is critical. Some firms sell beyond their capacity or misjudge a project's length, which can push your project beyond its deadline.

Make sure your vendor has extra capacity or will guarantee your deadline. The calling crunch begins several weeks before election day, when there are usually too few phones available.

Does the vendor follow, record, and recall changed or new phone numbers? A changed number often means a voter has moved—sometimes out of your district. "Chasing" numbers in a statewide race may be appropriate if the new number has the same area code, but is rarely logical in a state legislative race.

Can you monitor calls in progress from a remote location? In the phone bank business, monitoring is a nerve-wracking task. Vendors often know who their trouble employees are and will refrain from monitoring them. If you want to phone in from campaign headquarters and listen to calls in progress, ask your vendor if they have the capability. Most do, although some will claim they don't.

Where does the firm get its labor force? (From a nearby college or ex-post office employees?) Labor pool is important. Some firms draw from nearby colleges, others from rural towns; in either case, knowing the quality and education level of your vendor's labor supply can help you understand the phone bank's quality.

What is the firm's ratio of supervisors to callers? Most firms have one floor supervisor for every 10 or 12 callers. As questions arise (or problems), the more supervisors on your project, the better the management.

How much will the calling project cost? Vendors should include a bid that itemizes each cost in the project.

Are there any hidden charges? Ask the vendor what other expenses might be incurred under special circumstances, such as last-minute project changes or cancellations.

What's your cost per contact or cost per hour? Ask your supplier what the cost per contact is and what he would charge per hour. Like piecework, cost per-contact relies on the vendor's ability to meet hourly production quotas. Flat hourly rates may let the vendor run up the tab.

If you are paying on a cost-per-contact basis, what does it include? Some vendors charge for reaching disconnected numbers, and others charge for wrong numbers. Be sure to get a clear definition of what your cost per contact includes.

What are the vendor's payment arrangements? Given the number of vendors that have been burned in the last hundred campaign cycles, don't be surprised if you're asked to pay in advance. Suggest a progress payment arrangement that won't tap out the campaign coffers at the beginning.

Most firms are reasonable... but beware of the mega-phone banks that customarily have rigid payment policies. They may create problems for your campaign when it gets down to the home stretch.

Choosing Strategies

As Kirk's first contact with voters, Spock might choose a "blind" identification call, which tells him how voters feel about Kirk's candidacy and allows him to segment his lists into a targeted voter base. In a blind identification call, no background information or pitch is provided on candidate Kirk—voters will be for, against, or undecided on their candidate preference. The blind ID call relies on the voters knowledge and does not bias their response.

Voters who are FOR Kirk (the favorables) are probably a little familiar with him. A blind identification call is a quick way to find out how Kirk's probable voting base breaks out. Since Kirk spent most of his money on his last five-year mission, he does not plan on follow-up with favorable voters. He will rely on the support these voters have shown in the identification call. Speck calculates that since they expressed their position without a formal pitch these voters will hold true and vote for Kirk. Later, Kirk and Spock may change their minds and decide to solidify their support once they see their polling numbers.

On the other hand, undecided voters will need specific follow-up mail to promote the Kirk candidacy. Voters who tell Kirk's phone bank that they are against him will be vaporized without additional contact. Once Spock completes the identification call, he is ready to begin the persuasion program—a barrage of mailings that hit on key issues and/or his opponents' weaknesses.

Tips On Developing A Script

Once you've drafted a script, call a few friends and try it. You'll often work out the kinks rather quickly.

1: Be brief and direct. In an advocacy ID contact, callers need to identify themselves immediately. "Hi Mr. Mudd, this is Lt. Sulu calling for Capt. Kirk."
2: Prioritize your campaign issues, and target each message to the demographic groups you plan to call: "I'm calling you today to tell you about Capt. Kirk—he's running for senator and hopes to do something about the Federation budget problem."
3: Repeat your candidate's name as much as you can, but don't go overboard. "Kirk believes that the Federation should balance its budget and be fiscally responsible."
4: Throw in at least two issues. "Kirk would like to get the government out of the pocketbooks of hardworking citizens."
5: Move in for the close. "Mr. Mudd, Capt. Kirk asked me to find out if he can count on your support on election day?" The voter is given some brief information about Kirk and asked if he or she will support his candidacy. If the voter says that he or she is undecided: "Well, I've just not made up my mind," add another line of response, such as, "Your vote really matters in this election. Capt. Kirk is a man with 30 years' experience in the Federation's bureaucracy, and he knows how to get things done. Will you consider casting your vote for Kirk on election day?"

After the second push, you will get your answer—voters will generally shake out into one of three simple categories: Against, For, or Undecided.

As the election machine reaches warp speed, Spock may want to contact voters who were identified as undecided in the ID call and ask them for their support. Chances are a mail program has already been developed to persuade undecided voters that Kirk is the man for the galaxy. An advocacy call convinces voters of Kirk's legitimacy and measures their commitment to the Kirk agenda. Depending on Kirk's voter turnout needs, the undecided electorate may be critical in the end.

If the pool of undecideds is large, persuasion programs must shift it to the Kirk side. Spock may want to save campaign dollars by combining an advocacy call with an ID call. Because the voter hears how qualified Kirk is, he's more likely to say he's FOR Kirk. Consequently, advocacy ID calls inflate the number of voters who tell you they will support Kirk's candidacy. These "soft" FOR Kirk responses increase the number of voters Kirk needs to turn out.

By applying the key messages for Kirk's segmented voter base, the goal is to sway voters. Depending on Kirk's opponent and his voter-contact program, Spock will decide whether to run a blind ID or advocacy ID call.

Once Spock completes his persuasion program and knows who will vote for Kirk, it is imperative that he reminds them to vote on election day. Get-Out-The-Vote (GOTV) calls inform voters that election day is just around the corner and that Kirk is counting on their support. All the mail and phone contacts in the Federation are space debris if voters don't go to the polls.

Well before this point, Spock would have bought a list of registered voters in Kirk's district from the state party or a list vendor. Spock should be able to get a demographic breakdown of voters including their past voting history. The most commonly available voter demographics are party, gender, age, ethnic origin, and year of registration.

With each additional data item, Spock will have more information from which to construct his voter communications plan. For example, age is helpful because it enables Spock to tailor Kirk's message to the voters' interests.

The persuasive pitch at the beginning of the advocacy call to seniors might read, "Capt. Kirk has a plan for a national health care system that will provide insurance for all citizens," while a younger voter script might read, "Kirk believes that all Americans should have the right to own a home."

Although most phone banks will indicate how quickly the project can be completed, Spock will want to run the numbers through his tricorder to ensure that his vendor can handle the projected volume.

Since Kirk is a Moderate—running in a district with 50,000 registered Moderates—he will want to call many of them and will need to purchase a list with telephone numbers. Spock expects to reach 60 percent, or 30,000 voters, by telephone. A list broker will tell Spock how many voters they have that meet his specified criteria, with and without telephone numbers. And for an extra charge, phone banks offer a manual telephone number look-up service—the vendor will call the local operator and ask for a voter's phone number.

Using directory-assisted telephone number searches, Spock might reach 65 percent or even 70 percent of the voter file. If the voter file does not have telephone numbers, Spock will contract with a list broker to "match" names with telephone numbers from a larger database. Each match will cost 3 cents to 7 cents per phone number located.

The campaign plan calls for an advocacy ID calling program in July. Spock calculates how long it will take using the following assumptions based on a manual (non-computerized) phone bank. Reaching 60 percent of 50,000 voters will run at an average rate of 15 contacts per hour using a 90-second script. That's 2,000 calling hours for the entire project. Some phone banks will offer per-hour rates—though per-contact prices are often preferable.

Typical rates can run from as low as $20 to as high as $35 per calling hour, translating into a range of $1.33 to $2.33 per contact. If the phone operation works Sunday through Thursday from 5:30 p.m. to 9:30 p.m., this leaves a 20-hour calling window (five days per week times four hours per day). By dividing the total number of calling hours by the calling window (let's assume two weeks), Spock can determine how many callers the phone bank must commit to his project—2,000 divided by 40 hours is 50 callers.

Thanks to modern technology, the number of voter contacts per hour that the phone bank can make has risen dramatically. Typical "predictive" dialing systems can contact 30 to 35 voters per hour, leaving the dialing process to computers that make dozens of calls a minute. Predictive dialing systems use a complex pacing algorithm to predict when the next caller will be available. These systems recognize busy, disconnected, and wrong number signals.

By providing an automated operation with a magnetic tape of voters and using predictive dialing technology, phone banks' daily productivity rises tremendously while per-voter contact costs drop dramatically. The same 90-second script might cost 90 cents per contact in an automated operation (at an hourly rate of $27).

Predictive calling technology reaps other benefits—data never leaves its magnetic medium, which means no data entry costs and fewer human recording errors.

There is one manageable disadvantage to automatic calling systems. If predictive dialing systems are calibrated improperly, some calls in progress may get routed to a tape-recorded message, and voters are likely to hang up the phone.

In an automated phone bank environment, Kirk's 30,000-voter contact program would be completed in half the time with a per-hour contact rate of 30. Only 25 callers are needed in a two-week calling window. Spock logically concludes that he could get the project done in half the time as compared to a manual phone bank.

However, contracting with a manual shop may be cost efficient when working with small voter files—2,000 to 3,000. A reminder: quality phone banks have other clients that pay their bills in the off-campaign years, so pad your schedule.

Telephoning is a personal affair. The telephone contact may represent Kirk's only relationship with the voters and should follow proper guidelines to disarm the average quick-to-hang-up American.

Using a complicated vocabulary and tackling complex issues will only frustrate the callers and shorten the voter's attention span. Most Americans loathe telemarketing sales calls... and place voter contact barely a notch above.

The script should be brief, conversational, and honest. While the script provides callers with what to say it doesn't provide details about their mission or Kirk's platform.

This is where the background sheet comes in. It might say, "You're working for Capt. Kirk who is running for Federation senator. As captain of the Enterprise, Kirk learned how to manage a diversity of beings. He knows what it's like to be responsible for the lives of his crew."

Tell the callers about their role: "The calls you will make are designed to help voters decide how they will vote and to persuade them to vote for Kirk." Keep the background sheet to one page, just enough information to make callers aware of the objectives.

In the calling process, questions inevitably arise that extend beyond the telemarketing script and training. You can supply the phone bank with a question-and-answer sheet covering the unexpected. Voters will ask IF callers questions such as, "Why are you calling me? Where did you get my name?" or "What is Kirk's position on the endangered Three-Headed-Orange Wooly Worm from the planet of Beta Carotene?"

The more prepared callers are for the frequently asked questions, the more effectively they will move voters to believe in Kirk. Send along some campaign brochures—enough art to distribute to the callers who will work on your project. As a part of Kirk's arrangement with his phone bank, he expects a combined daily and cumulative report on the calling project. The vendor provides him with calling summaries the day following each calling shift. Information in this report includes number of contacts made contacts per hour, number of calling hours, number of disconnects or bad numbers encountered, calls placed per hour, daily and total number of responses by category (for, undecided, and against).

Reviewing these reports will tell Kirk how much of a battle his campaign can expect. If his numbers look like this—31 percent for Kirk, 53 percent against Kirk, and 16 percent undecided—Spock might counsel Kirk to beam back to the Enterprise as an ensign or check the list to make sure he has the right set of voters.

This kind of report is bad news for Kirk as it means that voters have made up their minds—and not in his favor. Unless his opponent is caught in the middle of the Neutral Zone, Kirk will need aggressive tactics to pull away his opponents' supporters.

On the other hand, if Kirk's numbers look like this: 89 percent for Kirk, 4 percent against Kirk, and 7 percent undecideds, you can put the campaign money elsewhere (perhaps staff bonuses). If Kirk is using an advocacy ID script, approximately 25 percent to 35 percent of fors are soft Kirk backers whose support must be solidified in a direct-mail and telephone contact program.

Many close campaigns start with numbers that look like this: 20 per-contact is clear. The undecided 70 percent will need repetitive contact.

Working with phone banks is not the nightmare it once was. We now have automation, professional operations, and a competitive marketplace. A campaign manager can get top quality results without the worry and headache associated with traditional aerobic dialing techniques and carbon based systems.

In your next campaign, step into the world of automated phone banks and boldly go where no candidate has gone before.

✓ The Alternative: In-House Phone Banks
Cathy Allen

If you're planning to hire outside help to handle all of your phone bank duties: don't. You might be missing a sure bet. There are a number of important ways that an in-house phone bank is essential in a winning campaign, such as in following up on invitations to special fundraising events, or mailings for campaign contributions. Further, volunteer phone banks will help identify favorable voters in low-visibility, low-budget races.

Whenever you mail an invitation or a solicitation for money; you can expect about a 3 percent return with an average contribution between $20 and $25. If you supplement the solicitation with a phone call, you can probably double the rate of return for virtually the same base investment. The same amplified success is true with invitations. No campaign event will be fully successful without a follow-up telephone call after the invitation is mailed.

As you get closer to election day, you'll see another critical use of a volunteer phone bank as you are confronted with the awesome task of finding the right voters and ensuring that they will be going to the polls.

You need to determine those individuals who are most likely to vote for you and not those who have a demonstrated history of voting for candidates like your opponent.

Targeted phone calls for voter identification do two important things: they help raise the name identification of your candidate, and they allow you to whittle down the list of those individuals who need additional mailings or calls.

If you're convinced that you need the phone bank in-house, you have two daunting tasks: setting one up and finding the right volunteers.

Your phone bank should be centrally located. Campaigns usually look for law offices, insurance firms, local labor halls, travel agencies, or real estate offices. At worst, you'll end up at the local party headquarters. These kinds of locations are generally open only during normal working hours (9 a.m. to 5 p.m.) and have more than five telephones.

Having found the right friend to let you have the keys to his or her business, you then need to develop a memo outlining the goals and operations of the volunteer phone bank and how it will use the proffered space. Spell out the responsibilities as well as the days and hours the campaign will use the office. Identify who is responsible for the keys and for letting people in and out of the location.

The location should have ample parking, and it should be close to bus stops or rapid transit. In addition, it must be in a safe neighborhood where the volunteers will have no fear for their safety as they walk away at night. Choose offices that have pleasant surrounds. Remember, phonebanking is monotonous.

You do not want to encourage phonebanking from any of your volunteers' homes because there is less opportunity for the type of supervision you should be using, and you can't watch for problems that are related to the campaign as easily.

While volunteers working at home might be expected to be just as loyal to the cause, the record shows that phone calls seldom get made in the same volume as they would in an office environment. In a good location, the team spirit comes into play: an important intangible. Because phonebanking is usually a volunteer's least favorite chore, you have to find incentives that will appeal to volunteers. In addition, you have to realize that being organized lends credibility to the effort they are putting in. Tend to the care, feeding, and safety of your volunteers as you would to a family member.

With a location and agenda in hand, you then have to have a supervisor trained precisely in what tasks are at hand. The supervisor is responsible for bringing all of the materials to the location to be used. These materials include a targeted voter list with telephone numbers; pencils and pens; tally sheets; written sheets for every volunteer; phone scripts, and, of course, food and non-alcoholic drink.

With expectations for three-hour after-work shifts, you do not have to provide a five-course dinner, but light refreshments—and increasingly, healthy choices—are a must. Coffee and soft drinks are a staple, but consider juice and water too. As for food, sandwiches are usually healthy. In a pinch, there's pizza, cookies, and potato chips.

Inviting volunteers on the fly to a phone bank, showing them to an office, and giving them numbers to call is a quick way to discourage a seasoned phonebanker and a sure way to have newcomers dissuaded from returning. In addition, the impact the phone bank should have on your fundraising followup or your voter drive may be diminished.

Every phone bank should begin with a short training session. Volunteers should be introduced to one another. They should also be given an update on the campaign as well as insider strategy information. It is important to celebrate key milestones as the campaign reaches critical benchmarks. If you have identified 5,000 supportive voters, you should celebrate at every 1,000, for example.

The phonebank supervisor needs to be watchful for volunteers who are not hitting their mark. Those who are too talkative or disruptive, or those who simply do not follow instructions, should be reassigned to other campaign functions. It is not worth the dangers that using a bad worker can have.

Each phonebanker should be issued a brochure and biography explaining who the candidate is, who the key people are on the campaign (and their phone numbers), and written instructions about what they should do.

Callers should also be given a list of targeted voters with phone numbers and a tally sheet for recording the results of their calls.

There should be a list of precinct polling places (in the event that a prospective voter inquires about where to vote), and a sign-up sheet for the upcoming phone bank evenings.

✓ Telephone Fundraising
Vicki Ellinger

Money is the life-blood of a political campaign. While there are many different ways to fill one's war chest there is one that will fill the coffers and reach down into grassroots America to make average citizens politically active supporters. It's called *using the telephone*.

While many still think telephone fundraising carries the stigma of shady boiler-room operations, modern agencies are light years beyond that. Between state legislation and self-regulation within the industry, the medium has proven its effectiveness and reliability. Indeed, telephone fundraising has hit its stride, and it's a winner.

The best thing about telemarketing is that it generates income over and above the existing direct mail program. It brings in a higher average donation, generates more net revenue, and increases response three to ten times over direct mail, depending on the application.

Yet it works best in conjunction with a direct mail campaign, actually enhancing its effects and predisposing those called to be more responsive to future mailings.

Most importantly, use of the telephone allows direct conversation with donors, which has a personalizing effect. The intimacy and immediacy of a telephone call make it second only to a personal visit in terms of fundraising effectiveness.

The telephone initiates a bonding process between donor and the highly focused and personalized. We can see its effectiveness in the story of a man who lay dying in a hospital, and was asked if anyone should be notified of his terminal condition. The man replied that he had no family, but wanted to notify a prominent political figure from whom he had received "personal" letters for a number of years.

However, on the other end of the spectrum are those who perceive such offerings as "junk mail." This is where a telephone campaign is effective, either as a prelude to or a follow-up on a direct mail action. In addition, the time spent making a phone call bridges the perceived distance between yourself and the donor.

The next step is to close the distance further, so you are no longer "just another voice on the end of the telephone." This can be done with a well-crafted telephone script that takes into consideration that the donor has political organization. In a two-way means of communication, donors become better informed, and they can express their concerns. With proper cultivation, that list can grow into a powerful force that goes beyond money. It can become a base of grassroots citizens.

Converting Donors into Activists

The key to cultivating activists is building a relationship with your donors. Imagine a series of barriers that stand between any politician and the average citizen. There's the "us versus them" mentality, something which is formidable in an age when people have become disenchanted with their leaders. Other barriers may include an actual physical distance or a perceived one based on class, race, or other factors. The more that can be done to overcome these barriers, the closer your relationship will be with your base of support.

Unfortunately, personal goodwill is usually allowed to erode between elections. Direct mail can help, but it must be something important to say. By listening and empathizing with those you talk to, a bond is established.

Call to Action

The simplest way to do this is by adding a "call to action" to your fund-raising script. Ask your donors if they would like to put their name on a petition that will be sent to the President or members of Congress. If you are raising funds to distribute informational brochures, offer to send them a handful to pass out to their friends. Ask if they would be interested in putting up a yard sign. As a result, your donors will feel closer to your cause or candidate. They will have gone from passively donating funds to actually becoming involved.

What remains now is to deepen their level of involvement. Through a series of carefully planned contacts, you can upgrade both donor contributions and their value as active members of your organization. Use the telephone as a source of generating revenue and as an activator for these upgraded donors.

An activation call does not raise funds. Its sole purpose is to energize your carefully cultivated list and move them to action. The most typical is the "get out the vote" call, but many causes have gone beyond that. Now the phone is being used to encourage concerned donors, to alert them of meetings and rallies, to ask them to call elected officials on the eve of an important vote, even to search for volunteers for even further political involvement. The potential inherent in a list is limited only by how it is cultivated and the imagination of the campaign.

Making it Work

While volumes can be written about how to get the best results from a telephone fundraising campaign, keep in mind that your object is not just to raise funds but to groom donors for future activism. With that in mind, it becomes important to be aware of the "people skills" that will motivate people to work for your campaign.

Be respectful of your donor base. Treat your donors as equals. They care enough about their country to get involved. That makes each one important to you.

Treat them with intelligence and tailor your phone scripts accordingly. While you would never use the phrase "As you know" in a novel, it works wonders in a telephone script because it tells donors you think highly of them.

In addition, let your donors know that they are important. Thank them for their support and lavish praise on them. Telling them that they made a new TV spot or a newspaper ad possible lets them know they are an important part of the process. It generates enormous goodwill. Above all, don't be afraid to compliment them on their patriotism. Let them know they are doing their part for their country when they get involved.

Finally, do what you say you are going to do. In a time when political scandals are hiding around every corner, the last thing you want to do is reinforce ill feelings voters have toward politicians. If you're distributing Voter Guides, make sure they get a copy, and let them know how the distribution went.

The telephone is not some magic device that can bring in funds and volunteers quicker than Aladdin's lamp, nor is it a balm to cure all political ills. But when properly used, it is one of the most powerful campaigning tools available, in terms of money raised, goodwill generated, and volunteers recruited. All it takes for success is professionalism and attention to the details. It will make your efforts pay over and over again.

✓ Use the Telephone!
Karen Johnson-Parker and Tony Parker

When you throw a pass in football, you want your intended recipient to catch the ball and run for a touch down. In other words, you want direct contact. The same is true in politics: You want the voter to catch your message, run with it to the polls, and score for you at the ballot box.

What constitutes direct contact? The obvious way is to knock on everyone's door, but in most cases, that's not practical. A professional phone bank is a more efficient way to get through the door to voters.

First, hire seasoned professionals. Then devise the strategy that will best meet your needs. A telephone bank confers the ability to change your message or your mode instantly. Campaigns can be unpredictable; in a heated race, new variables emerge on a daily basis. By using telephones, you can adapt to these variables and tailor a new message—without making a big change in your overall script.

In the last days of a race, it isn't easy to change a TV spot or billboard advertisement. Even if you could, media ads only amount to indirect voter contact. It's also difficult to get a new piece in the mail a few days before the election. However, voter contact through a telephone bank allows you last-minute flexibility and control.

For, Against, and Undecided

Let's say you're embroiled in a statewide race, you've conducted a poll, you know how your voters feel about you, your opponent, and the issues. Your first task is to identify who is "for," "against," or "undecided" regarding your candidate.

Also ask if they want a bumper sticker or a yard sign. If they are undecided, ask permission to send them information about your candidate. Or, you could target all of your "undecideds" with a mail piece. Mail is an excellent form of direct voter contact. However, if sent blindly, a direct mail drop can amount to a tremendous waste. Direct mail is the most effective when it follows a phone call that identifies the recipient's views. You may want to send undecideds (fondly known as "persuadables") one mail piece, and "negatives" another.

It's a good idea to make your second call to those persuadables. In this call, follow a script that conveys the most positive information on the candidate. This information has the greatest power of persuasion for this particular segment of your market. You may have several scripts for persuadables, depending on the segment of your market you are trying to persuade.

Also call those who are against you. Some in the consulting business dismiss such efforts as desperate and futile. True, it's a last-ditch effort that some say doesn't work. They're wrong. We like to refer to such efforts as "combat calls." When election eve is upon you and you're down in the polls, you should call those identified "against" with negative scripts on the other guy. These scripts must be structured correctly; there's no room for error. It's dangerous territory, with the threat of a backlash if you overdo it, not to mention the waste of money if the people you contact are intractable.

Your aim is to create enough doubt in their minds to at least prevent them from voting for your opponent. You may not win the allegiance of these voters, but that's not the only winning situation. The other guy losing support is also a boon for you. Just as in the electronic media, negative calling works as long as you don't cross the line and get vicious.

Your favorite group—the "fors"—should receive a get-out-the-vote call right before voting day. Being for you doesn't mean much if they don't actually vote for you. Ask supporters who lack mobility whether they need a ride to the polls. Also ask the voter to remind friends and family to vote. Remember, family and friends tend to vote alike.

Also important on election day are reminder calls, to make sure the supporter has voted. The voter may be sick of your calls, but if handled with pleasant skill they'll understand that you're only calling because their vote is so important. You can also promise relief from your calls, once they've voted. Humor and style works well in the final tense hours of a campaign.

On election day, poll watchers can report to the phone bank about areas where turnout is low. The phone bank then bombards those low turnout areas with reminder calls.

Phone banks work—that's why so many campaigns use them. But you want to use the right one for your needs. Do comparison shopping and ask for referrals.

✓ Computer-Telephone Integration
Robert Garber

If you are not using computers hooked to telephones to assist in contacting your voters, you are probably falling behind your opponent. Campaigns with CTI (Computer-Telephone Integration) are able to do the work of 30 volunteers with just 10. If you resist automation, your opponent could be making up to three times as many voter contacts with the same number of workers. Moreover, the quality of his contact may be better than yours because of new integration with sound recordings.

The simplest form of CTI is using the computer to dial a voter. Many software packages can automatically pull a phone number from a database and dial the number, usually through a modem. This eliminates the problem of misdials and reduces the time necessary to make a call.

In a manual system, the caller decides what number to dial, dials it, marks the results of the call on a sheet of paper, and then hangs up the phone. In an automated system, the computer can decide which voter to call next from a list, dial that number, and pull the record onto the computer screen. When the call is finished, the computer automatically disconnects the call and brings up the next call. Of course, the computer records all results and provides instant tabulations.

A typical caller goes through about 28 households in an hour. With advanced dialing systems, it can rise to 70 or 90 an hour. Instead of spending 20 minutes talking to voters and the rest of the hour dialing numbers, the caller now spends 40 or more minutes talking to voters.

Another area of computer integration is voice response. Everyone has left messages on someone's voice mail or been confronted with a recorded message requiring one to press different keys on the phone before reaching an operator. The same technology can be applied to voter contact.

Using voice response with automated calling is a mistake that can only anger voters. People do not want to hear from a machine. The best use is to combine a live operator with a computerized recording system.

For example, a live operator finds an undecided voter and asks for the most important issue confronting him or her. The voter says "taxes." The caller records the answer, presses a button, and a pre-recorded message from the candidate comes on the line—"read my lips—no new taxes." Rather than the caller paraphrasing the candidate's position, the voter hears directly from the candidate.

Similarly, you may have a number of pre-recorded endorsements on the computer. You ask voters if the endorsement of Local 297 would influence their vote. If the voter says yes, you say, "Listen to this!" and play a ten second endorsement from the president of the union. If the voter says that the endorsement of Local 297 won't sway his or her vote, you go on and ask about the endorsement you have from the AARP, etc., until you strike a chord.

Computer technology today can digitize voice messages. Instead of recording a message on a tape, which can break or deteriorate, the voice message is recorded on a computer hard drive. The computer is then able to transform this back into the exact intonations of the speaker and play this message over the phone line. Digitized messages can be accessed randomly in an instant, pulling out exactly the sentence you need. Tremendous advances in the last few years make this technology now available on personal computers.

A simple 30-second message can require more than 500,000 bytes of data, taking up more space than a 90 page document. There are two concerns related to this: First, you need enough disk space for these voice files. Luckily, the price of hard drive storage has dropped dramatically.

The other concern is network software. Most networks are not designed to handle constant heavy traffic. The result will be a slow or unrecognizable playback of the message. If you are doing a phone bank, you will need specially designed software in a network environment to circumvent this problem.

What was impossible just a year ago can now be done on a standard PC workstation. The issue is which campaign is going to do the best job at harnessing this new technology, not to harass the voter, but to communicate with him or her more effectively and more responsively.

9

Television and Radio Advertising

★ ★ ★

✓ Effective Use Of TV
Doug Bailey

Who among the following does not belong?

- Andy Warhol.
- Fawn Hall.
- Victor Kiam.

The answer is Victor Kiam. Andy Warhol said everybody will be famous for 15 minutes. Fawn Hall proved him right. But Victor Kiam goes on and on forever.

Victor Kiam is the guy who liked the razor so much he bought the company. His ad has done for Remington in the 1980s what the hammer and anvil did for Anacin in the 1970s. If the Anacin ad was designed to give you a headache, the Remington ad seems designed to entice you to slit your throat.

But if Kiam proves for all time how TV can make anyone an instant celebrity, he introduces this article because he is the exception that proves a rule.

Most commercial advertisers, if you have not noticed, have moved dramatically away from the Anacin theory of the seventies and the Remington theory of the eighties—the notion that one ad should last a lifetime. And the political corollary is becoming clear as well: No candidate will do well who assumes one ad will last an entire campaign.

The fast-food chains have new gimmicks in their advertising every month. More and more advertisers link their promotions around different messages tied to the constitution, sports greats, or historic heroes in scenes that change weekly or nightly. Increasingly, individual products are sold with different ads, different theme lines, and different graphics in the same time frame. In the commercial advertising world, executives fear boring the consumer.

Television Dictates Changes

For the most part, political advertising follows and mimics the trends of commercial advertising. As a result, perceptive political advertisers now should recognize the dwindling "shelf life" of television messages. This new development is only the most recent in a long list of fundamental changes in our politics dictated by television. Others include the following:

- Communicating to the masses via television has made organization politics and party endorsements seem less significant.
- The money required for candidates to advertise on television has dictated an intense emphasis on fund-raising that dominates most campaigns.
- The personal attributes television best communicates attract to politics candidates better suited to public service by their smiles than by their substance.

The News Reshapes Campaigns

Television journalism not only has changed the way the people receive their news, it also has shaped the way people think about the issues that affect every political campaign. Television news has given the public greater confidence in its own ability to weigh the big issues of the day. First, the nightly television news audience is much larger than that of daily newspapers. Second, seeing the news on television (which engages most of the senses) imparts a far more emotional experience than does reading the papers. This increases the public's confidence that they understand specific issues. Third, the pictures on the screen give a sense of reality to the subject matter greater than any words on a page.

Consequently, even though television journalism is more sensational and less informative than print journalism, it also has made most Americans increasingly confident that, even with little knowledge, they know enough to make decisions on significant issues. The emotional and personal nature of television has created a generation of Americans confident that their judgment on issues and candidates is good enough upon which to base their votes.

All of these changes—caused by the television revolution of the last two decades—mean several rules that dominated political campaigning when John Deardourff and I formed our political-consulting business 20 years ago not only are no longer valid but could be disaster for any campaign that follows them.

Old Rule Number One: If you have one really good point to make, make it early, make it often, and never vary from it.

New Rule Number One: If you have an especially powerful point or issue to make, save it for the end when it will have the greatest impact.

Example: In the 1986 Senate race in Missouri, Democrat Harriet Woods had a potentially powerful point to make about Republican Kit Bond: His special economic interests seemed inconsistent with Missouri's hurting agricultural economy. By using the issue in controversial television spots in the early summer, she threw the issue away for potential impact at the end of the campaign when people were making up their minds.

Old Rule Number Two: A really good television ad is timeless and people will never stop wanting to see it.

New Rule Number Two: Be prepared to change your television spots weekly.

Example: In the 1986 Kent Conrad-Mark Andrews Senate race in North Dakota, each campaign was changing spots weekly—sometimes daily. One reason is that negative ads had to be answered, and once answered, had to be pulled. A second reason is that both sides were buying television time at such an extraordinary rate—up to 2,000 Adult Gross Rating Points per week—that heavy repetition of the same spots might have (and perhaps did) cost votes. The third reason is that in toe-to-toe television combat, to let the same spot run too long causes some voters to believe you have nothing new to say—which is a strike against you.

Old Rule Number Three: Beware of using negative ads; they generally are not credible and are seen as a sign of desperation.

New Rule Number Three: Because the public now seems to believe what it sees on television, negative ads against you must be answered.

Example: In that Conrad/Andrews toe-to-toe combat, Conrad had a critical advantage. He was willing to say anything, and the public was ready to believe him if Andrews did not answer. One disadvantage Andrews had was his assumption that the public would recognize nonsense for what it was. In at least two instances, the campaign was slow to answer Conrad's television thrusts—or used other media to parry—and paid the price.

By no means were North Dakotans unprepared to believe Andrews. But by not hearing from him, many of them assumed he had no answer, and that Conrad must have been right.

Old Rule Number Four: Use the good stuff early, because it takes a long time to reach everybody.

New Rule Number Four: Use it late so it's fresh—or at least put a new wrapper on it so it looks fresh.

Example: Proponents of a casino-gambling referendum on the Florida ballot in 1986 faced one overpowering issue. Since New Jersey adopted its own referendum, residents of Atlantic City faced one unmitigated disaster after another. We told the Atlantic City story in Florida, over and over again in every forum, in every speech, from the very beginning of the campaign. But we saved the best until the end. The issue was still fresh when we put on Florida television genuine man-in-the-street interviews from Atlantic City in the last ten days. Old issue/new package. Although the man-in-the-street material always was the most powerful we had, we saved it and used it last rather than leading with it.

Old Rule Number Five: Use very early television—when people are not resistant to campaign rhetoric and other campaigns are not on the air—to establish a base-level of support for your campaign.

New Rule Number Five: Stay off the air early and concentrate the dollars at the end.

Example: In Harriet Woods' 1986 Missouri Senate race, she not only squandered her good issue by using it too early, she squandered her money as well. She did not need early television; she had sufficient name identification and credibility; she should have saved it for the end when people were paying attention. There is little justification for any known candidate to spend early, because the public decides late.

Old Rule Number Six: Run negative ads early enough so they are not labeled as desperation measures.

New Rule Number Six: Use them at the end of the campaign, because negative advertising, whenever it comes, has a credibility of its own—especially if it goes unanswered.

Example: In the 1986 Pennsylvania gubernatorial election, Bill Scranton, with a slight lead in the polls and one week to go, eschewed all negative advertising. Bob Casey, his opponent, using fresh material, ran extremely negative ads over the last weekend and wiped out the lead. Ten to twenty years ago, the Casey last-minute tactic would have guaranteed a Scranton victory, because it would have been seen as desperation. Now, any negative ad that bears even passing homage to the facts tends to be believed unless a counter argument exists. Unanswered negative ads work.

Old Rule Number Seven: Candidates should write one set speech—hone it, perfect it, and never vary from it.

New Rule Number Seven: If the candidate is going to perform well on television, he or she must be prepared to vary the issue and style.

Example: If Johnny Carson repeated his same monologue night after night he would lose his audience quickly, and you would not need Carnac the Magnificent to know why.

Old Rule Number Eight: Undecided or inattentive voters are ready to make a decision after Labor Day.

New Rule Number Eight: Undecided or inattentive voters will not make their decisions until the end.

Example: No race better demonstrates the capacity for people to change their minds at the end than the 1978 reelection campaign of Senator Charles Percy in Illinois. The respected (and historically trustworthy) Chicago Sun-Times Straw Poll ten days before the election said Percy would lose by 18 percentage points. Ten days later, he won by 16 points.

The polls were not wrong. People changed their minds, and you could track it in the Sun-Times Straw Poll day by day. There was no single dramatic event. It was simply a matter of the Percy campaign having effective material in front of them when it became time for people to make up their minds.

Old Rule Number Nine: Use sophisticated polling techniques as a valuable predictor of things to come.

New Rule Number Nine: Remember that any poll is only a snapshot of things at that moment—and that polls tend to be verifiers rather than predators.

Tracking polls are, in fact, Polaroid snapshots, enticing in their immediacy—but dangerous in that they seduce campaigns into believing voter attitudes can be so precisely measured that campaigns can afford to focus on the trees rather than the forest. It is an inevitable conclusion of any analysis of the 1986 Senate races that campaigns on both sides of the aisle became so mesmerized with their own tracking data that they failed to see that voters more than anything, were (and are) looking for confident leadership.

It is difficult to follow the polls and lead the people at the same time.

Old Rule Number Ten: The first money you spend should go to reserving your last week's television time. This is still true, but now there is a corollary.

New Rule Number Ten: The first issue you want to use ought to be the last issue you do use.

Just as the precious asset of money should be reserved to pay for television the last week, so should the even more precious asset of an issue that will change people's minds. Keep it fresh by not using it. Or at least keep it fresh for the end by preserving the best packaging for Election Eve. If Andy Warhol said we each have 15 minutes in the spotlight, today's candidates better be certain that their 15 minutes come on Election Eve.

In the television world of instant gratification, the shelf-life of an issue can be very short. Air it too often, and it will spoil. If you do not believe this, ask yourself: Would you vote for Victor Kiam? For anything?

✓ Film vs. Tape: Choosing a Format For Political Television Ads
Deno Seder

Since 1968 the favorite topic of debate among political media consultants has probably been the choice of format for shooting commercials. Prior to that year all political advertising was shot in black and white, and b/w film production was still about as economical as video tape, then just entering its second decade of use.

By 1966 however, all network prime-time programming had switched to color, and the pressure to enliven spots with it led to the widespread use of tape. Some consultants wouldn't budge, despite the vastly improved economy and turn-around time offered by the new format. Video looked cheap, they felt, and lacked the feeling of detachment so critical to the capture of a viewer's fancy.

To this day, Charles Guggenheim—the great political filmmaker of the '60s and '70s—has committed not one of his entire collection of spots to tape. But the advantages and disadvantages of each format are so diverse, it's hard to imagine a full-scale modern media campaign that refused the flexibility of using both film and video. But when should you use which, and how?

Edgar ("Sonny") Mouton was the early favorite in Louisiana's 1978 gubernatorial race. A popular Democrat, he had intelligence, money, charm, powerful friends, a sense of humor—everything he needed to become governor. Everything except votes. Sonny Mouton finished dead last in a field of six.

Post-mortems in the local press attributed his political demise to natural causes: a changing electoral mood, a trend toward more conservative leadership, the end of populism in Louisiana, and other predictable bits of political pabulum. In my opinion, Sonny Mouton lost this election because he used a media campaign produced on video tape, while his five opponents used film.

From the start, Mouton's media looked cheap, while his opponents' looked expensive. Mouton spots had the look of small town newscasts, and—ironically—that was his strategy. Shoot on tape and make it look like news, media man David Garth figured, because voters believe newscasts while they are skeptical of political propaganda. But for Sonny Mouton, shooting on tape was bad news. Dave Treen was elected the first Republican governor of Louisiana since Reconstruction.

A Difference of Perception

Although film and video tape may appear on the surface to be virtually identical means of recording a message, each conveys a particular feeling that can have a subtle, yet profound effect on the voter—for good or ill.

A fundamental difference between film and tape is that video tape looks live—the action appears to be happening as you view it. In contrast, filmed action appears to have happened in the past, creating a different mood, a feeling removed from everyday reality.

Consider an instant replay of a sporting event: A viewer can't tell the difference between what was broadcast live and the replay, unless the replay is in slow motion. On tape, the live broadcast and the replay appear to be identical, both being perceived as happening in the present. Yet filmed highlights of sporting events always look as if they happened in the past.

The key difference is image clarity—a filmed image is softer, and has almost a dream-like quality which makes it appear momentous, historic, larger-than-life. Much of this has to do with audience conditioning. People are used to seeing high-budget theatrical productions and old classics on film. The harsher reality of video suggests soap operas, improvised live broadcasts and impromptu news footage. Thus, it evokes a feeling of reality and immediacy, but also the tawdriness of costume jewelry if it is used to shoot what should be an inspiring scene.

Many of the perceptual differences between film and tape are not fully understood by candidates or their consultants, but neither are they ignored. Knowing when to use one or the other is one of the important factors which make media consulting an established art. Making the right choice can spell the difference between effectively communicating with the voters and paying hundreds of thousands of dollars to destroy your candidate in their esteem.

One recent campaign I consulted with provides several good examples of how to make these choices wisely. The results on election day would appear to confirm their effectiveness: We defeated a generally well-regarded incumbent governor by a margin of nearly 2-1.

Portrait of An Effective Campaign

That incumbent was none other than the aforementioned David Treen. Four years after winning the race that witnessed the self-destruction of the Sonny Mouton campaign, Treen was challenged by Edwin Edwards, a former Democratic governor who had been forced to sit out a term by state law.

Edwards hired my firm to handle his media, and I prepared television scripts and storyboards for twenty commercials, hoping to get approval for three or four to start the campaign. This candidate had money, lots of money—he raised and spent more than fifteen million dollars—so I pushed for shooting on film, much of it 35mm.

After my presentation of the twenty storyboards, a seemingly bored and unimpressed Edwards finally looked up. "Within ten thousand dollars, "he asked," how much would it cost to produce all of them?" I gave him a figure and he wrote out a check on the spot for the full amount.

I produced 37 TV commercials for Edwards, shooting on 35mm film, 16mm film, and video tape. Here are brief descriptions of some of them, with explanations of why they were shot on film or tape.

The "Gandhi" spot. The spot opens with a medium/close-up shot of Edwards. The camera zooms back to reveal his wife and about a dozen supporters. The camera continues to zoom back and begins to boom up, revealing several thousand supporters standing behind and around Edwards. The camera continues to boom up to about forty feet, dramatically revealing the Louisiana State Capitol in the background.

Reminiscent of scenes from the successful film Gandhi then in the theaters, the spot was shot on 35mm film and was a real "production number" in that it literally had a "cast of thousands." Its heroic proportions demanded to be shot on film, enhancing the dramatic visual effect of a candidate surrounded by a multitude of supporters. Shot on tape, the sequence would have lacked the power and depth it had on film.

The "Piano Movers" spot. This spot featured two men in white uniforms attempting to carry a large upright piano up the steps of the Louisiana State Capitol. One of the men (representing Governor Dave Treen) kept dropping his end of the piano. His partner kept encouraging him, "C'mon Dave, get a grip Dave," but Dave simply couldn't handle the job. It was too big for him. The voice-over announcer told us how Dave Treen mishandled his responsibilities and lost his grip on state government. His remarks were punctuated by Dave once again losing his grip on the piano, which then tumbled down the Capitol steps.

This spot was shot on 35 mm film to make it reminiscent of a scene in an old Laurel and Hardy movie. Video tape would have been perceived as too real, too much in the present, considerably diminishing the effect of the satire.

The "Man/Woman-on-the-Street spot. About a dozen of these commercials were produced for the Edwards campaign. They were all shot on video tape using the Panacam, an excellent video camera by Panavision. These taped commercials were a nice contrast to the big-budget film spots. They looked inexpensive, but they were clean and crisp. They had a quality of immediacy that made the people appear more credible, allowing the campaign's message to penetrate the skepticism which usually greets political ads.

A Second Case Study

Another media campaign which dramatically demonstrated the differing uses of film and video was one I just completed for Alabama Lt. Governor Bill Baxley in his race for governor. Baxley didn't really understand the difference between the two formats, other than the cost, but he readily trusted my judgment when I recommended that we shoot on film.

The candidate was justifiably concerned about the constraints of filming: the great expense, the extensive time needed to light the scenes, the large number of crew members required, and the inability to replay and see what was just shot. These are concerns which lead many candidates to balk when they are about to be shot on film for the first time. The best way to put them at ease is to remind them that quality demands certain sacrifices.

Baxley's spots dramatized his funding of the state's kindergarten program, his record as Attorney General and Lt. Governor, his positions on several issues, and his personal background. After four weeks of paid media exposure, he picked up fifteen points in the polls and was propelled into first place. The spots did what they were supposed to and Baxley was happy he had committed to film.

The second wave of media was also produced on film. For this shoot, we included a "video tap" system which actually taps into the film camera and lets you see on a black and white monitor exactly what the film camera sees. Using a compact portable VCR, you can also record the action and play it back on location, eliminating an important advantage of tape over film. Although the picture lacks quality, it's very helpful.

For example, if your candidate is doing a "talking head" spot on film, the tape replay lets you know when you've got a good take, saving time and money. The tap is also an asset for the director. It helps to set up shots, check camera angles and moves, and follow the action as it's being shot.

Toward the end of Baxley's campaign, I started using tape, for though we had the money for film, we hadn't the time. Commercials that were being shot on Monday were scheduled to hit the airwaves on Tuesday.

The video commercials were simple and straightforward, featuring Baxley on-camera and consisting of one scene per spot. At this late stage of the campaign, it was important to get a particular message on the air as fast as possible. The time needed to process, transfer, and edit film was not available. Furthermore, film would not have contributed significantly to the effectiveness of these straightforward messages.

The hazards of video once again made themselves evident in this race, however. Former Lieutenant Governor George McMillan placed a dismal last in the primary, despite having nearly defeated Governor George Wallace in a runoff four years before. Pundits were bewildered at his precipitously declining fortunes, but an answer was readily apparent in his media campaign: McMillan's spots tried to make him appear inspiring—on video in a sterile studio environment.

Opinions From The Experts

Jim Eury, Director of the DNC's Harriman Communications Center, says if he had a choice, he would always produce commercials on film. He refers to the look of video tape as "sterile," and stresses the quality look of film, which "added its own dimension to the story being told" in some of his work.

Eury points out however, that as election day draws nearer and the campaign heats up, "The 'response' commercials are done almost exclusively on video tape because of the quick turnaround time in production and posting. We have turned around a 'response' commercial here in Washington in an afternoon for airing the next day in a midwest television market. That would have been impossible with film."

Many campaigns start out on film and end up on tape. Early spots promoting a candidate's background, experience, accomplishments, and family are often shot on film, for they demand an inspiring quality. They are designed to improve public image and visibility, raise money, and send signals to the press and the public that your candidate is viable, serious, and well-financed. Later in the campaign—when time and money tighten up—the switch to tape is usually made, often using the man-in-the-street or "talking head" techniques that are effectively communicated through the immediacy of video.

Some consultants and media people insist on using film or tape exclusively, but in many cases, it's a reflection of their background. Bob Cirace a former cinematographer, who now shoots almost entirely on tape, claims that "Many media people who have been used to working with film are insecure with video, and take the film route whenever possible. A lot of people who have had a great deal of experience with film and its techniques aren't willing to make the change." Cirace has made the change and has shot dozens of tape spots for my clients.

Other people in the business, including freelance cinematographers Tom Kaufman and Glen Pearcy, are willing to shoot on both film and tape. When asked to explain some of the technical differences between the formats, Kaufman points out that "in terms of sensitivity to light, film is about twice as 'fast' as tape, and captures a higher resolution image. There are a greater variety of lenses for film cameras, and personally, I find the film camera more mobile than the best ENG camera, because I am not linked to the sound recordist." Kaufman also explains that "film has more room for shadow and highlight detail, and film can handle highlights much better than tape."

First and Last

Both film and tape would appear to have a place in an effectively conceived media campaign. Of course, paid media cannot "make" a candidate; but in a tight election, even the right choice of format can make a difference in where he finishes on election day.

For Sonny Mouton and George McMillan, poorly-produced video spots helped make that finish last-placed. For Edwin Edwards and Bill Baxley, the right combination of good filmed and taped messages contributed to a finish on top.

✓ Focusing Your TV Commercials
Dean Rindy

Concentrate. We are approaching another presidential election. For 20 years, Republicans have been beating the crap out of the Democrats. One reason is that they have done better TV ads. This isn't always the fault of the ad people. The high command of the Dukakis campaign, for instance, never had a clue the 1988 election was all about. As a result, they prevented their own media staff from working well.

The GOP did it right. They assembled a team from several different firms and took a collegial approach. Evil geniuses like Lee Atwater and Roger Ailes presided over a grand strategy, while ads and concepts were farmed out to various producers. The result, as in 1984 and 1980, was frequently brilliant.

You and me, of course, never make mistakes. We will make great TV ads, whether for a presidential campaign or for our brother-in-law Harry's race for the State Fish Commission. And, fortunately, anybody with an IQ over 100 can learn how to make competent ads. You may not be Speilberg, but if you follow a few basic principles, you will be OK. Here's how.

The Big Picture

TV ads are tactical and should always be part of a larger strategy. Each ad should evolve from the basic campaign plan. Each ad should reflect the campaign's basic themes. Every time you read an ad script, ask yourself: "Which of our goals will this ad achieve?"

Let us return to the late, lamented Dukakis. In 1988, the voters didn't really like Vice President George Bush. They didn't agree with him on a lot of domestic issues, and they were ready for a change. The Republicans knew this. To win, the GOP had to hold on to the socially conservative "Reagan Democrats."

There was only one way to do this: Wage a campaign on "values" and turn Dukakis himself into the issue.

A devastating series of ads—featuring the pollution of Boston Harbor, the famous revolving prison door, etc.—questioned Dukakis' values and closed with the diabolical line, "Now, Michael Dukakis says he wants to do for America what he's done for Massachusetts."

Remember that all campaigns begin with two questions: "Which voters do we need, and how do we get them?" Every ad should aim at a crucial group of those necessary voters.

The Bush ads of '88 spelunked right into the subconscious of swing voters—the middle Americans who feared liberals and disliked everything Massachusetts stood for. These folks distrusted the Democrats on questions of national strength, and, yes, they feared that Dukakis' party was soft on crime, soft on patriotism, and soft on minorities.

The Dukakis people, by the way, made a fundamental error of strategy that infected their whole ad campaign. Bush's Achilles heel was Iran-gate. It was the perfect counter to the "values" issue. Reagan and Bush, after all, traded arms for hostages, then lied about it. They weaseled around with the Ayatollah Khomeini, the arch-fiend himself, and then they lied about that, too.

Creativity Begins With Questions

When you write a media plan, or even a single ad, always ask these questions:

1. Whom do we have to talk to? (That's the audience.)
2. What things do we have to tell them? (That's the message.)
3. What are the most important things? (Discipline that message.)
4. What is the best way to tell them? (Stylize the message.)
5. What is it going to cost? (Ascertain your cost effectiveness.)

It is surprising how often campaigns get bright ideas for clever ads but fail to answer these essential questions. Remember, each ad is just a delivery system for your message. It is a reality sandwich for voters to chew on. Even brilliant ads are useless if they don't convey the right message based on sound research.

Maybe your message is simple: "Our candidate, an intelligent, professional woman, is a nice person—unlike our lying, thieving, recently indicted, sleazy opponent." The candidate, as in so many races, is the issue. Put her on TV. Let her talk to the camera. Show her family. Recite her credentials. She is the safe choice. You do not need tricks, at least in this case.

You do not need to waste lots of swag, either. If you only have a $70,000 media budget, do not let the consultant talk you into renting two helicopters and spending $30,000 to film an epic about the candidate having new ideas on a mountain top at sunrise.

On the other hand, do not be a miser with your creative people. A lot of big-time campaigns are just plain stupid about this. They will spend a jillion bucks to buy air time from robber-baron TV stations. Yet they bitch and moan if their ads cost more than $1.79 a piece. Often a couple thousand dollars more will improve an ad's production value 100 percent.

The crucial question remains: Will it help tell the message more effectively? If so, spend the money, Bubba.

From Heaven to Hell

Religion makes Democrats nervous. That's too bad. America happens to be the most religious country in the industrialized world. Religious themes permeate our culture, and spiritual redemption is a recurring national theme. Americans think about politics as a moral drama.

American political campaigns often tend to be moral fables. "The New Deal," "The New Frontier," "It's Morning in America." These are great campaigns equipped with a great moral fable. They tell stories with all the classic elements—character, plot, symbol, and message. They present saviors and scapegoats.

A typical campaign follows this arc:

Phase One: "He's Just Like Jesus!"
Phase Two: "The Serpent in the Garden."
Phase Three: "The Return of the Prodigal Son."
Let's explore each of these.

He's Just Like Jesus

This introduces the so-called positive ads.

"Bill Clinton was born in a town called Hope," the voice of God intones, as sweet music plays and the screen fills with old snapshots of Mr. Bill as a barefoot lad with cheek of tan. He saved Arkansas; now he's going to save the world.

Sometimes a candidate becomes Jesus-like simply by dominating a key issue. Harris Wofford did it with health care in Pennsylvania last year.

The 1990 Texas governor's race is a case in point. Crime was big in Texas in 1990. Not one single candidate took an official pro-crime position. But a Republican, Clayton Williams, ran great ads to seize public imagination to prove he was more anti-crime than his competitors.

Clayton's TV producers built a mock chain gang camp for drug dealers. Clayton sauntered through it wearing a cowboy hat, sounding like an old-time Texas Ranger, and preaching fire and brimstone to the camera. He didn't just dislike criminals; he wanted to hurt them real bad. As for drug offenders, "Let's give 'em a taste of bustin' rocks," he smiled.

It worked. Williams became a savior by running away with the time issue. He trounced his colorless Republican Party opponents in the primary. Eventually, the public discovered that Clayton had the political IQ of a cold waffle, and Ann Richards swept to victory in November. But it was a good try.

Corny as the Jesus phase sometimes is, it is necessary to build a platform of credibility, so build your candidate can withstand the second phase.

The Serpent in the Garden

In politics, like life, a snake often slithers into Eden. Frequently, he is disguised as your opponent.

Few of us like to be mean. But you should remember that the United States itself was created by a negative media campaign against King George III. The Boston Tea Party was a brilliant attack ad. Going negative has a long tradition in our Republic.

Politics is about choices, and choices are about contrasts. The job of the media consultant is to visualize those contrasts. Phil Noble, the Mark Twain of opposition researchers, points out that every campaign tries to paint a picture. Eventually, the public is going to choose your picture or your opponents. The difference in portraits you paint can involve character traits or ideas or issues or experience.

The most famous negative ad of all time is the atom bomb spot Tony Schwartz did for Lyndon Johnson in 1964. It is the Citizen Kane of attack ads. A little girl is picking daisies in an idyllic peaceful field. Suddenly, the picture freezes, and we hear an eerie countdown as the camera zooms into an extreme close-up of the little girl's eyes. Out of the dark iris of her eye comes Armageddon, as the screen dissolves into a nuclear explosion. Moral: Vote for Johnson; Barry Goldwater is a missile-rattling nut.

That was picture painting with a vengeance.

Return Of the Prodigal Son

Few politicians are loved. Every candidate has faults. Most elections really come down to a choice of who the voters are most willing to forgive. "OK, Smith stole the money; but Jones stole money, too, and besides, we do not trust Jones on Social Security." Bingo.

Karl Struble, a Democratic consultant, points out that "most persuadable voters are not issue voters. They use issues ... as validators to draw a picture of the candidate's character, and they vote based on the candidate's character (i.e., cares about people like me, honest, effective, etc.)."

Voters did not love LBJ any more than they loved George Bush. The whole trick is to make people think your strengths are more important than your weaknesses. That is what campaigns are all about.

Story Telling

A good political campaign is a good story. Great movies are great stories put on film. Great ads are the same.

Character, plot, symbol, message. These are the fundamental principles of human communication. They have not changed since Neaderthals first grunted around the fire. They are present in the great Bible stories—Lazarus rising from the dead, Moses parting the Red Sea. They live in our memory because we can see them in our mind's eye. People think in terms of stories, not abstractions. If you put the classic story elements into your ad, then your candidates will ascend on high. You will become a power in the land and you will be interviewed on morning talk shows. Painful as it is, think back to the anti-Dukakis campaign of 1988. The lead character was the Gov himself, a hapless nerd little known to the American people. Supporting roles were played by godless liberals and welfare-addicted minorities.

The plot: The Gov and his liberal, Harvard friends were trying to infect America with their unnatural ideas. There were many powerful symbols of this: prayerless and pledgeless classrooms, the revolting prison gate, Willie Horton, the guck of Boston Harbor, Dukakis' head as it wobbled foolishly atop a tank turret. And the message? Our national family could not be entrusted to the weak, inept, un-American values of this man and his sinister allies. "America can't afford the risk," said the Bush ad. It was a powerful story.

In the Realm of the Senses

How do you communicate your best message? Be different when you can.

Political consultants operate under a lot of Victorian constraints. We can't do what the Madison Avenue people do. We can't use sex. We can't paint the candidate in day-glo colors. We have to be extra careful when we use humor, lest we offend anybody and generate those dreaded press accounts about how insensitive our campaign is to the concerns of the worm ranchers or the league of adenoidal fat men.

But great ads are different. They come at us from an unexpected slant. Karl Struble once did an ad in which he needed to convey the fact that Tom Daschle was one frugal SOB. He could have just said: "Tom is a fiscal conservative." Instead, he showed Daschle driving around Washington in his old, smoke-belching Pontiac. No BMW for Dacshle; he was an ordinary guy. The ad concluded with the line: "Maybe he's sentimental ... or just cheap." We remember stuff like that.

Lately, I've been experimenting with animation. For a lot of subjects, it is inappropriate, but in certain situations, it works like a champ.

One time, we added up all the money that lobbyists spent on the Texas legislature, then we calculated how many millions of martinis, golf rounds, and trips to Acapulco that sum would buy. We did a cartoon ad about ethics reform. If you saw it once, you would remember it forever. Prediction: This year, you will grow sick of ads featuring endless rows of animated bouncing checks. See what I mean.

Simplicity And Beauty

Most great ideas can be stated simply.

"No taxation without representation."

"$E = MC^2$"

"Government of the people, by the people, and for the people."

Ads are ideas. Great ads, like great ideas, are simply at their core. Simplicity is the road to clarity. Simple concepts. Simple images. Simple words.

Doc Sweitzer, the Philadelphia image doctor, says that "the job of the campaign manager is to take what is complicated and make it simple." That goes double for the media makers.

As to beauty, I am prejudiced in favor of it. Of course, it is silly to pretend that media consultants are great artists. We are not. We are, however, artisans who practice a craft. We make choices about the harmony and beauty of our products. These choices make the difference between good ads and bad ones.

I do not mean mere pretty pictures or beauty for beauty's sake. The pictures must advance ideas. I like visual hooks—strong images that reach out of the TV set and grab viewers by the eyeballs.

It makes a tremendous difference if an ad opens with a fascinating picture that sucks you into the message. If you give people an image that pulls them out of themselves and connects them to something beautiful or striking or interesting, then you have heightened reality for them. You have made your message memorable.

I have bashed the Dukakis campaign mercilessly, so I should point out that Dan Payne did a fine ad for them in the primaries. The ad attacked Gephardt for flip-flopping on different issues. We've all seen a million of these ads, but Payne did it in a crisp, striking way. They dressed an acrobat up to look like Gephardt, then filmed him tumbling through the air, flipping and flopping and jumping through hoops. It was fun to look at, simple, and memorable.

You Gotta Have Heart

Finally, there is the matter of heart. Good ads have it. They ring true, factually and emotionally. They are relevant to the voters' lives. They raise authentic issues in a believable, authentic way.

Ask yourself, "What is the true heart of our message? Do our ads express it? Are they visually and verbally and emotionally centered on what we absolutely have to say? Do they make people give a damn? Does the image fit the message? Is the emotion appropriate to the idea?"

Not every spot can be a zinger. Usually, you won't make your audience whoop, or cry. Simple persuasive facts work best most of the time. But the principle of heart applies to every ad. If your campaign has heart, you can connect with the mental and emotional life of the voters.

Do that and you are on the road to victory.

✓ Negative Ads: Rethinking the Rules
David Doak

Any analysis of new trends in negative advertising must start with the basics. Three rules govern "negative" or, more precisely, "comparative" advertising.

1. The statement of fact about your opponent must be accurate.
2. The allegation must be a fair representation of the factual occurrences.
3. The allegation must be about the "public" record of your opponent.

If you are thinking about deviating from these general principles, you should think long and hard. The more you deviate, the more you expose yourself and your client to counter attacks. It's also important to challenge an ill-conceived general rule that has gained widespread acceptance since the Dukakis for President campaign. That so called "rule" is that you must answer every attack.

That's wrong. If a negative ad isn't doing your client any damage, then it is a waste of your resources to answer it. Second, if the ad attacking your client has no "good" answer, then a weak response on your part that does not fully refute the charges will only help confirm that your client is guilty of the allegation. More importantly, a bad response spot that does not fully defuse the charge may only contribute to the momentum of the allegation made by your opponent.

In the political media business, we often talk of the strategic concept of "definition". Definition means that if you can control what the voters believe the election is about, you should be able to cast the voting decision in terms favorable to your candidate. Responding to negative ads that are not harmful or responding when there are no "good" answers contribute to losing control of the definition. First, because it depletes your resources, and second, because it focuses the attention of the electorate on your client's weak points without defusing the issue.

The best rules for response are as follows:

1. If a spot isn't hurting your client, do not respond.
2. If a spot is hurting your client, respond if you have a good answer, but always find a way to take the arguments back to your main lines of attack, i.e. answer and then counterattack.
3. If an allegation has a negative effect on your client and there is no good answer, do not respond. Instead use the opportunity to attack your opponent where he or she is vulnerable, on an issue that voters see as more important than the issue upon which your opponent is attacking your client. The best way to explain this is the way one of former clients did: "If someone is hitting you over the head with a 2x4, sometimes you just have to get a bigger 2x4 and hit him back."

New Trends

The most important changes in negative advertising have come in the areas of opposition research and polling. The development of opposition research as a specialty has provided campaigns more ammunition to use, and the widespread use of computer data bases have made the gathering of information much easier, particularly news articles and voting records.

With more information available, earlier, it is commonplace these days to pre-test the potential arguments against an opponent to find out which work best with the voters. This is done through both focus groups and polls so that qualitative as well as quantitative data can be evaluated.

It's a good idea to view focus groups in person, because "touch" or "feel" is important. It's useful to watch how people discuss the issues and react to them. This can give you an understanding of how far you can push a given issue. Remember, most good negative information has an emotional component.

When writing a spot, it's helpful to have actually seen voters react to the information that is being presented to them.

Negative Goes Respectable

Perhaps the most important new development in negative advertising is the discovery that you do not have to be mean, nasty, or unfair to produce spots that hurt the opposition. More and more campaigns are becoming debates. Advances in opposition research and polling, the proliferation of instant mass communication and the rise of constant coverage channels like C-SPAN has given us the ability to exploit mistakes made by an opponent.

Late in last year's Chuck Robb—Oliver North Virginia Senate contest, North called for making Social Security voluntary, a position opposed by most senior citizens' groups and by Senator Robb. Polling indicated that this was a powerful issue in a close race. We used it, it wasn't the only reason we won, but it helped.

In modern campaigns, negative ads are increasingly about the issues. For all the bad publicity negative advertising gets these days, it's important to recognize that most negative spots actually advance the knowledge level of the voter and therefore can be a positive force.

Documentation

In the early days of negative campaigning, people believed that Watergate had been the pivotal event that made negative ads work. The reasoning went that suddenly people were willing to believe the worst about public officials instead of giving them the benefit of the doubt. Today, while people are still willing to believe the worst about political candidates, they have also become cynical about negative ads.

In addition, news organizations have started "fact checks" on ads and have become much more willing to act as a "referee", calling fouls on offending parties if commercials are out of line. While this has made making negative ads more nerve racking, it has made response ads easier. If you are able to get a newspaper or TV outlet to call your opponent's ad inaccurate and unfair, you have the verification that makes your response ad effective.

In this cynical climate it is extremely important to document your ads, not only in the copy and on screen for the voter but also on background for reporters. Our firm prepares a documentation sheet on every ad we produce and we work with the campaign press secretary to make sure the facts in our ads are documented and presented pro-actively to the press.

Quick Turnaround

Turning a response around quickly has always been a necessity, but new technologies now make it easier. It's now possible to transmit an ad by satellite and save a few critical hours.

More importantly, for a quick turnaround you must get an audio or video copy of your opponent's ad as quickly as possible. To accomplish this, we ask our campaigns to get a volunteer in each media market to tape the various television dayparts and alert the campaign if any new ads are in the opponent's rotation. Sometimes you can get lucky and an ad will start in one market before it starts statewide, giving you a couple of days advance notice. Many times you can't see the spot before you respond but you can listen to the audio track.

This is critical because it's imperative that you respond to what your opponent is actually saying. Too often the description of a spot you receive from an excited supporter is much different than the actual copy. In quick response, rapidity counts but you must always balance time pressures against effectiveness.

Humor

More often, humor is being used in negative advertising. One of the ads we produced for U.S. Sen. Alan Cranston (D-CA) in 1986 is partly responsible for this. The ad featured a fictional disc jockey "Jack Man Wolf" selling Ed Zschau's Greatest Hits Album. As each of the greatest hits were introduced by "Jack Man Wolf" a singer sang a few bars of songs like "Do the Zschau Bop Flip Flop". It won the best spot of the year award and is still often mentioned when talk turns to negative ads.

It was a good spot and an effective tool, but it had been proceeded by months of serious negative ads that had softened Zschau. In that context, the ad worked. In another situation it might not. Humorous ads have their place and can be great attention grabbers for unknown candidates, but keep in mind these caveats:

1. The most effective negative ads are deadly serious; they work because they make voters mad at your opponent.
2. If you are making light of a subject, you run the risk that voters might think that you are not really angry about your opponent's actions but instead taking them frivolously.
3. Be careful if an ad is too mean (making fun of someone is mean); it can tell the voter more about your client's character than it does about your opponent's.

Today, negative advertising is more issue oriented. The content does the talking. It's well documented to protect against counter attacks. Consultants now see negative as an opportunity to counterattack, to go on the offensive; and increasingly quick turnaround is critical. But most important, consultants are now equipped with more tools because of professionalized research and polling.

Negative campaigning is now cleaner and fairer because of the actions of journalists in reviewing ads. All of this means voters get more information, both good and bad, about political candidates. That's a positive development.

✓ Campaign Commercials
John Witherspoon

The "science" of political advertising as practiced in the computer age is primarily concerned with counting, defining, and quantifying media buys and audiences in order to carry messages to the voting public in the most cost-effective ways possible. But without the "art" of political advertising, this technology is wasted. As Roy Spence, Mondale's media consultant, says, "Effective communication in political advertising is called winning. If your opponent gets more votes than you, you haven't effectively communicated!" The subject of this article is the art of winning: creating and producing a message that will capture the attention, imagination, and votes of its audience.

We are not campaign managers. But we provide professional services to political campaigns. Our job: "to form the image." That means that we do know something about advertising in general. But campaign advertising has some special concerns. First, there's the timing.

Suddenly, every two years, comes this great glut of political activity, crammed impossibly into a few months, absurdly under-budgeted, and for the most part, staffed with well-meaning, energetic young amateurs.

Usually we have difficulty in understanding the thrust of what we see going on. Much political advertising is self-defeating, obviously self-serving, and mainly . . . ineffective.

Old Commercials and New Politics

We did some homework. The first politician to use television to advertise, we discovered, was Gov. Tom Dewey in his 1950 New York Gubernatorial campaign. Dewey's "Man on the Street" program was a carefully rehearsed question and answer series among pre-selected passers-by. An on-air phone-in program took questions from staff members.

The idea of paid ads, first used in the 1952 Eisenhower-Stevenson campaign, was so new and unsettling that many stations flatly refused to run them. The Presidency, after all, is NOT a tube of toothpaste! Yet Ike's series of 10-second spots are considered by many to have been a major factor in his campaign success.

Commercial and Political Advertising

There are today about nine federal agencies which regulate the content of commercial advertising.

They have no say in political advertising. At one time or another the networks may turn down as many as half the commercials for products submitted to them for violation of one code or another, but First Amendment rights prevent application of these same codes to political advertising. The 1964 Johnson commercials portraying Goldwater as a warmonger would never be tolerated in commercial advertising.

As one ad man paraphrased Abe Lincoln, "In the free market, you can fool some of the people some of the time . . . etc. In a political campaign, you only need to fool half of the people once!"

This is by no means meant to be a condemnation of political advertising—nor of commercial advertising. Our belief is they are essentially the same: an effort to persuade the voluntary exercise of freedom of choice—one in the marketplace and the other at the polls. And like commercial advertising, political advertising that WORKS will put across an honest representation of the candidate. The Candidate is the Message.

As we pointed out, one big difference, of course, is timing. If all is not ready for a Grand Opening of a store, you can, as a last resort, postpone it. Grand Openings are never postponed in politics!

A commercial advertising campaign can have one, two, three years or more to increase a market share by, say, 11 percent. A political campaign has a matter of weeks to convince more than 50 percent of the voters to buy your candidate.

As in commercial ad campaigns, there are obviously many ways other than television to carry a message to the voters. Newspaper ads, pamphlets, direct mail, telephone banks, shoe leather, precinct meetings, and vans to haul voters on Election Day are all necessary, even fundamental, parts of the successful campaign.

But in Congressional and statewide races, television advertising can be a deciding factor. It is also very, very expensive; it requires research and, more important, strategy.

Beyond Research: Strategic Considerations

No one denies the importance of research. As Lionel Sosa, a well-known Hispanic marketing and political consultant puts it: "If you fly by your guts, you're nuts!"

The polls, daily trackings, focus groups, and the many other techniques of gathering, compiling and sorting numbers are the very stuff of which a persuasive communication effort—political or otherwise—is made. The 1984 elections will be the most computerized in history. Software companies, non-existent a few years ago, now provide campaigns on all levels with sophisticated technologies for fundraising, budgeting, polling, targeting, opposition research and media buys.

Everyone has access to the science.

And that is precisely the point. From this science, to which you and your opponent both have access, someone must extrapolate a creative strategy. Someone must decide what, when, and how much.

Political advertising production for television will fall basically into one of three categories:

1. Name/Face Identification
2. Positioning/Issue Spots
3. 11th Hour Blitz

Early Name Recognition

One of the early innovations that we translated from the commercial production world to politics was the animated campaign logo. By using your campaign print graphics—your logo—on television, you reinforce recognition of your candidate's name as seen in newspaper ads, signs, bumper stickers and so on. Bob Kerr, in his attempt at a U.S. Senate seat from Oklahoma, actually used a campaign button as his television logo.

When time and budget permit, consider animating the logo. My associate Bill Hayes has been animating logos for campaigns in Texas for at least a dozen years. Research by Dr. George Shipley, an Austin-based pollster and consultant, indicates a 30 percent increase in recognition when the logo is animated! This does not, of course, mean that recall equals votes, any more than recall equals sales. It does mean they know you are in the race. If you can incorporate a face into the logo, so much the better. The message here is name/face face/name, name/face.

Incumbents obviously already have a degree of voter awareness. The first priority for a challenger is early name recognition; the sooner the voters know the players, the sooner they can compare.

Animated logos, when produced with digital video units—squeeze zooms, line expansion character generators etc.—can be completed in a matter of hours at a post-production facility for well under $1000. Five to seven seconds of logo animation produced on film on an animation camera will require at least two weeks at a cost of $3500 or more. The difference is more than just technique, however. The film animation produces a better image on the screen, a more "finished" look. The vast majority of network programming and advertising is still shot on film.

Both techniques require talent. A well-designed, well-produced logo is far more than just fluff. It can significantly increase name awareness, which translates to more market penetration per dollar.

Early television advertising can be a "best-defense-is-agood-offense" situation. Pollsters for Senator Russell Long of Louisiana discovered prior to a recent bid for reelection that there was a potential "softening" of the solid position the Long family has held in Louisiana politics. "Solid position" is probably an understatement. Campaign leaders produced an extraordinary 30-minute program documenting the career of Huey Long, complete with seven or eight minutes of remarkable footage of the Governor in action, and continuing with the job that his son Russell was carrying on in Washington. Six months prior to the election, the show was aired with a substantial media budget. The result? Not one opposing candidate filed.

Positioning and Issues

The bulk of your production dollars will be spent in positioning your candidate in the field and clarifying and comparing, as best you can, his or her position on the issues. After your name identification dollars are spent, you face the big budgetary question. "How do I allocate my media dollars?"

In Congressional or statewide campaigns, it is not unlikely that 50 percent or more of your total dollars will be spent on media. Borrowing some guidelines from Madison Avenue, up to 20 percent of this figure may be spent on television production. Half of your total media buy will probably be in the last three weeks of the campaign. This buy will be made well in advance of air date based on projected dollars available. Competition for time is fierce in these closing weeks.

An important caution. There are never enough dollars, but a contingency production budget MUST be established for the unexpected in the "11th Hour." More on this later.

But first, let's look at the types of spots available—a smorgasbord of commercial options. Try them on until you find one that fits.

"The talking head"

As the name implies, the camera is aimed at the candidate and he talks. In the case of charismatic(and photogenic) candidates, such as Texas Senator Lloyd Bentsen or San Antonio Mayor Henry Cisneros, this is probably the most effective and definitely the least expensive type of spot available. It can also be the dullest for the viewer.

American flags and bookshelves full of leatherbound law books are common props to give "atmosphere" to a "talking head" spot. Texas District Court Judge Roy Barrera appeared in his judicial robes behind the bench to establish his incumbency and overcome a deceptively youthful look. Lloyd Bentsen's credible delivery was reinforced with three simple hanging placards visually strengthening the issues he was discussing. The three cards were then animated into the closing logo tag.

Production costs are minimal for this type of spot. A 30-second commercial, shot in studio with a minimum of props, can easily be completed in an afternoon at costs beginning at a few hundred dollars—if your candidate is not rushed with an overly busy schedule that interferes with his remembering his lines or reading the teleprompter. Remember, a tired, ragged-looking candidate on the day of taping will look that same way every day the spot is run!

"The candidate in action"

Not all candidates are trained actors. Although a public servant may speak for himself, he may not speak in a particularly viewer-appealing manner. Nothing can be more frustrating to campaign workers than a qualified candidate that just does not "come across" on the air.

A very viable option is to show the candidate among the voters, or, in the case of an incumbent at work. This is an excellent way to target voters and issues; a candidate among senior citizens cares about Social Security issues, a group of students shows an interest in education, soldiers in defense, ghetto scenes in urban concerns, farmers in agriculture, wilderness campers in the environment, and so on.

Whether your candidate actually speaks while addressing a group or you use a voice-over announcer, the candidate is relieved of the one-on-one with the camera situation.

This is a good point to reiterate the basic truth of political advertising: "The Candidate is the Message," or, "Don't Confuse the Essence with the Image.

Jim Mattox, current Attorney General of Texas, projects a "fighter for the citizens" kind of personality. To present him any other way would be deceptive and counterproductive. Shots of Mattox with his jaw jutting, making no-nonsense "I'm not going to take it" positions were used in spots that concluded with the campaign line "the tough DO get going!" Lloyd Bentsen is a dignified statesman and family man. Spots of Bentsen showed him fishing with his grandson, with a voice-over about the kind of America the boy would inherit. Bill Hobby is a comparatively quiet, hardworking Lieutenant Governor. He was shown working after hours through a lighted window in the statehouse, and at planning sessions with charts and pie-graphs.

In almost all cases, this type of spot is more expensive than the "talking head." Because they are shot on location, they require a crew, equipment, lighting and sound equipment, and extensive post production. While very effective, it would be difficult to produce a "candidate in action" spot for under $2,500, and they can cost as much as $7,500 or more. Nonetheless, these are your bread-and-butter vehicles for presenting your candidate and the issues.

"Man on the street"

Applied to politics, this is a version of the testimonial. It is risky in commercial advertising, and because of the time constraints, much riskier in politics.

The problem is credibility. Chances are, unless you are very lucky, the spontaneous "testimonial" will come across as rehearsed. And from a production point of view, it probably would have to be The odds on getting an honest "man on the street"; opinion worthy of building into a television commercial are far too high. That means dozens of interviews for one good one, or hundreds of feet of film or tape for a ten-second comment.

Predicting the cost of this type of spot is like trying to answer the question "how much is a piece of string?" If the first five testimonials are great, it's cheap. If not, when is too much?

"Slice of life: paid performers"

The practice of using actors, actresses and on-camera announcers may be one area where commercial and political advertising do not mix. It is difficult enough for the best minds in Hollywood to create realistic, believable dramatic situations; I have rarely seen it done in politics.

It is not the fact that the actors or announcers do not perform believably, it is that the viewer will correctly perceive it as a person getting paid to say something nice about the candidate.

It is also expensive. Using professional talent, sets, makeup and wardrobe can easily bring the cost of a 30-second spot into the $20,000-and-over range.

On-camera announcers, if they have a reason for being on camera, can be effective. In this year's primary for a County Commissioner's seat, the underdog, an "outsider" (hence, unobligated) candidate utilized a paid announcer walking among door-sized panels with news clippings about his opponent mounted on them. It was only at the end of the spot, when the announcer pushed one of the panels into another, that the viewer realized the panels were the back sides of dominoes. The closing cutaway of dominoes knocking each other over created a very powerful visual strengthening of the message. The domino props and the paid announcer were the main expense items. The cost was under $3,000 and the candidate pulled about 60 percent of the vote.

"Attack and compare"

The result of this type of production, at its best, is to create distinctions. We have produced countless variations of a split-screen check list, with Candidate A on the left and Candidate B on the right. In many cases, when the honest facts of voting record, experience, or accomplishments justify it, this comparison can clearly show the voter the alternatives. For the most part, a spot of this type can be produced rather inexpensively: from a few hundred dollars for text on the screen, to $1,500 or so for more advanced visuals.

At its worst, this type of commercial is simply negative campaigning, ranging from mild innuendo to outright slander. The tricky part is attacking your opponent without sending a message to the voters that your motivations are not petty, vindictive, or greedy. It becomes hard for the voter to believe you when you then turn to him and say "trust me."

We have produced some interesting variations. One "weathervane" spot, designed to illustrate how flaky the opponent was, actually used a weathervane spinning erratically as the voice-over announcer described the opposition's apparent change of positions. In another spot, a split-screen comparison showed four needles of a lie detector as a background. As various statements were read, the needles on the opposition's side of the graph went wild with deception. The word "liar" was never uttered. A recent "mudslinging" spot showed one candidate talking as handfuls of mud began to obliterate his image on the screen. And a commercial in a recent Texas race showed unidentified hands plopping a carpetbag on the table and removing momentoes of the opposition's past political and business failures. As if being a "carpetbagger" in the South isn't bad enough, this guy wasn't even a good one!

It is this last category of spots that is most likely to turn ugly in the closing hours, and the most hotly contested, closest races are the ones in which the "last hour blitz" are necessary.

The 11th hour: the media blitz

It is in the closing weeks, frequently the closing days, that the most frantic, volatile and downright nasty things happen in a campaign.

Some races, of course, have by this time been decided. Most have not. Frequently the daily trackings are showing mixed trends, inconclusive results, or confusing mixes of data. Rarely is anything sure at this point. The knee-jerk reaction is to unload with everything you have.

Anticipation—knowing this was going to happen—is small consolation. It may be the only one you will have, however.

This frenzy of activity can be the most exciting and fulfilling period of time for the creative strategist. The atmosphere lends itself to a creative combustion that can sometimes move more than mountains; it can move big blocks of voters. That is the right idea at the right time can (and, of course, with the right amount of money).

I am not about to challenge the majority of consultants, researchers and analysts who claim that "in all 200 campaigns, I cannot think of one where the ads made a difference!" I will relate some tactics we have observed, an example of excellent 11th Hour use of media, and one amazing case history, and let you decide.

Early Media Buys

If there is one constant in this 11th Hour equation, it is to start early buying time to air your media blitz. Your ads won't do you much good if you can't get them on. Your media-buying service or person should purchase all the air time you can afford many weeks prior to Election Day, because the September to November period is television's busiest season with commercial advertisers and other candidates putting a strain on availabilities. As mentioned earlier, it is not unusual for half of your television media-buy budget to be allocated for your final blitz. So, when buying time, "buy back from Election Day," buy heavy for the final week or two and add spots for earlier time slots if more money becomes available.

Early Production

There may be issues in your campaign, or last ditch tactics that lend themselves to anticipatory, or early, production. That means producing a spot and leaving it on the shelf "just in case." We have produced dozens of these, most of which were never pulled off the shelf until after the campaign. Then a campaign staff member hurries over to retrieve the tapes. (Are you sure there are no more copies? These are all the masters?) Professional integrity, and in some cases common decency, prohibit me from discussing any details of these. The visuals usually show large amounts of currency going into pockets or coming out of brown bags.

A more positive reason for producing spots that may never run would be anticipating an event that could go one of two ways and materially alter a race: a labor strike, pending legislation, an important endorsement, foreign events. The candidate may see an advantage in clarifying his position. In such an instance producing one or two spots early on is a prudent use of your most limited resources: time and money.

The point is that time is very precious as you approach Election Day. Even a single afternoon for a "Talking head" spot may be impossible to coordinate. The only advice seems to be to size up your race and, if there are issues such as these, consider anticipatory production, and plan ahead. There is the undeniable possibility that you may be spending money on something you may never use, but it's like insurance. You hope you don't have to collect it, but you thank your stars for your perspicacity when you have a loss to claim.

"Quick on the feet" spots

More than likely, your 11th hour blitz will include spots that must get on the air today. Or sooner.

During the last Texas Gubernatorial race, Democrat Mark White faced the most lavishly financed campaign in Texas history to reelect incumbent Republican Bill Clements. Early efforts to get a handle on an issue seemed to elude White. The strategic decision was made to zero-in on a few, among them education and the newly formed Public Utilities Commission. The strategy was to maneuver any public debate or media coverage into a discussion of these hand-picked issues. That was the strategy. The tactic was push, push, push.

It worked. The incumbent Governor, and some of his appointees, were forced into making some statements that became apparent contradictions to Clement's current positions. These appeared to be the first chinks in the armor of a not unpopular Governor.

Each time one of these apparent chinks would appear, White's campaign staff, headed by Roy Spence, would use a simply-produced TV spot to pry it into a gaping hole. The technique? They simply "scrolled" the contradictory messages up the screen, and let the obvious conclusions be drawn. This begat Republican denials, and they begat more mistakes, and they begat more spots, and so on, and so on to the Democratic victory.

This is how it should work: media as a function of campaign strategy

The above is an example of how it should work: media as a function of campaign strategy. When the strategy begins working, amplify it with media. The "production costs" are inconsequential. The timing is everything. The turnaround time on these spots was probably 36 hours from start to on-the-air. The cost could not have been more than a few hundred dollars per spot.

The Senatorial handshake issue

The story of the "John Tower Handshake" is quite another matter. It is now rather famous in Texas politics, and may be the best media campaign story of modern times.

The 1978 U.S. Senatorial race in Texas was one of considerable differences in style and substance. John Tower, a longtime fixture and powerful Republican presence in the U.S. Senate, faced Bob Krueger, an urbane, scholarly, eloquent contender. The race was heated and was evolving on many complex levels: old school vs. new, rural vs. urban, with Hispanic, defense, union, and other undercurrents.

A paper appeared, allegedly circulated by some overzealous Krueger campaign workers, and authored by an influential Baptist leader. The document made some rather uncensored allegations about the Senator's reputation in Washington. In fact, the Baptist had been referring to a different Senator, but the paper "appeared," and was "nondenied" by the Krueger staff. Tower publicly demanded an apology, Krueger publicly denied responsibility. End of Round 1.

At a well-publicized debate at the Houston Press Club, both men were face-to-face for the first time since the standoff. Krueger offered his hand to Tower in greeting. Tower refused and turned indignantly back to his dinner plate, Krueger standing above and behind with his hand extended in gentlemanly manner. The photographers caught the whole sequence, and two sequential photos—of the offering, and the refusal—were run side by side in every tabloid in the state and many outside it.

The result was devastating. Less than a month before election, the Senator's narrow margin began to erode. Efforts to reduce the significance of the event to "it's only a handshake" did not stop the slide. Attempts to change the subject and talk the issues could not penetrate the Handshake

Curtain. Insiders reported a certain resignation among the troops, and possibly in Tower himself, that it was over.

While at Hayes' San Antonio studios taping a five-minute, 11th-hour recap of "what-is-and-what-is-not-important in this race," Tower related a story to his media strategists, which included Lionel Sosa, the media consultant who specializes in reaching Hispanic voters, and Bev Coiner, of Coiner and Garcia, an advertising consulting firm in San Antonio. At a meeting of mainly Hispanic voters a few days earlier, and tired of answering the question about the Handshake, the Senator finally told the whole story, asked the audience if they would not do the same thing, and received—to his amazement—a standing ovation!

Combustion! Here was the solution. Enter the media. Coiner borrowed a secretary's typewriter, wrote a 30-second script, and took it back to the Senator who delivered it faultlessly in about two takes. The spot starts with Tower sitting on his desk saying, "Perhaps you have seen this picture of my refusing to shake hands with my opponent. I was brought up to believe that a handshake is a symbol of friendship and respect..." as the now famous pictures appear on screen, "not a meaningless, hypocritical gesture. My opponent has slurred my wife, my daughters, and falsified my record." The spot concludes with the zinger, "My kind of Texan doesn't shake hands with that kind of man! Integrity is one Texas tradition you can count on me to uphold!"

Every other spot was pulled and the new one ran in all available time slots. About ten days before election, the slide was reversed. It then started to climb. Daily trackings showed the Tower curve crossed the victory line two days before election in what must have been the closest election in the Senator's career. Coiner claims the trend was so strong the election would have been a landslide had it been held a week later.

No one can say that he or she "won" an election because of their television spots. But who, in a major election, would do without them?

✓ Innovative Use of Radio
Joe Slade White

Question: When is a political radio ad not a political radio ad? *Answer:* When it is successful. This may seem contradictory; it is not. Most innovations in political media occur when consultants break the established rules, and treat a given medium altogether differently.

This is precisely how John Marttila, a Boston-based political consultant, revolutionized the print tabloid in the early 1970s. Previously, print tabloids looked like tabloid newspapers, complete with headlines, columns of dense print, and small photos. But Marttila treated the tabloid as if it were a series of TV spots, with huge full page pictures facing pages with tiny amounts of print surrounded by seas of white space. The Marttila tabloid has since become the industry standard.

The same thing happened with direct mail. In the old days, persuasive direct mail meant letters—few of which were read, and fewer still which were effective. Then California consulting firms began to treat direct mail pieces as if they, too, were essentially printed TV spots. They featured bold graphics and large pictures that conveyed powerful messages simply and directly to various targeted audiences.

This same approach can also work with radio—so long as a campaign understands that the secret is to look at a radio ad as something more than just a radio ad.

The Radio Ad as Press Release

In the race for Seattle Rep. Mike Lowry's (D-Wash.) open seat, King County Assessor Ruthe Ridder, running against two well-known opponents, sought to increase her name recognition. Her polling showed that Contra Aid was a critical issue for Democratic voters in this ultra-liberal downtown district. The problem was that Ridder was practically flat broke.

With Congress poised for vote on Contra Aid, her campaign produced a radio spot featuring the candidate arguing against funding. (A position shared by both her Democratic opponents.) The campaign bought time on two extremely inexpensive FM stations for just three days—the day before the vote, the day of the vote, and the day after the vote.

Just before the ads aired, Ridder called a news conference to unveil the new spots and announce that she was the first candidate to air radio ads. All three Seattle TV stations and the two newspapers ran key stories on both the ads and their timing. Not a single reporter asked how much money the spots cost (the total came to a mere $450!). By staking out the lead on a pivotal issue, her credibility was instantly established; her opponents were left dumbfounded.

The campaign followed up by sending out the script of the ad as a direct mail piece, along with a fundraising appeal. Soon everyone thought they had heard the spot, when in fact only a few voters actually had. The candidate achieved great success by using a radio spot as a press release and a direct mail piece—instead of merely as a radio spot—and she now is a leading contender to fill Lowry's seat.

The Sounds of Silence

Another race in which an innovative use of radio turned a campaign around was the 1980 Idaho Senate race. Incumbent Democrat Frank Church was seeking reelection against conservative Republican Rep. Steve Symms. Having spent months fighting on Symms' ideological turf over divisive questions such as the Panama Canal treaty, Church had fallen behind. In order to win, he needed to shift the campaign's focus. After a little opposition research, his campaign learned that Symms had never authored a bill that was passed into law.

Sen. Church immediately took to the airwaves. A radio spot told voters: "You know, some people say that Congressman Steve Symms hasn't really done much of anything in eight years. But that doesn't seem fair. Well here's a complete list of every law Congressman Symms has ever written on his own and passed during the last eight years."

This was followed by ten seconds of complete silence. The announcer then returned and intoned: "Yep, that's the complete list." And then proceeded to list a few of the significant laws which Church had guided to passage.

People laughed—and the race quickly tightened. The spot worked because it was innovative; it demonstrated silence can be just as effective as words.

Radio: The David That Topples Goliath

If you cannot afford television and your opponent can, try to use your radio ads to dictate your opponent's TV ads—and make those TV spots work to your candidate's favor.

Another female candidate in a Seattle city-wide campaign did this with particular effectiveness. She had very little money and was up against a male candidate determined to pour hundreds of thousands of dollars into TV.

Her radio spots referred to his TV spots, directly criticizing his lack of experience before concluding with her own experience and qualifications. By answering his TV spots directly, she undermined the credibility of his ads.

Indeed, by mocking the very experience his ads purported him to have, her radio spots served as an effective counter to his more expensive TV spots. Before long, people began laughing at his TV spots; the more money he spent on television the more he dropped in the polls. Her radio spots essentially doubled as a TV buy because she was able to make his TV ads work for her.

Even Unwritten Ads Can Be Effective

In 1984, shortly after Gary Hart upset Walter Mondale in the New Hampshire primary, the Mondale campaign asked me to produce a radio spot criticizing Hart. I answered that it was too late to do anything for the Illinois primary, which was a week away, but that I would give it some thought.

The next day a friend on Capitol Hill told me the rumor in Washington was that Mondale was bringing me on as a hit man. I laughed and said that I had not been hired. He asked if I would do a spot about Hart's name change. I said no, though I remarked that an ad stressing how Walter Mondale's name had, over the years, come to stand for something would hurt Hart even more.

Apparently, someone overheard the conversation and the rumor game began. Word quickly reached Hart headquarters that I had been hired to do a spot about Hart's name change. By the time the rumor had passed through four more people, it included a script (which bore no resemblance to the one I had dictated off the top of my head).

As word passed from one person to another, the "spot" continued to grow. Within hours, Hart people reported the fictitious spot as having aired in two states. One of Hart's staffers reported this to the candidate, and Hart responded by calling an impromptu news conference, where he blasted Mondale for airing a radio spot that had never even been written, much less produced and broadcast. Within hours, Hart had to reappear before the cameras, admit his error, and apologize to Mondale. That blunder helped Mondale regain momentum and win the Illinois primary.

All of these stories have one common thread connecting them. In each instance, the campaign took a risk with an innovative radio spot and reaped the benefits. You can, too. The only barriers to effective media are those which you erect in your own mind.

✓ Wavelength Winners
Joe Slade White

Here are 12 rules for the effective use of radio for political advertising:

1. Radio ads are not print. That seems obvious, but the deadliest give away of a novice script writer is complete sentences that sound like they belong on the printed page. People don't talk that way. Remember, you're for the spoken word. Clue: talk your script out loud. If it sounds stilted, it is. Use contractions, incomplete sentences; give it freedom.

One of my favorite scripts began: "How ya doing. Y'ok?" In print it would have been: "How are you doing? Are you alright?"

2. Sound effects are the most abused element available to newcomers. And the first refuge of the unimaginative. Sound effects are only powerful when they are used sparingly and used well.

They're the spice—so don't kill the audience's taste buds. The best sound effects are ones you can evoke inside the audience's minds. within the ad itself.

3. Beware of professional announcers. More good radio messages are butchered by "professional" radio announcers or DJs than by any other hazard. You know the voices—smooth, perfect enunciation, and ... totally fake. Radio is like talking with someone—not talking at someone. It is deeply personal and intimate. Don't be afraid to audition voices until you find a real human being. TIP: Singers understand the nuances of emotion in a lyric and the rhythm and pacing necessary in a good script.

4. Ask questions. Engage the audience to draw it into the message. The best way, literally, is to ask questions—the answers to which are in fact the message you want to convey.

5. Radio is " invisible." It works at its best in a guerrilla tactical warfare. Often an opponent, political insiders, and the news media will remain totally unaware until its impact has already been achieved. Radio is your secret weapon to make critical and effective tactical moves. This allows you to move on two totally different tracks simultaneously with visible television and invisible radio.

6. Please, please, no more "Husband and Wife Over the Breakfast Table" radio ads. You know, the ones that begin: Wife: "Dear? Did you know that Congressman Smith's Subcommittee on Intergovernmental Smoke and Mirrors reported out two new bills, thus saving Western Civilization as we know it?" Husband: "Golly dear, I did not know that. It is amazing. I guess I will be voting to re-elect Bob Smith on Tuesday, November the 8th, from 7 a.m. to 9 p.m. And I will be sure to tell all my friends."

I don't know about you, but if such a couple exists, I want them done away with. If my wife said something like that to me at breakfast, I'd throw something at her, and vice versa. But I guarantee you every year a candidate calls up with a script featuring a husband and wife over the breakfast

7. If you want to drive an opponent absolutely crazy—use an ad to talk to them directly on the radio. It works. You talk to them, and the voters love to "listen in" on your conversation. It throws your opponent's campaign into a useless flurry of meetings—and inevitably, the opponent hears the ad while driving and goes ballistic.

8. Read Tony Schwartz's book, The Responsive Chord. It's out of print, so you'll have to search it out at a public or college library. It is the source, not just for radio but for communications theory at all levels and all media. The book was written 20 years ago, and today it is still 20 years ahead of its time. Tony is the father of "the responsive chord" that has revolutionized communications theory. He is my mentor and the best there is in effective radio.

9. Radio is electronic human emotion. A radio ad can "move" a person in a way that is nearly impossible in a newspaper ad and actually quite difficult in television. But be careful. The most powerful emotions can be touched quietly and simply. The emotion is in the audience. Your job is to touch that responsive chord.

10. Right below "Husband/Wife Breakfast Table" dialogues come political jingles. Resist the temptation, and your candidate's cousin the country music writer. This, too, will pass. (Exception: a brilliant TV ad in a Republican Senate campaign featuring a woman in a rocking chair singing her own jingle. It was charming, real, and on message ... a rare combination.)

11. If you can tell it's a political ad in the first 10 seconds, you've lost. Draw the audience in. They don't like political ads. But they do love stories; they care about real life issues. Start there. Be interesting. They will follow you to your point in due time. A friend once told me, "I didn't know where the hell you were going at the beginning of that radio ad." I, of course, took that as the highest compliment possible.

12. Break the rules. I do every chance I get; and I did when I was just starting out—which, of course, is exactly how I discovered these "rules." Break away—the secret is in knowing why you're breaking them. Above all, have fun with radio—if it isn't fun, none of the rules will help at all.

✓ Personalizing Generic Spots
Steve Shaw

In 1992, Connecticut politicians voted "yes" on a cost-effective, innovative approach in getting their messages across to constituents. Instead of spending $16,00 a piece on a TV spot and then buying expensive advertising time on broadcast television stations, 16 Democratic candidates for state Senate spent no more than $1,250 a piece by personalizing a series of four 30-second spots we developed for their use on local cable stations.

The state's cable systems closely match the outlines of the state Senate districts. This enabled each candidate to target only his or her constituents at a fraction of the cost of broadcast television.

The first 20 seconds of each ad featured a video segment on one of four topics chosen from focus group research: the environment, abortion, government spending, and jobs. The final 10 seconds of each spot showed a color slide of the specific candidate accompanied by a personal audio message to voters.

Since local political campaigns tend to be run very economically, we needed to create a strong visual image that didn't require enormous shooting or post-production time. We kept our images simple–ones that viewers would remember.

For example, the environmental ad showed a child playing on a beach, and the government spending spot was shot from inside a bank vault with the door slowly closing, leaving the viewer in darkness. With this approach in mind, it took only two days to shoot all four spots at a package cost of $16,000.

The first 20 seconds of the four videos was written and paid for by the Committee for a Democratic Majority, which then offered the spots as an inkind contribution to each senatorial candidate. The candidates were responsible for the cost of adding the personalized audio, color slide, and graphics to the end of the spot, and for arranging to air it on local cable or broadcast TV stations. (We offered the candidates a sliding scale, ranging from $650 for one spot to $1,250 for all four spots. The PAC supplied a media buyer to help the candidates purchase cable time, which ranged form $5 to $45 per 30-second spot).

Remember: The key to keeping this money-saving approach to campaign advertising from producing little more than generic, fill-in-the-blank political ads is personalizing each spot and airing them in separate cable markets.

✓ Reaching Voters Through Homemade Videos
Robert G. Berger

Once your campaign has made the tactical commitment to a mass distributed video, the challenge becomes mastering all the details that concern how to develop, film, edit, target and deliver the piece. This process includes five distinct phases: pre-production, production, post-production, targeting and distribution. Only if the campaign can successfully grapple with each of these five phases will the video be turned to the greatest advantage.

Pre-Production

Pre-production consists of determining the budget for the video, collecting the creative and technical talent necessary to plan and execute the video, and developing the concept for shooting.

If a campaign does not have an experienced volunteer to help, other sources of creative help must be tapped. Start by looking in a political guide or magazine for professionals in your region—many of whom will be experienced in creating videos for television commercials or for limited distribution use on the fundraising circuit.

A commercial advertising agency will have the technical know-how, though the campaign will have to provide the political overlay for all such professionals, whose services may cost a campaign between $25,000 and $50,000, the type of distribution, rather than the medium, is the innovation.

When dealing with professionals, the key to remember is to balance the need for the video to look well-conceived against the potential to look too slick (an instinctive judgment call in which both candidate and campaign manager must be involved).There are alternative technical and volunteer sources potentially available as a pool of talent from which to draw the creative team.

The personal camcorder lets the campaign staff do its own taping and rough-cut editing in-house. There are now commercial edit studios springing up for public use that will facilitate a more polished editing of homemade footage. The danger of doing it in house is that the production may look too amateurish. An alternative is to contact a local university or community college where film is taught. A professor or recommended student may have the technical and creative bent and enthusiasm to produce your video on a volunteer basis.

Some cable franchises provide the public with the opportunity to be trained as producers or technicians. From the cable company, the campaign may be able to obtain a list of those who have been trained and recruit a creative producer and cameraman. They may be able to use the cable firm's editing facilities.

Whether the campaign ultimately chooses to retain a paid professional or employ talented volunteers, the team and campaign in tandem must devise an appropriate concept and shooting script before moving forward. These steps cannot be rushed and may take several months.

Production

Once the creative team has been assembled—including a creative director, writer, cameraman and narrator—it is time to shoot the video. If video equipment needs to be rented, assume it will cost at least $600 per weekend. For a video that will run between 5 and 10 minutes, the creative team will likely require three to four days to get the necessary footage.

Remember, for much of this time the candidate needs to be available. Given the sizable financial commitment to the video, it is only reasonable to schedule as much of the candidate's time as is necessary to get the job done properly and forsake knocking on a few extra doors. In addition, members of the candidate's family and any others who may be asked to participate (such as in segments of group discussions) also need to have their availability scheduled in advance.

Make a few practical considerations, including having a contingency plan for rain. And plan to feed the creative team periodically.

Post-Production

Once filming is complete, the real creative challenge begins: editing. This includes adding the narrative 'voice-over, background music and graphics in the studio. If music other than that in the public domain is being used, a licensing fee of several hundred dollars may be involved, payable through your editing house. If you need a professional narrator, it will cost several hundred dollars to do a short tape.

If the campaign has retained a political consultant or commercial ad firm, they likely will select the edit house. If not, the volunteer creative producer will need to locate an edit house himself (start with the Yellow Pages), if the editing facilities at the college or cable outlet are not available.

Reproduction of the video normally can be arranged through the editing house. In our case, we arranged to have 7,000 VHS copies made at $1.85 per tape, including a descriptive label but without a sleeve. It'll be tough to do it for much less, and, depending on quality, may exceed $2 per tape. Remember that reproduction takes at least two weeks.

Targeting

The finished product should energize volunteers, excite voters and draw together different threads of the candidate's message. Now comes the big question: Who should get it? Clearly, given the expense involved, the campaign needs to target the recipients carefully.

In our case, we targeted prime voters who had voted in the Democratic primaries in each of the last two election cycles in our transient, virtually one-party district. Since we decided that we did not have the resources to mail the tapes, we eliminated all high-rise buildings where access for hand delivery would have been impossible.

This left us with roughly 7,000 reachable prime voter households. Given the vicissitudes of such a complex delivery effort, we initially split the 28 precincts in our district into groups: those crucial to our success and those easiest to access were given highest priority.

Precincts where we did not have a good potential or where the candidate had not been able to visit personally were a second-tier priority.

Those precincts that were highly transient (particularly those with large proportions of garden apartments) and with historically low voter participation in off-year elections constituted a third tier. The larger the electoral district, the tougher the targeting decision becomes.

In a countywide race, for example, you may have to realistically target prime households in only 20 to 40 key, or swing, precincts—a strategy that still may prove far more cost effective than the scattergun approach of a handful of television or radio ads that may not be seen or heard, or print ads which may go unread.

At all times, in making such decisions, it is crucial to remember that the video is a complement to all the ground work the campaign has laid through personal visits by the candidate, direct mail, phone banking, lawn signs, paid media and free media. In this environment, targeting swing precincts makes tremendous sense.

While the raw data necessary for targeting will be available from the local board of elections, a tremendous amount of time will be preserved if commercial lists—normally in the form of 3" by 5" computer cards split out by street and precinct—are purchased from political list brokers.

The investment of perhaps $1,500 in such lists will make information immediately available in a useful format, as well as for door knocking and phone banking. Volunteer time, always precious, is far better used in executing such activities than in extrapolating data from board of elections lists and manually adding phone numbers form a house list.

Distribution

Now that you have the tapes and you've talked someone into storing them in a cool garage, you have to get a group of volunteers to handle the distribution.

If the campaign can afford the additional cost of purchasing a mail sleeve, a full set of mailing labels and bulk rate postage—which can ton several dollars per tape—you're golden. Remember, this is the best way to ensure distribution to all targeted voters, rain or shine, while avoiding theft or campaign sabotage.

This involves either paying a mail house to process the video (another several thousand dollars) or organizing (and feeding!) numerous volunteers to process the tapes by hand. The downside to using the mail is that the campaign cannot perfectly time delivery given the uncertainty of bulk mail in a rushed political season.

The video may be delivered overnight or not until after New Year's. The alternative is to undertake the massive job with volunteers—in my case, 45 of them. Ten days before the mid-September primary in 1990, these volunteers spent a weekend delivering the tapes, working 10 to 12 hour days in 95 degree weather.

They worked in teams of two or three, with a driver and one or two runners, over a 24-square-mile region. (We fed the volunteers a simple breakfast, gave them T-shirts that cost about $5 each and offered profuse thanks.) While the volunteers are at work door to-door, so should the candidate be on the streets putting them out as well, along with his or her family. If the candidate is not willing to make that commitment, don't expect others to do it. As a practical matter, if the campaign does not have a lot of volunteers with young and well-conditioned legs, the job will never get done. We packaged our tape in a plastic bag emblazoned with our campaign logo, containing a letter that explained how it was cost effective, so as to deflect potential criticism about excessive spending, and hung it on doorknobs.

The letter with union bug cost several hundred dollars to reproduce on campaign letterhead. The plastic bags, purchased with two weeks lead time from a novelty shop, ran in excess of $500. A responsible person will need to coordinate the distribution center throughout the drop period, answering volunteer questions and receiving undistributed tapes from the teams.

Be sure to collect index cards with the addresses of those locations the volunteers did not reach. This can be a tedious job, for without attention to detail something will go wrong. You don't want to have the volunteers hitting the same doors or ignoring others.

The tape itself likely will be an event for the recipients, who should be encouraged in the accompanying letter to share it with family, friends and particularly with neighbors new to the area. Its impact can be maximized if it is simultaneously linked to a media event explaining the drop.

Tell the Media

Make sure that copies are sent to all local TV affiliates and cable operators as well as to print media. The press should be given a heads-up several days in advance.

Members of the electronic and print media should be invited to the distribution center to meet the volunteers and accompany a volunteer team.

If the campaign can both get the tape into the hands of all prime voters and make the evening news, the tape's impact will be doubled. Mass-distributed video is not for the faint of heart. First, voters simply may not like your product. If the candidate simply is not good on tape and comes across as ill at ease, uncomfortable or untrustworthy, or if the production appears alternately too slick or too amateurish, it likely will backfire.

Second, be prepared for the inevitable critics, including opponents who carp that you are trying to buy the election, that the video is expensive and you are spending wildly. Some may even say that the mass quantity reproduction of the tape is environmentally unsound.

If the campaign plans well in advance, strictly budgets both time and financial resources, and pays close attention to mastering the complex array of details, bringing the video—and the campaign—to a successful conclusion is an achievable goal.

In the process, participants may feel that they have achieved something unique.

My Experience With Home Videos

We were able to negotiate a per tape reproduction cost of $1.85. One lengthy editing session cost an additional several thousand dollars. The production was readily solved through the help of a close friend, Emilio Pardo of the Washington, DC-office of Fleishman & Hillard advertising agency. Pardo, a former press secretary for Sen. Ernest F. Hollings (D-SC), acted as my creative producer and recruited three friends to volunteer talents as a writer, cameraman and narrator.

Our cameraman did a rough-cut edit on his own equipment and there we did the final editing during a 6 p.m. to 3 a.m. session at Roland House in Arlington, VA. The creative producer had already laid down the narrative track and chosen the music. The editing house provides a skilled technician to do the actual editing.

The total cost, including the fee for music, was near $3,000. The cost to the door—including camera rental, the printed plastic bags in which the tape was delivered, and the accompanying letter—was $2.65 per tape. By using a large volunteer base to deliver the video, we avoided all postage expenses. As a result, we reached 7,000 voter households for about $19,000 (including a pizza for the production crew).

✓ Versatile Videos
Ron Faucheux

One of the hottest trends in political campaign communications is using mass-produced videos. Expensive television time placements, together with increased audience fracturing due to numerous new cable channels and independent networks, has forced campaigns to look for new ways to get across extended messages. A five, 10, or 15 minute video is one of them.

In the 1970s, the cost of purchasing a blank half-inch VHS or Beta video tape exceed 10 or 15 dollars. A copy of your favorite movie could run over 80 bucks. But that was the Stone Age of video. Today, you can have videos duplicated and box sleeves printed in volume for under two dollars each—the more the cheaper. Given the fact that 80 percent of voting households have VCRs, and that videotape home viewership is very high according to most studies, mass-produced videos offer an array of possibilities for campaigners that didn't exist just a few years ago.

There are many advantages in the political use of videos:

- They provide the full power of television and film—combining the emotional impact of sight and sound.
- They are not confined to a 30 or 60 second length, so they can be long enough to tell a complete story. It is difficult to place five, 10, or 15-minute television programs, particularly in time slots with large audiences. Videos give you the opportunity to communicate a lengthy message or tell a full story.
- You can target who gets a mailed video, pinpointed to the individual or household. You can't do that with broadcast television time.
- You can time the distribution of videos to create momentum or "bumps" in name recognition or voter approval, which is often important to candidates who need a quick show of strength in a particular area or among a specific voter group.
- They can add potency to a media mix that includes direct mail and telephone contact, as well as newspaper, television, and radio ads.

When to Use Them

There are five chief ways to use videos in campaigns:

Defining a candidate's image and central message. The length of a video allows you to show many sides of a candidate and to get to know that person, whether it's through the candidate talking and answering questions or describing his or her accomplishments and biographical background. Videos can be sent to a broad spectrum of registered voters, if budget permits, or can be targeted to energize a core base or to persuade undecideds.

Some candidates have trouble speaking in short soundbites or can't tell their story in 30-second bursts. The added time of a longer video can accommodate the specific needs of certain candidates and issues.

Videos are also being used to explain issue messages and to prompt legislative advocacy, from congressional action on health care reform to state consideration of tort reform to the siting of a local landfill.

Fundraising. With campaign finance regulation and lower contribution caps, there is a greater need to enlarge donor bases.

Videos are a perfect informational and motivational vehicle for that. When used in conjunction with personalized direct mail and telephone follow-ups, they can be very effective.

Recruiting and mobilizing volunteers. Videos can assist in building organizations. Because potential volunteers and block captains usually represent a small subgroup of the population, reaching them with videos is probably cost efficient for most campaigns. This is especially important in issue and grassroots lobbying campaigns where citizen activists are crucial to public official contact programs.

Targeting messages to special groups. As an example of this, let's take a candidate for Mayor who wants to convey a lengthy message to environmentalists about protecting a local parkway. That candidate could produce a simple 10-minute on-location video at the park site explaining his or her commitment on the issue with several respected environmental leaders on hand to express their support. The tape could be mailed to 5,000 environmentalists who are the most susceptible to the message to be followed-up with subsequent volunteer recruitment mailings and phone calls.

A candidate running for governor, who supports new tax breaks for economic development, could do a 12-minute video explaining his or her plan to improve the state's business climate with noted corporate CEOs and economists chiming in their endorsements. The campaign could send the video, along with a fundraising pitch, to 20,000 active business owners.

Videos can also be effective with absentee voters, especially in state's that have liberal vote-by-mail laws and for military personnel stationed out of the country.

Keep in mind: Some video consultants have found that older Americans are less inclined to use today's technology and most often do not have VCRs. To get the maximum impact and remain cost effective, some consultants suggest, the campaign should consider screening out voters over the age of 70. This screening process requires using voter tapes that include age data.

Reaching convention delegates. Party nominating conventions are tailor-made for using videos. They provide an ideal audience for video mailings, which can enhance the effectiveness of other direct, more personal contacts.

As you can see, possible applications are endless.

Caveat Emptor

What are the limitations and obstacles in using videos? Like any other campaign message carrier, there are down sides. Here's what they are and how to compensate for them:

Production costs and quality. The fact is, producing 15, 10, or even five minute videos can be expensive, so hold down excessive production gimmicks from the start. Nevertheless, keeping an extended program both interesting and informative often requires resources. The first is a good candidate who can handle one of a number of formats, from a simple talking-head approach to on-location narration to answering questions from average citizens. If you have a candidate who can carry a five- or 10-minute video, you can save a lot of money and reduce production complications.

Another resource is good photos and graphics. Even if you use the candidate extensively, it is important that you add graphics and perhaps some still shots to add depth and interest. Remember Ross Perot's charts? Pundits may have snickered, but they were very useful in simplifying complex information. While important, graphics do not have to be costly.

Music can add impact and life to a video as well. If the video is purely a candidate talking-head or an interactive Q&A session with voters, music may not be needed or even appropriate. But if it is a biographical program, or the telling of a story, music is crucial to its overall emotional appeal.

If you attempt to produce a 10-minute video using your home VHS camera without proper lighting, narration, editing, or music, take heed: unless the video is interesting voters probably won't watch it. Don't throw good money away duplicating and mailing a dud. That's true about any ad that allows poor production quality to destroy the impact of a message or a story.

Cutting cost. One way to save money producing videos is to open and close them with your already produced 30 and 60 second spots. If they have good production, narration, music, graphics, action visuals, etc.) they can add pop to a video without adding cost.

Other ways to save money on mailing videos include using third class bulk postage (when time isn't a big factor) or using a state party committee's non-profit postage permit (when your candidate has no opposition). Also remember, that the lighter the plastic shell and the shorter the length of the program tape, the lighter it will be for postage purposes.

Postage costs need to be budgeted carefully. The choice of first class versus third class bulk rate mail is one of the biggest cost factors in a video mail project. Is a first class mailing at $1.45 per copy affordable? Or does the campaign have enough time (usually 14 days) to mail the video third class at 22 to 45 cents for each video?

You can produce effective videos without draining your treasury if it's planned and budgeted properly in advance. Keep that in mind when you consult professional media consultants and independent production firms for advice and guidance.

Balance cost against other budget items. A candidate in Ohio, for example, would have to spend about $250,000 to air a statewide TV spot with 600 Gross Rating. For that amount of money, the candidate could reach over 125,000 households with a mailed video and appropriate follow-up. It's really a matter of reach versus the power of targeted impact

Many statewide and congressional candidates may find the cost of mailing videos to every household in their electorates prohibitively expensive. To reach 150,000 voting households in a race for the U.S. House, mailing videos could cost as much as $250,000 to $300,000, depending on production quality, box sleeve printing, and accompanying mail materials. Unless your name is Huffington or Rockefeller, that's a big tab.

To lower costs, congressional candidates can target their mailed videos to, let's say, 40,000 "swing" voters, or 30,000 women under 40, or 20,000 men over 65. That cuts costs dramatically and makes full use of a powerful weapon among critical voter groups.

Videos may also be cost-effective vehicles for small, local campaigns. A candidate in a City Council district with 5,000 voting households could send every one of them a mailed video as a district-wide introduction before he or she begins a door-to-door canvass, for example. That would have unusual impact in such a race and could be produced for a cost that many campaigns may find surprisingly affordable.

Check the quality of the tape and the duplication. There are varying kinds and quality of tape that can be used in videos. Ask your video duplicator to show you specific examples of tape that would be used in your video.

Even though many duplicators use only "grade A" tape, there are many duplication methods and modes: SP is the highest quality recording mode and the most expensive; EP is less expensive because it uses fewer frames of tape per second; and LP is the least costly but produces the lowest quality picture. There is also "real time" duplication, which takes one hour to duplicate a one hour program and is used only for smaller quantity jobs, and "high speed" duplication, which takes only about a minute to duplicate a one hour program through the use of lasers that ensure consistent quality from the first to the last tape.

Shop around. Video duplication has become a competitive business. Get your best deal.

Video Packaging Matters
Larry Purpuro

Indirect mail video, packaging makes the first impression—and that first impression will determine whether recipients actually watch the video.

That's why it's important to create a package design that sparks interest and starts to tell your message the moment the video is pulled from the mailbox. Plain vanilla wrappers, like the brown padded bag or other generic packaging, may not save money and they do nothing to convince the voter to watch the video.

A custom-designed sleeve that doubles as a self-mailer usually takes less than a dime of your project dollar. The design options are many, and should suit your message, strategy, and distribution methods.

- Person to Person. The packaging for a video distributed by hand should be similar to that of a brochure. In this case, the video is being used as a piece of campaign literature so the video sleeve should include copy, graphics and photography to sustain the candidate's message.
- Direct Mail. For political videos mailed unsolicited to voters, it's best to think of the sleeve not as a mini-brochure, but as a poster. Keep it simple: Choose a key message and image and avoid design clutter.
- "Blind" Package Designs. Candidates and managers never want to miss an opportunity to place their name, image and theme in front of voters. But in some cases, a "blind" package may be the best. If survey data show target voters to be up in arms about health care, but uninterested in an election and unaware of the candidates, a health care video is more likely to generate interest than a candidate promo. In that case, a candidate video could be mailed in a simple sleeve with the message: "What can you do to cut your health care costs next year? Watch this tape."

✓ Do-It-Yourself Media Consulting
Timothy John Walker

You are a candidate for public office with little media experience. The local TV political reporter fancies himself the next Mike Wallace, and your entire campaign budget is less than the price of an all-day media training session with Roger Ailes or Michael Sheehan. What do you do?

The answer is to become your own media consultant.

"If there is anything the American public is good at," observes Raymond Strother, a Democratic media consultant, "it is watching television." Think about it. You have already spent thousands of hours watching television. You know what comes across well on TV.

All you need to improve your on-screen appearance is a home video camera and a VCR. Borrow them from a friend if you cannot afford your own. Then ask your campaign manager to videotape you talking into the camera, and review the tape. You will be amazed at how much you can improve your on-camera presence simply by emphasizing certain aspects of your delivery and downplaying others.

Before sitting down in front of a camera, determine what message you wish to communicate. A media opportunity is worthless if you do not have a specific message to convey. It must be simple, clear and concise and should contain no more than three specific points.

Unless you are running for president, senator or governor, you need only one broad message for your campaign. That message must let people know why you are running. If you are running against an incumbent, it should tell voters why your opponent should be fired.

Keep in mind that your experience in community affairs is not a message. It is simply part of a resume. Besides, every candidate has leadership experience in some seemingly public-spirited organization.

Your message need not be elaborate or complicated; the only requirement is that it be direct and forceful in addressing voters' concerns. A city commission candidate in Florida wanted to communicate the idea that the commission had not been doing a very good job. Rather than simply saying, "Vote for me because the present commission is making poor decisions," he exploited people's dissatisfaction with the local cable TV company. He vowed to fire the incumbent cable-service and start a city-owned and-operated cable company. He won.

Lights! Camera! Action!

Once you have developed and refined your message you can start practicing your delivery. Sit down with your campaign manager and a couple of close advisers and draw up a list of questions to expect in any interview. First on the list should be, "Why are you running?" Do not take this question lightly. You will be asked it repeatedly, and if you cannot come up with a credible answer, your campaign will never get off the ground. (Remember how Sen. Edward Kennedy derailed his 1980 presidential campaign by failing this test in an interview with CBS's Roger Mudd.)

The next step is to hold a mock TV interview. Have your campaign manager pose as the questioner. While you sit in front of the camera, have him aim a light at your face and turn on the camera. He then should start firing questions as if it were a real interview. Your interview should last for about 15 minutes and should include one or two off-the-wall questions to try to unsettle you. Your goal is to return to your message as fast as possible.

After you finish, review the videotape. If this is your first time seeing yourself on TV, you may be surprised at how you look and sound. Once past the initial viewing, isolate the one or two most appealing aspects of your performance. Then run through the exercise again and review your performance with a more critical eye. Finally, try watching yourself without the sound on to scrutinize your non-verbal communication skills.

In that vein, there are a few basic rules to keep in mind when appearing on television:

- Sit up straight.
- Lean slightly forward.
- Rest your hands on top of your knee.
- Smile.
- Keep you eyes on the interviewer, not the camera or monitor.
- Use your hands to make a point, but keep your gestures high and tight.
- Be comfortable. Men may wish to cross their legs at the knees while women would do better to cross at the ankles. In any case, be sure to keep your legs under your chair.
- Do not freeze your head. Your natural head movement will allow you to come across as a more genuine person on TV.
- Dress as if you are interviewing for a job. That means wear fairly conservative clothes. Avoid wild colors, excessive jewelry and white.
- Shake hands and thank the interviewer when you are through. Even if you lack the charisma of Jesse Jackson, you still can come across as cool and confident on TV. The secret is to focus on a subject that truly interests you. If the topic is an arcane aspect of tax policy that thoroughly bores you, in all likelihood you will thoroughly bore your audience. But if you are genuinely interested in the subject, your voice will rise and fall, your hands will move, and people will be far more inclined to give you a fair hearing.

Be Clear, Concise and Repetitive

After you have run through the mock interview a few times, bring in a friend or two to review your performance. Show the videotape once without stopping, and see how many of your two or three specific points your viewer can name. If the answer is not "all of them," you need to refine your points. Unlike newspaper readers, TV viewers cannot go back and review the preceding paragraph. This makes it imperative that candidates be simple, clear and repetitive.

Once you have honed your message, you can concentrate on the tough issues, such as abortion, tax hikes and gun control. Try to give a 15-second response to each; your manager should time your answers on a stopwatch. You need to be able to discuss complex subjects in short, compressed sound bites. Otherwise, your answers will be ignored by the producer and the public.

These rules also apply to debates. To prepare, sit down with your campaign manager and a few close friends, and write responses to every conceivable charge your opponent can throw at you. Prepare for the worst. Expect him to unearth every possible mistake you have ever made—and to make up some to boot. It is much easier to devise your responses in advance, in the privacy of your own home, than to come up with spontaneous answers in front of thousands of viewers.

Once you have anticipated and formulated answers to every question and accusation the media and your opponent could possibly devise, practice giving those answers in front of the camera. It is also worthwhile to tape actual coverage—such as press conferences—to see what kind of progress you are making in a pressure situation.

One last exercise. Stand in front of the camera and explain why you are running for office. Then show the videotape to someone not intimately involved with your campaign. After the first 60 seconds, see if he can describe why you are running. When a first-time viewer can do this, you are ready for the bright lights.

✓ Great Media On a Shoestring
Christian K. Forrnan

Hurling slings and arrows at political opponents costs an outrageous fortune these days. The medium of choice is television, and airtime and production costs can quickly empty a campaign's bulging war chest. But to ignore the power of TV in the political arena is to perish by it.

Step One: Production On The Cheap

According to Republican media consultant Tom Edmonds, the best way to keep production costs low is to keep your ideas simple. "The more complicated it gets, the more expensive it becomes," he observes.

Edmonds suggests the following guidelines to keep your media production looking professional and under budget:

Maximize the Use of Voiceovers and Talking Heads. Campaign commercials get expensive when you have complex dialogue and numerous actors. To avoid high costs, either shoot your commercial without sound and add your message in the studio with a voice over or confine your dialogue to one person. In addition, if you use a voice over you can tailor or change your commercials without reshooting. Merely erase the sound, make a few small edits, and dub over the same footage.

Use Stock Footage. An affordable way to make your commercials look professional is to purchase film from a "stockhouse"—a video library which sells clips of news events, sporting competitions, humorous sequences and scenic panoramas. This professional footage can be spliced into your commercial to add context to your production. For example, if you want to illustrate your opponent's poor record on the environment, buy generic footage of landfills and toxic waste dumps and use a scathing condemnation as a voiceover. Such a spot could be produced entirely in the edit suite. The largest stockhouses are usually run in affiliation with one of the three networks (ABC, NBC, & CBS) and charge a hefty price for their wares. A more recent breed of affordable, independent stock houses is beginning to fill the demand at the low end of the market. Typical of this group is the eight-year old Video Tape Library (VTL) of Los Angeles, which offers an extensive library at competitive prices—$450 to $600 for a ten-second depending on the size of the market where the spot will be aired. If even that is too rich for your budget, give your ad a historical flare by using the National Archives; they can provide anyone with news footage up to 1962, and charge only for the cost of duplication.

Shop Around. A basically-equipped production crew can range in price from two figures to $500 an hour, and quotes can vary considerably—even in the same market. Comparison shopping can realize tremendous savings on post-production facilities as well.

Make the Most of Publicly Available Facilities. If the prices quoted above are too steep, don't lose hope. A number of community access stations have editing facilities and production equipment available for very nominal fees. You only must complete a 3-6 hour course to be certified as a Public Access producer. After that orientation training, you are eligible to use their equipment to produce your campaign spots. According to Steve Radic of the Cable Advertising Bureau, the availability of such equipment varies between cable systems. "In your big markets you will probably see greater opportunity to walk in off the street and use equipment; however, these opportunities are not uniform. It depends on who you talk to." Many schools and universities also have video production programs. If you can find students who are technically proficient, they may be willing to help you put together your spots.

Scroll That Script. If money is really tight, the cheapest TV spot you can produce is a scroll. This familiar ad technique usually starts with a still picture, newspaper clip or even a blank screen; a character generator is then employed to roll the voiceover script across the screen. A pure scroll spot does not require a film crew, any editing of consequence, or fancy equipment. Done properly, they can be the most effective way of communicating factual information, such as a candidate's record or platform. Scroll ads are so simple in their construction, rookie producers should be able to turn them out on Public Access equipment with little difficulty.

Don't Forget Radio. According to Edmonds "radio is the great equalizer. A small-time candidate can walk into a radio station and for a relatively small amount of money can produce something which will sound as good as the anything that the big guys can produce." In this video age, many well-heeled candidates overlook the simple, workhorse nature of radio. Small candidates should not fall into this trap. The primary objective of any media campaign is to let the public know who you are and what you stand for, and radio provides a cost-efficient way to achieve this goal. If your media spots are placed during peak rush hour times, you will be able to reach an astounding number of people.

Step Two: Buying Time

The biggest expense by far in most any media campaign is the purchase of air time.

Bruce Mentzer—a media buyer formerly with Robert Goodman Agency who now has his own firm, Mentzer Media Services—explains that "the secret to an effective media buy is research. For example, I was working on a campaign in Missouri's Eighth congressional district. In this district there are three television markets. Without looking at any past voter trends you might assume that the market viewing percentages would be how you should allocate your media resources. After looking at the GOP primary returns in the last congressional race, we learned that the percentage of the GOP vote by the market area was drastically different from the percent of district coverage."

Mentzer found that the largest market (which accounted for over half of the population) accounted for only 35 percent of the GOP primary vote, while the two smaller markets were much more Republican—home to 64 percent of GOP primary voters. Using this information, he was able to design a media campaign which adequately blanketed the Republican strongholds in the two smaller markets.

The following is a quick check list to help you follow Mentzer's lead and effectively target your media buys:

Define Your Target Audience. The best way to identify your target audience is through polling; however, polling is usually very expensive. If such an exercise is out of your budget, you can turn to your local party. According to Betsy Weinschel, of River Bank Inc. (the group that handled Pat Buchanan's media spots), "the locals know where the voters are. They can be an excellent resource." If your party officials do not have the information that you require, Weinschel suggests the campaign target people over 35—with a special emphasis on those over 65. She states that "history shows that people under 35 typically vote only if they are extremely upset with the status quo. Since it is difficult to gauge this level of dissatisfaction, I always concentrate on the people I know will go to the polls." Moreover, the elderly are always a safe electoral bet since" they vote no matter what. They have the time to really study the issues and they have the time to go to the polls."

Making the Buy. Once you have determined who you want to hit with your advertising, your next step is to contact your TV, cable, or radio station. Advertising executives for these venues will help you find programming which can deliver to your target audience. However, Weinschel has some basic placement advice. "CNN is always a sure bet. Anyone who watches CNN is current on the issues and is interested in politics. They will vote. If you want to hit a male audience ESPN is effective. To hit a female audience "Life time" is always good."

Once you have decided where to advertise the only remaining task is purchasing the time Experts suggest that even if you have bees handling the media campaign up to this point you should hire someone to make your time buys. The world of log books and pre-emptible time can be very treacherous—a novice could find himself falling into some serious problems.

A word of warning: the person you hire to make these purchases should have a clear understanding of your audience targets. A media buyer whose experience is primarily in the retail market might try to place your ads during the Young and the Restless—a prime slot to sell cosmetics, but not politicians. Either hire a political specialist or clearly communicate to your commercial buyer where you want your ads to be placed.

Pre-emptible Time. Air time which is "Pre-emptible" is not guaranteed; if a company agrees to pay a higher price than you are paying, your ad will be bumped. The advantage of pre-emptible time is cost. Such time slots are cheaper than guaranteed time; so a lot of campaigns buy large numbers of preemptible spots knowing only some will air.

Weinschel believes this reasoning may be faulty, arguing that buying fewer slots and knowing they will hit the airwaves is more effective than buying more spots that may not have any effect. There is no evidence to suggest that any one school of thought is better; however, this issue is one you must tackle in designing your media play.

Step Three: Community Access and Interconnects

If your budget allows you to run only limited schedule of campaign spots on television or cable, Public Access (PA) and LocX Origination (LO) stations will allow you to get substantial air time at nominal or no cost. Everyone has seen PA and LO stations when flicking through the endless number of cable channels—they usually run a screen announcement of the next bake sale at the church or feature aspiring rock stars jamming in the family kitchen. Yet, some candidates have found these stations to be a very effective ways to communicate with voters. LO and PA channels allow a great deal of program flexibility. Since the programming schedule is so open compared to the commercial networks, you can tailor your program length.

Spots can last anywhere from 30 seconds to 30 minutes, and since the time is free, you may want to produce a low-budget program (such as a speech with Q&A) to lengthen your exposure. The second major advantage is cost. PA stations are chartered to provide air time free of charge to residents of the cable system service area. LO stations are run by the cable company, and usually charge a nominal rate.

Critics of community television argue that even though air time is incredibly cheap, this venue has little political punch since viewers are allegedly so few and far between. However, as Lauren Steiner, a Beverly Hills cable activist, states, " Most cable viewers don't keep track of where they are on the dial. In this day and age they flip through scores of channels and stop on something that looks interesting."

Another argument against PA and LO stations is their balkanization. Unlike major cable stations or TV, PA/LO stations only serve local communities that are often quite small. As a result, you may find yourself running around in circles, filling out forms for air time which will reach fewer than 4,000 households. However, thanks to what as known as a "soft interconnect," small PA/LO stations can now be linked together allowing a particular program to reach a very large audience. The night before this year's Iowa presidential caucus, Jerry Brown bought a 30 minute time slot from an interconnect that reached 145,000 subscribers. The cost—just $100.

As the saying goes, "nothing in life is free and easy." Even though PA/LO stations can fit into any budget, a campaign must jump through a number of bureaucratic hoops before it can broadcast a spot. No universal regulations exist for these stations; each separate channel has its own quirks and stumbling blocks. In addition, even though political commercials are legally allowed on PA stations, many directors are weary of providing assistance to political causes which may be opposed by forces in the local government. These problems can be exacerbated when dealing with an interconnect, which may suffer from a "lowest common denominator" effect, reflecting a wide range of restrictions practiced by any of its members.

A directory of community cable channels is available for $40 from the National Federation of Local Cable Programmers in Washington DC. This guide purports to be a comprehensive listing of all channels—though it has not been updated in five years. If you want to save the $40, merely call your local cable operator or the Cable Advertising Board (212-751-7770). They will provide the names you need to start the programming ball rolling for your campaign.

✓ TV Production Checklist
John Franzen

The following is a checklist of topics that I tell my clients to keep in mind when creating TV commercials:

1. TV commercials come at us one after another in a continuous stream. Your challenge is to stand out from the crowd, to be remembered. Your competition is not only other political spots, but products ads as well.
2. Chances are you can't compete with national product ads in terms of production values (lighting, special effects, etc.,) The average production cost of such an ad today runs into the hundreds of thousands. Thus the low-budget campaign must generally come up with ads that don't rely chiefly on production values for their impact.
3. Production values, however are not an either/or proposition . Any script or creative concept has a certain budget threshold below which it will fail. The thing to remember is that different scripts and concepts can have vastly different thresholds.

4. Because of the threshold problem, and for many other reasons, political campaigns should hire creative talent with experience in political advertising, where budgets and schedules are almost always tight. Commercial advertising is a different world entirely.
5. The most important element in any TV spot is a strong controlling concept. The finest production values in the world won't save a dumb idea. Yet, less than stellar production will often be overlooked if the concept is sufficiently arresting.
6. Rhythm and pacing are as critical to the success of a television spot as they are to a poem or piece of music. One of the most frequent mistakes of the low-budget campaign is to cram as many words as possible in the 30 seconds available. Picture is generally more important than words in the television medium, and silences can often speak more powerfully than the most eloquent prose.
7. To save money, low-budget campaigns are often tempted to cover more than one issue in a spot. This almost always fails. Even a bio spot that lists a number of career accomplishments should have one controlling theme.
8. The so-called talking head spot is cheap to produce and need not be boring, as is often assumed. One of the most important rules of advertising is to "show the product,' and in an election campaign, your product is the candidate.
9. Testimonial spots are also relatively cheap, but they should generally not be scripted. These spots derive their impact from the credibility of the people featured, and very few "real people" can read a script effectively.
10. In attack and counter-attack situations, there is always the danger that viewers will be turned off because things have gotten so "negative." Probably the most effective means of avoiding this outcome is the skillful use of humor. It is also extremely important to document your charges, with on-screen footnotes, briefing of the press, etc.
11. Location shooting tends to be expensive. There are now many ways to avoid this step entirely, however, and still produce a spot that's visually interesting and attractive. Even still photos can be presented in interesting ways through the use of digital effects. Also, don't overlook the potential power of simply putting words on the screen.
12. Most producers will prefer to shoot on film rather than video tape. Film's advantages include richer color, better control over color during post-production, and less extreme light/dark contrast (hard shadows are softened, skin wrinkles diminished). But the notion that a spot can't be pretty unless it's shot on film is a myth. Video technology has improved dramatically over the past 15 years, and a crew that knows what it's doing can achieve very nice effects. Video tape's advantages over film include lower cost, greater portability, faster turn-around and quality playback in the field.
13. Partisan candidates may also consider taking advantage of production and editing facilities which are offered to most candidates by party campaign committees. Using party sources, however, is not a substitute for hiring the best available creative talent to handle strategy, writing and directing.
14. Pre-broadcast testing of spots (in front of focus groups and so on) is often viewed as a luxury of the well-funded campaign. But testing is even more important to the low-budget campaign where there's not a dollar to waste. Remember, clever spots are produced all the time that leave viewers completely confused or even persuaded in the opposite direction from the one intended.

Adding Up The Costs Of A TV Production

In pricing the various components of television production, *Campaigns & Elections* asked several reputable production companies around the nation for cost estimates by service. Here's what we found:

- Taping with a one person crew (director/cameraman), $800 to $1,200 a day or $400 to $700 a half-day.
- Taping with a two person crew (director/cameraman and soundman with boom mike), $1,000 to $1,400 a day or $600 to $800 a half-day.
- Studio production (one camera), $150 to $250 an hour.
- Studio rentals, $175 to $250 an hour (cold stage) and $350 to $500 an hour (hot stage).
- Audio booth, $50 to $100 an hour.
- Stock music usage, $50 to $150 per spot.
- Post production analog editing (1", Beta, or 3/4" VTRs), $200 to $300 an hour.
- Post production digital editing, $285 to $450 an hour.
- Post production Avid off-line editing, $100 to $150 an hour (with editor).
- Post production off-line editing, $50 to $80 an hour (3/4" to 3/4") and $100 to $150 (Beta to Beta) an hour with an editor.
- Graphics and special effects: digital composition with Quantel HAL ($250 to $500 an hour), Wavefront 3-D animation ($150 to $250 an hour), and Chyron graphics ($75 to $125 an hour).
- Narrator (varies greatly depending upon experience, voice quality, and celebrity status) for most state or local campaigns, $100 to $600 per spot.
- Make-up (most experienced local stylists will charge a minimum of at least $100 to $150 per job and for extended day rates, average $200 to $400 a day.
- Duplicating finished spot for television stations ($20 to $30 per tape per 30-second spot).

It should be noted that these prices vary geographically and according to the quality of available equipment and the experience of the production and studio personnel.

How does all this add up for a 30-second spot?

For a typical testimonial spot that involves shooting several person-on-the-street interviews on location with a 10 second head-on candidate tag, with interspersed graphics, you may need: (a) a full day of taping with a two-person crew ($1,200 average), (b) three hours of post production analog editing ($250 x three hours = $750 average), Chyron graphics (one hour, $100 average), announcer narration ($300 average), audio studio (one hour at $75 average), make-up ($125), dubbing of finished spot (1" to 1" averages about $25 per spot).

Base production cost for this spot already totals $2,575. It should be noted that this does not include: professional copywriting, story boards, or concept development; still photographs that may be used in the spot; hiring a creative director; renting additional lighting equipment, which is often essential; hiring lighting specialists; travel for on-location shooting, or bad weather contingencies.

✓ A Guide to Desktop Video Editing
Patrick Tracey

Paul Wilson was down to the wire. It was Monday night in Washington, DC, and the deadline was closing in. At stake was a smooth finish to a 30-second TV spot for a November ballot issue in Louisville, KY. The spot advocated easing access for the handicapped.

All weekend he had been staring at 36 minutes' worth of footage, cueing and viewing images "off-line" on a new computer he bought for his offices in Old Town Alexandria, VA. Now he was "on-line in downtown Washington, DC. He had only two hours of time booked in a post-production suite where a studio engineer had been hired to make the cuts Wilson had spent the entire weekend mulling over. The finished commercial had to be in Louisville overnight.

Wilson had a sinking feeling as he went to brew some coffee. Seventeen years of producing TV spots as a political consultant told him lots could go wrong in the stretch.

At $300 an hour, all-night editing sessions are a budget buster. Wilson thought about the sequence of shots he had selected. He worried about putting the dissolve between the third and fourth scenes. Or swapping the close-up of the boy in the wheelchair for the establishing shot of the library steps.

When he came back with his coffee, his worries were gone. Not only was the ad ill done, all the cuts were made exactly as he had planned them.

"I was literally gone two or three minutes," he says. "Back in the suite, boom! It was finished. I was stunned. It was a three-minute assembly. It cut like butter."

The computer being used to layout video sequences for political spots at Wilson Communications is one of the hottest pieces of hardware to hit the video industry in years. It is also a scheme by Bill Ferster and his colleagues at Editing Machines Corp., Washington, DC, to put affordable video on your desktop.

Ferster began his career as a graphic artist for ABC's "Good Morning, America" before winning first place in the Experimental Film Category in the 1979 National Association of Broadcasting contest. Eight years later he founded his own animation production company with an off-line editing system. "It became clear that there had to be a better way," Ferster says. "I began researching the idea of editing digitally, marrying the technologies and graphic capabilities of the computer industry to off-line editing."

What Ferster imagined was a computer editing system that would provide maximum flexibility, speed, and creative latitude. "We were looking to humanize the process of editing videotape," he says.

"Before non-linear editing, editing videotape was like editing a book with a manual typewriter. This system frees the editor and gives him the ability to change his mind. Desktop video, as it is known, is television's answer to desktop publishing. Just as word processors can move whole paragraphs around, desktop video lets you cut and paste film or videotape—mix sound tracks, and create titles and graphics.

Word processors and video processors are technologies that rely on the same basic feature: random access to any part of the digital memory. Videographers and filmmakers alike are discovering that this feature offers them unsurpassed creative control.

"I was looking at every shot on the screen," Wilson says of the Emc2 system he purchased. "You can look at all your pictures in a flash as you edit."

"If you're coming into a post-production suite with a project that is frame-accurate," says Wilson, "you increase your output tremendously."

At its best, desktop video is a superb system for electronic story-boarding. Its digital off-line editing offers a visual mapping for laying out editable timetables, cinematic pictures, and stereo sequences. Its digital memory provides random access to any part of the video, so there is precise control for instantly grabbing frames from any segment of the tape.

"We can cut three or four different ways if we want," boasts Wilson. 'We have much more flexibility, many more ways to make the images look good. You come out with a very tasteful spot.

"I've brought in people who know nothing about video, and they can start scanning every shot inside the storyboards," said Wilson. "From a creative standpoint, it's extremely powerful."

The small size of a desktop system makes it easy to locate in any corner of a campaign office. The beauty of the Emc2 system, which operates on an IBM-based personal computer, or a system developed by AVID Technologies, Burlington, MA (a Macintosh-based younger cousin), is its display. As many as five stills from scenes in your program can appear on the screen at once. Better yet, all five can be mixed and matched, solely as images or solely as chunks of digital time codes. Next, you cat dovetail each edit into a sequence and view it as a seamless motion picture.

No more stops and starts to cut ragged edges in the post-production suite. No messy dubbing sessions spent ladling sound over pictures. No more twisting your guts out because you're paying $300 an hour. Instead of controlling multiple analog machines to make a cut, or record the cut to tape, the Emc2 lets you instantly view, move around, and arrange pictures in any order. Ditto for audio, because computers can build and mix whole orchestras in perfect digital-audio stereo.

Just lay the time-coded pictures over the time-coded sound, both tracks exhaustively edited if need be, and you'll go into post-production with a frame-accurate decision list. Because computers encode the information in digital format, each copy of the video-tape is identical to the original. Copying—and copying is an inherent part of the editing process—is minimized. That cuts production costs dramatically.

The technology can even auto-assemble a master copy onto VHS if you want to avoid post-production. VHS is passable for direct-mail videos, although rarely for slicker broadcast productions, which demand a lower signal-to-noise ratio.

Cheap, they're not, at $34,000 each, including software and hardware. The hardware includes a greatly modified IBM or Mac system, which if you provide yourself can save you about $2,000. A color monitor will save you those costs as well. The system includes a set of six external disc drives for magneto-optical discs—similar to the laser discs used for giving you movies at home.

The Emc2 is still out of reach for smaller political consultants. But for high-volume users like Wilson, it is easier, faster, and in the longer run, much cheaper than paying for a roomful of equipment and techno-twits in a post-production studio 30 weeks of the year. Since Ferster developed the system three years ago, about 300 units have been sold, and the price is down from the $40,000 range. Technology is continuing to improve with upgrades.

While the Emc2 was originally designed around a standard hard disk drive, for instance, the final design includes a magneto-optical disk drive that holds erasable disks that can be removed from the system. Ferster says each disk on Emc2 can hold one to four hours of source material. That means with the six drives, the storage capacity would equal 24 hours, with the option to use additional disks for more storage capacity.

The only real limitation is the resolution of the digitized images when they are processed in real time—or as fast as the human eye can see film in motion. Until recently, companies like EMC have faced unacceptably low resolution and low compression ratios. This slightly distorts the picture to the untrained eye. But Wilson said focus group sessions he has held reveal that few average viewers are able to tell the difference between their TV picture and the Emc² screen.

He adds that broadcast quality isn't a problem when you're editing off-line and going back to your master tapes for the final assembly. Companies making big strides with each new generation of compression chips, meanwhile, are improving pixel averaging—an action that combines visuals pixel by pixel.

Some special features, such as flashy real-time effects for moving a video image off-axis or using a page-turn effect, produce more distortion. But where there's a problem, there are companies looking for solutions The Video Toaster, for instance, is made by New Tek. It offers flashy, broadcast-quality effects that are popping up in TV ads everywhere.

Built around a New Tek Video Toaster card and a Commodore Amiga 2000 computer, the system features television character generation, a 24-bit paint system and three dimensional modeling, rendering, and animation with 192 broadcast quality, realtime effects to choose from.

Political consultants say small campaigns may be lured to the Toaster as negative campaign ads continue to rise. At $4,000, the Toaster does a lot for a little. Still, some consultants caution that viewers might quickly burn out on cheap-looking Toaster spots where scandal sheet headlines roll out to viewers.

Wilson, who owns a Toaster, says it is a nice supplement to the Emc2 but he wouldn't rely on it solely. "We often get distracted by the bells and whistles. The best effects in the world are not going to save a dumb idea. "The Emc², on the other hand, lets you try out all the dumb ideas you want until you've got something you absolutely love."

✓ Planning Your Last-Minute Media
Ken Eudy and Chris Brown

20 tips to get the most out of your home-stretch media

Think Visually:

By November, reporters are sick of news conferences in your campaign headquarters. Hold a press conference at the local toxic waste dump, or hold up a half-dead bird at a local polluted waterway. The press will bring cameras.

Make It Easy:

Know the deadlines of local news media. Evening papers go to press about noon, so don't hold a news conference at 11:30 a.m. If you want TV cameras, hold your event in a place where the station's satellite-relay trucks can park conveniently. Some producers pick stories based on how easy it is to get a crew in and out.

Cross Your Opponent's Path:

If your opponent is dedicating a new highway, show up, and point out that he voted against the appropriations to build the highway in the first place. Focus the press on the criticism of the moment, and leave before they ask you about the gasoline tax hike you proposed.

Make an Entrance

Arrive in a helicopter if you can afford it. If not, buy yourself a fire engine. Look like the Second Coming every time you show up.

Build a Wall of Shame

Make a wall-sized poster of your opponent's contradictory statements, include the dates and sources, update it daily, and make it a permanent fixture in the front window of your campaign headquarters. The press will show up every day to check for tidbits.

Plan Your Logistics:

Make sure your producers and dub houses have your overnight shipping service number, plenty of courier packs, and a complete listing of street addresses, fax numbers, and phone numbers for all the media outlets you'll have them shipping to. Have them pre-address an emergency set of airbills and make sure they know exact deadlines for package dropoffs. Get home numbers of the sales managers at your TV and major radio stations.

Know Your Media Market:

If you plan to buy six spots a day for the last five days from a local TV station, make sure they have the spots to sell before you build them into your strategy.

Publicize Your Endorsements:

Endorsements are valuable, so plan to produce spots touting them. Work newspapers and other influential organizations to release their endorsements early so they can be can be reprinted, or cut it into existing broadcast ads.

Save Some for Later:

Reserve funds for last-minute production costs and air time. Unless you plan to be the aggressor, you'll need to respond to your opponent's ads during the last 10 days. When attacked late, you can either cannibalize time you've bought for positive ads and replace them with response ads, or run your counterattacks on top of your existing program. The first choice is suicidal. The second only works if you have money to get on the air.

Use Intelligence

If you insist on hunkering down to await the worst, at least make sure you have good intelligence from the outside. Call or visit TV and radio stations daily to ask about your opponent's new ad copy, trafficking instructions, and air-time buys.

Plan a Final Offensive:

In the last days of a campaign, the only defense is a good offense. If you suspect a surprise attack, why wait? Produce your own attack spots now, and do onto others before they do unto you. Once you start, stay ahead by launching a second strike just before your opponent recovers from the first.

Warm Up the Bullpen:

Your producers should be prepared to provide same-day production of response TV and radio ads. Keep their home numbers handy, and know where they can be reached t all times.

Put One In the Can:

A counterattack spot on a germane subject can be on the air in 12 hours. If you get hit, a canned ad can buy you some breathing space.

Respond in Kind:

Always respond to an attack in the media in which the attack was made. If you're attacked on TV, a radio counterattack will be missed.

Don't Panic:

If you go on the defensive, people will think your opponent has gotten the better of you. Instead, counter by saying your opponent's smear ad is really a cover-up for something he's done wrong. Call a press conference to respond the day the ad runs and get on the air with a paid response within 24 hours.

Question the Coverage:

Reporters will show up if you call a news conference to charge the press is skewing your position on issues. But this is a double-edged sword; be careful. You risk alienating some of the reporters covering the campaign, and even if you have a valid complaint, you may shift focus away from the issues and onto the news media. Always avoid having the press cover the press.

Bite a Dog:

The old saying, "It's news when a man bites a dog, not the other way around" still serves as an acid test for most editors. So do the unexpected. If you're a Democratic congressional candidate and President Bush comes to campaign for your opponent, hang a "Welcome George" banner outside your headquarters. When the press shows up to ask about it, start dumping on your opponent s voting record.

Celebrate a Milestone:

Passing out your 10,000th brochure, knocking on your 5,000th door, or driving your 50,000th mile are all suitable occasions for publicity stunts.

Be Humorous:

Always have a snappy quote in reserve. The press gives more ink to the wise and witty.

Be Consistent:

Remember, when you say something to the press, it's on the record and may wind up in print. If you change your mind on something, hold a press a conference and say so. Never give your opponent a stack of newspaper clips he can use against you.

✓ The Computer-Assisted Media Buy

Tom Edmonds and Sheliah Roy

Every candidate recognizes the importance of paid advertising. Often, the content and style of a candidate's advertisements achieve more intense scrutiny than any other aspect of his or her campaign. A 30-second television commercial can be the single most remembered, important and "glamorous" ingredient in a $100,000 or multi-million dollar campaign.

However, no matter how well-produced, a commercial will mean nothing if it is not seen by the right people, in the right environment, and at the right time. It is this crucial final link, the media plan and buy, that can make or break the communications chain from candidate to voter.

Most campaigns are spending over half of their total resources on media time and space, so decisions about paid media are among the most important campaigns make. Unfortunately, in many cases media planning and buying is not as sophisticated as it should or could be. Even worse, media commissions are often used as barter to compensate suppliers of other goods and services. It is false economy to pay a good consultant to make a bad media buy. It is equally counter-productive to compensate a television producer for excellent commercials by asking him to step outside his area of expertise and make the media buy. Campaigns must take advantage of the benefits of computer-assisted media planning and buying. Today, fast changing technology is forcing the political professional who is responsible for campaign communications to use the new technology or lose out to those who are.

It is amazing that until now there hasn't been more "public" excitement about the power and effect of computer-assisted campaign media plans and buys. For a long time, sophisticated polling data has been an integral part of most campaigns. Such data has become the foundation for well-thought-out, well-crafted advertising commercials. But too often polling data is not fully utilized as the foundation for establishing "target audience groups" to better plan and buy media. In a professional sense, it is hard to understand why the wealth of information available in most polls ends up prompting a media buy that contains no more targeting than simple skewing towards an age or sex demographic. Even households reached or targeted Gross Rating Points (GRPs = the sum of rating points; rating points = the percentage of an audience reached by a spot or show), numbers provided by stations and rating services like Arbitron and Nielson, give minimum additional assurance that a commercial is reaching the intended target audience. The computer's ability to compare and organize large amounts of diverse data permits greater flexibility and accuracy in targeting than was possible before.

Another major obstacle that the computer is helping to overcome is the structure and orientation of the media industry itself. The existing systems for planning and buying media, particularly radio and television, are not designed for political applications. The media is structured to accommodate the commercial advertiser. Examples of such problems are numerous. Most rating and performance information on the media does not take into account the boundaries of political jurisdictions. The needs of political advertisers are foreign to most sales representatives for media outlets and to stations' internal tracking and billing systems. Indeed, many advertising agencies do not understand political markets and frequently do not want political advertising because of the problems mentioned. If you have ever tried to determine what portion of a particular station's listening audiences are within a given congressional district, or have been offered a "make good" after Election Day, or received an invoice from a television station whose computer is not programmed to handle payment in advance, then you have an idea of existing system problems that a computer can help overcome to properly execute a political media buy.

Getting the Most for Media Dollars

Here are some of the factors that are needed to improve the quality of political media planning and buying:

1. Campaigns must recognize the importance of media planning and buying and stop treating it like a stepchild. Media commissions should never be used as a source of revenue to compensate suppliers of other goods and services.
2. Media targeting should use the new computer technology to improve its accuracy in matching the people viewing the candidates message with the carefully crafted message itself.
3. A campaign must realize that the media "system" is geared exclusively for commercial advertisers. A custom media system must be developed that is sensitive to political needs, from a definition of "markets" coinciding with political boundaries to a solution for the inadequacy of the standard "make good" arrangement.
4. Campaigns must employ a more effective and a much more efficient system of administering the masses of paper work and the numerous details involved in the media budgeting and buying process. A system that can accurately and quickly track and report the numerous components involved in the media plan and buy can provide the campaign with significant information advantages. A computerized system provides an information edge for monitoring cash flow, tracking spot rotations, performing cause and effect analysis (using tracking polls), utilizing campaign staff, and preparing accurate FEC reports more easily.

Using the New Technology

For quite some time there has been a great deal of information available to assist media planners. However, because there is so much information, it has only been used in its simplest form. In other words, at best, television was purchased against Household Rating Points in geographic areas defined by the rating services.

Now, with computerized media planning growing so quickly, two things are taking place. One, media planners are able to work more quickly, efficiently and accurately with the help of the computer. And, two, because planners have more "think" time, different rating, targeting and planning tools are being developed.

American Profile

Donnelley Marketing Systems has developed a profiling tool, American Profile,™ which is valuable because of its application to understanding and targeting both present and future constituencies and audiences. You can define the geographic boundaries of the area you want to be profiled—whether it be a state, congressional district or even a city block. The report contains 1970 Census data, 1980 Census data, 1983 estimates plus projections into 1988.

Among the valuable information contained in such a report are breakdowns by age, sex, race, income, home value, occupation, education, industry, travel time to work and much more. For each piece of information in the report, there is historical data, current data and future projections.

This type of information when coupled with polling data is extremely valuable in selecting key campaign issues and knowing the make-up of constituencies within political jurisdictions.

Clustering

Clustering is another powerful means to describe how voters live and how to reach them through broadcast media. Clustering has been utilized by direct-mail companies for quite some time, but it is relatively new in the broadcast arena.

In simplest terms, the assumption behind clustering is that "birds of a feather flock together." In other words, "like" people tend to live in "like" neighborhoods. Cluster groups like those developed for PRIZM™ (Claritas Corporation, Alexandria, Va.) and Cluster Plus™ (Donnelley Marketing Information, Stamford, Ct.) are defined by such brief thumbnail descriptions as: "Top Income," "Well Educated," "Professionals," "Prestige Homes" or "Poorly Educated," "Unskilled," "Rural," and "Southern Blacks." (See CAMPAIGNS & ELECTIONS, Vol. I, No 1, pp. 25-46; Vol. II, No. 4, pp. 4-18; Vol. III, No. 4, pp. 62-73.)

Clustering is valuable to political media in several ways. First of all, it can be useful in determining where the areas of support or opposition are located within a political jurisdiction according to the location of cluster groups. As a result, both the media utilized and the message delivered can be tailored to the type of voter that tends to reside in a specific cluster.

Secondly, clustering is valuable in that services such as PRIZM™ and Cluster Plus™ also relate lifestyle characteristics to television and radio rating information. Once target cluster groups are defined, their lifestyle characteristics can be linked to media habits through rating service surveys. Certain cluster groups tend to have distinct television viewing and radio listening habits. Having rating information for cluster groups for particular shows is a competitive edge in reaching the voters you have selected to reach with each message.

Zip Code Marketing

As mentioned earlier, the broadcast system's orientation with regard to geographic boundaries and ratings is geared toward the commercial market not the political market. Sometimes a congressional district's boundaries will cover parts of two different Arbitron or Nielsen rating areas or, in the opposite case, the district might represent only a portion of the standard rating area.

Through the use of computer services such as Arbitron's AID™ or Nielsen's NSI-Plus™, rating books for "markets" that exactly match the boundaries of political jurisdictions can be created using zip codes. In addition to establishing age/sex and household ratings that match geographic areas, you can establish ratings against specific groups within those areas. For example, if you wanted to reach professional, managerial men with high incomes within a given political jurisdiction, you could create ratings against that profile. Knowing this kind of information is invaluable in purchasing media although there can be less lifestyle data than with clustering programs. Still, AID and NSI Plus are valuable tools for geographically targeting media buys.

Reach and Frequency Analysis

Once target audiences are established, even if it is as generic as age or sex, knowing the percentage of the target audience reached and the number of times they're reached can be very beneficial.

But all too often, schedules are planned and analyzed solely against Gross Rating Points which do not provide an accurate estimate of who is actually being reached.

Reach and frequency computer programs, such as those we have developed, analyze individual media to determine the best combinations of day parts (show times) or stations to purchase for the money. They are also extremely valuable in developing a multi-media campaign. For example, if you are planning a schedule that utilized television, radio and newspaper, a reach and frequency analysis could provide you with data on the best combination of media to obtain the highest reach or greatest frequency against a target audience.

In addition to supplying you with the percentage of target audiences reached and the number of times they're reached, a reach and frequency analysis can provide information on the quality of frequency. In other words, 100 GRPs do not always equal 100 GRPs. If you purchase 100 GRPs on an independent station late at night and 100 GRPs on network affiliates, the "different" people reached with the same 100 GRP level will vary considerably. For example, 100 GRPs on the independent station would tend to reach the same people repeatedly and the 100 GRPs on network affiliates would tend to reach more people less times.

A frequency distribution demonstrates the frequency with which spots are seen by different segments of the target group (in this sample Households and Adults 18-49 computed in thousands). For the sample schedule the average frequency is 8.9 against households and 5.7 against adults 18-49. The frequency distribution (6) shows what number and percentage of the target audience saw the spot once, twice, etc. A frequency distribution guards against reaching the same persons over and over again.

Radio Optimization

In political media buying, time and money are two ever-present constraints. That is why computerized analysis such as radio optimization is particularly valuable. A radio optimization program builds schedules and reports on the best combinations of stations and spots to achieve ones campaign advertising objectives. Then the different options can be compared according to reach, frequency, cost per thousand, or a combination of the above depending on a campaign's goals.

Because the computer simply performs numeric calculations at a rate much faster than could be done by hand, it is useful to set limiting parameters. For example, stations with black formats can be deleted if black audiences are not part of your target audience mix.

The computer will tell you the best combination of stations to buy and where to place the spots on those stations. An optimization is an excellent place to begin the planning for a radio buy. The computer "crunches" the numbers and points you in the right direction.

Spill-in/Spill-out Analysis

A newspaper or a radio station often has coverage outside its home market. For example, newspapers such as The New York Times and The Washington Post reach readers outside of New York and Washington.

If, for example, you were planning a schedule in the New York market, but wanted to know the impact of the schedule in the Washington and Baltimore markets against a target demographic or target group, a spill in/spill out analysis would provide that information.

A computer program can provide you with the percentage of readership in the home market and the percentage outside the home market that you want to reach or provide the percentage of a radio audience in and outside the home market.

Computer-assisted buying

Political media buying is often a last-minute, "fast and furious" effort. To improve the speed and efficiency of the buy, a number of tools traditionally available in hard copy only, such as Nielsen or Arbitron ratings, are now available in computer format.

Because the rating books are either on-line or diskette, you no longer need to wait for the station to send you "avails." (The term "avails" refers to the programs that a station carries, and does not necessarily refer to the programs available at the time of your purchase.) And the rating information that you generate from the computer is accurate, whereas stations often send ratings for "avails" that are either grossly inflated or totally inaccurate.

To provide a quick picture of a market, the computer can rank programs or stations in the order of how they perform against your target demographics. For example, you can rank the performance of prime time programming against your target demographics. This type of information helps you focus on only the programming that does well against your target groups.

The computer also allows for more efficient tracking of the buy. Market goals are entered in the computer, which establishes a benchmark for the buy. As you are making the buy, the computer calculates how much money you have spent, how much you have left to spend and how much closer each additional spot brings you to your goal. Because the computer performs the additions and deletions and keeps track of your performance, the need for the traditional legal pad, pencil, and calculator are eliminated.

It is during the buying process that human judgment becomes critical. The computer is only capable of manipulating the numbers. But the politically astute buyer can assess the projected ratings for new programming or know that a show is trending downward or have the "inside" scoop that it is about to be canceled.

It is also the buyer who knows that the 11 P.M. break on a 10–11 P.M. show delivers less than the 10:30 P.M. break of the same show. However, it is the computer that can monitor and plot the break positions and estimate program delivery. This type of information is far too tedious to track without the aid of the computer.

Once the buy is made, the computer can generate several types of reports including client schedules by market and for a total campaign buy, while generating broadcast insertion orders that include a station's address and a contact's name. This saves a great deal of administrative time and the information is far more accurate.

Another advantage of computerized media buying is that tracking data is immediately available. If a campaign needs to know how much money it has spent through a given day, the computer can supply accurate totals in a matter of minutes.

And a critical political media task where the computer helps is the monitoring of spot rotation, which constantly changes during a campaign. Copy instructions are stored as part of the buy so that new instructions can be issued immediately to stations, and if what actually runs does not match rotation instructions, make goods or a refund can be requested. This is of particular value in an early buy.

Invoice reconciliation, though indisputedly desirable, is quite often a function left incomplete because it is such a time-consuming and tedious task. This is the type of task that is well-suited to microcomputers. In simplest terms, the station invoices (affidavits of performance) are entered into the computer and matched-up with the "original buy." The "original buy" would include any and all changes in a buy that were communicated to the stations.

The reconciliation process is one of matching what was received with what was ordered (see Table 5). The length of the commercial, the time it ran, program adjacency, day of the week, unit cost and even spot rotation are checked against the original order. A report will be generated which displays all matched spots as well as all unmatched spots. Knowledge of discrepancies is valuable information. As important as it may seem to receive a credit or refund for a station error, it may be even more important for a campaign to correct a rotational mistake quickly and thus assure that the correct commercial is running exactly as originally intended.

What's Right for You?

John Naisbitt, author of the best-selling book, *Megatrends*, clearly summarized the obstacle that must be overcome, "We are drowning in information but starving for knowledge." The computer is turning the vast amount of under-utilized information available to most campaigns into "information technology." Today, there are two basic alternatives available to a political campaign which wants to take advantage of the new media planning and buying technology. The campaign can contract to use the services of a political media planning and buying service with extensive computer expertise, such as Multi Media Services, or they may develop a computerized media planning and buying system of their own.

Unfortunately, developing a "system" of computer-assisted media planning and buying is not as easy as performing many other campaign functions which have been adapted to the computer. There is not a comprehensive software package available at retail stores or from vendors. Indeed at this stage of development, your "system" largely would have to be a custom-tailored package of various components obtained from a number of suppliers like those outlined in this article. A number of firms such as Arbitron and Nielsen have developed research data independently which is available in hard copy as well as on tape or floppy disks. Also, independently, a number of firms have developed computer software which can manipulate and manage the data generated by firms such as Arbitron and Nielsen.

As far as hardware is concerned, you have three options: 1) a terminal interfacing with a mainframe computer; 2) a micro/PC as a free-standing unit; or 3) a micro-mainframe system which combines the database access power of a mainframe (interfacing with a terminal) with the usefulness of a PC as a free-standing unit. The third option is required for a full-scale computerized planning and buying operation. Only a mainframe can perform the more complex planning routines such as those using lifestyle clusters. But many functions can be performed on a PC with data supplied on floppy disks downloaded from a mainframe.

Selecting the "correct" option depends on your individual needs and budget. But if you are a "selfstarter," are willing to research the media databases available today and have access to a micro or a mainframe, or both, your campaign can make a quantum leap forward in your media planning and buying.

✓ Cost-effective TV Buys
Bruce Mentzer

Getting your spots aired before Thanksgiving doesn't necessarily mean having to pay fixed rates. Despite what you might have heard, there are more than two rates on the political rate card.

Depending on your media market, you can choose between two buying strategies to ensure paying the lowest rate possible in the last two weeks of the campaign.

Television station rate cards have become increasingly complicated, with at least five or six columns of rates: fixed, pre-emptible with notice (two, four, or six days), fixed lowest unit, and lowest unit immediately pre-emptible.

What looks confusing is really quite simple, especially instates with low market saturation.

Place your initial order at the lowest unit rate (LUR), the absolute rockbottom price on the rate card. Usually it's the one that says immediately pre-emptible without notice."

You're probably thinking that not only are your spots going to be pre-empted, but you won't know about it until it's too late because the rate said "pre-emptible without notice." This isn't necessarily so. We've bee notified every time we were about to be blown out and, concurrently, were offered the opportunity to increase the rate to stay in the same time spot.

The trick? Actually, it's a necessity: stay in close communication with your salesperson and ask daily if your spots are clearing.

Go ahead, try it. Submit an order at LUR. Then, a few hours after you've placed your schedule, check with the station salesperson or representative to see if your spots are clearing at the lowest level. In many markets, most of your order will be accepted at this rate and will air.

Bruce Mentzer, president of Mentzer Media Services, Inc., based in Baltimore, MD, has handled the broadcast media research, planning and spot-placement for more than 50 campaigns since 1985.

If the station says some of your LUR orders won't clear, bring your rate up only one level on the rate card and resubmit your order for just those spots.

Once again, check back with the station or sales rep within a day or so to see if the new schedule is going to run at the slightly higher rate.

If the station tells you your spots are not going to run at the low rate and advised you to use a higher rate, ask for assurance that no candidate is running at the lower rate.

Once or twice during the campaign have a campaign staffer examine the public file at each television station and copy the political buys that are running concurrently with yours. If you originally placed at LUR and were bumped up by the station to the next level, compare all rates to make sure that no other candidate runs at the lesser rate.

Sound like something that couldn't happen after the Federal Communications Commission audits of 1990? Well, it can and does. Guard against it.

Keep in mind that policies regarding clearance of spots at lowest unit rate vary from station to station and are just as confusing for the station personnel as for the buyer. Never assume that all is being handled correctly. Do your homework and check it out yourself.

Coming Up for Air

In tight markets, however, you need to employ a slightly different buying strategy for stations that have already sold out the cheap seats.

In this case, you may want to use the slightly higher rates to guarantee airing with no or little chance of preemption. This may be worthwhile even in soft markets to secure news adjacencies or other desirable time periods.

Or, if a station tells you that some programming areas are sold out, you may be able to buy your way in by paying a higher rate or a fixed rate. If the station allows this, and only some do, you probably will be pre-empting another advertise who's still in at LUR.

The sold-out situation usually does not occur until the final week or two before the election. At this pint, you should have your LUR rates bumped up to pre-emptible, but with notice–one day or more. This will prevent your spots from being nixed without notice on the final weekend.

If you normally place your initial order at a rate higher than the lowest unit, don't assume that the station will rebate you if others run at LUR. You are responsible for entering your spots into the fray, and you will be held accountable for placing at a rate higher than you should have.

Stations will only rebate money if you enter at a rate that is the highest in a certain time period. For example, if your rate falls between the highest and lowest, you're probably not entitled to a rebate.

You'll need financial flexibility to rework schedules on a day-to-day basis. To combat a fluctuating buy-dollar total, create a reserve fund. Make sure you include the amount of the reserve fund—8 to 10 percent of each week's paid media budget—in the original media plan. You can use any leftover money for the final week's media.

In almost all cases, start at the bottom of the rate card and work up. With some minor leg work, you'll be sure you're getting the best rates possible and the most media for the money.

✓ Executing Your Own Media Buy
Pat Beall

First, the horror stories.

Did you hear the one about the time buyer who spent 90 percent of his candidate's budget on one TV show? How 'bout the Midwestern representative whose $6,000 cashier's check got tossed in the TV station's dumpster?

Incidents like these are the reason time buyers put on a happy face when candidates solemnly announce that they, or their campaign manager's girlfriend, or their best friend is going to handle their multi-million dollar media buy.

But campaigns with a modest war chest can, and in some cases, should, plan and execute their own one-week, single market TV time buy—provided they know the right questions to ask.

1. **"What is a rating point?"**

Something you need 300 of and that's a minimum. Rating points are the percentage of TV sets tuned to a specific show. If Murphy Brown has a 15 rating for adults age 35 and over, then 15 percent of adults in that age group who live in that TV market and own TV sets are tuned into Murphy.

Shares are a percentage of a percentage. If Murphy's 15 rating equals a 30 share that means 30 percent of all TVs that were on were tuned to Murphy Brown. If that's confusing, just remember: Ratings are based on total TVs; shares are TVs that are turned on.

2. "Why 300 points?"

Conventional wisdom has it that an ad's message will not register until the viewer has seen it at least three times. Since you want 100 percent of the audience to see your spot three times; you'll need a minimum of 300 points.

Media buyers tend to want to buy closer to 500 points, because we know the electorate tends to head for the fridge during at least one of the precise moments you have purchased to prod its political consciousness.

3. "Where do I find ratings?"

At the TV station. I'm not being cute. I am assuming you are buying in a single TV market and have no wish to subscribe to Arbitron or Nielsen ratings services.

Call the station. Ask for the person in charge of political sales. Commiserate about the general awfulness of political buys. Apologize profusely for being one of the people who will make his or her life so complicated in the very near future. Then get down to business. Ask for "rates and avails," how much time costs and how much is available.

Here's a script:

Her: "Do you want ratings or thousands?"
You: "Both."
Her: "What's your demo [demographic]?"
You: "Adults 35 plus."
Her: "Nielsen or Arbitron?"
You: "Either one is fine."
Her: "The last ratings period?"
You: "Okay."
Her: "What's your flight date?"
You: "One week before (election date)."

That conversation nets you a list of the station's programs, each program's ratings for men and women 35 and older, the cost of 30-second spots on those programs, the number of households—by thousands—that the specific program reaches. The information will be based on the last ratings "sweep"—a thrice-yearly assessment of the market—by Nielsen or Arbitron, whichever service the station uses.

4. "We're going to buy shows with the highest ratings, right?"

Maybe. A Cosby rerun with a seven rating that costs $700 is not as cost-effective as an Andy Griffith rerun with a six rating that costs $500. This is known as a cost per point—CPP. To get it, divide the cost of the ad by the rating. The Cosby CPP is $100. So at $84 per point, Andy Griffith is clearly today's special. CPPs, as much as raw ratings, should guide your time-buying budget.

5. "We're going to buy the 6 o'clock news."

You, and everyone else. Conventional wisdom doesn't know it yet, but tracking polls strongly suggest buying news in a crowded political field is like singing in a choir—your individual voice gets lost in the chorus.

So you wind up paying more money for more points, and all you get is the same level of recognition you would if you were buying other, less crowded, programs that also appeal to probable voters: Donahue, Oprah, America's Most Wanted, CBS Sunday Morning, and the programs that either immediately precede or follow newscasts.

6. "Well, what should I buy?"

Every market has its quirks. People in Lexington, KY, get up at 5 a.m. to watch the early morning news. In Lake Charles, LA, folks watch nothing on Saturday until 6 p.m. And in northeast Florida, Star Trek pulls better political demographics and bigger numbers than sly conventional shows. Study what's available—there are always bargains.

7. "Let's buy cable, because it's a whole lot cheaper."

It's also a whole lot less watched. That's first of our two cable cautions. Rating points for cable programming are frequently marked by an asterisk—which means there aren't enough viewers to create a single point. Still, if your message targets a narrowly defined audience, cable's specialized programming can work wonders.

But what if the target moves? That's our second warning: Many cable companies insert into their programming lineup just once a week, usually on Monday.

So where does that leave you if you wake up Tuesday morning to charges your candidate's been cheating on her taxes? Here's where. On Wednesday, you go to the cable outlet with your response spot, only to be told that they can't get it on the air for four more days. With the election on the following Tuesday, and 80 percent of your message dollars tied up in cable, you may as well kiss your sweet asterisk good-bye.

8. "The station says I can buy the same show for different rates."

The station wants to keep its license. God bless 'em. The most expensive rate for TV time is known as the fixed commercial rate. Once you buy an ad at this rate, you won't be preempted or "bumped" by another advertiser. But after you buy a few ads at this rate, you won't have any money left either. The other rate is the lowest unit rate—LUR—or the political rate. The FCC says the station can charge you, the political candidate, no more than it charges its lowest paying advertiser for a spot in the same program, in the same week. Hold it to this.

9. "This political rate is great. This isn't much money at all."

In a crowded political year, it's also not much good at all. The rate is usually immediately preemptible without any notice, which means you have a real good chance of paying not much money at all for ads that will never air—or that will air at 2 a.m. You'll get your money back, but that won't do you much good after the election. Like Goldilocks, you want something that's just right: a rate that is pre-emptible with one week's notice. These cost more than the LUR, and less than fixed.

With pre-emptible rates, if it looks like your ad is about to be bumped, the station will call you to find out whether you want to:

1. Take the money you spent on this ad and buy an ad in another time slot;
2. Pay the extra money it will cost to lock in this time slot at a higher, fixed rate or;
3. Take a refund and pay your pollster.

In a year with not too many folks in the field, you might just get away with buying ads at preemptible rates right up to the wire. Hope for the best. But since you are buying just one week, and these spots are your only shot, be prepared for the worst-case scenario of ultimately having to buy some fixed rate time in order to stay on the air.

10. "My third cousin, who owns a hardware store, tells me he buys spots on Meet The Press for $50. I pay $65."

Rebates. They're not just for Chrysler anymore. If a spot aired during the same show/time slot your spot aired, and if you paid more for your spot than the other advertiser, you are entitled to a rebate amounting to the difference between the cost of your spot and the cost of his spot. The station owes you $15.

11. "My best friend in public relations says TV stations give him a discount on ads."

A bona fide agency of record gets a 15 percent discount on broadcast time buys. At most stations, a bona fide political candidate is entitled to the same. However, if a station balks, there is a 15-percent solution. Are any of your contributors or staffers affiliated with an ad agency?

Would that agency be willing to place the buy for, say, 7 percent if your campaign did the real work: devising the schedule, completing the paperwork, making the tape/check deliveries, handling all the revisions?

Would they, in a nutshell, be willing to accept 7 percent of your perfectly legal tender for doing nothing? Probably.

12. "When should I buy?"

Yesterday. If you wait until the last week, there may be no time slots left to buy. Worse, even the puniest of LURs rise precipitously as election day nears. So not only is waiting risky, it's also expensive.

Buy time for the last week of the campaign as soon as you can, or as soon as the political rates go into effect. That's 45 days from the date of the election.

13. "I'm ready to buy. Do I call the station or what?"

Only to let your sales rep know the paperwork is coming. Each station needs:

1   A letter, on campaign stationary, authorizing the buyer to place ads on behalf of the candidate, signed by the treasurer or campaign manager.
2. A schedule of the programs and program time slots you want to buy, at the prices you are going to pay.

3. A completed NAB form, which the station will provide.
4. A dub or videotape copy—of your spot. And check the dub to make sure your whole spot is there before you send it out.
5. A check.

14. "How many weeks should I buy?"

If you have enough money to buy 800 points, you might want to buy 500 points in the last week and 300 points the week immediately prior to that. Or, you can place 400 points in each week. Whatever you do, don't go below 300 points in any one week.

15. "Do I trust the station to run my spot?"

No! Get some volunteers from the campaign and make it their job to watch the stations you bought time on during the appropriate slots. If the spot doesn't run, call the station and scream. You're entitled to a refund.

16. "So that's all of it?"

No, this isn't even the beginning of it. Did I mention every TV station in the country does this differently? Once you go beyond a single week, single market buy, many of these suggestions become counterproductive.

But if you plan your one week, buy early and carefully, and are demonic about detail, then you too can relax—sort of—for at least one week of your campaign.

✓ Targeting Voters Via Cable TV
John Power

By the end of this year, cable television will be in almost 50 percent of the nearly 90 million American homes with television sets. Although cable television is having a major impact on television-viewing habits, its effect on the political-advertising process, with few exceptions, has been almost negligible.

This is about to change. Cable television advertising will have a significant impact on campaigns in 1988; it almost certainly will be a decisive factor in some close elections. What makes cable television so attractive is that it is an efficient way for a candidate to reach a highly targeted audience with a specific message.

Cable television tends to be narrowcasting, an industry term that means programming on most cable networks is targeted to reach very specific audiences. It is similar in this respect to the way radio is formatted to appeal to distinctly different demographic groups. On cable television, for example, you can see a sports network, a weather channel, news, and music videos. But you also can see a variety of locally generated and locally produced special-interest programming.

Producing a Winner

Perhaps the most compelling example of a politician who successfully used cable television to his advantage is Representative Barney Frank (D–Mass.). In 1982, Frank, a freshman Democrat, saw his suburban Boston congressional turf redistricted. As a result, Frank was forced into a race against Republican incumbent Margaret Heckler, who had held the seat in an adjacent district for 16 years. Now they were forced to face off, and Heckler appeared to have the geographic and demographic advantage.

Frank and his campaign strategists reasoned that the only route to victory was to concentrate on taking the pivotal mill town of Fall River. Research disclosed Fall River had a very large Portuguese population that was served by its own local cable channel.

By tailoring commercials to the Portuguese and airing them on the Portuguese channel, Frank carried Fall River by a substantial margin and won the election. Frank's commercials were simple and direct. They featured local Portuguese businessmen and women talking directly to one another about campaign issues, community issues, and about Barney Frank's local town meetings, which the station broadcast.

By taking advantage of cable television, Frank accomplished two important objectives in political advertising: He had targeted his ads to a specific geographic area and had tailored their message to the demographics of the audience.

Cable television offers this sort of distinct advantage, because the boundaries of local cable channels correspond to political districts and/or municipalities. In other words, when a city council or county commission reviews cable-television franchise applications, it awards the contract based on its geographic jurisdiction. From the standpoint of a political campaign, this is ideal. Campaign strategists know exactly which voters the station reaches. There is no "waste circulation," as there is when a campaign buys time on a network's local affiliate, in hopes of reaching voters in a specific town. In this way, cable television has a unique capacity for dividing audiences and targeting programming directly to those divided markets.

Who Watches Cable?

Cable television also delivers audiences that are more affluent, better educated, and more likely to be registered voters and politically active individuals. MediaMark Research Inc., a highly respected national market-research firm based in New York City, recently conducted a 92-page survey of 20,000 Americans. Based on this research, which involved an array of lifestyle questions, I have determined that cable-television subscribers have the following characteristics:

- They are 25 percent more likely to have worked actively for a political candidate.
- They are 9 percent more likely to have taken an active part in a local civic issue.
- They are 13 percent more likely to have written a letter to the editor of a newspaper or magazine.
- They are 10 percent more likely to have written a letter to an elected public official.

Why, then, has cable television been largely ignored by political advertisers? One of the main reasons is that, until now, cable media planning and buying have been difficult to execute. No measurement of local cable audiences existed. An advertiser or political campaign might call up the station and ask to advertise and become lost in a game of telephone tag. The stations were geared to operations—to making sure their customers' sets were properly hooked up—not to selling advertising.

Today, however, planning for and buying cable is becoming much easier because of the emergence of far more effective audience research and better sales representation.

Cable TV Media Planning

A capable political strategist will assess the audiences available in an electoral district through cable in the same way Representative Barney Frank's people did. The objective is to target messages to specific groups—the elderly, women, sportsmen, Hispanics, and teens, for example.

Such advertisements must be placed in a fashion similar to the way ads run on radio; that is, the same ad is repeated at frequent intervals. The reason for this is that although cable audiences can be targeted precisely and tend to be cost efficient, the actual audience delivered by an individual spot is usually small—often less than half a rating point. In other words, even though you might not reach large numbers of people, the folks you reach will be the ones you have targeted.

To improve political media planning, National Cable Advertising, Inc., a Boston-based national cable representative, soon will make available to advertisers—and political candidates—powerful cartography service that merges data files (demographic information, such as income and historical data) with boundary files (geographic information, such as retail-trading areas, television-viewing areas, and congressional districts). As result, a potential advertiser will see colored maps that express relative values within a specific cable system service area.

This graphic representation can simplify judgments about the merit of using cable-television advertising, given specific set of media objectives. In addition, this also can help clarify decision making about the efficiency of using other media within defined geographic boundaries.

National Cable Advertising, Inc. also plans to merge political advertising, cable television with direct mail to provide cable subscribers with a direct-mail reinforcement message.

Cable TV Media Buying

Another reason cable television now is an effective medium for political advertising is that with the advent of cable interconnects, cable programming has become much easier to buy. An interconnect is the industry term that describes a physical distribution system that allows individual local cable systems to band together. As a result, media buyers are able to purchase local-market spot cable on multiple systems with one order in similar fashion to the way they buy spot television.

The concept of the interconnect is several years old, but interconnects have grown rapidly during the last two or three years. In practice, interconnects create super advertising vehicles enable advertisers to target their messages efficiently to a number of cable systems. The Cable Advertising Bureau in New York publishes the Cable Rep Interconnect Directory to facilitate buying interconnects.

In addition, several of the biggest, well-known cable networks, including Cable News Network, Life-time, and the Christian Broadcasting Network, have formed a sales-rep organization that offers advertisers a central point from which they can purchase a time on a national basis.

Political Opportunities

Advertising on cable television offers candidates a number of extraordinary opportunities. For example, cable is far structured than conventional television, and messages need not be confined to the 30-second and 60-second commercial lengths standardized by network television. It is possible, for example, to develop programs for fund-raising or for recruiting campaign volunteers. Programs of, say, 15 minutes may be produced to present a candidate's positions on important issues in far greater depth than most candidates could afford on broadcast television.

Although no hard-and-fast rules exist on the costs of purchasing time on national network cable television, you generally can expect to pay 30-50 percent less on a cost-per-thousand basis than you would for the same time on national network broadcast television. Local cable systems also offer significant savings. Again, such figures are difficult to discern, because many systems still lack a sophisticated means of measuring their audiences.

Another opportunity for the political community regarding cable television would appear to be the Hispanic market, a group that might hold the key to victories in states with sizable Latino populations, such as New York, California, Illinois, and Texas.

The innovations and advantages of cable television offer an edge that savvy candidates are just beginning to recognize. Some campaign strategists complain that the research data available on cable audiences does not equal that of broadcast television. Because cable operators cannot deliver the same audience research as network television, they reason, why should a campaign that must target voters bother to invest in it?

Any candidate or strategist who takes this sort of narrow, numbers-crunching approach to cable television is doing himself or herself a severe disservice. Advertising on cable television can make the difference in even the best, most effective political campaign. I have no doubt it will decide a number of races in the coming years. Ask Barney Frank. He'll tell you.

✓ Gauging The Cable TV Audience
Bruce E. Mentzer

Developing a cable television buy is not easy. Here's why you should persevere with a cable buy, and how you should do it.

Cable television reaches some 61 percent of American homes. You cannot afford to miss out on the strategic opportunity. By following a few simple steps, virtually any candidate can effectively use cable.

The first step is to do some in-depth research. Study the Nielsen and Arbitron ratings books, which you can get from a cable rep or a commercial outlet, to determine how much local viewing can be attributed to cable. In most cases you'll find cable accounts for 10 percent to 20 percent of viewing, but each outlet will have a minuscule share.

Now comes the hard part. You have to compare your target voters and where they are with the geography and viewing habits of cable subscribers. This analysis will allow you to match up the areas that you want to hit with cable. If there are no good matches, try something else. If there are, now you are ready to organize a buy.

While cable in most cases is not a substitute for commercial television, it'll help cut down your media waste factor by targeting only those voters within your district. Most cable operations are organized by county.

Compare the rates offered by the local cable outlets with those from the national reps for the channel you need, and go with the lowest offer. (They should be the same, but sometimes they are not.) Here's a quick and easy way to measure each system's cost efficiency. Find out the total number of households reached by the cable system—not actual viewer numbers, as in television. To figure the cost-per-thousand households in order to compare efficiency among the systems, divide the individual spot cost by the number of cable households. For example, if a system covered 160,000 households and each spot costs $85, your cost per thousand would be 53¢.

While this method gives you a standardized number, it does not tell you how many viewers will actually be watching your spot. You can roughly calculate a network's local cable rating based on the networks national ratings and the local system's penetration figures. But because cable systems and television stations cover different areas, the ratings cannot be directly compared.

The actual cost of using cable advertising will vary greatly depending upon the number of households reached and the time of year. If you plan to advertise before either of the political periods—45 days prior to a primary and 60 days prior to the general election—you'll need to negotiate lower spot rates. If a system splits between your district and another, there are a few things that you should take into account before deciding to use that particular system.

Find out from the cable rep how many cities and towns covered by the split system are actually within your region. Are the majority of the system's homes within your district? Look at the cost-efficiency factor of this system in relation to the systems that cover only your region.

Is the spot cost for the split system comparable to or less expensive than the in-district system? Will this area be effectively reached by other campaign media? Are these households, according to previous election precedents, worth targeting?

Once you've weighed these and other race-specific factors, make a judgment call.

In most areas, you'll discover that CNN, ESPN, and USA are the highest-rated outlets. CNN is tremendous for older and college-educated voters. You'll get men with ESPN and families with USA.

Still, look for local patterns. In the south, for example, the Nashville Network does very well. What about women, 25 to 54 years old? How about Lifetime, which offers a mostly female audience.

In conjunction with your strategists, to make sure everyone agrees on whom the campaign is trying to reach. Remember, cable homes have lots of channels—so the audience is very fragmented. It is better to run a moderate weekly schedule—21 spots—on a few networks than to run a heavy schedule on only one.

Each of your cable spots will probably reach 1 to 3 percent of the cable system homes, so spread your spots around and vary networks weekly to attract the largest possible audience. To build frequency, run spots on cable for several consecutive weeks.

You'll have to determine what spot rate to use as well as which programming areas. By signing up for the rotation-of-schedule (or ROS, normally 6 a.m. to mid-night), rather than prime-time ads (usually 6 p . m. to midnight), you'll save money and expand your impact. For example, a system recently offered us a prime-time rate of $15 per spot, and an ROS rate of $5 per spot.

In one case, we first secured a promise from the cable system that our spot would get equal rotation among all programming areas (you can ask for anything with cable). Then, we ran three times the number of spots using the ROS rate than we could have in the prime-time rate.

We reached our targeted prime-time viewers, and the morning and afternoon audience as well, for the same price. Planning was the key. Besides the traditional spots, you may also want to consider running an extended-length production on your local cable system. Each system has a local-access channel that can be used for just such a purpose. And, while the audience is usually very small, the cost is also minimal. Some systems offer a half-hour for as little as $50.

If you are going to use this unique option, promote the time and channel of the program either with free press or paid media. In creating your media budget, you must determine if radio, television, or cable is the most cost effective way to reach the groups you are trying to reach. Without this analysis, coming up with an arbitrary percentage of how much money should go into cable would be capricious.

Keep another couple of points in mind: While most TV stations can process a new order fast, many cable outlets cannot. Most have deadlines for the receipt of tapes and payment the Thursday or Friday prior to the week of actual airing. If you need to get your message on cable immediately, ask the system if you can pay a special edit fee to insert a schedule midweek. Some systems work with you.

Since putting your ads on cable midweek can pose a problem, so too can pulling them off if there is a change in strategy. You'll need to be especially careful when airing a rebuttal or negative ad. You may not be able to change your spot rotation instructions as fast as you would with other media outlets. In most cases, it may be best to leave the more controversial spots to conventional television and radio.

Cable may be best utilized by airing positives spots to buffer the negatives you put on the other media outlets. Once the cable spot schedule is airing, don't sit back and assume that everything is running perfectly. Take some quality control measures into your own hands. Ask the local campaign office, friends, candidates, and relatives if they've seen the cable ads and if they are running error free.

Call the cable system midweek and ask them to check to make sure your schedule is running without a hitch. You'll be surprised how many bonus spots and make-goods you can receive by simply keeping abreast of your buy.

Finally, regarding your overall cable strategy, don't play follow the leader and simply go along in the footsteps of your opponent's cable media plan.

While you should know what the opponent's is doing—and your cable rep is likely to tell you—your adversary may be making some very serious errors that will hamper the efficiency of your own cable buy. Take the time to do the research necessary. You will be miles ahead, and much closer to victory.

✓ Breaking Into Media Consulting
C.C. Case

Every political junkie at one time or another—dreams of becoming a media consultant, fantasizing about the money, the access to power, the chance to be Spielberg with a mission. Like other high-profile professions, political ad work is not as glamorous as it first appears.

Campaign consultants laze about lanquidly for long periods, then endure an extended season of 18-hour days when their undivided attention is in demand by a dozen or more VIPs. They do battle with the formidable forces of MTV, Reebok and Calvin Klein as well as the machete-wielding opposition. And for every glorious trot along the victory lap, there is a gauntlet of unrelenting blame to run through after a defeat. For better or worse, attribution for a campaign will nearly always fall upon the media consultant.

For those of you whose bubble hasn't burst, we've asked several top consultants how they broke into the field, and what made them do such a crazy thing. The good news is, although the industry has slowed of late, most experts feel the market's not saturated; spirited capitalist competition continues to expand opportunity in the system. The bad news is, the underlying factor in each success story is Lady Luck—getting that first big break. For what it's worth, here's a variety of blazed trails to her door.

Don Ringe (R)
Ringe Media
Purcellville, VA
Clients: Sen. Hank Brown (CO), Govs. Carroll Campbell (SC) & Jim Martin (NC).

I started studying the print medium at Columbia University's School of Journalism, then switched to broadcast. While I was still in school, David Wolper took me on as an assistant for a documentary series he was making with Teddy White, "The Making of the Presidents." I followed Wolper to L.A., where we made a documentary for ABC on Bobby Kennedy; then he sold his production company and I became a jack-of-all trades for the local PBS affiliate.

In 1969, when I was 23, Stu Spencer saw my work and asked me to start up a media arm for the Spencer/Roberts consulting agency, the stewards of Ronald Reagan's career. I did that for three years, then went off on my own, traveling the world, shooting nature films. The market for that stuff wore out in the mid Seventies, so I became a producer for network affiliates in L.A., San Francisco, and finally Boston.

In 1977, I was on a seminar panel discussion on political media with Mat McDougal, a product advertiser who had run herd over President Ford's campaign the year before. He urged me to start my own political media firm, so I called up Stu and got three big accounts right away, with his help: Ed Brooke, Bill Clements and John Warner. You can't ask for a better start.

Hank Morris (D)
Morris & Carrick
New York, NY
Client: Dianne Feinstein

I did a lot of local [political ads] in Long Island, actually spending three-quarters of my youth running campaigns against [Sen. Alphonse] D'Amato. Campaigns were always something I enjoyed, but never thought I could make a living out of it, so I went to law school at Columbia. Then in 1977, my third year, my professor, Jeff Greenfield—now an ABC News correspondent—told me that he had just left David Garth's firm, because he no longer could put in the time commitment. Greenfield was aware of my passion for campaigns, so he encouraged me to contact Garth. I passed the bar, but never practiced.

Robert Goodman (R)
Robert Goodman Agency
Baltimore, MD
Clients: George Bush (1980 presidential), Gov. Pete Wilson (1988 U.S. Sen., CA)

In 1954, fresh out of college, I got a job with the Joseph Katz Advertising firm of Baltimore, which was one of the premier agencies. That year I helped with a new client—the DNC. Everyone thought it was a little strange to have the Democratic Party as a client along side Amoco Gas.

When I was 28, I began my own advertising firm, and met a progressive Republican named Spiro Agnew. Since everyone in Maryland was a Democrat back then, and we had no money Agnew was a longshot at best. I'm an old show biz fan, so the thing I pushed for was to rewrite the lyrics of a popular tune to the candidate's name. Hence, "My kind of guy Ted Agnew is," was set to the popular

Sinatra tune about Chicago. After Agnew became governor, the RNC put me on tour to teach others about political advertising. It's funny, how we've gone from Broadway melodies to mud wrestling....

Ken Swope (D)
Ken Swope & Assoc. Boston, MA
Clients: Presidential candidates George McGovern (1984), Joe Biden (1987), Mike Dukakis (1988).

I was a young schoolteacher in Philadelphia in 1969, with a pregnant wife and bills to pay. I had always wanted to be a creative writer, and figured writing advertising copy would be both creative and lucrative. After I had sent a home-made portfolio around to the local ad shops, H.W. Ayer, one of the great agencies of the day hired me on. After a brief stint in the Philadelphia office, I was sent to the big time in New York.

They must have thought I was promising They asked me to do the Army account; I said no; they said "okay." They asked me to do the ROTC account; the same thing happened. Then they asked me to do [Republican] Josiah Spaulding's [1970] campaign against Ted Kennedy. I said no; they said "do it or you're fired." Apparently I wasn't THAT promising.

Spaulding had an offer of $200,000 from Chuck Colson at the White House contingency upon his airing spots about Chappaquiddick, which had happened the previous year.... I told him not to do it, that he would lose anyway and damage his own reputation in the process. He turned Colson down.... That campaign hooked me on politics.

Alex Castellanos (R)
National Media
Alexandria, VA
Clients: Govs. Caroll Campbell (SC), Bob Martinez (FL), Sen. Jesse Helms (NC)

When I was a political analyst [for pollster Arthur Finkelstein] in '79, I realized that the campaign advisers that had the most effect in the outcome of an election were the media consultants. TV is like having a precinct worker in every living room. I would constantly gripe, "Hey, I can do that." I was only 26 and had rarely watched TV, much less taken any film courses. I think that kind of technical training is far overrated. When you are a media consultant what really matters is a gut understanding for the results you need to produce and the numbers you have to move. If you know the function of a campaign, learning the technical stuff is a snap.

My first client was Terry Dolan of NCPAC in '80, who I knew through polling. Once I made that first spot I officially declared myself a "media consultant." After another cycle of NCPAC, I got the tremendous coup of the '84 Helms/Hunt election. It was my first big solo—the rest is history.

Bob Shrum(D)
Doak & Shrum
Arlington, Va
Clients: Sens. Barbara Mikulski(MD), Paul Simon(IL), Alan Cranston(CA)

I was a speech writer for Ted Kennedy during his '80 presidential run when [media consultant] David Sawyer asked me if I, along with Steve Smith, could help write the commercial scripts and define the overall campaign message.

In the early 80s, Bob Squier contracted me to write a couple of spots, but it wasn't until 1985 that I decided to pursue commercial politics full time, and began a company with David Doak and Pat Caddell. Despite our campaign experience, it sure was tough getting those first clients with no demo reel!

10

Print Advertising and Campaign Materials

★ ★ ★

✓ Printing: How to Get the Most for Your Campaign Literature Dollar

Lorene Hanley Duquin

The candidate hands out palm cards. Canvassers carry brochures door to door. Supporters display bumper stickers and lawn signs. The finance committee sends out tickets for the next fundraiser. Volunteers fold and stuff direct mail letters.

Printed campaign material. It's one of the most important parts of any political race. It can mean the edge.

Most large congressional and statewide campaigns use advertising agencies or political consulting firms to develop and produce their literature. But for the political novice or the candidate for local office who has limited financial resources, it's a do-it-yourself project which is often the cause of confusion, frustration, and expensive mistakes.

It doesn't have to be that way. A little advance planning and some knowledge of the printing industry will help you to develop and produce your material in the most effective and efficient way.

Determining your needs

No matter what office you're seeking, you will need at least one piece which states your qualifications and your position on two or three issues. For most candidates, this piece takes the form of a brochure.

The brochure doesn't have to be fancy. In some local races, a slick, expensive-looking piece can actually work against you if the voter perceives that you're trying to "buy" the election. Many school board candidates reproduce a simple typewritten 8½" by 11" sheet which is folded into a booklet form. For a larger race, you might want to have the brochure typeset and include photos. But don't print in a single color like blue—your halftone picture will look awful.

A well-written brochure is especially important if you'll be enlisting the help of volunteers to spread your message. In *Behind Closed Doors*, Edward Costikyan, the former head of Tammany wrote, "A captain will not ring a doorbell for a candidate unless he has a piece of literature to leave. Why? Partly because the captain wants to make up his own spiel from something in print—not just his own theories. The official line in print is an assurance that he is safe in saying what he says, and he has something to fall back on when he meets a truculent voter. Indeed, the piece of literature in his hand is a final protective line against the truculent constituent; there is no better exit when faced with a voter who is angry than to thrust a single piece of literature in his hand and say, 'Look, I know you feel strongly, but please read this before you make up your mind.' It covers a graceful retreat, and makes it possible for the shaken captain to leave with his dignity intact and ring the next doorbell with confidence."

Beyond the basic brochure, there is a wide variety of printed paraphernalia from bumper stickers and buttons to direct-mail letters and tabloids. No one can tell you exactly what to order for your campaign. Your needs will depend on a number of factors, including:

- the office you're seeking
- the number of voters in your district
- your name recognition level in the community
- the number of campaign issues and their complexity
- the types of campaign materials commonly used in your area
- your campaign strategy
- your budget

As you formulate your campaign strategy, keep a list of the printed materials that will help you get your name and message to the voter. Ask yourself questions.

For example, what should the candidate carry? What will the volunteers distribute? Should we schedule targeted direct mailings? Will we need raffle tickets or special letters for fundraising? Do we want pre-printed office forms or stationery for the headquarters? Should outdoor advertising such as yard signs or bumper stickers be part of the plan? Are campaign novelties important?

Setting up a plan

Once you have a good idea of the types of material you'd like to use, formulate a plan. A lot of guesswork goes into the strategy of a political novice. How much you can spend will depend on how much you can raise; and if you've never run for office before, you probably won't be able to answer either question exactly.

"But everything does depend on planning," says Sheila Kee, an Erie County (N.Y.) Democratic Committee member and political expert who has counseled candidates in local, county and state races. "People who don't have a plan find out in October that they have no money left. Then they're really in trouble. Once you have a plan, you can make adjustments depending on the amount of money you're able to raise. It's really worth the effort."

Ms. Kee recommends that the plan be structured in the following way:

Item	Month of Expenditure	Quantity Needed	Estimated Cost

Start at election day and work backwards forming a schedule of what you'll need and when you'll need it. Your local party leaders and former candidates might be able to give you some ballpark figures on quantities and costs. You could also develop your own quantity estimates by using census figures, tax rolls, city directories, and voter registration lists.

Now prioritize each of the items in your schedule. Distinguish between those which are absolutely necessary, which are nice to have, and which are luxuries. Add your printing plan to your total campaign budget. If cuts in your printing costs are necessary, your priority list will help you decide which items should be sacrificed.

Throughout the campaign, review your budget to make sure your quantities and costs are still on target. Miscalculating, whether you've overestimated or underestimated, can be expensive. The reason for this is that in the printing industry, the more pieces you order, the less expensive each item is. For example, 500 copies of a flier might cost about $15.00. But 1,000 copies might cost $20.00 and 5,000 pieces might cost only $50.00.

Chuck Swanick, a candidate for an upstate New York County Legislative seat who was running on a very limited budget, spent over $100 more than he should have because he underestimated his quantities and had to order additional copies three different times. Each time he had to pay for printing set-up costs which could have been avoided had he ordered one long run instead. That wasted $100 could have been used to pay for palm cards or extra drop pieces. On the other hand, ordering a large quantity is wasteful if you don't use it and it ends up in the trash can after the election.

Developing Your Material

Writing and designing your own campaign literature is not difficult if you know how to find expert advice when you need it. Start by getting some good black and white glossy photographs of the candidate. Photos should be taken with a 35 mm camera. Take both formal and informal shots. Pictures of the candidate's family and endorsement shots with business or political leaders are sometimes used. Look for action poses that tell a story. A photo of a candidate sitting at a desk is boring.

You can save money by asking your local photography shop to develop the film into a contact sheet. This is one sheet of photographic paper with a small print of each frame on the film. You can then decide which frames are good enough to have blown up into larger prints.

Good quality photos will have a light background without any white spots or blurs and without telephone poles or other objects sticking out of the candidate's head. You might also want to have the photo blown up and then cropped to focus in on the main figure and eliminate unnecessary or distracting background.

Using your photos and two or three key issues, develop a theme and a tag line or slogan. The slogan should appear in all your printed material. Sometimes your own name will lead you to a catchy tag line—"Rich is right" or "I love Lucey" or "Make the Swift Connection."

If it is at all possible, pre-test your ideas to determine voter reaction. If scientific polling procedures are beyond your financial or volunteer capabilities, then test your ideas on neighbors or in a random phone survey before you have large quantities of brochures printed.

Beware of using sarcasm in your piece. It can work against you. One challenger for a seat on the village board in a small northern community used the theme "Open Up the Club" in a race against incumbents who were all from the same political party. While many people responded positively to the need for two-party checks and balances in the village, they saw the slogan as a sign of bitter sarcasm and felt that the candidate's attitude might cause him difficulty in working on a bipartisan basis if he were elected. He lost.

When writing copy for your pieces, remember that short words and sentences make the piece more readable. Some people have the idea that if they're going to pay for a piece, they should cram as much information into it as possible. But the most effective literature is that which is attractive to the eye and has plenty of blank space. An individual is much more likely to read a piece with many photos and captions, interesting headlines and artwork, and short anecdotal-size paragraphs.

If you feel uncomfortable about writing your own copy, you can hire a freelance writer. As long as you provide the writer with the research and idea of what you want included, your costs should be nominal. Many newspapermen and women are permitted to freelance. Shop your local papers' staffs for reasonably priced assistance. If they can't do it themselves, they always know someone who can help.

What's Available?

Here's a checklist of some of the more common printed campaign materials used by local candidates:

Brochures: No matter what level race you're running, you will probably need some kind of brochure. Keep it simple. Few people will spend the time to read long, wordy explanations of your qualifications and stands on issues. In some small races, a brochure is the only printed literature used.

Canvass piece: Some candidates like to produce a separate brochure or flier which is used by the volunteers who go door-to-door in the district. This piece can be used to reinforce the main campaign issues, to raise new campaign issues, or to challenge the records or statements of the opponents.

Tabloids: These are larger pieces, printed on newsprint. They are used when a candidate has lots of information and photos. A tabloid tends to convey the impression that the contents have news value.

Newsletters: Smaller than a tabloid and printed on bond paper, these pieces usually have many photos and short newsy articles. Some candidates use newsletters to keep campaign workers informed and enthused. Incumbents use them to inform the voters of the issues and what's going on in government. You can save money on a newsletter because it doesn't have to be typeset. Most are printed on 11" by 17" paper and folded in the center to form an $8\frac{1}{2}$" by 11" size booklet. The newsletter can then be folded like a business letter and mailed in an envelope.

Leaflets or drop pieces: These pieces are usually $8\frac{1}{2}$" by 14" or smaller and printed only on one side. They are used to zero in on an issue or to create name and face recognition. They are dropped off at residents' homes, distributed at special community events, or slipped under windshield wipers in parking lots. They are less expensive than direct mail, but while you are distributing them you cannot differentiate between registered and unregistered voters, or between constituents and people who live outside the election district—so many will be wasted.

Palm cards: Candidates often use small cards, about the size of a postcard, which have their name and picture on one side and their qualifications on the other. Since it's important to keep your name in the voter's mind as long as possible, instead of qualifications, some candidates print a sports schedule or a list of important government phone numbers on the reverse side.

Direct-mail letters: Whether you will be mailing to all registered voters or doing specially targeted mailings to specific groups, direct mail has proven to be an effective campaign and fundraising technique. Computer letters, where the voter's name and address are typed onto the letter by computer, are more expensive but have the advantage of being more personal. Laser letter printers have dropped this cost for very large mailing lists.

Postcards: Many campaigns use postcards to generate personal endorsements. Supporters write short notes on the backs of the cards and mail them to their friends and neighbors. To cut costs, use your palm cards as picture postcards with nothing printed on the reverse side.

Thank-you notes: Ever since John Kennedy sent thank-you notes to the residents who signed his nominating petitions for Massachusetts Senator, candidates have been sending thank-yous to people who talked to them at the door, signed petitions, made contributions, volunteered their time or opinions, and for any number of other reasons.

Signs: Lawn signs, road signs and window signs have never won elections by themselves, but they do have the advantage of showing support and generating interest in the community. In some communities political signs are banned for aesthetic reasons. It can be a misdemeanor—which is a crime—to put a poster on a telephone pole. Signs are also sometimes prey to vandalism—especially around Halloween time.

Bumper stickers: Like signs, bumper stickers are a show of strength. They aren't worth the expense unless you have enough supporters who will use them. If you decide to use bumper stickers, order vinyl ones so that they can be easily removed from the car after the election.

Novelties: Buttons, combs, rulers, coloring books, balloons, and hundreds of other items can be printed with the candidate's name and given away to potential voters. The idea is to keep your name in front of the voter.

Fundraising supplies: Depending on your money raising strategy, you may need raffle tickets, fundraising tickets, direct-mail letters, programs, favors, etc. These items are essential to most campaigns and the expense falls under the old adage, "It takes money to make money."

Office supplies: Stationery, press release forms, volunteer cards, voter response cards, and other office supplies may or may not be important in your race. If you're trying to economize, order a rubber stamp with your name, headquarters address, and phone. Then make your own "stationery" by using your stamp on plain typing paper. But, budgets aside, be careful of the "image" that such a device will project.

Understanding Screens

"Screening" is the process by which "halftones" are made as opposed to "lineshots." A lineshot is a photorepresentation of a subject such as a pen and ink drawing of a person. It is all one weight of line—thickness of the lines may vary—solid areas can be put down—but there is no gradation in the "heaviness" or density of the line or area such as in a photograph.

Screening allows a newspaper or magazine to print a photograph, and in some cases, an artist's rendering—such as a water color—where there are varying shades of the basic color or colors.

In screening, a semi-transparent screen which has a dot pattern is placed over the material to be photographed, and the plate is made from a negative that has been shot through the screen.

The number of dots per unit area is proportional to the quality of the image desired, which is often a function of the paper, press speed, and press method—offset lithography, letterpress, rotogravure. Newspapers use a "70-mesh," fine fashion magazines "130-mesh." When developed, both the negative and the printing plate have broken up the photograph into thousands of those tiny dots, and the size (and frequency) of the dots is proportional to the density of the amount of ink desired. A lineshot is a simple thing to reproduce and print, a halftone much more difficult.

To get a good reproduction, it is important to have good pictures. In general that means clean, sharp, contrasty, glossy photos. Good printing of a photo—especially an action photo—is usually characterized by the statement—"it has 'snap'"—the printer has captured the tones in the original photo. "Snap" means that it jumps off the page at you. Very few printers know how to shoot a halftone, develop the plate properly, and then control the inkflow onto the printing plate in the press in order to get real "snap" into the reproduction. So before selecting a printer, make sure that you see some of his work. See if the pictures jump out of the page at you. (This can also be a function of the paper too. Coated stock has a tendency to give more "snap" to a picture than uncoated stock, although some matte-finish papers allow the ink to sit on top of the paper and you can get "snap.")

Preparing Your Material for the Printer

How your material will be printed will depend on the items you've selected. Signs, for example, are usually silkscreened. Tickets are often printed on a letter press. Campaign novelties such as combs, balloons, and pens are produced by specialty companies. To order these things you only have to let the printer know the quantity, what you want printed on the item, and the colors.

The rest of your campaign literature, such as brochures, fliers, office forms, and letters, will probably be printed with a photo offset process. This means that a photograph is taken of the material. The photo is developed on a metal, plastic, or paper plate which is put onto the printing press. The image on the plate is inked onto the paper during the printing process.

If money is of no concern, you can give your printer your photos, your text, and a rough layout (called a "dummy") of how you'd like your finished piece to look. The printer will then charge you for assembling all of the pieces into what is called a camera-ready mechanical or, for more complex pieces, a "set of mechanicals."

A mechanical is the finished layout of your piece with all of the artwork, photos, headlines, and typesetting glued in place on a piece of cardboard. Camera-ready means that the material is ready to be photographed and turned into a plate for the offset printing process, without any further work by the printer on the mechanicals.

If saving money is important, you can cut costs by having the mechanical prepared by someone other than the printer. This person must have some commercial art experience, however. Some local candidates enlist the help of a student intern from the art department of a nearby college or university. Professors are often willing to give these students independent study credit provided that you can expose them to practical work experience on your campaign. After the election, you will have to evaluate their performance.

For some items, a formal mechanical isn't necessary. When there is little or no artwork or layout, as in a direct mail letter, you could type the letter on an electric typewriter with a carbon ribbon and it would be "camera ready." But if you don't have access to a good typewriter and your finished copy looks unprofessional with smudged letters or uneven type, then it's worth the extra money to have the printer retype it for you. Remember, a confused layout and a sloppy printing job will immediately alert the voter to your lack of organizational and administrative skills. And remember KISS—keep it simple stupid—simply because printers do make mistakes; the less the complexity, the less chance for error.

Finding a Good Printer

Selecting a good printer is like finding a good doctor or mechanic. Start by asking around for names from political friends and associates. You'll want to find the best service for the lowest prices and you'll see that prices will vary considerably. When Georgette Morphis took over as newsletter editor for the Amherst, New York Democratic Committee, she found that it was worthwhile to pay a little more for a printer who would work closely with her and take the time to give her advice.

John Molloy was that printer. The cousin of Jimmy Molloy, the Doorkeeper of the House of Representatives, John was firmly ingrained in local, state, and national politics by the time he opened his small printing business in the suburbs of Buffalo, New York. John Molloy might not always have the capabilities to print what a candidate wants, but he can refer him to larger printers or specialists if necessary.

"But before I do," he says, "I'd probably first talk to them about other options. Sometimes they think they need something that might not be necessary such as prenumbered raffle tickets. I've never been to a political drawing where someone pulls a stub out of a hat and reads off the number. They always read the winner's name and address. I could print and perforate raffle tickets for them without numbers and save them $15 to $18 per thousand. For a small politician who never knows how much is in the coffers, saving that kind of money can be very important."

Because he knows his customers and is familiar with the image that they are trying to project, John Molloy can also raise important questions when he thinks the candidate is getting off track. "If someone asked me where they could buy novelty items, I could tell them," he says, "but first I might ask the guy if he thinks his image will be enhanced or destroyed by having his name on a balloon."

Aside from the personal touch, there are other important considerations in choosing a printer. One is whether to use a union or a non-union print shop. Union printers are usually more expensive, but the extra cost is worth it if your campaign depends on labor support and donations. If you decide to use a union printer, be sure to ask for the union "bug" or label to be printed on all your material. This is a little marking which shows that your literature was printed in a union shop.

Before a printer can give you an estimate, he will have to know exactly what you want. Here are some of the questions you'll have to answer:

Is the material camera-ready? If it's not, the printer will want to know whether it has to be typeset, if there will be any photos, whether he will have to do the final layout or mechanical, etc.

What kind of paper do you want to use? You will have to select the finish of the paper (glossy, textured, smooth, etc.) and the weight of the paper. In general, the weight determines the thickness of the paper (coated stock is the exception—it has a very low thickness-to-weight ratio). In general, the heavier the paper, the more expensive it will be. The printer should have paper samples for you to examine. If you need very short runs—100 or so—sample paper may be donated by the printer.

What size will the finished pieces be? You will save money if you use standard sizes—$8\frac{1}{2}$" by 11", $8\frac{1}{2}$" by 14", and 11" by 17". These standard sizes can be folded to create a booklet or brochure.

What colors will you use? You will have to select a color of paper and a color of ink. When choosing colors, keep in mind that different colors elicit different reactions from people. Pinks, blues and greens tend to be calming. Reds and oranges tend to be inflammatory. Red, white and blue looks patriotic and is very "political," but tends to be overdone. The more colors of ink you use, the more you'll pay. You can create a two-color effect by using colored ink on colored paper—for example green ink on yellow paper (but watch those head shots—yhccch!). Whatever colors you choose, use them on all of your printed campaign material with the exception of direct mail letters.

How long is the piece? The printer will need to know how many pages it will be. If you have too much copy, he might suggest having certain parts of your text reduced photographically or reset in a smaller typeface. This will cost extra and if you're trying to economize, you're probably better off cutting some of your verbiage.

Will the piece be printed on one side or both sides of the paper? This is important from a cost and a scheduling standpoint. Most small printers do not have "perfecting" presses that print both sides of a piece on one run through the press. If the piece is to be printed on both sides, the printer will have to do one side first, let it dry, then print the other side. For each side you will have to pay for printing set-up costs.

Do you want any finishing work done? Any additional work such as varnishing, numbering, perforating, cutting, folding, collating, stapling, and binding will cost extra. You can save money (but usually no time) by having your campaign workers do this extra finishing work.

When getting estimates, call commercial printers and quick-copy printers. Both use a photo offset process, but the commercial printer uses metal plates while the quick copy printer uses paper or plastic plates. The main difference between the two is cost and capability. The best of the small quick-copier's work will always be better than the worst of the commercial printers

Use a commercial printer for large quantity runs over 15,000 or 20,000, or when you want slick four color process work which reproduces flesh tones and a variety of colors. A commercial printer can print on larger sizes of paper than can a quick-copy printer and probably has wider capability to do signs, bumper stickers, and tabloids.

A quick-copy printer does not usually use skilled labor. It's usually a family-run business and, while their capabilities are more limited, they are often faster and less expensive.

Working with Your Printer

Always give your printer ample lead time to do your work. A printer has to schedule his press time and his set-up time. Don't expect 24 hour service.

If the printer has to typeset your piece, he'll want you to proofread the typesetting. It's a good idea to take someone with you to help. One reads out loud, including punctuations, from the original copy, while the other checks the accuracy of the typesetting. Be sure to show up to proofread when the printer tells you to. If you're a day late, your finished material will also be a day late. Also, because of "slotting" (his scheduling of your work), you may not get on press for a week—and that's lost time. Remember, once you've proofread the copy, the printer is responsible only for his errors. Double-check names and numbers, especially. Mistakes are embarrassing. They're also expensive if the piece has to be reprinted because of a glaring error. One final piece of advice: don't forget to check headlines—just because it's big doesn't mean it can't be wrong!

Don't be afraid to ask your printer for suggestions. He might have good ideas on how you can crop photos, change type sizes, or use different types of paper and color insets for the greatest impact.

Be prepared to pay cash for your material when you pick it up. Some printers will ask for a deposit and even all the money in advance. It's not unreasonable when you consider that most printers have had at least one bad experience with a candidate who ran up large bills and then never paid after a lost election.

Some Money-Saving Tips

Here is a recap of some of the money-saving ideas in this article:

- Figure quantities carefully. Under-orders and reruns cost extra money.
- Pre-test your ideas before you print large quantities to make sure that your message is clear.
- Use student interns to do your artwork and layout.
- Have your film printed on contact sheets and then decide which pictures you want to blow up.
- Always use standard sizes of paper.
- Ask your printer for money-saving ideas.
- Use campaign workers to do the finishing work on your pieces, such as folding, collating, stapling, etc.
- Don't let your material sit on the shelf. You paid for it. Get it into the hands of the voter.

Some Printing Terms You Should Know

Bleed: When the ink extends to the edge of the page.

Camera-Ready: When your material is ready to be photographed in the photo offset printing process. No additional artwork or preparation is necessary.

Color Inserts: A technique used for emphasis in letters and brochures. One color, such as blue, is used for the text except in certain areas where a second color, such as red, is used for impact.

Condensed Type: Type can be condensed or pushed closer together if there is a need to fit more words per line in either texts, headlines, or both.

Copy: The text of the written piece.

Crop: To cut off unnecessary parts of a photo.

Dummy: Any sketched or pasted-up preliminary layout of a piece to be printed.

Extended Type: Type that is wider than normal.

Four-Color Process: A printing process where four colors of ink are used on the press at the same time to create a variety of tones and colors.

Glossy: A shiny rather than a matte finish.

Gutter: The inside margin on a folded piece.

Halftones: A photo must be made into a halftone before it can be printed. The process reduces the picture to thousands of tiny dots which you can see only if you look at the halftone with a magnifying glass. The printer will take care of having your half-tones made for you.

Justified Columns: A typeset column that has even margins on both sides. Most typewritten pages are justified only on the left-hand margin.

Layout: A detailed sketch of how your finished piece will look. It shows placement of headlines, photos, and text.

Letterpress: A method of printing from letters or type rather than from an engraved or photographic plate.

Light Table: A special table used by some commercial artists, which beams light from a light source beneath the work surface up through the mechanical, to facilitate accurate paste-up.

Mechanical: The final layout of a piece on which the headlines, photos, and typesetting are glued in place, ready to be photographed.

Paper Stock: The type of paper, its color, weight, and texture.

Photo Offset: A printing process whereby a photograph is taken of the mechanical or original copy. This photo is then transferred to a metal, paper, or plastic plate. The plate is set up on the press and the image is transferred form the plate to a rubber pad and then transferred to the paper from the pad or "blanket."

Paste-Up: Another word for "mechanical" but usually confined to work to be printed by offset - lithography.

Reductions: Reducing the size of a photograph but retaining the original proportions. Also, if you have more copy than will fit on a regular page, the printer can photographically reduce it to make it fit.

Reverse: When ink surrounds the letters on the paper so that it appears to be white letters in a colored box.

Typesetting: A special process to set type in justified columns, print bold face, italics, and variety of type sizes.

✓ Choosing and Using Campaign Promotional Materials
Leonard L. Lucchi

So you're running for office and you say the reason is that you know how to fix the problems of your state; you're the one with the plan; you're Captain Sincerity! But we know the real reason you're running. You've always wanted to see your name plastered on the side of large, red balloons.

Don't be shy, that's a better reason than some. The day after filing, you will be deluged with requests from the vendors of political materials. Everyone claims to know the key to your victory. You will be swamped with unsolicited campaign advice from friends, acquaintances, and even total strangers who now say they are your friends.

"You must buy huge, full-color posters with extra strength cardboard." And even: "You can't win unless you pass out packets of sunflower seeds!"

Buttons, bumper stickers, signs, shirts, hats, balloons, pens, combs ... all that jazz: They're called campaign paraphernalia, novelties, or hoopla. They are accessories for the well-dressed campaign. But what is right for YOUR campaign? What is too little and what is too much? This is mainly a question of money.

Every campaign has to make critical decisions about how to spend its money, and for most campaigns, donations are very hard to come by. Every time you buy two balloons, you are choosing against sending one more piece of direct mail to one more registered household. Are you making those decisions within the framework of a strategic plan? In a campaign, you must:

A. Maximize the direct communication of your theme to voting households, primarily through television, radio, direct mail, and door-to-door canvassing, and
B. Get more resources (i.e., money and volunteers' time) to increase (A).

When making decisions about whether to invest in "all that jazz," ask how it will help maximize communication or raise resources. Here are some examples:

Energizing Your Supporters

Most people helping out your campaign will be working for free.

You want them to be happy. You need them to smile while handing out your brochures. And what do they want for their trouble (besides pizza)? Buttons! Bumper stickers! Baseball caps!

In one of my most recent campaigns, every election day poll worker was given a T-Shirt. For a few days, campaign headquarters looked like "the clothing store from Hell."

Get this straight—these hoopla items do not persuade voters. But, when used in moderation, they can improve campaign morale and increase the quantity and quality of your volunteer resources.

Creating a Campaign Image

Most voters of sound mind do NOT go around the district counting lawn signs to determine the relative merits of the candidates. But the press and political insiders, who affect endorsements and campaign contributions, are not required to be of sound mind.

While managing one race, I "targeted" a key newspaper reporter. Our campaign couldn't afford much, so I found out where he lived and plastered his block with signs. Surely enough, within one week he wrote a story about what a great campaign organization we had!

A candidate waving a banner at the morning rush-hour traffic will not persuade the weary commuter that she is an intellectual (in fact, it may have the opposite effect), but she will develop the image of an energetic campaigner.

Yard signs, car-top signs, and banners (a.k.a. "visibilities") rarely communicate a campaign theme, but they will make voters more likely to pay attention to your television, radio, and/or direct mail.

Leaving A Reminder

Many campaigns use "keepers." These are items like refrigerator magnets, notepads, pencils, calendars, or shopping bags. They are supposed to have some utility so that the voters will want to keep them around. If they keep the item, they keep the candidate's name. Keepers tend to be expensive, so don't waste them on non-voters. Either enclose them in direct mail or hand them out while canvassing door to door.

Of course, keepers are for long-term name recognition. So it does not make any sense to distribute them just a week or two before the election. Generally, give out keepers BEFORE the voters are paying attention to your race, and then when they start to tune in they'll remember your name.

Here are two exceptions:

A. Write-in candidates might distribute specially printed pencils on election day to help voters remember what and where to write-in, and

B. If you hand out small tree saplings door-to-door in order to underscore your concern for the environment, you might do it late in the campaign to ensure that they don't die before election day!

Raising Money

Major contributors don't write their checks in order to receive a trinket. But your fundraising heavy hitters deserve an exclusive reward for their efforts. It certainly will make them more receptive when you go back to that same contributor later on and ask her to max out.

One of our statewide campaigns had exclusive lapel pins made up for the largest donors. It became a status symbol and encouraged others to become big donors. Likewise, campaign balloons, fans and hats will not increase attendance at your next big fundraising event, but they may help your contributors have a good time and want to attend future events. Just remember, don't spend too much money on overhead for your fundraiser— you need that money for direct voter communications. No matter what the purpose, here are seven rules to live by when ordering buttons, stickers, and "all that jazz...."

Budget Smart: Don't drain your campaign coffers to pay for novelty items when you haven't yet raised the money for adequate direct mail, radio, and/or television. Novelties are like a cook's spices: if lightly sprinkled, they can lend a wonderful flavor to your campaign; if overdone, you can ruin the whole thing.

Use a Consistent Logo: Develop a unique, striking logo to be used on every piece of printed material, especially all campaign paraphernalia. Make it recognizable from a distance. Write your last name large because voters are most likely to remember just that one word.

Use Fresh Colors and Type Styles: You're never going to stand out from the crowd with posters painted red, white, and blue. Look at the Pantone color chart and hit the voters with colors that

Don't Copy the Other Guy: Don't do it because everyone else does. The worst reason for buying wooden nickels with your photo on the back is that the other side already did it. You have to do something different or you won't stand out. Make your campaign novelty items clever and different.

Don't Overbuy: A few years ago, I was involved in a well-financed campaign. We had all types of signs, stickers, and banners. But a search on the morning after election day revealed cartons holding thousands of unused items. These items didn't do the candidate any good— and they made lousy Christmas presents.

Be a Smart Consumer: Shop around and find the best price for the quantity you need. Don't be afraid to go out of state. Make sure you understand all the charges—typesetting, reverses, halftones, and color matches may cost more. National vendors of campaign paraphernalia are often cheaper than local printers, but do your own comparison.

Don't Expect an Immediate Reaction: You're in the heat of the campaign. You notice an opponent's bumper-sticker a block down the street. Voters do not notice. It takes repetition, and then more repetition, before they do.

Now is the time to take the pledge: "I will not buy campaign hoopla unless it is tied to a strategic objective of the campaign. "Before ordering anything, I will always ask myself WHYS. "If the answer is consistent with our campaign plan and budget, and if it will help maximize direct voter communication of our theme or increase campaign resources, then we'll GO FOR IT!

✓ Effective Campaign Photography
Jeff Crosby and Scott Newton

It was 10 a.m. and the Fed Ex package had just arrived.

The envelope contained our client's picture, which, according to the campaign manager, was a "great" 5 x 7 glossy.

We gathered around in anticipation as the envelope was opened. We screamed in horror as the photo came into view.

The candidate's smile looked more like a grimace. The camera's flash had cast a ghostly pallor on his face. He looked like a constipated corpse.

We wanted to trash it and get another photo, but election day was near and it was too late to change. So, a few days later about 5,000 voters were asked to vote for our constipated corpse. They didn't.

It didn't have to be that way. The gruesome shot could have been avoided—if the campaign had taken the time and money to hire a skilled professional photographer.

As a service to the electorate and our colleagues, the following is a primer on how to get powerful photographs of the candidate and avoid the constipated corpse.

Understand photography's purpose.

A political photograph must meet two tests:

1. It must be arresting enough to grab the readers' attention and lure them into reading the copy. Innovative angles, lighting and scenes help reach this goal.
2. It must deliver the campaign message. You don't have to be a brain surgeon to get this done, but you do need to think about it.

For example, if the candidate needs to look like a strong leader, show him or her talking forcefully to a voter. If, however, you want the candidate to look like someone who is in touch, show him or her listening.

In this anti-political era, avoid political clichés, which confirm that you are a politician. Get rid of the Lindsayesque coat over the shoulder. No more Jimmy Carter-grins; leave them to used car salesmen.

Instead, go for the approachable. Have him or her look directly into the camera. Or, perhaps, have the candidate talking with a voter, especially a person representative of your target audience. Make the candidate look like a real person, not just another Bob or Mary Forehead.

"A picture is worth a thousand words," according to the old maxim. It's up to you decide which words.

Decide what you need.

Assuming you have a message, now count the number of pictures needed. To answer that question, you need to know how many print pieces you are doing and their formats.

Are you simply doing one palm card? Then you only need a portrait of the candidate. Are you doing several mailers, each with a large format and several pictures of the candidate? Do you want to put the candidate in situations which illustrate his or her stand on an issue?

If the answer is yes, then you need to estimate how many pictures you need and start planning.

Hire a photographer who's a pro.

Once you've decided what you need, now you can begin looking for a photographer. Forget the candidate's brother-in-law, Billy Earl, who took just "darling" photos of little Billy Earl, Jr. last summer. Get a pro.

And not just any pro. The photographer needs to be able to work on-the-run like a photojournalist, yet also has the ability to capture political symbolism. And it helps if the photographer can work with politicians. Respectful, but unawed, is the best approach.

If you don't know someone who fits this description, check with local PR and advertising types, even the yellow pages. Assemble a list of three to five and start interviewing.

Before the appointment, tell them:

1. The number of different photos, or set-ups, needed.
2. Whether it's black and white or color photography. Likely, it will be black and white. Don't try to convert color photos to black and white.

3. You want to look at the photographer's prints and contact sheets (contact sheets show entire rolls of film on one page). Contact sheets are a good way to find out if the photographer "works" the shoot by using several different angles and lighting situations. The more the photographer works a shoot, the more likely a good shot will come out of it.

And ask the following questions:

1. What's the hourly rate and charge for film and contact sheets? Is there a minimum?
2. What's the turnaround time for producing them?
3. Given the scope of work, how long will it take to do the shoot?

In the interview, get an estimate of the time needed for the shoot and thus an estimated total cost. Assume the photographer will want a check for time and expenses upon delivery of the contact sheets. Prints will be paid for as needed.

Plan the shoot and schedule.

Now that you have the photographer, you need to set a schedule.

If you need several set-ups at different locations and with several people involved, you will need a few days to round up people and set the sites. Get signed releases from civilians.

Here's a rule of thumb on time. An outdoor set-up will take 30-45 minutes. Allow an extra thirty minutes to set up and tear down lights for an indoor shoot.

Consult with the photographer throughout to ensure that you have not created a problem in the schedule.

Do not let the candidate and the photographer go out without a keeper. The shoot should be supervised by someone with political sense.

Suppose that the candidate is making a big issue out of foreign trade. It's not the photographer's responsibility to know that the Nissan in the background will make the candidate look like an idiot. It's yours.

And here's a few other tips:

- Very few people—even candidates—enjoy having their picture taken. To put the candidate at ease, explain what you are trying to accomplish and how the schedule will work before the shoot.
- When shooting with people, avoid grip and grins, those old-style shots with the candidate shaking hands with someone and grinning at the camera. Instead, capture communication by shooting over the candidate's or voter's shoulder and focus on the other's face.
- When shooting with people, you need managed spontaneity. By that, we mean they need to be put in their places, but from there let them carry on a natural conversation. That way, you'll capture genuine facial expressions and body language.
- Don't let the candidate stand square to the camera. This looks stilted. Instead, have him or her stand with one foot forward, with a slight shoulder turn. This creates movement and dynamism.
- Glasses, especially the Coke bottle variety, are a big problem. Light reflects off them and they can make eyes look the size of golf balls. You might try getting duplicate frames without the lenses, although this trick sometimes renders the candidate dull-eyed.

- Be aware that mid-day light is tough for outdoor shots. Early morning or late afternoon provides the best portrait lighting.

If you have found the right photographer and planned and managed the shoot well, you should come out with some good photographs. You are not out of the woods yet, however.

Several years ago, a candidate running for Texas State Senate (not one of ours) put out a tabloid which contained a picture of him standing beside his prized stallion. Changing the names to protect the silly, the caption read: "Representative Snort on left, his horse Trigger on right."

Pay attention to details and plan thoroughly, and you'll avoid getting your candidates confused with horses—or constipated corpses.

✓ Maximizing Use of Your Logo
Becky West

Voters base their decisions on issues and the competence of candidates, right?

Wrong. In the real world, how a candidate is packaged often matters more. In the voter's mind, image carries as much weight as experience, and effective packaging begins with the candidate's logo.

Between TV commercials, direct mail, newspaper ads, signs, bumper stickers, lapel pins, and solicitation letters, a candidate's logo is a common denominator that ties the campaign together visually. And with so much exposure, it's vital that a logo convey the proper image. That image can imply that your campaign is well-financed and organized, and that you're going to win. It can even help scare away possible opposition early on.

Plan for simplicity. An effective logo needs only the candidate's name, the office sought, and possibly a simple graphic symbol such as a star, a check-mark or a flag. The name should be the most prominent element. If a symbol is used, be careful that it doesn't distract from the candidate's name. Campaign slogans, even short ones, should be saved for brochures and other materials.

Typefaces often impart messages themselves, so pay particular attention to the type style used to highlight the candidate's name. Consider your voting audience in the formula. Is the typeface businesslike and professional, or is it casual and artsy? Is it masculine or feminine? Does it look conservative and traditional, or progressive and innovative? Will it look equally good on signs, campaign fliers, lapel stickers and contribution letters? Is it legible, up close and from a distance?

The choice of logo colors will enhance your logo design. Again, the key goal is legibility, but as with most campaign decisions, cost must be considered.

Where printing costs must be held to a minimum, a one-color logo in a deep, rich shade is often best. Almost as cost effective is the two-color logo, with black and another color. Most campaign literature with photos, unless printed in expensive four-color process, will require the use of black for the halftones. (Few candidates look their best in shades of blue, green, red, or purple.)

In newsprint, the judicious use of spot color with black copy is both powerful and cost effective. (The logo color can also be used to highlight a strong headline or the campaign slogan.)

Probably the most conspicuous use of your candidate's logo will be on signs. Here, the background color, and how it works with the logo's color, is important. Will campaign signs be located mostly in grassy lawns, along the highway or on cluttered city streets?

We've found that—especially in residential suburbs—white is a good, clean background that "pops" well amidst foliage and other signs.

However, for campaigns waged primarily in urban districts, a brighter color such as yellow stands out better. And, along dusty rural backroads against brown farmland, a richer background color with reversed type is most effective.

Keep in mind that background color is also important on miscellaneous items such as lapel pins and bumper stickers. Lapel pins with white backgrounds are not only easily read in person, but also often show up clearly in newspaper photos.

Whether or not your candidate has future offices in mind, design the logo for long-term use. In future campaigns, this strategy will pay off in voter recognition and will save valuable marketing dollars and time for other projects.

Logo No-Nos

- District I.D.s are a logo clutterer, as many voters don't know offhand what district they're in. All signs, direct mail, etc., are distributed in the candidate's district, anyway, so unless the candidate is running for an at-large position, don't include "District #94" on the logo.
- Watch for sexist terminology. For instance, substitute "City Council" for "City Councilman."
- In choosing colors, consider local sports rivalries. In Alabama, for instance, diplomacy would dictate staying away from the Crimson Tide's red/white and Auburn's blue/orange combinations.

In a competitive political climate, informed citizens may vote for a candidate based on issues. However, uninformed or undecided voters will often choose the candidate whose name and packaging are most memorable. To make sure your candidate has that "top-of-mind" voter awareness, a powerful logo is the best place to start.

✓ Crafting an Effective Personal Image
Larry Cole

Political campaign materials have interested me since I was a boy. At one time, I even collected campaign buttons. However, few campaign advertisements have ever entertained me as much as the one circulated by a candidate for the Tennessee Public Service Commission in the 1990 general election.

On the front of the card, which is about 4 inches by $6\frac{1}{2}$ inches, there is a picture of a genial-looking older man with a broad smile wearing a large, knotted tie. His name is at the card's top, and his first ambiguous statement is at the bottom. It reads: "Red Tape Is Killing the Little People."

Now I think I know what the candidate was trying to imply by using this phrase. However, in my mind I still have visions of midgets smothering in yards and yards of giant red tape. Then I wonder what this candidate thought the PSC could do about smothering midgets.

On the card's back are some really dubious statements. The first one that caught my eye says: "Stop small trucker harassment, which already has driven many small men out of business." Does this mean that large trucker harassment should be allowed to continue?

But, more important, how tall can a trucker be? Would this candidate, had he been elected, have asked the PSC to set out in its rules and regulations the dimensions of a small trucker? And how did he know that harassment has driven many small men out of the trucking business? Could the reason they left, if they did, really have been that their little legs just weren't long enough to reach the pedals?

Another statement that probably caused the then-existing Public Service Commission employees a great deal of concern is this line: "Immediately restore good employee moral by inserting Civil Service." Unless this is just a typographical misspelling of the word morale, the candidate must have thought that the employees were immoral and therefore hell-bound. But the candidate's remedy sounds like a terrible thing to endure. As he says, he wants to "insert Civil Service." My Webster's New World Dictionary definition of the word insert says: "to put or fit (something) into something else."

The fact that the candidate did not get the opportunity to bring his remedy about must have given the employees great relief. No doubt some employees had a horrible vision that, if this candidate had been elected, one day a Supervisor would come into the office and say, "Bend over everybody, today they're coming to insert civil service." One statement by the candidate sent me to the dictionary. His proposal was to "Get the mollycoddlers out of the PSC." I guess he had planned on doing this between insertions of civil service.

Not being familiar with this word, I imagined that the mollycoddlers were some kind of inspectors who were being nice to big— railroads and big truckers. But I was surprised to discover that Webster's says a mollycoddler is "a man or boy used to being coddled, or protected, pampered, etc.; milksop." A cross-reference found milksop defined as "a person who is timid, ineffectual, effeminate, etc."

It's probably a good thing that some of the more rugged-type PSC employees didn't bother to get out their dictionaries and look up this definition during the campaign, or the candidate might have found himself the object of some manly physical abuse. But what does it matter now?

The election is over. He lost. He is not a commissioner. All the inserting that he proposed to do will not be done by him. And I hope nobody else will do it either.

✓ Paper Drive: Seven Ways to Use Newspaper Ads
Ron Faucheux

"Do you realize we're living in a time," recently posited a cynical media observer, "when almost everybody reads a newspaper, and the only thing they believe are the ads?"

As television exploded in importance as a political communications medium, newspaper ads waned as a tool of campaigning. But with cheaper and faster desktop print production capability and new discount plans for political candidates, newspaper is getting a second look around the country as campaigns and their media buyers move toward election day.

As you plan for your final two, three, or four-week push before election day, here are some ideas for effective use of newspaper ads:

1. Endorsement Listings.

If you need to show that your candidacy has won important endorsements, particularly when their number exceeds single digits, then newspaper is an ideal way to display this broadened support.

Examples abound. If you had primary opposition that has since come on board in the general election, a newspaper ad is a good way to show party unity. If you're labor-backed, and want to show that you also have business support, an ad cataloging the signatures of key corporate leaders would be a good way to accomplish that task. If your opponent is supported by large environmental groups, you may want to use a newspaper ad to highlight the endorsements you've received from credible environmentalists who may not be affiliated with those groups. The possible strategic usage's of endorsement ads go on and on. It depends on your situation and strategy.

2. Attack document

Ever try to write a 30-second attack TV spot that needs to contain complex charges and convincing documentation? It's a tough job squeezing into that short time frame the information necessary to explain your argument and to back it up with pertinent facts and source citations.

The ideal way to launch an effective media attack is to do a mix of electronic media (TV and radio) plus newspaper advertising. Newspaper ads can provide details and documentation, in easy-to read, believable black and white text, the way short TV and radio spot announcements can't hope to do.

3. Comparison shopping.

Newspaper ads offer a perfect vehicle to provide point-by-point comparisons between you and your opponent. If you want to show, for example, the many qualifications you have as a candidate as opposed to the scant credentials of your opponent, a newspaper ad provides an excellent visual frame. Candidate A who has 15 lines of copy next to his or her "civic involvement" section makes a strong counterpoint to Candidate B who has only three lines of copy for the same thing.

4. Targeted appeals.

As campaign communications becomes more targeted, direct mail has gained favor as an instrument for individualized campaign messages. But direct mail, when used in large quantities, can be expensive. In some cases, when you're trying to reach a specific region or audience segment, a targeted newspaper ad can be an efficient and less expensive substitute.

For example, if you want to tell voters who live in Madison County that you are opposed to a proposed hazardous waste site in their area, and there's a strong weekly or daily newspaper that covers the entire county, then doing an ad in that paper may be the most cost-effective way to get that information out to those voters.

5. Always on a Sunday.

The advantage of direct mail is its ability to communicate individually targeted campaign messages by household. When you have the available funds and the right lists for direct contact campaigning, it can be extremely effective. But it has its limits as does every medium. If you're timing a mail piece to hit in the last few days before a Tuesday election, you may find that Sundays—when no mail is delivered—creates a problem. Dropping a mail piece timed to hit on the Saturday or Monday before the election may be a tricky proposition. An ad in the Sunday newspaper, on the other hand, provides security in that you'll know when your message will hit.

Depending upon budget constraints, newspaper can be used as a substitute for direct voter contact where appropriate or it can be used as part of a weekend media mix along with direct mail and even telephone contact follow-up for maximum impact.

6. Advertise last-minute TV programs or rallies.

As election day approaches, many campaigns will purchase TV program time to air 5, 15, or 30 minute programs on network affiliates or even longer town-hall type meetings produced for lower cost cable TV slots. In the right setting, these programs can be effective. But for them to be, they must be seen. In many cases, candidates have found newspaper an efficient way to promote TV programs, particularly because they can often be placed in the TV section of a local weekly or daily paper.

Newspaper is also a good way to invite people to attend rallies and other public events that are more likely to attract large audiences in the last weeks before election day.

7. Turnout messages and election information.

Voters often turn to newspaper articles, editorials, sample ballots, and voter guides to fill out their own tickets either on election day or right before. If for no other reason, running ads in election day newspaper editions may be the best way to deliver your final message at the voter decision point.

Newspaper ads geared to voter turnout can also be effective, particularly since many voters read newspapers early in the morning and it serves as a prod to vote. Newspaper also provides enough space to list election information such as absentee voting rules, polling place location, dates and times.

In elections with a large number of state and local ballot propositions and bond issues, newspaper advertising is important because it gives voters a chance to see the actual ballot, to hold it in his or her own hands, and to become familiar with the ballot line-up before walking into the voting booth.

✓ Do It On Your Desktop: Using Electronic Publishing
Karen Booth

Back in the mid-80's, desktop publishing (DTP)—the ability to write, design and print final output of publishable material with computers—was a cottage industry that seemed destined to become the sole domain of computer nerds, resume typesetters and aspiring artists eager to doodle in new creative avenues. With those new programs you could draw boxes, manipulate type a little, and do simple illustrations, but not much more. For those of us at ground zero, it was nearly impossible to envision government, universities and big business ultimately embracing something we thought was just... well, fun.

Today, electronic desktop publishing has grown up and gotten serious. The technology has become faster, more sophisticated and more affordable, even for the smallest office or campaign. The computer industry has spawned an incredible array of software programs that morph images, edit videotape and sound, and lay out pages with full-color photos, complex illustrations and thousands of different typestyles. Anyone can become a one-person publisher with a computer, scanner, printer and the right software.

Publishing and Politics

In many ways, DTP is ideal for the world of political campaigning. Whether you decide to invest in the equipment and staff to produce all materials in-house or to hire a service bureau to do the design for you project by project, desktop publishing is the fastest, most cost-effective way to design and print your material. It's a technology that every campaign and political professional should be taking advantage of now.

Two key issues will help you determine how best to desktop publish: quantity and complexity. Simple projects, such as a one-color flyer on colored paper or a black and white newspaper ad, can be put together with the simplest hardware/software combination.

Ongoing projects that require more expertise and fancier software, like direct mail pieces with photos or a two-color newsletter, should prompt you to think about buying your own system. If you can answer 'yes' to most of the following checklist, you may be a candidate for investing in your own DTP system:

- Will I need daily or weekly design of flyers, invitations, forms, direct mail letters, print ads, press releases, signs, bumper strips and other materials?
- Will there be an ongoing use for the system after my campaign/project is over?
- Can I find a staffer to do in-house design?
- Will I spend less money doing desktop publishing in-house than hiring an outside service bureau or designer to do it for me?

Of course, not everyone can or should shell out thousands of dollars to buy a DTP system and hire a designer. In fact, many larger campaigns who could, shouldn't because of infrequent need or existing consultants. Your DTP needs should be carefully evaluated before you consider making such an investment in equipment and staff.

Modern campaigns must be nimble and able to respond rapidly to the day's events to gain a competitive edge. Desktop publishing can contribute enormously to the adaptability of your campaign. Three different ways to utilize desktop publishing are outlined below:

Do it yourself with your own computer system. Buying and using your own DTP system has obvious advantages: control, proximity, and turnaround time. Both Macintosh and PC systems (IBMs and compatibles) are fully capable of desktop publishing, although some older PC models are not. You can set up exactly the type of system you need for the design you'll be producing and have much greater control over the final product.

Do it yourself with someone else's computer system. A second option is to use a rent-by-the-hour DTP system. Many full-service bureaus and copy centers also offer self-service computer rental by the hour. You can hire a staffer who is proficient with graphic design software on a DTP system to do the work as needed. This is a good relatively inexpensive choice if you'll only need occasional design work.

Remember: in addition to the hourly rental rate, service bureaus will charge you for every piece of paper you use, every scan, and (often) any help required from their staff.

Hire an outside designer. A costlier way to publish using desktop computers is to hire a service bureau to typeset and design your materials. Many copy shops now have full-service DTP departments and can design anything from the smallest flyer to books and special-fold brochures. Service bureaus typically charge less for design than freelance graphic designers, but the quality of their design work can vary drastically. Ask to see samples of their work before you hand over your project.

Setting Up Your Own System

If you decide to buy the computers and software to create your own in-house desktop publishing system, here's a quick list of recommendations to get the ball rolling. One indispensable piece of advice: rely on word of mouth.

1. Find a reliable computer vendor. Get a recommendation from a friend or colleague whose company does in-house desktop publishing and find out where they bought their equipment. Nothing beats word of mouth when looking for trustworthy computer sellers.
2. Decide which type of computers you want—Macintosh or IBM/compatible. If you don't already have a preference, you'll find vociferous advocates for both types of machines. Most high-end digital artists are loyal to the Macintosh, but in truth, both types of computers can perform design functions equally well. What type of computer system you decide on will determine the bells and whistles like the scanner, CD-ROM drive, etc. and the type of software you'll buy.
3. Decide what type of software you'll need. You'll need the three basics: word processing, a graphics program for scans and illustrations, and a page layout program to pull it all together. For the Macintosh, the combination of Microsoft Word (word processing), Quark Xpress (page layout), Adobe Illustrator (illustration) and Adobe Photoshop (scans, photo manipulation) has devout users world-wide. These four programs can span the spectrum of design, form a basic postcard to the most complex four-color layout with photo manipulation. IBM designers tend to stick with CorelDraw for illustration, Quark Xpress for page layout and WordPerfect for word processing.

4. Hire someone to be your designer. Although there is no magic formula for finding the right person, most recent college graduates (and many other folks, too) have at least a working knowledge of the most common DTP programs.

Too many people make the unfortunate decision to literally do it themselves because it looks easy. Resist that temptation unless you're schooled in design or want a new career as a digital designer. Rome wasn't built in a day ... and PageMaker can't be learned in one either.

After you've made the decisions and jumped onboard the desktop publishing bandwagon, you'll wonder how you ever got along without it. And, you'll find those ghastly old rub-on letters and blue-lined art boards to be quaint reminders of an era (thankfully) gone by.

11

Candidate Preparation and Presentation

★ ★ ★

✓ Looking Good: Why a Candidate's Appearance Makes a Big Difference
Lillian Brown

When all eyes are upon you, your clothes have the first word. They silently introduce you before you say anything. Their purpose is to form a framework to present you and your message. Your clothing should not overpower you nor detract from your message.

Practice good investment dressing. You need a few good, plain garments that can go anywhere, anytime and adapt to many situations. Select good fabrics, perfect fit and classic look. Keep your image in mind at all times, choosing clothes that fit your present and future positions.

Use color to enhance the color of your eyes, skin and hair. Variations of light and dark blue are pleasant and stable colors, especially for the cameras. Other good choices are grey, burgundy, teal, purple, rust, taupe, and olive green. (Some of these colors, obviously, are for women only.) Red bleeds on camera and is overpowering; black is harsh and makes one look older; white flares, glares and adds weight.

Stay with one color scheme when you travel. Carry a variety of mix-and-match accessories to take you through the entire day's activities. List every function from morning until night, and carry only what you need. To eliminate baggage hassles, carry everything in a bag on wheels that fits into the overhead compartment on the plane.

A note about glasses: light can be a "kicker" on your glasses that will obscure your eyes. Have the lenses coated with a non-glare material. Choose frames with a dull finish that are not shiny. Heavy frames may obscure the cheekbones, so consider those that are rimless on the bottom. Heavy black plastic frames should be avoided. Also avoid tinted lenses; they make anyone look like a "shady character," especially on camera.

Dressing the Female Candidate

You need a few good suits with a variety of blouses and scarves to take you from breakfast to dinner. A navy blue blazer is a good, reliable addition to any political wardrobe. Grey outfits may sound boring, but can actually provide an attractive neutral frame for your face. Keep in mind the appropriate color choices for the still and television cameras.

Strive for an unbroken line, with the same color value from head to toe. Avoid bare arms, white hose and spike heels. Also, no stripes, polka dots, bold patterns, big flowered prints or fancy frills. All of these contribute to a "chopped-up look" and subconsciously draw the viewers attention away from your message.

Skirt lengths are a personal thing. You should find the one that works best with your body build and ignore the dictates of fashion. Select skirts that enable you to sit comfortably when facing a room full of people. Remember, you don't want to be distracted with the need to fuss with a hiked up skirt. You want your audience's attention to be on your message and your eyes, not on your thighs!

Wear real jewelry rather than gaudy, eye-boggling costume pieces. Gold-colored jewelry should have a matte, not shiny, finish. Earrings should not be too large. A few good pieces—button earrings, a modest neck chain and a tasteful watch—should suffice. Bracelets can rattle into the microphone. And while pins can add an attractive fashion element to an outfit, they are distracting and bring the viewers' eyes away from your face. When you are dressed, stand in front of the mirror and squint your eyes. If any of your jewelry "jumps out" at you, take it off.

Dressing the Male Candidate

You will need one dark grey suit and one dark blue suit to carry you through a variety of activities. A navy blue blazer can be your best friend when combined with a pair of light and dark grey pants. Checks, plaids and many houndstooth patterned jackets cause a moire pattern on camera and drive the television audience nuts! So even if you like them, give them up during the campaign.

Ties give you a chance to express your individuality; however, they should be discreetly patterned. Choose dark backgrounds with monotone blended colors such as paisleys and foulards. Avoid shiny fabrics, stripes, checks and bold prints. Carry a tried-and-true "television tie" at all times.

Somehow red became fashionable as "the power tie," but red ties bleed on camera and overpower you in person. It is wise to avoid them.

Believe it or not, the appropriate color for shirts is pale gray. Blues and whites don't look as good as gray on the new television cameras. Pale gray photographs white and does not glare against your skin tone. Splurge on a few tailored shirts that fit perfectly at the neck, chest and arms. Select a smooth neat collar, avoiding button downs, which tend to bulge and look rumpled.

Long black socks complete the look—no bare shins should show between the sock and the pants' cuff. Select comfortable black shoes.

Hair for the Female Candidate

Have your hair shaped and layered to fit your head. Adopt a style that you can care for yourself, so you are not dependent on a hairdresser. A natural look is most flattering.

Excessive hair spray will give your hair a stiff "barbed wire look" that is unflattering in camera lights. Hair that clears your shoulders will move with your head and will not break up. Hair that falls below the shoulders carries the eye downward, away from the face.

The ideal hairstyle will withstand wind and adverse conditions.

Never fidget with your hair. If you have to push it out of your face, or endlessly rearrange it, get a new hairstyle.

Allow at least ¾" of space between your hair and eyes so both eyes can be seen. If you color your hair, touch up the roots frequently.

Hair for the Male Candidate

Keep your hairstyle neat and well-trimmed. A good hairstyle should be layered to fit your head, just off the collar in back and covering the top third of your ears. A well-trimmed beard can be effective. It should follow the jawline and widen slightly at the temples where it meets the hairline.

If you choose to wear a mustache, trim it so that the upper lip is visible. People see what you say, as well as hear what you say. Keep the mustache slightly turned upward and confined within the natural laugh lines—it should not droop downward. Also keep it trimmed evenly or your face will look "lopsided" on television and in photos.

Accept baldness graciously. Never pull a long lock of hair across the bald spot. Avoid sunburn and hair spray. To reduce glare, use a touch of invisible translucent powder. Transplants and hair pieces are seldom successful and hard to keep secret.

Makeup for the Female Candidate

Let your makeup enhance your own natural beauty. If you look "made-up," it is too much. Less is best. Emphasize your good points. Indent the cheekbones by placing blush under them, not on them. Enhance the jawline by using a darker contour just under the chin—this is especially important if you are overweight or have a full, round, facial shape.

Use liquid or cream stick base a shade warmer than your face (white-skinned women) or very close to your natural shade (Native American, Asian or African-American women). Many female candidates also like the convenience of the newer creamy bases that come in a compact container.

Eliminate circles under the eyes with a soft creamy liquid or concealer one shade lighter than your base color: Avoid the chalky white look. Circles under the eyes are enhanced by shadows cast by bright top lights. Tilt the chin level with the floor to let the light under the brow.

Make the eyes look larger by using dark gray or warm brown shadow and liner on the upper lid. Never wear bright blue or green eye shadows. Avoid dark smudges and liner on the lower lids. Apply mascara on the upper lash tips only, thereby preventing your mascara from flaking when you blink.

Apply translucent oil control powder for a soft, dull matte finish. Dark-complexioned women should use a matte-finished powder as close to the natural skin tone as possible.

Choose a lipstick color that blends with the inside of your mouth, so that the inside and outside move as one. Avoid the "scarlet slash." In general, a brownish-rose color is the most flattering for fair-skinned women, and a brownish burgundy-red for darker skinned women.

Exaggerated high-fashion makeup does not work well on television. Close-up cameras demand soft, natural, more invisible makeup. Shiny lip gloss catches the light and makes the mouth look abnormally large. Dark lip pencil can be plainly seen, and attracts undue attention to lip movement. Similarly, too much brow pencil can often look odd on camera.

When you are going to do a TV interview, never assume that there will be a makeup artist in the studio. Many stations do not offer makeup services to their guests. Many a candidate has arrived at a studio with a "just washed" face and no makeup in her purse, only to find that there is no makeup artist.

Lights and lenses add 10 pounds and 10 years. They flatten and distort the face and figure. Compensate with soft makeup and carefully selected, plain clothes.

Television Makeup for Men

Television makeup is a necessity to cover a heavy beard, eliminate circles under the eyes and even up the gradations of skin color. Cameras emphasize the beard (even if you've just shaved), perspiration, sunburn or redness.

When no professional makeup person is available, carry a translucent powder compact in medium shade to eliminate the shiny forehead and nose.

Keep hair spray off your skin: it shines like cellophane and resists powder. If you need to use it, spray your fingers instead and use them to smooth the hair.

To control perspiration, try applying a little witch hazel with a cotton ball before makeup. Limiting liquids (especially hot coffee or tea) an hour before your appearance will also help.

If you have a broad brow, sit tall into your key light. Do not lean or hunch over the table or lectern.

✓ Techniques for a Winning Public Image
Drew Kugler

In preparing for a campaign, keep in mind that voters want to support an individual who has communicated competence, composure, and character. Almost every communication behavior affects two and possibly all three of the dimensions simultaneously. Voter perception can be influenced by something like appropriate attire in addition to straight answers and eye contact.

If candidates understand why media communication consultation and coaching are as important to their program to communicate views to voters as paid television advertising, they will be more successful. Surveys show that people believe character is the greatest shortcoming of most politicians. While this stereotype may be unfair, it is a dominant perception.

One character-killer is an indirect, rambling answer to questions. Red flags will continue to wave in the minds of voters until candidates eliminate opening phrases such as "well, let me say this" followed by convoluted answers that are seen as dodging the question.

The voter does not trust such responses. Direct and logically structured answers will go a long way to change the stereotype. candidates who choose their strategy carefully will benefit by verbally standing apart from their rambling counterparts.

Additionally, eye contact is critical. Great value can be found in creating the perception of "looking someone squarely in the eye." How is a voter supposed to feel anything but distrust when a candidate's eyes seemed yanked by a bungie cord to the pages before him?

With major political addresses, from the Oval Office to the Convention dais, the prompter is strategically placed so as to create the perception of eye contact with the viewing voter. Unfortunately, many candidates do not have the good fortune to suspend the reality of eye gaze with a teleprompter. Candidates lacking such a weapon must increase their preparation and coaching efforts.

A candidate must demonstrate a controlled physical image, especially when put under the white light of pressurized communication. Performance under communication pressure can make or break credibility. The reaction to stress, whether speaking, debating or meeting face-to-face with the public or the press, are moments of truth and must be closely coached and prepared. Competence is the belief that candidates have a grasp of the facts. There are techniques for enhancing this perception in the voter's mind.

The importance of eye contact cannot be overemphasized. Averted glances back at the written page make the candidate seem unprepared. It should, therefore, be the candidate's goal to avoid speech reading, therefore sustaining eye contact. If not, there is the risk of defeating the purpose of giving the speech in the first place—that of enhancing leadership perception.

Another area for concern is the organization of a speech. Voters often criticize candidates for never getting to the point. This perceived inability to clearly explain a position creates negative feelings. Candidates should state a position and then provide explanatory details, not vice-versa. Restrict the initial position summary on an issue to one or two clear sentences, and follow up with supporting explanations.

✓ Effective Speaking Skills
Jeanette Alexander

"What? Presentation skills!?," cry some in the political class, campaign managers included, who still believe the myth that good speakers (and thus, good candidates) can only be born that way. After all, when a campaign's candidate has the quick-witted speaking skills of a four-year-old with his hand caught in the cookie jar, it can only be explained by genetics, right?

Yeah, sure. Let's be realistic. Speaking effectively is about as inherent as driving a car or reading music. It is simply a matter of making an effort to increase one's awareness of what works and what doesn't.

What is effective speaking? Simply put, it isn't what your candidate says—most of the time the voters have heard it all before anyway—it's how he or she says it!

Skills Are Learned, Not Inherited

All successful presentation is the result of specific actions, or causes, which, by virtue of Newton's Third Law, "For every action there is an equal and opposite reaction," unavoidably provokes specific and predictable effects. Regardless of whether those actions are created accidentally or intentionally, when causes are put in, it is impossible not to have certain effects come out. A glass will still end up broken whether it slips accidentally from one's hands or is thrown with intent against a wall. Which means that, invariably, the heretofore elusive character known as "perception" is really just an effect that is caused by a candidate's own personal presentation.

As it is obvious that the required skills are learned rather than inherited, then exactly how does one learn the most effective way to say something? Well, like every other kind of learning, there are two ways of going about it: by self-teaching, fashioning ourselves after others believed (often misguidedly) to be more adequate, spending years of trial and error until the basic idea settles in; or, when considerable time and energy are at stake, finding someone else who's spent years researching it, and learning what they know. Which means that what an effective campaign manager needs more than a word-creating communication consultant is a "word-rescuing" presentation advisor.

Contrary to popular belief, presentation training is painless—or at least, should be—as it is merely the creation of a greater awareness of specific presentation causes and effects, where there was less awareness before. Telling a candidate to stand in a certain way, or dress a certain way, or speak a certain way is not creating awareness, it is merely bullying. Describing logical reasons why a speaker should do something a certain way to create a specific effect, and having it make perfect sense to that speaker, is the only successful way to improve presentation skills.

To Be Trusted, Meet the Audience Norm

Since the dawn of mankind, people have been primarily communicating one-on-one. It's what they know best, and how everyone is most comfortable receiving information. It's the one kind of communications Lyndon Johnson and George Bush were evidently able to master, but couldn't transfer to a group situation.

The causes and effects that make up every one-on-one communication have, over the millennia, become the established "norm," or what people have come to subconsciously expect to experience during the transfer of human information. This norm is made up of hundreds of unconscious elements, including, among many other factors, the vocal patterns, such as pitch, pace, pausing, and volume, and the physical movement, or body language, which accompany them.

When a presentation meets the norms, the audience will trust it. When it doesn't, it's all over for the presenter, and nothing more the presenter says will help. Unfortunately, the moment most speakers are faced with a group, they believe they must adopt a different set of norms, a "speech" set, and proceed to neglect all that would occur during a normal one-on-one communication. Always use the same volume.

Ronald Reagan, regardless of the size of the group to whom he is speaking, always behaves as though he is conversing with one person in his own living room. Every listener, even in a crowd of thousands, comes away with the distinct feeling that "he was talking to me, directly to me." This, of course, should be the ultimate goal of every presentation. It is also one lesson Bill Clinton has yet to learn, although he has been improving.

While there are many factors which create Reagan's one-on-one effect, the most noticeable element is in the volume. Whereas many speakers feel the need to step up into "speech mode" reminiscent of the days when electronic amplification had yet to be invented, Reagan always uses exactly the same volume he would use were he standing directly in front of us at a social occasion. Such a simple thing, yet tremendously important to the psyche of the listener, who no more wants to get shouted at in a crowd than he would in his own living room. Yet volume is one of the first aspects of vocalization to go by the wayside when a speaker presents before a group.

Eye Contact on Focal Points

Eye contact is essential for achieving effective communications. Unfortunately, most speakers interpret that to mean, "Try to catch the eye of as many people in the audience as you can." In effect, the speaker splashes his eyes around the room, desperately trying to make eye contact with anyone who's looking back at him! The result, of course, is that the speaker actually looks unnaturally shifty-eyed to the rest of the listeners, which is unavoidably interpreted as nervousness, insincerity, and, of course, untrustworthiness. Remember, whether the causes are intentional or accidental, the effects on the listener will be the same!

The solution, then, is to forget about trying to make eye contact with everyone in the it, it is impossible anyway). Instead, mentally divide the room into three sections, the ce sides, finding one easily-spottable person (or camera) in the center of each section, then speech only to those three people.

Depending on the size of the room, dozens, even hundreds, of people near that focal point will think that the speaker is actually looking directly at them, and feel the strength of that one-on-one communication. In fact, with well-placed focal points, almost everyone will feel the effects of this method.

Simply by maintaining a single focus toward these three different points in an audience, a speaker can replicate the same impression.

The next question then becomes, "How long does a speaker stay at one focus?" The answer, of course, is, "For as long as it is comfortable." Once again, we each have an established "norm" as to what is an acceptable time to speak to one person while another stands by. Imagine two people conversing at a cocktail party, when a third comes along, expecting to join them. It will be very short order before the one who is talking will feel compelled to finish what he is saying and turn to welcome the newcomer. It is that sense of timing that comes into play during a speech. When a speaker begins to feel he is neglecting his other focal points, it is time to turn to another focal point.

The most important thing to remember about this element, however, is that the speaker must finish that element of the speech before changing focus, as this is the one-on-one norm to which everyone adheres out of ordinary courtesy.

These are just a few of the most basic and fundamental presentation considerations a speaker must make in order to replicate the strength of a one-on-one communication, yet even these simple and sensible strategies are very often ignored by so-called "good" speakers. Make no mistake, the absence of these and the dozens of other fundamental considerations will constitute a cause which will create an effect, and invariably, they will be negative ones. When the desired effect is a positive perception of the candidate, that candidate must consciously put in the appropriate presentational causes to get the effect. It can come from no other source.

✓ 20 Tips for Better Public Speaking
Michael Shadow and Greg Peck

Both incumbents and challengers have assets and liabilities that they must either dodge or take advantage of when they speak to a crowd. Here are 10 tips for each to keep in mind when announcing your candidacy.

Tips For Incumbents

1. Know Your Message. You're not a voting record on legs, so don't just read a list of bills you voted for or sponsored when you speak to a crowd.

Explain what your voting record, bill sponsorships, and committee memberships mean to the people in your audience.

2. Create a need to hear your record. Before you say what you did, paint a crisp and vivid picture of the need. Your votes and sponsorships are meaningful only to people who know that a problem existed in the first place. Someone who hears that you voted to spend $750,000 to build a pedestrian overpass might think you're a big spender if he or she doesn't know that children had been hurt because there was no safe way to cross the street.

3. Satisfy the need. Tell audiences what you did to solve a problem. But don't lose votes by overselling yourself. In other words, don't brag.

4. Visualize the benefits. Illustrate how people's lives, a neighborhood, or a small business district was improved by action you took. As an incumbent, you probably have drawers full of letters from people you helped, recollections of remarks made in person, or newspaper articles praising your achievements. Use them to remind your audience of the benefits they have gained from putting you in office.

5. Don't rest on your laurels. Focus your message on the future. Although experience and knowing how to get things done are automatic assets, relying on past accomplishments is an automatic liability for an incumbent. Identify future challenges, and show that you have the energy to take on those challenges. Otherwise, you'll be in a poor position to clash with a dynamic, forward-looking challenger.

6. Begin with a claim, not history. Don't respond to a question on your vote to cut funds for power resource development with a short history of electric power regulation in your state. Leaders are expected to state what they see as a problem and then propose a solution one that usually equals putting them in office. Make your claim first, and then explain it to your listeners. Leave historical narration to the historians.

7. Be simple. In our culture, truth is seen as simple, not complex. Leaders are expected to take complex material and boil it down into something everyone can understand. Look at the bottom line of each issue that's critical to your campaign. Your job is to articulate what is important, and fundamental, about an issue and to state your position on it.

8. Demonstrate your responsiveness to your constituents. How? By referring to letters received ("More than 50 of your neighbors wrote to describe the problems they were having..."); or people interviewed ("Yesterday I spoke with a young single mother and what so impressed me was..."); or community meetings attended ("Every neighborhood council meeting I've attended from Lakeside to Maple Leaf to Beacon Hill, the response has been unanimous..."); or groups met with ("I knew I needed to hear from those most affected, so I asked for a meeting with people from Mothers Against Drunk Driving"). Try to make sure that members of groups you mention are in the audience you're speaking to.

9. Have echo power. Having listeners remember—and repeat—something you've said benefits you. That's echo power. Repetition of your words creates a pattern for your listener. A vivid statement can ensure that you will be remembered and quoted. So use figurative language, and don't be afraid to occasionally say something outlandish.

10. Create the context before you attack. How people see a political attack is greatly influenced by the context in which it occurs. Counterattacks are perceived more favorably than initial attacks. But whether you attack first or second, use the context of the attack to position yourself as a dynamic leader who's working on behalf of his constituents.

Tips For Challengers

1. The speech has to be with you. Delivering a white-collar speech with a lot of nice, white-collar words when you're a blue-collar candidate in a working-class district is like buying a nice blue wool suit that doesn't fit. The speech has to be sincere; otherwise, no one will believe that you have any convictions.

2. Use personal anecdotes and illustrations. Somewhere in your life are events that made you want to change the world through politics. Use one or two of them to illustrate your objectives. This will help your audience see you as a real person instead of just a statue on a stump.

3. Killer lines are a double-edged sword. If you use them, keep them aimed directly at the opposition, and don't be too abrasive. Bob Dole's frequent zings at George Bush during the 1988 Republican presidential primaries were seen as below the belt. But by the same token, don't forget Sharon Pratt Dixon, the only mayoral candidate in Washington, DC, who would take on the issue of how ill-run Marion Barry's administration was. She brought down the house when she said she would use a shovel—not a broom—to clean out City Hall.

4. Use humor with care. The golden rule of joke telling is "The longer the setup, the better the punch line had better be." So unless you're an exceptional joke teller, stick with one-liners. And if you're so stilted that you can't even handle a one-liner, don't bother trying. In the end, your voters will thank you for it.

5. Keep it simple. Don't lay out your entire agenda in one speech. This will overtax the audience and make your speech read like a shopping list. Instead, leave them with a couple of clear messages.

6. Educate your audience about you. Tell them who you are. And give them some key points on your background. This is the only way you can raise the audience's acceptance level of you as the best person for the job.

7. Don't make promises that you can't keep. A precautionary measure. When you run for re-election, people will go back over your earlier speeches and look for promises you didn't deliver on.

8. Be informal. Speak as you speak, not as you write. Design your speech for delivery. Use contractions and colloquial language, but avoid clichés. They usually don't fit into your delivery and can make you trip over the best parts of your speech.

9. Tailor your speech to the audience. Do some research to find out where the audience stands on certain issues. Tailor your speech to stress the similarities between your positions and theirs. Visualize yourself as a member of the audience.

10. Tone is important. The tone you use to announce your campaign will carry over into the campaign. Remember, people usually recall the tone you use more than they recall the words you say.

✓ Candidate Debate Checklist: 15 Handy Tips
Ron Faucheux

There was a time when candidates spent countless hours agonizing over whether to debate. The old rule of thumb was that front-runners had everything to lose by debating, and underdogs had everything to gain. Since most elections have front-runners, debates were often shunted.

But in recent times, debates have become a fixture of campaigning. Unless you're an incumbent running against only token opposition, debating has become something most candidates can't avoid. Ever since 1984 when incumbent President Ronald Reagan, who enjoyed a big lead in the polls, consented to debate his underdog opponent, Walter Mondale, the incumbent/front-runner no-show excuse was obliterated.

Now, voters and the news media expect all candidates to debate, whether you're running for town alderman or president. When a candidate won't debate, he or she becomes suspect and subject to attack. Candidates who have good reason not to debate have to weigh the damage done by refusing alongside the risk of doing it.

Meeting one's opposition in debate can be the scariest thing a political candidate is called upon to do. Experienced campaigners, as well as newcomers, usually get the jitters before they walk on stage to debate. Fear of being surprised with an unexpected attack, or being hit with a question for which you don't know the answer, sets off butterflies in the stomachs of even the toughest combatants. In prep sessions, campaign staff and media consultants should be sensitive to the dread and trepidation with which most candidates approach debates.

It has been said with substantial justification that you don't win debates, you only lose them. Most debate injuries are self-inflicted. That's why carefulness and preparation are critical. However, in your attempt to be careful and prepared, don't become too timid or stiff, either.

The following are lessons that have been gleaned by observing debates among candidates in races small and large, local and national:

1. Know the rules. A candidate must be fully briefed on the rules of the debate before it begins. That includes knowing the amount of time available for opening and closing statements, answers, and rebuttals. It also includes knowing whether and how prepared notes may be used and what visuals (charts, photos, documents, etc.) may be displayed. The rules will directly affect your presentation strategies.

2. Know the physical format. Your biggest enemy in a debate is surprise.

Do everything possible to reduce the possibility of shock. That includes making sure the candidate is fully aware of the physical format. Whether you will have a podium or table in front of you will affect how you use notes. Whether you will be standing or sitting will influence how you can relate to the opposition.

3. Insist on a say in the format and think about it carefully. Your campaign should always have influence in debate arrangements and should require final approval of the format before you agree to debate. In making format decisions, you will be asked to consider the following: Will the candidates stand or sit? Will there be a podium or a table? How many people can each candidate invite to be part of the audience? If televised, who sets up the camera angles and the lights? What kind of microphones will be used? Will reaction shots be allowed? How long will opening and closing statements last? How long will you have to answer questions? Who will ask the questions? Who selects the questioners? Will candidates have the right to ask questions of the opposition? When are rebuttals allowed and how long can they be?

Addressing these issues may have a serious impact on the political consequences of the debate. For example, short candidates may not want to stand near their taller opponents. Contenders who have trouble making a point in quick sound bites may want an opportunity for longer answers.

A classic case that underscores the importance of this point occurred during the second presidential debate in 1992. This debate was arranged around a town hall format where members of the audience were allowed to ask questions. It was a big mistake for George Bush, who requires the protection of a podium while he debates, to agree to such an arrangement which served the interests of Bill Clinton, whose touchy-feely style better fit the situation.

4. Prepare your opening. In most debates, candidates are given an allotted time usually two to five minutes to open. Don't wing it. Prepare what you're going to say before you walk into the room. Before you open your mouth, know the words that will come out of it. Your opening will set the stage for the rest of the debate. In laying the foundation for your debate strategy, keep in mind that the opening statement must relate to your campaign's overall message and is one more opportunity to convey that message.

5. Prepare your close. This can be a little tricky. While it is important to know how you want to close, and to prepare some closing lines in advance, you also need to remain flexible enough to adjust to the circumstances. For example, if either you or your opponent stumbles during the debate, you may need to deal with that in your closing. Or, if an opponent levels a serious charge against you and you don't have adequate opportunity to answer it, you may want to use some of your time at the end to do that.

6. Prepare soundbites for difficult issues. In most debates, you will be able to predict most, if not all, of your opponent's pitch as well as questions that may come up. Since debates usually limit statements and responses to short 30 to 90 second lengths, you need to have some memorable and politically pertinent one-liners prepared. These one-liners can be used to deflect a tough question, handle a sore point, or respond to an opponent's attack. In 1988, vice presidential candidate Dan Quayle, when responding to questions about his youth and qualifications, used a line which favorably compared his own experience to that of John Kennedy when he was elected president. It was a good line, but it had been overused. In the televised debate between the candidates, Quayle's opponent, Lloyd Bentsen, was ready for it. When Quayle popped the Kennedy line, Bentsen came back with the crushing rejoinder: "I knew John Kennedy. John Kennedy was a friend of mine. And Senator, you're no John Kennedy."

Another example was the first 1984 presidential debate. Mondale was prepared when Reagan recycled the famous debate line he had used against Jimmy Carter in 1980, "There you go again." In response, Mondale turned the line against Reagan, asking him if he remembered the last time he used the line and reminding him of his own weakness on the issue at hand—in this case, Medicare. Reagan's reaction was uncharacteristically lame and raised serious doubts about his advanced age. Then, in the second debate, when Reagan's age was brought up, he shot back with calculated wit, saying tongue-in-cheek that he would not use "my opponent's youth or inexperience" against him. It was a big hit and in one fell-swoop, it put the age issue to rest.

One temptation candidates have when they come up with a good one-liner is to run it into the ground. In most cases, if you sting the opposition with a good hit, let it go. Often, when good lines are repeated too often, they lose their punch.

7. Address the right audience. Most political debates are covered by the news media. In bigger elections, many are televised live or rebroadcasted. Always remember that the wider news audience is the real audience you're addressing, not the dozens or even hundreds of people who actually attend the debate. In some cases, the actual live audience may be heavily skewed to certain kinds of voters (students, seniors, liberals, conservatives, business people, teachers, lawyers, etc.) while the wider media audience that will read about the debate in the next day's newspaper or watch sound bites from it on the evening news will represent a much different audience.

Also keep in mind the televised audience. If the debate is being carried only in one part of a state or district, make sure your performance is geared to the political dynamics of that area. But in trying to make targeted appeals, in no case should you say one thing to one audience and something contradictory to another one, regardless of the pressures of the moment to do so.

8. Get ready for candidate-to-candidate Q&A. In many debates and forums, candidates are allowed to ask one another questions. This is an opportunity and a risk. Candidates often wrestle with the choice of whether to ask the opposition a tough, embarrassing question (and risk looking mean) or an easy question (and risk letting the opponent off the hook).

Before you prepare your questions, and possible answers, make sure you know the format and the rules. Usually, the questioner is given a chance to respond to the answer. If that's the case, drop your bomb in the response, not in the question. Make sure you set a trap for your opponent, and then close the trap in the comeback. Try to get your opponent to talk about something that you can smash in your response. But if, as a questioner, you can't comment on the answer, then make sure your question is asked with that limitation in mind.

9. Open aggressively. Generally, open on the offense and stay there. From your first utterance, take the lead, frame the issues, and make your opponent react and dance to your music. This is as much an attitude as it is substantive content.

10. Prepare for all possible questions, even easy and light-hearted ones. In most elections, candidates are asked the same dozen questions, over and over. Candidates should never, ever walk into a debate without being prepared to handle at least those questions. They should also be prepared to handle variations of them.

In addition, also prepare for simple, funny, or off-beat questions, such as: Why are you running for this job? Will you say something nice about your opponent? Can you name your political hero? What's your favorite book? Movie? TV show? Professional football team? How often do you go to church? What charities do you support? These may seem irrelevant or trivial, but prepare answers, anyway. Make sure that when a surprise question hits you, you don't look like a deer caught in headlights. Use of wit can also be extremely effective as long as it isn't corny, silly, or mean spirited.

11. Talk to the audience, not your opponent. As a general rule, you should address yourself to the audience—to the voters. The classic example of this was the first 1960 Kennedy-Nixon debate, in which Nixon seemed weak and insecure largely because he kept addressing Kennedy, as if he were trying to get his opponent's approbation, instead of reaching the millions of voters viewing him on TV. Voters don't want to watch politicians bicker. They want to be talked to directly.

There are exceptions, of course. Occasionally, you may need to address your opponent when you make a point, ask a question, or answer an attack. However, depending upon the format, these should be rare occasions.

12. Surprise the opposition. Remember: Your opponent is as scared as you are. The last thing you want is to be surprised, to be thrown off stride. Conversely, do something early to rattle your opponent, whether it's a new attack, raising a previously untouched issue, or displaying documentation. Attitude can be a powerful weapon. Walk into the room where the debate is being held with an air of ease and confidence. You may be able to surprise your opponent by how cool, polite, and in control you are.

13. Know the difference between two-candidate and multi-candidate debates. In a multi-candidate forum, it is usually important to figure out a way for your candidate to stand out from the crowd, to make a singular impression. Some candidates have attempted to stand apart through the positions they have taken on issues or by attacking their opponents. Others have tried physical gestures, like the time Bruce Babbitt stood up and challenged his opponents for the 1988 Democratic presidential nomination to stand with him in his admission that new taxes would be needed to reduce the deficit.

The dynamic of a multi-candidate debate can be considerably different from a two-way match-up. Two rules to remember: First, if two of your opponents are fighting between themselves, let them have at it. It will behoove you to hold their coats while they slug it out. It gives you a chance to rise above the fray. Also, watch for an opening when you can sweep in as the great statesman and clean up their mess with a well placed bon mot. Second, if you get into a two-way verbal contest with one of your lesser adversaries, and there's no way to easily extricate yourself from it, quickly drag your major opponent into it. Don't let him or her off the hook.

A major issue when there are more than two candidates in a race is which ones will be allowed to debate. It is usually to the disadvantage of an incumbent or a front-runner to have too many opponents on stage. On the other hand, if you're stuck with them, it's unwise to appear as if you don't want them there. Remember how petty George Bush looked in 1980 when he and Ronald "I paid for this microphone" Reagan were tussling over who would be included in a New Hampshire debate?

14. Be careful when leveling an unprepared attack. If you're going to attack the opposition in a debate, make sure you're on sound footing and have thorough documentation. Avoid cheap shots and retain a sense of personal dignity and overall fairness.

Often, candidates are tempted to respond to a surprise attack by hitting their opponent with a broadside that has not been thought through or lacks proper evidence to support the claim. Be careful. As Democratic media consultant Michael Sheehan advises his clients, always stop short of where you're tempted to go when making an unprepared attack. Don't paint yourself into a verbal corner that you can't escape. Nothing looks worse than taking a jab at your opponent and then being forced to either back down from it or to split hairs over what you really meant to say.

15. Avoid fighting with the moderator or panelists. For the most part candidates look mean and petty when they get into a fight with a debate moderator or with a panelist. Remember, you're not running against them no matter how much they may irritate you. Sometimes, however, if a moderator or panelist goes too far in something they say or skirts the rules to the opposition's clear advantage, it may become necessary to point that out in a way that doesn't look too priggish. If you make such a challenge, keep in mind how it will look to the viewing audience, so avoid being obnoxious, annoying, or pedantic.

Haggling over debate rules and making excuses why you can't properly get your point across doesn't communicate well to a mass audience. That mistake was made by Ross Perot in his 1993 debate with Al Gore over NAFTA.

✓ Problems Faced by Business People as Candidates
David B. Hill

Herbert Hoover once speculated that, "American business needs a lifting purpose greater than the struggle of materialism." In 1990, more than a dozen prominent American businessmen responded to that challenge and offered their services to voters, running for the office of governor.

The result was not very uplifting for business. Prior to developer Fife Symington's belated victory in Arizona last February, only two businessmen had won their state's highest office in the 1990 electoral cycle.

Republican businessmen, representing the quintessential party of commerce, took the brunt of the losses. Every GOP business candidate except for Symington failed in his quest to become governor. Sheffield Nelson, a former utility chairman, lost a bid to unseat Bill Clinton when he was governor of Arkansas. Manhattan economist Pierre Rinfret was drubbed by New York's Mario Cuomo in 1990. Republican challenger Jon Grunseth, a corporate public affairs executive, dropped out of the Minnesota gubernatorial race in its final weeks on account of a sex scandal. Telecommunications entrepreneur Jim Gallaway was unsuccessful in the Nevada governor's race despite heavy personal spending in support of his own candidacy.

Perhaps the biggest embarrassment of all for the business community was Republican Clayton Williams' multimillion dollar debacle in Texas. The west-Texas millionaire businessman with extensive oil, banking, and telecommunications interests, squandered a 20-point lead and was beaten by a populist female career politician hampered by unanswered allegations of illicit drug use.

Ironically, the only businessmen to win gubernatorial contests in 1990 were both Democrats—Bruce Sundlun in Rhode Island and Ben Nelson in Nebraska—each of whom benefited from having singularly unpopular Republican incumbents as opponents. Sundlun won the two-year term post on his third try, finally beating DiPrete, the victim of violating a no-new-taxes pledge, involvement in an investment scandal, and a crippled state economy. Campaign spending also made a difference; post-elections reports indicated that millionaire Sundlun's campaign spent $6 million from the candidate's own deep pockets over the last six years and a total of $4.1 million from all contributors in the 1990 race alone, better than twice the amount spent by DiPrete.

Nelson—a lawyer and insurance specialist—defeated Gov. Kay Orr despite fierce attacks by Republicans on his directorship as a major corporate junk bond holder. Other candidates with business credentials lost primary bids or dropped out of gubernatorial races in about a dozen states, including Alaska, Connecticut, Iowa, and Oklahoma.

Amidst the carnage of these businessmen's dashed hopes and dreams for high office are some lessons for those that follow them—including construction executive Kirk Fordice of Mississippi, who stepped down from the national presidency of the Associated General Contractors in January 1991 to launch a successful challenge to Governor Ray Mabus (D).

Time For The Effort

The first chore for businessmen/candidates is to get their corporate affairs in order so they can devote full time and attention to politics without nursing lingering business problems. Restaurant franchisor Vince Orza, a close loser in Oklahoma's GOP runoff primary for governor after garnering 40 percent of the first primary vote, was said by the media to interrupt press interviews with business calls. "I have to take care of my business," he explained. "If it craters, they (opponents) will use it against me."

Orza's words were prophetic. In a runoff election campaign, his opponent and major newspapers hammered him repeatedly for not having made a profit in the three years since he took Eateries, Inc. public. The demands of running a multi-state franchise that *INC.* magazine ranked as America's 19th fastest growing company and opening a half dozen additional restaurants in the election year of 1990, were clearly incompatible with a sustained run for his state's highest office.

Even the busy T. Boone Pickens entertained thoughts of a race for governor of Texas in 1990. Early on, his business aides justified the required time off from corporate affairs by describing Pickens' businesses as being on "cruise control." Later recalculation of time commitments caused Pickens to declare that his stockholder battle with a Japanese auto parts manufacturer would preclude a gubernatorial bid.

Despite careful corporate planning made prior to the race, contingencies can still arise even after the campaign is underway. Clayton Williams almost abandoned his quest when, in the midst of the primary campaign, a private plane crash resulted in the deaths of several of his highest corporate executives. While some career pols were puzzled at Williams' prolonged leave-of-absence from campaigning in the wake of the crash, the business class understood.

Skeletons In The Closet

Businessmen must also assess the skeletons in their corporate closets. Williams didn't look hard enough before he leaped into the race that Pickens wisely bypassed. In the closing weeks of the campaign, Williams' campaign was besieged by a grand jury investigation of a credit insurance scam allegedly perpetrated by auto dealers and his Midland bank. He never stopped defending those charges. Up to then, the archetypical Claytie backer had been the blue-collar Texan who was stung by credit insurance; Democrat Ann Richards finally had yet another issue to undermine the millionaire businessman.

Oklahoman Orza was skewered by charges that he kept his publicly-reported corporate salary artificially low in order to fool shareholders while his company was paying large fees for "consulting services" to a separate Orza-controlled company where he presumably took another salary.

Personal skeletons can come back to haunt too, as Minnesotan Jon Grunseth painfully discovered. After almost recovering from charges—vehemently denied—of nude swimming parties with the adolescent girlfriends of his stepdaughter, Grunseth got stung by public admissions of a long-time mistress.

Business Success

The importance of a successful record in the business world cannot be ignored either. Responding to Sheffield Nelson's persistent claims that he could cut the fat from the government, opponents retorted that the candidate's successor at Arkansas Louisiana Gas Company "cut 500 jobs, saved millions in gas waste, and whittled down the company's mammoth gas supply costs." Too bad, they chortled, that Nelson's successor was not running for governor on the cut-waste platform.

Cynical responses to businessmen's calls for businesslike government are common. Some voters feel that candidates who want to run state government like a business ignore the central role of government, which they say is protecting the health and safety of the public, not making a profit. Or they conclude that the work forces and managerial styles of the two sectors are so different as to preclude successful crossover of leadership talent.

Texas Republican candidate Jack Rains—founder of a large successful international design firm in Houston and once a Secretary of State under Governor Bill Clements—often needled Boone Pickens and Clayton Williams about this issue in his 1990 campaign speeches. "You certainly can't run government like a business," he argued knowingly after serving in both sectors. His one-liner inevitably got applause, even among GOP voters.

In addition to mediating calls for making government like business, it would apparently behoove corporate candidates to abandon business-like scrutiny of politically-charged issues.

Nevadan Jim Gallaway found this out the hard way. He naively suggested that Nevada could - benefit from a scientific study of the safety risks associated with a proposed high-level radioactive waste dump. His opponent, incumbent Democratic Governor Bob Miller, pounced on this slip-up with vengeance. Gallaway protested, saying that a scientific study by skilled Nevada experts would put the matter "out of the hands of the politicians and in the hands of scientists." What Gallaway failed to appreciate adequately is that people would rather entrust some emotive issues to pandering politicians than to value-free scientists.

Lowering The Sights

Such naiveté about the harsh realities of politics, typical among corporate campaigners, can be overcome with a little experience, however. Two early candidates for governor came to this conclusion in 1990 and both redirected their campaigns at lower level offices, hoping to live for another day to mount a later shot at the top spot. Also, in Alaska, a GOP gubernatorial candidate accepted a late opportunity to run for lieutenant governor.

New Haven, Connecticut developer Joel Schiavone switched from a gubernatorial bid to a race for state comptroller after spending more than $1 million of his own money to be governor. Concluded Schiavone, "The odds of my being governor are less than my being comptroller. You don't have to be a governor to do something for the state." The entrepreneur also said that service as comptroller was a better use of his financial expertise.

While Schiavone eventually lost even the lower-level race, better results were achieved by a Nebraska welding supply company owner, another businessman candidate who sought to parlay his financial expertise into state service. Democrat John Breslow switched from a gubernatorial bid to a race for state auditor and upset a 20-year incumbent Republican, promising a watchdog style that would go beyond traditional auditing requirements to require performance auditing unlike anything Nebraska has seen before. With that message and campaign expenditures of over $500,000, including $320,000 of his own money, Breslow outspent the incumbent 20-to-1 and got his political career off to a fast start. And doubtless he will get around to a race for governor at some future date, wise for having been patient.

Building supply millionaire Jim Campbell, a narrow loser in Alaska's 1990 GOP primary for governor, accepted a late opportunity to be Arliss Sturgulewski's candidate for lieutenant governor when her running mate, State Senator Jack Coghill, switched to ex-governor Wally Hickel's independent effort. That move by Campbell, even after losing to Sturgulewski in a tough, nasty primary race, probably will give Campbell a leg up with many GOP loyalists should he decide to make a run for Alaska's top job.

✓ Overcoming Postelection Depression
Jim Crounse

Post-election blues, that time after an election when many people feel burned-out, down and out, and downright exhausted. Candidates, campaign workers, consultants—the postelection blues hit everyone, and it hits hard.

After 14 years of running campaigns, consulting on campaigns, and running for office (I ran and lost an energetic but cash-poor legislative race in Nebraska in 1978), I've learned that after election day, win or lose, I am exhausted and blue for a month. I've also learned I am not alone.

Yet those of us who make our living around the election process are slow to admit these kinds of problems and even slower in trying to break the cycle that causes them.

But there's always hope.

Occupational Hazard

Let's face it, if you're in politics, what you do for a living is different. You work feverishly toward a kind of D-Day. Months and sometimes years of work and intense activity culminate in a single day. You're not like 9-to-5 people who can leave their jobs and go home. Your work spills over into your personal life, and other people find this very difficult to understand or accept. Sometimes you don't even understand it yourself.

When your work is done on election day, it's measured by an excruciatingly public report card with a pass/fail grading system. We are much like athletes or actors who prepare for months prior to being publicly judged moments after a performance as winners or losers. Fifty percent of us win, 50 percent of us lose. Adding primaries into the equation brings the loser category to 80 percent.

Toss in the inherent craziness of a campaign and you become very vulnerable to all sorts of things. You gain weight, lose weight, drink and smoke to excess, become irritable and push people away, have a campaign romance, scream and yell, and get screamed and yelled at.

Don't Put Your Real Life on Hold—Too Much

Campaign season is a time when you naturally put your "real life" on hold. You see your family and friends less, telling them, "See you in November," and then you find that you weren't exaggerating.

You put off big and little decisions that affect your life and future. Your dry cleaning and laundry stack up (and, admit it, once you even bought new underwear and socks instead of washing them).

I know several people who neglected to pay bills on time during a campaign and had their credit cards canceled. This can be very embarrassing when taking your friends out to dinner—friends you haven't seen because of the campaign—and the waiter takes away your card as if you are a white-collar criminal.

Because you are constantly rushing around and always late, dealing with trifling details like plugging a parking meter or parking in legal spaces is beneath you since you, of course, are on a mission to save the world. However, only when my friend Bill had to pick up the candidate at the airport for an important debate and went to get his car—finding it had been towed for non-payment of parking tickets—did he learn firsthand that bad things always happen at the worst possible time.

Another friend rented a car for four days during a campaign. Too busy to return it, she ended up keeping the car for three weeks and having to personally pay $1,200 for it.

Psychotherapist Bayla Kraft of Arlington, VA, puts this kind of "life" into perspective: "No candidate, campaign staff person, or consultant will ever go to their deathbed saying, 'If I could have won one more election, put out one more yard sign, or aired one more great negative TV spot.'"

"People are more likely to say, 'I wish I could have spent more time with the people I love or with my friends.'"

So the question is not only what can we do while the campaign is going on to make our lives better and more balanced, but also what can we do when it's all over to keep our exhaustion and blues from escalating into full-blown depression?

✓ The 24-hour Candidate
Nick Winter

Traditionally, grassroots activities are considered a wasted effort for statewide races in large, heavily populated states. But you can put your candidate on a diet of "24-hour" days that generate significant free media coverage. The ensuing local and statewide coverage magnifies a candidate's voter contact.

U.S. Senator Barbara Boxer (D-CA) is a case in point. In 1992, not only was she running statewide in a country-state like California, but she was competing in a three-way primary against one opponent who was better known and another who was better funded.

That she had voted for congressional pay raises and had overdrawn her account 143 times at the House bank increased her vulnerability dramatically.

Yet Boxer has an intense personal magnetism and an ability to inspire people, both one-on-one and in crowds. Clearly, she needed a way to capitalize on these strengths and minimize those weaknesses.

While the Boxer campaign could not afford to focus significant financial resources on grassroots activities, it could use another crucial resource for this task: the candidate's time.

The week before the primary election was devoted to a tour of the state that was climaxed by a "24-hour" day in which Boxer attended rallies, met with voters, toured hospitals, and discussed the race—nonstop.

Having several hundred people attend a rally at 2 a.m. makes a powerful statement of campaign momentum for those who watch and read the coverage of the tour.

Having won the primary, Boxer used late August and early September to expand the 24-hour day into a 24-day highway tour of the state's small, rural counties. Boxer capped her campaign shortly before election day with a "28-hour" day.

The tours were designed to bring Boxer into contact with voters during the period surrounding each election, when persuadable voters are paying attention to the race and making up their minds.

Though the tours included the major media markets, they concentrated on the rural counties where statewide candidates rarely travel and are thus guaranteed significant local press coverage. As a bonus, the tours received statewide coverage from major media reporters.

Boxer's three statewide tours allowed her to reconnect to the voters of California in a direct and personal way. This reconnection was crucial for a candidate—any candidate—who needed to overcome the stigma of incumbency, involvement with the House bank, and voter disillusionment.

✓ How to Conduct Your Own Political Physical
Earl Bender, Michael Grant, and Nancy Nagle

Those of us who advise political campaigns regularly hear candidates attempt to justify personal style over effective campaign strategy. We are admonished: "That's just not the way we do things around here."

Incumbents tell us they would not have been elected if their past campaigns were not correctly run. So why should they change? And challengers puzzle over everything—from whom they should trust, to which high-tech campaign tools fit their needs. As a result, candidates and campaigns often turn inward, creating a self-reinforcing group-think among insiders that can block new ideas and constructive organizational change. In a closely contested election, such a situation can lead to defeat.

We have developed a campaign-assessment tool to help candidates, campaign managers, political consultants, party committees, and PACs take an objective look at campaign organizations.

The assessment functions as a "political physical," providing a campaign with much the same service a doctor provides a patient in a routine examination. It gives a view of the campaign's current health and, when necessary, suggests where improvements can be made. It has been applied to the campaigns of incumbent members of Congress (see the accompanying story on the DCCC Assessment Project), to challengers and incumbents in executive and legislative races, and to initiative campaigns.

The Assessment Mechanism

There is no great magic involved in conducting this assessment. Simply stated, a complete assessment consists of four basic tasks. Task #1 determines what the campaign needs to do to win and what resources it has in hand to do so. Task #2 applies resources to needs: which configuration of resources will maximize the campaign's effectiveness. Task #3 conveys this information to the campaign. Task #4, by far the most difficult, makes a persuasive argument that these objectively formulated recommendations can improve the internal operation—that it indeed is worthwhile to expand from the comfortable way things always have been done.

It is important to realize that the best you can do is show "the truth" in a manner most digestible to the candidate and staff. You cannot make them comply—nor should you spend substantial effort trying to make them see the light. The old adage holds true: You can lead a horse to water, but you can't make him drink.

Completing the assessment as early as possible in the election cycle allows plenty of time for the candidate to understand the recommendations and to implement them successfully without disrupting the campaign effort. With sufficient time and the campaign's internal discipline, your assessment can lead to significant improvement. Here are the steps you need to follow to conduct your own political physical:

Step 1: What type of campaign is this anyway? At the beginning of this effort, you must be certain you understand the campaign you are assessing. Just as you would not prepare your candidate to run against the wrong opponent, it will to you no good to prepare a campaign for a beauty contest when you are about to face a high-dollar media war and a house-to-house turnout battle. The following broad categories can help you focus on the specific race you are assessing:

- Is it a candidate election or a ballot measure? One obvious difference between these is the presence of a candidate. Ballot measures have no incumbent, and there is no public "record" at issue. Candidates have personal styles, strengths, and weaknesses.
- Is this a competitive or noncompetitive election? If it is noncompetitive, you can stop right now. Either you cannot win it or you cannot lose it; the quality of your assessment skills is moot.
- Are you assessing the incumbent or the challenger? They are vastly different. The incumbent has the assets and liabilities of an electoral history, a public record, a staff, the ability to generate news coverage, and an established political base. Challengers frequently have little or no record to defend and must start from scratch to build a political operation.
- Is the race for an executive or legislative office? Executives—governors, mayors, the president—have clear images to voters; they are held accountable. Every time they make a decision, it disadvantages some person, group, or interest. Through time, people remember what their officials do to them, and not necessarily what they do for them. On the other hand, individual legislators often can take credit within their districts for good things the entire legislature does and usually can avoid the blame for unpopular legislative action.
- Is this a large or small election? Judging this requires some common sense; the answer is not always as obvious as it seems. Among the indicators of a large race are the presence of full-time professional campaign staff, outside consultants, and a campaign season that lasts longer than two months. A rule of thumb: If it takes $250,000 or more to be serious about winning, it is a large race.

Now that you have determined what kind of campaign you are assessing, you can proceed. Let us assume you are assessing an incumbent state representative's legislative and campaign operations.

Step 2: What should you look for? The following nine subject areas account for the universe of political phenomena surrounding our state legislator:

1. Themes.
2. Press/Free media.
3. Communications.
4. Scheduling.
5. Computer operations.
6. Lists and list management.
7. Research.
8. Fund-raising.
9. Campaign operations.

Now, in analyzing these specific functions, overlay the following political elements:

1. the legislator as candidate;
2. the incumbent's office operations, including all capital and district offices;
3. fund-raising;
4. campaign operations.

Keeping these four larger considerations in mind will help you apply a broader political perspective to each specific function. For instance, in examining the scheduling function, determine if the scheduling meets the needs of each of the four components and if they are working in harmony.

The following are the analytic criteria for each of the nine assessment components:

1. Themes. Is the entire campaign enterprise organized by a single unifying idea? This is the most important question you can ask. Themes organize thinking and lead to planned, concerted, organizational effort aimed at winning the election. If a single theme ties together every action—from the way the candidate uses his time, to the activities of his office and staff, to the specific language and graphics used in the campaign materials—election is more likely.

When a campaign theme exists, everyone knows how his individual job or role fits into the overall effort. Legislative staff knows what to emphasize in official activities. As a result, the entire effort more effectively communicates the message to the voters. Without a theme, the legislative office and campaign are frequently a beehive of well-intentioned but uncoordinated activity. There is not likely to be a campaign plan or, if there is one, it is unlikely to be implemented.

2. Press/Free media. Press coverage, or free media, is fully one-third of the campaign offense, and it is free. The campaign always should emphasize the press operation and the resulting free peerage of the candidate.

The press operations of the legislative office and the campaign should be aggressive, garnering maximum—but not random—coverage of the legislator/ candidate. Press should reinforce the campaign themes sufficiently so that voters and constituents understand that the legislator is saying to them and doing for them.

Answer these questions when evaluating the press operation:

1. Is the message planned and integrated throughout the operation? Government and politics are two sides of the same coin; they must work together.
2. Is the press effort active or passive? If the campaign waits for press coverage, busy reporters will never quite get around to covering them. Just as the campaign must tell the legislator's constituencies how they are being served, it also must show the press what the legislator is doing for the public.
3. How well does the candidate or campaign communicate through television, radio, and the print media?
4. What communications devices does the press operation routinely use? Radio actualities? Press releases? Teleconferencing? Employing the most modern techniques is one way of letting voters know the legislator stays on top of their business for them.

3. Communications. What sort of routine mailings, newsletters, announcements, birthday cards, and sundry other mechanisms does the legislator use to communicate with his voters? Are they active or passive—that is, does the legislator write whenever he has done something of interest to the citizen, or does the office only respond to letters and requests that arrive in the mail? Are the graphics lively and interesting? Is the prose deadly dull or is it written in "news you can use" form? Is it keyed to the interests of the people who live in specific communities, or is it the type of policy-speak usually quarantined within C-SPAN and Sunday morning talk shows?

Good communications programs stress frequent contact with constituents, are well written, interestingly presented, and targeted to reflect the demographics and issue interests of the district. They waste neither people's time nor public money. And—surprise!—they stress the campaign themes.

4. Scheduling. You carefully must assess how the legislator/candidate uses his time. The candidate's time is another third of the campaign's offense and, unlike the other resources, it cannot be expanded. No matter how much money it raises, the campaign cannot buy another 24 hours between now and Election Day.

All officeholders, but especially long-term incumbents, tend to spend their time doing what they like to do and avoiding what they do not like to do. This is bad enough when the incumbent stays in the legislature working on committee business or shepherding legislation through the chamber. It is doubly dangerous when he spends more days playing golf in Florida than he does in his district.

The schedule must balance all of the candidate's competing political needs: first, the need to do a good job as legislator; second, as campaigner; third, as fund-raiser; and fourth, as the ultimate manager of the legislative and campaign staffs. Additionally, each legislator needs adequate private time to think, reflect, rest, and be a spouse and parent.

Among the questions to ask about the scheduling are the following: Is it thematic, supporting other official and campaign activities? Is it targeted to voters? To key constituencies? To contributors and potential donors? To specific geographic areas?

Do individual schedules make sense? Does the candidate proceed in an orderly manner through the district, or is he hopscotching madly from one corner of the district to another?

5. Computer operations. Take a deep breath. Now, momentarily forget every byte of binary you know. This is about computers and common sense. You want to evaluate whether the computer capability serves the political needs of the incumbent's offices and the campaign. That is, do the machines work for the people? Do they do the job they were intended to do, or do the humans work for the machines? If staff members spend all their time programming or simply swearing at broken printers, the system has gone awry.

Computers are supposed to do the most brutal and menial tasks efficiently and cheaply. They should assist the campaign in list acquisition and maintenance and with all routine clerical and writing chores. They should facilitate targeted and blanket mailings and keep track of the myriad things that every governmental and political operation must know and remember.

Evaluate whether the computers and their programs are political. That is, are they set up to store and process information with the same political criteria that you expect the office and campaign staff to use? Are they flexible and easily adapted to the campaign's changing needs? Do the official legislative and campaign computers store information in the same manner, so a person can easily understand information from each one? To the extent legally allowable, can the campaign and official computers communicate with each other and share information? Is all of this affordable?

6. Lists and list management. Every campaign junkie knows no substitute exists for accurate, comprehensive lists that subdivide every fact and every person by every characteristic possible. Evaluate whether the political and official lists are stored and maintained in a way they easily and flexibly may be used. The advent of highly targeted direct-mail communications reinforces the need for incumbents to be able to communicate with every group within their districts. Communications programs should code every available piece of information about a citizen to permit targeted communications with each constituent.

7. Research. Research is divided into two categories: opposition research and support research. Almost every campaign understands the importance of researching the opposing candidate's voting record. But high-quality opposition research is broader than this. It analyzes all of the opponent's official travel, governmental office expenses, campaign-expenditure reports, public statements, and the records of business and financial dealings that are matters of public record.

Support research frequently is ignored by incumbents who claim, "I know my record." There are two significant disadvantages to this cocksure attitude. First, although the incumbent might know his own record, staff members and campaign supporters and volunteers do not know it that well. Second, although the incumbent might know his positions on every issue, he is unlikely to recall the significance of a ten-year-old procedural vote in subcommittee.

A good support-research program investigates and answers all the same questions as the opposition-research program. It arrays all the votes (often in separate binders) by each significant constituency and interest within the district. This permits staff members to tell the residents of Anytown, U.S.A., or local environmentalists what their legislator did about the town's sewer problems.

8. Fund-raising. Fund-raising depends largely on the candidate, but they involve the effort of every part of the campaign. You need to assess every discrete fund-raising activity and whether it is integrated into a successful program.

First, evaluate the candidate. Does he have the ability and willingness to be a good fund-raiser? What is he lacking? Does he like to raise money? Has he made the time commitment necessary for a successful fund-raising effort?

Next, is there a fund-raising plan for the campaign? Is it realistic? Can the campaign fund-raising team execute it? Is the fund-raising plan matched to the campaign's cash-flow needs? It does no good to raise all the money in October if the television buys must be made before Labor Day.

Determine where the money is supposed to come from. Are the targets for the high, medium, and low-donor groups realistic? If the campaign is conducting direct-mail fund-raising, are the lists sufficient to raise the amount of money expected from this effort? Is the campaign mailing to a proven list of previous donors, or is this a cold, prospecting list?

Is there a finance committee? Does it adequately represent the breadth of the candidate's political support and the diverse economic interests within the district? Are the finance committee members producing? Have they donated money themselves?

Is there a PAC fund-raising effort? Is the dollar target for PACs too high? Too low? Who is responsible for asking for PAC donations?

Cross-check the answers to these questions with everyone knowledgeable about the campaign's fund-raising operations.

9. Campaign operations. Assessing the campaign operations frequently is the most critical component of you'll evaluation. You need to determine if all the campaign operations effectively support the entire campaign and whether all the aforementioned activities support the campaign and its objectives.

First, does the campaign have a strategy? In other words, does the campaign know how many votes it takes to win, and does it have a simple, coherent idea how it is going to persuade that number of voters to turn out and elect you legislator? If someone can express the strategy to you in one paragraph, and it makes sense, this is a good indicator that the strategy is understandable and can be executed reliably. Does the campaign leadership understand and believe in the strategy?

Second, is there a campaign theme? (Yes, we have returned to the same concept with which we started.) The theme derives from the strategy and summarizes the ideas being used to convince voters to choose your candidate and to help you organize every activity of the campaign. The theme is not a slogan. Nor is it the idea that, "We're gonna win." It is the central precept that defines the candidacy and tells voters what the candidate and his campaign offer them.

Is there a written campaign plan? Can it be executed? Does the plan include a cash-flow campaign budget that reflects when the campaign must spend the money, not just how much money the campaign must spend?

Does the campaign employ a professional team of staff and consultants? Today, even many low-budget state legislative races employ professional campaign managers and some consultants—especially pollsters, media consultants, or direct-mail consultants

Is there a polling program? Are sufficient, timely polls planned to guide the campaign's strategic and tactical decision making?

Does the targeting and demographic analysis of the district identify the vote by population subgroups and geographic areas that must be captured to implement the campaign strategy? Is there a voter-contact plan to identify, persuade, and mobilize this vote? Do the volunteer and professional resources exist to implement the voter contact plan?

Do all these operational components fit together? Does the campaign staff work well together? Do they work well with the legislator's official staff?

Now that you have a complete description of what you are looking for in your evaluation of the legislator's political and campaign operations, we will actually get down to the assessment.

Step 3. Conducing the assessment. Analyzing the foregoing political operations requires that you interview the candidate, key staff members, campaign principals, and informed political sources outside the campaign. You also must evaluate all the relevant, current campaign documents you can obtain.

In every interview, you should use an open-ended interview technique. Introduce each of the topics, and lead the interviewee to discuss all the subjects in his or her own idiom. This way you can capture the information you need and begin to understand how each person thinks about the issues you are investigating.

Interview the legislator/candidate first. We recommend that you conduct two separate meetings. The first of these is a "ceremonial high tea," in which you sit down with the candidate and describe the general purpose of the assessment. If you are being sponsored by a party committee or some other institution, you should have the leader of this group attend the meeting with you to demonstrate the significance of the assessment.

The second meeting is an extensive interview of the legislator; it might last as long as three hours. You have several objectives in this interview: (l) to obtain the incumbent's views on each of the assessment components, (2) to form an initial impression about the candidate and his style, and (3) to establish a rapport with the candidate and determine what he hopes to gain from this analysis.

You then need to reshape your planned study to incorporate the questions and needs of the legislator. Fitting your methodology to his needs will go a long way in creating mutual trust and furthering the ultimate success of the assessment.

The only thing you should not agree to do is determine which staff members to fire. No one will cooperate with you in the assessment if they believe you are the hatchet man.

Analyze all the documents you receive according to the criteria in Step 2. This is tedious, but it reveals much about a political operation that your personal interviews cannot or will not. Schedules, polls, and campaign plans (or lack thereof), for example, frequently identify critical political problems and suggest the candidate's strengths and weaknesses. Contributions and expenditures reports display spending priorities as well as the balance and pacing of the entire fund-raising apparatus.

You must visit the district. During this visit, interview district staff, and observe their office operations. Determine their political responsibilities and how they work with the campaign staff. You also should interview the key campaign team members and the political sources that have been provided to you by the legislator and his staff. Cross-check this information with your own independent political sources within the district.

Step 4. Recommendations and implementation. Now what? First, prepare a formal written analysis with an executive summary of the report for any reader who wishes to skip the analysis and read only the recommendations. Submit the recommendations to the legislator.

As soon as the legislator has had a chance to read the report, schedule two meetings. The first one should have the same ceremonial tenor as the initial meeting, and the same participants should attend—especially the leader of any institution sponsoring the assessment. At this meeting, discuss your findings and recommendations, as well as any resources or assistance the sponsoring institution might provide to implement the recommendations.

One way to hasten implementation of your recommendations is to make any financial or other political resources the sponsoring institution has to offer to the legislator contingent upon the implementation of the recommendations.

Next, schedule a second meeting with the legislator. During this meeting, you should take sufficient time to discuss fully all the findings and recommendations. If the legislator disagrees with any findings, pay close attention to his alternative view. At this time, discuss an "implementation timeline."

The Secret

Candidates and public officials are human beings. If you strive during the assessment to understand their personality and approach to political problem solving, you greatly increase the chance your assessment and recommendations will lead to organizational change.

The trick is to tailor the writing of the report—not your objective analysis—to the individual legislator. Try to determine the best way to give written and verbal advice to this individual, and format your report accordingly. In baseball parlance, pitch the ball where the batter likes to hit it. In this analogy, the game is Home Run Derby, and you are both successful when the legislator hits a home run and implements your recommendations.

✓ 10 Questions to Ask Yourself Before Running
Ron Faucheux

There's nothing quite like running for office. It's an unforgettable experience that most who do it would rather forget. That's because only about one in seven political candidates ever win. But when it works and ends in victory, it's exhilarating; like nothing else on Earth. Noted one wag, flushed with the jubilation of an election night victory party: "If God invented anything better, he kept it for himself!"

Deciding to run is an easy equation for some, a logical next step. Occasionally, circumstances create candidacies. But for most newcomers and challengers, the decision can be complex and anguishing.

Even though it's easy to get caught up in the ego trip of being the center of attention, the intense personal commitment required of candidates is a matter that demands reflection and sober assessment. Candidacy brings high ups and low downs—every day. In fact, every hour. At two o'clock, you can feel like The Master of the Universe. At three, you're looking for Dr. Kevorkian's phone number.

The instability and uncertainty of campaigns, even the carefully planned ones, and the extraordinary mix of emotions tangled within them, strain the candidate, often making him or her feel like a piece of meat for everybody to cut up and chew.

Once you make the decision to run, it can be a relief. It may even be the most enjoyable moment of the entire campaign, matched only by the elation of victory. Those first few days when you tell yourself, "Yes, I can do it! Yes I'm gonna do it!" are remarkably fanciful. But once the novelty wears off and the slugfest begins, feelings shift. It begins to seem as though a sword is hanging over your head, dangling on a thin thread, just waiting for any loon with a printing press or a fax machine to clip it, and your career, in one fell snip. Just ask Bill Clinton how he felt when he heard that Gennifer Flowers was calling a press conference.

Making it through a strategically tricky race is like walking across a mine field. You may have lucked out here, but watch out! They may get you over there. When things are going well, you feel very, very well. When things turn a little sour, you feel very, very sour. The pendulum swings wider for candidates than it does for lesser mortals.

Political campaigns provide a unique view of society, revealing a cross section you cannot see anywhere else. They bring out the best and worst in people. When it's the best, it's touching; when it's the worst, it's excruciating. You haven't lived until a young child hands you his or her weekly allowance of quarters, nickels, and pennies to help your campaign. You haven't lived—and may not want to—when you find out that your second cousin has been caught passing out leaflets for the opposition because he thinks you're a loser and wants a favor from the winner.

In making the decision to run or not, there are 10 questions you should answer:

1. Do I want the job?

Too often, candidates run just to be running, simply to get into public life, without much regard for the job itself. When this is the motivation, it usually shows. Once the press and the voters begin to sense a candidate's lack of interest in the job, it becomes increasingly difficult to be taken seriously.

Many public offices are not for everyone. A middle-aged business executive who enjoys managing large organizations may love being mayor of a big city, but may hate serving in the state legislature. A young idealist who's motivated by strong issue commitment may find serving in Congress a dream-come-true, but may abhor being sheriff or clerk of court.

2. Do I know what I want to do with the job?

At the end of "The Candidate," young Bill McKay (played by Robert Redford), having just been elected to the U.S. Senate after a storybook come-from-behind finish, looks up in puzzlement and asks his campaign guru, "What do we do now?"

Unfortunately, many candidates run without a clue as to what they want to do with the job. A good example was Ted Kennedy's unsuccessful bid to capture the 1980 Democratic presidential nomination. Sure, Kennedy wanted it. But because he hadn't decided why he wanted it, his early days on the hustings were disastrous. His poor performance in the celebrated CBS interview conducted by family friend Roger Mudd, when he couldn't give a coherent argument as to why he wanted to be president, sharpened the point. Many candidates want the job. Too many don't know what they want to do with it.

3. Can I take the time?

The naive believe they can simultaneously run for office and keep their jobs and businesses going at full speed. They don't understand that few things in life are as all-consuming as politics. Unless it's a lopsided contest or one for a low-level office in a tiny district, campaigning takes time. A lot of time. Usually, more time than you have. There's always something else you should be doing: one more hand to shake, phone call to make, dollar to raise, news article to read, thank you letter to write, or strategy meeting to attend. If you think you can run in a tough, competitive election and be a part-time candidate, think again. Be prepared to live, breathe, eat, and sleep your campaign. Or be prepared to lose.

4. Is this the right time?

Right person. Right office. Wrong time. The classic example was Hubert Humphrey. He mounted a spirited campaign for president in 1960, but that was John Kennedy's time. In 1964, fate catapulted Lyndon Johnson to the party's top spot on the ticket, relegating Humphrey to second banana. When he finally did win his party's nomination for president in 1968, it happened to be a ghastly year for Democrats—war, urban unrest, a crisis in confidence in national leadership. He barely missed.

By 1972, Humphrey's time had passed and the liberal wing of his party rejected him in favor of a new face, George McGovern. For Hubert Humphrey, the White House was not in the cards. Not because his party and his country didn't want him there, but because the time was never right. Just like time passes some candidates by, others fall flat when they jump too, soon. Albert Gore's 1988 presidential bid was a case in point, although the stature he gained from that campaign served him well four years later as Bill Clinton's VP pick.

5. Can I take the name calling, lies, and gossip?

This may be the single biggest reason why more good people don't run for office in the 1990s. No candidate is perfect. Everyone has flaws, has made mistakes, and is susceptible to being embarrassed or misunderstood. In politics, every crack of imperfection is magnified into a bottomless canyon. Thanks to television, those cracks can be exploited by the opposition day in, day out—100 times a day—in living color, uncivilly in the living rooms of your family, friends, and neighbors. Add to that an increasingly snoopy news media, where every piece of personal conduct is under the microscope of self-righteous analysis, and being a candidate starts looking less and less appealing.

Hence, the Halloween Rule of Politics: if you have a skeleton in your closet—even just a small bag of disconnected bones—expect it to jump out before election day, and count on it to look uglier than you ever imagined.

Even though some candidates escape the sledge hammer, don't bet on being so lucky. A 1992 example was that of Lena Guerrero: a smart, capable rising star in Texas. But she saw her fortunes for statewide office go down the tubes when it was discovered that she had fudged her resume and had, in fact, not been the Phi Beta Kappa she professed to be, or even a college graduate, as she had repeatedly claimed she was. She had used the same deceptions in her earlier and successful races for the state legislature, but her luck could not last forever.

Always expect the worst in politics. You'll never be disappointed. Remember: if the skeleton is too big and ugly, you may do well to pass on running at all. If you do run, make sure your business and personal affairs (unpaid taxes, unsettled lawsuits, hiring of illegal aliens, criminal investigations, etc.) are in order.

6. Can I win?

You need a sense of objectivity and good research to answer that question. Most candidates buy the latter. But few are blessed with much of the former. Wannabees often exaggerate their chances because they don't understand political arithmetic or human nature. There have been legions of hardware store owners, little league coaches, and car salesmen who think, because they meet hundreds of friendly people during the course of their work that (a) these people add up to an electoral base and (b) all those smiling faces will actually vote to put you into public office. Not so. In large electorates, the number of people you know isn't even a blip on the screen.

Many prominent civic leaders are shocked to find out in a poll that they have single-digit name recognition and are even more shocked when they learn that their share of the vote in a trial heat is marked with an asterisk signifying less than 1 percent. Candidates shouldn't run if they aren't running to win. Getting exposure for your law firm is fine, but adding useless noise to the clutter of politics is distracting to the democratic process.

Candidates also hate to admit that many of those nice people who tell them to their faces that they're with them are, in fact, liars. Follow the One Third Rule: Plan on one-third of the people you meet on the street who say they're going to vote for you to actually vote for you, one-third not to give a damn one way or the other, and the final one-third to vote against you. Those are the people who tell you they're for you. Imagine the range of feelings in the many voters who don't say anything?

7. Can I afford to lose?

Some people, because they've already lost elections, or because of the circumstances of the race, may not be able to survive a loss with their careers intact. This is particularly important when it comes to money. If you figure the only way you can finance a campaign is largely with your own money or on your own borrowing power, make sure if you lose you can afford to still feed your family. Some candidates who throw caution to the wind are elected; others have their houses repossessed.

8. Can I afford to win?

This is a relevant question in those contests for public offices that will take you away from your job or your business without adequately compensating you for your time, expertise, or lost wages. Every lawyer one time in his or her life dreams about being a judge. But many lawyers, when faced with a decision as to a possible judicial candidacy, forfeit the shot because they can't afford to give up a $200,000-a-year law practice for a $68,000 judgeship. Many legislators who are responsible for large businesses, budding law practices, insurance agencies, or full-time employment, find it hard to take the time off to go to the state capitol several months out of each year.

Another factor to consider is the bite of the political bug. Victory usually stirs ambition to go farther up the career ladder. What may begin as a part-time commitment to serve on a local school board may grow into a desire to run for county supervisor, then Congress, then governor, and then president. Beware of the bite! The toxin it spreads has few antidotes.

9. Can I raise I enough money?

Financing is another obstacle that keeps a lot of good people—particularly women and minorities—out of public office. For some, raising money can be an experience that falls somewhere between having a root canal and an enema. Most candidates hate it. They wake up each morning dreading that they have to bleed strangers and, even worse, friends and relatives, for cash. If you're not a Rockefeller, or an unbeatable chairman of the House Ways and Means Committee with lobbyists begging for the chance to write you a PAC check, fund raising is a tough business. If you have no easy money sources, and you detest asking for money, think twice about running.

10. Can I do this to my family?

Politics is hard on families. While close family members share few of the ego pleasures of candidacy, they suffer many of the slings and arrows that come with political combat. Remember Ross Perot ranting about Republican dirty tricksters disrupting his daughter's wedding? Candidates and their families are subject to cruel jokes, gossip, and innuendo. It's open season on the way they look, act, think, dress, and talk. Everything they do is going to be ridiculed by some jerk somewhere.

The long hours of hard work and being away from home don't help either. Losing, after taking all that abuse, can rack otherwise well-adjusted, sane people with bitterness and deep emotional scars. In politics, there's pain with every gain.

Whether you have the temperament and skills for political life is a question only you and your close friends and advisers can answer. Most importantly, it is a question that needs an answer before you enter the fray. The excitement of running for office and winning is incomparable. But so is the depression of being in the wrong place at the wrong time and losing. Think about both possibilities, and get ready for anything.

✓ Determining Whether You're Ready To Run
Cathy Allen

You have schmoozed at every holiday reception you could find. You have endured relentless boosterism from friends urging you to run. And you have importuned just about everyone you know about your prospects as a candidate. Now it is time to make up your mind. Are you or are you not in the running?

If December is for hobnobbing with key people to test the waters, January is for laying your actual political plans. Only nine short months remain before a new crop of political leaders takes over. Will you be among them? Your constituents, to say nothing of your potential opponents, want to know. Members of your family have put a winning campaign on their lists of New Year's Resolutions. Your friends and colleagues await their campaign assignments. You must decide now.

The question is: How do you decide to run?

This first step is a good self-analysis though some might recommend psychoanalysis, in which you ask and answer a series of tough questions. As part of this reality check on your prospects, take the questions and answers to a trusted friend, a reporter if you have bad public exposure, and to others who can be candid about your failings. One of the most difficult messages to hear is that you might not have the right stuff to run for office—especially when you want to hear the best.

The Desire: Why do you want to run for office? What do you offer people that is deserving of their respect? What do you want to do to change life for the better for your prospective constituents? What is it you feel strongly about, and can you convey that to others?

The Style: Can you face a crowd and convey your convictions? How well do you hold up under television lights? Do you have a sense of humor? Do you have good experience handling 18 matters at once? How well do you perform with little sleep? Are you good with people? Are you good at delegating responsibility? Can you attract a strong team?

The Background: Is there anything in your past that might be magnified to hurt your chances? Drunk driving, tax evasion, dope smoking, abortion, a messy divorce, a prolific sex life, dismissal from a job for ethical reasons, lying or cheating about your performance in college—you get the idea. Is your resume strong enough to reflect experience, stability, and knowledge? Have you put in adequate time learning about your community?

The Family and Job: Will your family support your candidacy? Do they want you to run? Can they survive well with you gone most of the time? What effect would losing have on your children? Can your bank account afford the drain of a campaign? Will your business allow you a leave of absence, or can your schedule at work be tailored to suit a campaign schedule? If you lose, will you have a job to return to?

The Physical Stamina: Can you maintain a neat, attractive appearance? Are you physically healthy enough to run? Can you cut out the cigarettes and cut down on the alcohol? Can you go 15 hours a day in the public eye and sleep six hours a night without showing the wear and tear on your personality? How well do you hold up to criticism and piercing press inquiries? How well do you handle setbacks?

The Community Quotient: Do you know what the electorate thinks about you? What have you ever done for them? Do you draw your supporters from a close-knit group of friends; or do you enjoy support of a cross-section of the community? Do the movers and shakers know who you are and consider you one of them? What does the local media have on file about you? Have you received much press?

These are a sample of serious questions that need serious answers. Usually no one answer to one specific question will eliminate you from making a race, but if you answer honestly, the ledger might weigh heavily toward one side. Spend time with people who will tell you the cold, cruel truth. Then assess your positive and negative attributes. Generally, the less agonizing the decision-making process, the better suited you are to run.

Know Your District

Basic information about your election district may be found in a variety of places. The municipal clerk, state elections office, the lieutenant governor's or secretary of state's office, or even some newspaper's files will have basic information about how many people are registered to vote and how many of them traditionally vote. Other demographic information you will need includes the female-male breakdown, party registration, and how often specific voters cast ballots.

In addition, direct-mail and computer businesses frequently have "teaser" sheets they mail to prospective customers giving free samples of what they offer. Check with these businesses and ask if they have demographic information they release for free. Look for clues about age, occupation, income levels, education, special interests, religious, and ethnic and racial breakdowns of your constituency.

Another source of demographic information is former candidates, major contributors to your party, or the party itself. Check recent polls that have tracked the profile of your election district. In some cases, local newspapers, ad agencies, or universities conduct polls that might be available to you with relatively little effort. Your local chamber of commerce and the U.S. Census Bureau have useful population breakdowns you will need.

The best option, of course, is to commission your own poll with a bona fide pollster who knows your turf. A good poll will cost anywhere from a few thousand dollars to serious thousands of dollars, depending on the sample size. A "benchmark" poll is the traditional first step in evaluating the voters by issue identification and demographic breakdown. This first poll give you a basic outline of the district and is the initial planning tool to target your prospective voters.

If your campaign is painfully tight about its cash, you might want to piggyback polling services with another candidate also running in the area (but obviously not against you). In these piggyback polls, you generally buy the right to ask few questions in a much larger poll that also yields a good demographic breakdown of the district.

Getting a snapshot of your potential constituents is crucial, but it also is good to know the physical setting of your electorate. Hop in a car or small plane and view the entire area. Drive the boundaries. Know the big industrial plants and the small playground parks. Know all the natural landmarks and visit the problem neighborhoods. Check out the libraries and the local newspapers. Count the schools and drive the back roads.

Know Who's In Charge

Assessing the power structure is not so easy as driving the district or reading the poll information. Who are the community leaders? Talk with them in person. Attend the chamber of Commerce luncheons, Rotary meetings, your local women's political caucus, the environmental group's banquet, and so forth. Schedule meetings with union, minority, parents, business, recreation, and other leaders. Ask about their goals for the community—and ask for their help. One of the most frequent reasons newcomers win support from the power structure is that they ask for the help first. One important reason to announce early is to be the first to ask for a person's, group's, or organization's support.

The track record of the incumbent (if it is not you) is critical to know. Talk with local reporters. Most are not so difficult to approach as you might think. It is unlikely a reporter will allow you see his files concerning the incumbent, but most will talk freely about an incumbent's record and style. Reporters can provide a wealth of objective information not only on your opponents but also on the issues that might surface during the campaign. Tact and charm might convince a reporter to level with you about your own chances. In your effort to create a positive relationship with a reporter assigned to cover your race, listen more than you talk.

Some preliminary research about your opposition is important. Outline the strengths and weaknesses of any prospective candidates for your race. Talk with people who might have worked on their campaigns to find out about their pet issues and campaign styles. You can be sure your opponents are doing the same.

It also is important for you to research the functions of the office you plan to seek. Do you really know what the job is all about? Are you qualified to handle the duties? Speak with former officeholders and party leaders to help you answer these questions.

The Legal Picture

During the winter months, there is ample time to do the most boring task of the campaign: reading and understanding all the rules, regulations, ordinances, laws, and procedures that accompany each race. In these days of public disclosure about where each candidate receives and spends mash, regulation is part of the game. In most states, some form of campaign restrictions apply, usually regarding who can contribute and how much. You also might find that a tradition in your community dictates from whom you might want to take contributions.

Even though you might have scads of lawyers and a campaign manager who have dealt with election law, read the rules yourself even though you might not understand them all.

Talk with local election officials about the most common abuses of the regulations. Obtain any applications, forms, and explanations. In many states, an election official will speak personally with a campaign team to answer questions and explain the laws. Such a session will help you become at ease with the laws and reporting deadlines. Be sure to note these filing and reporting deadlines and be certain to review any paperwork at least two days before official deadlines.

Other self-imposed restrictions are worth considering, although each time you restrict the amount of money you will receive, be sure you have a good reason. Many candidates refuse money from political action committees; others refuse money from regulated businesses, such as insurance companies and banks. You might want to limit contributions from government employees you might supervise should you win. Some candidates limit contributions from minors to $25. Still others limit the amount of money they personally will contribute to the campaign, especially if they are perceived as being rich enough to "buy" the election.

Find out if your opponents plan to limit the money each will take, check out other races in your district where campaign contributions might be an issue. Check with party leaders to see what might be important to them. Check with your own team to find out what limits you might want to impose and whether such restrictions might fly in the face of your strategy or common sense.

The Role Of Campaign Committees

Axiomatic of campaigns is that the candidate is the boss—even though everyone agrees the candidate is the person least likely to be objective about problems, especially during stressful times. As campaigns have evolved, however, we are seeing an ever-increasing series of committees that have varying degrees of control and responsibilities. These committees traditionally are composed of prestigious individuals you want actively working for you and giving you feedback on how the campaign is proceeding.

No committee should make decisions, nor should it be calling the shots your professionals (if you have hired any) are trained to handle. Maintain this control, and you will spend less time reigning in your committees and more time benefiting from their help.

No single committee is imperative for any campaign; many varieties are worthwhile. All are time consuming; too many can waste time or be uncontrollable. Each committee you consider should have a specific role, a regular meeting time, and a clear mission ask part of the organization. The time you spend organizing your committees is critical. Make sure the composition is representative of your constituency, and be sure to add people who are likely to be the devil's advocate as well as those who are blindly supportive.

When you meet new supporters, especially important representatives of special-interest groups, do not immediately ask them to join a committee. Determine what you think they might add, and ask others who serve on the committee for advice before you make the offer.

The Steering Committee. This group meets once or twice a month and includes community leaders, constituency representatives, mentors, longtime friends, former or current elected officials, the chair of the finance committee, and key campaign staffers. Although candidates usually attend most of these meetings, valuable give and take occurs at some meetings where the candidate is not present.

The purpose of this committee is to gauge the campaign's progress and to report on how the strategy is working. Agendas for committee meetings should be written, and a secretary should be appointed to call members about meeting times and to follow up on suggestions made by the group. Steering committees do not run campaigns; they generate advice and ideas. The members are your trusted guides through the confusing and hectic times of a campaign, but they do not speak for the campaign, unless directed to do so. Committee members should attend all the major functions of the campaign; especially at low-turnout fund-raisers, these loyalists always help make the room look full.

Some steering committees work well by plowing through full reports of everything going on in the campaign; others simply respond to the agenda prepared by the candidate and campaign manager. Meetings are good times to divvy up pressing chores and critical phone calls to community leaders. Steering committees often add valuable insights on opponents' campaigns and should always act as energetic rallying points for campaign staffers and the candidate. You know you are missing the boat if these meetings become draining interrogations or rambling reviews of your staff.

The Finance Committee. The finance committee is the most important committee of every campaign. Its members are people who have money and/or can raise lots more of it. These people need not meet frequently so long as checks are coming in. The best way to ensure this happens is to meet as often as possible to encourage more searching for bucks. Because finance committee members often are business people, breakfast is a good time to meet.

Again, have an agenda, a specific meeting date once every other week, and a list of all members and their telephone numbers. Each meeting should discuss an up-to-date schedule of all campaign events, as well as current totals of money raised and money needed.

There can never be enough people on a finance committee, and you should add freely to the list. Seek out people from the special-interest groups you have targeted for support and contact finance committee members from past campaigns. Your finance chair should be an experienced fund-raiser who can command respect in the political community. This person should know how to run a meeting and be prepared to carry out the agenda without your presence. The chair needs to be a spark plug that can motivate newcomers to solicit money from their own mother and strangers alike.

The finance committee should know the cash-flow chart by heart and be told what the big money of the campaign will buy. Different finance committees require different levels of campaign formation, but in general, simple explanations of where the money is going should suffice. The finance committee should not make any decisions expenditures, but it should be told cash is being handled and what will be the priorities for spending should the money slow to a trickle.

Also, finance committees are the first place some campaigns discuss poll results—the horse-race numbers can be valuable in encouraging new contributions.

Make sure the finance committee is properly trained in how to accept contributions. You might want to schedule a meeting with local election officials so your finance team can ask questions about contribution limits, reporting requirements, and so forth. Often, such officials are pleased a campaign ask questions early; knowing you started out on the right foot, they might be more willing to help you with future problems.

The Kitchen Cabinet. A critical issue to settle right now is deciding to whom you will listen during the course of campaign. Historically, campaigns include a "kitchen cabinet" of friends and family to rely upon advice and key decisions. The structure usually is informal, or it can involve regular meetings and take on some of the functions of the steering committee. Generally, the kitchen cabinet meets as time warrants and crises arise.

If there is a major, radical turn of events (entry of an unexpected strong contender, the firing of a key campaign worker, press coverage of a scandal involving the candidate), you need to know now how you will react. The group by its nature should be small. A close friend or two who is not involved with the campaign, a key member of the finance or steering committee, the campaign's pollster are frequent players on such a team. To prepare for a crisis, know whom to call to rally the kitchen cabinet.

Shifting Into Gear

This is a big election year; people are running in virtually every political jurisdiction. You cannot start soon enough. There will be competition for competent, paid professionals as well as for hard-working volunteers. Start scouting out the paid consultants that share your style and politics and are within your budget. (Naturally, whether you hire consultants depends on the size and demands of your race, as well as your bank account.)

Your pollster will give you the numbers that help analyze the district and keep you in tune with what your constituents are thinking. There are many kinds of polls and several ways to use them; determine what you can afford and find the most professional help available. If you plan to hire a pollster, talk to more than one to make sure you speak the same language. Find out which campaigns a pollster has handled in your geographic area as well as those races that shared your strategy characteristics. List any concerns you might have about polls or pollsters now; your pollster will be the key information broker as the campaign days dwindle.

If you plan to use television, your media team must be able to capture you and your campaign theme in 30-second spots. Media consultants are costly and require major disruptions in every campaign schedule, and you must trust them to translate your electability to your constituency. Choose carefully and deliberately. Find out the costs up front and understand what you will be paying for with each consultant you consider.

A political consultant is an experienced campaign professional who can help you respond to crucial situations in ways that limit your liabilities or make good news even better. The consultant's job is to help devise a strategy that fits your personal and political style and to troubleshoot in-house problems that might hurt the campaign. Hire a consultant who has had direct experience in your district or with candidates similar to you. Shop around and shop early—there are as many styles and approaches to campaign consulting as there are candidates.

Staffing choices for the day-to-day operations of the campaign are just around the corner. Now is not too early to think about hiring the campaign personnel you will need. A campaign manager, a scheduler, and a press person are the three standard ingredients in most campaigns. Depending on how strong you believe the finance committee will be, you might decide to hire a fund-raiser.

Other talents you need to round up for the campaign include managers, lawyers, bookkeepers, accountants, and people who have dealt with sign construction and placement in other campaigns. It is unlikely these people will be full-time volunteers to the campaign, but all will be required to lend professional expertise. It is important to identify these people and their specific roles early in the campaign.

You might need office space, equipment, supplies, computers, and phone systems, depending on your race and budget. Start scouting now for the material and equipment. Every time you walk into someone's office, look around to see what you might be able to borrow later in the spring.

Limiting The Competition

It always is worthwhile to attempt to "scare off" other candidates from entering the race. Once you have determined you will run, conventional strategy is to announce quickly and present as strong an image as possible. Print small cards with your name and office you seek and hand them out to everyone you meet. Let reporters know you are running and keep reminding them.

You might want to talk to potential competitors directly to show them you mean business and already have a campaign organization and strategy. You also might want to solicit early support from key advisers to people who are considering a race against you. Whatever the approach, preemption strategies are designed to give you an early push and make other candidates think twice about jumping into the campaign waters. Such a strategy can backfire, however, prompting fence-sitters to take the plunge in order to shore up their own campaign coffers.

With the holidays behind you and the election in front of you, now is the time to decide whether to run. The time for hand wringing is over, and the time for planning your campaign has begun. The work you do now cuts down on work you will have to do later. Think carefully about this important decision. Postpone it and you will conduct the process in haste.

✓ Political Humor
Robert Neuman

While their ideologies differed, U.S. Rep. Morris Udall and U.S. Sen. Henry Jackson had a good deal in common when they sought the presidency in 1976. Both were from the West—a region where the Democrats needed to broaden their appeal. Both were widely respected by their colleagues as well as the media.

And both lost.

The failure of Mo Udall and the late "Scoop" Jackson to achieve their party's highest prize underscores the importance of humor and its proper use at all levels of political endeavor. One did himself injury when he sought to employ humor; the other undermined his credibility when he failed to.

Jackson was without peer in his knowledge and authority on defense and foreign policy issues. He was admired for his work habits and integrity. And yet, there was something missing that prompted questions about his ability to move up: The man simply could not tell a joke.

Jackson's "humor gap" plagued him throughout an otherwise distinguished career. His staff despaired at the media's persistent references to the senator's tiresome speeches and stultifying delivery (the phrase "dour Norwegian" appeared regularly in profiles of Jackson). The senator's aides used coaches and technicians to enliven his style. And they urged him to pepper his speeches with one-liners in the manner of rival Mo Udall, an unquestioned master of political wit.

Jackson finally followed their advice, much to everyone's later regret.

In 1975, the senator went to a luncheon and heard a joke that struck him as topical and funny; he considered it a sure-fire winner for a speech he had to give that evening. The story went as follows:

Shortly after his emotional resignation from the presidency, Richard Nixon paid a courtesy call on Gerald Ford at the White House. As he entered the Oval Office, he tripped and bumped into a startled Ford.

"Pardon me, Jerry," said Nixon.

"I already did, Dick," replied Ford.

That night, Jackson was on the road. Introduced to an adoring audience as labor's friend, a staunch anti-Communist and a committed social liberal, Jackson had the crowd in his hand. He decided to show the press corps traveling with him that he could do as well as Mo Udall, and he proceeded to tell the story:

"President Nixon was visiting the White House after his resignation, and as he entered the Oval Office, he tripped and bumped into President Ford.

'Excuse me, Jerry.'

'Already did, Dick'."

The audience was stunned. The disbelieving press corps eyed each other with looks that betrayed genuine embarrassment for the man. And Scoop Jackson took another step away from the White House.

Udall, meanwhile, was as uncomfortable with negative campaigning as Jackson was with humor.

In the crucial 1976 Wisconsin primary, he watched as his opportunity to defeat Jimmy Carter was being eaten away by other candidates cutting into Udall's support among liberals and union members. Udall's advisers told him that he had to go on the attack—especially against Jackson, long a favorite of organized labor. But Udall resisted, arguing that he could counter an opponent better with a joke than with a gun shot.

"There is no time for jokes, Mo," his advisers cried. "Jackson is going to kill you . . . you have to take him on."

Udall protested that would be out of character.

"Mo," his consultants pleaded, "the bottom line is simple. No one is taking you seriously. How are you going to talk about the economy when everyone is waiting for the punch line?"

So Udall held a press conference in Milwaukee in which he unmasked Henry Jackson as a hawk (big surprise), hostile to the environmental movement (big deal), an opponent of school desegregation (which did not go over well in South Milwaukee) and unfriendly on women's issues (ditto).

Udall was ill at ease, and his heart clearly was not in the attack. The press, accustomed to Udall flaying an opponent with a gentle barb and a joke, were shocked at Udall's assault and lapse of form. Columnist Robert Novak summed up the effort neatly in a dispatch filed from Milwaukee:

"Congressman Mo Udall tried to do a hatchet job on Henry Jackson today, a task to which he is spectacularly ill-suited."

There is an old politician's prayer that says, "Oh Lord, teach us to utter words that are gentle and tender, because tomorrow we may have to eat them." Udall had to eat his words, to say nothing of watching his chances of winning the presidential nomination taken off the table by a 7,000-vote Carter victory in Wisconsin.

Udall and his advisers learned a lesson: If you can tell a joke and are known for your sense of humor, take advantage of it—and, for God's sake, don't turn negative.

There are few people in politics today as funny as Mo Udall, as there are some who are as "dour" as Scoop Jackson. For the latter group, the lesson is: If you don't have the timing and the touch to tell a joke, don't try.

There is, however, a large group in the middle. These are politicians whose private wit could be used to advantage in their public lives, but who are simply afraid to try:

Excuse No. 1: I feel jokes detract from the seriousness of an issue or the campaign.
Excuse No. 2: I don't know any jokes that haven't been told a hundred times.
Excuse No. 3: I just can't get a joke over to an audience (memories of "Excuse me, Jerry").

Pardon me, but one does not have to be a bore to be substantive. In fact, the case can be made that politicians who use humor are more likely to be taken seriously. Such successful presidents as Abraham Lincoln, Franklin D. Roosevelt, John F. Kennedy and Ronald Reagan are a testament to that.

And the two highest-ranking Republicans in the U.S. Senate—Minority Leader Robert Dole and Minority Whip Alan Simpson—also are two of that body's wittiest members (excepting those occasions when Dole has squashed his image on national television with some dark statement).

Lincoln's use of humor during the Civil War did take some heat from political opponents and press critics. The story is told of a conversation during that terrible conflict in which two Quaker women were speaking of the protagonists, Lincoln and Jefferson Davis. One said, "I think Jefferson will succeed." Said the other, "Why dost thou think so?" Replied the first, "Because he is a praying man." "But so is Abraham a praying man." "Yes," said the first, "but the Lord will think Abraham is joking." (The Lord never would have suspected Michael Dukakis of joking.)

What Lincoln and some of his wittier successors have done is to frame their messages carefully with laboriously crafted humor, thereby building acceptance from the audience. Most of the above mentioned political wits also have used self-deprecating humor as a way of inspiring affection from the crowd.

That lesson sometimes escaped Jimmy Carter. Early in the 1976 campaign, Carter—having finished fourth in the Massachusetts primary—was in a surly mood. On the campaign plane, Carter was stopped in the aisle by *Boston Globe* reporter Curtis Wilkie:

"Governor, why don't you use deprecating humor like Mo Udall?" asked the reporter. Snapped Carter: "If I had written the legislation creating the Postal Service like Udall, I'd have plenty to be self-deprecating about."

Udall's classic in self-deprecation came during the same campaign. He told of walking into a New Hampshire barber shop on the first day of his longshot effort. Sticking his head in the door, he introduced himself to the barber and a shop full of townsmen: "Hi, Mo Udall of Arizona, I'm running for president." The barber looked up, nodded and said: "We know, we were just laughing about it this morning."

That brings us to Excuse No. 2 for not using humor in politics: originality.

Do not be afraid to steal jokes; they are in the public domain upon being told for the first time. "Buchwald's Law" (named for columnist Art Buchwald) mandates that you give credit to the author the first two times you use someone else's joke. After that, the hell with it.

Udall's barber shop joke was "borrowed" by U.S. Sen. Albert Gore, Jr. in New Hampshire during Gore's presidential bid in 1988. Gore changed the locale to a grocery story, but kept the punch line intact. The joke had such widespread currency in New Hampshire that, within 24 hours, Gore's theft had been reported in the press. That prompted a written apology from Gore to Udall, who replied that Gore was free to use that and any other joke. Udall also expressed the hope that Gore would have better luck with the jokes than he did (Gore didn't).

Finally, there is Excuse No. 3. How can a politician learn to tell a joke and avoid the Scoop Jackson syndrome?

In short, it takes hard work, practice and some self-confidence. There are few natural comedians; being humorous is a skill that can be acquired. Delivery—which includes body language, voice inflection and timing—is about three-quarters of the art. And there are now media coaches who claim the ability to turn sow's ears into silk purses.

Perhaps the most notable transformation of the 1988 campaign involved former Arizona Gov. Bruce Babbitt. In early televised appearances, Babbitt resembled a cross between Ichabod Crane and a gecko lizard; he had an unnerving manner of darting his tongue out of his mouth. By the time he left the race, Babbitt had become a candidate of polish and wit whom the press corps regularly described as the class of the field.

Babbitt's Cinderella act was the work of media trainer Michael Sheehan; in the process, he provided a glimmer of hope to every candidate who freezes on camera or stumbles over punch lines.

At the same time, there is a danger of being overcoached. When he sought the presidency in 1984, U.S. Sen. John Glenn was plagued with the Scoop Jackson Curse—he was alternately described as humorless, wooden and downright boring. To combat this, the ex-astronaut's advisers arranged for Glenn to be one of the featured speakers at the annual Gridiron Dinner, whose audience of Washington insiders provides one of the toughest tests for political wits.

Glenn's consultants left nothing to chance. They recruited the most accomplished speech writers and political wits, and met long into the night selecting appropriate jokes and refining the senator's presentation. On the night of the Gridiron Dinner, Glenn was very, very good—but received little credit for his performance. Wrote one member of the press: "It took more people to get John Glenn up on stage than it did to get him to orbit the Earth."

Even politicians who are masters of delivery must continually worry about the content of their humor. Jokes about ethnics, women, the poor, religion and Dan Quayle just about have been frozen out of politics, and more is the pity (about the only ethnic group safe to belittle are WASPs, because—as columnist Mark Shields points out—there is no Episcopalian Anti-Defamation League).

If you are tempted to take on any of the above individuals or groups, keep in mind Neuman's Fourth Law: "Nobody can take a joke anymore." For example, there was the time in 1984 when I was working on a Gridiron speech for former Democratic National Chairman Robert Strauss—who was being mentioned as a possible presidential candidate. As the presidential race heated up, Jesse Jackson had caused a great stir with comments (reported in the Washington Post) that were widely considered to be anti-Semitic.

With that background, I offered the following joke for delivery by Strauss: "You know, a lot of people have been talking about my running for president. And I kind of like the idea. I would work hard all week. And then, after, I would take my wife Helen by the arm and walk out of the Oval Office, across the South Lawn to the Marine Corps helicopter—and we'd fly off to Camp Hymie."

Strauss laughed until tears came out of his eyes. Then he put down the joke and said, "Too bad we can't use it." It was too Jewish, too black, and too "inside-the-Beltway."

But do not be scared off; there are plenty of targets that are inbound for the politician who wants to warm up his audience with some humor. For starters, there are the rich, George Bush, stockbrokers and journalists.

Of course, the best targets for political humor are politicians themselves, particularly those who work and live in Washington. As a public service to the aspiring novice, I offer a couple of sure fire jokes, free for the stealing, that feature politicians as targets. These have the advantage of being constructed so that the most prominent (or notorious) public figures of the moment can be inserted to make the joke topical.

Recommended for a Democratic audience.

The president was spending the weekend at Camp David after a particularly trying time; Congress was rebelling and his staff was riddled with internal conflict. He stole away from his Secret Service detail for a solitary walk in the woods. Suddenly, he came upon a cave entrance covered with brush. Upon entering the cave, he encountered a hermit.

"Old man," said the president. "Give me a sign. If John Sununu, James Baker and Lee Atwater jumped off the Washington Monument, who would land first?"

The old man thought a moment, and replied: "It is not important which of them would land first. It is important that they jump."

Recommended for a Republican audience.

A jogger running through the nation's capital was accosted recently by an armed robber. After taking the runner's watch and Walkman, he put a gun to the jogger's head, and demanded: "Who do you want to be the Democratic nominee in 1992—Cuomo, Nunn or Jackson?"

The jogger thought for a long moment and finally replied: "Go ahead shoot."

✓ Announcing Your Candidacy
Randy Thompson

Campaigns are not won or lost on announcement day just started or stalled. The day's events set the tone for the weeks and months of campaigning that will follow.

There is no magic formula or set of rules for announcing your candidacy, no checklist for success. There are only guideposts to steer you around hazardous waste dumps of defeated candidates and silly ideas.

Don't announce before you have at least the framework of a campaign assembled. This begins with the backing of your family and friends. You will need all of their moral support during the dark days that befall every campaign. The last thing you need are those closest to you saying, "Boy, I wish you hadn't entered this race."

Determine your message and put it to a test. You may have solutions which will end world hunger and stop war. But if your constituents are more concerned about BMW's and garbage collection, don't waste your time on global issues. Good research will be the backbone of your campaign. Also, while the logistics are being ironed out, work on a speech that outlines the message of your campaign. Don't make it a position paper. If it's longer than 10 to 15 minutes you will lose your audience. And don't assume you can deliver a good speech. You're a performer. Rehearse.

Site selection is key. Where you announce, especially for television purposes, is sometimes as important as what you say. If you are running in a blue-collar urban district which is heavily union, don't announce at a country club. Get it? Determine your audience and put yourself in surroundings they understand. Also, depending on the type of race you are entering, it may be necessary to announce at more than one location. All must match your message.

Keep your schedule tight. The press corps and your supporters are doing you a favor by attending your events.

Not only is it rude to keep them waiting, but it will become part of the story: "John Smith, who was 30 minutes late, announced for Congress today, saying..." You may also wish to schedule fundraising events or tours of places like malls, schools and work sites. The key here is to make this a day of activity. Don't just give a speech; show some energy and momentum.

Play to a packed house. After you have selected your location, it is up to your campaign to fill it up. Think visually. This will be one of the few free television days you will receive. The set should not be empty.

Make life easy on the press corps. Prepare a press kit that includes a copy of your speech, a press release, a schedule of the day's events, a current photograph, a biography and any prepared position statements. For the television stations which do not attend, provide video clips of important segments of the speech. These can be delivered by hand or by satellite uplink the day of the announcement. Also, if you are traveling, offer transportation. You don't want anyone to get lost.

Milk the story by selling it in advance. Do one-on-one interviews with key reporters, send out a press release announcing the announcement, and call all members of the media twice, once to notify them, and a second time to ask if they will be attending. Mail press kits to all media outlets. Then, if they don't attend they will have information in house.

Don't panic. Announcing your candidacy for public office will be one of the most important events in your political life.

At least look like you are having a good time. After all, you volunteered for this agony.

✓ Creating an Effective Speaking Style
Michael Sheehan

In this era of electronic campaigning, it's easy to overlook the oldest element of a candidate's repertoire—the stump speech. Now—whether you are nine months or a year and a half out of an election—is a good time to focus on the fundamentals. Here's how to start:

Everyone polls to construct a message and focus his or her paid media, so why is polling an afterthought to the stump speech? Unless your autobiography is enough to carry you, you must poll and use the results to construct your stump speech. Even if you know you'll be talking about health care, for example, your polling will direct you on how to talk about it.

For inspiration, don't read the speeches of Winston Churchill, John F. Kennedy, or Franklin Delano Roosevelt. Their speeches may be inspirational, but they are bad models for you. See, those guys were already in office—leaders of nations—when they gave those speeches. I'm guessing that most of you are not.

Phrases such as "And so my fellow Americans, ask not..." become history when delivered by an elected president. When delivered by you, especially if you are a local-level first timer or a challenger, such language sounds pretentious and out of touch.

Better models are Madison Avenue, Dale Carnegie, even the family counselors on PBS. Don't overreach on rhetoric...until you win.

It's a truism because it's true—practice, practice, practice! Rarely does a politician take it seriously enough, and too often it shows. Actors rehearse four-to-six weeks for a supporting role in a play. I'm appalled by how little rehearsing candidates do. And pen to paper isn't practice; aloud, maybe with a hand-held dictating machine, is.

Professional athletes in every sport intensely review their game films. What are candidates so shy about? The only way you can see and hear the same sights and sounds as your audiences is to practice that way. Perform, record, and play back. Your neighbor's home video camera is good enough. If not, just a mirror and a tape recorder are an adequate start. While advanced coaching is a highly developed skill, basic self-critique is effective, too.

The basic checklists are easy:

- Visually, look at your eye contact (is it steady enough?), gestures (are there any?), posture (is it fairly comfortable yet neat?), and facial expressions (do you look like you're undergoing a root canal?).
- Vocally, listen in the playback mode for the following: volume (is it modulated?), pitch (is your emphasis short of whining?), pacing (slower is better), and inflection (is it varied enough?).

Stump speaking is like vaudeville. Work up an act, rehearse it, and take it on the road. Don't change what works—if it gets a response, keep it. Your only real enemy is your own boredom brought on by repetition.

✓ The Basic Rules of Working a Room
Lorene Hanley Duquin

For local candidates, going to community events, shaking hands, and talking to people is still one of the most effective methods of swaying voters. People like to meet candidates. But some candidates are better at meeting people than others. Some radiate charm, wit, and trustworthiness, while others appear overly aggressive, nervous, or insincere.

What is the secret of success? Is it luck? Is it that mystical quality we call charisma?

Perhaps. But many successful candidates also admit that throughout their professional careers, they have developed a few special techniques for working a room and meeting voters. And these simple techniques make a real difference in the effectiveness of their personal campaigning. Here are some of those secrets of success which have been gathered from elected officials across the country.

Assessing the Situation

One of the most difficult things about personal campaigning is learning how to walk into a room with confidence and begin introducing yourself. Some local office holders rely on staff members who arrive at an event early and make a few advance preparations. These staff people hand out campaign literature and buttons, determine the mood of the crowd, their interests, their ages, and their protocol. If the opponent is present, the staff members make notes on what issues are being discussed. They also make lists of the important people in the room who should receive special attention by the candidate. Then they brief the candidate before he or she enters the room.

Staff members for Eileen R. Anderson, Mayor, the City and County of Honolulu, Hawaii all plan in advance her circulation route through the room in order to maximize her visibility. "They identify the group leaders and the key individuals present who can assist in introductions," she says. On the other hand, some candidates never use advance people. "My campaigns have always had a grass roots flavor," says Chuck Swanick, a local legislator from Kenmore, New York. "So I usually go to these events alone. But before I start shaking hands, I stand in the doorway for a few moments to observe the crowd and plan my route through the room."

Swanick mentally divides the room into four parts and decides in advance where he'll start and where he'll finish. "I also watch for people that I know will try to monopolize my time and for people who are likely to try and embarrass me or give me a hard time about something," he says. "With a little practice, it gets relatively easy to determine the nature of the group and who is there just by watching. And those few minutes at the doorway before I start shaking hands seem to bolster my confidence and restore my interest and enthusiasm for meeting people."

Creating a Positive Impression

Successful candidates know that meeting as many people as possible is the lifeblood of a political campaign. They also know that they'll be meeting most of these people for the very first time and they probably won't have a chance to meet them again before the election. So when they do meet someone, they make sure the impression they create is a good one. Here are some of the important dos and don'ts which candidates suggested for making a positive impression:

- Always have a firm handshake. No one likes a limp fish handshake.
- Be prepared for those hard handshakers that nearly break your hand. Don't wince. Grin and bear it. And remember, the pain is less if you don't wear a ring on your shaking hand.
- Maintain eye contact with the person you're talking to. Don't look around the room or at another person while talking to a voter.
- Give each person your complete attention and interest. Make them feel like they are the only person in the room.
- Be energetic. Stand up straight with your head up, shoulders back, and stomach pulled in.
- Don't be overbearing or effusive.
- Don't ever wear dark glasses.
- Have clean hands and well-manicured nails.
- Don't ignore anyone—especially youngsters.
- Be honest and always be consistent in talking about issues.
- Be yourself.

It was also suggested that you try to consciously observe yourself and make a mental note of any nervous mannerisms or annoying habits that you might have. If you can't recognize your own behavior problems, then ask your campaign manager to observe you. Be especially alert to irritating little quirks such as clearing your throat, sniffling, rubbing your nose, pulling your ear, tapping your fingers, shuffling your feet, pointing your finger at people, scratching your head, wrinkling your brow, or making other facial expressions that imply nervous tension. Then concentrate on breaking those bad habits.

Barbara Bennett, Mayor of Reno, Nevada notes that even something as positive as a smile can create a negative impression. "If the situation calls for a smile, do so," she advises. "But don't walk around with a glued-on smile." And never smile when discussing serious matters.

As you work the room, try to create the impression that you are sincere, friendly, and accessible. "You have to get to know the voters. Convince them that you are aware of some of their needs and that you're trying to determine all of their needs," says Richard Arrington, Jr., Mayor of Birmingham, Alabama. "Talk, but spend some time listening, too!"

While you listen, be sure that you are really paying attention to what the person is saying. Don't fall into the trap of thinking about what you are going to say or do next while someone else is talking. If you find yourself stuck with someone who is talking excessively, learn to cut that person off without appearing rude. The best way of doing that is to find an appropriate place to interrupt and politely excuse yourself. For instance, you might say, "I think you have a very good point there and I appreciate your bringing it up. But I'm afraid I have to move along now."

The key is not to be phony. Be honest. Be yourself. And always try to leave the people feeling good about themselves and feeling good about you.

Avoiding blunders

"I like to place my hands on people's shoulders and inject humor into the conversation," says Barry L. Robinson, a County Legislator from upstate New York. But while Robinson's easy, familiar style is highly effective, it is not a technique that every candidate can use successfully. Humor and touching can be a real plus or a real minus. And smart candidates are able to determine when these techniques are appropriate by paying close attention to the non-verbal messages that voters relay.

For example, kissing someone on the cheek or putting your arm around someone's shoulders is obviously a more personal gesture than a simple handshake. While some people are receptive to personal contact, others are more reserved and dislike being touched by strangers. Although they probably won't say anything to you verbally, their body language will be telling you to BACK OFF! A person who doesn't want to be touched might inch backwards, or break eye contact, or become stiff and rigid, or exhibit other signs of nervousness. The smart candidate knows how to recognize these types of signals and reacts accordingly.

Humor is another technique that must be treated with caution. What might seem like a cute little remark to you could be interpreted by someone else as being insensitive. Never joke about serious matters. And never belittle anyone else—especially your opponent.

As you develop your own style, keep in mind that even the most polished and experienced candidates still make embarrassing mistakes. James D. Griffin, Mayor of Buffalo, New York, is well known for his Irish charm and his ability to say exactly the right thing to each person. Yet even Mayor Griffin admits to at least one of these embarrassing situations on the campaign trail. "I asked a woman when she was expecting," he recalls. "She gave me a dirty look and said she wasn't!"

In situations like that one, the only thing you can do is apologize and keep on moving.

Another common faux pas is overstaying you welcome. Even worse is the candidate who barges in where he isn't welcome at all. "There is a time and a place," says Betty Hoffman, Mayor of North Tonawanda, New York. "Don't overdo it. For example, if you're at a private dinner or benefit, don't table hop."

It's a good idea to have someone from your campaign staff check with the organizers of a community event beforehand to make sure that political candidates are welcome and to get a feel for how long you can stay without creating a problem or bad feelings.

Remembering Names and Faces

One of the most embarrassing blunders a candidate can make is connecting the wrong name to the wrong face. Some candidates recalled situations where they had carried on an entire conversation with the wrong person. They found out later the person had absolutely no idea of what the candidate had been talking about. It's the kind of occupational hazard that led the mayor of a large city in Ohio to quip, "The best advice I can give to a political candidate is to pray that everyone in the room has a name tag on."

Popular self-help books abound with advice and elaborate techniques for remembering names and faces. Most of these systems tell you to associate the person's name with a phrase that sounds like the name. Then you're supposed to pick out a distinguishing characteristic about the person's face and create a mental picture which associates th facial characteristic with a phrase that sounds like the name.

For example, suppose you meet a Mr. Sullivan. You associate the name Sullivan with the phrase "Stole a van." Then you imagine that the lines on Sullivan's forehead are the road map he used to drive the stolen van away from the scene of the crime.

If this all sounds very complicated and somewhat ridiculous, you're right. It is. And it can sometimes create more problems than not remembering the name in the first place.

The best advice for remembering names is to listen. If you don't catch the person's name when you're being introduced, ask the person to repeat it. It's never in bad taste to say, "I'm sorry. I didn't catch your name when we were introduced." And in most cases, the person will feel complimented that you cared enough to ask.

After you've been introduced, learn to use a person's name throughout your conversation. It will help you to reinforce in your mind the name and face of the person.

In some cases, you might want to ask the person for a business card or maybe jot down their name and telephone number for future reference. Later you can make a note of where you met the person and why it is important for you to remember the name.

Keep in mind that we all have a tendency to remember things that we perceive are important. Remind yourself constantly that meeting voters is one of the most important activities a political candidate can engage in. Then concentrate on people's names and faces as you meet them. And if you do happen to forget a name, don't ever try to guess it. Swallow your pride and admit that the person's name has slipped your mind.

Handling hostile voters

"I was at a community event where a hostile group was planning to ask questions that they hoped would be embarrassing to me with the media present," recalls Eleanor J. Kesim, Mayor of Elkhart

Indiana. "Having been forewarned by a friend, I said that because of another closely scheduled appearance (which was true) I would be unable to answer questions that evening, but perhaps another time. Those who were hostile were plainly disappointed."

It pays to have good contacts who can keep their ear to the ground in situations like this one. But not all candidates are lucky enough to be forewarned about troublemakers. If you find yourself in a hostile situation, don't get angry and lose your temper. It will only make matters worse. Stay calm. Don't argue. And get away from that person as quickly as possible.

"It's important to learn to take rejection," says Rep. Geraldine A. Ferraro of New York. "If someone refuses literature or won't shake your hand, go on to the next person. Keep moving and introducing yourself."

You can avoid a lot of hostility if you learn not to make promises that you cannot keep. Try to make general statements if asked for favors. If you don't know the answer to a question, say you're not sure but that you'll find the answer. If someone is baiting you on a hot issue that you'd rather not take a stand on, ask what that person's opinion is. Your willingness to listen is especially important when the other person is obviously upset. Then make a graceful exit. Many candidates mentioned that they rely on campaign staff members to keep them moving through the crowd and to arrange for swift exits.

Following-up after the event

While meeting people may be an important part of a political campaign, it is also an exhausting one. But after you leave the event, your work is not finished. Many candidates dictate notes to staff members or jot down important information that they want to remember. For example, you might want to make a note to send a thank you letter to the organizers of the event or to those individuals who were kind enough to introduce you to other people. You might want to jot down the names of people who said they'd like to help on your campaign. If you offered to send literature or information to someone, make sure you've made a note of it.

Since shaking hands can be rough on the skin, some candidates also take a moment to rub a little lotion on their hands after an event to prevent callouses and rough skin.

Last but not least, after the event is over, it's a good idea to reinforce your confidence with positive thoughts. Review in your mind the good things that happened. As one candidate recalled, "The most touching thing that ever happened to me when shaking hands at an event was when a woman came up to me and said: I'm voting for you because I believe in you. Don't ever let me down. I've always remembered that."

✓ Campaign Spouses: Trials, Tribulations and Triumphs
Janet M. Taliaferro

When the phone rang I was standing in the kitchen. The conversation was short and unforgettable. "Janet?" said my husband's campaign manager, "Who's going to run this campaign, you or me?"

"You are," I said.

"Thanks," he answered, "that's all I wanted to know."

That conversation set the scene for one of the most distasteful and yet one of the most enlightening jobs I have ever had in twenty-five years of being a campaign manager, political fundraiser, consultant and all-around political junkie. I was the "candidate's spouse."

Being the spouse of a candidate is a role—not a job. Like actors and actresses, no spouse is going to play the role quite the same as any other.

During the presidential "primary season" of 1976 a seminar was held at Mount Vernon College in Washington, D.C. One of the most poignant moments came when Ann Lewis, who was with the Bayh campaign, firmly defended Marvella Bayh's right not to participate in the campaign: in short, her right to be ill.

If a candidate is married to a famous spouse, there is often the opposite problem: just how much exposure should the mate get? In Virginia, during Chuck Robb's race for lieutenant governor in 1977 and John Warner's Senate race in 1978, a great deal of time and energy was absorbed in discussions concerning the reaction of Virginia's conservative voters to someone married to Lyndon Johnson's daughter, or to someone married to a famous but oft-divorced movie actress.

Virginia voters acted like normal Americans. They loved having celebrities around and rushed out to shake hands. The outcome of both elections proves there was minimal negative impact. The charge that either man was elected simply because of his more famous wife seems irrelevant. Chuck Robb went on to be elected governor quite on his own record, and no one was predicting Warner's political demise this year, without Ms. Taylor at his side.

Actually, campaigns where the wives are as well known in their own right as a Lynda Robb, an Elizabeth Taylor, a Jane Fonda or a Phyllis George, have some definite advantages. First, the women all like people, were used to being in the public eye and were at ease speaking before crowds or on camera. Second, the wives were a vehicle for instant name recognition. This freed the campaigns and their media people to proceed directly to presenting the candidate, without having to get the public's attention first. These are extreme cases.

But, famous or obscure, a campaign alters the basic way in which any family is organized. Every campaign manager should be aware of these changes. The most important are:

1. A new authority figure, symbolized by the campaign manager, is introduced
2. The existing financial structure of the family is threatened
3. The allocation of family time is profoundly altered...and
4. Finally, there is the loss of family privacy.

Losing the Household Vote

Since it is the manager's job to budget the candidate's time and resources to maximum advantage, he must step directly into the family decision making process. The weight of this decision-making process inclines decisively to the side of the Candidate/Manager. If a spouse disagrees, she inevitably loses, unless she can persuade either her husband or the manager into an alliance with her. Whatever else, if there is any disagreement, it becomes a continuing game of two against one. Such disagreements can run the gamut from deciding whether father is going to be allowed to fit the school play into his schedule, to deciding whether or not to take out a second mortgage on the house in order to finance the campaign.

The Financial Threat

The threat to the financial stability of the family is too often ignored.

Granted, it is difficult to get any candidate to concentrate fully on the financial aspects of a campaign. If, as a manager, you do get it through the candidate's head that he may indeed end up with considerable personal debt, the long-term consequences and their solution are likely to be ignored until after Election Night.

I remember being at a "note-burning" party one evening. The host was a United States Senator. The note had been taken out twenty years, three statewide, and three local races before; for his first run for the state house of representatives.

The problem is not simply one of just another debt. Often the entire financial structure of the family shifts. A candidate may be giving up the security of a well-paying lifetime job for the insecurity of low-paying, temporary public position. If both partners have been employed, income is suddenly halved, at least. A wife who may already have shifted roles from "working wife of student" to "wife of professional man" is just beginning to relax and enjoy the fruits of their joint labor. If the spouse is a husband, he may now be faced with the prospect of having to underwrite her "doing her own thing!" to the tune of a considerable amount of money just when, financially, their heads are comfortably above water for the first time.

There is a particular problem when either the husband or wife of a candidate is personally wealthy. The press and the electorate is going to speculate that the spouse is "buying the election" for their mate.

This tends to make candidates defensive. On the other hand, the spouse might have secret (or maybe not-so-secret) feelings that their money is being spent not wisely and well, but rapidly, excessively and randomly.

May all managers be blessed with candidates of independent personal wealth, and all candidates and spouses with managers who help pay off campaign bills!

More Work, Different Work

The physical and psychic demands of campaigning are a burden to any family. The candidate, naturally, bears the greater load. The manager and staff must insure that the candidate works to maximum capacity. The spouse is faced not only with taking on extra chores, often with no real staff support, but may be the only one with real concern for the health and well-being of the mate. He or she must also confront decisions alone which were shared before in balancing the needs of the family, their own jobs, children, and campaign assignments. It means coping with enormously enlarged tasks and responsibilities.

With more and more women running for office and holding jobs, shifts in the division of labor demanded by campaigns can be even more disruptive and burdensome than in the past.

Losing Privacy

The loss of privacy can be devastating to a family and a marriage. The intrusion of the press is almost impossible to explain to children. They must learn to live with everyone having an opinion about their parent. That means they might have to learn to live with hate.

Once during the turmoil of the early seventies, the media had been making quite a thing about the bad blood between two office holders. The two in question lived within walking distance of each other and their children were friends. One evening, one of the fathers noticed that his eight-year-old daughter was very quiet. When he questioned her, she asked about what she had heard on the television. He explained the controversy as best he could, but finally she blurted out what was really on her mind: "Daddy, does this mean we can't play over at their house anymore?" The father made the mistake of telling the story in public... and the local newspaper quoted the child's remark!

Sexual infidelity on the part of either the candidate or the spouse is a particularly painful problem. If the infidelity pre-dates the campaign, what had been a dirty little family secret suddenly becomes at least semi-public knowledge. The offended spouse has to live with the knowledge that now "everyone knows." The same is true if someone in the family has had a drug or alcohol problem. During a campaign all family members are subjected to negative gossip, slanted press, and idle judgements on almost a daily basis.

Public exposure and demands on time and resources generate anxieties which a candidate's family as a whole must endure. But there are additional pressures arising from the dynamics of the husband and wife relationship itself. The spouse undergoes a process of personal reorientation which begins when he or she asks: What am I doing here? And if I am important, what's my job?

What am I doing here?

If campaigns were logical events, inhabited by totally controlled and rational people, most of the problems could be worked out with relative ease. Campaigns would also be very dull. In reality, it is the quintessential humanity of campaigns which draws people to them. Not only is one doing something for his/her country and contributing to "the system by which we govern ourselves," but one is also involved in a truly exciting, unpredictable, gut-level, winner-take-all experience.

Such a large dose of stressful human interaction can overwhelm a person who is involved in a campaign simply because they happen to be married to the candidate.

The bummest of bum raps on a spouse is that the candidate is running because the husband or wife "pushed them into politics." That messianic gleam in the eye of someone running for office springs directly from the ego of the candidate—any candidate and every candidate. Even if a committee of ten has called to encourage the guy to run, the decision to put oneself through such madness springs only from inside.

One dear friend, who was often a candidate, had a personable and outgoing wife who was accused of urging her husband into public life. I well remember one Sunday afternoon when he was holding an agonizing session with a group of friends to determine if he should run again. Finally, after three hours of indecision, the wife slammed out of the room, shouting, "I don't give a damn if you run or not, but for God's sake make up your mind and let me know!"

A classic case on this point is the telegram sent by Muriel Humphrey to the former vice president in 1960. Although they had been criss-crossing the country together "testing the waters," she was surprised by the timing of the announcement that he was entering the presidential primaries. In fact, she heard it on the radio! She good-humoredly wired from their home in Minnesota, "Congratulations. Let me know if I can be of any help!"

Am I Important?

An attractive, articulate spouse who sincerely likes public life can be a tremendous asset to a candidate. Just as important is the truly supportive spouse who willingly adds to the family image of love and stability, but who may not care for speaking and glad-handing.

But with more women running for office and more wives of candidates having professions or businesses of their own, we are beginning to see greater obstacles to the spouse being able to play the traditional supportive role in a campaign. If the spouse is a doctor, lawyer, teacher or has a going business, she cannot afford to stand around and "look interesting."

Too often spouses, instead of being made to feel a part of the campaign, are made to feel that if they smile and stay out of the way they will be tolerated; so long as they take any family problems elsewhere! It is hardly surprising that spouses react with some gut-level feelings of their own: anger, resentment and guilt. On the one hand they are usually truly proud of their mate and sincerely want a win. (After all, isn't that a nice reflection on the spouse?) The price paid for all this reflected glory can be the near loss of personal identity.

Of course, husbands are just as prone to emotional reactions as wives. The two campaign husbands who stand out in my own experience exemplify the best and the worst. The first managed to give graceful little speeches which clearly showed his love and admiration for his wife. He learned about campaigning with her and from her, and listened attentively to advice. He supervised two teenage children and continued in his own profession. When she lost, he was a comfort. He then encouraged her to run again! She won and still holds public office.

The second fellow was so opposed to what his wife was doing he was a continual nuisance. He didn't interfere with the campaign, he just complained constantly and refused to take any part. Election night, he emerged from his office at home just as the returns showed his wife had lost. Instead of saying anything about the election, he demanded to know when the equipment and campaign paraphernalia would be removed from the house. My first reaction was to consider moving a particular calculator to a permanent location between his teeth. However, since judges in that state did not run for office, I was afraid the act would not be considered a justifiable assault.

The husband or wife who has had real campaign experience before their mate announces for public office is at particular risk. They know a great deal about the process. One young woman whose father had been in public life was contemplating her husband's recent announcement for public office. She did not want to participate in the election process at all, but as she said, "There are really no choices. You either accept and endure or get a divorce. Those are the options." She had been reminiscing at length about her own childhood, her feelings that she had been neglected by her parents, the fact that her mother often had had to choose between the interests of husband, his public and the children. Now she was contemplating the loss of a comfortable life and facing the prospect that history might surely repeat itself for her own children. "Children always want more love and attention than any parent can give" is an easy theory to mouth, but one that didn't provide much reassurance in this instance.

Another wife, who was one of the best campaign field operations organizers I ever met, learned a different lesson. Since I was the campaign manager, I had something of the same conversation with her that my husband's manager had with me; albeit at greater length. About ten days before the end of the campaign, we were having lunch. She said, "You told me I would be incapable of thinking logically at the end of the campaign, and I didn't believe you. It's true. I am so emotionally involved and so exhausted, my judgement is no good to anyone. Now I know why doctors don't treat their own family."

Building a Productive Role for the Spouse

So, how does a campaign manager begin to build a productive role for the campaign spouse? First is the one big DON'T... DON'T let them run the campaign. (This "DON'T" actually applies to any family member.)

On the other hand, there are lots of things ONLY a spouse can do:

...they can brag about the candidate in public;
...they can criticize the candidate in private, and get a hearing;
...and, they are the most credible surrogate for the candidate.

There is, of course, the campaign spouse who is simply a complete pain. There is not much managers can do about them except to "manage" them out of the way.

However, most candidates are married to basically decent folk. If a manager gives the situation a little thought, there is a lot which can be done for spouses and by them. Here's a checklist which should help a campaign manager deal with these new stresses in an old relationship:

- First of all, do think about the trials and tribulations of campaign spouses.

Many managers simply try to ignore the spouse, probably because they know that a husband or wife is the greatest real threat to their own authority over the candidate.

The development of a good relationship between manager and spouse can result in a valuable ally for the manager. Also, if a manager spends as much time getting to know the spouse as he does getting to know the candidate, the manager can make use of what may have been hidden talents.

- Talk about how the campaign will affect the candidate's family and spouse.

Both the candidate and the spouse need to spend some time with the manager discussing the financial and personal pitfalls which are naturally going to come along. Often spouses are antagonistic simply because they are unsure of their role and unfamiliar with the process. If a spouse has been involved in politics before, he/she is really going to feel slighted if ignored. For a manager, remaining firmly in control of a campaign is not incompatible with, and in fact requires, the inclusion of a spouse in the process. But it takes thinking and talking!

- Try to identify areas of real conflict and set priorities early.

Take into consideration the background, experience and talents of the spouse, the ages of any children involved and the way in which family schedules will be disrupted.

- Watch out for real emergencies.

Children get sick. They can have accidents and be hospitalized. Parents and relatives can die. Be prepared to be flexible.

While the campaign may be the most important thing in the world to you, the candidate and the staff, the spouse and the rest of the world don't necessarily feel that way. At times of family crisis, the needs of the spouse should be first. And cynically, the manager should remember that at such times the first question asked by the general electorate is "Where was the candidate when the accident happened?" The second question is always, "Where is he now?" The answer had better be, "at the hospital!"

- Watch your candidate's behavior toward his/ her spouse and children.

In doing some survey research a few years ago, I found the electorate amazingly tolerant of some of the most egregious past personal behavior of a candidate. What they could not forgive, however, was his present treatment of his wife.

- Understand the role the husband or wife has played in the past successes of a candidate and try to utilize that role or create a new positive role.

Use the talents of the spouse. One candidate's wife didn't know beans about politics or care very much. She did, however, think her husband would make the greatest living public servant. She became the volunteer chairman and spent all her time recruiting. She was marvelous. Her enthusiasm made it impossible for people to turn her down.

- Give some time to organizing for the spouse.

This is especially critical with a statewide campaign. The usual complaint is that insufficient staff time is given to coordinating husband-wife schedules, and that there is no support staff for a wife or husband who suddenly has mail to be answered and a dozen new jobs to take care of.

Sometimes a really good friend of the spouse is a godsend as a volunteer staffer. Often this is a friend who doesn't give a damn if the mate is elected and may not even like the candidate. But that person does care very much about the spouse and is willing to put in long hours to help him or her.

- Keep the spouse informed and take the time to do some training if there is a need.

Many wives especially live in terror that some constituent will ask about their husband's position on an issue. Spouses need to know how and when to answer such questions. They are in the public eye too and need some coaching on appearance, style and substance. But advise and coach, don't dictate, or you will get nowhere.

Re-election Blues

Remember, the problems for the spouse don't go away after a campaign. Losing a campaign is like death. After the funeral, most people don't show up again. I remember with deep gratitude those who remained with my husband and me in a postelection depression. Somehow we all got through it, learned a lot and went on to bigger things.

If you win, you really have problems. I am always delighted when I can hand my newly elected candidate into the tender care of an Administrative Assistant, and I can attend to the campaign cleanup happily swapping war stories with the rest of the staff. But... after about three weeks, the problems of re-election surface.

The way the entire family adjusts to the new life of an "elected official" will greatly affect the next campaign. If you think you may want the role of manager in a reselection effort, this would be a good time to help the spouse with problems of readjusting the time schedule, paying off the campaign debt, and relocating the family if a move is necessary. A little thought after the first campaign will make it easier on you the next time around.

Of course, some husbands and wives are impossible. So are some candidates. Luckily for campaign managers, we usually don't get two in the same family!

✓ Door to Door Campaigning
Lorene Hanley Duquin

Angry constituents, barking dogs, tired feet, worn-out shoes, and blisters. Door-to-door campaigning can be hazardous to a candidate's emotional and physical well-being. But in many local races, it can also mean the difference between winning and losing.

Why? Because even in these days of sophisticated campaign techniques, voters are still impressed and complimented when a local candidate takes the time to deliver his or her message in person. That personal visit allows the voter to see you, to hear you, to ask questions, to shake your hand, and then tell all his or her friends and neighbors about it. One visit can create a positive ripple effect throughout the district.

But too many political newcomers and many incumbents don't use door-to-door effectively. Many start walking without a plan and waste valuable time trying to reach every voter when they should be concentrating on finding the right voters.

Others give up before they even begin because the thought of walking up to even several hundred homes is appalling—and it may mean several thousand.

And then there are always a few who assume door-to-door is a magic formula for success when they would be much better off using other campaign tactics.

Effective door-to-door campaigns are carefully planned and systematically executed. They are specially designed to best utilize a candidate's time in his or her district. Then the door-to-door contact is reinforced by other campaign tactics. While it may appear to be very informal, smart candidates know that their successful door-to-door program is just one small part of their overall campaign strategy.

"No matter what political level you're on, it's important to realize that in a campaign, time, money, materials, and workers are limited resources," says Jeff Spencer, now a Buffalo attorney. "The problem every candidate must face is how to maximize those resources so they have the greatest impact on the electorate."

Spencer was a Syracuse University graduate student in 1973 when he developed a successful door-to-door program for New York State Assemblyman Robin Schimminger. Although Spencer is no longer involved in professional politics, his theories on strategy and door-to-door as a campaign tactic can be applied to any political race because they are based on military principles.

"I've always been interested in military history," Spencer says. "When I was active in political consulting, I would take military strategy, decision theory, and organizational theory and apply them to political campaigns.

"For example, in the military, if you're in a defensive position, you'll need fewer men than if you're in an offensive position. It takes a whole company or four platoons on the offensive to overcome one platoon on the defensive. Now if you apply that to a political campaign, and you're the incumbent with a strong base, you can see that you don't need as many resources to hold your territory and win the election. But if you're the challenger, the greatest amount of your campaign resources must be spent attacking your opponents territory and capturing enough of it to win. But while you're attacking, you still have to keep a minimum amount of resources in a defensive position to protect your own base and whatever new territory you've captured."

In many cases, door-to-door campaigning can be an effective means of attacking an opponent's base. But a good overall campaign strategy makes the best possible use of all campaign resources. So in addition to door-to-door, it's essential to have a defensive strategy which will reinforce and protect your base.

While door-to-door is a good offensive tactic, it is not the only offensive tactic. And sometimes, it is the least efficient method of reaching the voters (any good book on marketing will tell you exactly the same thing—don't get locked into one method of reaching the market).

The Pluses and Pitfalls

Whether you should use door-to-door or not will depend on the size and character of your district, your personality, and the amount of time left in the election.

For example, in a race for school board in a large district where there is always a low voter turnout, door-to-door would be a less efficient way to use a candidate's time.

It would be better to locate the people who would be most likely to vote in the school-board race: teachers, parents of school-age children, members of taxpayer organizations, senior citizens. Since the chances of zeroing in on these people in a door-to-door campaign is slim, the candidate would be better off planning hand-shaking campaigns at PTA meetings, senior citizen centers, and other community events that attract these probable voters.

Similarly, in a higher level race, a candidate's time is often better spent meeting large numbers of people. For example, when Rep. John LaFalce of New York first ran for Congress in 1974, he already had good name and face recognition because of his previous elections to county and state legislative seats. Since the congressional district was large, LaFalce's time was better spent shaking hands at plazas, businesses, industries, and community centers in the area. People already knew him, so having the opportunity to shake his hand was impressive because he had political celebrity status. A door-to-door campaign would have limited the number of people LaFalce could have reached.

Chuck Swanick, on the other hand, was a political newcomer when he first ran for an upstate New York county legislative seat in 1979. Unlike LaFalce, no one knew Swanick. Since there was a good chance that a voter who met Swanick at a plaza would consider it more of an annoyance than a privilege, his campaign strategy emphasized door-to-door where voters would be impressed by an energetic young man who was taking the time to walk to their homes.

Determining What's Right For You

Before you decide whether door-to-door should be part of your political strategy, ask some questions and do some investigating. Here are a few suggestions:

- Drive around the district. Examine the types of homes, the neighborhoods, the number of apartment complexes. Going door-to-door is difficult in rural areas and impossible in some apartment buildings, co-ops, and condominiums where soliciting is prohibited and tight security prevents anyone but residents from entering.
- Know your opponent. If he or she has a history of using door-to-door successfully, you may have to follow suit.
- Talk to people who have run for office before. Ask them why they did or did not use door-to-door and whether they think it would be effective.
- Ask your political party leaders for advice. Is door-to-door expected in your community? If not, would it give your campaign an edge?
- Take a look at the physical size of the district. Is door-to-door realistic? Or could your time be better spent in other ways?
- Study the voter enrollment in your district. Do you have the political advantage or are you the underdog? Would you use door-to-door as an offensive tactic to turn votes or as a defensive tactic to hold your base?

Setting up your plan

Once you've decided to use door-to-door, formulate a plan. Start by determining how much time you can spend on canvassing each day and how many days of the week you can walk. Some candidates might be able to walk every day, while others might have only weekends available.

A good quality door-to-door contact that will make an impression on a voter usually lasts between three and five minutes. At that rate, you could make about 15 good contacts an hour. Multiply 15 by the number of hours you plan to work each day to find the average number of homes you can reach daily. Then multiply that by the number of days that you'll be walking between now and Election Day.

For example, let's suppose you planned to spend two hours a day on door-to-door campaigning. Multiply that by 15 contacts an hour and you've got an average of 30 homes you can reach each day. If you planned to walk every day and there are three months or 90 days left until the election, you'll be able to reach 2,700 homes at best.

But remember, that means walking every day for two hours no matter what the weather conditions are and no matter how you're feeling any particular day. And it doesn't take into consideration the fact that at many of the houses no one will be home.

Doing this little calculation does have one advantage though. It will give you a basis for developing a door-to-door plan.

For instance, let's suppose there are fewer than 2,000 homes in your district. You now know that you have a pretty good chance of reaching every home if you spend two hours a day for the next three months. But if your district is larger than that, you'll either have to increase the amount of time you can spend on door-to-door or find some other way of getting the most out of the time you can afford to spend.

Targeting

Finding a more efficient way to reach the voters is called targeting. Instead of walking to every home, you walk only to the homes of those voters who you decide must be contacted in order to win. Targeting is usually based on three theories:

1. There are many homes in the district where residents are not registered to vote. Since they can't vote in the election, it's a waste of the candidate's time to stop at their door. But if you want these homes contacted someway, you'd be better off sending a volunteer with registration forms who might be able to convince these people to register. If they do and they know the forms came from you, they'll probably vote for you. If they don't, you haven't lost any of your valuable time and you have nothing to worry about because they won't be able to vote for your opponent either.
2. In every district there are some homes where only one registered voter lives, homes where two voters live, and homes where three or more voters live. A smart candidate who doesn't have much time will focus his or her efforts on those homes where the most voters can be reached.
3. In every district there are people who do not vote along strict party lines. If you can identify them and convince them to vote for you, it may provide the extra votes you need to win.

Putting the theory to work

Dennis Ward, an Amherst, New York attorney, used these theories when he developed what he calls a "Swing District Targeting Program" for his brother Dan, who was elected to a county legislative seat in 1975.

"Our goal was to reach 80 percent of the voters," Ward says. "In order to do that we had to start in March and work right through to the November election. We also realized that it was more important to contact some voters than others. So we took a comparison of five previous elections to see how the Democrats and Republicans in each district voted. Since my brother was running on the Democratic line, we looked for districts where the Republicans had a history of swinging over to the Democratic lines. Then we rated each district.

"The districts where the Democrats and Republicans tended not to deviate from party line were classed as low priority. We figured the Democrats would vote for us anyway and the Republicans probably wouldn't. The swing districts had a high priority."

In Ward's high-priority districts, the candidate walked to the home of every registered voter. He carried voter affiliation sheets so he knew where the registered voters lived, what political party they were enrolled in, and how many registered voters lived in the home. Each person the candidate spoke to received a telephone directory of important government services. The directory was designed so the candidate's name appeared in bold type. After he left each home, the candidate put a plus mark next to the name of the person he had spoken with. Each week, a campaign worker would send a hand-written thank-you note to the people who had pluses next to their names. The thank-you note was designed to reinforce the visit in the mind of the voter.

"Since we started so early, we had to adjust our strategy because the voters we reached in March are not as attuned to the election as the voters in September or October. But we figured that the candidate makes the best possible contact and even if the early ones were not as effective, since we had touched the voters, they would remember it nonetheless. We always reinforced those early contacts later in the campaign with phone calls and other campaign tactics that built up our name recognition and momentum in the district."

Sometimes a candidate appears to be going door-to-door, when in fact, he or she is only going to very special doors. Len Lenihan waged that kind of campaign for a seat on the county legislature in Erie County, New York when reapportionment left him in a district where he was at a 5,000 vote disadvantage.

Lenihan's door-to-door campaign was so finely targeted that there were often streets where he would actually visit only a few homes on the entire block. So instead of walking through the neighborhoods of his district, Lenihan had a campaign volunteer drive him to his targeted homes. This idea of using a driver would also be advantageous in rural areas or in suburban communities where homes are spread far apart. And if there should be an unfriendly dog, you can always jump back into the cart.

"Once you understand that time won't permit you to walk to everyone's home, you have to sit down and decide exactly where you want to go and where you have to go," Lenihan said. "At first, I was opposed to using a driver because I wanted to be seen walking down the streets informally. I didn't want it to look like I was picking and choosing the houses I went to. But in terms of productivity and effectiveness, a driver is the best way—especially in the fall when it starts to get dark early and you want to hit as many targeted homes as possible."

Lenihan also used thank-you notes to reinforce his visits at the door. His notes were pre-printed but he always took the time to jot down a personal message on the note with a blue FLAIR.

"To me, the most effective thing about the note is that personalized message," he says. "I might write Thanks for the iced tea or Your dog was cute. In some cases there wasn't anything particularly different about the visit so I'd just write, Mrs. Smith—I enjoyed talking to you."

Getting Ready to Go

In addition to winning votes, walking door-to-door is great body exercise. When you walk you tone your feet, ankles, legs, thighs, hips, back, and arms.

Each day before walking do a few stretching exercises to limber up and improve your body alignment. Remember even the best of skiers do stretching exercises before hitting the slopes—it prevents injury. Repeat those stretching exercises after you walk to keep your muscles from tightening up. Here are a few simple exercises that are often used by joggers and long-distance walkers that will only take a few minutes of your time:

- Stand up on your toes, swing both arms overhead, and reach for the ceiling.
- Standing straight with arms overhead bend over and touch your toes. Don't worry about not bending your knees. Keeping them locked can give you lower back problems.
- With feet spread apart, stretch your arms overhead. Then bring both arms over to your left side and then back over to your right side concentrating on stretching the muscles in your side and waist.
- Holding onto the back of a chair, raise your leg and rotate it to improve flexibility in your hip joint. Repeat with the other leg.
- Raise your leg and rest it on a table or the back of a chair. Hold onto the ball of your foot and gently pull your foot toward you to stretch the muscles in the back of your legs. Repeat with the other foot.

Finally, remember that after walking, there's nothing like a hot bath to relax you. Together with a short nap you're ready for your evening campaign events. No one likes a tired-looking candidate of any age or party—don't overdo it!

Putting Your Best Foot Forward

Here are several tips for putting your best foot forward on the campaign trail:

- Make sure you're walking properly. With correct gait, each foot lands heel first on the ground. Keep both feet pointed straight ahead. If your feet point inward or outward as you walk, it's very likely that you'll tire more quickly and you may also develop backaches and other minor pains.
- Buy yourself a good pair of walking shoes. Leather shoes with a dark cushiony sole are the best. The leather allows your feet to breathe. The cushiony sole is more comfortable, absorbs bumps in the pavement, and provides better traction. Look for a wedge sole. It will give you greater support.
- Purchase your shoes late in the day after you've been on your feet for a while. Feet tend to swell as the day goes on. In warm weather you might also need a larger size shoe.
- Measure each foot. They may be different sizes. The larger foot should always determine the shoe size you purchase.
- Make sure that there is 1/2 inch between your longest toe and the end of the shoe while you're standing up. The widest part of the shoe should fit the widest part of your foot. If it's off slightly, the shoe will be uncomfortable.
- The heel of the shoe should fit snugly. The shoe should have enough height so your toes don't rub against the top as you walk.
- Keep your shoes shined and don't let the heels wear down. In addition to a poor appearance, worn down heels will alter the way you walk.
- If your shoes get wet, don't dry them by a heater or they'll shrink. Instead, use shoe trees or stuff them with newspaper or tissue and allow them to dry slowly.
- If your feet get cold or sore, don't soak them in hot water. Always use warm water.
- Wash your feet daily with soap and water. Dry thoroughly and apply talcum powder.
- Avoid nylon socks or stockings if your feet tend to perspire excessively. Buy full-fashioned heavy socks. Watch for lumpy seams at the toes—they can be uncomfortable and can cause blisters.
- Blisters are caused by friction. Stop wearing problem shoes or socks. You can treat a blister yourself by soaking in warm salt water for 10 to 15 minutes two or three times during the day. The blister will disappear by itself. It's dangerous to break a blister unless you have sterile conditions. If the blister persists or becomes infected, see a doctor.
- Corns and callouses are also caused by friction from ill-fitting shoes. Never try to trim corns or callouses yourself. Apply olive oil, castor oil, or baby oil to callouses or dry patches of skin after bathing to help soften them.
- Go into training early and build up your walking strength and speed—especially if you're going to be working hilly country.
- Watch the weather. Ten dollars will buy you a pocket radio tuned to your local U.S. Weather Service Forecast Office. Use it to modify your clothing—both internal and external.

Perfecting Your Technique

"I always fall back on my experiences as a part-time mailman when I was in college," says New York Assemblyman Robin Schimminger who has used door-to-door campaigning in every political race he's entered. "The first cardinal rule of door-to-door is: Train your eye to spot the ominous chain or rope. It's a sure sign that the home is also inhabited by a dog.

"Cardinal rule number two is: No vote is ever worth a fight with an angry dog. It's always better to skip the house than to run the risk of being bitten."

Schimminger also suggests that after you've rung the doorbell and you hear barking that you wedge your foot against the outside door so the dog can't come jumping out at you if the latch is not properly hooked.

Terry Wegler, a Legislative Aide to Assemblyman Schimminger, suggests that candidates be alert to neighborhood happenings. "One day I started canvassing for Robin in a neighborhood where a murder had taken place earlier in the week," she recalls. "Residents were hesitant to open their doors and they acted irritated. It only took a few stops before I remembered the murder incident and I realized that it was not a good time to be canvassing this neighborhood."

Here are several other door-to-door tips from successful candidates:

- Introduce yourself and briefly tell the voter what office you're running for and why. For example, you might say, "I'm running for Town Supervisor because I think the office needs more attention than a part-time administrator can give it. I plan to work full-time at the job."
- It's a good idea to wear one of your campaign buttons or a name tag for identification and name recognition.
- Always apologize if it's apparent that you've interrupted a resident's nap, meal, or other activity.
- Don't ever get into an argument with a resident at the door. If the person doesn't agree with you, leave.
- Always give a piece of campaign literature or a campaign novelty to the voter. It's best if the item has your name or photo displayed prominently. Sports schedules, phone directories, and library schedules have an added advantage because the voter tends to keep them longer than he would a brochure listing your qualifications.
- Never canvass after dark. People don't like opening their doors to strangers after sunset.
- Avoid canvassing during important televised football games. If you must canvass during a game, keep a small transistor radio in your pocket so you won't make the mistake of ringing a doorbell in the middle of an important play.
- Don't dress too formally. But don't dress too casually either. Never appear eccentric or sloppy.
- Don't take notes about your visit while the resident can see you.
- Keep your message short. Remember three to five minutes at the door is best.
- Never walk by a person who's working on the lawn or sitting on the porch. Even if you've not targeted to visit this home, it's a good idea to stop briefly and just say hello. Don't spend a lot of time there, however. The person might not even be registered to vote.
- Don't take it to heart if someone slams the door in your face. It's unreasonable to expect that everyone will vote for you. Just shrug it off and keep on walking.

12

Dealing with the News Media

✓ Establishing Effective Press Relations
Monte Williams

The last four weeks of the campaign can be a wonderful and exhilarating experience, but over the course of a lifetime you get to enjoy campaigns about as often as you get to perform the Heimlich maneuver in restaurants.

Therefore, let's focus on the grinding, desperate downballot races that hardly ever make their way into the popular press. Maybe there's a little money for a TV spot, maybe the local news has done one story on the race. It's close, emotions inside the two camps are running high, and you're a month away from the election.

What happens next depends on how much you've done up until now. (For the sake of this article, I'm told to presume that you're a traumatized ex-reporter/first-time press secretary.) Here's what to do.

Get Out Your Filofax

Make a four-week calendar, and begin to fill it up. Consider debate invites, financial filing deadlines, newspaper endorsement dates, upcoming public polls that might mention your race, the beginning of the inevitable candidate profiles, travel schedules of your ballot-mates, your opponent's scheduled public appearances, early or absentee voting, the commencement of any paid advertising, and travel plans of reporters covering the race.

Casing the Fourth Estate

Touch base with every reporter covering the race. Be quite candid with them if it feels right, and ask for an honest assessment—"Are we going to get any coverage or not?" It's been my experience that they'll give you accurate information.

If you're involved with a race that desperately needs press, resist the urge to gain instant popularity by telling your candidate a reporter is going to do a story. If a reporter does a story on your race, there will be plenty of time to take credit. But if you claim a story is in the works—or more commonly, that an upcoming story "ought to be good"—and then are proven wrong, you will be a bitter disappointment to everyone, worthy of their scorn.

A Pressing Issue

If you haven't determined this next part, call the staff together and resign in disgrace. Do you need all the press you can get? Or is it perfectly acceptable if not a single word is written about your race?

First, Do No Harm

Apply the answer in step 3 to the calendar in step 1. If you need press, these are your available dates to get it. The only problem is, that's when the larger, more interesting campaigns will also be trying to get press.

Remember that news in these campaigns is largely the reporting of conflict, so don't be skittish in the final weeks. However, if you hope to put reporters to sleep in your race, then these are the dates you can expect to be attacked. Try to inoculate reporters against being infected by these attacks. But remember that a common side effect of inoculations is to end up with the very ailment you're trying to prevent. In other words, don't talk reporters into doing a story when your goal is just the opposite.

Divide and Conquer

Lay the press calendar over the scheduling calendar. See where you're going to be on those critical days. Begin planning.

Repeat After Me...

Every day, from now until the election, have this sign above your desk and this note written on the palm of your hand and this mantra to mumble: I WILL NOT INFLATE MY COLLEAGUES' EXPECTATIONS OF THE PRESS COVERAGE. It's fine to inflate a little with supporters, but it can make you look very stupid to your co-workers. You can follow these steps, but campaigns are rowdy and unpredictable. So in trying to fill in the gaps, let's look at three cases.

Situation A

You work for an incumbent state representative; you've never seen a poll on your race because it's too small; you live just outside a large city and so have no television coverage of your race; you sense the race is close, and you have a local debate coming up that will be covered by your local radio station and suburban newspaper.

Recommendation: Situation A is the most challenging because there is little press coverage or, for that matter, interest. But explaining to the candidate your lack of work product by claiming there is no interest in the race will likely produce unexpected results.

One thing to try in this situation is approaching the major daily in the proximate big city. Contact the capital bureau rather than the city desk. If you're with a state rep candidate, you may at least get the capital reporter to contact the city reporter. That's assuming you want any coverage at all.

Other than that, make sure your candidate has met—personally—every reporter, every editorial page editor, every local radio news reporter, and every other whoever in the small universe of your race. This is not an attempt to get press, so don't present it as such. Your candidate, as the incumbent, should make sure all local media rings are kissed. Ignore this advice at your peril.

Situation B

You work for a statewide challenger; the state has five media markets, one big and four little; your candidate is way behind—but she is the darling of nearly every newspaper editorial board in the state, and you honestly think you may get every major paper's endorsement; your opponent is ducking a debate.

Recommendation: Since situation B involves a statewide race, I'm assuming the campaign has TV spots, so as press secretary it's vital that you stay on top of newspaper editorial endorsements. The only time editorials are good is if one candidate gets nearly all of them, because you can use them to make an effective TV spot. Appeal directly to editorial page editors, in essence trading on your candidate's popularity, and plead your case for an editorial chiding your opponent for not debating. If you get one, you can turn that into news as well by traipsing your client out with the editorial in hand.

Situation C

You work for a challenger; your opponent is the mayor, and things seem to be going his way—he got the endorsement of the paper and a published poll has him leading; your campaign is demoralized, and there are only six days left until the election.

Recommendation: Prepare a resume and reserve a U-Haul. But between now and the time you sneak out of town, consider this: The press will give you until 48 hours before the election, then it will really clamp down on stories, probably even embargo any attacks. Therefore, you've got about four days.

Choose four sections of the city, either from poll data or some other reasoning. Announce to the press that, for the final four days of the campaign, your candidate will visit four different areas of the city and explain each day how that area will suffer under your opponent's administration.

If for some reason you haven't launched everything by this point, launch your strongest attack as soon as possible. And pray to God your GOTV works.

✓ How to Survive Your Trial-by-Camera
Robert Wechter

During this campaign, you have probably skirted with the TV news; a few quick interviews, perhaps a talk show or two. It's hard to keep the egg off your face, isn't it? Especially if you draw some blow-dried wonder fresh out of Mass Communications school with his/her eye on the big markets and network stardom.

If you managed to win, your brushes with TV will probably be more frequent, as camera crews dog your steps to and from sessions of your governing body. If you lost, TV may have done you in, leaving you a place in the classroom of effective presentation. Either way, here are a few tips to make the medium work for you in the future:

Be on time. Punctuality is critical. Don't keep a TV reporter and care waiting—they are not a patient lot. TV news is a business where people live and die by immovable deadlines. If you are running behind schedule and think you will definitely be late for an interview, someone on your staff should immediately telephone an assignment editor at the TV station with your estimated time of arrival.

Set your gaze off camera. Look at your interviewer or the producer. Do not talk to the camera unless you have been specifically instructed to do so, are on a satellite feed or are making an urgent, personal appear to the voters. Looking and talking at the camera will usually make you look ridiculous. When in doubt about where to look, ask the camera person, producer, or reporter.

Leave cosmetics to the pros. If you are doing a studio TV interview, let the hair and makeup artist do their job. Makeup and hair spray are absolutely necessary (for either sex) when you are appearing under thousands of watts of bright studio lights. Refusing cosmetic preparations is the real course of vanity. If the interview is out in the field, do not worry excessively about your appearance. Viewers are fairly sophisticated about context; when you are giving a speech in 95 degree heat and humidity or during inclement weather, they don't expect you to look like Ken or Barbie.

Respond to questions directly. Listen very carefully to the question that you are being asked and then answer the questions! Focus specifically on responding to what you are being asked. Candidates who do not listen to questions often get in big trouble. You can avoid unnecessary problems by carefully listening to and responding directly to the questions. If you're not sure about the question don't hesitate to ask for a repetition or a clarification. If the questions aren't lending themselves to your central messages, devise rhetorical bridges to work them in.

Use subdued body language. The non-verbal message that you send to your viewers is as important as what he/she says. Sitting still rather than rocking or fidgeting in the chair, using natural hand and facial gestures rather than exaggerated gestures, and looking directly at the interviewer will help convey a calm and calculated demeanor. As Richard Nixon learned in the 1960 presidential debates, non-verbal impressions can be more profound and lasting than any other form of communication.

Always stay on the record. Absolutely nothing is off-the-record. Unless you are saying it to yourself in the shower consider it to be for attribution. Most reporters will not broadcast off-air remarks, but some producers and reporters don't even know what OTR means. You are "on" from the moment you leave your front door in the morning until you are back home or in your hotel room for the night. The political graveyards are filled with those who carelessly made what they thought were casual remarks—only to end up being hounded for their carelessness.

Deliver substantive sound bites. Interview clips for the evening news must be pithy and concise, but don't expect to make the cut by mouthing platitudes. Your sound bites will never be repeated unless they say something substantive. Provocative remarks will also draw attention, but you'd better have thoroughly researched their content and impact beforehand.

Rein in the humor. Unless Johnny Carson's writers have found work on your staff, leave the jokes for openers on the rubber chicken circuit. Reactions to humorous remarks are difficult to gauge in advance. They can often backfire or make you look silly. Captured on videotape, a poorly-received joke will be seen by thousands of voters, and may continue to haunt you from the clip file. If you must reach for levity, self-deprecation is usually the safest form, but avoid any off-the-cuff witticisms.

Throw out that script. Nothing is more boring than listening to a candidate "read" their remarks. Use brief notes or nothing at all. During media training sessions I routinely trash the person's script and their on camera performance immediately takes a quantum leap for the better.

Sex. Lies, and videotapes. Have an aide record or get copies of every TV appearance you make and systematically log the tapes. Campaign staff can critique the candidate's performance and make suggestions for improving their on-camera technique. The tapes may be useful in the production of campaign spots.

✓ Anatomy of a Successful Media Event
J. Brian Smith

The seemingly enviable position of front-runner in a political race is not always a blessing in the long run. Voter interest wanes rapidly if a race appears to become uncompetitive, and the news media often seems more than willing to try to correct the situation by focusing their critical scrutiny on the favorite. Maintaining a leading campaign's momentum and positive image in the face of an apathetic public and an adversarial press can be a difficult challenge for any candidate.

One way to avoid "front-runner's syndrome" is to put the election beyond the context of a race between politicians, casting the popular candidate as a friend/hero impossible not to like. Enthusiasm-generating "media events" can provide the necessary means if they are handled skillfully. Years ago I succeeded in staging such an affair—but not before suffering a few anxious moments.

In 1986, Republican Congressman John McCain of Arizona looked like a prohibitive favorite in the race to succeed retiring U.S. Senator Barry Goldwater. The Democrat who would have presented McCain with a tough challenge, Governor Bruce Babbitt, had decided to forego the Senate contest to concentrate on his presidential ambitions. Taken aback by the governor's decision, Democratic leaders finally turned to a young former state senator and chairman of the Arizona Corporation Commission, Richard Kimball. Statewide polls taken in January showed McCain leading Kimball by as many as 25 percentage points.

With two hotly contested congressional districts and the governorship up for grabs, the attention of the public, party workers and news media was shifting away from the McCain campaign. It seemed the conservative congressman was doomed to become but the latest victim of the "front-runner syndrome" of inevitably declining fortunes. Yet McCain managed to widen his lead in the next four months—without the benefit of any major miscues by his opponent—and went on to win.

How can momentum be maintained by a runaway favorite? Perhaps the most effective means is by presenting the candidate in settings that will command the attention of the media and—as a result—the electorate.

Fleshing Out The Concept

To meet the challenge of getting people excited about John McCain's front-running campaign, we reached into the past and resurrected a colorful campaign format that has long since been made obsolete by modern technology: an old-fashioned whistle-stop train tour. Our objectives for the day-long event were three-fold: to (1) create interest and excitement in the McCain campaign; (2) generate positive electronic media coverage in the state's two largest media markets; and (3) permit our own film crews to record the excitement and interesting visuals for later use in McCain television commercials.

We selected a Saturday, February 1, as the date of the whistle-stop tour. Promoted as John McCain's "campaign kickoff," our plan called for a morning rally at the Tucson train station and an afternoon rally in Mesa—a suburb that happens to be the largest town in McCain's congressional district.

To make an event as elaborate as the McCain whistle-stop tour succeed, you need to have a number of ingredients; among them are money, hard work, organizational skill—and luck. The McCain campaign was blessed with all these ingredients.

The railroad industry, we learned, is reluctant to provide special trains (and special routes) to political candidates because of the time and effort required. It is worth their while if you are the President of the United States (the Reagan-Bush campaign used a train in Illinois during the 1984 campaign), but of questionable utility if you are merely a candidate for the U.S. Senate.

Lucky for us, John McCain was well-liked by Southern Pacific Railroad executives, and they willingly talked to us about a whistle-stop tour. Another fortuitous development: Southern Pacific's two business entertainment cars would be heading west after the Super Bowl in New Orleans.

But "renting" the train would not be inexpensive. The price tag for six hours with two stops came to almost $13,000—not an insignificant amount for a Senate candidate. On top of that, an additional $5,000 was needed to pay for a $2 million personal liability insurance policy that Southern Pacific required to operate the train.

Insurance companies these days are reluctant to provide coverage for "specialty items" such as train rides. Even the famed Lloyd's of London—which at one time would insure everything from Betty Grable's legs to Jimmy Durante's nose—is essentially out of the specialty market. Strings had to be pulled at high levels before we could find an insurance broker willing and able to obtain the policy we needed. (In fact, we received confirmation that coverage would be forthcoming only 48 hours prior to the trip.)

An Organizational Challenge

The details associated with planning an event as elaborate as a campaign whistle-stop tour seem endless. It was a test of the McCain campaign staff's ability to juggle a range of details simultaneously and then work as a team in executing the event.

The first detail was the train itself, and Southern Pacific came through admirably: two bright burgundy-and-gold engines were freshly painted and hand-waxed for the occasion. There was a "VIP" lounge car—the interior of which resembled a swank private club—and an elegant, 50-year-old parlor car outfitted with kitchen, formal dining room, several bedrooms and a comfortable seating area at the rear.

Named "The Stanford" for Leland Stanford (one of the founders of Southern Pacific as well as a former governor of California and namesake of Stanford University), the parlor car could qualify as a museum piece. Used by President Truman during his famous "give 'em hell" whistle-stop campaign of 1948, it also served Presidents Eisenhower, Kennedy and Johnson at various times. One of the stewards on board had worked on the Stanford for 40 years, and recalled for us his experiences serving four U.S. presidents and a range of other famous people.

To enhance the train's visual impact, both sides of the engine were mounted with large flags (the Arizona state flag and Old Glory). The rear platform of the train, from where John McCain would speak, was beautifully decorated with custom-made red, white and blue bunting and an oval, hand-painted plywood sign that read, "McCain Victory Special."

Both campaign rallies were meticulously planned and advanced. We decided to provide free refreshments (hot dogs, popcorn and soft drinks), and recruit bands to provide music at each location. Each rally had a "master of ceremonies" to warm up the crowds and introduce the candidate. Thousands of helium-filled balloons and small American flags were distributed to the people. At the Mesa rally, an elaborate "balloon rise" took place on cue at the high point of the candidate's speech.

Minimizing The Risks

Much effort was expended to turn out people at the rallies, as the entire concept would have broken down without adequate turnout. Film footage of enthusiastic crowds would be impossible to get—and the news media would report that McCain's campaign kickoff was a flop—if attendance was perceptibly poor.

The plan to get people to attend the rallies consisted of the following elements:

- A mailing to all McCain supporters (volunteers and contributors);
- Newspaper ads that appeared the Wednesday before the event;
- Telephone banks the week before the event to reach identified McCain supporters and party workers;
- Organizing GOP party workers who could be trusted personally to deliver groups of 10-20 people.

Two film crews were hired to record the day's activities. The crew director and the chief cameraman went to Arizona several days early to scout the locations, inspect the train and determine camera positions. A helicopter operated by a Phoenix station was engaged to shoot aerial footage of the train in motion, and arrangements were made for the use of other special equipment, such as a Hollywood-style camera crane. So elaborate were the preparations that the filming of the whistle-stop tour became a well-orchestrated "event within an event."

The night before the event, McCain's staff went to bed tired but excited by the prospects of a truly memorable day ahead. That feeling of elation quickly turned to fear as an unusually severe weather front moved into Arizona. Friday evening, the sky over Tucson opened up as it had not in years, raining steadily throughout the night and the next morning.

Arizonans are not used to rainfall; merely having rain in the forecast is enough to keep most of them indoors. There was a real concern over whether the inclement weather would keep people from attending the rally, particularly in Tucson where John McCain was not yet well known and where we were relying on legitimate public interest in the whistle-stop concept. Although he had survived more than five years in a Vietnamese prison, the candidate confessed to being terrorized by recurring nightmares of empty train stations.

Fortunately for the mental health of all involved, the rain stopped by 9:30 Saturday morning, and the clouds began to break up. We still were concerned about the size of the crowd, but at least the whistle-stop could proceed.

Perseverance Rewarded

The candidate boarded the "McCain Victory Special" at a location just outside the Tucson train station. With him for the ride were about a dozen supporters who paid $1,000 each for the privilege of accompanying the candidate, enough to pay for roughly one-half of the total cost. Had we focused earlier on ticket sales (a major fundraising dinner held just two weeks prior to the whistle-stop tour dominated the time and attention of the campaign staff), there is little doubt that we could have sold tickets for every seat on the train.

At the appointed time, the "McCain Victory Special" started toward the Tucson station. As it rounded a bend and approached the platform, we could hear music, then cheering. By the time the train pulled to a halt, we were looking at approximately 300 enthusiastic, flag-waving, sign-holding people—a heartwarming sight for all aboard.

The scene in Mesa later that day was even more spectacular. A large hot-air balloon and beautiful weather made a vividly colorful backdrop for the home-district crowd. From 500 to 600 loud and enthusiastic people gave us precisely the feeling we had hoped to capture on film for television commercials and television news programs.

As in Tucson, the candidate gave a rousing speech and descended from the rear of the train to mingle with the crowd. People surged around him as if he were a rock star or a major celebrity which—of course—he was on that day.

There was little doubt among any of the people who witnessed or heard about the whistle-stop tour that John McCain's Senate campaign was in high gear. The excitement had returned.

✓ What Makes a Press Release Sing
Steve Snider

Most reporters say the value of a press release has gone up in recent times—thanks to the advent of newsroom recycling. But your release can get to the box marked "in" before it goes into the one marked "bin" if it shows that you know your message and your media.

Trashing an ambitious politician is a cherished rite in the news business, and showering reporters with too much paper is a sure-fire way to be called before the bar and grill after hours.

In an age when satellite coverage and on-line services advance further down the journalistic food chain, the press release can seem less relevant.

But, like it or not, reporters and the people who assign them still rely on press releases. Campaigns are often quickly graded by the quality of the information the press section puts out. Good reporters will never follow your road map all the way. But if you establish your credibility early, the press will work with you, not around you.

To keep your campaign's releases in play, make them essential to the story you want to see. Start by making sure your press people are an essential part of the campaign team, with access to the candidate and the other senior staffers at all times. They need to know what's up with polling, paid media, and mail strategies, not just the overall campaign game plan.

The best press release makes the job easier for reporters, editors, and news directors. The clock is unforgiving to them, and you always get credit for helping them beat it.

Take a hypothetical campaign event: the endorsement of Candidate Jones by Friends of Law Enforcement.

Although much of what a campaign does to earn free media around an event happens on the phone, it is especially important to make sure the right piece of paper gets into the right hands at the right time. So let's concentrate on the paper itself. It should be white, should include black ink, the name and telephone number of a press contact, including an after-hours number, and the campaign address. Most important, it should include the name of the candidate. Most of the coverage that a campaign receives focuses on what a candidate does.

At least a week in advance, the campaign should send a schedule to the press, listing all events and telling reporters where to find the candidate. At the same time, a brief news story written by the campaign should go to weeklies in the area of the event with a lead discussing the substance of the event. Quote the candidate directly. Radio reporters—especially those with major news programming—should get a calendar item suitable for broadcast and an audio feed. Television is key. Focus on the news director and a specific reporter at each station you want to reach. They should receive a release that plays up the visual elements of the event, an approximate script, and an expected running time.

If this sounds like spoon-feeding, it is. But keep in mind, of the three questions that decide TV coverage, the least important is: "What is the issue here?" The most important are: "What does it look like?" and "Can we get it on the air in time?" Your release should answer all three questions every time, in order of importance.

With the tightest deadlines, the shortest stories, and the toughest competition in all of newsdom, television doesn't care what Jones' position is on habeas corpus unless the reporter wraps a story around your event.

At the event, supplement your advisories by distributing a one-page release that ties the event to your message in the first two paragraphs. Don't be shy: say it plainly. For example, write: "Joining the ranks of thousands of law enforcement officers across the state who have endorsed Candidate Jones, the Friends of Law Enforcement said today that Jones is the clear choice on Nov. 6."

Reporters at the scene won't use that lead, but those words and the facts behind them will be sitting next to the word processor when the story is typed, and your release is an active reminder of the most significant single message of the day.

In this, and any, release, be sure to include the names and titles of the principals and background about the site. If Candidate Jones is making a speech at the event, make sure an advance text is available and highlight the key sections for television and radio reporters.

Don't forget to report the event yourself after it has happened. Write down the important quotes that other individuals may have said about your candidate and prepare your own story to send to weeklies, as well as to the dailies that didn't show up. This is a two-pager, complete with headline, lead, quote, and background. This is designed as a cut-from-the-bottom wire story, a release that often makes the weeklies untouched and sometimes is even printed as a filler or campaign brief by the daily press.

If you can afford it, hire a photographer and have the film developed at a local one-hour print shop. Deliver these prints, in black and white whenever possible, with a caption taped to the back. The greatest danger of the press release is its overuse, especially if you rely on them to carry your message without linkage to events, reporter access to candidates, and regular personal contact with the press. One of the most satisfying columns I ever read was a piece about our opponent's releases being used as scratch paper by a columnist's three-year-old.

In a campaign where our opponent over-seeded the media with paper, the opposing campaign manager—we'll call him "Smith"—frequently used caustic, personal quotes against our candidate.

After several of these attacks, we sensed the fatigue of the press and wrote a one-line release quoting our press secretary: "Sounds like Smith has bitten through his leash again." It was picked up across the state. Our opponent may have kept up his release barrage, but we never heard it reported again.

✓ Garnering Newspaper Endorsements
Larry Purpuro

To be sure, some campaign consultants will disagree on the overall value of newspaper endorsements. Not one, however, will argue that it's not valuable to have support from a respected local newspaper. Newspaper endorsements, which represent the single greatest free media effort in the race, always come very late in the election. Therefore, using endorsements effectively requires lots of planning. Here are a few steps to maximize your opportunity for favorable endorsement support.

Taking Inventory

Call both the daily and weekly publications to find out whether or not they will be issuing an endorsement in the election. Find out when the paper anticipates having the editorial board session with candidates. Equally important, find out when the endorsement will be made. Most newspapers by tradition have a preset day on which they issue endorsements.

Bottom line: You can't use the endorsements effectively if you don't know when they are going to be published.

Wooing The Daily Planet

Six weeks or so prior to the editorial board session, conduct a public relation s campaign aimed at those who will sit on the editorial panel and review your candidacy.

Call the editorial page editor and ask who will participate. Usually, this group includes editorial writers, editors, senior political reporters, publishers, and managing editors.

Do not make the mistake of sending your position papers and press releases only to the political reporter covering the race. Make sure that others on that newspaper know the kind of "issue-oriented" campaign you are conducting.

Routinely send the editorial page editor copies of statements with your card attached, marking it "FYI." If the publication has written an editorial with which you agree, take the time to send a complimentary note.

Rehearse, Rehearse, Rehearse

Treat the upcoming editorial board session like an audition or a job interview. You would not walk on stage without knowing your lines, nor would you enter a prospective employer's office without being able to state clearly your abilities.

Give editorial boards the same attention you would a candidate debate. Conduct a rigorous Q&A with your staff before you meet with an editorial board. Editorial board sessions are almost always on the record; often a member of the editorial board review panel will have a tape recorder present.

Ready, Set...

Endorsements aren't worth the paper they're printed in if nobody reads them. And not too many people read the paper these days. So, prior to the newspaper endorsements ever being published, you should sketch out a rough layout of your voter handout. This flier should include the following elements.

A title that reads: "What respected papers are saying about John Smith for Congress." Listed below this headline should be room for four to six favorable quotes from various newspapers. Use the masthead of each paper as artwork above each quote.

You need not quote an entire paragraph to make your point. Ellipses are the greatest PR tool since the fax machine. The quotes themselves can be one sentence, a phrase, or just a word. (Read any movie review and it's easy to see that the endorsement does not have to be long to make its point.)

The point of an endorsement handout is to show that a number of recognized authorities think your candidacy has merit. Therefore, if a voter simply glances at this handout, he should be able to see the names of four or five recognized newspapers with favorable quotes.

Go!

Since newspapers do not release their choices until very late in the campaign, you need to consider in advance how you will distribute such a flier.

One of the easiest and most effective options is the personal handout in well-populated centers. Therefore, prior to election day make sure to have every train station, bus stop, supermarket, and newspaper stand staffed with a volunteer handing out this flier.

Positive Bad Reviews

One does not have to win the endorsement of a paper to win votes from an endorsement. Assuming a candidate has shown substance, commitment, and talent throughout the campaign, most newspapers will make an effort to write something positive about the candidate they are not endorsing. It is that one line referring to you as "thoughtful, hardworking, aggressive, issue driven," etc., even in the losing endorsement, that can be used effectively on your behalf.

In summary, to overlook newspaper endorsements or not to maximize their use is to ignore one of the most valuable, free promotional opportunities in any campaign.

✓ The Keys to Crisis Management
Cathy Allen

It is 30 days before the election. The clock reads 4 a.m. and you are still sitting behind your desk at the office. Your stomach is tied in knots and your face bears a cold sweat. Sleep is something other people do.

Your list of problems seems endless: Your opponent just dropped off new radio spots at the local station and you have no idea what they will say; your phone bank supervisor has just fallen in love with your scheduler and they are taking off for the weekend; you cannot remember who has the helium tank and you promised to supply balloons for the 7 a.m. breakfast; the telephone company is turning off the phones at the end of the day unless it receives $1,000—which you do not have and have no idea where to obtain; your computer data base is inaccessible and the person who devised the system is on vacation

No wonder you cannot sleep. Welcome to the world of crisis management—the term that best describes the hundreds of decisions a campaign manager must make each day to survive the last push of a campaign.

Running out of yard signs, missing a scheduled event because you failed to call for directions or not receiving a particular newspaper endorsement are not crises. But if all this bad news comes in one day, the net sum may throw you into a crisis mode.

Granted, it is hard to be upbeat when your lights are being turned off or the city is taking down the posters you attached to utility poles. But it is important to isolate each situation and keep the campaign in perspective. Minor bad news that comes in threes can take your focus off the big picture and thereby affect the entire campaign.

The key to making the last 30 days run smoothly is to differentiate between crises and problems. When a canvasser is complaining incessantly about the field director, or the candidate's business partner thinks he is the campaign scheduler, that's a problem. Crises are events that prevent voters from receiving your message in the final days or, worse, actions that cause voters to receive a bad message. To the extent that you can distinguish between crises and problems and place priorities on your time and attention, you will be able to guide your campaign through troubled waters with minimal trauma.

A Crisis Checklist

To prepare yourself for upcoming crises, you need to make some quick assessments. What response system is in place to handle press inquiries? Is your scheduler tough enough to tell the field coordinators they cannot have any more of the candidate's time? Can your field director literally lock the office and push exhausted volunteers out onto the street for door-to-door canvassing?

You need to take a preemptive look at such elements as:

Budget

Money is the largest single cause of campaign crises. In these days of negative campaigning, you should expect a media attack—either in form of a paid spot or earned coverage—if you are ahead or if the race is tight. If you have not budgeted for paid media to counter that hit, you are in a crisis you may not be able to finesse.

You need to know how much cash you have on hand, how much you plan to raise, and how much you intend to spend in the closing weeks before Election Day. What was a guesstimate in April and an estimate in July is now a bill in October. You have to know where your account stands.

Start by spending a few hours on Sunday night devising a zero-based budget to take the campaign through Election Day. Instead of looking at all those neat little columns of numbers apportioned for each month, look at what it will take to pay for media, office expenses, an intensive GOTV effort, critical salary commitments and tracking polls.

At the very least, compute a bare-bones budget for your most important expenses—those tasks that absolutely must be carried out. And do not avoid bill collectors. In fact, you should talk to them the first day they call. If you are honest enough, you can enlist their help in taking you through those last critical 30 days.

Income

If you do not have enough money to finance all of your essential projects, it is time to call your heavy hitters and have them spend two hours a day on the telephone reaching other large donors. It also would help to have the candidate make a round of one-on-one calls, along with a few conference calls. If you are really in a financial bind, you may want to consider taking out a loan.

But do not panic. If necessary, resolicit the family and friends of both yourself and your candidate. And do not forget your mother.

Campaign Staff

Now more than ever you need weekly staff meetings to make sure key aides are up for the final push—and to let everyone know what is going on. Although you may think there is a clear chain of command about how decisions are made, it helps to have a chart so everyone can see who reports to whom.

Supplies

Know what you have, and what you lack. Stash a few supplies in the trunk of your car for peace of mind. Do not panic at a dwindling inventory and do not succumb to screaming field coordinators who insist on 100 additional (expensive) yard signs.

Find out to what degree your printer and suppliers are backed up with other orders. As November 8 nears, you will have trouble finding enough new supplies—even if you have the money to buy them. Try to mass-produce last-minute flyers instead of more costly brochures. With so many new desktop publishing programs on the market, you should be able to turn out something attractive in a short time.

The Candidate

Is he sleeping enough and eating reasonably well? Be on the lookout for blank stares and a telltale nodding of the head that may look to others like he is listening when in fact he is not hearing a word. And be sure to keep in mind each of the candidate's pet peeves. Have each staffer do something each day to cater to the candidate's particular habits and—in more than a few cases—eccentricities.

But you need to think about more than the candidate's physical health. Few candidates lack political vulnerabilities ripe for exploitation by the other candidate in the closing days. It is much easier to deal with such developments if a plan for doing so has been formulated in advance.

And check to see how the candidate's family is holding up. An unwatched, ill-informed family can explode into a major problem at the most inopportune time. Ask key family members how they see things and what problems they consider most serious. You may not agree with—or, for that matter, be interested in—their opinions, but you can bet the candidate hears them each and every night. Do a little PR on your own behalf.

Sample Problems and Solutions

There is not much you can read to prepare you for all the crises to come, but there are some basic solutions available if you simply plan ahead:

Problem: Both you and the candidate will receive at least 50 calls a day, and if you are not careful, you could easily spend your entire day on the telephone.

Solution: Train others to take those calls and answer their requests within 24 hours.

Problem: Scores of decisions will line up at your door, all of which must be made immediately.
Solution: Handle the most pressing and timely problems, and learn to delegate the rest. Do not be afraid to say to a trusted staffer, "Handle it your way."

Problem: Personality conflicts in the office will occur, and you will have to mediate them before they impede performance.
Solution: Address these problems directly and only once. Take the warring parties out of the office, let them air their grievances, make a decision, and move on with the campaign.

Problem: The candidate will say something wrong at the most inopportune time.
Solution: Keep your press list with reporters' home numbers nearby. Do not be afraid to call them to clarify the candidate's remarks.

Problem: The press will write an inaccurate, poorly researched, biased story precisely when it hurts most.
Solution: Errors often occur after a reporter has called about a story criticizing the candidate, and the official response is either poorly conceived or delayed past a deadline. This is the time for all good press secretaries to come to the aid of their candidates: sit down and agree on answers to any sticky questions, then discuss the questions that might confront the campaign in its final days. Write out both the questions and your responses.

Extracting Yourself from a Crisis

The most important aspect of crisis management is having a system in place to deal with crises as they arise. The candidate, his immediate family, the campaign's inner circle, and key volunteers are too close to the action to be objective. If your campaign has consultants, this is the time to call them. Make sure you know where your consultant, pollster and media buyer can be reached; with Election Day closing in, these busy professionals are hard to find. Keep a copy of their schedules alongside the candidate's schedule.

This also is a time when the steering committee can do some real work. When framing the problem, do not exaggerate the severity of the crisis, and do not leave any doubt that these people are gathered with a specific purpose in mind. You also should make certain that representatives from your target audiences are present. Many campaigns assemble a steering committee of great thinkers but have no one actually representing their target groups.

If the crisis centers around devising a response to negative TV ads, frame the agenda to center around possible solutions. Determine how much your opponent's spots are altering your message, then plot your response. Have budget documents, research files and relevant information at your fingertips.

No matter how traumatic the crisis, the greatest danger is overreacting. If there is a late-breaking media spot or a press story slamming your candidate, try to focus the debate. Conventional wisdom dictates that you respond immediately, accurately and directly in the same medium that the charge was issued. Have a response ready to blunt the attack and saturate the market.

Think twice before slashing back, however. Charges followed by counter charges followed by more charges can confuse a fragile, undecided voter. If your race is tight, stay on course and focus on your strengths.

Finally, from the "it's your friends who will kill you" department, beware of supporters who, with the best of intentions, write a letter to the editor that sends exactly the wrong message. The more you can keep your supporters reading the same script, or at least clearing their actions with you beforehand, the better your chances of minimizing unexpected disruptions.

To recap, your most important tasks are as follows:

- Keep to your overall plan, while making adjustments along the way.
- Never stop raising money.
- Watch your opponent's every move as best you can.
- Reduce stress levels when you can.
- Save yourself for big crises; avoid small, annoying problems.
- Most important, think through all your actions. Rather than reacting immediately, set your procedures for handling crises into motion. A little humor, always in short supply during the last push, also helps. Remember, others have lived through worse.

Now that you know what to do, start tackling your problems one by one: listen bravely to the radio spot, tell your scheduler and phone bank chairperson that they cannot run off together until the campaign is over, check your volunteer coordinator's home for the helium tank, ask the telephone company for another 24 hours to pay the phone bill, track down your computer whiz in Hawaii, and get some sleep. You have only one more hour before all hell breaks loose.

✓ How to Win Rural Press Coverage
M. Darrell Williams

In a campaign year, hundreds of candidates in rural districts will stage large events and give newsworthy speeches. But most voters will not read about them in the newspaper, hear about them on the radio, or see them on television—because the candidate never gave them the opportunity.

And this will happen over and over again until candidates think ahead about media coverage.

As part of your basic campaign strategy, you need a plan for scheduling, door-to-door contact, fundraising, paid advertising, events, speeches, direct mail, and literature drops. Your plan also must include earned media. This involves what messages are to be released, when, and to whom.

Your first step is to build a complete up-to-date listing of local media, including the names of news directors, news editors, and reporters.

The Rules of the Game

In dealing with rural media, you need to be aware of seven basic rules:

Inform the media. A candidate for public office is a bona fide and legitimate news source. Local media have time to kill and space to fill. The more news releases, tapes, and calls you make, the more opportunities for media coverage you have. But do not assume local reporters will know about you, your campaign, or your event. You must tell them.

Be aggressive about seeking coverage. Do not be rude or pushy, but darken media doorways as often as you have something intelligent—and new—to say. And do not give up your earned media efforts because the media fails to show up. Quitting sends the media (and the voters) a defeatist message.

Realize reporters are not the enemy. They are real people who share the same values as everyone else. They have opinions (who does not?), but most strive to maintain objectivity. It is a reporter's job to seek out opposing points of view, so do not discourage him or her from reporting your opponent's views. If your position on a given issue is not better than your opponent's, you should not discuss it.

Be your own spokesperson. The candidate is the one running for office, not the staff; if there is an opportunity for earned media, the candidate should be the one to capitalize on it. Voters will find only the candidate's name on the ballot; a good staffer seeks name recognition only for the candidate.

Show them who signs the check. Whenever you purchase time or space from a local radio or TV station, or local newspaper, always hand deliver the check yourself. Small town reporters understand from where their paycheck comes. It also gives you an opportunity for an interview.

Do not be greedy. Too often, candidates become greedy—and lose their credibility. In their quest for more press, they often say, "I want three press releases a week." Nothing destroys media confidence faster than pabulum releases labeled "news."

Never argue with the media. If you feel you have been wronged by a reporter, assess the damage, assemble your facts, and then only if absolutely necessary, calmly discuss the facts with that reporter. Do not seek public confrontation.

As a legitimate candidate for public office, your announcement speech and related events will in all likelihood be well covered by rural media. A post-announcement speech, however, carries no such guarantee—even if it details your position on a major issue.

To attract attention, call each of the area radio stations and the local newspapers and brief them on the thrust of the speech. Also, invite the appropriate reporters to attend the event.

Even if the regional television stations may not cover the speech, call them—if for no other reason than to remind the news directors that an active political race is in the making within their viewing area. And, although a station may not be able to staff the event, it may be interested in having a reporter interview the candidate the next time he or she comes to town.

Working with Reporters

Having made all of the appropriate contacts, your next task is to ensure reporters receive the same message the candidate wants to convey to the voters. The candidate has three basic options: allow reporters to "interpret" the speech; give reporters a hard copy of the speech; or provide a copy of the speech accompanied by a written news release.

The last option is best. Most reporters hate taking notes (though few would ever admit to it). They would much rather mingle with the audience than actually listen to a speech and have to concentrate on note-taking. A prepared text accompanied by a news release makes it a breeze for reporters to write their stories.

Given the importance of your speech and your need to garner media coverage, it is a good idea to write the news release first and then draft the speech text. Write the news release in the same way you would want to see the speech covered in the newspaper. Lead with the "impact points" of the message, then fill in the background material.

Few people actually enjoy writing speeches, and the beginning usually is the toughest part. By writing your news release first, you make drafting an outline a piece of cake. Writing the speech then becomes as easy as filling in the blanks. If you have great difficulty writing news releases, you may find a sympathetic reporter (in need of Saturday night beer money) to help you.

Do It Yourself Radio Actualizes

When you arrive for the luncheon speech, give a copy of the text and news release to each of the reporters in attendance, and let them know you will be available to answer questions afterward. In many rural areas, there will be no radio reporters at a luncheon. They are usually tied up with the noontime news hour and farm report routine.

Accommodate them by using a standard size cassette recorder and an external microphone to tape the speech ($100 at the local Radio Shack will get you into the radio racket). Then hand deliver the tape to radio stations in time for their afternoon news programs. Radio reporters love tape, especially from a live event in front of "real people." But remember that radio is an instant medium; yesterday's news will not be broadcast today.

Two other advantages to taping: It provides a built-in critique mechanism to help you analyze your speaking style, and supplies potential material for radio commercials (complete with crowd applause). Speech commercials have credibility because they sound real, in contrast to staged commercials, which sound fake.

The payoff for this work is increased name recognition, as the combination of earned and paid media delivers your message to the voters. You know it is working when you hear people on the morning coffee crew at Bertha's Bakery say, "Oh yeah, I heard you on the radio," or "I read about you in the paper."

By Election Day, they may even greet you with those resounding words, "Hey, I think you're gonna win this thing. People are talkin' about ya."

✓ Right Sound Bites
David R. Voss

How do you get reporters to pay attention? How do you get them off your back? Different problems, same theme: Managing the media. Out of all the frustrations that politicians have experienced over the years with the press, a few basic guidelines have emerged. Practice breeds confidence; once you're confident, performance rises.

Regardless of your strategy or your personality, you have to understand your local media, warm up to the key players and adapt accordingly. Just as all politics is local, so is all media.

The following guidelines can help prevent media hassles, especially as you try to control your message and gain favorable coverage. I call them the "Ten B's."

1. Be realistic. The press is not your PR machinery. It faces time and space limitations, lots of races to cover and a penchant for digging up dirt. Before peddling news, understand news values and try to think like a journalist. The average television sound bite for a politician is 12 seconds; when speaking in front of the cameras, make the most of your time. These facts of media life are immutable, so accept them and move on with your strategy.

2. Be prepared. Know the hot buttons and hot-shot reporters in your community. Understand their organizational structure and which editors are really calling the shots. Never do an interview unless you're ready. If you need a delay—even if there's a microphone in your face—ask for their deadline, tell them you have to collect some information and offer to get back to them at a precise appointment. That buys you time without putting them off.

3. Be accessible. Work on long-term media relations; they're really human relations. That means being there when they need you, so they'll be there when you need them. Avoid saying "no comment"—it makes you look guilty or you're hiding something. Answer these questions by explaining why you can't comment, discussing general policy (instead of the specific issue) or by switching to something you can say.

4. Be honest. Admit bad news and move on to corrective action. It shows character and moves the media on to something else. Lying will come back to haunt you.

5. Be quotable. If the media is giving you a chance to be quoted, make it memorable. Try to create a catch phrase, putting your issues into plain English that connects with the voter. That is why I advise delay in certain circumstances; you must take the time to prepare a message designed for your targeted audience.

6. Be in control. Once you say something quotable, make sure it's quoted. This is accomplished by changing your pace when you get to the good part, delivering it slowly and distinctly, and couching it in a 20-second sound bite. When the reporter wants to talk about something else, segue back to your quote—that means working your key phrase into the answer no matter what the question. Use short lists when you need to convert a complex issue into a digestible explanation.

7. Be liked. TV is an emotional, subjective medium. People will remember how they feel about you more than what you say. Remain your normal, lovable self, don't sound "official" or pompous. Talk to reporters before going on camera and then pretend you are continuing the conversation, using conversational language and looking the reporter straight in the eyes. Stand or sit up straight, wear clothing and accessories that fit the occasion and don't distract from the real message—you.

8. Be innovative. Getting press is the toughest challenge for local races; you can't accomplish it in a routine way. You have to step out of the crowd. Press releases about promotions and positions on issues won't cut it. Remember earlier when we talked about knowing your local press and thinking like a journalist? Here is where that advice comes into play. You need action, extraordinary examples, prominent figures, children, human interest and timeliness. In other words, do it, don't say it.Create media events, not press conferences. Attach yourself to a national or state story with a local angle. Provide news tips (a story idea rather than a complete press release) to the reporter who already has an interest in the subject.

9. Be assertive. Don't lay back and hope media coverage just happens. Make it happen! Forcefully volunteer information and counter-quotes when the reporter obviously has a bias or slant. Talk to the City Editor about problems with your coverage or the Editorial Board about issues. Seek editorial endorsements; to get them, you'll often have to ask for meetings with the local editorial honchos.

10. Never screw up on a slow news day. Remember that news is relative. The importance of your news depends on what else is going on that day. Use it to your advantage. Create news when weekend TV reporters are looking for an angle and get rid of bad news in the middle of the week when there's a lot going on.

✓ The New Electronic Politics
Michael McCurry

"Reaction time, lads, reaction time is everything," my then-boss, Sen. Daniel Patrick Moynihan of New York, was fond of saying in the midst of his 1982 campaign for re-election. However, even for a politician with Moynihan's keen sense of news and nuance, "reaction" in those not-so-distant days consisted largely of scanning the front page of The New York Times and composing a response that could be on the desks of political writers when they arrived at the office around mid-morning.

Little more than a half-decade later, everything about the process of political communication—how information is formulated and dispersed by office seekers and how it is received by the press and voters—has changed dramatically. Politicians and campaign operatives who expect to remain competitive in the 1990s need to understand and to take full advantage of the technologies that have set a new, dynamic tempo for American politics.

Political information now bounces around the globe so quickly that well-defined news cycles no longer exist; daily newspaper deadlines and twice-a-day wire service deadlines have given way to the "all the news all the time" deadlines of 24-hour news on radio and cable television. Within minutes of a major announcement or development, opinions are formed, positions are staked out by the principals, and any response that sounds "conventional" will likely be ignored or treated as something other than wise. This breakneck pace puts a premium on the ability to react swiftly to news, adapt quickly to the changing landscape of a campaign, and find the right means and media to put your particular "spin" on an issue or development.

The bad news is that many a good campaign strategy memo will find its way to the wastebasket—a victim of events and developments that now move too rapidly for careful advance planning. But there also is good news: The technology of modern politics makes it possible to fine tune your next move, determine your audience, and deliver your message on target—and to utilize a variety of multi-media options suited to the voters you are trying to reach. From satellite broadcasts to VCRs to home computers to direct mail to targeted phone banks, technology is defining a new "high tech electronic politics" that is transforming American campaigns—perhaps for the better.

Of course, there is a dangerous side to the technology of modern politics. To the extent that it centers debate on the "matter of the moment," politics can become awfully trivial. Remember the "Great Dope Debate" of the 1988 campaign, when hundreds of journalists and campaign operatives attending a Democratic dinner in Des Moines one weekend were mesmerized by the question of whether the presidential candidates had experimented with drugs in their youth? That was followed by the microscopic examination of allegations, apparently baseless, that Michael Dukakis had once been treated for depression—to say nothing of the frenzy over George Bush's love life and war record.

In the era of electronic politics, when too many reporters are chasing too little news with too much available technology, the off-beat and the inconsequential can quickly dominate campaign coverage. Reporters send tidbits to anxious editors, printouts of stories from far-flung newspapers are faxed to campaign headquarters, rumors of disclosures are spread by mobile phones, and television crews with satellite trucks stand ready to beam reports to control rooms across the state or across the country. In response, candidates and their staffs compound the frivolous by crafting meaningless "sound bites" and one liners that transform political debate from something substantive to something merely designed for instant replay.

Indeed, journalists are not alone in responsibility for the problem. Campaigns are now adept at producing 30 second commercials that machine-gun the opposition in a matter of days. Overnight polling, feedback schemes with focus groups, and hand-held "people meters" capable of recording an instant thumbs-up or thumbs-down on a particular line of attack give an electronic aura of respectability to arguments which ought rightfully to be labeled nonsense. Before anyone has time to reflect on the simple question "Does it really matter", the new technology can send the dialogue of a campaign spinning off in a remarkably unpredictable and unsatisfactory path.

So the cost of electronic politics seems all too obvious. But in their new book, *The Electronic Commonwealth*, authors Jeffrey H. Abramson, F. Christopher Arterton, and Gary R. Orren argue that we need not be victims of this new age of politics. Instead, they say, we could use those technologies which now speed the processing of political information to attract more voters into a methodical, community-based discussion of issues and positions.

"This is the politics of the electronic commonwealth and the televised town meeting," the authors write. "The congregating or conferencing capacity of the new media can put such politics into practice. The choice between racing democracy and slowing democracy is ours. Only politics, not machines, can make that choice."

How can participants in the campaign process—candidates, staffs, consultants, and the press—make this choice a wise one? It will take sober reflection on the lessons from our most recent campaigns, and an understanding that voters—through their increasing non-participation—already have indicated that they are disturbed with some of the new trends.

Lessons for Candidates, Consultants and Operatives

Electronic politics, for all its short-comings, is quite capable of unmasking exaggeration in the blink of an eye, and of rooting out the indecisive and superficial among those who seek the public trust. To succeed, candidates must know who they are and what they are saying. As every candidate learned from Joe Biden's experience with an intense questioner in a New Hampshire audience, from now on there will be someone present with a camera to record every moment of every campaign at virtually any level.

It goes without saying that, in the age of high tech politics, staffs must know how to capitalize on a sudden opening and how to limit the damage of a suddenly-revealed weakness. Consequently, campaign structures—often laden with bureaucracy and hampered by imprecise decision-making—must be streamlined to allow fast action.

Above all, campaigns must understand that their best asset in managing their message lies at their very fingertips: phone calls quickly returned, press releases rapidly produced and distributed, targeted mailings instantly sorted for the right households, interviews arranged on a moment's notice to set the record straight, talking points electronically distributed to a national or statewide network so that every functionary knows the correct "line of the day."

The most important change in political technology is the microcomputer. In 1984, some news organizations used computers to transmit stories and there were some attempts to computerize campaign operations on a broad scale. But, with the exception of an occasional fundraiser, delegate tracker, or accountant, few operatives knew the first thing about computers.

By 1988, it was standard procedure in most campaigns to share data files between laptop and portable computers in the field and headquarter hard-disks. Campaigns transmitted speech texts and memos to candidates on the road, advance staff raced ahead with data disks to load remarks electronically into teleprompters, and press secretaries utilized portable printers to distribute speeches to the press well in advance of deadlines. Able to edit and revise remarks on the spot, candidates and speechwriters produced the staple of all campaign stops—The Speech—minus the sloppy typos and awkward phrases common in the hunt-and-peck days of typewriters and mimeograph machines.

Personal computers also sorted and organized lists of supporters, press contacts, fundraisers and friends—while researchers arranged data on the opposition for instant retrieval, loading up an opponent's record into user-friendly databases. In the foreseeable future, no campaign—be it for the White House or for town council—will reach its potential without incorporating the personal computer into its day-to-day management plan. That means a host of job opportunities for those specializing in information management rather than the rawboned work of field organizing.

Between 1984 and 1988, campaigns recognized and took advantage of second major change in political technology: the communications satellite. Everything from debates to press conferences to fundraising appeals broadcast via satellite to audiences and newsrooms around the country. Those that could not afford "going up on the bird" mass-produced videocassettes for distribution to potential supporters and contributors.

In one celebrated case, the capabilities of the home VCR produced an interesting lesson in truth-in-packaging—when the Dukakis campaign spliced together segments of similar speeches from Joe Biden and British opposition leader Neil Kinnock. Biden left the race, Dukakis campaign manager John Sasso left his job, and left behind was the realization that the new electronic politics forever had altered the age-old tradition of "leaking" to the press.

Besides creating a new generation of campaign specialists familiar with the exotica of transponder coordinates and video technology, the ability of campaigns to record and produce their own videotapes and live broadcasts has blurred the traditional boundaries between the politician and the press. Even campaigns at the local level have the growing resource of cable television at their disposal, allowing them to bypass the political press when it comes to delivering their message.

In turn, the job of the press—to sort out the multitude of messages and point the dialogue in the direction of truth—has become more difficult. There is just too much information for any one news organization to digest and report.

In 1984, you could count on a few news organizations (and an even smaller number of individual reporters) to set the tone for most political coverage. By 1988, political journalism still had its stars, but (with apologies to George Bush) there were a thousand new points of light. C-SPAN followed you to a reception, watched you schmooze, and even listened in as you raised money from a fat cat. Local TV affiliates hired their own analysts, sent their crews on the road, and—thanks to the satellites—beamed back national politics with a down-home twist.

Around the country, political reporters—veterans and newcomers alike—continued to cover local, state and national campaigns for a local audience. But instead of being limited to that audience, their work suddenly gained national currency through the *Presidential Campaign Hotline*—which collected the news of the day and dispatched it by computer to virtually the entire political community.

Stories that previously took days, maybe even weeks, to circulate became white hot in hours. For political junkies and campaign staffers, Hotline was a godsend. But, for journalists looking for news, having everyone instantly in the know meant that there was little left to tell. With the difference between a good story and stale news shrinking rapidly, reporters developed a new specialty: "news-analysis," a hybrid article conveying both news and analysis.

Daily coverage of "spot" news was supplanted in large part by longer think pieces which sought to put the intricate debate of a multi-candidate race into context. In fairness, this approach was a good faith effort by a good reporter to boil down to manageable length the reams of relevant political news. But the tendency towards "summing up," along with almost instantaneous electronic access to each other's reporting, often left journalists repeating the same conventional wisdom.

Consequently, we are left with a paradox when examining the new technology and the new politics: What is good for candidates and political professionals may not be as good for reporters. The very techniques which make the new electric politics more precise and focused may be making it easier for reporters to rely on each other, leaving them with fewer incentives to find out what is really going on in voters' minds.

Lessons from the Voters

Again, there is some good news. In campaigns to come, the new political technology will make it easier for politicians and the press to measure voter reactions. That, in turn, will give voters more say in the on-going tug of war between the positive and the negative in campaigns.

Voters clearly respond to targeted, precise information, effectively delivered by either the press or the candidates. Today's realities leave little room for error in a candidate's organization and presentation. But, as always, a candidate with a provocative message can break through the resistance of a skeptical press and the attacks of his opponents. With all those free electrons bouncing through the media, the victorious will be those who focus their message laser-like on the issues and concerns that touch the lives of average citizens.

For those who cover politics and try to sort out fact from artful fiction, the lesson may be this: Everything about the new technology of politics and communication increases the speed at which we see and hear the news, but not necessarily our understanding of what is important. The difference between good reporting is the same difference between a good movie and a good book—they can both be entertaining, enlightening, and easy to comprehend. It just takes longer to make it through one than the other.

✓ Targeting Your Most Influential Constituents
Cathy Allen

In these days of increasing media influence, campaign managers and candidates are constantly attempting to catch the eyes and pens of political reporters. Why not catch their attention by highlighting those issues which the press feels passionately about? For example, attract their attention with a call for more open meetings at every level of government, campaign spending limitations, campaign reform, a challenge for more candidate debates, ethics in government and public disclosure of all special-interest dollars that may influence campaigns or legislation, and access to more information in the government files.

Candidates should never be advised to include issues in their rhetoric that they do not believe in. However, there is a close correlation with candidates who espouse these kinds of issues and those who seem to enjoy favorable press attention. And at the very least, these stories—when proposed as campaign stands—always get covered, if you are the first to adopt them publicly.

Seduce Them With Style

Complementing the issues, there are candidate styles that attract more press. Constant accessibility—particularly on deadline and at times of high stress and negative attacks—can be more important to the long-term relationship between a key political reporter and candidate (or manager) than waiting until you have devised the perfect quote or response. "Quotability," the talent of always having something clever to say no matter what the question, is more innate than learned but it can be learned. Collect little gems of wisdom and practice situations when they would best work. Anticipate the issue and prepare a few "sound bites."

Letting reporters talk and offer suggestions (as they invariably want to do), is critical. So many candidates will respond to a reporter's thoughts by saying, "Yeah, well, we're already doing that." A better response is simply to say, "That's a good idea." If the reporter then sees one of her offhand suggestions carried out in the campaign, she is flattered.

Dare to talk about what's wrong with your campaign. Honestly. If your campaign coffers aren't filled to the brim as you expected, say so. Allow reporters to hear something other than "everything is fine."

Candidates and managers always act like the campaign is perfect when they are around reporters. The reporters know better. If you tell them about the little things that are not perfect, chances are they will believe you when you talk about the big things.

Leaking nasty information about your opponent used to be a way of endearing a campaign to reporters. Not so any more. Most reporters tend to regard stories about the opposition as self-serving and gutless. If you have a charge to make, handle it up front or face retaliation. Remember, the media's product is news. Helping them make their product helps you.

Find 'em in the Field

Reporters are voters, and they live in neighborhoods you can target. A little bit of extra effort can go a long way to give a reporter a look at your field operations.

Check out the home addresses of reporters and send them your direct mail, whether they fit the exact target or not. You know that political reporters will read and probably save all political mail that lands in their mailboxes.

When the yard signs go up, make sure the entire neighborhood where the important press people live is targeted. If you are doing phone banks, make sure the reporters' home telephone numbers are on your list. The spouse of a reporter will always remember to tell his wife about the call. And, when your field force is going door-to-door to hand out leaflets, target the reporters' homes as well. They should see firsthand what your personal approach looks like on the streets.

And by the way, it doesn't hurt to personally choose the person who will be knocking on the chief political writer's door. Send your best.

Share Your Strategy

Preview all your print, broadcast and even direct mail ads with the press. As a candidate, stop by local newspapers, radio and TV stations to see the reporters you seldom hear from.

And train yourself to remember their names. Invite them to stop by the office and spend a day, any day, on the campaign trail with you. Invite them to a steering committee meeting and open up your books if you must. After all, the real success of a campaign isn't the written plan, it's the implementation. When filing campaign spending and contributor reports, have extra copies made and delivered to the press. Have a separate tally sheet for them that records other information that the official reports don't require: how many contributors do you have, how many contributions under $100, how many are over $100, how many contributors have given the maximum and who are they (this usually is better to reveal first then to have the press "discover" later).

Tell them how you are spending your money (readily used information includes what percentage of the total amount spent was paid for media, staff, direct mail, office expenses).

If you tally and present the information that shows your campaign in its best light, the press may buy it.

All of these hints are devised to give you ideas for working with the press for your advantage. Nothing, however, beats the basic, old-fashioned way to get press: always tell the truth.

✓ Handling the Press: 20 Rules Never to Break
Kevin Shaw Kellems

Candidates should bring this with them to every media interview.

1. Never lie to a reporter.
2. Exude confidence, trust and truthfulness, not fear, trepidation and evasiveness.
3. Develop thick skin and a sense of humor.
4. To win, view reporters positively, not disdainfully. Treat each one as an informational lifeline to voters.
5. Err on the side of being accessible to the press.
6. Don't try to be something you're not.
7. Know who you are, what you believe and why you're running before announcing for office.
8. Stop to think deeply about your won biography and ensure that bio info in all campaign literature is accurate.
9. During interviews, emphasize biographical elements that lend credibility to campaign themes.
10. You must believe in yourself, your purpose, your very candidacy to be a credible salesman of your message.
11. Think big thoughts beyond the office sought. Reveal your enthusiasm for big ideas. If you feel emotion, show it.
12. Resist the temptation to brag about the brilliance of your own campaign strategy. Discipline yourself to issues that reinforce your campaign themes, rather than tactics, money.
13. Look for ways to weave your two or three core themes through most of what you do or say. Know them cold.
14. Master the mechanics and nuances of how the media works (deadlines, personal quirks/interests, inter-office relationships).
15. Don't dress down a journalist unnecessarily, and avoid gong over their head to an editor with a beef, if possible.
16. Establish the terms of the interview before it starts. Avoid off-the-record commentary.
17. Mean and nasty is out; funny and constructive is in.
18. Be a positive advocate for constructive change, not only because it will help you win, but because what you say in interviews and press releases has real consequences.
19. Have the word credibility in mind as your constant goal during every speech and every interview.
20. Interviews should be two-way informational exchanges. Listen to the reporter, answer your way, and ask questions.

✓ Damage Control: Prepare for the Worst
Morgan Stewart

You could hear the impact reverberate across the political landscape. Like a punch from Michael Tyson to an opponent's ribs, the blow struck with nauseating effects. Bloodied and bruised, Republicans feared one of their rising stars was down for the count. U.S. Rep. Jim McCrery, a north Louisiana conservative, was being "outed" by a national gay magazine, The Advocate. The cover story featured an accuser who claimed to be McCrery's former gay companion and charged the young Congressman with hypocrisy for his strident anti-gay stance. Plain brown envelopes containing the article were anonymously distributed to news organizations in McCrery's district. High dollar donors, and anyone with a McCrery lawnsign received it on their doorsteps.

The story threatened McCrery's tight re-election bid against neighboring incumbent Jerry Huckaby, a Democrat who was reapportioned into the same district. Said Grace Wiegers, McCrery's campaign manager, "We came to a conclusion that we would do one thing and one thing only, and that was to issue a statement to the effect that the allegations were untrue, we were disgusted by the fact that they were brought up, and we would no longer address the issue anymore."

While the press continued to prod, McCrery and his staff refused to stray from the original statement or to talk about the issue any further. Despite the insidious manner of the attack, the campaign routed the attackers with textbook efficiency. McCrery crushed Huckaby by 26 points.

As political experts know, damage control connotes the need to manage a crisis, to minimize a problem that suddenly raises its ugly head and can't be ignored. The McCrery campaign controlled their case well, but it is never as easy as it sounds.

When The Shot Is Fired

Politicians have been getting into trouble as long as there have been politicians. Even our nation's founding fathers, august leaders that they were, on occasion scurried for ways to contain the consequences of mistakes, scandals and embarrassments. Damage control is not a wholly political phenomenon, corporate execs and movie stars try to smooth over their indiscretions every day; but it is something politicians have become very good at, which is why so many non-political moguls are looking to campaign professionals for crisis management counseling.

Successful damage control operations usually depend upon two things: first, preparation, and second, the ability of the candidate to hold up.

There is nothing more important than preparation. Experienced political consultants recommend that you "game plan" every possible eventuality and have a ready explanation for every possible problem. Don't ever let your candidate be caught off-guard or unprepared. Candidates who do not think quickly on their feet and who do not know when to talk and when to keep quiet are time bombs in campaign crises.

If you question the value of preparation, ask Gary Hart's handlers. In the spring of 1987, they witnessed the evaporation of their frontrunning candidacy in a single week of sloppy damage control. The fact that Hart dared the press to follow him to prove he was not womanizing, and then did it anyway, raises the issue of not only preparedness, but stupidity as well.

There is a certain art to damage control. And sometimes it requires plain old experience to work its magic. Often it takes luck. Usually, it takes clear thinking and good strategy.

- Once the shot is fired, most pros suggest that smart campaigns gather only a few of their best advisers to decide on a response. Democratic media consultant Dawn Laguens says devising damage control responses should be kept deep within the campaign. "The one thing that creates additional distrust among voters is a campaign publicizing the inner machinations, the strategy to control damage. Stories about damage control teams make the candidate look insincere and fake. Keep the team small and keep the strategizing quiet." (This could explain why press coverage of teams of political advisors flocking to Hyannis Port after Chappaquiddick hurt more than helped Ted Kennedy's career.)
- Once the message is devised and disseminated, move to the rest of the campaign. Sometimes it is hard for the candidate to hold up. Republican public relations consultant Craig Shirley said handling the candidate is often the toughest job: "I've seen some of them just lose it completely, while others have ice water in their veins and know what to do. With some candidates, it is best to keep them busy with other things. With others you should either isolate them or just give them a dose of Prozac."
- After coordinating the plan of attack, come up with a statement and stick to it. Do not give the press, or the opposition, anything to fuel the fire after the initial response. "Anything you say keeps the issue around and gives it more credibility," Wiegers says. "You never win talking about it too much."

Press Response

In politics, damage control usually centers on dealing with the news media and explaining allegations about untoward sexual conduct, financial corruption, or getting caught in a big lie. It may arise out of a baseless rumor or it may be a disclosure that is partly true.

Consultants and reporters have varying ideas for dealing with the press, but the underlying theme remains the same—the press must believe the spin. "The press responds most positively to the individual truth meter," says McCrery advisor Elliott Stonecipher, "that is the relative degree each member of the press thinks you told the truth, the whole truth and nothing but the truth."

For CNN correspondent Ken Bode, the key to spinning reporters is credibility: "We're a tougher lot to convince. We happen to be a lot more cynical than most." A good example at failed credibility was the spin attempts after the 1988 presidential debate in which Bernard Shaw asked Democratic contender Michael Dukakis, "If Kitty Dukakis were raped and murdered, would you favor an irrevocable death penalty for the killer?" Dukakis answered in a detached and unfeeling manner. After the debate, Democrats tried to declare victory but convinced no one. "It was just crazy," said Bode. "There was nobody in the entire auditorium or in the entire globe who thought he won that debate."

Spinners should also add new information. But if that information turns out to be false, says Bode, "not only is the candidate harmed in that instance, but the spinner is harmed permanently."

When Gennifer Flowers came out with her allegations of a 12-year affair with then-governor Bill Clinton, consultant James Carville effectively steered the press away from the story. "He said, 'Look at the source of this. This is cash for trash, this is sleaze.' He spun reporters away from the story, including the New York Times," recalled Bode. "And that was a smoke screen in my view."

Carville told an audience at a recent *Campaigns and Elections* seminar that in a case like this, "You intervene early and you intervene big and loud."

Some other damage control tactics include:

- Admit it and move on. In 1884, Grover Cleveland's paternity of an illegitimate child became an issue which he diffused, not with slick one-liners or deceitful double-talk, but with straightforward admission. Cleveland not only set an admirable example for today's pols who find themselves in the soup, but also an effective one: he won the presidency despite the scandal. (His supporters sang on election night, "Hooray for Maria, hooray for the kid, we voted for Grover, and we're damn glad we did!")
- Admit it and move out. Tony Coelho, the rising star Democratic Congressman from California, had a problem with a shady S&L deal. Realizing he faced a long, drawn out series of embarrassing news stories and political troubles, he ended the controversy before it started—he admitted his mistakes and promptly resigned his public office. Now he's working in New York city as an investment banker, earning more money with less headaches, and is still a respected Democratic party player.
- Admit it and throw yourself at the mercy of the voters. Asking for forgiveness is often a useful tactic. Although, as Laguens pointed out, "they may forgive you, but they may not necessarily elect you."
- Fuzzing the admission. When Bill Clinton admitted to smoking pot, he added what he thought would lesson his sin, "I didn't inhale." What it did was make him look silly.
- Stonewalling. This is the attempt to tell the press there is no problem, no story. Nixon tried it with Watergate. Clinton tried it with Whitewatergate. You be the judge of how well it works.
- Inoculation. This is often the best defense. Go to the voters before they come to you. During the 1988 presidential campaign, contender Al Gore admitted to smoking marijuana after Supreme Court Justice not-to-be Douglas Ginsburg admitted to smoking the illegal narcotic as well. This requires a little known campaign tactic—opposition research on yourself. Many candidates do not realize how much baggage they carry. As one consultant said, "It's not the nature of our society for secrets to survive."
- Snowballing. This favorite among corporate damage control teams is the strategy by which spinmeisters throw out so much complex information, reporters get bowled over and taken along for a ride. Presidents do this with budgets. And it often works.
- Deny the charge and demand proof. Roger Stone, a Republican spinner for Ronald Reagan and Jack Kemp, has been quoted as saying, "If you deny it and demand proof, be sure your opponent or the press doesn't actually have the goods."
- Statute of limitations. You can put the problem back in time when you were young and foolish, but now you are older and wiser. This often works if the indiscretion occurred before one was a public figure or when the candidate was college age.
- Ignore and evade. Sometimes voters do not hook-in to damaging stories. If that is your preferred tactic, the next step is to pray the issue doesn't catch up to you until after election day. Don't count on it though.

Four Nightmare Scenarios: Some Advice from Top Pros

Political consultants from around the country were presented with four hypothetical scenarios and asked to present their plan for handling the damage. They are: Dane Strother (D), of Strother/Duffy/Strother; Mark Weaver (R), vice-president of Wilson Communications; John McLaughlin (R), of Fabrizio, McLaughlin & Associates; Craig Shirley (R) of Craig Shirley & Associates; Dawn Laguens (D) of Seder/Laguens; Jim Farwell (R) of the Farwell Group; Donald Fields (R) of DFA...Public Relations, Inc.; Leslie Israel (D) of Politics, Inc.; and Cathy Allen (D) of Campaign Connection. This is what they said:

Scenario 1

Your gubernatorial candidate's brother, who is not a well-known public figure, calls a press conference (covered by the statewide press) two weeks before the election and announces his support for your candidate's opponent. He accuses his sister, your client, in general terms of being "dishonest" and "an incompetent lawyer and businesswoman"—his animosity resulting from an internal family fight involving inherited real estate. There's also a pending civil lawsuit against your client, which had not gotten any press notice, in which her brother and a real estate broker accuse her of double-dealing and incompetence as an attorney. The latest poll showed your client five points ahead, which is down from an 11 point lead she had a month earlier. How does your client respond to her brother?

Weaver: Produce a high quality film spot. Show the candidate in her living room, by a family photo. In a warm way, to camera, she would say (partial script): "Since Dad died, there have been many disagreements in our family. Like many families there are strongly held and differing views. What's sad for me is that these private disagreements have become public. I'm running for Governor to make a difference in our state. Don't judge me on the squabbles in my family—judge me on my vision for our state."
We would immediately air the spots in a 50/50 rotation with the spot already airing until polling shows it has done it's job.

Israel: Go public with a fully honest press conference. Do not let the half-truths and innuendoes drag on. I would probably suggest a "more in sorrow than in anger" approach, sharing your pain over this sad family feud. Make it clear that you will have no further comment on the situation, since you still love your brother and hope for a reconciliation. "Sometimes money makes people forget what really matters, but I'm not going to make things worse by continuing to dwell on this." You may need to cut a sincere candidate-to-voters TV spot to this effect. Then get on with your campaign.

Farwell: Check the facts. Have your candidate call a press conference and express compassion for her brother's confusion and difficulty in dealing with personal problems, and treat the matter as an internal family problem. Voters know that everyone has family problems. Don't let the controversy spread beyond those parameters.

Allen: Hold a press conference in front of the old family home. Her response: "You know, I think that everyone who's ever had a brother has probably had a fight with him. I can remember growing up when he first took my toys and wouldn't give them back. I can also remember a lot of good times we had—summer camp, watching him win his first Little League game... despite it all, I still love my brother.

But now, it's with great sadness that grown-up fights make the news. This is a family affair and it has nothing to do with the campaign.

"It's two weeks before election day. You decide what's more important... the issues of education, crime and the economy, or a fight between a brother and a sister."

Don't get into double-dealing accusations, rather just wrap them in the blanket of a family squabble.

Strother: Turn the other cheek. Release a statement saying, "I love my brother and this pains me. We obviously have a misunderstanding, but this is a family matter and I will deal with it privately. Families quarrel, but we will be friends again." Take no other questions on this subject.

Scenario 2

Your married male candidate (who's running for attorney general against an incumbent) is named a defendant in a paternity and child support suits filed one week before the election by a woman who claims to have had a long, secret relationship with him. A local reporter tells you his newspaper is running the story, and they have talked to the woman. Your client tells you privately that he had sex with the woman many times, but the last time was well over a year before the child's birth, making his paternity impossible. So far, he has said nothing publicly about the matter. The latest poll showed your client three points behind, but rapidly moving up. What do you advise him to do?

Strother: Release a statement saying there is no way the child is yours and the courts will determine that the day the child is born. But we, as society, must do more to help single mother families. And until our education system is improved, then all the children in the state suffer.

Laguens: If his wife won't stick by him, he's toast. If she will, do a Clinton. "Admittedly, Bev and I have been through some tough times, but we have worked hard to solidify our marriage. I am unequivocally not the father of Ms. Johnson's child."
Other choice: Avoid it long enough to attack your opponent HARD to create distraction and "air" cover. You can fudge this for a week. But you'll have to deal with it sooner or later.

McLaughlin: Since modern science would provide a definitive answer and the candidate is sure of his responsibility, the newspaper should be implored to hold the story pending the outcome of the test. Whether or not the newspaper would agree to that would be a very important variable. If they don't, they weaken their credibility.
The second variable is the reaction of the candidate's wife. If the spouse doesn't "stand by her man" á la Hillary, there may be a similar reaction in the electorate.
The candidate should be honest with voters and try to put his personal life back in place. If he is able to win, a video tape of Fatal Attraction and a medical analysis of John Bobbitt's operation should be appropriate gifts for reflection.

Shirley: This guy's got a problem, but... hey, so did Bill Clinton.

It would seem, in fact, to call for a modified Clinton: complete with an understanding wife, admission of past problems and denial of recent affairs. The woman is obviously bitter and is simply trying to hurt the candidate. The wife, who is key here, must stand by her man and should be outraged that the press would even consider giving credence to these charges.

Five years ago this guy would have been doomed. Now... who knows?

Farwell: If the facts hold up, try to kill the story by getting to the editor the facts and threatening libel. Agree to a blood test and take it. Expedite the results. A blood test is definitive. New York Times v. Sullivan won't protect a newspaper against this type of story—a fact publishers know, and which can cause them to stop the story, if you have given them the facts. Be ready to accuse your opponent of a dirty trick and be prepared to use paid media to document it.

Scenario 3

Your client is running for re-election to the City Council in a tight race. Your client voted for an anti-gay rights ordinance and incurred the wrath of the local gay community. A month before election day, your candidate is accused in a local gay publication of being a "closet homosexual" and the article has a grainy photo of your client partying at a prominent gay bar. Your client is a 50 year old man who is in the middle of a nasty divorce from his wife of 15 years; he publicly and privately denies the allegation that he's gay but privately admits to you that he did, in fact, visit the bar at the invitation of gay and non-gay supporters. An opponent has just mailed the article to all the voters in the district. How do you handle this?

Weaver: Mail a four color, oversize postcard refutation. It would feature our candidate in separate photos with African American, female and Jewish supporters. The headline: "John Jones represents everyone on the City Council. Just because he meets with them doesn't mean he's one of them." The piece would attack the bigotry and McCarthyism of the opponent. It would end (showing a photo of John and his family) with an appeal for unity.

Shirley: Assuming for a moment that his wife isn't divorcing him because he is gay, this is one of those instances in which the truth might prove a viable option.
The candidate should handle this himself. He should be outraged at the fact that his opponent would stoop to such tactics and demand an apology. Personal mud slinging rarely works.
He can reiterate his earlier position on issues involving gays, but say that as a candidate for public office he has an obligation to listen to the views of all voters and that he was doing just that in visiting the bar in question. He must do this with a straight face. He should produce those who took him there who should also condemn the attempt by his opponent to twist a legitimate campaign appearance to damage an honorable man.

Lafuens: Get signed affidavits from supporters stating that they accompanied him to this bar where he in fact did campaign. Attack the opponent for sleazy campaign practices, for having launched a patently untrue personal attack to cover that he (1) had nothing to say about himself and (2) wanted to cover up [insert negative information here]. Point out our candidate represents all the voters in the district.

Fields: Use the "I'm trying to do what's best for the community" approach. I would advise the candidate to admit that he might have been somewhat insensitive albeit unintentional, towards the rights of all citizens including the city's gay citizens, and I would advise him to simply deny that he's a "closet homosexual" and state that for 15 years he was happily married and committed to his wife and their family. He would also seek the understanding of the community while he and his family endure this very painful ordeal.

Regarding the appearance in the gay bar, I would advise him to categorize it as one of his many campaign appearances hosted by gay and non-gay supporters of his campaign, simply that and nothing more.

Israel: Since your opponent has used the mail, I would follow suit. Use an envelope with an overprinted tagline like "The truth...from Councilman Doe." Enclose a short, dignified letter in which he explains briefly the facts of his visit to the gay bar, where he had a chance to meet with and listen to the members of that community. Then make your opponent the issue. Skillfully handled, you can even win the respect of the gay community if you avoid lifestyle comments and attacks. Overlay this will strong, positive radio and TV, if your budget permits.

Scenario 4

Your client, who is running for an open congressional seat with a large lead over three primary opponents, told you that he received a masters degree from an obscure out-of-state university and had graduated "with honors" from undergraduate school. You put this information in campaign literature that has already been distributed. Three months before the election, your candidate tells you that he fudged his bio and does not have a masters degree and did not graduate with honors. Apparently, a local alumnus of one of the universities noticed this duplicity and called the candidate and is threatening to go to the press but won't if he's paid $10,000. Your candidate tells you he wants to "come clean" before it blows up. How do you handle it?

Strother: Either stonewall the issue until election or Adios—Remember Lena Guerrero (the 1992 Texas Railroad Commissioner who lost the election because of a faked resume.) Lying about something that is easily proven will kill a campaign quicker than anything.

McLaughlin: Before "coming clean" on this one point, all bios and resumes should be reviewed with the candidate for full accuracy. Then they should be verified by others. A second "fudging" could be fatal.

From that point on all materials should be re-done. The blackmailer should be reported to the police and the decision to go public with this threat should be made with the advice of legal counsel. Upon going public the candidate would have to be totally honest to re-establish credibility with a good explanation.

Laguens: I would be tempted to resign the campaign. His only choice is to admit it, try to make it a mistake of years ago that just never got corrected and pray he is so far ahead that he can survive.

Fields: Oh Boy!!! Explain that in our candidate's zeal to serve the community as their congressman, he inadvertently exaggerated his accomplishments. For this indiscretion he is genuinely and personally sorry.

He extends his apologies and hopes that by asking voters for their forgiveness and compassion that he might be allowed to move past this "human error" to serve them in the congress.

My client further pledges to continue his educational pursuits towards the completion of his masters degree, and further pledges to personally establish a scholarship fund, to enable at least one inner city youth the opportunity to pursue a higher education.

Allen: Destroy all the old brochures and redo the pieces, specifically mentioning, "Though I never received a graduate degree, and even though my grades in college weren't perfect, I know the value of good education, which is why it's one of my top priorities." Get them distributed immediately.

Meet with the person and explain what will be done to correct the problem and ask if that will be enough to satisfy his concerns. Give no hint that we are already racing the clock to get this brochure on the streets. Wear a wire to get the bribe on tape, if it's repeated.

If the alumni member does not relent, then keep the conversation going for another week or two, allowing time for the brochures to drop.

After the brochures have been distributed, the candidate does a public mea culpa press conference and admits that things just got out of hand, and even though he meant to tell the truth the first time his resume was misinterpreted, he never did until someone tried to blackmail him. Play the radio tape of the bribe, and come clean.

✓ Handling Damage Control: Look Right, Sound Right
Michael Sheehan

During her first press conference after the Nancy Kerigan incident, skater Tonya Harding read a prepared statement to the press about her troubles. Her intention was to rally support and understanding from the world viewing audience. No Olympic judge would have awarded her anything more than a 3.0. Her expression was grim, her voice pained, and her eye contact mechanical. It did not help when she mispronounced "represent my country."

In the scenarios presented, each of the consultants laid out damage control responses. These responses would work only if the candidate is able to carry out the strategy in all public appearances—in person, on the stump, during a press conference, or television interview. To paraphrase Marv Levy of the Buffalo Bills: the best game plan in the world is useless if the players can't execute it properly.

Scenario 1

Most of the consultants' responses call for a "warm and fuzzy" approach. It's tough to achieve that standing up behind a podium on a raised state, or booming into a microphone.

I suggest this strategy be executed with the candidate sitting down in an informal setting. An example might be the President seated across from a foreign dignitary during a photo opportunity, fielding a few questions in a low-key fashion. If the candidate is relaxed, speaking slowly in modulated tones, with an understanding expression on his/her face, any of the suggested approaches will work.

Scenarios 2 and 3

Some of the consultants would take similar approaches to the second and third scenarios—setting the record straight without being defensive in scenario 2, or appearing insensitive to any group in scenario 3.

Here's the dilemma: The candidate will want to assert his/her position with confidence. That very assertiveness which might exhibit itself in a loud voice, stem expression, and rigid gestures is likely to make the statement sound overly defensive, which would undermine the strategy.

The key is to run the candidate through the statements so many times that he/she sounds somewhere between matter-of-fact and boring. You do not want the candidate to come off combative or defensive. That would only attract additional attention to the response itself with the possibility of having it picked up on the evening news.

Ms. Laguens takes the opposite approach and wants to employ a strong counterattack to override the denial/admission. In this case, she will take candidate in exactly the opposite direction: making the attack particularly loud, harsh, over articulated and overly gesticulated. (Five cups of double espresso would help, too!) In this case, the attack would generate more attention than the defense.

Scenario 4

The consultants suggest varying strategies.

Dane Strother's approach requires the development of a Reaganesque stiff-arm runaway: the ability to walk easily past reporters while pleasantly pretending not to hear their questions, with perhaps a sprinkling of joshing one-liners: "Degrees? Oh, I'd say it's about 75 degrees right now."

Donald Fields has developed an approach that would be difficult for the candidate himself to affect. As sketched out, this approach is best affected by a third party—be it a press secretary or the campaign manager. In that case, see next month's issue on stylistic points of press secretaries and campaign managers covering for their candidates.

Ms. Laguens' response would call for a lawyer who's good on tort law: someone good at canceling contracts.

13

Initiatives, Referenda and Grassroots Lobbying

★ ★ ★

✓ Media and the Initiative Campaign
Robert Nelson

I don't know which I dislike more: politics or warm beer. That's why I especially enjoy running initiative campaigns. These campaigns have little relation to politics in any conventional sense. An initiative has no political party, no public record to defend or promote, no personality to charm or disgust the voters. And there are no brothers-in-law who need a job.

An initiative is just waiting for you to define it and give it life. Initiative campaigns are *mano a mano*—it's just you and the voter. It's the only real test of pure communications skill in the campaign world. It's war.

In handling media and communications for an initiative campaign, there are a number of differences from a Conventional campaign. You need to be aware of them and how they affect the way you'll do your job.

Your client—usually a committee of financial or volunteer interests—deserves your loyalty. You should never do anything that damages their image or portfolio of concerns. But you can't win a tough election if you focus on issues from their perspective alone. You've got to make the voters your co-equal client.

Think the way the voters think. View life from his or her perspective, not from the lofty intellectual perch of an environmental leader or the capitalistic focus of a corporate public affairs officer.

Most voters care about neither the perpetuation of the spotted owl nor about job and profit losses at Intergalactic Inc. The voter wants to know how the issue will affect her taxes, or the safety of his family, or the family's health care, education, environmental quality, or cost of living.

Voters want their laws to make sense—to follow some coherent policy that fits well with other laws and policies. If you can divide your mind and respond simultaneously to the interests of both your paying and your voting client, you're on your way to winning. Use pollsters who understand how to correctly survey on an initiative. Many pollsters will lead you astray in an initiative campaign.

In a large county election in California in 1984, a respected national pollster told me on Friday that we were "five points behind and closing."

On Election Day, the next Tuesday, we lost by a 70 percent to 30 percent margin. We haven't used this guy again. Although I like him a lot, he doesn't understand how to survey for an initiative. Planning strategy and media for an initiative forces you to reexamine everything you've ever learned in candidate campaigns. The most significant factors in candidate races are party affiliation, name identification, personal image, and agreement on issues, in that order.

But an initiative has no party. Your candidate's name is either "vote yes," or "vote no," so name identification is largely irrelevant. Your candidate is a piece of legislation, so there is no personality imagery—no charisma factor.

In the beginning, all you have is the issue. Everything we know about winning candidate elections tells us that issues count least. A major hurdle in an initiative campaign is to first abandon your preconceptions and formulas. Plastering the city with "Vote No on Measure Z" may raise your name I.D., but it won't work like it might for a candidate.

You have to grapple with the issue first, not last. You need to get inside the voter's head and find out how this can be made important to him or her.

Find ways to make the issue one of cost, or personal freedom, or jobs. Look for the classical election themes.

In November '93, all published polls and private pollsters for the gubernatorial candidates showed us losing a major statewide initiative by 10 to 30 points Our own polls showed us winning by 20 to 30 points. On election day, the tally was 69 percent to 31 percent in our favor. Why were they all wrong when we were so right? Because of the precise wording used to ask voters how they planned to vote on this specific question. Unlike candidate or product surveys, minor nuances in initiative ballot questions can make huge changes in response.

When polling for a candidate, you get consistently accurate results by giving the candidate's name and party I affiliation. But when polling for an initiative, how do you describe the proposed law without coloring the response?

For that moment, the pollster's question is the entire initiative, and every word used to describe it has the potential to change the voter's feeling about it.

If you are using focus groups to "test" commercials, you are wasting your time and your client's money. Voters hate political commercials. If you show them an effective spot that threatens to change their preconceptions, they'll tell you how rotten and manipulative and false it is.

If you show them a "vote no" spot, they'll complain about negative advertising and start talking about America's inevitable decline because of commercials like this. If they love your commercials, you have succeeded in giving them something that reinforces all the beliefs they brought into the room with them. In other words, you persuaded no one of anything. So, do you think we hate focus groups? Surprise! Absolutely not.

We consume vast quantities of focus groups, and I travel tens of thousands of miles each year to personally view them. We used 40 groups last year alone, but we don't test commercials there. Focus groups are a place to listen to our "clients"—the voters. Our goal is to find out the whys that lay behind the whats that a survey reports. Our goal is to glean the words, the phrases, and stories that real people use to talk about the issue at hand. If we showed them a commercial, it would not be to find out whether they liked it or even remembered it.

We are looking for ways it changed the way they talk about the initiative, to find out if it put new things in their heads. Hal Larson, the David Ogilvy of initiative advertising, has the definitive instruction for understanding a focus group: "It's not the words, it's the music." Listen for the rhythms, the volume, the tone of discussion, not the reasons people give.

If you can force the election debate to focus on your issues, you win. If the debate is about the other side's issues, you lose. We often begin major advertising three months before an election. It usually works, keeping in mind your paying client's resources. In 1986, we had a sure winner initiative when our committee's finances unexpectedly ran dry six weeks before election day. For five of these six weeks, we had no advertising at all, watching impotently as Ralph Murphine, Bob Goodman, and Pat Caddell hammered our brains in. We lost statewide by one vote per precinct.

The lesson: controlling the debate early must be secondary to dominating the media at the close. "Money is the mother's milk of politics," is true in initiatives as in candidate campaigns. The basic rule, however, is that money is more important for a "no" campaign than a "yes" campaign. If a strong majority of voters don't start the campaign in favor of a proposition, it stands little chance of winning, even with a generous campaign war chest. Money can be the crucial factor in defeating an initiative.

Money gives you the ability to create strong advertisements—creative that can compete in the increasingly sophisticated world of television and direct mail. It can enable you to start early and sustain your message to the end. It can let you hire staff to mount an aggressive press and speakers bureau program.

If you have the advantage of a well-funded campaign, money will be an issue itself, and it can be your undoing if not handled properly. If your funding source is from corporate interests—from land developers to tobacco companies—the press will write headline stories about it, and the voters will be suspicious about your campaign's credibility.

Some basic rules to prevent your campaign spending from becoming the focus of debate:

- Never try to hide whom the money is coming from.
- Never say in advance how much you plan to spend, but always obey legal requirements about disclosing how much you have already spent.
- Never explain your contributors' motives for donating funds, but help them anticipate how to answer such questions when they are asked.
- Most important, build a strong local committee of people who have no financial stake in the outcome and create high visibility for these persons throughout the campaign.

The best advice I can give to anyone is to start your planning effort early.

We start to plan major campaigns up to 18 months before the election. Over time, your plans will change as new information comes to hand.

But if you dedicate significant resources to the planning process, you will build a strong working team, learn your strengths and weaknesses, find new and more potent ways to present your arguments, and be better prepared to meet the unexpected.

As Eisenhower said, "Plans are worthless, planning is everything."

✓ Winning the Referendum Game
Ron Faucheux

"Let me tell you about the very rich," wrote F. Scott Fitzgerald, "They are not like you and me." In the same vein, referendum elections are not like candidate elections. They are as different from one another as rich and spoiled Jay Gatsby was from the simpler Nick Carraway.

Aside from the obvious—that in a referendum, there is no flesh-and-blood candidate—there are many differences between the two types of balloting that bear heavily upon how campaigns for each should be run.

There are a number of strategy rules that have been developed from working on many statewide and local referendum campaigns. Though every rule has exceptions, the following points should be remembered as helpful guidelines:

1. It's easier to kill an issue proposition than it is to pass one.

Proponents have to provide compelling reasons why a ballot issue needs to pass (i.e. more police on the streets will cut crime; added property taxes will save schools; term limits will make politicians more accountable). Opponents, on the other hand, merely have to raise doubt about a proposition to kill it.

A flawed candidate can win if his or her opponent has even more conspicuous flaws. To pass a referendum, the issues flaws must be overcome, there are nobody else's negatives to run against.

In 1992, if there had been a national ballot proposition that read, "Is Bill Clinton the best person in America to become president" it would have gone down in flames, losing at least 57-43. But in the real election, Clinton's negatives were viewed relative to those of his opposition. Clinton didn't have to prove that he was the best person for the job, only that he was better than the alternatives.

2. A chain is as strong as its weakest link.

In a multi-part proposition, the vote in favor of the issue will usually not exceed the favorable support for the weakest of its parts. Often in controversial propositions, proponents put in sweeteners (e.g. tax cuts) to mask unpopular features (e.g. tax hikes). Unless the sweeteners become the central focus of the campaign and the more controversial points ignored (unlikely if there's organized opposition), it is rare that they can carry the whole issue.

That's why it's so difficult to pass complex issue propositions. Complexity scares voters. They fear the devil in the details. Complex propositions are rarely passed by selling specifics. Generally, they can only be passed when the overall thrust, the wider message (i.e. "Let's get rid of a failed system and build a new one from scratch") is so timely and popular that it becomes bigger than the sum of its parts. This requires a rare electoral chemistry.

3. Endorsements from politicians can hurt more than help.

To pass a proposition, keep the politicians away from the public campaign. It's usually better to have citizens and civic groups carry the banner than a bunch of elected officials.

Don't pile negatives too high. Each issue has its own set of negatives. When the negatives of a politician (even a popular one) are added to those already carried by the issue, the load gets awfully heavy.

Once, during a campaign to kill a bond issue, the opposition aired a new spot featuring an impressive list of public officials who supported the bond issue. As the ad ended, one person glanced forlornly and, anticipating an "Oh shit!" response, asked how the spot would be received. The response surprised the campaign worker, "If that doesn't kill the bond issue, nothing will." Of course, the bond issue went down to defeat (why else would the story be here), but the point is made: most ballot issues can't carry the baggage that elected officials bring with them—so leave them home!

There are, however, three extremely "important things" public officials can do: They can raise money. They can work to hold down organized opposition (see point nine about how important this is.). They can be used as "expert witnesses" confining or contradicting statements of fact that back up important argument.

4. Tell the truth about what the proposition will and won't do.

Don't overstate the case. Don't exaggerate the facts. Don't be afraid to present information in a straightforward manner. Voters should feel satisfied they're getting the whole story.

When the truth is obscured, it's an open invitation for the opposition to attack the credibility of the entire campaign, raising critical doubts. It's hard enough to win a controversial issue without a credibility problem; with one, forget it.

Honest use of statistics is important. For example, if a proposition is estimated to create 10,000 to 15,000 jobs (depending upon which economist you listen to), use the lower, more defensible figure.

Don't get too cute. Ads that stretch the truth or inappropriately portray an irrelevant political message expose a glass jaw that's easy to crack. Inexperienced media producers who don't understand the subtle nuances of referendum politics will often go for flashy, over-dramatized ads that set themselves up for counter attack. Keep ads simple and information-oriented; build them around a central message that works strategically. The point of a political ad is not to win a Pollie or advertising club award, but to win an election.

5. Make sure the campaign hires professionals with varied issue election experience.

Not all media consultants, campaign managers, and pollsters—even those with strong candidate-campaign track records—are seasoned issue election specialists. Hire only those who are. Political consultants like referendum campaigns. They give them a chance to directly impact public policy and to make money between regular candidate elections. There are also personal reasons. As one consultant put it: "Issues don't have egos and they don't have spouses."

6. Public opinion on ballot issues is usually unstable and subject to abrupt change.

In candidate elections, voters rely on "cues" to help them make their choices. These cues, such as the candidate's party, ideology, region, age, gender, and race, help voters sort out the "good guys" from the "bad guys".

In a referendum campaign, these cues don't exist, except as they are represented by visible supporters and opponents of the issue. Consequently, voters are more often swayed by the last argument they hear that they agree with. In a referendum, the power is in the argument; the message wins or loses on its own, untainted by candidate characteristics. This makes possible wide shifts in public opinion.

The volatile nature of issue elections is why referendum ballet language can be so important. In most cases, the ballot language is already written by the time political consultants are hired. That's a mistake. Ballot language is your advertisement in the voting booth, the last word. In some cases, legal requirements limit wording leeway, particularly with constitutional amendments or bond issues.

7. Don't misread early polls.

Rule-of-thumb: If the "for" position at the start of the campaign doesn't have at least a two-to-one lead over the "against" position, then the proposition is probably in jeopardy, particularly if there's organized opposition.

In referendum contests, polls better measure "against" sentiment than they do "for" sentiment. When tracking voter attitudes, keep your eyes glued to the negative number. If it ever exceeds 35 percent, the issue is in big trouble even if the "for" position polls what would normally appear to be a comfortable 10 or 15 point margin over the "against" position.

8. The lower the voter turnout, the better chance a thus proposition usually has to pass.

There are many exceptions to this rule. Political observers can cite numerous examples when tax proposition passed in large turnout elections and lost in low turnout ones. But generally, at the local level, lower turnouts help pass taxes. That's because there are clearly defined constituencies that have a large financial stake in the passage of a local tax issue such as school teachers, police and firefighters, road builders, unions, and civil servants. When trying to pass a tax proposition, consider not only the message but the means to communicate it. Direct mail and telephones in low-turnout special elections can be more effective than television in terms of lulling opponents to sleep while targeting a base constituency for election day turnout.

In one school tax election, we overcame the desire on the part of some of our supporters to concentrate on converting the opponents and undecideds, and instead canvassed and phoned only those households that contained our natural base: public school parents, employees, or teachers. We left the rest of the electorate alone. It worked. Core supporters turned out while many of our adversaries stayed home.

9. If there's no organized opposition, you may be able to ignore points one through eight—and still win.

Many of these strategy guideposts assume that there's organized opposition with the resources to deliver its own messages. If no such opposition exists, a win may be possible no matter what goes on. But don't plan on that being the case. Opposition can materialize instantly and inflict its damage the last few days before the election, at a time when it's too late to make a case, much less respond to attack.

✓ The Grassroots Explosion
Ron Faucheux

Information technology now speeds along with such velocity, it has transformed American culture—and our politics—in ways that few are able to comprehend. This unstoppable force has popularized the methods of acquiring political power and has put vital public issues on the same level as Madonna's sex life and O.J. Simpson's cutlery.

In the modern world, few major issues are merely lobbied anymore. Most of them are now managed, using a triad of public relations, grassroots mobilization, and lobbyists.

There was a time when lobbying was strictly a backroom affair. Affable men in suits would hang around swarming, sweaty legislative chambers, buttonholing lawmakers as they swaggered through lustrous bronzed doors, whispering in ears, slapping backs, winking knowingly. These were the same men who were always good for a free lunch, a round of cocktails, and at election time, a check from their fainthearted clients.

Much lobbying is still done this way, up close and personal. But new rules, both written and unspoken—surely to get even tighter since the November 8th massacre—have either restricted the lunches, cocktails and checks, or at least have required that they be publicly reported when they become a bit too generous.

As the balance of power tips from one party and branch of government to another, as campaign finance is increasingly regulated, as interest groups expand and professionalize, as the news media intensifies its spotlight, and as technology makes building volunteer organizations as simple as writing a check, issues from federal lawmaking to local zoning fights, from franchise competitions to contract procurements, are going public with a vengeance.

But going public is only one aspect of this phenomenon. The other side is the planned and orchestrated demonstration of public support through the mobilization of constituent action. This is what grassroots lobbying is all about, and it is one of the hottest trends in politics today.

Grassroots lobbying is really nothing new. Mass public campaigns on behalf of civil rights, unionism, and a variety of other causes have influenced policy-making for years. What is new is how hundreds of private businesses and over a thousand trade associations are using these populist techniques. As a result, professional grassroots lobbying has become an $800 million industry unto itself.

Power Shifts

We're entering the Golden Age of grassroots lobbying according to the field's top consultants. Only a decade ago, it was the exception rather than the rule. But now both sides of most major issues have a grassroots component. Interest groups that don't play the game risk becoming political eunuchs.

Glenn Lebowitz, president of Optima Direct, Inc., a Washington-based public affairs consulting firm, sees "power shifting towards the grassroots as populist politics becomes more prevalent" and predicts a steady rise in grassroots activity at the federal level and an explosion at the state and local levels.

Association executive Robert Hoopes attributes these trends to the increase of primary political and public policy information now instantly available to the citizenry through cable TV, on-line electronic services, and fax machines. He also believes that restyled legislative bureaucracies have increased the available targets for citizen input.

There seems to be a consensus that lobbying reforms and increased legislative turnover resulting from public discontent and term limits will propel even more grassroots activity. Taking a more cynical view, some ascribe this trend to the election of more blow-dried candidates who have few deep convictions, only care about re-election, and are highly attuned to every slight change in public opinion. Regardless of perspective, one thing is certain: As old relationships and power channels change, so do the techniques.

The grassroots trend will accelerate, observers concur, despite the fact that many public officials don't like it. "Politicians hate pressure," says a top assistant to a California legislator. "Nobody wants an avalanche of mail and calls advocating an opposing view. But smart legislators realize that the more letters and calls they get, the bigger and richer the mailing lists they can compile. And that's pure gold when it comes to re-election."

Though some businesses and associations are still grassroots hold-outs, the recent health care battle broke the back of resistance among many. Insiders expect this higher level of activity to remain if and when health care reform fades in the public eye.

In the end, there will be more grassroots activity because advocacy groups are rapidly learning the lesson that John Davies, a California-based political and public affairs consultant, tells his clients when dealing with the public sector: "Every decision is political, and people are politics."

Models of Advocacy

A host of corporations, ad hoc coalitions, and trade associations have developed a wide range of grassroots strategies. Some of the most effective involve the most controversial issues, from smoking bans to waste disposal to gun control. Tobacco giants Philip Morris and R.J. Reynolds, for example, are noted for their lobbying prowess and full-blown grassroots programs. Waste firms such as WMX Technologies and Browning Ferris Industries, because of the constant governmental involvement in their businesses, are also major players. The National Rifle Association has set an example for other single-issue organizations in its sophisticated mastery of grassroots mobilization. In addition, there are various models of advocacy used by others. Here are some examples:

• National Federation of Independent Business (NFIB). One of the largest and most sophisticated associations is the 617,000-member NFIB. According to vice president of government relations John Motley, this massive national network is well-equipped to use grassroots lobbying tools "from a bludgeon to a scalpel."

The NFIB has built a state-of-the-art information system that contains data on its members including names, addresses, phone and fax numbers, geographic region, legislative districts, number of employees, type of business, issue positions, and political backgrounds. This computer network is connected to laser printers and broadcast faxes, making instant communications possible. National and state executives will soon have on-line access to membership files which will make it possible for them to target activists for overnight faxes sent straight from their desks.

The NFIB's expansive reach can be seen in its numbers. In addition to 50 state directors, they employ over 600 field representatives whose primary job is membership growth but who also handle lobbying chores. Their membership is divided into the 400,000 "A" list (members who re-sponded at least once to a direct mail activation), the 200,000 "AA" list (members who responded to more than one direct mail activation), the 40,000 "guardian" list (most active members), and the 3,000 "Key Contact" list (members who have close relationships with public officials such as George Mitchell's brother and Lloyd Bentsen's cousin).

Targeting is critical. "We can't afford to mail or call all 617,000 members every time we have a problem," says Motley, "which is why we have a flexible system that we can quickly segment."

Even though the NFIB focuses heavily upon direct mail activation of its membership, they also do extensive "tele-lobbying" using telephone patch-throughs that connect individual members to their elected representatives. Because their membership is already preconditioned for political involvement, Motley says their high response rate of over 66 percent has reduced costs for completed phone patch-throughs from nine to ten dollars each to five to six dollars.

Another technique the NFIB uses is "rolling" their direct mail. If they're going to do a 150,000 piece mailing in 100 congressional districts, for example, instead of doing entire districts at a time, they space them out and randomly select only a portion of the total, say 25,000, to be mailed each week. This constant flow evens out peaks and valleys which helps eliminate the astroturf effect.

• Health Insurance Industry of America (HIAA). The HIAA was a highly visible player in the health reform war. Buttressing their TV "air assault" was an extensive "ground effort" coordinated by Leslie Gianelli, external affairs director.

During the health care battle, the HIAA hired field directors in six states—Texas, Louisiana, Kansas, New York, North Dakota, and Oklahoma—and sponsored a coalition grassroots program that covered all 50 states. In addition to an extensive in-house lobbying apparatus, the HIAA hired The Clinton Group for telephone contact, the RTC Group for direct mail, and Direct Impact for grasstops field organizing. Democrat William Hamilton and a GOP firm, Public Opinion Strategies, did polling.

• Independent Insurance Agents of America (IIAA). Grassroots lobbying has been "the cornerstone of our public affairs agenda since 1987," says IIAA grassroots pro Robert Hoopes. His group activated nearly 140,000 of the nation's 280,000 insurance agents during the health care battle. Out of that, he estimates they have a core group of reliable activists that now exceeds 5,000, and growing rapidly.

Using computerized information systems, the IIAA links its members to legislative committees and individual legislators, powerful weaponry when quick action is needed. Their programs are managed in-house, which includes publishing a regular newsletter, an inbound 800 information number, production of video tapes and training manuals. Grassroots techniques are driven by the legislative calendar, says Hoopes, who prefers to time the most intense activities around major presidential speeches when all eyes turn to Washington. He views constant follow-up as fundamental to the process. "After our agents contact their legislators, they need to know what happened, how their work helped. They also need to be thanked."

• National Restaurant Association. Representing over 100,000 business units, this association runs an aggressive grassroots program. Although they directly represent one-eighth of the restaurants in America, their grassroots scope encompasses non-members as well, a common tactic for many trade groups that champion the causes of broad-based industries. "We tap the whole universe," says grassroots chief Patricia Stinger, "because they share a common interest and give us additional numbers."

In addition to traditional mail and phone contact programs, Stinger's group has employed newer, high-tech methods. In one lobbying onslaught, they used satellite technology to transmit three live shows in one day to 200 sites around the country reaching over 5,000 people. Their BITE-BACK program uses an inbound 800 number to inform members of impending issues. They've also set up interactive kiosks at trade gatherings to facilitate member contacts with legislators. Advised by political consultants Gannon, McCarthy, and Mason, they reportedly spent nearly $2 million during the last Congress on a grassroots and advertising program that was widely acclaimed for its effectiveness.

• National Association of Life Underwriters (NALU). "There's a lot of competition for the ear of each congressman," says David Winston, executive director of political involvement at NALU. "You have to go beyond the Beltway to get attention."

NALU began its political involvement program with 600 activists, a number that has tripled in recent years. They have also built a network of over 10,000 members who serve as contacts in 521 of the nation's 538 congressional districts. Local coordinators routinely meet with each Member of Congress three or four times a year.

Even though they maintain their own data base and manage most of their grassroots functions in-house, NALU employs consultants for specialized projects, such as strategist Kevin C. Gottlieb, and uses political software products to manage mailing lists.

Last year, NALU organized 954 face-to-face meetings between Members of Congress and local life underwriters and sponsored "Capitol Hill Days" which brought hundreds of members to the halls of Congress. They also use a "contact tree" for phone and fax communications and send out over 8,000 action alerts newsletters to keep key members informed of legislative happenings. These activities generated over 24,000 telegrams to Members of Congress last year.

Since 1992, NALU's grassroots lobbying budget has increased six-fold, a steep rise typical for an association heavily involved in health care reform.

• American Association of Retired Persons (AARP). The AARP uses a variety of methods to mobilize its vast 33 million membership. Much of its grassroots effort is locally-based, run by state leaders and district committees. Even though non-partisan and without a political action committee, they regularly use direct mail, monthly publications, telephone trees to involve as many as 400,000 activists in lobbying programs. To rally their troops, they've also used paid ads, volunteer speakers, video teleconferencing, and community meetings. They have a 10-person grassroots lobbying staff in Washington, DC plus nine staffed field offices around the country.

The AARP's grassroots programs are run in-house. According to chief lobbyist John Rother, "We beefed up our grassroots efforts for health care reform, but will keep them beefed up because of other looming issues such as entitlements and threats to Medicare."

• American Nursing Association (ANA). "Last year, we experienced a grassroots revolution," says Daniel J. Lerner, the ANA's political outreach director. Not long ago, they had a small network of 560 volunteers who kept in regular contact with legislators through action alert newsletters and informal phone trees. They now have 35,000 trained activists and expect that number to grow to 50,000 next year as part of their "N-STAT" (nurses strategic action team) program.

Organizing nurses for political participation has unique challenges. "All nurses have a story to tell. They're able to say this is what I see every day' and that makes a difference to public officials on medical issues," says Donna Richardson, director of governmental affairs. The ANA has hired outside consultants such as APCO Associates, a full-service public affairs firm based in Washington, D.C. that was once an arm of the Arnold and Porter law firm, to help with media training and materials production. At a recent national convention, over 20,000 letters to public officials were gathered from 5,000 nurses in attendance.

In one crisis, they needed to activate a major contact effort late on a Friday afternoon after most people had already left work. Responding quickly, ANA operatives hit the telephones, directing many of their calls to beepers since most nurses wear them on and off duty. It was something to see, recalls Richardson, who says the project proved to be very effective.

• National Education Association (NEA). Representing over 2.2 million public school teachers and employees, the NEA's grassroots strategy is in transition, according to Dick Vander Woude. Once, they relied upon a cadre of 485 congressional contact teams to carry the load. But now, they're moving into wider contact universes using more volume-oriented programs in addition to their existing district contact mechanism.

One of the more intriguing strategies employed by the NEA was in 1992 when they ran TV advertising that delivered a pro-public education message. The spots artfully reinforced similar pitches that were being delivered by mostly Democratic candidates who were arguing that domestic priorities must prevail in the post-Cold War era. "It was a slick way to impact the political environment without ever saying 'vote,'" remarked a Republican media consultant who admired the strategy. "Others should take a lesson."

Personal Touch

Everyone agrees about one aspect of grassroots lobbying: the more personal, the better. Even though mass-produced form letters, postcards, mailgrams, and petitions are still rated useful in some situations, the trend is away from impersonal "astroturf" devices toward higher quality contacts such as individualized letters, direct phone calls, and personal visits. As one political consultant sums it up: Personalized is better than mass, but mass is better than nothing.

Lobbying is a process of looking for the button to push that moves a legislator toward your position, explains Vic Kamber, who has advised labor unions, private corporations, trade associations, and non-profits on legislative strategies. The pressure point may be an editorial in an influential home town newspaper, the endorsement of a particular organization, the opposition of a popular radio talk show host, or it may be 5,000 postcards or 500 phone calls. Kamber rates personal visits—eye contact between a legislator and a strong advocate—as the most effective weapon. "Nothing beats a personal visit. Nothing."

Glenn Lebowitz says the most effective grassroots programs allow constituents to communicate in their own words to their elected officials. "Tools used depend upon the issue and the situation. The strategy needs to be set first."

Political consultant Wally Clinton, president of The Clinton Group, echoes this assessment and grades the power of grassroots techniques according to their function and purpose. "It depends on the level of government, timing, and nature of the issue."

Clinton has found that at the federal level, a combination of techniques is usually needed. At the state and local levels, postcards and mailgrams are still useful, particularly if they're from constituents with addresses that prove they're real voters and are timed as part of a steady stream of contact. Better voter files and new software products has made the execution of all of these procedures much more efficient, he adds. "There was a time when name, address, phone number, and district boundary matches had to be done by hand, and that was murder. Now, we can rapidly match names and addresses with nine-digit zips in each district, and it's very accurate."

Liz Welch, who manages Clinton's Louisville, Kentucky, telecommunications center, says vendors must be able to activate citizens overnight because of sudden legislative developments. But Welch cautions that there is a difference between quick-turnaround capability in a crisis and one-shot programs that are short-lived. The best efforts, she says, involve educating, sensitizing, and mobilizing people over time.

Grassroots specialist Jack Bonner, whose gold-plated clients have included General Motors, Citicorp, Merck Pharmaceutical, GTE, General Electric, Hershey Foods, Aetna, Exxon, and Boeing, believes high quality contact is where it all began and where the industry is now headed. Grassroots works best, he formulates, when you "activate politically important home district constituents who can demonstrate they understand both sides of an issue and can explain in their own words how this issue will impact their district."

"The old politics was based on individual contact. That's what works." Having said that, though, Bonner quickly admits that mass-produced contact programs can also be effective, depending upon the issue. His firm produced over 6,000 postcards per day during the heat of the health care battle in 1994, for instance, punctuating his point that volume still counts, too.

"Grassroots is getting back to basics. Astroturf is out. Now, it's real people, real issues, real victories," says Pamela Jones-Lee, president of National Grassroots & Communications, Inc. "Clients need to take time to educate their constituencies so the constituency is still there after they leave."

Jones-Lee, who has attracted a large following of corporate clients, advises customers to start by mobilizing their own employees, officers, shareholders, and vendors. The focus, she says, should be on quality not quantity, which is why she doesn't often use mass-generated phone calls or postcards. The exception is when "it's at the bottom of the ninth and quick action is needed."

Most public affairs pros agree that the best "hits" are the most personal ones, and that they lose effectiveness as they become less individualized. Daniel J. Lerner at the ANA says his association stays away from automated efforts such as pre-printed postcards, and favors personal letters. "We've tried all the methods. We've learned that quality works best." Paralleling this viewpoint is RTC Group executive Jeanne Herman, who says her company is now concentrating on personalized direct mail.

Les Francis, of Winner, Wagner, and Francis, says the most effective grassroots effort uses a balance of field operations, free media, paid ads, direct mail and phones. Like others in the business, Francis stresses that personalization matters and mentions drumming up attendance of articulate advocates at town hall meetings as an especially effective technique.

Capitalizing on this trend, consultant John Brady offers clients a variety of field recruitment programs that rely heavily upon personal meetings between constituents and public officials. His firm maintains a network of field operatives in all 50 states. During the past year, they had as many as 140 local operatives working on various projects. They hire people who have expertise in politics and a Rolodex they can immediately tap. This grasstops approach to lobbying is nothing magical, insists Brady, "The real magic is having a quality network in place and ready to go. The nuts and bolts are simple, it's quality control that matters."

Brady said the first step in a typical grasstops program is direct lobbyists identifying swing legislators who need to hear from constituents. His local operatives then develop a list of volunteer advocate prospects, usually business people, and hold one-on-one 30 to 60 minute meetings with each of them. If that person can articulate reasons for support of the issue, he or she is asked to either call, write, or fax their Congressman or state legislator, or schedule an office visit or a lunch meeting, whatever is appropriate to their relationship. Usually, between 20 and 60 advocates per district or state are recruited this way.

Dealing with siting and land use issues is a particularly thorny predicament for many environmental firms, manufacturers, and real estate developers who often get clobbered by neighborhood protests. John Davies, president of a political and public affairs communications firm based in Santa Barbara, California, has counted among his clients cellular communications companies that often face "Not In My Backyard" (NIMBY) opposition to new tower sites. At a *Campaigns & Elections* seminar in San Francisco, he made the point that in siting controversies, companies must find their friends, make new ones, and disarm opponents. The first step to making friends, he says, is to do something many business people are afraid to do: Ask for help.

Making friends is one thing. Keeping them is something else. That's why Mike Malik, a grassroots consultant, thinks groups and businesses should get to know more about the people they're recruiting and put more attention into activist education. This means the building of data bases that can be enriched over time, and not just collecting mailing lists.

Dan Siwulec, vice president of Below, Tobe, & Associates, a national direct mail and data base management firm based in California, agrees with Malik's emphasis on support maintenance. "It's critical to keep supporters active and interested even when things aren't hot. Many times people will be recruited, participate in one event, and then they'll be forgotten completely. Direct mail is the most effective and inexpensive way of not only recruiting but retaining supporters."

Air Assaults

Not all grassroots lobbying is restricted to personal contacts. Paid ads can play a role as well. For example, a key component of the HIAA's health care campaign was its $15 million television advertising effort which featured the now famous "Harry and Louise" spots. This media blitz was very closely coordinated with the organizational aspects of the grassroots push.

A crucial part of the "Harry and Louise" commercials was the 800 number provided at the end of each spot. It generated over 350,000 phone calls out of which 40,000 grassroots activists were recruited. It is estimated that these volunteers produced 200,000 contacts with Members of Congress. Most of the $2 million spent on grassroots organization went to fulfilling information packets sent in response to inquiries from the TV spots.

Ben Goddard, president of Goddard*Clausen/First Tuesday, the firm that handled the media for the HIAA, underscores the importance of a multi-faceted effort. "The Harry and Louise ads were only the tip of the iceberg. The grassroots component was critical. The combination of targeted mass media with high-quality grassroots contact is a powerful hammer."

Goddard, whose firm produces both media and organizational campaigns, explains that media-buying for such efforts is usually targeted to reaching 10 to 15 percent of the public most likely to contact legislators. In the TV campaign they produced for the HIAA, Goddard's firm targeted most of their budget outside of the nation's capital to strategically selected local markets. They also bought heavily on cable TV and CNN, placing no spots in prime time and focusing, instead, on news and public affairs programs.

Goddard said buying ads in magazines and newspapers makes sense for clients with a message that is targetable to specific reader profiles. Even when buying mass media, emphasizes Goddard, targeting is still important because most clients can't afford national time buys.

Public affairs consultant Earl Bender has found that paid media campaigns have one advantage over large grassroots lobbying programs in that they're more controllable. Another advantage: they're still enough of a novelty to be able to punch through.

Paying Attention

A Gallup Poll, commissioned by Bonner and Associates after the 1992 elections, interviewed 150 new and returning Members of the U.S. House and Senate. The survey found that communications from constituents are by far the most influential means of getting a message to a Member and that there is a large difference in the attention paid to personal, non-form communications as opposed to canned communications.

Over 70 percent of the lawmakers said they pay a great deal of attention to (a) personally written letters from constituents, (b) meetings with heads of groups, (c) CEO visits representing companies with a job presence in the district, (d) personally written letters from heads of groups in the district or from company officials with a job presence in the district, and (e) phone calls from constituents; between 60 and 69 percent said phone calls from heads of groups in their districts; 20 to 25 percent said postcards and mailgrams from the district; and 19 percent or less said issue papers, form letters from constituents and company officials, editorials, CEO visits from a company without a district job presence, and advertisements.

One pollster who reviewed these findings said they "make perfect sense because politicians want to get across that they listen to people from their districts." However, she continued, "This survey, while valid and interesting, doesn't really measure what influences a Member's vote but only what a Member is willing to admit influences his or her vote. Even though congressmen may not want to say they are influenced by editorials or advertising, it's inaccurate to conclude they don't work. The "Harry and Louise" spots proved that a sustained media presence can create a favorable political environment in which grassroots pressure can thrive."

Inside Jobs

A big trend in corporate public affairs is the internal mobilization of company officers, shareholders, employees, and vendors into a grassroots lobbying force. While many companies have moved into this area, others haven't scratched the surface. One government relations consultant estimates that fully one-half of Fortune 500 companies haven't even sorted their people by congressional or legislative districts—which is considered the crucial first-step in developing internal lobbying capacity.

Pamela Jones-Lee sees a bright future in this area, as the success of her firm attests. "Many companies are finding themselves up against a network of non-profits and unions. They have no choice but to educate, motivate, and activate their own people." Since 1990, her corporate business has increased 300 percent and has included clients such as Wal-Mart, McDonald's, and Food Lion.

Internal business organizing isn't always an easy chore. It requires employee sensitivity and knowledge of legal requirements. Jones-Lee warns that companies must be careful that they don't coerce employees or violate union contracts. Even though the National Labor Relations Act protects workers against employers who lean on them too hard for political purposes, Jones-Lee believes it's more than a legal problem. "Coercion destroys volunteerism," she says, "grassroots support needs to be caught not taught."

Related to this is a question now being pondered by many public affairs executives: Should we maintain an internal grassroots operation or hire outside consultants and vendors?

As part of the answer, Jack Bonner cautions against what he sees as "a big trap". "Most companies with large employee rolls already have a strong political presence in the areas where they are located. Legislators know who their big employers are. But often, there's a need to go beyond this base and that usually takes outside help."

John Brady—whose client list includes the American Petroleum Institute, Chemical Manufacturers Association, the National Association of Realtors, NYNEX, RJR Nabisco, and Tenneco—adds that even when groups run in-house programs, outside consultants can do useful tweaking. He has found that organizations that have the best in-house capacity are those with large sales forces.

Jones-Lee says that most clients usually need both an in-house team and outside consultants and vendors. She explains that "many of them start off thinking they can do it in-house through their human resource departments but quickly learn it's hard for existing personnel to treat public affairs activities with the time and priority that's needed."

Resolution of this issue depends on whether the client has a pre-existing grassroots infrastructure, the way most labor unions do, says Vic Kamber. The AFL-CIO, with 390 local building trades councils spanning the nation, already has "the infrastructure and the contact mechanism in place," he points out. "Where they and other groups like them may need outside help is to prepare materials and do other things that are more efficient to farm out."

Kamber also argues that it's cheaper for a company, an association, or a union to hire outside consultants if they're only concerned about one or two major issues. "It makes no sense for most of them to fund a full-time, full-blown mechanism like we maintain if there are not enough ongoing issues to deal with." His firm employs 100 people who at any one time may work on 25 or more issues. To help address these questions for potential clients, Kamber's firm does an initial "image audit"—an assessment of their internal abilities, strengths, and weaknesses. The cost for this first step, he estimates, is about $25,000.

Another way many companies and associations deal with structural concerns such as these is through the formation of temporary ad hoc compacts that use a combination of in-house personnel and outside consultants to run grassroots programs. Michael J. Kerrigan, president of The Advocacy Group, a nationwide network of federal, state, and local lobbyists, dubs this concept an "adhocracy"—the bringing together of talent only for as long as is necessary to solve the problem at hand—and sees it as a wave of the future for lobbying public issues.

Business Style

A big hindrance to effective grassroots lobbying is timing. Most consultants feel strongly that businesses and advocacy groups err when they wait too long to make their move. Frequently, a grassroots lobbying campaign is an after-thought, something that's only done at the end of the game after its already fallen apart. Complains one political consultant, "CEOs and corporate types don't understand how fast politics and legislation can move, and they can't comprehend the need to frame issues before the enemy does."

He continues, "Gradually, clients are starting to realize that it ultimately costs the same whether you start early or wait until the last minute. Starting early can save big dollars at the end."

When dealing with business people, it's the bottom line that counts, says Jones-Lee, who offers clients public relations as well as grassroots services. One way she ensures client accountability is by keeping track of press clips of weekly and daily newspaper, magazine, TV, and radio stories that her firm helps generate. Through a Florida-based company named ADI PressTRAC, Inc., Jones-Lee provides her clients with detailed analyses of press coverage. This information is cross-referenced by state and federal legislative districts, which links press coverage on an issue to targeted legislators.

The interaction between direct lobbying, public relations, and grassroots organizing is reflected in the organization of many modern public affairs firms.

Take Winner, Wagner, and Francis, for instance, a Washington-based grassroots lobbying firm that's run by Les Francis, former director of the Democratic Congressional Campaign Committee. An affiliate, Winner, Wagner & Associates, was founded in 1975 by Chuck Winner and Ethan J. Wagner as a public affairs and communications strategy firm, which now has offices in Los Angeles, New York, and the nation's capital. Another affiliate, Winner, Wagner, & Mandabach Campaigns, founded in 1985 with offices in New York and Los Angeles, specializes in ballot proposition campaigns.

Francis first realized the potential of a widening public affairs advocacy field along with partner Pat McGinnis as they worked in the Carter Administration to create the Department of Education. "We saw how a combination of outreach, press relations, and field-based organizing could be brought together to advocate an issue. We saw how political campaign methods were applicable to a legislative context."

A model for public affairs firms of the future may be Cassidy & Associates, also headquartered in Washington. Under one umbrella, Cassidy offers governmental relations, public relations (through its arm, Powell-Tate, headed by former Carter Press Secretary Jody Powell and Nancy Reagan adviser Sheila Tate), and grassroots lobbying (through its arm, Beckel-Cowan, which is run by Bob Beckel, a respected political analyst and former Mondale for President campaign manager, and partner Glenn Cowan).

The RTC Group is another multi-service firm that has reflected industry trends. It was created by the merger of Reese Communications, which was founded by legendary political consultant Matt Reese, and Targeted Communications. Reese is credited with originating in the 1960s the instant volunteer organization concept upon which grassroots lobbying programs of today are based. The combined entity is owned by a London-based holding company, WPP, that also owns public relations and advertising giants Hill and Knowlton and Ogilvy & Mather.

Call the Dogs Off

What do traditional lobbyists think about grassroots lobbying? After all, large-scale grassroots campaigns can exhaust funds that lobbyists could have otherwise used to pay for personal entertaining, travel, and PAC contributions.

Powerful Texas lobbyist Buddy Jones says that grassroots lobbying is a viable force in the Lone Star State and will be for a long time to come. "It was the factor in a number of battles." He says in recent years issues such as interstate banking, seat belt regulation, tort reform, health care, and telecommunications all involved large grassroots efforts.

Jones believes emotional issues are best suited for grassroots campaigning. "They present more fertile ground, as opposed to purely technical business issues." From his experience in Austin, Jones ranks personal visits by constituents the best grassroots tactic. After that, he picks personal letters and then phone calls.

Lobbyist Randy Haynie, whose Louisiana-based firm represents national blue chip clients such as Philip Morris USA, Waste Management, Inc., Corrections Corporation of America, Webbcraft Games, and Alamo Car Rental, believes grassroots lobbying in the 50 state capitals will continue to increase. Haynie anticipates that within a few years, all major state issues will have a strong grassroots component.

Even though Haynie cites this evident trend, he believes that traditional lobbying will continue to play a key role. "Lobbyists are essential in targeting which legislators need to be reached through a grassroots campaign. Lobbyists are also the people legislators go to when they want the dogs called off."

Haynie says his firm does targeting research on each issue he's promoting and develops a rating system based on past voting records and electoral variables that may affect legislative voting. Once that's done, "we divide legislators into three categories: supporters, opponents, and swing votes. It is on the swing districts that we focus grassroots. We then decide if a district will receive a heavy grassroots push, a medium effort, or a light one. We also overlay Senate and House districts geographically to determine degree of activity, putting added emphasis on areas that overlap."

Haynie believes old tensions between consultants, and lobbyists are diminishing. "Government relations people now realize that each issue brings with it three cost centers: lobbying fees, PAC costs, and expenses for grassroots programs." Haynie predicts that in the future more lobbyists will offer grassroots programs as one of their own in-house services.

Florida lawyer-lobbyist John French, whose law firm represents major national corporations and local trade associations, agrees with Jones and Haynie that grassroots campaigning is a growing state trend. "In Florida, we've mostly seen first generation grassroots operations that focus on the quantity of response without much focus on the quality," says French. "Future campaigns will need fresh ideas targeted more to opinion leaders and campaign contributors as potential advocates."

One successful grassroots effort that caught French's attention was the campaign recently mounted by the Florida business community on behalf of their position on joint and several liability legislation, which pitted corporate interests against plaintiff-oriented trial lawyers. "The business community had a broad-ranging effort, with faxes, phone calls, letters, and newspaper ads that generated a lot of response, both in volume and quality. They kept up the drumbeat throughout the entire session, and turned it on and off when needed." French cautioned that such an effort, though, may not be easily duplicated. "It's something that can only be done so many times and still work."

He was also impressed with the internal grassroots program implemented by one of his clients, Burger King, which generated thousands of phone calls and hundreds of personal visits on health care issues. "By working through its franchises, Burger King was able to do a high quality, incredibly effective program."

French, who once viewed public relations as "fluff" when it came to lobbying legislation, now believes there can be a natural synergy between public campaigning and insider lobbying. "Both sides need to understand what each other is doing, there needs to be mutual respect." He cited his dealings with Atlanta-based PR firm Cohn and Wolf, a subsidiary of Burson-Marsteller, as an example of a cooperative relationship that turned out well. "The key is for lobbyists and PR people not to try to do one another's job."

Donna Richardson says there is no friction between direct lobbyists and grassroots at the ANA. "Our lobbyists push for grassroots back-up," she says, "They know our power is our 2.2 million nurses—and that means grassroots."

Some associations have put control of direct lobbying and grassroots in the same hands, as has the National Retail Federation. John Dill, who oversees both functions, says "The days of old-time backslapping lobbying is over. Legislators make decisions more on information and a read of their constituents." Pam Stanziani, who handles grassroots programs for retailers, makes a distinction that underscores the complementary roles of each. "Direct lobbying produces information. Grassroots lobbying produces constituencies."

Back to the Future

On the horizon, Earl Bender envisions grassroots lobbying benefiting from new technologies such as the pentium chip and CD-ROM, plus other tools "we can't even now imagine." He foresees more interactive communications, such as E-mail, internet contacts, phone patch-throughs, and video taped constituent messages. "Those who use new techniques first will have the highest impact. Once the tools of the trade are used too often, they lose novelty and punch."

When assessing untested techniques, Bender warns clients that flash does not equal effectiveness. "Americans love to buy high-tech toys, and some buy them without regard to their productivity. That's something business people who don't have in-depth political experience must keep in mind."

Echoing this theme is John Brady, who argues that technical bells and whistles don't substitute for genuine communications, and Frank Howard, Jr., senior vice president of National Grassroots & Communications, Inc., who maintains that in the future, smart grassroots lobbying will use technology to add effectiveness and speed, not slickness.

Looking ahead, most participants predict that more grassroots services will be deliverable with overnight speed and that they will become more integrated with overall corporate image and marketing operations. This will enable companies to reach out to customers at the same time they accomplish legislative goals.

Healthy Sign

Does grassroots lobbying have a good or bad influence on democracy?

While some see it as another weapon in the arsenal of the rich and powerful to gain and maintain influence, others see it as a healthy sign of democratic reinvigoration and a cause of greater electoral competition. Says Vic Kamber, "The less voters know about the issues, the easier incumbent re-election is. Grassroots activities inform the public and make them more aware of issues. That's good for the system."

The ability to mobilize citizens and get them to contact their public officials is the pivot upon which a democratic nation rests. That is why the U.S. Constitution, in its First Amendment, put high value on protecting the freedom of "the people to peaceably assemble, and to petition the Government for a redress of grievances."

Critics who decry the artificiality of grassroots campaigns and disparage the manufacturing of public sentiment by well-heeled corporations and interest groups miss one point: grassroots lobbying, when done honestly, is a legitimate tool of direct democracy and is a valid way to increase public awareness and participation in the governmental process. In failing to make that point, though, they suggest an even more telling one: grassroots lobbying works.

Most observers agree that "schlock operators" who try to use trickery and deception in grassroots lobbying won't get very far. They'll likely be rejected by clients and colleagues.

Private sector decision-makers who fear or ignore modern trends toward populist constituency-building, and who want to continue doing business in the backrooms and boardrooms of yesteryear, will likely come up short, too.

After all, we live in an age when every affair is a public affair.

✓ Earl's Pearls: Grassroots Lobbying

Earl Bender, president of Avenel Associates, a Washington-based public affairs consulting firm, has worked on a variety of issues such as the super-collider, deauthorization of the cross Florida barge canal, and public education. Bender has analyzed grassroots efforts and reached conclusions about their effectiveness. The following, he says, *always* works:

- Real citizens talking to legislators about their direct interests. As long as the legislator's district has a stake in the issue that is represented by the constituent doing the lobbying, a key connection is made and the exact techniques used to accomplish it aren't all that important.
- Local opinion leaders working with the press to encourage favorable hard news attention and supportive editorial comment.
- Knowing key legislative staff members and communicating with them. Often, contacts with staffers can be more productive than with elected officials.
- Using originality and occasionally humor to break through the clutter. It's important that your written messages to legislators catch the attention of staffers so they separate them out from the "body counts" of daily mail.
- A sustained organizational program where a few well-informed, articulate people repeatedly contact a legislator, particularly if they were key supporters in that legislator's *first* campaign.

According to Bender, the following usually *don't* work:

- Any contact effort that looks like purely bought-and-paid-for mass pressure. Even though these programs may seem to work temporarily, they usually hurt in the long run and leave a bitter aftertaste.
- A confrontational style that attempts to win over votes through physical harassment. In one controversy involving social security, impassioned advocates jumped and beat on the cars of Members leaving the congressional parking lot—a good example of what *not* to do.
- When citizens don't know what they're talking about when they talk to legislators or staff. It's alright for constituents to have highly idiosyncratic opinions as long as they're rooted in an understanding of the proposal being discussed, but if they seem like wound-up robots without any knowledge or feeling for the issue, their views won't be taken seriously.

Grassroots Lobbying Glossary

Grassroots lobbying: the process by which an interest group identifies, recruits, and activates citizens to contact public officials (usually legislators) on behalf of their shared public policy views. Citizens who are mobilized are often affiliated in some way with the lobbying organization, such as members or employees, but may also include wider constituencies not directly tied to the group but who have propensities to support their governmental goals. The total pool of people from which recruits are sought is called the **contact universe**. Once a person is recruited and agrees to support the cause, that person is called an **activist**, (an **advocate**).

Telephone patch-through: a contact technique, also referred to as **direct-connects** or **third-party calling**, in which a phone bank for a lobbying organization gets an agreeable activist on the line and directly contacts him or her to the targeted public official or staff member so that the activist can deliver a personal message.

Mass or volume grassroots programs: those that involve getting activists to sign petitions, pre-printed postcards, form letters, or authorizations to send "mailgrams" (printed letters that are designed to look like a telegram) that are addressed to public officials.

Grasstops: those that involve the identification, recruitment, and activation of a small number of influential citizens and opinion makers to contact public officials through personalized letters, phone calls, or visits.

Bounce-backs: direct mail response vehicles, often pre-printed, postage-paid business reply cards, that are signed by the activist confirming that they have completed their lobbying task, be it writing, faxing, visiting, or calling a public official.

Mobilization: the overall process in which individual constituents or groups are organized to provide a show of strength to a public official on a certain issue as part of grassroots lobbying.

District matches or data base matches: a process where the addresses of potential or recruited activists are sorted by local, state, or federal legislative districts. Lists can also be **purged** of duplications and lists with only names and addresses can be **merged** with lists that have phone numbers. This process was once done by hand but now can be accomplished rapidly through off-the-shelf or customized software programs.

Interactive kiosk: an exhibit booth, usually displayed in a public place or at a convention or association conference, where citizens or members, through a touch-tone phone or computer terminal, can authorize or transmit messages by mail or other means to public officials.

Satellite conferencing: an electronic meeting in which a group of constituents in a legislator's district can discuss upcoming legislative issues with a lawmaker who is at a state capitol or in Washington, D.C.

Coalition partners: interest groups or individuals who have common public policy goals who come together, either in formal structure or ad hoc arrangement, to support specific issues through cooperative efforts such as cost or information sharing, public endorsements, or coordinated lobbying activities.

Astroturf: a mass or volume grassroots program that involves the instant manufacturing of public support for a point of view in which either uninformed activists are recruited or means of deception are used to recruit them.

Action alert: a letter, newsletter, mailgram, phone call, fax, E-mail message, or other communication from an interest group to supporters designed to activate a specific contact response.

✓ Take the Initiative
Richard Arnold

Step-by-step tips on how to put an issue on the ballot

Last year, the political process seemed to catch the public's fancy for the first time in at least two decades. The phenomenon led to a burst of activity on the initiative front, with a record 69 qualifying for statewide ballots. The emphasis of initiative campaigns also shifted, from high-dollar fund raising to volunteer driven activities.

In the wake of talk show campaigns, and the Perot movement, far more people are now willing to involve themselves in the making of public policy; they want to have more direct influence over political decisions and are volunteering in record numbers. Many of last year's ballot issue drives collected most of their petition signatures with volunteers, reversing a long-term trend toward the use of private companies and paid canvassers.

These developments call for a reappraisal of strategies for qualifying questions for the ballot, suggested steps are outlined here.

Three Phases to Weave

Initiative efforts have two preliminary stages, the pre-circulation phase and the circulation phase, before the customary electoral phase begins.

During the pre-circulation phase, the coalition is formed around a specific goal. The laws and ballot rules must be thoroughly researched and understood.

State election agencies will provide information on the number of signatures required, deadlines for filing, petition format, etc. Study the rules and follow them to the letter throughout the campaign. Often, popular initiative movements are kept off the ballot by

the courts, on technical objections.

Once there is agreement on the objective, the exact wording of the initiative must be agreed upon. This complicated task should include the best political and legal advice available. Frequently, focus groups and polls help determine the best way to phrase the initiative in terms of persuading voters. Start early! Time is truly money in initiative campaigns.

When we handled the circulation phase for the Colorado Educational Voucher Initiative (CEVI) last year, we had less than 12 weeks to collect about 80,000 raw signatures. The measure—which would have given parents vouchers that could be exchanged for tuition at public, private, or religious schools—was a controversial one, mightily opposed by the teacher organizations. Validation would be sternly contested, and competition for signatures was fierce—10 issues qualified for the ballot and three others came close.

We ultimately succeeded, using five steps along the way:

1. Raise Money—The most successful petition campaigns have financial commitments and a time line already in place before they begin circulating. For the 1990 ballot in California, successful signature campaigns spent an average of $1.14 per signature. Colorado state law requires nearly 50,000 valid signatures for ballot qualification; because of the difficulty in matching signer qualifications, a general rule of thumb is to get eight raw signatures for every five valid ones required. Therefore, we calculated we needed to collect at least 80,000 raw signatures, which—at a unit cost of $1.14—would require a petition budget of about $92,000.

Ultimately, we collected more signatures for less money.

Fortunately, the sponsoring organization, Coloradans for School Choice (CSC), had done all the pre-circulation work prior to contacting me, including raising a significant amount of money. The issue had been attempted in 1984 and 1988 and much of those support networks were still intact.

2. Print Petitions—Since the wording had already been completed, the initiative was immediately filed with the secretary of state. A printed copy of the petition must be approved by the secretary of state prior to circulation. As in most states, the approval process takes several weeks. When the petition was finally released for circulation, we had only 58 days to collect 80,000 signatures.

   A petition packet should be created that includes petitions, fact sheets, circulator instructions, circulator rights, local contacts, voter registration information, and deadlines.

3. Establish an Office to Process Signatures—We established a headquarters that was responsible for planning, coordinating, printing, distributing, retrieving, processing, validating, storing, and submitting all petitions.

   All contacts were placed in the computer. Contact with circulators was direct, in person, by telephone or by fax. Short on money and time, the campaign did only one mailing during the circulation phase.

   Because Colorado requires that each petition section be signed by the circulator in front of a notary, it was not possible to get signatures through a mailing. This requirement always makes it harder to get volunteer signatures; the paid circulation unit of our effort simply arranged to have a notary in the office at turn-in times.

   Each signature block must be checked at HQ for legal compliance. A small random sample of the signatures should be checked against the voter roles to determine what percentage are valid registered voters.

4. Plan the Signature Campaign—On May 5, 1992, we prepared a proposal based on collecting at least 30,000 signatures with volunteers. The mix would be heavier on the paid side because of the limited time available. Most paid signature drives are less expensive and more successful than volunteer efforts, unless you already have a very strong volunteer organization.

   An organizing committee should be made up of people who are not only enthusiastic about the issue, but who also wield financial, political or organizational clout. CSC assembled a diverse group of supporters including two state senators, home-schoolers, private school representatives, and church groups.

5. Organize Volunteer Structures—Volunteers need to be recruited, trained, supervised and rewarded. The best volunteer structures are built around existing organizational units that have a stake in the results. Polling can help identify which groups will make the best recruiting targets. Our plan had three arms: individual volunteers; private schools (including home-schoolers); and churches.

   Individual volunteers are the hardest to recruit, supply, and retrieve completed petition sections from. To get the word out, we used an 800 number and disseminated information through talk shows, speaker bureaus, letters to editors, news articles, press conferences, church bulletins, newsletter advertisements, and special interest publications. The process is a slow one. Most of these signatures will come in near the deadline.

Private schools were not as fruitful a source as we had hoped. Classes were no longer in session and not all such schools supported the initiative. Success requires a dedicated volunteer for each

Private schools were not as fruitful a source as we had hoped. Classes were no longer in session and not all such schools supported the initiative. Success requires a dedicated volunteer for each school—finding the right person was not easy. Sending packets home with the children had a low rate of return.

There are several steps required to organize churches. Through the use of local and regional church organizations and directories, we were able to contact several congregations at once. We obtained permission from often reluctant churches to have members of their congregations circulate petitions on Sunday morning after the services. Friendly competition between congregations inspired higher signature totals. Ultimately, we circulated about 100 churches. Individuals in rural areas acted as contact people to their local churches, accounting for almost 10,000 signatures.

Winding Up

On July 3, 1992—with four weeks remaining in the campaign—we had collected just over one-fourth of the 80,000 needed signatures. The paid effort was on target, but with little room for error. The volunteer effort—which had only four weeks to organize—was falling short of projections. The consensus was that we might fall as many as 10,000 signatures short of that goal.

We agreed that we would take steps to both increase the paid signatures by 10,000 and to provide additional money to beef up the staff for the volunteer effort. On Sunday July 12, the volunteer staff was able to target over 20 churches in Denver and Colorado Springs. That was the turning point. Over 5,000 volunteer signatures came in that weekend alone. More importantly, we had recruited enough volunteers and new churches to do even better the next Sunday. The paid effort had also picked up steam, collecting over 12,000 signatures that week, bringing the paid total to 40,000.

After a second big weekend, the effort was cut off a full week early on Monday, July 27. We had collected over 91,000 signatures in seven weeks—41 percent from volunteers. The total cost for the drive was just over $80,000. Paid signatures cost $44,000, an average of 82¢ per signature. Volunteer signatures cost $33,000, an average of 90¢ per signature. The remainder of the budget was spent on printing the petition sections.

The Gallows Poll

Our short circulation time frame had forced us to take drastic measures, such as putting more money into the signature effort than originally planned. But while the additional money spent in gathering signatures could have been used to help win the election, there would have been no election if we had fallen short of valid signatures.

Hamstrung by a lack of funds in the voter persuasion phase and hammered by the teacher unions, CEVI was turned back at the polls by nearly a 2:1 ratio. The phrasing of the initiative also proved to be a burden, as its opponents were successful in gaining credence for the notion it would cost the state $79 million in its first year—an obvious problem in this age of shrinking budgets.

14

Recruiting, Mobilizing, and Activating Volunteers

★ ★ ★

✓ Volunteers Working Overtime So Your Consultants Don't Have To

Frank J. Vresics and Stephen P. Jones

How can a statewide campaign committee afford the services of consultants during a tough fundraising year? The Pennsylvania House Democratic Campaign Committee (HDCC) came up with an innovative approach to contracting with consultants this cycle that other committees may want to consider using.

The HDCC had the deck stacked against it from the start. We were trying to maintain Democratic control of the state House for an unheard of sixth straight term. Adding to the challenge, the House Democrats had recently passed the largest tax increase in Pennsylvania history.

Other factors working against us: the anti-incumbent mood of the electorate, the unusually high number of open seats (due to early retirements and redistricting), and fundraising competition from the presidential campaign. In short, there was too much to do, too little money with which to do it, and no room for error.

Though we had managed to maintain a majority in the House after the '90 elections, we knew there were several gaps in our coordinated campaign. The two most important weaknesses were strategic planning and opposition research. It was obvious we needed help. It was equally obvious, however, that we couldn't afford to purchase the full services of professional consultants for each targeted race. Our solution was to contract for the intellectual resources and seasoned experience of a consulting firm while employing trained campaign volunteers for as much of the actual campaign work as possible.

In essence, the consultants would not be wasting time and resources attending to minor details in a specific election district and the HDCC would not have the consultants' meter running overtime. We contracted Campaign Design Group (CDG), which had done multiple targeted legislative campaigns in other states, as the general consultant. The cornerstone of those efforts was the development of an individual campaign plan for each race. This level of direct involvement was more than we could afford. So CDG developed a comprehensive "Campaign Planning Workbook" to facilitate campaign planning in the targeted races. The workbook included a series of forms and worksheets that took the volunteer plan writers through the process of thinking a campaign through on every level, and summary forms that defined the plans.

Ten local volunteers were trained to use the workbook to develop a comprehensive plan for each targeted campaign. These plan writers were people who had some relationship with the candidate and relatively low-level campaign experience. They were not, by and large, experienced campaign managers or operatives.

In addition to training the plan writers, a two-day seminar was held for all the candidates, campaign managers, and campaign workers in all legislative races in Pennsylvania.

With specific workshops on each aspect of a campaign, the training gave an overview of designing and executing a successful campaign.

Working under CDG's supervision, the plan writers were able to help the candidates establish a detailed series of goals and objectives for each part of their campaign, including fundraising, voter contact, communication, and earned media. In other words, a clear, coherent, and integrated campaign plan that reflected a winning strategy was developed for each targeted race.

Once the plans were completed, the progress of the individual campaigns was monitored against the goals established in the plans. CDG did the monitoring, helped manage the flow of the overall project, and worked with the candidates to ensure the communication—primary mail, radio, and TV—was "on message" and consistent with the strategy.

Another important example of HDCC's strategy occurred with opposition research.

Phil Noble & Associates was hired to train the volunteers to research legislative journals, court records, newspaper articles, and other public documents. The volunteers then sent the collected and organized information back to PN&A, which analyzed the extensive data and wrote a short report with strategic and tactical recommendations. In structuring and developing this research project, three basic goals were met. One, our staff and volunteers were trained in the skills of campaign research. Two, a large database was assembled that can be built on and expanded for subsequent campaigns. Three, a large number of races were provided with professional quality research that would not normally have been available. We were thus able to benefit from professional help without having to pay the hourly cost for field research.

There are two critical steps to this overall strategy. First, contracts between the HDCC and each consultant had to provide a clear and detailed understanding of what was being purchased and at what cost. It took four months of negotiations to work out these arrangements with the consultants. Second, we needed to identify volunteers with some previous training in effective campaign techniques. This was important because of the volunteer staffs new involvement in campaign planning and opposition research. Fortunately, we had already organized ongoing campaign schools for volunteers during the previous two years. Approximately 20 volunteer staff members were selected to participate in the program.

As in any election year, we still thought there was too much to do and too little money with which to do it, but this approach to contracting with consultants kept our margin of error razor sharp without causing our budget to hemorrhage. The result: higher quality campaigns at lower costs and maintaining Democratic control of the House.

✓ The Carter Brigade: Keep Your Volunteers Happy and Active
Doreen P. Conrad

In 1976, when I was Mid-Atlantic volunteer coordinator for the Carter presidential campaign, I was often asked how we recruited volunteers. I was puzzled because we never had to recruit; our volunteers recruited others. It helped that we were backing a frontrunner.

Since most campaigns can not operate without volunteers, our premise was that volunteers would join if made to feel welcome. Everyone who came was given a specific task to match their skills, available time, and interests. We found that they would stay if they were treated like responsible grownups and had fun. We developed a simple multiple choice sign-up sheet and an orientation blurb, both updated frequently. There are other selling points. After all, campaign volunteering offers definite benefits to job-hunters, students and retired people: an office, a business telephone number, professional experience, and/or new contacts.

For example, a recent law school graduate joined the campaign. Because of his outstanding research on a campaign criminal justice project, he was hired by the U.S. Department of Justice. Guided by a retiree, student interns organized a voting pattern study that aided campaign planners. Then they helped design and promote a popular college political campaign seminar. They got school credit for their work in the bargain.

Then, there is the intangible "fun" benefit. Working closely, friendships and romances develop. Campaign volunteers often feel like family. As volunteer coordinator, I served as a surrogate for the youthful paid campaign staff. Fortunately I had received on-the-job training from my young daughter.

It helps that my personal style is supportive, outgoing, and easy going and that I can talk to almost anyone. I love inventing systems to fend off disaster. My cubicle door was always open. Probably my most useful talent is to remember up to 400 people's names and life histories and match them with faces. Beyond 400 my powers flagged so that I had to choose 10 volunteers as my assistant moms and dads.

Here, from the secret files, are some cautionary war stories:

One of the lessons I learned was not to blow anyone off: that pest may be your savior. An hour after arriving in New York City to set up Carter's Democratic Convention volunteer unit, an advance man ordered 300 warm bodies to prepare for the candidate's arrival at Madison Square Garden. When we hotfooted it up to the Carter Convention Office, we were dismayed to find out that they had ignored local volunteers. But there is this one guy over there who has been bugging us for days they said. Get him off our hands. After some polite background questions, I discovered that he headed a major New York Democratic organization. Could I use, he asked, 300 people? After that, I bound him to my side.

Then there were several unconventional volunteers who organized ethnic, arts, and other groups. They also founded a speakers bureau. Two dear old duffers came daily to do boring tasks shunned by everyone else. It turned out they were two rich old duffers and helped raise money among their old money friends.

The second lesson was that the right people show up when you need them. Using their skills imaginatively can have remarkable results. When trying to design and conduct a secret poll, an unemployed pollster, a statistician, and a retail store manager appeared and put together the survey. Next five good talkers showed up and conducted the poll. The results were remarkably accurate. A bright fourteen-year-old volunteer who knew the D.C. contingent was brought up to New York to act as go-between. Without him, much would have fallen through the Convention cracks. A volunteer who was a local ethnic organization young turk helped us solve a damage control problem.

Writers were assigned to the busy correspondence desk where answering requests for campaign literature and corresponding with the lonely was punctuated by threatening letters passed on to the FBI. Sometimes, the mail brought resumes accompanied by full frontal nude photos. These certainly brightened dreary days. Our volunteers discovered a spy in our ranks. Brawny maritime volunteers assisted the Secret Service at the Convention and volunteers alerted them to a serious death threat against one of our regional directors.

I could tell you about the "Citizens for Carter" charmers who worked the fundraising phones, headed by a kind and generous man who later inexplicably became a shlock TV celebrity. There was even the sad story of an assistant who had to be let go (yes, I even "fired" volunteers) to avoid a damaging campaign sex scandal.

But I won't.

Whatever we did, it worked. Our volunteer staff grew, and our candidate won.

✓ Priming the Pumpers
Johnny Allem

While Democrats gathered in New York to nominate Bill Clinton and Al Gore, the campaign assigned me to design and produce a field management system for use in the Fall campaign. As a consultant, creator of political action programs for unions, and author of numerous handbooks on practical politics, it had been my experience that political campaign volunteers become a viable and measurable force for winning elections when (1) significant numbers of activist voters become motivated toward a candidate or cause, and (2) the organization tailors its work system specifically for volunteer personnel.

The Clinton-Gore campaign benefited from maturing voter dissent and a populist message to attract volunteers in unprecedented numbers. But the conversion of this energy to real electoral power took a commitment by the campaign to do business on citizen turf to a degree unknown in modern presidential campaigning. Our system—"Putting People in Charge!"—accomplished that task by incorporating these important directions:

- Be suggestive: The volunteer action programs were to channel energy, talent and resources—rather than impose control and manage hourly work.
- Be flexible: Each project was designed to give field managers maximum latitude and numerous options in order to meet both the level of volunteer commitment and the local political agenda required for victory. In addition, projects were designed for both; computer-assisted and manually maintained data bases.
- Be task-oriented: Campaign objectives were to be broken down into easily managed tasks. Yet these tasks had to appear vital to victory from the viewpoint of the volunteer.
- Be relevant: Traditional political organizations are "vertical" in that they work within precincts. Today's social fabric is more often "horizontal" as people build personal relationships on non-geographic factors; i.e., craft, issue interest, profession, health/sports activity, etc. The Clinton-Gore campaign endeavored to tailor volunteer assignments for both.

The resulting system had three specific action projects and was implemented by state-level Clinton-Gore managers in conjunction with managers of the Democratic coordinated campaigns within each state. The projects included the SIGN-UP CAMPAIGN, TEN MORE FOR CLINTON-GORE and the DOORSTEP CAMPAIGN. They were outlined in a 46-page manual constructed so that various task descriptions could be copied as "stand-alone" instruction sheets for training and assignment.

Recruiting

The SIGN-UP CAMPAIGN was the recruitment device. Pollsters and social researchers have long pointed out that the most significant reason people do not volunteer in campaigns is simply because they are never asked. And even though the market for Clinton-Gore campaign workers was good, we believed a specific method of asking for workers was essential to organize the recruitment in a business-like way and to provide easy data entry on prospects.

The key retail element of the project was the tear-off recruitment card, leaving the volunteer with a message piece and an 800 number, but giving the campaign a response document that could be tracked nationally, by state or locally. The handbook outlined procedures for recruiting at candidate events (including the bus tours), recruiting by mail and handling responses for eventual assignment.

One of the more popular uses of the recruitment card system was their distribution at rallies. Campaign workers wearing special hats and carrying baskets or barrels stood at the crowd perimeter and/or exit-points to collect prospect cards on the spot.

Public Site Outreach

TEN MORE FOR CLINTON-GORE proved to be the most popular campaign tool at the grass-roots level. It was designed to facilitate outreach in non-precinct based environments.

The retail element was a four-page document which included: (a) instructions on how to recruit support, (b) a one-page flyer that the worker was asked to photocopy for "self-published" literature, and (c) a record sheet for registering the recruited support. Again, the manual offered various management options and suggestions to managers for planning the effective use of the "Ten More For Clinton/Gore" kits. This tool was also used by nationally-based Clinton/Gore support groups—including woman's groups, teachers, union members, etc.

One method of implementing the Ten More concept resembled an informal "Tupperware" party and was utilized at company lunch rooms and similar gathering spots: a host or hostess invited a few associates, gave a Clinton Gore pitch and gathered signatures. Another method found campaign volunteers using the photocopied flyers in individual "hits" in offices, at Happy Hour, at the gym, after class, etc.

Residential Outreach

The DOORSTEP CAMPAIGN was the most sophisticated project, and offered the most options for building classic field organization at the neighborhood level. Using a basic organizational model, a volunteer manager could place emphasis on either persuasion or turn-out objectives.

The premise of the project was dividing targeted precincts into working blocks of 25 to 50 households. Within these constituencies, the project furnished geographically sequential voter print-outs and established a work schedule for electioneering within each unit. Project coordinators also maintained adequate supervision, material supply, data feed-back, coordination between field and phone-bank contact, output phone/mail/lit drop options, and volunteer reward mechanisms.

Using the management handbook, Clinton/Gore operatives used this program in a wide variety of ways—with and without computer assisted databases. In some cases, the project was specific to the presidential campaign; in most, the workers promoted the entire Democratic slate.

In several instances (including New York City), state and local candidate organizations managed DOORSTEP on behalf of Clinton-Gore and the state coordinated campaign as a means of establishing future grassroots alliances and networks.

Professionalizing Volunteers

In all three volunteer programs, the Putting People In Charge! handbook urged managers to observe some classic rules in dealing with volunteer power, including:

1. Organize work into manageable tasks.
2. Make people believe their effort matters.
3. Train volunteers professionally for professional results.
4. Re-enforce, reward and measure—then repeat the cycle.

"The doorstep campaign personalized the politics of the Clinton message," according to Michael Whouley, coordinator of the Clinton-Gore field effort. "It dramatically demonstrated that Bill Clinton not only talked about change, but that he enlisted people in the process, empowering them in their neighborhoods and in their work environments to make change happen from the grassroots up."

A previous weakness of the Clinton campaign was the rather feeble way training aspects of the field system were executed. While the grassroots system was widely accepted and enthusiastically distributed, time pressures prevented textbook implementation in many areas of the country. Where classroom training occurred, volunteer attendance was high and results significantly more disciplined and professional.

Training for systems like TEN MORE and DOORSTEP will certainly increase productivity. But even more important, training results in better voter feedback, more accurate records, and—therefore—more powerful implementation.

Modern political action volunteer systems—driven by computer-based data and tracking capability—have dramatic potential three specific applications in the 1990s:

1. membership-based interest groups,
2. political party re-building efforts, and
3. local campaigns unable to compete in major media markets.

In the Television Age, political effort has tilted away from personal voter contact and volunteer organizing. At the same time (perhaps not so coincidentally), alienation by voters soared to catastrophic heights. The professionalizing of volunteer systems—through enlightened leadership AND modern technology—is clearly a trend to watch in succeeding election cycles.In the Clinton/Gore campaign, the message of "putting people first" was substantively reinforced by campaign action: "Putting People In Charge!"

✓ Recruiting and Managing Volunteers
Catherine Webb and Joseph Mockus

Corralling volunteers is only the first step in loosing an effective slave labor force on the electorate. Kate Webb and Joe Mockus emphasize the importance of structure and planning in the process of marshalling volunteer work for the campaign. The article explores methods of recruiting and coordinating a happy, and productive group.

A volunteer is a creature who tends to come late and longs to leave early, who telephones to say, "I'm on my way," then never shows up. Ask a volunteer to take a vital mailing to the post office, but don't be surprised to learn, a few days later, that the mailing is still in the trunk of his car. Place a group of volunteers in the same room to work, and each will be convinced that the others have been given sharper pencils, more comfortable chairs, and better light.

Volunteers are a pain in the neck. But, like getting out of bed in the morning, they are an essential pain in the neck. First of all, despite their deficiencies, they do some work and they do it for free. Effective use of volunteers can reduce a campaign's payroll by 20 percent. In a statewide race this can mean substantial dollar savings. Equally important is the fact that the presence of volunteers gives a campaign visibility and the appearance of momentum. Volunteers suggest to voters that the candidate is worthy of commitment.

Volunteers, in other words, not only help deliver messages to voters—by licking envelopes, writing notes or telephoning friends—they are messages in themselves.

Volunteers—Are They Out There?

Novice candidates consider volunteers their due and are always optimistic about collecting their due at the outset of a campaign. Aunts, uncles, and godparents galore stand eagerly ready to roll up their sleeves. And, of course, somewhere in the drawer of a desk there is a file with the names of hundreds of people who have offered, unasked, to help in the campaign. (This is invariably the file that is never found; on the day before the election the candidate is still looking for it.)

The candidate's optimism is soon replaced by despair. Once he envisioned an army of volunteers streaming in the doors of his campaign headquarters. Now he sees only a void.

But, according to a nationwide poll sponsored by D.C.-based Targeting Systems, Inc. and conducted by W. R. Hamilton and Staff, also of Washington, D.C., the volunteers are out there. Eleven percent of respondents in the May 1980 poll claimed to have served as a volunteer in a political campaign within the previous two years. The high response was neither a regional nor party phenomenon. Most volunteers, however, cluster in the 35–49 age bracket and are somewhat wealthier than the average citizen. The poll suggests that professors and students can be considered volunteer "types." Blue collar workers seem to be the third most likely source of campaign workers. The potential volunteers are there. Asking people to serve is the key to volunteer recruitment.

Targeting Recruitment Efforts

Targeting is the discipline that, through the study of past election results, polling data, demographics, and related information, helps a campaign determine which voters are worthy of attention and which are best ignored. The most likely volunteer prospects can also be targeted. The easier targets are:

- Individuals with a personal stake in the candidate. This group includes the candidate's friends family, associates, acquaintances—and the friends' family, associates, acquaintances.
- Groups which identify with the candidate positions on issues. Organized single-issue groups are sources of potential volunteers.
- If the candidate has run before, past volunteers can be re-recruited.
- The candidate's political party.
- Labor unions.
- Students, especially political science majors.
- People who have contributed small amounts of money to the campaign.
- Anyone who can be perceived in any possible way as "owing" the candidate something.

The Volunteer Coordinator

In any volunteer recruitment effort, the first person who must be added to the campaign team is the volunteer coordinator. The coordinator recruits volunteers, prepares their projects, and supervises their work. It is generally a salaried post—and it should be. It is a demanding job.

The coordinator must set up the work so that volunteers can fulfill their commitment with as little hassle as possible. A space for each worker must be prepared, each with its ball-point pens, consignment of envelopes and stamps, list of names and addresses for mailings, and other essential materials. If this sounds a bit like a kindergarten teacher getting ready for class, the analogy is not entirely inappropriate.

Since most groups of volunteers contain a healthy percentage of conspicuous eccentrics, there will often be minor quarrels to settle. This must be done with the tact of a Dinah Shore. Yet there are times when even Dinah Shore must be stern. The point, after all, is to get the work done. The volunteer coordinator does have the option of easing a volunteer out of the effort—graciously and firmly. Successfully coordinating volunteers requires the ability to organize and motivate, attention to detail, respect for deadlines, an agreeable personality, and a knack for making the most routine activities enjoyable.

Every employment application for a volunteer coordinator should include the question, "Have you ever been a martyr?" Martyrs do not succeed. Martyr volunteer coordinators attempt to do all the work themselves—work that volunteers should be doing. Martyrs begin to sink about a month after they join the campaign. Soon they arrive at headquarters in the morning with uncontrolled twitching.

Two months before the election they have nervous breakdowns, leave the campaign, and are thereafter spoken of in hushed voices. Because a volunteer coordinator must be available to the campaign at all hours of the day and week, this is often also the fate of non-martyrs.

A volunteer coordinator must be perceptive About people—and like them. One important duty is to unearth and assess the talents of volunteers. Most volunteers are destined for responsibilities no more taxing than mailings. But volunteers often include sign painters, researchers, writers, photographers, and persuasive speakers. Gems do exist. It just takes a lot of looking to find them.

Recruitment Methods

In most campaigns, the need for volunteer help is so pressing that a number of methods should be used simultaneously. Direct recruitment is the simplest. With this method, the first essential is a list of people to recruit. Such a list should be drawn from the sources discussed earlier under the heading "Targeting Recruitment Efforts." It should include the name, address and telephone number of every prospect to be contacted. The other basic ingredients of a direct recruitment effort are a system—including instructions, tallies, recruitment cards, reports—and a "pitch," a telephone, and a telephoner. At its most elaborate, direct recruitment takes the form of a paid telephone bank working either under the direction of a paid supervisor or out of campaign headquarters. At its simplest, direct recruitment can be accomplished by unalienated members of the candidate's family calling from home or from an office that has donated the use of its telephones.

Are there large numbers of refusals? Yes. Do myriad individuals profess ignorance or indifference? Invariably. Will the process yield volunteers? Without fail.

The telephone call in the direct recruitment process is more than an aid to recruiting volunteers. It is also a "hit." A call drives the candidate's name a little deeper into the consciousness of the person contacted.

Organizational recruitment relies on a pyramid structure to make an unwieldy job manageable. Suppose that a campaign needs 500 volunteers for a specific purpose. To corral that number, the volunteer coordinator needs help. He gets it through the following process:

1. He recruits ten "deputies."
2. Each deputy enlists from among his own friends, relatives, and acquaintances ten recruiters, for a total of 100 recruiters.
3. Similarly, each recruiter brings in ten volunteers.

This gives the campaign 1,000 volunteers when only 500 are needed—in the spirit of the most important of the Mockus/Webb rules of recruitment: always aim for twice as many as the number required, for only half are likely to put in personal appearances.

Examples of other recruiting methods include:

- The president of a local union is given 100 volunteer recruitment cards and asked to recruit campaign workers from union ranks.
- Recruitment tables are set up whenever the candidate makes a major appearance, or when volunteers are passing out campaign literature at a shopping center.
- The coordinator contacts local activists and says, "You are a good friend of a lot of people who are doers. How about signing 25 of them up for the campaign?"

In the end, the most necessary element is the ability to recognize and seize quickly a recruiting opportunity when it arises.

The Three Rules of Recruitment

What we have discussed up to now is nothing less than a blueprint for disaster and chaos. Imagine it. The candidate's Aunt Millie says she has lined up 52 volunteers. Of course she's written down their names, addresses, and telephone numbers on a list—do you take her for a fool? Unfortunately the list is in her other purse, which she left at her daughter-in-law's last Friday. But there's nothing to worry about. She'll collect the purse sometime next weekend. Uncle Morris has promised to talk with 25 volunteer prospects and will begin doing so as soon as he figures out what to say. The pyramid structure has spawned hundreds of recruiters, and, as far as we know, they're out there recruiting. Has anyone heard from them lately? We have set up a formidable recruiting machine but, no matter how impressively it rumbles and roars, there is the danger it will produce nothing.

There is a way of imposing order on the process of recruiting, as well as that of voter contact. The key to productivity has three elements:

1. Strict Accountability
2. Rigid Systemization
3. Creative Informality

Strict Accountability

Everyone involved in a volunteer recruitment effort must be given goals and deadlines. It is not enough to say to a person, "Your job is to recruit a couple dozen volunteers in the next few weeks. I'm depending on you. Call me when you've got your volunteers." Instead, the message should be: "Your goal is 20 volunteers. You must recruit them by Sunday, August 24. That gives you ten days. In the meantime, I will be telephoning you every other day to check on your progress."

The second message imparts a sense of urgency. Its promise must be kept; the top of the recruitment pyramid must demand progress reports from those beneath them in the structure. Those on the lower levels must know their performance is being monitored.

Rigid Systemization

People do not generally take on volunteer responsibilities frivolously. When they promise to recruit volunteers and contact voters, they have every intention of keeping that promise. But often some thing happens. They become shy. They don't know what to say. They feel "funny" about contacting others—awkward and inadequate. And so they put the job off. They become evasive when reports are demanded: "I call and call, and nobody's ever home."

Rigid systemization is a way out of this dilemma. Everyone involved in a volunteer recruitment effort must be given step-by-step written instructions. Suppose your assignment is to recruit the volunteers. With rigid systemization, you would be given a kit with the following materials:

The step-by-step instructions just mentioned

The instructions should leave nothing to chance, and should anticipate potential problems. There is a deadline for each step. For example: Step 1—Compile a list of prospects to contact. You are expected to recruit ten volunteers. For that you will need a list of 40 prospects. Consult sources such as your Christmas card list and the membership lists of organizations to which you belong. Include friends, relatives, business associates, neighbors. Begin compiling the list on Tuesday, August 26. You will be telephoned on Thursday, August 28 for a report.

- Forms for recording the results of contacts.
- Report cards, used to report progress to campaign headquarters.
- Background information on the candidate and his stands on the issues. Such information aids the recruiter in answering questions and selling the candidate.
- A script to guide the recruiter when approaching prospects.
- A name and telephone number where questions can be answered at any time.

True, the job of volunteer recruitment is not especially complex. But to the uninitiated it can seem intimidating. With rigid systemization, the recruiter is never in the dark and never at a loss. He feels competent because the instructions demonstrate how really simple his assignment is.

Creative Informality

This is the element that keeps the process from becoming oppressively totalitarian. Some find comfort in preplanned rigidity, but others may bridle and say, "I don't want to telephone all the people on my list. I want to get them over to my house on a Saturday night, get a couple of drinks in them, then ask them eyeball to eyeball to volunteer for the campaign." Stifle such an individual approach and you risk stifling the recruiter's enthusiasm. Allow the recruiter to adapt the system to his own personality—and the personalities of those he plans to contact.

How to Use Volunteers

What should a volunteer be asked to do for a campaign? The most fundamental answer is: something. A volunteer who spends an evening at campaign headquarters wandering about with empty hands and vacant eyes is unlikely to return. A volunteer who is not given something to do feels abused. He thinks, "They tell me it's so important that I come down to headquarters, and then they haven't got any kind of job for me. I've got better things to do." There is always plenty to do in a campaign. Idle volunteers are invariably a sign of disorganization in the upper levels of the campaign.

The most important use of volunteers is in voter contact programs. Volunteers

- address, stamp, and stuff the envelopes that carry the candidate's message to voters
- telephone or write short notes to friends and other voters
- host small parties or coffees at which the candidate can meet the volunteer's friends and neighbors
- build audiences for candidate appearances by inviting 25 friends to attend such functions
- knock on doors to distribute literature
- recruit other volunteers

A Good Word for Volunteers

The beginning of this article painted a grim picture of the role of volunteers in a campaign. And so it is only appropriate to close with a few encouraging words. Volunteers are sure votes. If a volunteer has worked for you, he's sure to vote for you. Volunteers influence their friends to vote for the candidate. Many people go to the polls with no strong feeling about the majority of races. Voters often cast their ballots one way or another for reasons more whimsical than substantial: "This is the guy George worked for. I might as well vote for him."

They do important work—for free. And they bring a rare enthusiasm and vitality to a campaign. So, once a campaign has volunteers on board it pays to treat them well, to give them safe, clean, adequately appointed places in which to work, to provide them with free coffee and a snack once in a while, to thank them repeatedly both by mail and in person. They may drive "seasoned professionals" up the wall, but they are one of the elements that can make the difference between a winning and losing campaign.

✓ Building Blocks: Solid Organization Starts With Precinct Volunteers
Dick Schneider

No matter how popular you are, and how much media attention you're getting, your election is likely to be won at the precinct level, the smallest geographical piece of political real estate of an electoral district. Forgetting that fact may spell doom for any campaign, be it for state representative or mayor. True, the tactics may be different, but the goal is the same—find someone or some group who knows, or can contact, 1,000 neighbors and get them to the polls on time.

Here in Louisiana, most precincts have 1,500 to 2,000 residents and some 500 registered voters. A legislative district here may have 10 to 15 precincts. This will be different in every state.

Your goal, from the moment you decide to run, is to turn out enough voters to give you a majority. To do that, you need to have an organization in place that can contact the masses and bring the right people—your supporters—to the polls on election day.

Building an Organization

At election day minus 90 days—at least—you need to have a precinct operations coordinator in place in your headquarters. This individual should be good at working with people and be very familiar with the geography of the election district.

The coordinator should immediately set up a "war room" in some part of the office where the precincts in the election district are posted. A wall map should be used and should become dotted with pins showing where you have installed precinct captains. Accompany the wall map with a list of the names and phone numbers of the precinct captains as they are selected. Remember to keep this in a secure area; you never want the opposition to know what you are doing if you can help it.

The precinct coordinator is responsible for obtaining a precinct list from the campaign staff and making sure each precinct or block captain has the correct jurisdiction. Check with the local registrar of voters or buy a list or tape to find out who are the registered voters in the electoral district. Have at least three copies, including one for use by campaign staff for other purposes—such as fundraising and mailings.

Precinct Captains

Precinct captains, the key to a successful election, should be selected by the precinct coordinator in every region where you are expecting to have an impact.

The captain should generally be chosen from the registered voter list. Select up to 10 names in each precinct from the list of people who you believe would be able to serve either as precinct captains or as block captains. Call the list until you have enough acceptances. The time frame for the coming election and the time commitment during that period should be the first order of business when contacting these individuals.

You'll probably end up with a precinct captain for every region in a small race, and 5 to 10 block captains underneath each of them. The time commitment involves enough hours to execute the jobs of the precinct captain outlined below—which may run up to 20 hours a week, if not more during crunch periods.

Who are these people? Generally, someone on your campaign staff, and their extended families, may know people who can serve the campaign as precinct captains. In addition, you may reach out to some of the prominent interest groups that support your candidacy and ask them to look at their membership for likely candidates. Use every resource; play out every lead.

Once the precinct captains are selected, the precinct coordinator should call a meeting to outline the job and conduct several training sessions to go over each task and how it should be accomplished. The precinct captain has seven major tasks:

- Phoning each household in the assigned area on behalf of the candidate;
- Visiting each household, answering questions, leaving literature, and placing yard signs;
- Accompanying the candidate on door-to-door visits;
- Arranging informal get-togethers to develop support for the candidate;
- Setting up a neighborhood phonebank to contact each favorable voter as close to election day as possible. You also need to make sure that these voters turn out;
- Maintaining contact with the polling place on election day via telephone to monitor turnout;
- Reporting to headquarters total votes tabulated on machines after the polls close.

Precinct captains should try to set up hierarchical organizations that include block captains who have the responsibility for smaller, arbitrarily designated segments of the precinct rural areas, these regions will be geographic patches in which people can come together in a common place for a meeting or a coffee, but won't actually constitute a block.

How the Organization Works

Under the supervision of the coordinator, the precinct captains are given the job of making contact directly—or through block captains—with those folks who are likely to be favorably disposed to voting for your candidate. The heart of this program is a door-to-door identification program that may take more than a month and will provide a key building block to your electoral victory. The block canvass should for on getting answers to specific questions. In an ideal situation, a block captain will go from door to door with a list of registered voters and try obtain three goals:

- At each household where someone is home, introduce him or herself as a supporter working on a volunteer basis for a particular candidate;
- Ask the householder how he or she feels about that candidate;
- Record the response an move on to the next household. The response should be classified in one of three categories: favorable, unfavorable, or undecided.

Given the unfamiliarity with turf, the first time this process is carried out, it may take some time to reach all 1,000 registered voters you want to solicit. Take the time; it will be well worth it. The precinct captains should collect information from the block captains and pass it on to the precinct coordinator in a digestible fashion.

Outside of the traditional poll, this canvass provides you with critical grass roots-level information about your expected support. The data you collect will be important in helping the campaign staff develop and target its message. Remember, on the first pass, you have to have your data collected no later than 60 days before the election in order to go to the next stages.

Keep in Touch

After you have refined and aired your message soliciting support throughout the district, begin a second pass at each household. This message might be a television advertisement, a radio broadcast, or some form of direct mail. The result of this canvass will give the campaign an indication of how the message was received. If each precinct captain has been given a target vote to seek, then the third visit by a block captain should be all that is necessary to firm up a solid figure of how many people are likely to vote for the candidate. You'll know whom is still undecided—likely targets for further persuasion tactics. This should occur about 20 days from election day.

During this window, you'll want to get the candidate out to many of the precincts to sway the undecided voters. This door-to-door effort by the candidate is essential in virtually any election. There is no reason—except time—why the candidate cannot visit every precinct in the district in a well-designed local campaign. Be sure to schedule the time of the candidate.

Door-to-Door

If the door-to-door effort is coordinated with a block captain or precinct captain, particularly in target or critical precincts, then there will be a synergism of a little-known candidate and a neighborhood individual who has been there before. This is a very effective use of the candidate's time and energy in many elections.

This process requires little money, and if properly designed, uses the volunteers in a better fashion than if they were sitting around the campaign headquarters waiting for the phone to ring.

At the end of the process, the grass roots organization you have built is going to shift into high gear and turn out the vote. This get-out-the-vote initiative generally turns out to be the winning move if the voters are familiar with the organization already.

Depending on the depth of the precinct captain organization, you may have identified each and every household—or voter—who plans to vote for your candidate. You never want to keep coming back to those who are unfavorable. Leave them alone. Don't try to persuade them they are just dead wrong. They don't need to hear it from you or your volunteers, and the constant rejection will discourage the volunteers.

Get Out the Vote

On election day, use your organization to find out how you are doing. The precinct captains will become your poll watchers, monitoring whom, comes to the poll and who doesn't. They will cross off the names of whomever shows up. Since you already know which folks are yours, and which aren't, you'll get a good feel for the outcome in each precinct.

You may even be able to have runners collect this information every few hours, returning the data to the central phone-banking operation. Call the voters who have not made it out by midday and ask them to vote. Offer transportation if the voters are hesitant. The importance of casting the vote for your candidate should be re-emphasized. If each precinct has identified enough voters for a victory, and done their job to bring them out to vote, you'll win. If the count is correct, then the campaign is won.

Relax, it will only be a few years before you have to set up the operation all over again.

✓ Taking Advantage of Free Support
Jim Kainber

It's 11:30 a.m. and another morning of putting out fires is coming to a close. The intern, still full of energy, bounces into the campaign manager's office to see if he can start that important project that was promised him two weeks ago. The campaign manager, just finishing a call, looks up, smiles and says, "Boy, am I glad to see you...."

Adrenaline rushes through the intern, finally a real project. "I'm starved; can you go pick up something for lunch? Here's a ten. Be creative."

Before the kid can protest, another important person calls.

It's 12:30; do you know where your intern is?

With May around the corner and thousands of young eagers ready to flee the confines of academia for life on or near the campaign trail, you should be thinking about how to take advantage of interns. That's different than exploiting them.

First, find them. Put up signs on college and high school campuses. Advertise in free classifieds. Appeal to their curiosity and they'll call.

In recruiting, define what an intern with your campaign will do, even if it includes "and the intern will pick up all the details everyone else is too busy to catch."

Once on board, the intern should start out with goals outlining what he or she wants to accomplish during the course of the campaign. Everyone wants to learn about strategy, but why can't an intern learn about targeting, writing press releases, and fundraising? Include an intern in these loops. The result may be a fresh approach and some valuable side effects. For example, if a manager stops to explain targeting to an intern, the side effect is a brief moment to think about the project.

There are many projects interns can handle in addition to filing, and getting coffee. Good projects include: organizing press clips; keeping the candidate's family informed; set-up for fair booths; organizing students; setting up recycling of office trash; organizing child care for volunteers; learning how to fix problems with the FAX, or copy machine; desktop publishing of flyers; and checking with fundraisers to make sure the event checklist are followed.

The point here is that an intern who has a specific assignment, project, he can call his own, will have more energy for the little tasks that traditionally come with the job.

15

Voter Registration and Turnout Programs

✓ Grassroots GOTV

Cathy Allen

GOTV—Get-Out-The-Vote—is universal political shorthand, but it means something different to everyone in a campaign.

To the experienced campaigner, it means the seemingly insurmountable list of things to do in the last few days of the campaign. To the candidate, it means a final new task at the end of a long line of projects. And to volunteers, who gravitate to the campaign as the momentum picks up, GOTV is the tangible connection to voters that puts them eye to eye with the democratic process.

GOTV should not concentrate on all the people who live in the district. It should concentrate only on those who will vote and are likely to vote for you. If you consider that in nonpresidential years, especially in states that have only local contests, or no statewide candidates or initiatives, voter turnout could be as low as 25 percent of the registered voters, the importance of a strong GOTV program cannot be underestimated. Time and again, it has been proven that strong GOTV can make the difference of a couple points in the final outcome.

At every level a well-coordinated GOTV effort should concentrate on moving at least 10 percent of the votes you need to win. If you are running a state legislative race and need 15,000 votes to win, you must have at least 1,500 identified supporters whom you will push to the polls. Whatever combination of direct mail, phonebanks, doorbelling, or meetings with the candidate you use, inform targeted voters, repeat your message, and persuade them to vote for you.

Establish Your GOTV Organization

At least 30 days before the election, the campaign manager should have a list of all the activities, principal players, and timelines for a comprehensive GOTV plan.

You won't find yourself short of help in the closing weeks. Expect your loyal workers to take time off from their jobs. Other volunteers will devote far more hours than they have for ordinary projects. Don't wait to decide what to do with these people until they all show up at once. Be prepared:

- Determine how many voters you need to reach and the number of volunteers needed to reach them. Your assessment should contain a budget and a list of supplies. Include a timeline for action.
- List the names and the hours that each volunteer is available to work at least a month before the GOTV plan swings into effect.
- Have a range of part-time and full-time project assignments ready to dole out.
- Post a central calendar. Critical to the operation is a calendar which shows the times, dates, locations, and leaders for each of the GOTV projects.
- Assign a GOTV coordinator. There are dozens of little decisions that will need to be made in the pressure-filled atmosphere of the last week of the campaign. Only one person—preferably not the manager—should coordinate how all the pieces work together.
- Don't be caught short on supplies. Last minute door-hanging pieces, phone lists, balloons, yard signs, postcards for mailing, maps, T-shirts, campaign buttons, and other materials need to be gathered from all storage locations, including car trunks and basements. Check everywhere before you order anything new.
- As the final hours near, pull the team together for a rousing GOTV kick-off. These Friday night or Saturday morning rallies can build spirits and draw needed free press.

The GOTV coordinator can outline all the projects and get last-minute volunteers signed up. Packets for doorbelling can be handed out and yard signs for the last sign blitzes can also be distributed. (Don't worry about security; you can announce every activity.)

Make Those Phone Calls

Nothing gets out the vote like a telephone. If you have been meticulous and organized during your campaign phonebanking, you have already identified hundreds or thousands of voters you are counting on to vote for you. These supporters should be in a data base, but in smaller campaigns they might well be circled on walking lists or on phone lists. Depending on how many volunteers you have, begin recalling those voters Saturday in order to reach them all before the polls close on Election Night.

It is very important to figure out how many calls have to be made so you can secure enough phones. Let's say you have 3,000 GOTV calls to make and your phoners will complete approximately 20 per hour. That means it will take 150 hours of phoning to complete all the calls. If you want to complete these calls in a three-hour shift, you will need 50 phone lines.

If you do your phone banks over two nights' time, you can cut your need down to 25 phone lines.

Start looking for phones early. Finding existing multiple lines takes time—and persuasion—and new installation of temporary phones is too costly for most campaigns. However, some special-interest groups—unions and even some law firms—may rent phone lines as part of their in-kind contribution to the candidate.

Don't Knock Door-To-Door Drops

In precincts where your targeted voters live, you have already sent mail, placed yard signs, and had the candidate spend lots of time doorbelling and attending meetings. Now, it's time to remind these folks to vote. A popular piece many campaigns choose is a small doorhanger which can easily be affixed to doorknobs and screen doors. This simple printed flyer might have the candidate's picture, the campaign message, and the specific name and address of voting locations listed for easy reference.

Around 4 a.m. the morning of the election, assemble a group of dedicated volunteers in the targeted neighborhoods to distribute doorhangers.

Take Advantage of Visibility

Although you think there is nothing going on in the hours prior to the opening of the ballot boxes, it is time for some hoopla.

Sign-waving at key locations helps raise the visibility of both the candidate and Election Day. Start between 6:30 a.m. and 7 a.m. on Election Day and wave through morning drive time, during the noon lunch hour, and again throughout afternoon drive time. Have key volunteers gather at major intersections to wave candidate signs, and have the candidate wave at voters en route to work.

In some states signs and other candidate identification are not allowed if they can be seen from the actual precinct polling place. Check the local ordinances. If there is no restriction in your area, try to place yard signs as close to the polling places as possible.

Where legal, get roving vehicles with loudspeakers to travel through targeted precincts and announce that Election Day has arrived. Some campaigns have caravans of colorful cars with signs and balloons that drive around raising attention for the campaign. But, be careful that visibility projects do not anger people. If a voter misses an appointment because she is stuck behind your candidate's car caravan, you may lose a vote.

Do You Need Poll Watching?

In most areas election reform and civic interest in ensuring a fair election have made poll watching obsolete. But if you think your opponent will try to cheat, assign a poll watcher to each precinct. The campaign attorney should set the rules for monitoring the polls, arid train all the poll watchers. In addition, the attorney should be accessible all day, particularly after the polls close as the votes are counted.

Check Off Voters

More important than poll watching is getting the list of those voters who have cast their ballots. You can pick up the list of people who have voted by noon and check them off against your list of identified supporters. You can then re-call those supporters who have not yet voted and remind them to go to the polls. Do the same thing at 5 p.m. Because this process is slow and tedious, some campaigns with fewer workers will simply re-call everybody. If they've already voted, say "thanks" and hang up.

Provide Rides To The Polls...

Providing rides to the polls is a service that every campaign traditionally offers. There is no guarantee that a free ride will earn you a vote, but it usually works out that way. But don't worry, you don't need a fleet of limos to pull this off. The service is seldom requested more than a half-dozen times during the entire day.

And Day-Care Services

You will have far more volunteers if you provide day care on Election Day. A central location with a few qualified day-care providers should be all you need. Keep it simple and make sure that there are very responsible, experienced people in charge. Do not offer extensive recreational or feeding services, as you want to limit your responsibility. Do not attempt to offer everyone services, particularly if the only baby sitters you have are teenagers who agree to watch kids while their parents vote.

Give Directions to Polling Places

On Election Day there are always voters who have no idea where they should go to vote. Always have someone familiar with the town map near the headquarters phone on Election Day. You will get a few dozen calls about where to vote. Make sure you have both a road map and a precinct map, in addition to a list of the polling places and precinct numbers.

Celebrate Victory

Getting out the vote also requires a great victory party. Keep it inexpensive and hold it at a location where people want to gather. Where some campaigns prefer high-priced campaign party at a local hotel or banquet hall where the returns are phoned in, other campaigns opt for less expensive celebrations and turn their headquarters into the campaign party.

In all circumstances, the victory party should not be on anyone's list of responsibilities until the polls are within minutes of closing. Phone calls should continue until an hour before the polls close.

Of course, even a party won't shorten the hours between the closing of the polls and the awaiting of returns, but the hours are easier to bear if you know you have produced a well-organized field, absentee ballot, and GOTV operation.

So keep your cool; good fieldwork means the champagne is on its way.

✓ Turning Out the Vote
Lou Peck

In politics, few terms conjure up a more negative and illegal image than does "street money." The practice of using street money, which still exists in the rough-and-tumble politics of some urban areas, is perceived by many today as a cover for such unsavory activities as vote-buying.

In reality, making use of street money—when done properly—is not only legal, but can be critical in winning elections in heavily populated areas. In many municipalities, voter turnout is the key to victory. To guarantee this turnout, it is necessary to stimulate voters' interest and help them get to the polls by making this act of citizenship as easy and painless as possible.

The precise manner in which you do that will determine not only whether you stay on the right side of the law, but also how effective you will be in turning out your vote.

How did street money get such a bad name? Just like passing out turkeys at Christmas, street money long has been associated with ward bosses of flexible ethics. Though it grew out of the machine-style politics of a bygone era, candidates in many urban areas still have to budget generously for "Election Day expenses" to accommodate local custom. Even in major races, one will still find an account for street money amid allotments for such modern campaign items as polling, television and radio ads and direct mail.

"It has become an accepted practice, and people have come to expect it," says Jacky Grimshaw, an aide to the late Mayor Harold Washington—who stressed the money in Washington's campaigns went to hire workers to bring voters to the polls, not to buy votes. At the same time, Grimshaw admits that the line between hiring workers and buying votes can become blurred.

"When the machine committeemen handed their precinct captains some cash, they told them merely to use it to get out the vote," she says. "And some undoubtedly did... buy votes."

On the other hand, there are numerous Election Day activities that are not only legal, but necessary, for winning in urban areas. When street money is used today, it is most often used for the purpose Grimshaw describes—to hire workers. Paying people to work on Election Day is often essential in turning out the vote.

Workers have legitimate expenses such as food and gasoline for transporting voters to the polls. There is nothing illegal about advancing and reimbursing workers for such expenditures. To ensure "street money" is actually enhancing voter turnout, several guidelines must be kept in mind:

Pre-GOTV Campaign Activities

It is almost impossible to create an effective GOTV operation overnight in a given district or precinct. Even in those areas where the electorate tends to focus on the candidates only on the last weekend before voting, it can generate interest in your candidate two to three weeks prior to Election Day. Beyond the obvious advantages of enabling the candidate to become better acquainted with the voters, this type of effort can distinguish the people in the district who are the workers from those who are the talkers.

Planning Meetings

For workers to be effective, they must understand the basic Election Day plan and how they fit into it. Meetings prior to Election Day will not only accomplish this purpose, but they also will serve as a good indicator of who will actually show up for work when the voting begins.

Proper Methods

In the frenzied atmosphere that accompanies the last few days, many campaigns overlook the obvious step of requiring receipts for expenses paid. Adherence to proper business practices will provide workers with an important message: that you are running a fiscally responsible political operation.

Method of Payment

Handing a person a stack of cash to pay other workers encourages what might charitably be called middle-man surcharges. It also increases the likelihood that some campaign money will end up in the wrong place. To protect against such occurrences, it is highly advisable to pay each worker in person—and by check. This will ensure that proper records are kept for the benefit of federal, state or local election authorities. And, since these types of activities are legal, there is no reason not to keep accurate records.

Timing of Payment

If you want to make sure you receive a full day's work from an Election Day recruit, it is wise to pay at the end of the day. That is the strongest incentive for a person to work until the polls close.

In this day of sophisticated phone bank operations and highly targeted campaigns, some of the less attractive uses of street money are on the decline. Old-time political organizations are less brazen, chastened by the increased scrutiny of law enforcement organizations. They also fear indictment. In one Indiana county, for example, several local political operatives were nabbed by the federal government for liberal use of street money.

Utilizing street money and staying on the right side of the law involves careful record keeping. In some urban areas, candidates have decided the accounting burden is not worth the return in votes and have abandoned the practice. But street money, if handled properly, is not a sin. The trick is to plan ahead, to treat it as conservatively as you would your personal funds—and to make sure it is dispensed in a manner that ensures you are paying for actual performance.

✓ The Limits of Polling Place Persuasion
Robert Brett Dunham

Every state in the country has enacted some limitation on electioneering in or about the polls. These regulations, which the United States Supreme Court refers to as "campaign-free zones," run the gamut from Vermont's prohibition of political activity within the polling place itself to Hawaii's ban on electioneering within 1,000 feet of the polls.

Despite the great strides in political communication techniques and computer-generated personalized mailings, direct one-on-one communication between voters and the candidate or campaign workers is still among the most effective tools in influencing voters. Moreover, precinct persuasion is disproportionately effective in low-visibility races, off-year elections, and primary elections.

Consequently, any last-minute information or persuasion a precinct worker can provide will disproportionately influence voter choice.

In low-visibility races and in primary elections in which a voter cannot pull a straight-party lever, a good campaign organization can reduce fall-off and disproportionately influence the voter simply by convincing voters who have come to the polls for "more important races" to vote in a "less important" race.

The effect of campaign-free zones is to suppress this form of political advocacy. While a large campaign-free zone will hinder the efforts of any well-organized field operation, the zones disproportionately disadvantage candidates with fewer resources, candidates for lower-visibility offices, and grassroots political campaigns and initiatives that cannot afford other means of communications and must more heavily rely on election day volunteers.

A Matter of Interpretation

Although state and federal courts have ruled that campaign-free zones in eight states violate the First Amendment as applied to the media, state restrictions on political advocacy or solicitation outside the polls have rarely been challenged.

In 1988, a federal court in Florida invalidated that state's 150-foot campaign-free zone as applied to the solicitation of signatures to place a referendum on the ballot. Two years later, the Tennessee Supreme Court overturned Tennessee's 100-foot ban on electioneering, also on First Amendment grounds.

This spring, in Burson v. Freeman, a badly divided U.S. Supreme Court reversed the Tennessee ruling, holding that states may ban electioneering within 100 feet of the polls.

Burson's effect on precinct persuasion in the fall election may well be more theoretical than actual since the court's opinion did not overturn any existing statute.

More than 25 states have statutes establishing campaign-free zones of 100 feet or less, and Burson makes clear that campaign workers risk arrest and prosecution if they violate these restrictions. Even though Burson upheld the Tennessee electioneering statute, it left a number of important questions unanswered. For example, the court recognized that, even though a 100-foot campaign-free zone is constitutional, a campaign-free zone will become unconstitutional at some unspecified but nonetheless measurable distance from the polls.

This strongly suggests that statutes still on the books in Minnesota and North Dakota, which prohibit all election day literature distribution and electoral persuasion, respectively, are unconstitutional. However, Benson does not clarify at what point a campaign-free zone slips over the line and is transformed from being constitutional to violating the First Amendment.

One federal district court in Florida has already ruled that a 150-foot campaign-free zone is unconstitutionally large. And even if Burson can be read as having overruled the Florida decision (and there is no indication one way or the other whether it has), the court would probably still conclude that campaign-free zones that greatly exceed 100 feet—such as those in Hawaii (1,000 feet), Louisiana (600 feet), and Wisconsin (500 feet)—are unconstitutional. Consequently, campaign organizations in those states, whether supporting candidates or taking sides in referenda, may be able to successfully seek injunctive relief that would permit their precinct workers to influence votes closer to the polls.

While the Supreme Court has said 100 foot campaign-free zones are not facially unconstitutional, it has hinted that these statutes may nevertheless be unconstitutional as enforced in certain precincts. By this, the court has in mind the mostly urban precincts in which campaign-free zones tend to extend beyond intervening public streets and sidewalks, thereby denying campaign workers access to voters and any real opportunity to electioneer.

Though the court wrote that a constitutional challenge of this son "should be made by an individual prosecuted for such conduct," it would be highly irresponsible and politically counterproductive for any campaign to subject its campaign personnel to the possibility of arrest and conviction. Apart from a campaign's legal obligations to its field workers, precinct workers are in the field to persuade voters—and they can't do that from a jail cell.

The only effective and responsible way to challenge the constitutionality of a campaign-free zone is through a lawsuit seeking to enjoin the enforcement of the statute. Finally, Burson does not address the constitutionality of multi-tiered campaign-free zones.

Maryland and Tennessee have enacted campaign-free zones that are larger in rural counties than in urban counties, and in Burson the court specifically declined to review the constitutionality of Tennessee's outer zone.

Florida, Arizona, and Texas, among other states, have instituted another type of multi-tiered zone that establishes separate boundaries for different types of speech, such as speaking to voters, soliciting signatures, distributing literature, conducting exit polls, and using loud speakers.

The Burson opinion permits a state to establish a campaign-free zone of 100 feet without violating the First Amendment. It says nothing, however, about whether a state may establish multi-tiered zones that themselves discriminate among or between different types of political speech.

These multi-tiered zones are especially problematic; by creating different zones, the state implicitly assumes certain kinds of speech must be restricted—but only in an inner zone—while other political speech must also be prohibited throughout a larger outer zone or zones.

Challenging Your State's Zone

If your campaign is dependent upon precinct persuasion and you believe you are unfairly and unconstitutionally disadvantaged by your state's campaign-free zone, you should mount a legal challenge to the statute as soon as possible. This is particularly true for any facial challenge to the constitutionality of the larger campaign-free zones.

In such a challenge, there is no excuse for delay because the facts necessary to bring the suit are clear. Although there is no bright line date before which you should file such a suit, you must file far enough in advance of the election that, if you win, your state has enough time to educate the precinct election officials as to the new rules of conduct before the election. The prospects of a court hearing your challenge become increasingly dim over time, and a court will almost certainly deny injunctive relief in the final two weeks before the election. Similarly, you will want to lay the groundwork for any "as applied" challenge immediately, even though you may not be able to file that action until local election officers officially announce the polling locations.

The economic reality that impels lower budget campaigns to rely heavily on precinct persuasion also makes it unlikely that these campaigns will be able to challenge these zones. Consequently, if this nation's democratic traditions are to be upheld, and unconstitutional election day practices are to be curtailed, the burden of doing so will likely fall on the political professionals.

✓ Handling a Recount
Chris Sautter

When razor-thin margins separate candidates on election night, the final outcome often turns on complex legal maneuverings and an arduous vote recount conducted in the weeks that follow. If your campaign is unprepared to challenge results, it doesn't stand a chance.

Preparing for a recount begins before Election Day. If you believe there will be vote-buying, notify the U.S. Attorney's office prior to the election and request the presence of U.S. Marshals at polling locations. On Election Day, assign lawyers to each county or ward to observe voting and handle election-day problems. Take notes of challenged voters. If you have good reason to believe they are yours, attempt to persuade election officials to allow them to vote.

You should have a reliable, experienced person observing the tabulation of votes at each County Board of Elections on election night. Your observer should be prepared to "eyeball" precinct-by-precinct numbers for errors made in transmitting returns. He or she should note tallying or counting procedures which may hurt your candidate.

Finally, each campaign should determine prior to Election Day what type of ballot each county uses: paper, machine, punch card, or electronic. The mode of voting is critical because it affects the types of challenges available in a recount. Many counties use more than one mode of voting, so you may have to break it down by precinct. Also note that frequently, absentee balloting is tabulated differently from Election Day voting.

The Morning After

Immediately after a close election, contact local officials to determine if all ballots have been properly secured. You need to know how, when, and where the machines, ballots, poll books, and election materials are being stored. Also, find out if they're under lock and key and who controls access (usually it's the county clerk).

Contact your observers for reports of problems during voting or tallying. If you are behind and there are reliable reports of problems—such as fraud or eligible voters being turned away—which could affect the outcome, invite the press to investigate complaints.

Be sure you obtain the official, certified precinct-by-precinct returns. Certification usually occurs several days after the election, so this may take time. Compare them with your own election-night returns, and do the arithmetic to determine if the tally is accurate.

The Rules of a Recount

In recounts, sometimes the rules determine the outcome. If you are ahead, you want to limit the recount to a simple review of the arithmetic. If you are behind, you will want to examine as many individual ballots as possible.

Some states provide for uniform procedures, and grant authority to certain state officials, frequently the Secretary of State, to oversee the recount and issue administrative guidelines. In others, the circuit court for each county determines the procedures for recounting votes in each county, resulting in a variety of recount rules. All recount laws are open to some interpretation, and both sides will spend considerable time fighting over their meaning in order to obtain a favorable set of rules.

Typically, the major battle revolves around a candidate's ability to challenge ballots. The apparent loser will want to check the validity of each ballot, and challenge those he believes were improperly counted. Many states have separate contest statutes under which candidates may challenge the legality of the election itself.

Another significant issue is whether state law requires each ballot to be verified by Election Day judges from each party. Some states hold that ballots not initialed by a judge may not be counted. Thus, large numbers of voters may be disenfranchised when election judges fail to properly sign off on ballots. Candidates who are behind going into a recount argue for strict enforcement of such statutes, while apparent winners counter that it is unfair to toss out ballots on technicalities.

Typical Election Night Mistakes

Mistakes, if they are caught, can result in changes of dozens of votes. There are five typical types of mistakes to look for. Most recounts focus on:

Arithmetic. Election officials, in the press of election night, make simple errors. Some are caught in the post-election certification or official canvass process, but many are not found until a formal recount is conducted.

Counting. Ballots which are counted manually (usually paper) are sometimes miscounted. Such mistakes may result in a change of as many as 20 votes or more in a given precinct.

Transposing numbers. Election officials may invert or otherwise incorrectly record returns. For example, 27 may become 72.

Uncounted ballots. Practically every recount turns up missed ballots. More often these are absentee ballots which have been properly stored but never counted.

Voter intent. Sometimes ballots are hard to read and mistakes are made in determining a voter intent. Thus, bad ballots are incorrectly counted and good ballots incorrectly voided on election night.

Absentee Problems

In many states, the counting of absentee ballots may occur after election night—sometimes days later. In 1988, Rep. Denny Smith (R-OR) was the loser on election night. But absentee ballots counted later gave him the victory.

If you are in such a state, you should try to use the process to your advantage. Assign trained observers to each county to ask that votes be counted as you believe they should.

Other issues concerning absentee ballots include:

- whether the ballot envelope is properly verified with the voter's signature;
- whether the ballot is postmarked in time (usually prior to Election Day);
- whether the ballot was received before the statutory deadline (not always Election Day).

The best advice to give any candidate unlucky enough to be caught in a recount is to hire a good lawyer. But you can't conduct a recount without organization. Many recounts—like many close campaigns—are won in the trenches with dedicated, low-paid field staff and volunteers fighting for votes one at a time.

✓ How to Prevent Fraud in the Polling Booth
David W. Childs

The goal of any campaign is to produce the votes necessary to win. Unfortunately, some organizers spend more time manufacturing votes than in registering voters. Most candidates are familiar with the usual methods of turning out a favorable vote. Phone banks, mailings, billboards, yard signs, door-to-door contact, polling, issue identification, and dozens of other tactics are constantly analyzed, debated, and updated. Yet, one area of vital importance to vote production—for Republicans and Democrats alike—is often ignored, swept under the rug, or dismissed: vote fraud.

Vote fraud gets no respect. It often seems that its sole purpose is to provide comic relief stories for political gatherings. We all have our favorite punch-lines: the votes that turn up a week after the election, more votes than registered voters, persons with name tags to remind them which registered voter they are impersonating, poll watchers being given Ex-lax, and the "repeat voters" who take their sacred right to vote seriously—very seriously.

My own favorite was related in 1980 by a Dallas poll watcher. In mid-afternoon, a woman entered the polling station, expressing her desire to vote. By this time of day the poll watchers had convinced the election judge that all voters must verify their registration. When confronted with this unexpected inconvenience, the woman produced credit cards, which were rejected. When informed that she must produce a voter registration card or take an oath that she was a registered voter, she stormed from the building explaining as she left, "I don't understand what your problem is! The other three places let me vote."

But vote fraud is really no laughing matter. In 1980, I worked for a Congressional candidate whose "Ballot Security" program contributed to the prosecution and conviction of six people, the first vote fraud convictions in the history of Dallas County. Following that election, a careful analysis of documented abuses led us to believe that at least five percent of the vote had been illegally cast or obtained. In 1983, following the Chicago Mayoral election, U.S. Attorney Dan Webb said that his election monitoring staff had documented a fraud rate of seven to eight percent in that election. These figures of five to eight percent of the total vote refer only to fraud that has been documented in highly secure elections. How much fraud occurs when there is no program to prevent it, or what has gone undetected, is anyone's guess.

Obviously, considering these facts, a ballot protection program needs to be an integral part of most campaigns. I developed the following program by researching how fraud is perpetrated, developing deterrents, testing them in elections, then analyzing and refining them.

Targeting Precincts

Determine which precincts need to be watched. There are two important factors to consider. One is traditional voting patterns. Any precinct in which candidates from your party generally received under 20 percent of the vote should definitely be fortified with poll watchers. If you can recruit enough poll watchers you should observe precincts in the 20 to 40 percent range as well. Another way to target precincts is to research the conduct of election judges in previous elections. Interview previous candidates and poll watchers to find out which precincts are problem areas.

Remember that you are not concerned with precincts where the actual vote total never exceeds the number of registered voters, for example a legitimate 500(—) 100(+). You want poll watchers in those precincts where that 500(—) might mysteriously become an 800(—) if watchers are not present. In 1980, upon hearing about our proposed ballot security effort, one opposing election judge said to our candidate, "You can bring in the national guard and I'll still fake 200 votes." Those are the precincts to target.

Clean Up Those Rolls!

Long before your campaign begins, work toward cleaning up the voter registration rolls. If your area maintains computer records of voter registrations, purchase the computer files and contract for a "merge-purge" search for multiple registrations and cross-precinct registrations. If the information is not available on computer, purchase the voter registration rolls for your targeted precincts and have them checked by volunteers for multiple and cross-precinct registrations. The multiple registrations are obvious.

They show Chris Jones of 123 Elm listed three times in succession. However, without a computer, cross-precinct registrations are more difficult to identify. The best, but laborious method, is to have the volunteers fill out a 3x5 card for each registered person, last name first. When all of the registration rolls and 3x5 cards are completed, begin filing the cards alphabetically. If you have a card for Sam Jones, age 26, in one precinct, and Chris Jones, age 26, in a neighboring precinct, then Chris may be a repeat voter.

If you have the time, or sufficient volunteers, you may also wish to select five or ten of the most notorious precincts, and arrange the registered voters street by street, block by block. Then, drive the precinct checking for registrations at vacant lots, evacuated buildings, and sides of houses, cornfields, etc. This type of sorting will also reveal those addresses where eight, ten, twelve, and fifteen names have been registered. Often, election judges themselves use their own address, or an address on their block. Check this area first.

You may also wish to contact your state's Bureau of Vital Statistics for death records from the past five to ten years, and check these names against the registration rolls. On one election night in South Texas, campaign workers were frantically checking grave stones, seeking last-minute voters while a friendly election judge held out his votes.

Once your research is done, submit it to the local election official and the Secretary of State, requesting that invalid registrations be stricken from the rolls. If these false registrations are not removed, people posing in these names can vote. And they do vote. There are several documented cases in Dallas of persons being registered and signed in as having voted on Election Day, even though they did not reside at a given registration address. How many such votes are actually cast in any election is anyone's guess, but in January 1982 when the Dallas County Election Administrator mailed out 748,000 updated voter registration cards, drawing mailing addresses from the current registration rolls, 105,000 cards were returned due to wrong address. Roughly one of every seven voters in Dallas was not residing where the voter registration rolls said they were, meaning that up to 14 percent of the vote in Dallas could have been impersonated or forged.

As a final precaution before Election Day, prepare a list of the invalid names that appear as registered voters in each poll watcher's assigned precinct so that the poll watchers are prepared for the appearance of these persons, or someone posing as these persons, at the polls. Recording the appearance of these people provides excellent evidence for post-election challenges.

Getting Fair Judges

Biased and partisan election judges and clerks can influence, alter, or fabricate literally thousands of votes. Forging names onto sign-in sheets, stuffing ballot boxes, keeping a separate ballot box in the car trunk and turning it in rather than the actual box, gouging hundreds of punch cards with a small nail or straight pin, circling names on the machines, breaking certain candidate's levers, allowing anyone to vote, telling people how to vote, physically and verbally abusing observers, carrying guns; all are common practice in many precincts.

Laws regarding the selection of election judges and clerks vary from state to state, but the basic goal is to get as many fair election judges appointed as possible. In those precincts where you fear that you are not going to get an honest election from the judge, make sure that you are represented by at least one friendly election clerk. In most states clerks have little legal power, but they can serve as an additional observer, and you need as many different observers as you can get.

Be sure that you are very familiar with the election laws in your state. For example, Article 3.01 of the Texas Election Code states that if a political party submits two names to an election judge at least 30 days before the election, the judge is required to select at least one as an election clerk. Therefore, in Texas, we make sure that each opposing election judge receives a list of two names at least 45 days before the election, and we send the names by return receipt requested mail to ensure that the judge does not claim they did not receive the list. Make sure that every such subtlety is allotted for.

Machines that Work

Your top priority in this area is to ensure that machines and/or ballots are allocated on the basis of previous precinct voter turn-out. This will help prevent under-allocation in your strong areas, lest hundreds of your voters leave the polls without having voted.

In areas that use machines, especially lever machines be sure to:

1. Check the maintenance and repair records of the machines to find out which machines are allocated to which precincts. Make sure that the old, damaged machines are not all allocated to your strong precincts. A few machine failures can create long lines and encourage your potential voters to go home.
2. Before the election, research the protective counter number for the machines allocated to your targeted precincts. Include this information in your poll watcher materials so that the poll watchers can check the counters for tampering on election morning.
3. On election morning, have the poll watchers make certain that all levers are working and that none, especially your levers, are jammed or broken.

For areas that use punch cards, in addition to assuring sufficient machine and card allocation, have poll watchers make certain that all slots are open and can be punched; make sure no slots are jammed. Throughout the day, be certain that no cards are pre-punched before they are handed to the voters. Straight paper clips or small nails can punch a hole through a stack of fifty cards in an instant.

As for the greatest ballot security nightmare, paper ballots, make sure that the ballots are marked only by the voter, and that none are premarked or torn. In addition, check the ballot cans to be certain that they are empty when the day begins.

Nursing Homes

Most nursing homes display a roster of residents in their foyer. It is common practice among some politicians to send volunteers to copy these names, then request and vote absentee ballots in the name of these persons. To deter such action, compile a list of the nursing homes in your district. Before absentee voting begins, visit the homes, not merely to shake hands, but to meet privately with the home management. Inform them that the voting rights of their residents have been abused in the past. Educate them as to the election laws that pertain to absentee voting and absentee voter assistance. Provide them with your campaign headquarters phone number, the Police Department phone number, and the phone numbers of the local media. Ask them to report anyone attempting to perpetrate improper election activity. You might even suggest that some of your campaign workers may make a follow-up visit to ensure their diligence in this important matter.

Absentee Voting

Monitoring absentee voting is difficult because it is not as glamorous as Election Day activities and involves a longer period of time. Therefore, volunteers are difficult to obtain. However, you should try to accomplish the following assignment goals at a minimum:

- at least one supporter as election judge or clerk at each absentee voting location.
- at least one poll watcher at each voting location.
- at least one watcher at the location where ballots are mailed in.
- at least one poll watcher assigned to observe the absentee vote count.

Also, be sure that the chief election official is compiling a precinct-by-precinct list of absentee voters, and that this list will be available in the precinct on Election Day so that poll watchers can remain alert to absentee voters trying to vote again on Election Day. Achieving these goals will prevent a great deal of absentee abuse and deter even more. In one election, a poll watcher assigned to a suspect absentee voting station slept late and arrived at the polls as a bus-full of people was unloading. When the election judge noticed the poll watcher's arrival, she signaled to the bus to reload and move on, which it did. Without observers present, the number of bus-loads that may have voted is anyone's guess.

Inspecting the Inspectors

In addition to poll watchers, you may wish to contact your Secretary of State, or the U.S. Justice Department, and request that state or federal election inspectors monitor the election. Inspectors serve several purposes. Their arrival alerts the opposition that you have organized a serious fraud prevention program. Their appearance in the precincts carries more weight and commands more respect than poll watchers. They are flexible and free to move from one trouble spot to another while poll watchers are bound to one precinct. Finally, they are unbiased, non-partisan agents who can observe and verify your charges of improprieties.

Poll Watchers

A quality poll-watcher program has three aspects: recruiting, training, and assigning. As for recruiting, sources for quality poll watchers include:

- political party clubs
- college students
- churches
- service clubs (Rotary, League of Women Voters, etc.)
- veterans
- senior citizens
- dentists
- lawyers
- real-estate and stock brokers
- off-duty police and firefighters
- politics-related organizations (Gay Rights, National Rifle Association, etc.)

If you contact all of these sources, and use your own Rolodex, you should tap into a sufficient supply of helpers.

To train poll watchers in a ballot security program, first establish a flexible training schedule, with day and night sessions at several locations throughout your district. The training sessions should be clearly structured and accompanied by "follow along" material. Each session should be less than an hour in length.

As the recruits arrive, have them sign their names, addresses, phone numbers, and the names of those who recruited them. These sheets serve two purposes. They may help identify members of the opposition who are there to monitor your program, and they will serve as your address notations when you deliver poll-watcher packets.

The training session should begin with a discussion of the Poll-Watcher Packet, which includes five basic items:

1. Poll-watcher certificate. The legally accepted form—generally provided by the Secretary of State—that poll watchers must carry with them to the polls. Once again, be certain that you are aware of all the pertinent state law. For example, in Texas, the certificate must be signed by a sponsoring candidate, and no precinct can have more than two poll watchers for a given candidate. So, even in precincts where we have recruited more than two poll watchers, we make sure that only two of them have a given candidate's signature on their certificate. (Caveat: in Texas, candidates have been known to send two poll watchers with forged certificates, thereby giving the forewarned election judge the opportunity to throw out the two legitimate poll watchers.)

2. Poll-watcher badge. Design an authoritative looking badge that will command visual respect. (Tip: Cite an election code article, such as OFFICIAL POLL WATCHER appointed under article 7.02 of the State Election Code. Such special touches make the badge a bit more imposing.)

3. Challenge and Violation Sheets. These should include: the date of the election; the County; the precinct number; names of election judges and clerks; the name, address and phone number of the reporting poll watcher; the names and numbers of other friendly poll watchers in that precinct; and considerable space to cite in detail all violations noted. These sheets will provide the bulk of the legal, written evidence on which to base any challenges. In addition, they will provide a wealth of information on which future campaigns can determine which precincts need to be observed and what tricks need to be prepared for. Be sure that these forms are on two-part paper, one copy for the campaign and one copy for the poll watcher to retain.

4. Poll-watcher's handbook. (This is the poll watcher's bible.) Preferably arranged in flip-chart form, the handbook has a page of instructions for each of any number of circumstances that the poll watcher may be faced with. Our last ballot security handbook began with a cover page featuring assistance phone numbers, such as election headquarters, the Secretary of State's election office, and the Sheriff's office. Our flip-chart was arranged with the following headings:

- Your Status As a Poll Watcher (what you can and cannot do)
- Important Reminders ("Dress professionally," "Take your own food and drink," "Don't leave under any circumstances")
- Before Election Day ("Vote Absentee," "Call your fellow poll watchers and prepare your car pool)
- Opening the Polls ("Make sure the counters/ cards/ can is/are at zero")
- Signing In a Person
- Person Does Not Have Registration Card And Is Not On Poll List

- Registration Card Has Another Precinct Number
- Voter Has Moved
- Assistance To Voter
- Closing the Polls
- Turning In Materials ("Follow the judge to the courthouse to make sure the same numbers are reported there that were agreed on in the precinct.") This may sound ludicrous, but judges have taken poll watchers on high-speed chases in an attempt to lose them. We have also had poll watchers leave the precinct with a given vote tally and discover a different set of numbers appearing in the morning paper.

5. Vote Tally Sheets. These should include:

- Date of the election
- County
- Precinct number
- Number of voters on the sign-in sheets
- Last two names on the sign-in sheets
- Number of voters by head count
- Votes for each candidate
- Poll watcher's name, address, and phone number

Concerning tallies, tell your trainees that if the voting method is paper ballots or punch cards, they may include a count of total ballots, ballots used, unused, and mutilated. If lever machines are used, they may want to record the total vote for each machine. This form will be on two-part paper so that the poll watcher may turn in one copy-and retain a copy. After filling out this form, the watcher should follow the judge to the courthouse, monitor the reporting of the vote totals and turn in all materials to your headquarters.

Once all of this has been discussed, you may throw open the discussion for a few questions. Conclude with some fraud horror stories to reinforce the poll watcher's importance.

Finally, assign the watchers to their precincts. Pair teams of watchers according to proximity to targeted precincts, personal strengths and weaknesses, and personalities. On the weekend before the election, deliver a Poll-watcher Packet to each person with a description of their precinct assignment, directions to the precinct, and names and phone numbers of their fellow poll watchers. Wait until the last minute so that your opponent will have no time to counteract your efforts.

On Election Day, have someone trained in the entire program at your headquarters to handle poll watcher requests for assistance or advice. On election evening, as the poll watchers arrive at headquarters to turn in their materials, you may find their Vote Tally Sheets to be a rapid and efficient source of returns. In a recent governor's race, as I took returns from poll watchers, the media began relying on me as their fastest, most organized source of information.

Once the Violation Sheets and Vote Tally Sheets are all in, you can begin analyzing them, either to prepare a challenge, or to file as a source for future programs to refer to.

Obviously, a quality ballot protection program involves more of a commitment than it generally receives. But the effort can be well worth it. Not only can you affect as much as five or ten percent of the vote and come out a winner, but you will encourage real, not manufactured, voter participation.

16

Perspectives on Modern Campaigning

★ ★ ★

✓ The Birth of Modern Campaigning
Keith Melder

Those who engage in political campaigning today must cope with rapidly changing technologies. They try to keep informed of the most recent developments in data processing, computer software especially designed to implement political strategies, and countless other changes which appear almost daily. But at the same time that modern campaigners adopt new techniques and adjust to technological change, they still are working within a basic framework of political action which developed in the nineteenth century. The modern political campaign really originated in the second quarter of that century, concentrated in presidential contests during the years between 1825 and 1840.

The "new" politics of the 1820s and '30s grew out of a revival of the two-party system with its national partisan enthusiasm and organization. Historians identify this development as the rise of the second American party system.

A few definitions are essential at this point. The term modern campaigning refers to what historian David Potter and others have called the "hurrah" campaign, which generates intense activity and enthusiasm in order to win voters and influence election results. Modern campaigning is, of course, especially evident at the presidential level where it is highly organized, national in scope and comprehensive in effect. Involving broad participation, it utilizes available media of mass communication, appealing to the interests and emotions of the electorate by emphasizing issues and images. Modern campaigning aims to communicate with voters in order to persuade them, but it also serves to reaffirm the electorate's attachment to political institutions.

The Formative Years

One of the critical elections in bringing on the new "hurrah" politics was the 1828 presidential contest. Several political developments of the time influenced this campaign. In the years before 1828, the two-party system of the early republic which consisted of Federalists and Republicans had largely disappeared. The Republican party had evolved into a loose collection of personal and regional factions, while the few remaining Federalists possessed little influence. Thus the nation had essentially a "no-party" system.

Two changes in electoral procedures encouraged the development of popular campaigning. In the early 1820s suffrage qualifications were extended so that nearly every white male could vote in most states. Between 1824 and 1828, four states made elections more democratic by giving the voters rather than state legislatures direct choice of electors. Both of these changes gave more power to ordinary voters, giving impetus to the development of presidential popularity contests.

Like many twentieth-century presidential campaigns, the contest of 1828 began immediately after the preceding election. Andrew Jackson had run for president in 1824 and, although he ran ahead of three other candidates, without party support he failed to secure an electoral majority. Under the Constitution, the House of Representatives had to choose the president, and the House picked John Quincy Adams rather than Jackson. In 1825, believing he had been robbed of the presidency through a "corrupt bargain" between Adams and Henry Clay, Jackson began to campaign for the office. Jackson contended that Clay had maneuvered Adams' election in the House in return for being chosen secretary of state. He vowed to defeat the dour New Englander in the 1828 election.

Andrew Jackson was made-to-order for the political arena. Already a semi-mythical figure on the American scene, he was known as the nation's greatest living military figure. Called "Old Hickory" and the "Hero of New Orleans," he had led a frontier army over the British at New Orleans in 1815. At the end of the War of 1812, a struggle that resulted ingloriously for the United States, Jackson's victory was identified as one of the few bright occasions in the struggle. Jackson was also the embodiment of rugged individualism and frontier courage, a hot-tempered duelist and old Indian fighter. He represented and appealed to the spirit of the new West.

Determined to win another great victory, Jackson unwittingly promoted the formation of a new political party. Shortly after Adams' inauguration, Jackson and his cohorts began corresponding with state political leaders, convincing them that he had been cheated and that the only way to redeem the nation for the people was to elect the "Hero president." From these communication efforts, a Jacksonian party gradually appeared. Emerging first in Tennessee, the new Jackson organization spread into other states. With increasing momentum, the Jackson party established a network of political newspapers strategically placed at the state level. Party newspapers and their editors were at the center of new Jackson political machines in several states. Presses were supplemented in many areas by intensive organization of party committees to attract political workers and facilitate communication.

In 1827 the Jackson party acquired one of its key leaders in the person of Martin Van Buren, senator from New York. Van Buren had worked his way up in state politics until he was acknowledged as leader of the Albany Regency, the governing machine in New York state. As an experienced operator in one of the nation's roughest political environments, Van Buren represented a new generation of professional careerists in politics. His knowledge of how to pull together a tight political organization, enforce loyalty and distribute rewards became a solid asset to the Jacksonians. Attracted by the general's reputation and his support of limited government and states' rights, Van Buren made his talents available to Jackson's national party.

Fundraising and Image Strategies

Gearing up for the campaign, Jacksonian editors and orators issued a barrage of rhetoric that today would be called imagemaking. Jackson was described as the candidate of the people in opposition to the aristocratic Adams, who only worked in the interests of the rich. The contest was between the vast majority of ordinary people and the minority of well-born and wealthy. In reality a well-to-do landowner, Jackson was pictured in the political press as a simple, brave and pious frontiersman. Propagandists reinforced the candidate's image as a hero who was larger than life. Adams, in contrast, was presented as a figure of effete corruption. Editors made up stories debasing the president, accusing him of spending money for gambling devices and luxurious accessories for the White House. Adams was even described as a pimp and a procurer for the Czar of Russia.

As they learned to present their hero in vivid imagery, the Jacksonians also learned how to raise and spend more money than had been expended in any previous presidential contest. The political press alone probably spent half-a-million dollars (many millions in today's dollars). Funds were raised at all levels, from the few pennies and dollars collected by local groups to large contributions given to city and state committees. Fundraising events, such as dinners and banquets, were good for party treasuries and reinforced political attachments. Many thousands of volunteer man-hours went into committee work and electioneering. One of the campaign's greatest expenses, the cost of mailing, was shifted to the government through the use of franking or free mail privileges available to members of Congress who sent out quantities of propaganda literature at no cost.

In the summer of 1828 the campaign reached its climax, becoming a national mass celebration. Adapting devices from religious and patriotic ceremonies to traditional participatory political events in order to season them with contagious enthusiasm, Jacksonian Democrats managed to create a new kind of political experience. Issues were subordinated to barbecues, parades and processions, mass rallies and marathon speechmaking. Capitalizing on Jackson's "Old Hickory" nickname, his partisans erected countless hickory poles in village squares and alongside roadways throughout the country. Campaign music appeared to help the populace celebrate, and gimmicks made of ceramics, metal, glass and other materials reminded the people of their hero's exploits. Political propaganda issued forth in thousands of printed forms emphasizing Jackson's towering personal qualities.

Mudslinging and Negative Advertising

Compared to the Jacksonians, partisans of John Quincy Adams, known as National Republicans, were political amateurs. Adams himself thought the presidency should be above politics and he disdained to compete at the level of popular electioneering. Desperate to find ways of combating the Jacksonians' successful campaign techniques, National Republican editors resorted to mudslinging. One story, widely published across the nation, accused Jackson of murdering six militiamen under his command during an Indian War in 1813. This accusation gave rise to the celebrated "coffin handbills" depicting the six murdered victims, issued in several varieties during the contest. The most lurid anti-Jackson propaganda accused him of bigamy and adultery for having married his wife, Rachel, before her legal divorce from her first husband. Not simply an attack on Jackson, this story dragged the name of Rachel through the mud. From both sides such tales continued to circulate, making this one of the most vile and "dirty" campaigns in American history.

The lesson discerned by political leaders from the campaign of 1828 was that new campaign tactics worked. Jackson won a landslide victory over Adams, but did his success result from campaign efforts itself or were other explanations possible? Observers could not be sure, but they were impressed by the techniques employed by the Jackson forces. The outcome of the election assured that the new campaigning was here to stay.

Institutionalizing the Process

Jackson's winning campaign in 1828 was a first giant step toward the modern presidential contest. Successive elections in 1832 and 1836 continued the development of presidential campaigning as a highly-organized, mass-participatory experience. In 1832 the first significant third-party movement, the AntiMasonic party, ran candidates for president and vice president and captured seven electoral votes in Vermont. This same party held the first national party nominating convention in 1831. Both the National Republicans and Jacksonian Democrats followed the Anti-Masons in holding national conventions to nominate candidates and rally their party legions for the election of 1832. These conventions grew out-of-state party conventions which had been common before the 1830s. In 1832 the National Republicans proclaimed the first semi-official party platform of an American political party. Thus, several other ingredients of the modern campaign appeared.

Between 1832 and 1836 an old party disappeared and a new one made its first tentative drive for the presidency. The National Republicans, by the early 1830s only a name representing the old Jeffersonian coalition, dissolved. Out of its wreckage opponents of Jackson formed a new organization known as the Whig Party. At first the Whigs were more united by their hatred of Jackson than by devotion to positive goals, but some common purposes appeared in a few years. Supporting positive action from the federal government rather than restrictive programs favored by the Jacksonians, the Whig Party worked for internal improvements, a national bank and a protective tariff. By 1836, the Whigs were well on their way, to becoming a national party able to compete for the presidency in every state.

Jackson retired from the presidency in 1837 but his influence lingered on in his hand-picked successor, Martin Van Buren, who succeeded him as president. Without Jackson's charisma and image, Van Buren ran a close race against four Whig candidates. Not yet organized nationally, the Whigs held no party convention but relied on state nominations which produced regional candidates. Although not able to match the well-organized Democratic campaign, the Whigs made a healthy showing in many states. The strongest Whig vote-getter, William Henry Harrison of Ohio, had been, like Jackson, a general in the War of 1812 and an old Indian-fighter. In the aftermath of Van Buren's election in 1836 the second American party system completed its formative stages. Two parties, the Democrats and the Whigs, were organized not as regional entities, but to oppose one another on a national stage. With the presidency the focus of political competition, the elements of modern party competition were in place.

Like the Jacksonian Democrats with Martin Van Buren, the Whigs had their master of campaign organization. Thurlow Weed emerged during the 1830s to guide the Whig Party to ultimate victory. An arch-rival of Van Buren in New York state, Weed had taken on editorship of the Albany Evening Journal for the AntiMasons. Shifting his support to the Whigs when that party formed, Weed planned and maneuvered to undermine Van Buren. In 1838, rehearsing for the presidential election of 1840, Weed managed the campaign of William H. Seward to be the first Whig governor of New York. He hired Horace Greeley as the able editor of a special campaign paper, the Jeffersonian, and skillfully coordinated the state's Whig forces.

Seward's victory under Weed's management portended the outcome of the next presidential race.

The Whigs brought all the new campaign developments to bear in the great "Log Cabin and Hard Cider" presidential campaign of 1840.

✓ Looking Ahead: The Next 25 Years
Joseph R. Cerrell

We recently celebrated the 25th anniversary of the American Association of Political Consultants. As one of its early members, I have watched the business evolve from a small gathering of so-called "hired guns" into a field that is diverse in its composition and utilizes the latest campaign technology.

So what can we see in the crystal ball over the next 25 years? There's no doubt the industry will explode with opportunities. Many of the young consultants who worked on national and local campaigns in recent years will become more specialized to respond to the growing diversity of the country's electorate and its candidates.

No longer will political campaigns be a one-person or even a one-group effort. Specializations will continue as our technology becomes more advanced and campaigns become more detailed in nature. We will see consultants whose specialties include buying satellite radio feeds, designing campaign computer software, and targeting ethnic groups. The Nintendo generation will address the needs of a fragmented electorate through technology.

Consultants also will have lots of business through the increase in term limit initiatives, which have been growing in many states all over the country. Whatever your personal feelings are about term limits, incumbents will give way on a regular basis to new candidates and campaigns. These candidates will create opportunities for consultants to apply the latest knowledge on advanced campaign technologies. Issue-oriented groups will create plenty of opportunities for political consultants. Taxes and the economy will still be dominant issues in future campaigns, but we will also see the growth of single-issue candidates running on health care, education, or the environment. With the political agenda becoming larger and more complex, single-issue candidates will be able to employ specialty consultants to grab the interests of targeted voters.

The last election cycle saw the emergence of many "new" faces. Women and ethnic candidates captured seats at the local, state and national levels. The ability of new candidates to break through the "glass ceiling" will continue as they successfully mobilize the traditional groups of voters while generating energy and interest from individuals who never before participated in the electoral process.

Women and ethnic candidates such as Carol Moseley Braun, Barbara Boxer, Diane Feinstein, Ben Nighthorse Campbell, and Jay Kim, among others, captured the attention of their core constituents and set precedents for future minority candidates. Women and minorities proved in unprecedented numbers that they will continue to strengthen their roles in the political system. Supporting them will be a new generation of voters who will propel new leaders and agendas to the forefront. All of these candidates will use advanced technology and bring in both "young Turks" and old pros to manage their efforts.

Diversity has become a catch word in our society and it will roll over into the political arena. Our nation has become increasingly diverse in its racial and ethnic composition. This change will alter the traditional rules of the campaign game. Cities have become cultural "mixing bowls" with electorates as diverse as their ethnic makeups. The composition of these political arenas will require special skills and an understanding of the changing electorate. The old ways just won't cut it any longer.

The results of the changing demographics of the electorate will demand many more consultants who are able to penetrate and mobilize untapped markets of voters. Needed in the future are individuals who will not only be more technically sophisticated but will also be culturally sensitive. Opportunities in this arena are endless and suggest growth throughout the '90s.

American politics could be dramatically altered in the next 25 years as the high technology revolution in campaign management finds new issues and audiences. The hopeful result is an increase in participatory democracy with an explosion in opportunities for our business. This development will be great to observe, especially for all of the veterans in this ever-changing industry.

✓ Earning Votes with Irreverence
C.C. Case

Perhaps it has more to do with the perverse personality of a campaign junkie, than a last-minute, desperate attempt to ruin one's opponent. However, it's a fair assumption that at one time or another, you have "beautified" an opponent's yard sign, or placed your candidate's bumper sticker on a highway toll booth; such common campaign practices go almost unnoticed by your opposition . But what if you were to assault your opponent's headquarters with hordes of your own zealous human billboards, partisans dressed in patriotic colors, all doing the wave—just to shake your opposition up a little? That type of behavior will qualify you as a genuine campaign prankster.

Campaign pranks have been going on since Brutus stuck it to Caesar. Today, although pranks rarely result in death, the desired result is pretty much the same.

In the 1886 gubernatorial campaign in Tennessee, Democratic nominee Bob Taylor toured the state with the GOP standard-bearer—his own brother, Alf. The internecine warriors slept in the same railroad car and delivered competing addresses from the rear platform of the caboose. The night before a major joint appearance, Bob slipped the intended speech from his brother's coat pocket, committed it to memory and delivered it the next day before a flustered Alf had an opportunity to speak. (Political rhetoric was interchangeable even then.)

Forty years later in the same locale, middle Tennessee warlord Luke Lea ran a fake telegraph wire into the headquarters of arch-rival "Boss" Crump of Memphis. When Crump's ticker finished reporting the boxes from Lea's rural strongholds, the urban godfather calculated the needed margin and released his "Big Shelby [County]" vote. Lea then had his lieutenants report the real returns, leaving Crump's gubernatorial candidate a much-surprised, 1,500-vote loser.

An opponent's communications are still a popular target, particularly in-house phone banks. One former field operative boasts that he once snipped the phone line of the opposing headquarters early election day.

One wonders why a campaign would leave campaign-central unattended on election morning; no doubt they were still out placing door hangers.

A more common telemarketing prank is to plant a volunteer in the opposition's voter-ID phone bank. The spy then relays the bank's phone numbers, in code, to an opposing volunteer force tucked away at phone booths in the local shopping mall. The mall-agents then simply call back the numbers and leave their receivers off the hook to tie up enemy lines. One phone bank prankster confessed that occasionally your volunteers want to chat with opposition volunteers, which can obviously lead to problems, but for the most part it successfully shuts down your opponent's calling for the evening.

Herein lies another popular political gag—planting moles. Moles are ordered to stuff the wrong answer to an issue request or as one Republican put it, "just find out as much as you can." That can be a tough request. How much can someone learn licking stamps at the donut table?

One ex-mole describes the hardships of living a double-life. "It's thankless work that I couldn't even share with my immediate family, if but it's all for the cause, right?" This card-carrying liberal Democrat lived in constant fear of being exposed as he juggled his tangled duties: 1) getting good information; 2) acting poised at all times, even while reliving highlights of the Reagan Era; and 3) signing up for a walk-a-thon sponsored by the Young Americans for Freedom. Though his efforts were wholehearted, he was eventually exposed.

"It was in a bar in Derry, New Hampshire when my guard was down. We were relating our best campaign experiences and, I mentioned the time I had to buy new stockings for Geraldine Ferraro."

Due to the nature of the act, the success rate of "disguised" volunteers will probably never be determined. However, one seasoned volunteer coordinator became so paranoid of moles that he described how each volunteer underwent a lengthy screening process similar to that of the National Security Council. It's a serious operation that interrogates every Jane Jefferson who baked for your holiday picnic, just because some blueberry pie filling spilled onto the candidate's tie.

Security reaches paranoiac levels around the candidate for a good reason: his persona is the favorite target of opposition practical jokesters.

Ohio Republicans sent a six-foot, singing chicken to a posh reception at the DLC meeting in Cleveland to present a state rep. with the "Liberal of the Year" award. One Italian prankster posed as a candidate during the Labor Day parade in a heavily Italian district, to distract attention from the legitimate WASP candidate. Another claimed he got the candidate subpoenaed for jury duty the week before the election. But the most personally painful experience was a Young Republican who trekked through every college dorm in the district and distributed the opponents congressional business cards to pretty coeds—asking each one to dinner.

The blue ribbon of personally-oriented pranks, however, goes to a group of San Diego women who found an effective vehicle for high-lighting Congressman Jim Bates' alleged practices of sexual harassment. The weekend before the 1988 election, they bought up every red bra in the downtown area, then stapled them to scores of 4x8 Bates signs posted along the district's freeways. To get more mileage out of the mischief, they uprooted one sign and replanted it in front of the San Diego Tribune office.

Second to phone banks, direct mail seems to be an easy hit. "Dear Occupant" letters to your opponent's finance committee is a popular stunt.

The mailer denounces the candidate for several unrelated reasons, and the opposition is forced to schedule a rebuttal press conference because they think the piece has gone to every household in the district. Likewise, one GOPer bulked a Lyndon LaRouche-type letter throughout Greenwich Village, endorsing the Democratic candidate. The prank was not a strong enough hit to make lower Manhattan vote Republican, but at least the turnout was low.

Is the approach effective? "Absolutely," cries a current Senate committee staffer who once amused himself by writing "gag" letters. "Fake mail, is not only entertaining during the tough months, it works wonders." His superiors seem to have agreed; his postal creativity earned him a raise to $250/week.

One high-profile media consultant confesses that he once produced a fictitious "man on the street" radio spot in which all "observants" claimed that his client had won a prominent statewide debate. (Of course the spot was recorded three days earlier so it was ready for the next morning's drive time.) Also before the debate, the consultant lined the opponent's driving route with signs rehashing the kicker of his negative spot. The press isn't immune from pranks either.

How about faxing out fake press releases to every news organization, nightly, on the letterhead of the opposition? It's called the "cry wolf" prank, as it conditions reporters to automatically round-file anything from your opponent. Ever work in a campaign where you made no waves in print, despite all efforts short of making your candidate bungie-cord off a bridge? Maybe this gem was employed against you.

Not withstanding, there's a fine line between political pranks a dirty politics. Is it defaming the process to engage in political prank or just a mischievous way to blow off steam? Ralph Murphine, chairman of the ethics committee of the National Association of Politic Consultants, confesses it would be impossible to legislate a code behavior along these lines, but offers a warning to would-be pranksters:

"I'd hate to see all the humor purged from politics; if it's legitimately funny, involves no fraud and does not interfere with the opponent's campaign, a prank is a form of free speech and can be funny and effective. But such practices can very easily slide into viciousness and criminality, practices which do damage to the political process and easily backfire on the perpetrator with disastrous results."

Other campaigners are not likely to be so cautious. To these political Peter Pans, performing campaign pranks is like reliving junior high school stunts against substitute teachers. "Most 'pranks' are just that, it's nothing to get worked up about," says an ex-staffer. "I'm optimistic about the future of new and creative pranks and will personally continue the legacy."

✓ How to Topple an Incumbent
Daniel M. Shea and Stephen C. Brooks

If you were asked to handicap a candidate's chance in the next election, and could use only one piece of information to make your guess, what would that be—party label, gender, or ideology? Perhaps you would inquire about his or her finances, or prior campaign experience. In truth, the most important question is whether the candidate currently holds the seat.

Defeating a member of Congress, state legislature, or even a city council is a rare event. Since the 1960s, roughly 95 percent of those who sought reelection were returned to office.

At first glance, the 1992 and 1994 elections would seem to have weakened, if not shattered, this trend. Weren't scores of polls displaced by insurgent "outsiders?" What about the backlash against "business as usual," the "Washington establishment?" Certainly the groundswell of support for term limits and the Perot movement had an impact on incumbent

success rate?

Not really. Nine out of ten members of Congress were returned to office even in these "historic" elections; it just so happens that all of the defeats in 1994 were Democrats, and most were in open seats. If you want to send a member of Congress, a state legislature, or a city council packing, you had better have your ducks in a row.

The list of usual advantages afforded incumbents is vast, including better finances, higher name recognition, the ability to dispense favors and greater access to the media. There are a few pluses these days to being a newcomer (even the most consummate insiders struggle to be seen as fresh faces), but it pales in comparison to the scores of resources available to candidates already holding that office.

In a nutshell, little has changed—the odds are dramatically stacked against challengers. But incumbents can be beaten. Here's how.

Three Keys

Opinion polls rate politicians below used car dealers, yet at the same time over 90 percent are reelected. To make the electoral system more open and fair, several campaign reform initiatives are under discussion, among them term limits, campaign finance adjustments, and open access to media for all federal office candidates.

We asked the best and brightest in the campaign field to provide ideas and tips on how to knock-off incumbents within the existing electoral system. Three themes emerged:

- Some, but not most, incumbents are beatable. They are still popular with the folks back home and challengers have a long row to hoe, but their reelection today is less assured. (At the very least you can give them a good scare!)
- Successful challengers are often aided by the incumbents themselves. Caution, overconfidence, and the reliance on worn-out campaign techniques are all part of a spreading illness, termed by one pro as "incumbentitus."
- Successful challenges take hard work and smart campaigning. The anti-incumbent tide sweeping American politics will do little if the challenger does not have the smarts, preparation, and resources to capitalize on it. Certainly the mood of the electorate has changed, but that does not mean challengers have it easy.

Handicapper's View

In the wake of the 1994 election, practitioners and students of the electoral process seem to be asking "what changed?" Stuart Rothenberg of the Rothenberg Political Report conveys the groundwork for understanding incumbent defeat. Rothenberg points to changes he has seen in the political environment that make defeating incumbents somewhat easier and made Michael Patrick Flanagan's upset of former Ways and Means Committee Chairman Dan Rostenkowsi possible.

First, he suggests that the nationalization of politics is challenging the "all politics is local" dictum. Second, the benefit of name recognition and experience is increasingly discounted. An extensive record by a candidate may be as much a liability as an asset. Likewise, Rothenberg points out that Republican Flanagan's capture of Rostenkowski's House seat in heavily Democratic Chicago goes against the common notion that "you can't beat somebody with nobody."

He has also observed shifts in the strategy of campaigns. The rise of attack advertising poses risks for opponents. In past years, incumbents have ignored opponents unless the race became close. Yet, effective attacks can harm an incumbent and the damage may be done before it is recognized. In part, these effects may be due to following the traditional campaign strategy of starting positive, going negative, and then ending on the positive. Modern campaigns, according to Rothenberg, have a simpler strategy—all negative.

Another shift is the rise of social issues. "The 'vote your pocketbook' mentality of voters has broadened to the point that candidates must also address important social concerns like crime," he says. "The ability to defeat an incumbent has as much to do with changing political rules as it does with any specific strategy or technique."

Successful Challengers

Although Rothenberg suggests it is indeed possible to beat somebody with nobody, several consultants argue the right incumbent and the right challenger can make a big difference.

Cathy Allen, a principal with Campaign Connection, consultants in Seattle, provides a check-list of attributes most commonly found among winning challengers. Topping the list are swing districts, the ability to raise a large war chest early, and high name recognition prior to the race. "With all respect to my good friend and client Patty Murray, you don't get a lot of 'moms-in-tennis-shoes' running and winning," she says.

Another key element is control of an exclusive base of support. "Challengers need a group of supporters that will be there for them and not some laundry list of candidates. There's no need to share your base with labor, small business, or any other group."

Allen also underscores the importance of extensive opposition research. "All challengers I have worked with had great opposition research. They knew the four main Achilles heels of incumbents: they've lost touch, are too arrogant, just don't get it, and are not connecting with voters. Research into these areas pays big dividends."

Successful challengers, according to Allen, are not afraid of the media: "They must be willing to stand in front of the camera and refuse to be ignored." They also know their own job description and stick to it, make the phone calls and skip the meetings, spend money on the right things (no bumper stickers, thank you), and rely upon strategic plans. "If it's not in writing, it's not a plan," she says. They also know how to inspire, excite, and energize. As she puts it: "Challengers must have fire in their gut. The public knows if your faking—the public knows big time!"

Contrary to popular wisdom, Allen sees primaries as a plus for challengers: "You need a strong primary to show you can fight, to learn how to do this job called campaigning, and to get people up and organized." Very much related, challengers must, if possible, put together a campaign team that has worked together in the past. This helps put the gears of the campaign in sync much quicker.

Finally, successful challengers have timing on their side and stress core values over issues. "It's the broad themes that work," suggests Allen, "not the complex issues." It's the lazy incumbents who don't get it. They have the polls, but not the passion."

Add to the list of strong challenger characteristics "candidates who have a big heart—those not afraid to show it," says Jim Murphy of the New York State Democratic Assembly Campaign Committee. "When you're looking for challengers to back, the depth of their conviction says as much as anything." He added that women make superb challengers because they often come to politics in unconventional ways, and, as such, have greater sensitivity to the issues that affect voters.

Successful challengers stay focused, adds James Wray, president of Wray and Associates, consultants in Washington, DC. "They should find two or three messages and drive them home. Challengers must develop an environmental check—that is, take the blinders off and see what is truly on the minds of voters. All consultants lose control the minute the candidate steps behind the podium, so the more well-rounded the challenger is with peripheral vision and an awareness of what they are getting into, the better. This is the main factor for a successful challenger."

Knocking Incumbents Off Their Pedestal

Switching the focus somewhat, Ed Brookover, political director of the National Republican Congressional Campaign Committee, provides a profile of vulnerable incumbents. Topping the list are those who have committed, in his words, "a deadly sin." These include excessive absences, numerous junkets, office internal budgets, misuse of public funds, nepotism, cronyism, and voting consistently to raise taxes. "Look for any of these and you've got a head start," he says.

Another important characteristic to look for is what he terms "defenders of the status quo." As he puts it, "Voters base their decision on what the candidate can do in the future. Incumbents defending the past, as opposed to what they can do in the future, are very vulnerable."

Two other items to look for are those incumbents failing to understand the changing electorate and excessive use of surrogates in defending their record. "Voters today are demanding new issues, new solutions, and new ways of thinking about government. George Bush certainly learned this. You have to keep ahead of the pack." Moreover, voters expect straight-forward answers from the candidate, "not trotting out someone else to talk about the record."

Finally, according to Brookover, there's nothing more pleasing, from the point of view of a strategist, than to work against an incumbent who runs the same campaign again and again. Referring to his days in Ohio, he suggests that "the old days of three yards and a cloud of dust may have worked for Woody Hayes at Ohio State, but off-tackle play after play can be deadly in politics. It makes it easy if you know how they will spend it."

Once you have the right candidate, how do you put together a winning strategy? Consulting big wigs Jerry Austin, Neil Newhouse, Ed Goeas and Richard Schlackman all highlight the need for a clearly defined challenger-centered strategy. To be a true challenger, you need to think like one, and the main difference between the challenger and the incumbent is that the challenger is not the incumbent.

Jerry Austin, president of Gerald J. Austin and Associates, Columbus, Ohio, gives two words of advice for running campaigns against incumbents: guts and luck. "You need guts for making decisions in a campaign when it goes against everything everybody says you should do or not do. While the campaign cannot control luck, it can work to take advantage of the good luck and minimize the bad luck."

Austin cites his work in several races where luck and guts merged to help defeat an incumbent, including the defeat of Rudy Boschwitz in 1990 at the hands of U.S. Sen. Paul Wellstone (D-MN), and the primary upset victory in 1992 of U.S. Sen. Carol Moseley Braun (D-IL). "Braun won with only $39,000 because of guts and luck," Austin says. "It took backbone for her to run in the first place, and we were lucky it was a three-way race. We sat there and watched the front runners beat themselves up. That race set politics in America on fire."

While acknowledging the importance of those two factors, Neil Newhouse, with Public Opinion Strategies, a GOP polling firm in Alexandria, Virginia, argues campaigns are not won by single events, but from a well-developed strategy. Debunking the notion that challengers must cozy up to the positions of the incumbent to draw-off some of their supporters, Newhouse says "you don't win against an incumbent by being more like the incumbent."

Instead, a challenger must demonstrate how he or she is different from the incumbent. This is much easier if the incumbent suffers from 'incumbentitus'—the tendency of an incumbent to look upon a past successful campaign as the model for all future campaigns, assume all the voters know him and his positions, rely upon PACs from outside the district, no longer walking door to door, and ignoring challenger attacks. "In today's politics the burden of proof is on the incumbent—why they should be reelected."

Newhouse goes on to list the ideal conditions for beating an incumbent. Challengers must be hardworking and believe passionately in an agenda. They must have sufficient funds—not tons of money but enough to communicate the message. They must also be in a district that is at least somewhat competitive "or undergoing turmoil." And finally, challengers must have a potential, identifiable base of support to begin the campaign. In all, incumbents can be beaten by demonstrating differences and sticking to careful strategy.

Ed Goeas, with the Tarrance Group, another GOP polling firm in Alexandria, details how challengers can define themselves. He notes that much of the recent Republican success is due to a change of strategy.

Goeas argues that no longer do Republican candidates attempt to get the "50 percent plus one" number of voters by piecing together supporters in many different sub-groups of voters. Instead, the strategy is to "prevent opponents from getting 50 percent of the vote, by going after all potential voters." He adds, "for individual candidates, the best way to accomplish this is to have clear definitions of themselves and their opponents, as well as know how the opponents will be doing the same."

Goeas takes issue with Austin's faith in guts and luck. "The biggest problem I see in campaigns is that they are always putting together a 'what if' strategy. If you don't get the campaign in the position of making luck happen, it doesn't matter how much luck you get."

One way of positioning your campaign to capitalize on sudden changes is to develop a strategic team—people who have worked together and know how the pieces fit. Moreover, candidates have to remember, suggests Goeas, that campaigns must constantly readjust as developments unfold. "Strategy is a thought process, not a set of rules you put together in the beginning of the campaign that you are stuck with."

Richard Schlackman, president of the Campaign Performance Group, a Democratic media firm, provides a final perspective on strategy and tactics. Picking up on the theme of candidate definition, he talks about the importance of research. "In modern campaigns, opposition research is most important—especially on your own campaign," he says. "God forbid a campaign manager discovers, well into the race, that the candidate hasn't voted in the last ten years or paid taxes in the last three." What's more, "candidates often exaggerate their accomplishments—but it doesn't matter if it is true; if it isn't believable, it won't work."

As for what to look for in vulnerable incumbents, Schlackman notes that long-time legislators are often set in their ways. "They run the same campaign each election," he says. "They are what challengers use to be, ignorant of the process. These people are much easier to beat."

Money and Organization

In every campaign, especially challenger campaigns, there is never enough money—at least that's the common notion. Challengers, it seems, are always strapped for cash and getting more is no simple task. According to the experts, however, they can gather sufficient money and volunteers—if they know how to do it.

Taking issue with Rothenberg's claim that money was less critical in challenger victories during the 1994 election than in previous years, Michael Malbin, of the Rockefeller Institute of Government, State University of New York at Albany, insists that the money raised by challengers remains a strong predictor of their success.

"You might be able to beat somebody with nobody, but you can't beat somebody with nothing," he says. Malbin further notes that the amount of money spent by incumbents often, contrary to traditional wisdom, indicates their vulnerability—not necessarily their invincibility. "It makes sense that as incumbents get into trouble, they spend more money."

There are three factors that challengers must keep in mind to be successful at fundraising, say Mary Sabin, with the consulting firm Fundamentals, in Perrysburg, Ohio. "They are work, work, work. If you're not feeling anxiety and stress, you're not doing your job." She adds that this is especially true in challenger races. "This isn't rocket science or brain surgery. What it is is working hard, staying at it, and concentrating on raising the money while feeling completely obsessed about it."

Challengers, notes Sabin, are at a disadvantage when it comes to raising money because they usually do not possess a donor list and are up against the special interests linked to the incumbent. However, with fresh ideas and hard work they can overcome these limitations. "Ask yourself, who hates the incumbent, who wants to beat him as bad as I do. This starts the donor list process." She also points out that incumbents have a tendency to relax, "so your hard work can make all the difference."

Incumbents, unlike many challengers, have voting records. According to Kim Scott, president, Kimberly Scott and Associates, Washington, DC, this simple fact should guide challenger fundraising efforts. "Look at the voting record of the incumbent and go to the organization on the other side. If the incumbent has not defined where he or she stands on an issue, then the challenger needs to provide that definition to the PACs."

Challengers must keep in mind PAC fundraising is like a courtship: "There is a lot of care and attention to your appeal and a bit of manipulation involved," Scott says. She also notes that "every campaign needs an information broker—a political liaison to meet with PACs. This person must have intimate knowledge of the issues and be able to articulate their candidate's position."

Scott also points out that fundraisers should know the kind of groups the candidate will not accept money from. "Remember, it can be used against you down the road," she warns.

In terms of other campaign resources, James Nathanson, president, Nathanson and Associates, Dayton, OH, explains that political parties are "resource centers and service bureaus that challengers should tap into."

Moreover, parties often provide direct contributions, coordinated expenditures, non-allocable contributions, and most importantly, channel funds from other groups. "Parties have been completely underrated, unknown and under-utilized as a resource for challengers who are likely to be weak in most traditional resources," he says. "If the party does its job, it's a ready-made pool of volunteers, as well as a strong coalition builder."

Getting Your Message Out

One of the hottest political issues today is the extent to which challengers must rely on attacks to unseat an incumbent, and whether incumbents should sit idly by while getting attacked.

Marilyn Roberts, professor at the University of Florida's College of Journalism and Communication, suggests that negative attacks, in both directions, have strong psychological affects. "As much as voters don't like them, they are given greater weight, are seen as more creditable, leave a more lasting impression, and are difficult to challenge," she says. "Incumbents can no longer ignore attacks. What we may see in the years ahead is a growing number of incumbents attacking challengers right from the get-go. The traditional notion that incumbents are above the fray is rapidly becoming outdated."

Gary Nordlinger, president, Nordlinger and Associates, Washington, DC, sees little choice for challengers. "In order to pry voters from the incumbent, challengers must convince them that he is in office for personal gain, or not addressing the issues," he says. "The only way to do this is with 'comparative' campaigning. When most challengers only have one-fourth the money that the incumbent has, he needs to concentrate on the sleeping giants."

Nordlinger believes this process is in one sense much easier today, since voters can be easily convinced that it is time for a change and they are less likely to give incumbents the benefit of the doubt. On the other hand, it may be more difficult to bump off an incumbent because they are less likely to fall asleep at the wheel. "They know there's anti-incumbent sentiment out there and they're ready."

Mark Weaver of Wilson Communication Services notes that the key to challenger success lies in extensive research, the repetition of a central message, the ability to draw the opponent in, and preparation for the coming attack.

"The idea is to use paid media to raise charges related to the incumbent's strengths, and use earned media to bait him on his weaknesses," Weaver says. "An important point to remember is to predict the counter attack and be ready, because it will come. By then he's on the defensive and you're pounding home the message that you have designed. You have succeeded in changing the agenda of the race, precisely what challengers need to do."

According to Weaver, incumbents still have numerous resources over challengers. But when it comes to the "message arena," it's a level playing field. "There is no advantage in who can be more creative or effective with a message. This is precisely where challengers need to concentrate."

John Franzen, president of John Franzen Multimedia, seconds this idea, noting that "message discipline is exceedingly hard to achieve in practice, but the short attention span of the voter and the expense of paid media highlight the importance of this simple, yet basic, strategy for challengers."

Stephen Clouse, president, Stephen Clouse and Associates, of Marshfield, WI, highlights the importance of smart radio and TV buying. "Challengers are often, by definition, less experienced and are inclined to waste money," Clouse says. "Paying attention to market share, programming, demographics, and geography will help them get the biggest bang for the buck."

Media relations, not just advertising, are crucial for challengers who live or die by their exposure. Providing a campaign outsider's view, Edward Lifson, of National Public Radio, says challengers must cultivate the press as assiduously as any incumbent.

"Candidates think reporters are looking for a sound bite that will make my job easier, so they give us 30 second answers and don't open up," Lifson says. "I toss this stuff out. Challengers, like all candidates, need to have good relations with the media, reporters in particular. This means you have to be open, honest, and accessible."

✓ Internet Bonanza: 15 Reasons Why You Should Go On-line
Karen Booth

At a recent dinner party in Washington, the conversation turned to the Internet. One of the guests, a congressman from California, admitted that he had a modem at his Capitol Hill office, but nobody knew how to use it to get online. Then he added, "Actually, I know everyone in my district is probably online." He looked around the table sheepishly. "But I have a fax . . . isn't that enough?"

Not anymore. Granted, some of us probably feel the way folks felt back in 1893, when talking on the telephone between Boston and Chicago was considered miraculous. The real forward thinkers knew that the telephone would change their lives forever. It's not much different in 1995, when revolutionary new avenues of communication are unfolding before us and (once again) transforming the way we live and work.

The question every candidate should ask is: What can "going online" do for me? For political professionals—be they politicians, candidates, party officials or consultants—now is the time to make peace with the online world, learn what's relevant to your business, master it, and put it to work for you.

The first step is to forget almost everything you've ever read about "cyberspace." Those visionary portraits of a global society linked by computers from Boca Raton to Borneo may take your breath away, but they don't mean much to most of us. The world of the Internet is vast and confusing—kind of like a cable TV system with thousands of channels but no Cable Guide—but there's a place there for you.

And what is politics about if not communication? Success in this business depends, in part, upon who the best spinmeisters are, which candidate stays "on message," and which party can put its finger on the pulse of an increasingly cranky electorate. How voters consume information is urgently important to the way we campaign, and the Internet may provide just the edge you're looking for in the hyper-competitive world of political campaigning.

Here are 15 real-world reasons why you should get online now:

1. Become a real road warrior. While on the road, send and receive instantaneous, private e-mail messages and documents (unlike faxes, which anyone can pick up) from your laptop computer to your office, clients, campaign offices and home. Review strategy memos, send out candidate schedules, e-mail polling results and more. If you go online for no other reason than this, it's probably worth it.

2. Get real-time returns on election day. Last year, California's Secretary of State teamed with Digital Equipment Corporation to provide automated election returns in the World Wide Web. A DEC spokesman said that the returns were "very real-time"—actually 15 to 20 minutes ahead of the state's official tallies—and that the company is talking to a "high percentage" of other states about setting up similar electronic vote tallying in time for the 1996 election.

3. Find out the best bargains on airfare, then book your airline reservations directly from your computer. America Online, for example, offers an extensive (10-page) up-to-the-minute list of the most incredible airline bargains available, including deals on all those little discount carriers. Most other services offer direct access to the airline industry's database of scheduled flights and fares.

4. Find solutions to your design problems. For direct mail and print ad folks, the Internet offers bulletin boards where designers can communicate with each other and with technical support specialists to solve software problems, learn design tips, and buy and sell equipment.

5. Get something for nothing. Online services are a treasure trove of free fonts, graphic images, searchable databases, software and more. In fact, many major computer companies are now putting new software releases on-line, so you can download directly onto your hard drive instead of waiting for a new disk to arrive by mail.

6. Send your direct mail job to your printer online. Many direct mail firms use printers all over the country, which translates into a lot of money in FedEx and airplane delivery charges. Some printing companies can now receive camera-ready artwork digitally via modem, and more are sure to catch up in the future. Many service bureaus are now receiving files on-line, too.

7. Find out what's on your constituents' minds. Last year Senator Barbara Boxer (D-CA) published a health care reform questionnaire on the World Wide Web and received over 1,000 responses in 10 days. Think of all the creative ways you can communicate with the folks back home—with quicker results and no franking costs.

8. Get daily legislative schedules for both houses of Congress. You can also download copies of full legislative transcripts from the Internet. There are many areas of discussion and browsing to interest political junkies. Congress has its own Web site called "Thomas," after a certain president of the same name. (Thomas' address is: "http:/Icweb.loc.gov/homepage/lchp.html")

9. Tell Bill Clinton and Rush Limbaugh what you really think. You can e-mail the President and Vice President directly, although you'll probably get an automated response. But staffers who run the White House e-mail system claim that they regularly read all e-mail and present Clinton and Gore with summaries and selected correspondences weekly. (President Clinton's e-mail address: president@whitehouse.gov. Vice President Gore's e-mail address: vice_president@whitehouse.gov). Rush Limbaugh reportedly reads his e-mail every morning before his radio show for ideas. (His e-mail address is: 70277,2502@compuserve.com)

10. Get the latest FEC PAC contribution reports for every member of Congress. Federal Election Commission reports for every sitting member of the U.S. Congress are residing on the Internet, along with up-to-date House and Senate Committee members and their phone numbers, and roll call votes from the 103rd Congress and the 104th Congress.

11. Access to political campaign products, services, and consultants, offered by *Campaigns & Elections* magazine. If you need a pollster or a printer, a video duplicator or a software supplier, a direct mail specialist or a media consultant, a mailing list broker or a data base manager, *Campaigns & Elections* magazine is updating information on all of these products and services, and more, on the Internet. Information includes firm profiles, buyer's guides, classified listings, seminar and training programs, and employment opportunities through The Political Jobline. UAL is http://www.infi.net/camelect. Complete text of current and back issues of *Campaigns & Elections* may be accessed through Lexis-Nexis.

12. Find people across the country (or globe) who share your interests and talk to them regularly. These discussion groups are called "newsgroups," and you can find them on nearly every subject imaginable. Amateur chefs, Vince Foster conspiracy theorists, gardening enthusiasts, gun control opponents . . . all have a happy home together, oddly enough, on the Internet.

13. Download the text of all the bills of the Contract With America. Finding it hard to keep up with those zesty Republicans and their break-neck legislative agenda? The full text of the CWA is available on the Net, along with the text of all CWA bills as they are introduced.

14. Reinvent your next campaign. Imagine a campaign where the pollster, media consultant, campaign office, fundraiser and candidate and staff are all online. Imagine coordinated rapid response like never before, private strategy memos that will never make it into the wrong hands, outreach to online voters, daily updated candidate schedules zapped to the entire operation at the touch of a button, e-mailing the latest draft of a direct mail piece to all the right people at the touch of a button. Sound revolutionary? It is. Get online . . . or eat your opponent's dust.

15. Check your stocks, send your mother flowers, file your taxes. Shopping online may sound like a computerized version of the Home Shopping Network, but you can send a dozen red roses, buy a C-SPAN coffee mug, have your prescription drugs delivered to your office, or buy a rare artifact from the New York Museum of Modern Art without ever leaving your computer. The Internet also provides the latest tax news from the IRS, reams of information about tax filings and regulations, and copies of any current IRS tax form you need to file your taxes. Then you can file your taxes electronically.

✓ Putting the Internet and E-Mail To Work
Frank Tobe

Political consultants are thirsting for knowledge about E-mail, electronic communication, the Internet, and how all these innovations can benefit their businesses and their immediate campaign practices. They're aware that this technology is a trend that is infiltrating their workplace and will probably affect them directly during the next election cycle. They want to know more now so they can adapt in time for the forthcoming political season.

But for a small handful of computer techies in our midst, political professionals are way behind the progressive corporate learning curve. Do you know what a Web-site is? Do you have a fax/modem? Does your company use E-mail? Do you know your E-mail address? Do you have it printed on your business cards?

Remember when just a few businesses had telecopiers, using instead the wrap-around-the-drum QWIP machines? Then, almost overnight, everyone had a fax machine and added their fax phone number to their business cards. Now we cannot live without them! The fax phenomenon is analogous to the development of E-mail and electronic networking.

It's incumbent upon each of us to come out of denial and recognize the opportunities that await us; to quickly master these new technologies and make them part of our arsenal of tools when we begin the '96 campaign cycle. The principle advantages of becoming Internet savvy will reduce phone, fax, courier and FedEx charges for office-to-office, home-to-office and office-to-major-client communications.

Other benefits include:

- The creation of bargain international links that may open new markets and consulting opportunities.
- Access to huge amounts of research data at extraordinarily low rates including being able to regularly monitor the tone, content and magnitude of on-line political discussion groups.
- Inexpensive direct contact with electronic activists, donors, clients and vendors—plus friends and family.
- The ability to run grassroots programs to newly emerging niche-market electronic audiences.

Side-benefits of becoming Internet savvy include upgrading your PC, being able to fax from your desktop, and the functions of Windows and its software. Another major side-benefit is that you will reduce touch-tone voice-mail messaging, phone tag, and curled-up and smeared faxes.

Six Steps

Begin the conversion process right away—in the next 30–60 days. Here are six suggestions on how to accomplish that transition:

1. Determine equipment and software already available to you.
2. Compute the overall cost for additional equipment and software to decide where you will need to upgrade and/or add equipment and software. Then allocate the funds and get the ball rolling.
3. Decide whether you or someone else will be doing the upgrade and installation. If you did steps 1 and 2 yourself, you can do the rest; if not, you will probably need help.
4. Conclude the acquisition/installation process and then self-train and explore not only the Internet and America Online, but also your new Windows word processing and faxing software. Invest a few h ours in becoming proficient in all your new capabilities.
5. Think ahead. Set goals that involve the Internet, electronic communications, networking and your business.
6. Implement those goals.

We're not talking big bucks here. What you'll spend is peanuts compared with the advantages and savings. These costs are necessary business investments that must be made to keep your company competitive and cost-efficient.

Assuming you already have an office PC or a traveling notebook computer, all that is needed is a fast modem, software, installation, training and an electronic network service subscription.

To upgrade WordPerfect from DOS to the current Windows version is only $99 (most other Windows word processor upgrades cost similarly), another $249 for a fast fax/modem, $49–$84 to upgrade the fax software to WinFax—a very proficient, easy-to-use package; a subscription to America Online; and possibly for the adventurous and curious, Internet-in-a-box and a $49 subscription to an Internet service provider—about $129 for both.

That's only $430 with a monthly subscription cost of $7.75 for America Online and $40 a month and $550 for the more adventurous alternative. You'll save that—and more—in reduced fax, FedEx and courier charges in the first few months!

Attention, Shoppers

If you need to buy a PC, a wonderfully capable color laptop costs about $1,999 these days. You'll need to add software, modem and monthly subscription costs to fully outfit it. Then you'll be a true road warrior!

After the system is all set up and running, you'll need to invest two to three hours of self-training—your time, no cash-out-of-pocket. After a week or so of exploring, you can start doing business differently, electronically, and economically.

After you're experiencing the initial benefits from the switch-over to electronic communication, you may want to take advantage of the wealth of other productivity and cost-saving tools available to you. Here are a few options:

- An internal network and E-mail system so that everyone, at every desk, has an ability to E-mail everyone else and electronically participate.
- An electronic storefront—a place on the Internet where some of the repetitive questions that people ask can be answered graphically and electronically and from where you can encourage people to read your electronic brochure(s) and other persuasion material. From that electronic storefront, prospects can be culled out and forwarded to the right person in your company for follow-up.
- Helping grassroots campaigns get their operations up and running.
- Collecting critical campaign data and setting up an economical 24-hour data collection and processing capability.
- Helping commercial clients market their catalogues of goods and services electronically.
- Upgrade one of your PCs to be multimedia compatible, so you can listen to and watch full-motion video played from a CD-ROM drive attached to your computer; download multimedia files from the Internet; utilize massive libraries of data stored on CD-ROMs that are easily accessible and quickly searched; etc.

Ours is a high-speed, high-tech, high-touch business. Let's start E-mailing one another right away. It'll make our profession more productive and it'll revolutionize the way we conduct our businesses and campaigns.

✓ Great Slogans
Ron Faucheux

A campaign slogan is like a soufflé. A good one rises to perfection. A bad one falls like a stone off a ledge. Take Ronald Reagan's re-election theme in 1984: "Leadership That's Working." Simple, easy to understand, and on target, this catch phrase succinctly summarized what the American people already believed, that Reagan, in contrast to his predecessor, was a strong leader who had made things better at home and abroad.

For bad slogans, consider Barry Goldwater's 1964 motto "In Your Heart You Know He's Right." Sounds fine, but for someone who was fighting an image as a right-wing extremist, the inevitable play on words was a net loss. Opponents countered with, "In Your Guts You Know He's Nuts."

Slogans force campaigns to define themselves in short statement consisting of simple and clear language. They crystallize the image of a candidate's strengths.

"Good slogans have rhyme, rhythm, or alliteration to make them memorable," writes columnist William Safire. "Great slogans may have none of these, but touch a chord of memory, release pent-up hatreds, or stir men's better natures."

A campaign's slogan should not be confused with its message. In modern politics, The Message is the central strategic rationale as to why a candidate or issue position is the right one at the right time and is preferable to other alternatives. A slogan, on the other hand, is a shorthand way to explain the various aspects of The Message to the public.

Slogans have been around a long time. The Oxford English Dictionary traces them back to 1513. Slogan styles have varied with the temper of the times. "Tippecanoe and Tyler, too" was one of the earliest presidential campaign mottos which spotlighted William Henry Harrison's victory at the Battle of Tippecanoe in 1811, and notable because it's one of the few that even acknowledged the existence of a vice presidential nominee.

Plagiarism

Like old soldiers, winning slogans never die. In fact, they rarely fade away. In literature, it's called plagiarism; in politics, it's called experience. For example, when Harrison's grandson, Benjamin, ran for the presidency in 1888, he dusted off the old man's winning line and used it again. "Tippecanoe and Morton, too" may not ring quite as loudly in the ear of history as did the earlier version, but it was ultimately as effective. Benjamin Harrison won his race, too.

Candidates have to be careful which slogan they purloin, however, Patrick Buchanan, when running for the 1992 Republican presidential nomination, used the theme "America First." These words, on face value, seem about as safe as you can get. But Buchanan's enemies drew unflattering comparisons between his slogan and the same one that had been used a half-century earlier by the "America First" committee, an isolationist group that opposed U.S. entry into World War II.

Over time, slogans became more issue-oriented. In 1856, voters were treated to: "Free Speech. Free Press. Free Soil. Free Men. Fremont and Victory." Here, John C. Fremont unabashedly laid out a platform as well as a catchy lyric.

In 1896, William Jennings Bryan's slogan had nothing to do with either his name or his background, but instead was directed at his issue: free silver. "16 to 1" was the Democratic battle cry, underlining Bryan's populist proposal to increase the money supply by coining 16 ounces of silver for each ounce of gold. Republican William McKinley took the opposite stance: "In Gold We Trust" and "Sound Money." McKinley also campaigned on the theme of "A Full Dinner Pail"—an attractive promise for workers and families struggling through the Industrial Revolution.

Perhaps the most unpretentious issue-oriented slogan was the one used by a local candidate in Washington: "Dog Litter—An Issue You Can't Sidestep."

Turning Liabilities Into Assets

Crafting campaign messages that turn a candidate's liabilities into assets is nothing new. Ulysses Grant may not have been an illustrious president, but his image as a military victor was vital to his appeal in 1868. His rallying cry "Let Us Have Peace" was the strategic equivalent of a home run. It sent an important signal that a general-as-president wouldn't necessarily plunge the nation into another bloody conflict.

Campaign themes are also designed to reassure voters. This can be a risky tact, however, when the adage centers on a weakness in your own candidacy. The perfect example was Woodrow Wilson's desperate 1916 campaign that hinged on his ability to maintain the peace. "He Kept Us Out of War" was his theme. It was phrased retrospectively, as a statement of fact, and not a promise for the future. There was no explicit vow that, if re-elected, Wilson would continue to keep the country out of war, but only a declaration of the obvious that, up to that point, he had kept America out of war. Crafty old Woody had pulled a fast one. Only months after his re-election, America was very much in the war.

Some slogans are time bombs. If America had entered the world war before election day, Wilson's campaign pitch would have been a mockery. Any campaign theme that can be undermined by uncontrollable events is a gamble. Nelson Rockefeller's assertion in 1968 that he was "The One Republican Who Can Win in November," was shattered when poll results on the eve of the GOP convention showed Richard Nixon running better against the prospective Democratic nominee than Rockefeller.

Occasionally, slogans miss the strategic mark and end up hurting the candidate they're designed to promote. Standing for re-election in 1932, hapless Herbert Hoover wrapped himself in the status quo and asked voters to "Be Safe With Hoover"—right in the middle of the Great Depression! When Birch Bayh used "It Takes a Good Politician to Make a Good President" in the 1976 New Hampshire primary, it fell flat. Watergate era voters wanted nothing to do with traditional politicians, good or otherwise.

Most large campaigns have more than one slogan. Eisenhower used "I like Ike" on buttons and banners, but his central theme "It's Time for a Change" packed the strategic punch. Lyndon Johnson's 1964 campaign—arguably the first modern media-age presidential campaign—used "Let Us Continue," asking voters to carry on with John Kennedy's unfinished agenda, as well as " All the Way with LBJ" and "LBJ for the U.S.A." as rhymes used in songs and on signs. "Vote for President Johnson on November 3. The Stakes are Too High for You to Stay Home." was the TV spot tag line, a get-out-the-vote pitch that was important because only an abnormal election day turnout could have eliminated Johnson's large lead.

George Wallace always came up with solid slogans for his losing presidential bids. In 1968, "Stand Up for America" shifted attention from his racial politics toward a more uplifting, patriotic theme. "Send Them a Message" was the perfect pitch for a protest candidate to use in the 1972 presidential primaries. Four years later, Jimmy Carter successfully countered him with "Send Them a President."

Ins and Outs

For "outs," most slogans center on change. When voters are ready to oust an incumbent regime, it's a tough theme to beat.

There are many ways to phrase the change message. In 1946, Republicans asked the question, "Had Enough?" In 1960, Kennedy used "Let's get this country moving again!" In 1968, Hubert Humphrey found himself cast as the candidate of an unpopular status quo. To remind voters of his long record of legislative accomplishment, his campaign made the case that "Some Men Talk Change. Others Cause It." In 1976, Carter and Walter Mondale tied concepts of change and leadership together and came up with "Leaders, for a Change." In 1980, Reagan focused on the incumbent's economic and international misfortunes as a backdrop for "Let's Make America Great Again."

During the 1992 presidential primaries, Democratic candidates tried to one-up each other on the change issue. Bill Clinton talked about his "crusade for change" and cast himself as "The Change We Need." Tom Harkin proposed to "Build a New America." Bob Kerrey started with "Fight back,

America" and then settled on "Courage for a Change." Tsongas went even further, calling himself "The Big Change."

Change isn't always the magic word. It can be an unacceptable path when the "ins" are popular. America did not want change in 1936; they wanted FDR and his New Deal to "Carry On," just as they wanted the Kennedy-Johnson prosperity in 1964, and Reagan's "Morning in America" in 1984 to continue. Often, the stay-the-course theme has an added dimension. "Connecticut Works Better Because Ella Works Harder" was Governor Grasso's way of linking job performance to visible improvements.

Experience is a central focus of many re-election slogans. Lines like "Keep (candidate's name) On the Job" or "Keep (candidate's name) Working For You" have decorated signs and brochures for incumbents from dog-catcher to governor. "Experience Makes the Difference" was Nelson Rockefeller's theme in 1970 (in addition to the unadorned but potent "Governor Rockefeller for Governor") and "Experience Counts" was used by Vice President Nixon against the less experienced Kennedy in 1960. "Re-elect the President" and "Now More Than Ever" were Nixon's successful re-election slogans in 1972.

On occasion, geographic identifications are apt, such as Governor Martha Layne Collins' "Experience Counts, Kentucky" and Martin Schreiber's "Experience Makes Wisconsin Work." In running for re-election as governor of Kansas, John Carlin based his message on the notion that "Running for office is one thing. Running the office is something else." In 1986, Governor Michael Dukakis told his state's voters "Massachusetts is in good hands," Governor Madeleine Kunin explained her rationale for another term with the phrase "Results for Vermont," and Senator Tom Daschle characterized himself as "South Dakota's Best."

Personal Qualities

Along with experience, other personal qualities have been used as slogans. Words like honest, integrity, qualified, fair, and tough have called out from billboards and bumper stickers across America. Sometimes, these words don't fit the candidate or the situation and are merely empty rhetoric. Using "integrity" presents a sharp contrast if your opponent is under federal indictment for bribery, but may not mean much when personal trust isn't an issue. One campaign that did use its candidate's personal qualities effectively was produced by consultant Dan Payne for Detroit's mayor: "Strength. Experience. Pride. The Right Stuff. Coleman Young. The Mayor." Another viable slogan strategy has been "Common Sense—Uncommon Courage," a theme used by senators Henry "Scoop" Jackson and Phil Gramm, as well as many others.

Possibly the best incumbent "mea culpa" came from New York's telegenic Mayor John Lindsay in his rough-and-tumble 1969 re-election. Lindsay's flaws were too well known to hide. So hometown media consultant David Garth came up with a theme that didn't even mention what Lindsay had done or promised to do as mayor. It simply said: "It's the second toughest job in America." The implication: being mayor of this ungovernable city is so difficult, don't expect anybody to do it very well. It did the job. Lindsay won a second term.

Ironically, one of Lindsay's city hall successors, Ed Koch, was elected in 1977 on the theme, "After eight years of charisma [a shot at Lindsay] and four years of the club house [a swipe at incumbent Abe Beame], why not try competence?" The author of that provocative line was none other than David Garth, the man who had previously sold the eight years of charisma to the Big Apple.

Some slogans accent the sound of a name. To clarify an unusual surname spelling, William Greenhalgh, a candidate for county executive in Maryland, once used "Get On the Balgh With Greenhalgh" and "This Falgh, Vote Greenhalgh." To rhyme with the unexpected pronunciation of his name, Congressman Bill Schuette entreated voters to keep him "on duty." The closing line of a television documentary for unsuccessful Virginia gubernatorial candidate William Battle was fitting and powerful: "A Man Worthy of His Name: Battle." After his defeat as a presidential candidate in 1964, and his retirement from the Senate that same year, Barry Goldwater made a sentimental comeback in his home state in 1968 when he regained a Senate seat with this slogan: "Senator Barry Goldwater. Doesn't that sound great?"

Populist Appeals

Many slogans associate candidates with average voters. "People First" was particularly effective in Bill Clinton's race against George Bush largely because Bush was viewed as being out of touch with ordinary folks. Michael Dukakis' last-minute pitch in 1988 that he was "On Your Side" was a populist appeal many observers thought he should have developed much earlier. Hubert Humphrey was fond of calling himself "The People's Democrat." Texas Senator Ralph Yarborough's re-election theme, "He fights the people's fights. And he wins." stressed not only populism but effectiveness.

Getting things done is a common theme for office-holders. Messages crafted by David Garth for Congressman Richard Ottinger's U.S. Senate campaign and Congressman Hugh Carey's gubernatorial campaign are good TV-age examples. It's easy to promise. It's a lot tougher to deliver. Ottinger delivers." was a successful pitch that won Ottinger his party's nomination even though he ultimately lost the general election. "This year, before they tell you what they want to do, make them show you what they've done" was Carey's way of making the point that political promises should be viewed in the context of a track record. It worked and Carey won. Presumptuous, open-ended slogans are delicate. When you say a candidate "has done a lot" or ask voters to "look at the record," you're inviting the opposition to turn these words on their head. "Senator Smith says he's done a lot. Let's look at what he's done. He voted against pensions for police widows. Then he voted to raise his own pay." Make sure a clever line isn't too clever by half. The one thing worse than running against your opponent is running against yourself.

Candidates with controversial records or philosophies slightly to the left or right of mainstream often run as "fighters." John Tunney, son of a famous boxer, won a California Senate seat by asking voters to "Put a fighter in your corner." Frank Bellotti's earthy gubernatorial theme was "Massachusetts is worth fighting for." Incumbents have frequently used the generic "(candidate's name) Fights For Us." One candidate, who wanted to make sure he was seen as a battler for what's right, claimed he knew "how to fight, who to fight, and what to fight for." He'll make your fights his fights" is a popular line that combines a fighter-populist image.

Sometimes, though, fighting isn't enough. John Lindsay's failed 1972 presidential bid used the argument, "While Washington's been talking about our problems, John Lindsay's been fighting them." Given his poor showing in that race, voters apparently wanted a president who would do more than fight problems; perhaps they wanted someone who would solve them.

The Unslogan

Slogans can stress what a candidate is not. "Unbought and unbossed" was Shirley Chisholm's banner. "Not just another politician" has been fashionable for newcomers running against established politicos.

As electronic media began to dominate electioneering, so did slogan creativity. "Let's do something about the state we're in" was the piquant double-entendre consultant Joe Napolitan used for underdog Senate winner Mike Gravel in Alaska. "Joe Tydings never ducks the tough ones" was used by an incumbent senator from Maryland who had cast a number of liberal votes out of step with his more conservative constituents. (Tydings was defeated by Glenn "You know where he stands" Beal). "He's for real. The quiet man nobody owns, everybody respects." was successful for William Winter's gubernatorial run in Mississippi, largely because it was true.

Classic examples of hip slogans were the two used in the late '60s by New York senate candidate, Paul O'Dwyer: "He doesn't cop out" and "Elect a man who gives a damn." These tough-talking, down-and-dirty phrases seemed daring at the time, but now appear to be relics of a Tom Wolfe narrative about Manhattan's radical chic.

Gender references in campaign slogans have also undergone a transformation. As recently as a few years ago, candidates were still calling themselves "the man for the job" or "the right man for Cincinnati." One city council candidate ran on the slogan "Let a man do a man's job." Apparently, nobody in that 1969 election ever asked why male testosterone was considered to be the most important qualification for a city council seat. Don't expect to see many slogans like that any more.

On the other hand, women are often elected on themes that emphasize gender as a symbol of change, honesty, or independence. "She's not just one of the boys" was a common slogan for women running for office in the late '70s and throughout the '80s. "Put the state's purse strings in the hands of a woman" was another.

In the end, candor is perhaps the most endearing quality in any political slogan. The 1991 gubernatorial runoff in Louisiana pitted racial extremist David Duke against Edwin Edwards, a much-investigated ex-governor with a well-earned reputation for Las Vegas high-rolling. Many unhappy voters were confounded by what they saw as a choice between a "Nazi" and a "crook". To address this dilemma, an Edwards supporter came up with this masterpiece: "Vote for the Crook, It's Important."

Now, there's a reason to go vote if there ever was one!